Switzerland

written and researched by

Matthew Teller

WITHDRAWN

ROUGH GUIDES

NEW YORK • LONDON • DELHI

www.roughguides.com

Contents

Swiss cheese and chocolate insert following p.216

Mountain excursions insert following p.392

◀◀ Alpine flowers ◀ Snowboarder, Mürren

Stuttgart   Stuttgart   Stuttgart

Munich
Innsbruck
Landeck

GERMANY

Kempten

Schaffhausen

Konstanz
Kreuzlingen
Friedrichshafen
Bodensee
Romanshorn
Rorschach
Bregenz
Rhine
Winterthur
Baden
St Gallen
St Margrethen
Limmat
ZÜRICH
OSTSCHWEIZ
Appenzell
Feldkirch
Reuss
Zürichsee
Santis
2502m
AUSTRIA
Zug
Walensee
Einsiedeln
Vaduz
LIECHTENSTEIN
Vierwaldstättersee
Schwyz
Glärnisch
2914m
Klosters
Scuol
SCHWEIZ
Altdorf
Flims
Chur
Davos
Inn
Titlis 3238m
Klausenpass
1948m
Ilanz
Flüelapass 2383m
Pass dal Fuorn
(Ofenpass)
2149m
Sustenpass
2224m
Disentis/
Mustér
Thusis
Filisur
GRAUBÜNDEN
Furkapass
2431m
Andermatt
Oberalppass 2044m
Albulapass
2312m
Müstair
Pso. del
S. Gottardo
2108m
Lukmanierpass
1914m
Grimselpass
2165m
Splügenpass 2113m
St Moritz
Nufenenpass
2478m
Passo del
S. Bernardino
2065m
Julierpass 2284m
Pso. del Bernina 2328m
Biasca
Malojapass 1815m
Peschiavo
TICINO
Chiavenna
Locarno
Bellinzona
Valtellina
Tirano
Domodóssola
Lago di Como
Lugano
Lago di Lugano
Lago Maggiore
ITALY
Varese
Como
Lecco
Bergamo
Malpensa
Ticino
Brescia
Novara
MILAN
Linate

0   25 km

Introduction to

Switzerland

"In Italy for thirty years under the Borgias they had warfare, terror, murder, bloodshed, but they produced Michelangelo, Leonardo da Vinci and the Renaissance. In Switzerland they had brotherly love; they had 500 years of democracy and peace. And what did that produce? The cuckoo clock."

Orson Welles as Harry Lime, in *The Third Man* (1949)

Never has one throwaway movie line done so much to damage the reputation of a whole country. Even now, despite being one of the most visited countries in Europe, Switzerland remains one of the least understood.

The facts are that until national reconciliation in 1848, Switzerland was the most consistently turbulent, war-torn area of Europe (so much for brotherly love), and yet, both before and after it found stability, it brought forth luminaries in the arts and sciences of the calibre of Hans Holbein, Jean-Jacques Rousseau, Albert Einstein, Paul Klee, Hermann Hesse and Alberto Giacometti. So much for the cuckoo clock – a Bavarian invention, anyway.

But two centuries of tourism have left their mark: faced by an ever-increasing onslaught of visitors, these days the Swiss are content to abide by a quaint stereotype of Switzerland that's easily packaged and sold – the familiar Alpine idyll of cheese and chocolate, Heidi and the Matterhorn – while keeping the best bits for themselves. Come for a "Lakes and Mountains" package, or a week of skiing, or a short city-break, and you'll get all the pristine beauty, genteel calm and well-oiled efficiency of the Switzerland that the locals deem suitable for public consumption.

The other Switzerland – the one the Swiss inhabit – needs time and patience to winkle out of its shell, but can be an infinitely more rewarding place to explore.

Within this rugged environment, **community spirit** is perhaps stronger than anywhere else in Europe. Since the country is not an ethnic, linguistic or religious unity, it has survived – so the Swiss are fond of saying – simply through the will of its people to resolve their differences. Today, a unique style of "bottom-up" democracy ensures real power still rests with the people, who seem to vote almost monthly on a series of referenda affecting all aspects of life from local recycling projects to national economic policy. The constitution devolves power upwards from the people to municipal governments and up again to the regions (known as **cantons**), only as a last resort granting certain powers to the federal government.

This kind of decentralized structure means that the cantons – which are, in essence, tiny self-governing republics who have volunteered to join together – have mostly held onto their own, unique flavours. Although Swiss people value their shared Swissness above all, they also cherish their own home-town identity and their differences from their neighbours. Tensions exist between the four **language** communities, as they do between Catholic and Protestant, or between urban and rural areas, while **regional characteristics** remain sharply defined and diverse.

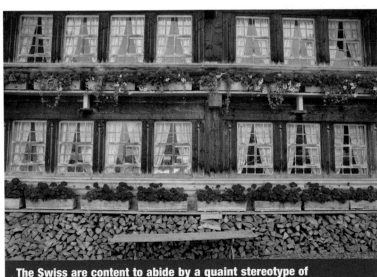

▶ Chalet, Emmental

The Swiss are content to abide by a quaint stereotype of Switzerland that's easily packaged and sold. The other Switzerland – the one the Swiss inhabit – needs time and patience to winkle out of its shell.

Schweiz, Suisse, Svizzera, Svizra

For such a tiny country, Switzerland is remarkably polyglot. There are four official languages: about two-thirds of the population have German as their first language; about a fifth French; six percent Italian; while Romansh, a direct descendant of Latin, has clung on in pockets of the mountainous southeast. Around one in ten people use English every day, and many Swiss are comfortably tri- or quadrilingual.

These language divisions are reflected in divisions of culture and identity. In the centre and the east, the old isolation of tight-knit mountain communities lingers on in Swiss German *Kantönligeist* ("little cantonal spirit"), a stubborn parochialism leavened by down-to-earth rumbustiousness.

To the west lies the *Röstigraben*, a comical but slightly discomfiting name given to the invisible language border – a *Graben* is a military trench – between French-speaking Switzerland, where they don't eat the traditional potato dish *rösti*, and German-speaking Switzerland, where they do.

Local pride is fuelled by a range of traditional **folkloric customs**, most of which stem from pagan or medieval Christian festivals. Most prominent of these is **carnival**, held around the country on or around Mardi Gras, the last day before Lent. The most exuberant celebrations, held in Luzern, Bern and Basel, feature bands, masked parades, street dancing and spontaneous partying that belie the stereotype of a placid, unadventurous Switzerland. A host of smaller events fills out the calendar and it's still easily possible to stumble on village festivals that have been staged by local people for centuries past.

This sense of cultural continuity sits oddly with the fact that Switzerland has grown into one of the world's **richest** countries. Its economy is small-scale but thoroughly modern: traditional industries such as watchmaking and textiles now thrive by focusing closely on the luxury end of the market and have ceded prime position to engineering, pharmaceuticals and service industries. **Tourism** has been a high earner since the mid-nineteenth century, when the Alps became both a fashionable destination for wealthy travellers and a prescribed retreat for sufferers from respiratory diseases needing curative sunshine and fresh mountain air. And yet the country still stands alone. In the 1940s, Switzerland was surrounded by hostile Axis powers; these days, it's encircled by the "friendly" EU. Switzerland's dogged **neutrality** rings ever more hollow – and yet, far from embracing a wider perspective, the country has collectively taken a step into conservatism. Commentators are noting sadly that Switzerland is only now embarking on the kind of multi-ethnic social integration that its neighbours began in the 1950s.

Having taken centuries to bolt their country together from diverse elements, the Swiss seem instinctively to return to their sense of community spirit, expressed most tangibly in the order and cleanliness you'll see on show everywhere. Yet the sterility so decried by Graham Greene (who wrote Harry Lime's jibe about brotherly love), if it characterizes any part of the country, applies only to the glossy, neatly packaged tourist idyll of lakes and mountains. The three great Swiss cities of Geneva, Zürich and Basel are crammed with world-class **museums** and galleries.

▶ Appenzell

Fact file

• Switzerland covers an **area** of 41,285 sq km – roughly the size of Wales or West Virginia. At the most it is 220km from north to south, and 348km from west to east. The highest point is the Dufourspitze at 4634m above sea level, the lowest is Lago Maggiore at 193m. The total **population** is around 7.4 million, of whom 5.9 million are Swiss citizens.

• The Swiss Confederation is ruled by a seven-member government called the **Federal Council**, with the presidency rotating annually between all seven members. Both this and the **Supreme Court** are elected by the bicameral **Parliament**. Constitutional amendments can be proposed by Parliament or by popular initiative, the latter requiring 100,000 signatures; in either case a referendum ensues, and a double majority – of votes cast both nationally and canton-by-canton – sees the proposal becoming law. 50,000 signatures can also put any existing law to a referendum.

• Each of the 26 **cantons** has its own constitution, parliament, government and courts, and there is also a good deal of autonomy vested in the 2942 **communes**, which vary in size from small, crowded city districts to thinly populated tracts of mountain terrain.

▼ Arosa Express

In Zürich and Lausanne, there's a humming arts scene and underground club culture that feeds **nightlife** as vibrant as anything you'll find in much larger European cities. The **landscapes** are dominated by the Alps and their foothills, but mountains aren't the only story. In the north and centre are lush, rolling grasslands epitomized by the velvety green hills of the Emmental, traditional dairy-farming country. Vineyards rise tiered above Lake Geneva, the Rhône valley and the Rhine. The southeast is cut through by wild, high-sided valleys, lonely, dark and thickly forested. Most surprisingly of all, bordering Italy in the south you'll find subtropical Mediterranean-style flower gardens, sugarloaf hills and sunny, palm-fringed lakes.

Switzerland may be a small, little-regarded mid-continental country with a serious image problem, but it has plenty more to offer than most visitors suspect.

Where to go – and when

Although Switzerland is best known for its mountain scenery, there are any number of hooks on which to hang a visit, whether you choose to stay in one city or resort, explore a region, or tour the whole country. Getting about is easy, with an unrivalled network of trains, buses and boats. You'll find places to stay and get a hearty meal wherever you end up, even in the wildest of mountain valleys.

CH

UK websites are suffixed .uk, France has .fr, Italy has .it – but Switzerland has **.ch**. For internet domains, as well as international postal services, vehicle registration and all sorts of other matters, Switzerland dodges the issue of its multilingualism and resorts to its Latin title: Confoederatio Helvetica, meaning the Helvetic (that is, Swiss) Confederation, universally abbreviated to **CH**.

The cities

Switzerland has no big metropolises on the scale of Paris or London. Swiss towns and cities were preserved from bombing in World War II, and all of them retain medieval alleys, houses and churches at their centres.

Geneva is positioned at the tip of the idyllic **Lake Geneva** in the south-west, a short distance from the graceful lakeside city of **Lausanne**. In the northeast, **Zürich** too is set on its own lake, within striking distance of the peaceful **Bodensee** (Lake Constance). The diminutive Swiss capital **Bern** has a fine cobbled Old Town, while equally attractive **Luzern** (Lucerne) lies in the centre of the country on its own, famously beautiful lake. **Basel** is located on the Rhine at the point where France, Germany and Switzerland

▲ The KKL, Luzern

▲ Château d'Oex balloon festival

meet, while at the opposite end of the country, **Lugano** basks on the shores of an azure lake a few kilometres from the Italian border.

Any of these – or smaller but no less characterful regional towns such as St Gallen, Schaffhausen, Neuchâtel, Chur, Fribourg, Sion or Bellinzona – could serve as a base for a relaxing short break, especially during the temperate **summer** months (June–Sept). At other times they can get distinctly chilly, although most receive generous dumps of **snow** in the winter, which, combined with glittering sunshine and frozen lakes and rivers, paints the most romantic of urban pictures.

The mountains

There are almost limitless possibilities for exploring the great outdoors. The **Alps** run in a band across the centre and south of the country, with resorts big and small – plus stunning scenery guaranteed. The two main **seasons** run from June to October, and from mid-December to mid-April; between these times, most mountain resorts close down altogether (see "Basics" p.72 for more).

The best-known Alpine region is the **Bernese Oberland**, focused around the tourist hub of **Interlaken** and boasting such famous names as **Wengen** and **Grindelwald**. To the south, in Valais, sit **Verbier**, **Crans Montana** and, at the foot of the iconic Matterhorn, **Zermatt**. In Graubünden in the southeast are **Davos**, **Klosters** and **St Moritz**. Justifiably popular, all these places boast some of the best winter skiing and summer hiking in Europe.

It's relatively easy in even the busiest centres (which are still nothing like the mega-resorts of the French and Italian Alps) to head off the beaten path and explore alone, or to aim for smaller, more manageable satellite resorts in adjacent side-valleys. However, you may prefer to shun the big names altogether and seek peace and quiet in the less frenetic hinterlands. Two regions stand out: in the northwest, the scrubby **Jura** mountains are an ideal landscape for long lonely walks and bike rides; while in the south, the wild valleys of **Alto Ticino** lace the southern foothills of the Alps with little-known hiking trails, a world away from the chic lakeside resort of **Locarno** nearby.

▲ The Eiger, Mönch and Jungfrau mountains, Schilthorn

Switzerland's climate

The table shows average monthly minimum and maximum temperatures (in °C), and average monthly precipitation (in mm) Precipitation patterns vary widely, with the northern cities (Bern, Zürich) experiencing more overcast skies than, for instance, Lugano, which tends to have long periods of sunshine occasionally punctuated by short downpours.

Average maximum and minimum daily temperatures and monthly precipitation

	Jan	Feb	Mar	Apr	May	Jun	July	Aug	Sep	Oct	Nov	Dec
Bern												
Av min °C	-5	-3	-1	3	8	10	11	11	8	4	-2	-5
Av max °C	0	4	9	13	18	20	21	20	17	11	5	0
Precipitation, mm	56	49	62	77	97	120	118	114	96	71	68	65
Davos												
Av min °C	-11	-11	-8	-4	1	4	8	7	4	0	-4	-8
Av max °C	-1	-1	3	8	10	14	18	18	14	10	7	1
Precipitation, mm	71	60	57	60	66	121	140	135	90	69	63	70
Geneva												
Av min °C	-2	-1	0	4	8	10	12	13	11	7	3	0
Av max °C	3	5	10	14	19	20	22	22	21	15	9	5
Precipitation, mm	63	57	55	50	67	92	64	96	102	77	84	59
Lugano												
Av min °C	-2	-1	2	6	9	11	14	14	11	9	5	0
Av max °C	6	8	11	17	20	23	28	29	25	19	13	8
Precipitation, mm	61	64	96	148	217	199	183	196	160	172	152	95
Sion												
Av min °C	-6	-3	1	3	8	10	11	10	9	4	0	-3
Av max °C	3	6	9	14	20	21	25	24	21	15	9	5
Precipitation, mm	51	45	40	37	39	46	50	64	65	50	53	62
Zürich												
Av min °C	-5	-2	0	3	9	11	13	13	11	8	2	-2
Av max °C	0	4	9	15	20	22	25	23	20	14	9	3
Precipitation, mm	75	70	64	81	108	137	144	135	110	80	76	64

26

things not to miss

It's not possible to see everything that Switzerland has to offer in one trip – and we don't suggest you try. What follows is a selective and subjective taste of the country's highlights: beautiful cities and lakes, top mountain resorts, spectacular train journeys and secluded Alpine getaways. They're arranged in five colour-coded categories to help you find the very best things to see, do and experience. All entries have a page reference to take you straight into the guide, where you can find out more.

01 **Winter sports** Page **72** • St Moritz offers some of the most scenic skiing and snowboarding anywhere in the Alps.

03 **Adventure sports** Page **379** • The area around Engelberg in Central Switzerland is one of the top destinations for canyoning, bungee-jumping and paragliding.

02 **Carnival** Page **369** • Switzerland has a long tradition of carnival, the best of the bunch being the Luzerner Fasnacht, a hedonistic weekend when thousands pack into Luzern's old town for parades, music and raucous merry-making.

04 **Lake Luzern** Page **366** • The most dramatically sited of all Switzerland's lakes, ringed by mist-wreathed cliffs.

05 **Walking** Page **69** • The high-level route from Schynige Platte past the Bachalpsee and down to Grindewald is just one of many memorably scenic walks throughout the Swiss Alps.

06 **Rösti** Page **58** • Nothing is more warming after a day out of doors than rösti, fried grated potato, here topped with melted cheese and an egg.

07 Bern Page **230** • Switzerland's uniquely attractive federal capital, loomed over by a giant cathedral tower, has a medieval street-plan that has survived unchanged for five centuries.

08 St Gallen Page **466** • The library of St Gallen's ancient abbey has one of the most impressive secular Rococo interiors in Europe.

09 Davos Page **498** • Boarders and freeriders will find that there are few better destinations in the world than Davos.

11 Montreux Jazz Festival Page **154** • Stellar annual music event in this ritzy lakeside resort; Isaac Hayes is just one of the top-drawer names in soul, dance, rock, world music, jazz and blues to have played in recent years.

10 Alto Ticino Page **534** • Giornico, with its picturesque bridge, is one of a string of attractive villages in the lush, high valleys of this Italian-speaking region that offer long, lonesome countryside rambles.

12 **Lake Geneva** Page **140** • From the vineyards of St-Saphorin on the Swiss shore of Lake Geneva, stunning views look westwards up the valley of the Rhône.

14 **Appenzell** Page **469** •
Endearingly old-fashioned dairy village, tucked away amidst hilly countryside that is ideal for long walks.

13 **The Matterhorn** Page **344** •
No mountain in the world is so immediately recognizable, dominating the horizon above the world-class skiing, snowboarding and hiking resort of Zermatt.

15 **Lugano** Page **549** • A chic lake resort spectacularly surrounded by sugar loaf hills.

16 **Bernese Oberland** Page **271** • You can enjoy classic Swiss Alpine scenery from Wengen village, one of a trio of beautifully sited resorts in the mighty Bernese Oberland that includes Mürren and Grindelwald.

17 **Geneva** Page **94** • At the centre of this most discreet, hard-working of cities stands a monument to Calvin and the Reformers, who proclaimed Geneva a "Protestant Rome" in the sixteenth century.

18 **Lausanne** Page **117** • Tiered above Lake Geneva and crowned by a stunning Gothic cathedral, Lausanne is Switzerland's most visually dramatic city.

19 **Rhätische Bahn** Page **484** • The southeastern corner of Switzerland is the setting for some of Europe's most spectacular train rides aboard the RhB.

21 Château de Chillon
Page **158** • Grand medieval castle, majestically located on the Lake Geneva shore.

20 Wine Page **60** • Switzerland's wine industry is modest but Swiss wines – some of the best of which come from near Sion – can compete on equal terms with better-known labels from around the world.

23 Schaffhausen Page **452** • This quiet, little-visited market town, replete with medieval frescoed mansions, stands just upstream from the mighty Rhine falls.

22 Stay in an igloo Page **379** • Either build your own and spend a night in the icy wilderness, or opt for a ready-made and more luxurious version.

24 **Zürich** Page **417** • Beneath a medieval cityscape of spires and steeples, Zürich's old town is filled with cobbled lanes and courtyards to explore.

25 **St Moritz** Page **511** • Switzerland's sunniest mountain resort, boasting outstanding skiing and snowboarding as well as the infamous Cresta Run luge course.

26 **Basel** Page **201** • Ancient Rhine-side city straddling the French and German borders, enhanced by fine medieval architecture and one of Switzerland's best art museums.

Basics

THE SWISS CANTONS

GERMANY

FRANCE

LIECHTENSTEIN (FL)

AUSTRIA

ITALY

N

0   50 km

Schaffhausen · SH

Basel · BS

Liestal · BL

Delémont · JU

Aarau · AG

Solothurn · SO

Zürich · ZH

TG · Frauenfeld

St Gallen

Herisau · AR · AI · Appenzell

SG

Luzern · LU

Zug · ZG

SZ · Schwyz

Glarus · GL

Neuchâtel · NE

Bern · BE

Stans · NW

Sarnen · OW

Altdorf · UR

Chur · GR

Fribourg · FR

VD

Lausanne

GE · Geneva

Sion

VS

TI · Bellinzona

Given is the date of accession to the Confederation, the name (in the local language only), the standard two-letter abbreviation, and the cantonal capital.

1291	**Uri (UR)** – Altdorf	1501	**Schaffhausen (SH)** – Schaffhausen
1291	**Schwyz (SZ)** – Schwyz	1513	**Appenzell Ausserrhoden (AR)** – Herisau
1291	**Obwalden (OW)** – Sarnen	1513	**Appenzell Innerrhoden (AI)** – Appenzell
1291	**Nidwalden (NW)** – Stans	1803	**St Gallen (SG)** – St Gallen
1332	**Luzern (LU)** – Luzern	1803	**Graubünden (GR)** – Chur
1351	**Zürich (ZH)** – Zürich	1803	**Aargau (AG)** – Aarau
1352	**Glarus (GL)** – Glarus	1803	**Thurgau (TG)** – Frauenfeld
1352	**Zug (ZG)** – Zug	1803	**Ticino (TI)** – Bellinzona
1353	**Bern (BE)** – Bern	1803	**Vaud (VD)** – Lausanne
1481	**Fribourg (FR)** – Fribourg	1815	**Valais (VS)** – Sion
1481	**Solothurn (SO)** – Solothurn	1815	**Neuchâtel (NE)** – Neuchâtel
1501	**Basel-Stadt (BS)** – Basel	1815	**Geneva (GE)** – Geneva
1501	**Basel-Land (BL)** – Liestal	1979	**Jura (JU)** – Delémont

Basics

quotes here include taxes and charges. For the cheapest fares, always book online.

On any of the **no-frills airlines**, if you book far enough in advance – several weeks at least – you should be able to find a ticket for £50–70 return, but these rates often apply only to midweek early morning or late evening flights, and are generally non-refundable and non-exchangeable. For more convenient flight times, you may be looking at £100–150 return, a price the **full-service airlines** can often match or undercut.

Airlines in the UK

bmibaby ☎0871/224 0224, @www.bmibaby.com.
British Airways ☎0870/850 9850, @www
.ba.com.
Darwin Airline ☎00800/1771 7777, @www
.darwinairline.com.
easyJet ☎0905/560 7777, @www.easyjet.com.
Flybe ☎0871/700 0535, @www.flybe.com.
Helvetic ☎020/7026 3464, @www.helvetic.com.
Jet2 ☎0871/226 1737, @www.jet2.com.
Ryanair ☎0906/270 5656, @www.ryanair.com.
Swiss ☎0845/601 0956, @www.swiss.com.

Flight agents in the UK

Cheapflights @www.cheapflights.co.uk.
ebookers @www.ebookers.com.
Expedia @www.expedia.co.uk.
Lastminute.com @www.lastminute.com.
Opodo @www.opodo.co.uk.

By train from the UK

Travelling by **train** still has much of its old leisurely romance and can be a scenic and relaxing way to get to Switzerland – although rarely as cheap as flying. Time is also a factor: the fastest route London–Geneva (which still involves changing trains in Paris), takes about 7hr 30min.

Eurostar runs passenger trains from London through the Channel Tunnel direct to **Paris-Gare du Nord**. Until 2007, they depart from **London Waterloo** (journey time 2hr 35min). After 2007, they depart from **London St Pancras** (journey time 2hr 15min).

From Paris, many trains serve Switzerland, but not from the Gare du Nord, and also not from one single station, meaning you have to plan your route in advance and be prepared to lug your bags through the Paris metro. From **Paris-Gare de Lyon**, high-speed

TGV trains (for which you must pay a small supplement) depart throughout the day on three different routes: to Geneva (3hr 25min); and under the Lyria brand (@www.lyria.biz) to Lausanne (3hr 45min) – continuing on some trips to Martigny and Brig (6hr) – or to Bern (4hr 30min) and Zürich (6hr). From **Paris-Gare de l'Est**, handily situated beside the Gare du Nord, non-TGV trains depart frequently to Bâle/Basel (5hr).

There is complete **timetable information** on all trains from London to any station (or bus stop, cable car or ferry halt) in Switzerland at **@www.rail.ch**.
Eurostar ☎0870/160 6600, @www.eurostar.com.
Rail Europe ☎0870/837 1371, @www
.raileurope.co.uk.
Swiss Federal Railways Freephone
☎00800/100 200 30, @www.rail.ch.

Driving from the UK

Switzerland is just about within reach of the UK on a day's *drive*: the Swiss border is very roughly 850km from the Channel coast and, given an early start and clear *autoroutes*, you could be in Basel, or even Bern or Lausanne, for dinner.

It makes most sense to aim for Calais. This route benefits from rapid Eurotunnel service and avoids large cities in France, but the motorway runs out as you approach the Jura mountains, forcing you onto main roads instead.

Eurotunnel runs shuttle trains for vehicles between Folkestone and Coquelles, near Calais, via the **Channel Tunnel**. You can just turn up and go, though booking is advisable. Boarding is quick and easy – there are frequent departures, 24 hours a day – and the journey takes a smooth, hassle-free 35–45 minutes. **Ferries** and **catamarans** between Dover and Calais are operated by a changing roster of companies – currently P&O and Sea France.

Fares vary a lot; travelling between 10pm and 6am can cut costs, while travelling at weekends, or in July and August, adds a premium. Booking ahead, a return ticket by ferry or Eurotunnel during the summer peak could be as low as £100 per car, though last-minute fares are much higher.
Eurotunnel ☎0870/535 3535, @www
.eurotunnel.com.

P&O Ferries ☎0870/598 0333, ⓦwww.poferries
.com.
Sea France ☎0870/571 1711, ⓦwww.seafrance
.com.

From Ireland

From Ireland, the daily nonstop flights from
Dublin to Zürich on Swiss are around €200–
250 return, matched by Aer Lingus's less
regular service to Zürich and Geneva. On
Swiss, transfers which fly you to Zürich and
then double back to Geneva or Basel might
seem counterproductive, but connection
times at Zürich are so well coordinated that
they can save time on other airlines' routings,
such as BA via Heathrow. Flying Ryanair
into Stansted, then on to Friedrichshafen in
Germany (from where eastern Switzerland is
a ferry ride away) saves little.
Aer Lingus ☎0818/365 000, ⓦwww.aerlingus
.com.
British Airways ☎1890/626 747, ⓦwww
.ba.com.
Ryanair ☎1530/787 787, ⓦwww.ryanair.com.
Swiss ☎01/806 7430, ⓦwww.swiss.com.

From North America

From North America several airlines fly
nonstop to Switzerland, and many others
have flights via other European hubs. Swiss
(a subsidiary of Lufthansa) is first choice,
flying into Zürich daily from a fistful of US
cities plus Montréal. Swiss codeshares
with American out of JFK and United out of
Washington, giving access to both carriers'
domestic networks, as well as Air Canada
out of Toronto. The lowest **fares** – always
found online – are around US$500–700
round-trip from the East Coast, perhaps
$250–450 more from the West Coast. Flying
in peak season adds $350–550. You may find
cheaper deals than this on routings via other
European hubs – for example Air France via
Paris, or British Airways via London.
Air Canada ☎1-888/247-2262, ⓦwww
.aircanada.com.
Air France US ☎1-800/237-2747, Canada
☎1-800/667-2747, ⓦwww.airfrance.com.
American Airlines ☎1-800/433-7300, ⓦwww
.aa.com.
British Airways ☎1-800/AIRWAYS (247-9297),
ⓦwww.ba.com.
Cheapflights.com ⓦwww.cheapflights.com &
www.cheapflights.ca.

Expedia ⓦwww.expedia.com & www.expedia.ca.
Lufthansa US ☎1-800/399-5838, Canada
☎1-800/563-5954, ⓦwww.lufthansa.com.
STA Travel ☎1-800/781-4040, ⓦwww.statravel
.com.
Swiss ☎1-877/FLY-SWISS (359-7947), ⓦwww
.swiss.com.
Travel Cuts US ☎1-800/592-CUTS (2887),
Canada ☎1-866/246-9762, ⓦwww.travelcuts
.com.
Travelocity ⓦwww.travelocity.com & www
.travelocity.ca.

From Australia and New Zealand

From Australia and New Zealand there
are no direct flights to Switzerland, although
there's plenty of choice to Zürich via major
Asian hubs. The most convenient routings
going west are with Thai or Malaysian, who
both codeshare with Swiss from Australian
cities and Auckland to Bangkok and KL,
and on to Zürich, or on Qantas (also a Swiss
codeshare partner) from Sydney to Zürich via
Frankfurt and either Singapore or Bangkok.
Going via London may be cheaper, but adds
several hours onto your journey time. Heading east with Qantas, Air NZ, United or American to Los Angeles, from where Swiss fly
nonstop to Zürich, is another viable option.

Fares vary tremendously. Expect A$1800–
2800 from Australia, roughly NZ$2000–3000
from Auckland. Thai and Malaysian fall at the
lower end of this bracket, Qantas, BA, Swiss
and the rest at the higher end.
Air New Zealand Australia ☎13 24 76, NZ
☎0800/737 000, ⓦwww.airnz.com.
American Airlines Australia ☎1300/650 747, NZ
☎0800/887 997, ⓦwww.aa.com.
British Airways Australia ☎1300/767 177, NZ
☎09/966 9777, ⓦwww.ba.com.
Malaysia Airlines Australia ☎13 26 27, NZ
☎0800/777 747, ⓦwww.mas.com.my.
Qantas Australia ☎13 13 13, NZ ☎00800/0014
0014, ⓦwww.qantas.com.
Swiss Australia ☎1800/883 199, NZ ☎09/977
2238, ⓦwww.swiss.com.
Thai Airways Australia ☎1300/651 960, NZ
☎09/377 3886, ⓦwww.thaiair.com.
United Airlines Australia ☎13 17 77, ⓦwww
.united.com.

Flight agents in Australia & NZ

Cheapflights.com ⓦwww.cheapflights.com.au.

Fly less – stay longer! Travel and climate change

Climate change is a serious threat to the ecosystems that humans rely upon, and air travel is the fastest-growing contributor to the problem. Rough Guides regard travel, overall, as a global benefit, and feel strongly that the advantages to developing economies are important, as is the opportunity of greater contact and awareness among peoples. But we all have a responsibility to limit our personal impact on global warming, and that means giving thought to how often we fly, and what we can do to redress the harm that our trips create.

Flying and climate change

Pretty much every form of motorized travel generates CO_2 (the main cause of human-induced climate change) but planes are far and away the worst offenders, not just because of the sheer distances they allow us to travel, but because they release a selection of greenhouse gases high into the atmosphere. The statistics are frightening: two people taking a return flight between Europe and the US will contribute as much to climate change as an average household's gas and electricity over a whole year.

Fuel-cell and other less harmful types of plane may emerge eventually. But until then, there are really just two options for concerned travellers: to reduce the amount we travel by air (take fewer trips – stay for longer!), and to make the trips we do take "climate neutral" via a carbon offset scheme.

Carbon offset schemes

Offset schemes run by climatecare.org, carbonneutral.com and others allow you to make up for some or all of the greenhouse gases that you are responsible for releasing. To do this, they provide "carbon calculators" for working out the global-warming contribution of a specific flight (or even your entire existence), and then let you contribute an appropriate amount of money to fund offsetting measures. These include rainforest and other indigenous reforestation, and initiatives to reduce future energy demand – often run in conjunction with sustainable development schemes.

Rough Guides, together with Lonely Planet and other concerned partners in the travel industry, are supporting a carbon offset scheme run by climatecare.org.

Please take the time to view our website and see how you can help to make your trip climate-neutral.

Ⓦ **www.roughguides.com/climatechange**

CIT Australia ☎02/9267 1255, Ⓦwww.cittravel .com.au.
Flight Centre Australia ☎13 31 33, NZ ☎0800/243 544, Ⓦwww.flightcentre.com.
Lastminute.com Ⓦwww.lastminute.com.au.
STA Travel Australia ☎1300/733 035, NZ ☎0508/782 872, Ⓦwww.statravel.com.
Travelshop Ⓦwww.travelshop.com.au.

Packages and organized tours

Package tours cover a wealth of possibilities. In addition to fully escorted, many agents can put together very flexible deals, sometimes amounting to no more than a flight plus car or rail pass and accommodation; if you're planning to travel in moderate or luxury style, and especially if your trip is geared around special interests, such

packages can work out cheaper than the same arrangements made on arrival.

Ski packages

Most agents offering **ski** holidays in the Alps include at least one or two Swiss destinations. Packages tend to include flights, transfers and half-board accommodation (breakfast and an evening meal), but exclude lift passes. Prices vary tremendously depending on the operator, the resort, the style of accommodation and the time of the season. For more, see p.27.

Accommodation is almost always of high quality: standard two- and three-star resort hotels abound, although deals in Verbier, for instance (which doesn't have a great range of hotels), or Zermatt, can include a choice of **catered chalets**, which sleep anything from two people to a group of fifteen or more. Free or discounted **extras** to look out for include lift passes, equipment, lessons, train passes and reductions for children. Most UK operators also offer car-rental that can cut well over £100 per person off a package price if you choose to drive to and from Switzerland.

"Lakes and Mountains" and other packages

Most travel agents tout packages to Switzerland, often under a "Lakes and Mountains" title. The most famous destinations are Interlaken and Luzern, which offer a wide choice of hotels; prices drop if you choose self-catering accommodation, or stay in less famous lakeside resorts.

Specialist companies worldwide offer summer **walking holidays**, mostly following the high Alpine routes around Mont Blanc and the Matterhorn, and also in the Bernese Oberland. These can be a great way for experienced hikers and novices alike to get well off the beaten path. Some put you up in campsites, others use mountain huts and refuges, and a few may include vehicle support or porterage. All stick to small groups of 10–15 people. In the same vein, **cycling holidays** are becoming more popular, taking advantage of Switzerland's extensive cycle-path network and high degree of trail support. Some operators make use of the outstanding Swiss public transport system to offer holidays that link together series of **rail journeys** on classic Alpine routes.

A few UK operators offer **city-breaks** in summer or winter. For minimum hassle, these can be excellent value (especially in low season), often including a discount travel card. Favoured destinations are Geneva, Lausanne, Bern, Luzern and Zürich, but some operators go to Lugano or Basel, as well as mountain resorts such as Zermatt, Wengen or Mürren.

Tour operators in the UK

British Airways Holidays ⓦ www.baholidays .com. Year-round city-break packages.
Crystal Holidays ⓦ www.crystalholidays. co.uk. Well-respected winter sports specialists, with

destinations including all the top names plus less well-known resorts. Also standard summer city-breaks and "Lakes and Mountains" deals.
Exodus ☎ 020/8675 5550, ⓦ www.exodus.co.uk. Experienced adventure tour operator running excellent small-group walking tours in the Swiss Alps at all levels of difficulty, plus novelty expeditions such as snowshoe trekking.
Great Rail Journeys ☎ 01904/521 936, ⓦ www .greatrail.com. Specialists in train tours, with a full range of classic Alpine journeys.
Inghams ☎ 020/8780 4433, ⓦ www.inghams .co.uk. Major operator with summer and winter packages of all kinds, competitive prices and plenty of experience. Especially strong on ski deals.
Interhome ☎ 020/8891 1294, ⓦ www.interhome .co.uk. Has a massive, easily searchable database of self-catering holiday homes and apartments in towns and villages all over Switzerland.
Keycamp ☎ 0870/700 0740, ⓦ www.keycamp.co .uk. Specialists in summer camping and mobile-home holidays at Alpine sites, with good deals for families.
Kuoni ☎ 01306/747002, ⓦ www.kuoni.co.uk. A wealth of flexible summer and winter package holidays around Switzerland, taking in all the major resorts and most of the minor ones, with good family offers.
MyTravel ☎ 0870/238 7710, ⓦ www.mytravel .com. Standard, cheap package deals.
Naturetrek ☎ 01962/733051, ⓦ www.naturetrek .co.uk. Acknowledged leaders in birdwatching and botanical holidays worldwide, offering sympathetic, expert guidance for small-group summer tours to the Alps.
Plus Travel ☎ 020/7420 4900, ⓦ www.plustravel .co.uk. Commercial arm of the official Switzerland Travel Centre, with city-breaks, fly-drives, tailor-mades and combination possibilities around the country. Options include train itineraries, bike or adventure holidays and gourmet tours, as well as plenty of more orthodox packages and skiing at resorts big and small.
Powder Byrne ☎ 020/8246 5300, ⓦ www .powderbyrne.com. Slick, upmarket ski and summer operator, with a Swiss office and plenty of choice at major hotels in top resorts.
Snow Line ☎ 0870/050 7025, ⓦ www.snow-line .co.uk. Major ski operator, with a good, diverse range of options.
Swiss Travel Service ☎ 0870/191 7145, ⓦ www.swisstravel.co.uk. Specialist tour operators with a wealth of experience and local knowledge. Almost limitless choices around the country, covering one-centre and two-centre packages, city-breaks, train tours, walking weeks, golf holidays, adventure excursions and biking, farmhouse stays, health and beauty holidays, even open-air painting tuition for

budding Alpine artists. Winter skiing possibilities are equally comprehensive.

Waymark ☎01753/516 477, ⓦww
.waymarkholidays.co.uk. Small operator specializing in walking and cross-country skiing packages to lesser-known resorts around Switzerland.

Tour operators in North America

Abercrombie & Kent ☎1-800/323-7308 or 630/954-2944, ⓦwww.abercrombiekent.com. Five-star guided sightseeing tours and customized tours with a heavy accent on resort towns like St Moritz and the scenery of the Alpine rail routes.
Above the Clouds Trekking ☎1-800/233-4499 or 802/482-4848, ⓦwww.aboveclouds.com. Summer trekking tours in the Swiss Alps.
Adventure Center ☎1-800/228-8747 or 510/654-1879, ⓦwww.adventurecenter.com. Lots of different trekking trips in the Swiss, French and Italian Alps; be prepared to camp the whole way.
Adventures Abroad ☎1-800/665-3998 or 360/775-9926, ⓦwww.adventures-abroad.com. Adventure specialists, with plenty of Swiss options.
CBT Tours ☎1-800/736-2453 or 312/475-0625, ⓦwww.cbttours.com. A variety of mountain biking tours, some including hiking.
Ciao Travel ☎1-800/942-2426, ⓦwww
.ciaotravel.com. Jazz festival specialists, with tours to the Montreux Jazz Festival and others.
Euro-Bike & Walking Tours ☎1-800/321-6060, ⓦwww.eurobike.com. A good selection of cycling and hiking holidays.
Europe Train Tours ☎1-800/551-2085 or 845/758-1777, ⓦwww.etttours.com. Plenty of options for seeing Switzerland from the rails.
Himalayan Travel ☎1-800/225-2380 or 203/743-2349, ⓦwww.himalayantravelinc.com. Independent and guided hiking trips on various routes in the Swiss Alps.
Maupintour ☎1-800/255-4266, ⓦwww
.maupintour.com. Luxury tours by train through Switzerland and Austria.
Mountain Travel Sobek ☎1-888/MTSOBEK or 510/527-8100, ⓦwww.mtsobek.com. A broad selection of mountain hiking tours, including, unusually, in the Ticino.
Rail Europe US ☎1-877/257-2887, Canada ☎1-800/361-RAIL, ⓦwww.raileurope.com. Rail, air, hotel and car reservations.
Switzerland Tourism ⓦwww.myswitzerland
.com. From the horse's mouth: a vast range of tours and breaks of all kinds, from art and culture to inline skating to spa and wellbeing retreats.
Wilderness Travel ☎1-800/368-2794 or 510/558-2488, ⓦwww.wildernesstravel.com. Supported hikes in the Swiss mountains.

Tour operators in Australia & NZ

Adventure World Australia ☎02/8913 0755, ⓦwww.adventureworld.com.au, New Zealand ☎09/524 5118, ⓦwww.adventureworld.co.nz. Agents for a vast array of international adventure travel companies.
CIT Australia ☎02/9267 1255, ⓦwww.cittravel
.com.au. Tours of the Swiss and Italian lakes.
Explore Holidays Australia ☎02/9857 6200 or 1300/731 000, ⓦwww.exploreholidays.com.au. Accommodation and package tours to Switzerland.
Ski and Snowboard Travel Australia ☎02/9955 5201, ⓦwww.skiandsnowboard.com.au. Customized skiing holidays.
Swiss Travel Centre ☎1800 251 911, ⓦwww.swisstravel.com.au. Far and away the widest choice and sharpest knowledge. Specialist operator for escorted tours and ski packages, and can book car rental, train passes and inexpensive accommodation.
Switzerland Tourism ⓦwww.myswitzerland
.com. See above.
Travel Plan Australia ☎02/9958 1888 or 1300/130 754, ⓦwww.travelplan.com.au. Top choice ski operator, with a wide choice of packages to Swiss resorts.
Walkabout Gourmet Adventures Australia ☎03/5159 6556, ⓦwww.walkaboutgourmet.com. Classy food, wine and walking tours.

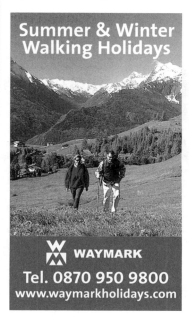

Summer & Winter Walking Holidays

Red tape and visas

All EU nationals and citizens of the US, Canada, Australia and New Zealand need only a valid passport to visit Switzerland and Liechtenstein, neither of which are members of the EU. In theory, stays are limited to a three-month maximum per trip, and six months total per year, but in practice border officials rarely stamp passports unless asked.

Duty-free allowances for visitors are 2 litres of alcohol under 15 percent, 1 litre of alcohol over 15 percent, and 200 cigarettes or 50 cigars or 250g of tobacco (for visitors arriving from Europe) or 400 cigarettes or 100 cigars or 500g of tobacco (for visitors arriving from outside Europe). There are no restrictions on the import of currency. ⓦ www.zoll.admin.ch has full information.

Swiss embassies abroad

Full listing at ⓦ www.eda.admin.ch.
Australia 7 Melbourne Ave, Forrest, ACT 2603 ☎ 02/6162 8400, ⓦ www.eda.admin.ch/australia. Consulates in Adelaide, Brisbane, Darwin, Hobart, Melbourne, Perth and Sydney.

Canada 5 Marlborough Ave, Ottawa, ON, K1N 8E6 ☎ 613/235-1837, ⓦ www.eda.admin.ch/canada. Consulates in Edmonton, Halifax, Montréal, Québec, Toronto, Vancouver and Winnipeg.
Ireland 6 Ailesbury Rd, Ballsbridge, Dublin 4 ☎ 01/218 6382, ⓦ www.swissembassy.ie.
New Zealand 22 Panama St, Wellington ☎ 04/472 1593. Consulate in Auckland.
UK 16–18 Montagu Place, London W1H 2BQ ☎ 020/7616 6000, ⓦ www.swissembassy.org.uk. Consulate in Manchester.
USA 2900 Cathedral Ave NW, Washington DC 20008 ☎ 202/745-7900, ⓦ www.swissemb .org. Consulates in Atlanta, Chicago, Houston, Los Angeles, New York, San Francisco and other cities.

Information and maps

Information on Switzerland is easy to come by: the Swiss tourist industry has had 150 years to refine its approach to visitors, and the efficient, super-helpful tourist offices in Switzerland, abroad and online are only too happy to regale you with exhaustive detail on any city, region or the whole country.

All cities, virtually all towns, and a size-able number of villages have a **tourist office** (*Verkehrsverein, Verkehrsbüro* or *Tourismus, Office du Tourisme, Ente Turistico*), pretty much always located next to, opposite, or within five minutes' walk of, the train station, and invariably signposted on approach roads. Most staff nationwide speak at least some English and are scrupulously helpful. They can provide you with city or town maps (free, or costing a franc or two), lists of hotels, restaurants, campsites and apartment rentals, and information on local sights and events, as well as detailed hiking maps and guides to the surrounding area and transport informa-tion. Some sell transport tickets and parking permits. Most offices will phone around local hotels to book a room for you for free, and some extend the service nationwide (for which a fee – Fr.10 or so – is usually charged).

Beware of **seasonal opening hours**: in the low season (in the mountains this means mid-Oct to mid-Dec plus April & May; elsewhere Sept–June), most tourist offices outside major cities and resorts operate on limited hours, perhaps only Mon–Fri 9am–noon and 2–5pm, plus two or three hours on Saturday morning. Outside these times, it's still worth going to the office: many keep racks of leaflets outside for passers-by to take and almost all post lists of hotels, restaurants and forthcoming events in the window. Alternatively, you could check the local tourist office website for information, or ask at the train station, where staff generally keep a small stock of maps and pamphlets behind the counter.

Switzerland Tourism

Worldwide ⓦ www.myswitzerland.com.
UK & Ireland 30 Bedford St, London WC2E 9ED. Freephone ☎ 00800/100 200 30.
US & Canada 608 5th Ave, New York, NY 10020. Toll-free from US ☎ 1-877/SWITZERLAND (794-8037), toll-free from Canada ☎ 011800/100 200 30.
Other countries PO Box 695, CH-8027 Zürich. Either call the international toll-free number ☎ +800/100 200 30 (add your international prefix: 0011 from Australia, 00 from New Zealand, etc), or call direct to Zürich ☎ +4144/288 1111.

Online

There's a vast quantity of useful information **online**. Switzerland Tourism, the national tourist organization, has an encyclopedic homepage at ⓦ www.MySwitzerland .com, with virtual tours around every resort, weather and snow forecasts, live pictures,

stacks of background information, booking details, special offers and tons more. "Hôtellerie Suisse", the Swiss Hotel Association, has a full listing at ⓦ www.swisshotels.ch of their thousands of quality-controlled hotels nationwide, and last-minute offers for cut-price multi-night deals.

Most individual cities and resorts run efficient and informative sites geared towards tourists, which we've flagged in the guide text where relevant (often they're just the town name prefixed by "www" and suffixed by "ch").

The best source of Swiss news is ⓦ www .swissinfo.org, which also has a massive archive of background material and features. For detailed weather forecasts, go to ⓦ www.meteoswiss.ch.

Maps

Our **maps** of town centres and regions should be fine for most purposes; otherwise tourist offices always have town maps to give out, either free or for a franc or two.

The best-respected commercial series – which depicts Switzerland's varied terrain superbly well – is that published by the Federal Office of Topography (ⓦ www .swisstopo.ch); they do a full range starting at 1:1 million, including an excellent full-country two-sheet set (1:200,000) updated annually, detailed 1:100,000 regional maps and 1:50,000 and 1:25,000 hikers' maps, as well as specialist maps on different scales detailing cycling and inline-skating routes, ski runs, historic sites, vineyards, cultural attractions and more. All can be ordered online; major map bookshops worldwide (such as Stanfords in London) stock most sheets, and

Swiss Museum Passport (SMP)

The **Swiss Museum Passport** (*Schweizer Museumspass, Passeport musées suisses, Passaporto musei svizzeri*) gives free entry to roughly 400 museums, galleries and castles around the country; full details are at ⓦ **www.museumspass.ch**. The pass, plus a little booklet giving addresses and opening days of all the places included, costs Fr.111 for a year. An Adult Plus pass (Fr.122) covers one adult and up to five children; a family pass (Fr.202) covers two adults and their offspring.

However, if you buy a Swiss Pass or Swiss Flexi Pass (or their youth versions) for travel by public transport – details of which are on p.41 – the full benefits of the Museum Passport are automatically included.

In the guide chapters, we've indicated those museums and attractions that offer free admission to Museum Passport holders with "**SMP**".

many general bookshops in Swiss towns and cities sell a wide selection.

Hallwag and **Kümmerly & Frey** are two major Swiss cartographic publishers with worldwide distribution and a host of products on many different scales.

Map outlets

UK and Ireland

Blackwell's Map Centre 50 Broad St, Oxford ☎ 01865/793 550, 🖳 maps.blackwell.co.uk. Branches around the country.
The Map Shop 30a Belvoir St, Leicester ☎ 0116/247 1400, 🖳 www.mapshopleicester.co.uk.
National Map Centre Ireland 34 Aungier St, Dublin ☎ 01/476 0471, 🖳 www.mapcentre.ie.
Stanfords 12–14 Long Acre, London WC2 ☎ 020/7836 1321, 🖳 www.stanfords.co.uk. Also at 39 Spring Gardens, Manchester ☎ 0161/831 0250, and 29 Corn St, Bristol ☎ 0117/929 9966. One of the best travel bookshops in the world, with expert knowledge and worldwide mail order.
The Travel Bookshop 13–15 Blenheim Crescent, London W11 ☎ 020/7229 5260, 🖳 www .thetravelbookshop.co.uk.

North America

The giant US map wholesalers Map Link (🖳 www.maplink.com) has a useful list of specialist map/travel bookstores in every US state, as well as some worldwide; click on Retail Partners.
Book Passage 51 Tamal Vista Blvd, Corte Madera, CA 94925 ☎ 1-800/999-7909, 🖳 www .bookpassage.com.
Globe Corner Bookstore 28 Church St, Cambridge, MA 02138 ☎ 1-800/358-6013, 🖳 www.globecorner.com.
Longitude Books 115 W 30th St #1206, New York, NY 10001 ☎ 1-800/342-2164, 🖳 www .longitudebooks.com.
Travel Bug Bookstore 3065 W Broadway, Vancouver, BC, V6K 2G9 ☎ 604/737-1122, 🖳 www .travelbugbooks.ca.
World of Maps 1235 Wellington St, Ottawa, ON, K1Y 3A3 ☎ 1-800/214-8524, 🖳 www.worldofmaps .com.

Australia and New Zealand

Map Centre 🖳 www.mapcentre.co.nz.
Mapland 372 Little Bourke St, Melbourne ☎ 03/9670 4383, 🖳 www.mapland.com.au.
Map World 371 Pitt St, Sydney ☎ 02/9261 3601, 🖳 www.mapworld.net.au. Also at 900 Hay St, Perth ☎ 08/9322 5733.
Map World 173 Gloucester St, Christchurch ☎ 0800/627 967, 🖳 www.mapworld.co.nz.

Insurance and health

Even for travel in a supposedly "safe" country such as Switzerland, it's advisable to have good travel insurance. Aside from absorbing the horrendous costs of medical emergencies and treatment (break an ankle on a mountain path and you might need a Fr.50,000 helicopter rescue), insurance also covers the loss or theft of your property, flight tickets and money. Many companies will tailor policies for you if you plan on going skiing, or if you want to take part in other "dangerous" sports or adventure activities.

Before paying for a new policy, it's worth checking whether you're already covered: some all-risks home insurance policies may cover your possessions when overseas, and many private medical schemes include cover when abroad. In Canada, provincial health plans usually provide partial cover for medical mishaps overseas, while holders of official student/teacher/youth cards in Canada and the US are entitled to meagre accident coverage and hospital in-patient benefits. Students will often find that their student health coverage extends during the vacations and for one term beyond the date of last enrolment.

After exhausting these possibilities, you might want to contact a specialist travel insurance company, or consider the travel insurance deal offered by Rough Guides (see box). A typical policy usually provides cover for the loss of baggage, tickets and – up to a certain limit – cash or cheques, as well as cancellation or curtailment of your journey. Many policies can be chopped and changed to exclude coverage you don't need: sickness and accident benefits can often be excluded or included at will. If you do take medical coverage, ascertain whether benefits will be paid as treatment proceeds or only after your return home, and whether there's a 24-hour medical emergency number. When securing baggage cover, make sure that the per-article limit – typically under £500/$750 – will cover your most valuable possession. If you need to make a claim, you should keep all receipts, and in the event you have anything stolen, you must obtain an official statement from the police.

Health

If you're arriving from Europe, North America or Australasia, you don't need any jabs. Virtually all travellers' afflictions arise from a lack of awareness of the impact of the high Alpine environment on those used to lowland life.

EU citizens are entitled to discounted emergency medical care in Switzerland and Liechtenstein on production of an **EHIC** (European Health Insurance Card), available in Britain from post offices and online at ⓦ www.dh.gov.uk (click on "Health advice for travellers"). You normally have to pay the full cost of treatment upfront – which never comes cheap – and claim it back when you get home (minus a small excess); make very sure you hang onto full doctors' reports, signed prescription details and ALL receipts to back up your claim.

Every village and town district has a rota system whereby one local **pharmacy** (*Apotheke, pharmacie, farmacia*) stays open outside shopping hours: each pharmacy will have a sign in the window telling you where the nearest open one is, or you could ask your hotel reception to phone the operator on ☏ 111 to get an address. Local newspapers also have details. Virtually every Swiss **hospital** (*Spital, hôpital, ospedale*) has some kind of 24-hour emergency service. Wherever possible, seek advice from your embassy in Bern as well as your insurer at home before getting hospital treatment.

Health issues

You can get **sunburnt** very quickly in the mountains, due to the combination of a thin atmosphere and reflection off snow, ice and/ or water. High-factor sunscreen, a hat and total sunblock for lips, nose and ears are essential. Reflection of the sun's glare can

Rough Guides travel insurance

Rough Guides has teamed up with Columbus Direct to offer you travel insurance that can be tailored to suit your needs.

Readers can choose from many different travel insurance products, including a low-cost backpacker option for long stays; a short-break option for city getaways; a typical holiday package option; and many others. There are also annual multi-trip policies for those who travel regularly, with variable levels of cover available. Different sports and activities (trekking, skiing, etc) can be covered if required on most policies.

Rough Guides travel insurance is available to the residents of 36 different countries with different language options to choose from via our website – ⓦ **www.roughguidesinsurance.com** – where you can also purchase the insurance.

Alternatively, UK residents should call ☏ 0800 083 9507; US citizens should call ☏ 1-800 749-4922; Australians should call ☏ 1300 669 999. All other nationalities should call ☏ +44 870 890 2843.

also damage your eyes, so always wear UV-protective sunglasses or a ski visor.

Hypothermia, when the body loses heat faster than it can conserve it, is most often brought on by a combination of cold, wind and driving rain, with hunger and fatigue also playing their part. Symptoms include exhaustion, lethargy or dizziness, shivering, numbness in the extremities and slurring of speech. In these initial stages, you must get the sufferer out of the elements and under cover, replace any of their clothing that is wet (with your own dry garments if necessary), give them hot liquids and high-calorie sugary

| **Ambulance emergency** ☎144 |

foods such as chocolate, and encourage and reassure them by talking. Despite the Alpine heroics of brandy-laden St Bernard dogs in the past, alcohol is a bad idea at such a critical time.

Virtually all high-altitude walks in Switzerland stay below 3000m, the rough cut-off point above which **altitude sickness** can kick in. If the symptoms of headaches, dizziness and breathlessness don't pass after a day or two, the only treatment is to head down.

Costs, money and banks

Contrary to the stereotype, it's no more expensive to travel in Switzerland than in parts of Germany, Italy or England – and Swiss standards of service and facilities across all budgets far outstrip those elsewhere. The country's reputation for priciness is misleading: value for money is the national motto, and in most situations you get what you pay for.

Switzerland is the wealthiest country in the world, nursing an average per-capita income of around £28,000 a year – and that's *after* paying taxes of some thirty percent. The country is infamous as one of the safest places to stash a fortune, hard-earned or otherwise, and it's been estimated that there's about £1,000,000,000,000 squirrelled away in the anonymous numbered accounts of the various Swiss banks. The Swiss franc (CHF) is renowned for its stability and is one of the benchmarks against which international standards are set.

Currency

Prices in both Switzerland and Liechtenstein are in **Swiss francs** (*Schweizer Franken*, *francs suisses*, *franchi svizzeri*). The most common abbreviation is "Fr." – but you may also see "fr", "sFr", "Sfr", "SF", "FS", or the official bank abbreviation "**CHF**". Each franc

is divided into 100; these are called *Rappen* (Rp.) in German-speaking areas, *centimes* (c) in francophone areas, and *centesimi* (also c) in Italian-speaking areas. There are coins of 5c, 10c, 20c, 50c, Fr.1, Fr.2 and Fr.5, and notes of Fr.10, Fr.20, Fr.50, Fr.100, Fr.200 and Fr.1000.

The currency in all the neighbouring countries – France, Germany, Austria and Italy – as well as elsewhere across Europe is the **euro** (€), divided into 100 cents. Design of the coins may vary, but all euro currency is legal tender in all eurozone countries. Across Switzerland, you'll find vending machines, ticket dispensers and phone booths which may accept euro coins as well as Swiss coins, or which may accept only one or the other; they'll be clearly marked either way. Tourist brochures and hotel lists often quote prices in CHF and EUR, generally side by side: check which column you're reading. For exchange rates, check ⓦwww.xe.com.

Carrying money

The best advice, since there are still some places where you can't use debit/credit cards, is to carry your money in a mixture of **cash** and **plastic**. Fees on plastic transactions can often work out less than commissions on purchases of **travellers' cheques**.

Debit and credit cards

Every corner of Switzerland is plastered with banks, almost all of which have English-language **ATMs** (cash machines) which accept foreign **debit and credit cards** in a panoply of brands including Visa, Master-Card, EC, Maestro, Cirrus and Plus. You can pay for most goods and services around the country using a foreign debit/credit card, although there may be a lower limit of Fr.20 or Fr.30, and some shops and supermarkets don't accept foreign cards at all. As usual, **charge cards** such as Amex or Diners Club are less widely accepted. There's a growing push nationwide to reduce the reliance on cash: you'll see stickers at supermarket checkouts and on lots of vending machines (such as transport ticket machines, which increasingly often don't accept banknotes) for a domestic Swiss cashless smart-card, known – rather confusingly – as "**CASH**". This often has wider acceptance than international brands of plastic. Before relying on being able to pay for goods or services with your own card, it's always a good idea to check with staff.

Changing cash and cheques

Invariably, the best place to change foreign **cash** or **travellers' cheques** is the desk to be found next to the ticket counters at virtually all train stations around the country: rates are identical with the banks, no commission is charged (except at some airport locations), and they're usually open seven days a week for long hours.

Some basic costs

If you're prepared to cut all corners by walking or cycling your own bike around the country, staying in hostels or campsites, and never eating out, you could scrape by on

Fr.40–50 (£18/$30) a day; add in one cheap meal and a beer, and Fr.55–65 (£26/$42) is more realistic, while budgeting something for visiting a few sights or museums (average Fr.5–7 per place, or £2.50/$4) would mean you might actually enjoy your trip too. If you don't have a bike, you'd have to factor in transport costs on top of this (see p.41 for more).

Staying at simple inns or guesthouses in one or two rural areas, avoiding cities altogether, and spending your days hiking or just relaxing in reasonable comfort is unlikely to set you back more than Fr.100/day each (£42/$67), but going up a mountain – which may be the whole point of your visiting Switzerland in the first place – can wipe out a day's budget. A journey to the Jungfraujoch, for instance, costs roughly Fr.120 (£50/$81): hiking part or all of the way up or down can bring big savings. If you're planning a skiing holiday, you should book an all-in package from home, which costs a fraction of the equivalent over-the-counter rates.

A comfortable double room in a two- or three-star city hotel is on average Fr.130–160 (£62/$100), depending on the season and the city. Two people using this kind of accommodation, eating lunch and dinner in modest restaurants, taking in a scattering of sights, the odd boat trip or train ride, and a luxury or two, are likely to shell out, on average, roughly Fr.320 (£140/$215) a day between them.

Youth/student ID cards soon pay for themselves in savings, principally on international air, rail and bus fares, admission to larger museums and attractions and on some resorts' lift passes; crucially, however, not on Swiss public transport. Full-time students are eligible for the International Student ID Card (**ISIC**); anybody aged 26 or less qualifies for the International Youth Travel Card; and teachers qualify for the International Teacher Card – all carrying the same benefits. Check ⓦwww.isic.org for details of outlets selling the cards. **Children** get in half-price or less to many museums in Switzerland, and can travel free with their parents on a Family Card, issued free alongside any kind of Swiss travel pass (see p.41).

Getting around

The efficiency of the massively comprehensive Swiss public transport system remains one of the wonders of the modern world. It's hard to overstate just how good it is: you can get anywhere you want quickly, easily and relatively cheaply; everybody relies on it as a matter of course; and it's clean, safe and pleasant.

Services always depart on the dot, and **train** timetables are well integrated with those of the **postbuses**, which operate on routes not covered by rail, including the more remote villages and valleys, as well as **ferry** services on Switzerland's many lakes (and some of its rivers). **Cyclists** are well served by the Swiss instinct for encouraging green thinking in all things; see p.73 for details of cycling routes and bike rental.

Tickets and ticket machines

One point can't be stressed enough. Swiss people virtually never pay full fare on their own public transport systems, and you should follow suit: unless you're planning to drive or cycle everywhere, you will definitely save money by travelling on a **Swiss travel pass** (see opposite). All give free or discounted travel on trains, buses, boats, cable cars and funiculars nationwide, and some are also valid on urban tram, bus and metro networks in nearly all Swiss cities.

If you're based in one resort, investigate the terms of the local **guest card** (*Gästekarte*, *carte des visiteurs*, *tessera di soggiorno*), issued for free when you check in at your hotel; these often give free transport on local buses and trains and – sometimes – cable cars and funiculars. Lift passes at ski resorts invariably give free valley-floor transport to and from outlying cable-car stations.

Unless you're holding the Swiss Pass (which is almost universally valid; all you have to do is show it on demand), you're likely to find yourself tangling with **automated ticket machines** at some point, even if only to buy a ticket for a cross-town tram. Most urban transport networks are divided up into **zones**. Note that these never follow the system – familiar from, say, London – of concentric rings with consecutive numbering:

in Zürich, for instance, the most central area is Zone 10, bordered on various sides by zones 21, 40 and 54. Fares are calculated by how many zones you travel in, and you nearly always have to buy your ticket before you board from the machines located at every stop. These generally follow a pattern, but are rarely marked in English and can be frustratingly difficult to fathom. First, press a button for your **journey** – either a destination code or an option to let you travel across, say, one, two or three zones. This choice often incorporates a **time validity** (a short-hop ticket may be valid for unlimited changes within an hour), or you could instead select a full-day pass. You may then need to choose either **one-way** (a single arrow) or **round-trip** (a double arrow). Then, press a button for yourself – adult or child. Some machines (in Zürich, for instance, where tickets are also valid on class-segregated trains and boats) give you the option to choose **1st class**. You'll also see an option for "**1/1**" or "**1/2**"; press the latter if you hold a pass that permits you to travel half-price. The readout will then show the fare. With the rise of the smart-card payment system "CASH", you may not have the option to pay with a banknote, but coins are always acceptable – either Swiss francs or, in some areas, euro coins. Some machines selling long-distance train tickets let you pay by **debit/credit card**.

Trains

The Swiss are the most frequent **train** users in Europe – not surprising, given the quality of the network. Travelling through Switzerland by train is invariably comfortable, hassle-free and extremely scenic, with many mountain routes an attraction in their own right. Swiss Federal Railways, or **SBB**

CFF FFS (*Schweizerische Bundesbahnen, Chemins de fer fédéraux suisses, Ferrovie federali svizzere*), retains a monopoly on most of the network. Fares are affordable, equipment and rolling stock are state-of-the-art, and staff motivation is high.

SBB covers virtually the whole country, but there are some routes, especially Alpine lines, which are operated by the individual rail companies which constructed them often a century or more ago. Two of the largest of these are **BLS**, which runs the pivotal Bern–Lötschberg–Simplon route between the Swiss capital and Milan; and **RhB**, the Rhätische Bahn, which operates trains within Canton Graubünden. There are dozens more, often tiny concerns used by local people to get to and from their nearest town, sometimes (such as the Bernese Oberland's **Jungfraubahnen**) massive enterprises ferrying thousands of tourists from valley to summit and back again. However, ticketing systems are well integrated, and you don't really need to know which company is which, since each route has only one company providing services: you never have to shop around between competing train companies.

All trains, apart from local stopping services and mountain lines, have **first-class** and **second-class** sections, and are **no-smoking** throughout.

Fares and passes

The wide range of Swiss **passes** offer the most economical way to get around the country on public transport. With no barriers on the platforms, inspectors on the trains are the sole method of **fare-enforcement**, and they'll move through the whole train more or less between every station: get caught without a valid ticket or pass for your journey and they'll slap a Fr.60 **fine** on you, to which a surcharge is added if you can't pay on the spot. Most regional and local trains are marked with a prominent **swirly eye pictogram**: this means that there's no conductor and that you're trusted to either hold a valid pass or buy a ticket. Roving bands of inspectors may board at any point to check tickets. If you intend using any kind of multi-day pass or undated ticket, you must stamp it before you board in the little boxes marked with the same swirly eye pictogram on platforms or near escalators.

Swiss travel passes

There's a confusing array of different **Swiss travel passes**. All are good value, also bringing a discount on bike rental from train stations (see p.74): it just takes some untangling to see which is best suited for your trip. Consult ⓦ**www.swisstravelsystem.com** for full details and purchasing.

Top of the pile is the **Swiss Pass**. This gives free unlimited travel on 4, 8, 15, 22 or 30 consecutive days on all SBB and most other trains, as well as on all boats and postbuses and most city tram-and-bus networks. Where travel isn't free (eg on cable cars and mountain railways), discounts of at least 25 percent apply. The **Swiss Flexi Pass** gives the same privileges as the Swiss Pass on any 3, 4, 5, 6 or 8 days within a month. These are available online, from Swiss tourist offices abroad and, in francs only, from major stations within Switzerland on production of a foreign passport. Two or more people travelling together (up to a maximum of five) all get 15 percent off the cost of a Swiss Pass or Flexi Pass under the "**Saver**" scheme. The **Swiss Youth Pass** is a standard Swiss Pass discounted for people under 26 on the first date of travel. All these also include the benefits of a Swiss Museum Passport (see box p.35).

The **Swiss Transfer Ticket**, only available outside Switzerland, gives one free journey from the airport or border to anywhere in the country, and back again within a month – ideal for skiers. The **Swiss Card**, buyable abroad and at airport or border stations within Switzerland, extends the terms of the Transfer Ticket: as well as a free journey at the start and end of your holiday, it gives a month's travel by train, postbus and boat at fifty percent discount (plus partially reduced fares on most mountain railways).

The **Family Card** is a **free** add-on to any of the above: kids up to 16 accompanied by their parents travel free, while kids without their parents go for half-price.

Note that although the convenience and universal validity of the Swiss Pass or Flexi Pass is alluring, it pays to do some sums before you splash out on one: depending on the kind of journeys you're liable to take (all

Excursions by train, bus and boat

Although few Swiss journeys are short on scenery, there are a handful of exceptionally beautiful routes around the country which are marketed as unified single journeys. On most – after having **reserved** a seat the day before for a few francs – you just sit back, flash your travel pass and drink in the views. Some require you to change from train to boat, or bus to train, but you never have to walk more than the length of a station platform, and timetables always allow enough leeway that you're never in a hurry. Plus, of course, you can always send your heavy bags ahead.

Some of the more spectacular routings run special **panoramic** train carriages, either with partial or total glass roofs, or (in first class) with some raised seating inside a transparent bubble in the roof giving 360° views, but for these – and for extras such as onboard lunches – you always pay a **supplement**. For information, timings and routings, check well in advance at train stations, online or at larger tourist offices.

Note, too, that it's easy to follow the same routes on ordinary trains and pay no extras, or to get on or off at intermediate points: the Centovalli line, for instance, is worth exploring regardless of its marketed Lötschberg add-on. And, it should be added, these are only the trips in the spotlight: equally spectacular shorter rides such as Chur to Arosa, the tiny Lauterbrunnen to Mürren line or the celebrated Swiss Chocolate Train, are just as deserving of your attention. Details of these and others are at ⓦ **www.rail.ch** (search for "Scenic Routes").

We've described the journeys in one direction, but you could just as easily travel in the other direction instead. Most need advance reservation, and some cross international borders (in which case, you'll need your **passport**). Note that some tour operators will let you add these excursions to a package holiday at the time of booking for bargain rates.

- **Bernina Express** and **Heidi Express** ⓦ www.rhb.ch. Various routes from Chur, St Moritz or Davos over the high Bernina Pass and through the stunning Val Poschiavo to Tirano (Italy), where – in summer only – you switch onto a postbus and skirt Lake Como to Lugano. Total, including a couple of hours in Tirano, 8hr. Daily. Panoramic carriages. Reserve at any station.
- **Glacier Express** ⓦ www.glacierexpress.ch. A spectacular and understandably popular route, and – given its ups and downs – the slowest express in the world (average speed 30kph). From St Moritz (1775m) or Davos down to Chur (585m), then up the Rhine valley to the high Alps, crossing the Oberalp Pass (2033m) to Andermatt, through the tunnel beneath the Furka Pass and down the Rhône valley to Brig (671m), before climbing to Zermatt (1604m). Total 8hr, 291 bridges and 91 tunnels. Daily. Panoramic carriages on most trains. Reserve seats and dining-car places at any station.
- **Golden Pass** ⓦ www.goldenpass.ch. Flagship panorama route from Luzern, running over the Brünig Pass to Interlaken and the glorious countryside around Gstaad, then a spectacular descent through vineyards to the lakeshore at Montreux, with a variety of different panoramic carriages on various legs of the journey. Total 7hr. Daily. Reservations needed for some stretches; ask at any station.
- **Lötschberg–Centovalli** ⓦ www.bls.ch & www.centovalli.ch. South from Bern beneath both great Alpine ranges, courtesy of the Lötschberg tunnel into Canton

of which are fully researchable online), you may well find that you can save substantial amounts by getting a humble Swiss Card and shelling out for half-price travel tickets each time, rather than buying an expensive Swiss Pass and travelling for free.

If you're planning to concentrate on one area of the country, but still want the flexibility to visit local sights, it might be more economical to get a **regional pass** for your particular region. These vary across the country in both price and validity, but

Valais, and the Simplon tunnel from Brig to Domodossola (Italy), where you switch to the little trains which ply the wild and gorgeous Centovalli east to Locarno. Daily. Total 4hr. No reservations needed.

• **Mont Blanc Express** ⓦ www.momc.ch. Dramatic narrow-gauge route climbing from Martigny to the French border and then on into the high Alps to the resort of Chamonix (France), on the slopes of Mont Blanc. Swiss tickets are valid only to the border station of Châtelard; you can buy add-ons to Chamonix on the train. Daily. Total 1hr 30min. No reservations possible.

• **Palm Express** ⓦ www.postbus.ch. Postbus from St Moritz over the Maloja Pass into the dreamy Val Bregaglia, crossing the border to Chiavenna (Italy) and the shores of Lake Como, then crossing back into Switzerland to end at Lugano. No train-track exists on this route. Total 4hr 15min. June–Oct daily; rest of year Fri–Sun only. Reservations mandatory (see website).

• **Rhône Express** ⓦ www.rhoneexpress.ch. Memorably diverse scenery, with a boat ride from Geneva to Montreux, and a train running the length of the Rhône valley up to Brig, changing again for the rack railway to Zermatt. If you take the whole package (with a hefty supplement), you get a ride on an old-time paddle steamer with three-course lunch, and first-class train transport; otherwise, it's easy to link ordinary boat and train services together to form the same ride without supplements. Total 9hr. Mid-May to mid-Sept daily. Reservations needed for some stretches; ask at any station.

• **Romantic Route Express** ⓦ www.postbus.ch. Linked series of postbus journeys on some of the highest roads in Europe – from Andermatt over the Furka Pass and past the Rhône glacier to Gletsch, then the tortuous route up and over the wild Grimsel Pass to Meiringen, from where the final leg takes you through some lovely scenery in the Grosse Scheidegg Pass and down to Grindelwald at the foot of the Eiger. Reservations mandatory (see website).

• **St Bernard Express** ⓦ www.momc.ch. Narrow-gauge trains from Martigny climb south to the terminus station of Orsières, from where buses (summer only) continue up to the high Grand-St-Bernard Pass. Daily. Total 1hr 30min. No reservations possible.

• **Voralpen Express** ⓦ www.voralpen-express.ch. Route between Romanshorn on the Bodensee (Lake Constance) and Luzern, scheduled trains speeding through the pretty countryside of the Prealps around St Gallen, the Zürichsee and the Rigi. Hourly. Total 2hr 45min. No reservations possible.

• **William Tell Express** ⓦ www.lakelucerne.ch. Another incredibly beautiful journey, from Luzern by boat across the whole of Lake Luzern to Flüelen, then a train south, corkscrewing its way up into the Gotthard tunnel beneath the Alps and then down again through the Ticino to Lugano. If you go for the whole package, you get a three-course lunch in a lake paddle steamer, plus first-class panoramic seating on the train (supplement payable). Avoid the supplement by making your own way on scheduled trains and boats. First-class package available on north–south travel only. Total 6hr. May–Oct daily. Reserve at any station.

normally give 5 days' free travel in 15 within a limited region, often including discounts for the other 10 days. Regional passes are most popular in the Berner Oberland, the Gstaad–Château d'Oex region, Central Switzerland around Lake Luzern, and the Lake Geneva shoreline, but are also offered by many other regional tourist offices. Contact the Swiss tourist office in your home country for details.

The passes above are targeted at foreigners staying less than 30 days. If you intend being in Switzerland for longer, check out the amazingly good-value season tickets and passes at ⓦ www.rail.ch.

Timetables and information

The national **timetable** (*Kursbuch* or *Fahrplan*, *indicateur* or *horaire*, *orario*), covering all rail, bus, boat and cable-car services is consultable at most main stations, and online (in English) at ⓦ **www.rail.ch** – where you'll also find fare details, full arrival and departure boards for every station in Switzerland, and complete information on every train, down to platform numbers and the kind of onboard refreshments available. Check times carefully if you're travelling in December, when the timetable is revamped each year. Ask ticket-office staff how to get from any station to any other and they'll print out an itinerary for you showing exact connection times. The national train enquiry number is ☏ 0900 300 300.

Train and bus timetables posted on station hoardings are always colour-coded: the **yellow timetable** always shows departures

(*Abfahrt*, *départ*, *partenza*), while the white one always indicates arrivals (*Ankunft*, *arrivée*, *arrivo*). Train and bus timetables look alike and it's easy to mistake one for the other: check in the top corner for the relevant pictogram.

Trains are identified on the timetable by an alphabet soup of initials, which denote where, when and how fast they go. **CIS** are tilting express "Pendolino" trains run by Cisalpino between Switzerland and Italy; **ICE** are Inter-City Express services between Switzerland and Germany; **TGV** are high-speed trains between Switzerland and France. Sleeper services are either **CNL** (CityNightLine) or **EN** (EuroNight). Day trains between major European cities – that may stop at only two or three places in Switzerland – are denoted **EC** (EuroCity). If you're holding an ordinary ticket or train pass, all of these are free of any surcharges within Swiss borders; you must pay supplements only if you cross an international frontier, or if the train is marked in the timetable with an R in a square box. In

Swiss passes – some sample prices

The few **sample prices** given here for Swiss, Youth and Flexi passes are for **second-class travel**. Add about 50 percent to travel first class. "Individual" means the price per person travelling alone; "saver" means the price for each person when there are two or more travelling together (maximum of five). For full details, see ⓦ **www.swisstravelsystem.com**.

	£	US$	Fr.
Swiss Pass			
– 4 consecutive days, individual	115	185	250
– 4 consecutive days, saver	98	158	212
– 8 consecutive days, saver	141	225	308
– 15 consecutive days, individual	202	322	440
– 15 consecutive days, saver	172	274	374
Swiss Youth Pass			
– 4 consecutive days	86	139	188
– 8 consecutive days	125	198	272
Swiss Flexi Pass			
– 3 days/month, individual	110	176	240
– 3 days/month, saver	94	150	204
– 5 days/month, individual	155	248	338
– 8 days/month, saver	175	281	383
Swiss Transfer Ticket	57	88	124
Swiss Card	82	133	178

these cases, a seat reservation costs a few francs.

Within Switzerland, **IC** InterCity expresses cross the country stopping at larger cities only; those marked **ICN** tilt round corners for extra speed. **IR** InterRegio trains ply between regions, stopping at a few more places in between. **RX** RegioExpress services are one step slower. Something misleadingly described as a *Schnellzug*, *train direct* or *treno diretto* goes from village to village; while a *Regionalzug*, *train regional* or *treno regionale* stops at every haystack on the way.

Platforms are marked out in **sectors**, from A to D: beware of truncated one- or two-carriage local trains departing from Platform 3 Sector A while you're standing 150m away at Platform 3 Sector D tapping your watch. For mainline services, the PA announcement (and a detailed plan in blue posted next to the timetable boards) tells you which sectors the first- and second-class carriages will arrive at, saving you running up and down the train. Sometimes two short trains will depart in opposite directions from different sectors of the same platform.

Stations and services

It takes something of a leap of faith to realize, but in Switzerland a **train station** (*Bahnhof*, *gare*, *stazione*) isn't the dregs-of-the-earth place it might be in another country. Many Swiss stations harbour genuinely good restaurants alongside their formica-table buffets (going out for a nice meal at the station is a new experience for most visitors) and many also shelter the only shops and supermarkets in their town open late.

Just about the only people you'll see lugging suitcases or rucksacks through train compartments are foreigners. Most Swiss register their bags (each up to 25kg) at the station **baggage counter** before boarding, for Fr.10 per item per journey: SBB's team of baggage-handlers take the strain, and the bags are ready for collection at your destination station a day later. This is a great service to take advantage of if you want to see a lot of things in a day but don't fancy carting your gear from locker to locker. You can pay more for a same-day service. Several hotels (listed at ⓦ www.rail.ch) will deliver your bags to your room if you arrive by public transport.

You can find many convenient facilities at just about all train stations. **Luggage lockers** are universal, found at all but the tiniest country halts, and normally come in two or three sizes: average prices are Fr.3 for a small one (into which you can just about stuff a full rucksack), Fr.5 for a large and – only at main stations – Fr.8 for an extra-large. Once they're locked, you can open them only once. After a week or two staff may open the locker, impound your property at the left-luggage office, and require you to pay through the nose to get it back. Ask at the information counters beforehand what the time limit is. Access to lockers may also be prohibited between midnight and 5am.

Virtually every station also has a staffed **left-luggage office** (around Fr.5 per item per day), invariably open daily for long hours, and often combined with a **lost-property office**, a **bike-rental counter** (see p.74), and the **airport check-in** service (see box p.46).

Train-station **lost property** offices are linked by computer, so they can all run a nationwide check for you; it costs Fr.5 to retrieve a small item, Fr.20 for a large or heavy piece. Other services you'll find in all stations are **bureaux de change** and money-wiring facilities, invariably spotless toilets (free or Fr.1–1.50) and, in city stations, equally spotless shower cubicles (Fr.10).

Buses

Backing up the train network is a yet more comprehensive system of **buses**, which get to every single village and hamlet in the country, covering ground – such as in the high mountains or deep countryside – left untouched by the trains. Many travellers don't even consider using the buses, imagining them to be too slow or too much hassle to figure out; this is a shame, since buses are not there to compete with the trains but to complement them, and they can get you to all kinds of out-of-the-way places – and some essential ones – quickly and easily. All Swiss travel passes are valid for travel on buses as well as trains.

Bus stations are nearly always located in the forecourt of train stations. Even more handily, the bus and train **timetables** are coordinated together, ensuring watertight connections from one to the other. Swiss

Airport check-in at the train station

This is the outward-bound flipside of the "Fly Rail Baggage" incoming service (see box p.28), and is just as useful, letting you **check your bags in** ahead of time for Fr.20 per item at any one of several dozen Swiss train stations, from where they're transported independently to your departure airport and loaded onto your flight; you don't have to lay a finger on them until the baggage-reclaim carousel in your home airport. At the same time, and for no extra cost, you can make a seat reservation and receive a **boarding card**, cutting out all hassle at the airport and letting you proceed directly to your departure gate.

You'll need to show the station staff your flight ticket (with an "OK" reservation), and – most importantly – a train ticket or pass to prove that you'll be travelling to the airport by train; otherwise, you pay a surcharge. Virtually all flights out of Zürich and Geneva are served, but all US flights and easyJet are **excluded**, as are bulky items such as bicycles.

You can do a station check-in at the **earliest** 24 hours before your flight departure. Station staff and ⓦwww.rail.ch have details of the **latest** possible check-in times for all stations, which vary depending on which airport you're flying out of and what your scheduled take-off time is: for a morning or lunchtime take-off, you may need to check your bags in at the station the day before to ensure they reach the airport in time.

---

buses stick to their schedules with utter reliability.

Most long-distance bus lines are operated, in an endearing remnant of pioneer times, by yellow **postbuses** (ⓦwww.postbus.ch), with *Die Post*, *La Poste* or *La Posta* on the side. Various regions have their own local bus companies, either instead of or as well as postbuses, but all are equally reliable. Note that some longer, more difficult or direct bus routes – such as over the Alpine passes – require either advance **seat reservation** and/or a small supplement around Fr.10 to be paid: check online or with bus-station staff ahead of time.

Boats

All of Switzerland's bigger lakes, and many of its smaller ones, are crossed by regular **ferry services**. Most run only during the summer season – which can vary, but at its broadest covers the period from April to October – and are primarily pleasure-oriented, duplicating routes which can be covered more cheaply and quickly by rail. However, if you have the time, a leisurely cruise through the Alpine foothills to Interlaken, for example, or between the three lakes of Neuchâtel, Morat and Biel/Bienne, or from shore to shore along the length of Lake Geneva, beats the

equivalent train journeys hands down. Apart from on Lago Maggiore (which is mostly in Italy), travel by boat is covered by all Swiss travel passes (see p.41). The **Swiss Boat Pass** (Fr.35), valid for a year, knocks fifty percent off fares on fourteen of Switzerland's bigger lakes; the **Swiss Family Boat Pass** (Fr.50) has the same benefits and also lets the kids travel free.

Most of Switzerland's **rivers** are too young and fast-flowing to be navigable. However, boats ply a scenic, wooded section of the **Rhône** west of Geneva before the French border, and northeast of Biel/Bienne, there's a lovely stretch of the **Aare** navigable until Solothurn. Best of all, and one of Europe's great river journeys, is the uniquely peaceful part of the **Rhine** between Konstanz (or its neighbour Kreuzlingen) and the falls at Schaffhausen, the sole stretch of that river that is free from any kind of bankside industry. The falls merit a journey in themselves.

City transport

The most common form of transport within cities is **buses**, whether the ordinary petrol-driven kind or electric-powered **trolley buses**. Many cities also have **trams**, and a few hillside ones have a **funicular** or two, but the only true **metro** system is in and around Lausanne. Larger cities have dense networks of suburban commuter trains (**S-Bahn** in German, **RER** in French), which may extend to neighbouring towns.

Within each city or local area, all transport is integrated under one **ticketing system**, with no limitations on changing from buses to trams or even some boats within the time validity of your ticket. The Swiss Pass and Swiss Flexi Pass cover free travel within most cities across the country (listed on the card); tourist-oriented regional passes give free travel within their allotted area; and city tourist offices sell various **day passes** of their own giving free or discounted travel, which can be excellent value. You must always hold a valid ticket before boarding. Ticket inspections are common within cities.

There are plenty of metered **taxis** sharking around every town and city in the country, but given the density of public transport they're pretty much unnecessary, and besides you need to be on a Swiss salary to afford them: flagfalls of Fr.6, plus per-kilometre rates of up to Fr.3, are normal.

Driving

Driving obviously gives you extra freedom to explore nooks and crannies that others zip past without stopping. Switzerland's road network is comprehensive and well planned, and although the mountainous terrain can make for some circuitous routes there is, of course, the compensation of impressively scenic – if sometimes hair-raising – mountain drives. However, Swiss transport policy means that cars are slowly being given the squeeze, with tough city parking regulations and strict law enforcement.

Driving your own vehicle

Minimum driving age is 18, international licences are recognized for one year's driving in Switzerland and, as across Europe, **third-party insurance** is compulsory. It's obligatory to carry both a red warning triangle and the registration documents of the vehicle. If you intend driving on Swiss motorways, you have to stick a **vignette** inside your windscreen. These cost Fr.40 for any vehicle up to 3.5 tonnes, are bought most easily from the customs officials when you first cross

the border (also at post offices and petrol stations, and at ⓦ www.swisstravelsystem .com), and remain valid until January 31 of the following year. Trailers or caravans must have their own, additional vignette. Getting caught without one lays you open to a Fr.100 fine.

However, it's quite easy to avoid motorways altogether and stick to ordinary main roads, which are free and – outside urban centres at least – reasonably fast.

Renting a car

Car rental in Switzerland can be expensive. You can significantly cut costs by renting in advance from the big international agencies; they all cover Switzerland, with offices in all major towns, most minor ones, and at all airports. **One-way rentals** are simple to arrange, although they may attract a handling fee. Hertz has a deal with SBB whereby you can reserve, pick up or drop off cars at any of 700 train stations across the country for a small surcharge. There are dozens of local rental companies in most towns, usually operating out of ordinary petrol stations or garages, with mostly trustworthy cars at prices that undercut the big agencies' walk-in rates: find them in the phonebook under *Autovermietungen* or *Mietwagen*, *location des voitures*, *noleggio di automobili*.

To rent a car, you need a valid, clean UK, EU or international **driving licence** that you've held for more than a year. Minimum driver's age is 20 or 21, occasionally 25, depending on the rental company. All rental cars have the annual motorway vignette prepaid and, in winter, are fitted with snow tyres and supplied with snow-chains (and even a ski rack) for free.

Although it's usually no problem to drive **across borders** in most Swiss rental cars you should always check the rules with your rental company in advance: Switzerland is not in the EU, although it's surrounded by EU countries. Border controls are a formality but can be time-consuming, especially at heavily used crossing points; you'd do well to be certain, before you depart Switzerland, that you're not going to inadvertently break customs regulations or passport/visa requirements on your way back in.

Principal Swiss Alpine passes

There are 72 **Alpine passes** in Switzerland that are open to motor traffic, and hundreds more that are for hikers or cyclists only. We've given the names (in alternative languages where necessary) of the most important ones; their altitude above sea level; the approximate period during which the pass road (and any tunnel road) is open to traffic, barring significant weather disruption; and the main towns/regions on either side of the pass. Approach roads to all passes have large signboards displaying whether the pass, and the high-altitude towns or resorts on the way, are **open** (*offen, ouvert, aperto*) or **closed** (*geschlossen, fermé, chiuso*).

Albula/Alvra 2312m; June–Oct; Tiefencastel GR, La Punt GR

Bernina 2328m; all year; St Moritz GR, Poschiavo GR

Brünig 1008m; all year; Sarnen OW, Brienz BE

Croix 1778m; all year; Villars VD, Les Diablerets VD

Flüela 2383m; June–Oct; Davos GR, Zernez GR

Forclaz 1526m; all year; Martigny VS, Chamonix (France)

Fuorn/Ofen 2149m; all year; Zernez GR, Val Müstair GR

Furka 2431m; June–Oct; Gletsch VS, Andermatt UR

Grand-St-Bernard 2469m; pass June–Oct, tunnel all year; Martigny VS, Aosta (Italy)

Grimsel 2165m; June–Oct; Gletsch VS, Meiringen BE

Jaun 1509m; all year; Bulle FR, Simmental BE

Julier/Güglia 2284m; all year; Tiefencastel GR, St Moritz GR

Klausen 1948m; June–Oct; Altdorf UR, Linthal GL

Lukmanier/Lucomagno 1914m; May–Nov; Disentis/Mustér GR, Biasca TI

Maloja 1815m; all year; St Moritz GR, Val Bregaglia GR

Mosses 1445m; all year; Aigle VD, Château d'Oex VD

Nufenen/Novena 2478m; June–Sept; Ulrichen VS, Airolo TI

Oberalp 2044m; June–Oct; Andermatt UR, Disentis/Mustér GR

Pillon 1546m; all year; Les Diablerets VD, Gstaad BE

San Bernadino 2065m; pass June–Oct, tunnel all year; Thusis GR, Bellinzona TI

St Gotthard/San Gottardo 2109m; pass May–Oct, tunnel all year; Göschenen UR, Airolo TI

Simplon/Sempione 2005m; all year; Brig VS, Domodossola (Italy)

Splügen 2113m; May–Oct; Thusis GR, Chiavenna (Italy)

Susten 2224m; June–Oct; Meiringen BE, Andermatt UR

Car rental agencies

Avis UK ☎ 0870/606 0100, ⊛ www.avis.co.uk; Ireland ☎ 01/605 7500, ⊛ www.avis.ie; US ☎ 1-800/331-1084, Canada ☎ 1-800/272-5871, ⊛ www.avis.com; Australia ☎ 13 63 33, ⊛ www .avis.com.au; NZ ☎ 09/526 2847, ⊛ www.avis .co.nz; Switzerland ☎ 0848 811 818, ⊛ www .avis.ch.

Budget UK ☎ 0800/181 181, ⊛ www.budget .co.uk; Ireland ☎ 0903/27711, ⊛ www.budget .ie; US ☎ 1-800/527-0700, ⊛ www.budget.com; Australia ☎ 1300/362 848, ⊛ www.budget.com.au; NZ ☎ 09/976 2222, ⊛ www.budget.co.nz.

Europcar UK ☎ 0870/607 5000, ⊛ www. europcar .co.uk; Ireland ☎ 01/614 2800, ⊛ www.europcar.ie; US & Canada ☎ 1-877/940 6900, ⊛ www.europcar .com; Switzerland ☎ 0848 808 099, ⊛ www .europcar.ch.

Hertz UK ☎ 0870/848 4848, ⊛ www.hertz.co.uk; Ireland ☎ 01/676 7476, ⊛ www.hertz.ie; US ☎ 1-800/654-3001, Canada ☎ 1-800/263-0600, ⊛ www.hertz.com; Australia ☎ 13 30 39; NZ ☎ 0800/654 321; Switzerland ☎ 0848 822 020, ⊛ www.hertz.ch.

On the road

Switzerland and Liechtenstein drive on the **right**, **seatbelts** are compulsory for all, and penalties for **drink driving** are tough (one glass of beer has you at the limit). For safety reasons, always drive with **dipped headlights**, day and night. Beware of driving with sunglasses on, since there are hundreds of **road tunnels**, plenty of them single-bore with one lane in each direction and no central divider: you can be plunged from sunshine into scary blackness with little warning. Usefully, all tunnels have a small plaque at their entrance stating their length. If you're in a traffic jam in a tunnel, waiting for temporary traffic lights at roadworks or at level-crossing barriers, copy the locals and **switch your engine off**.

Swiss motorways/freeways are **signed in green**, while main roads are signed in blue; it's common to see a green sign and a blue sign to the same place pointing in opposite directions. A motorway (*Autobahn, autoroute, autostrada*) has two sets of identifiers, the national system (N) and the pan-European system (E): the main route through the Gotthard tunnel, for example, doubles as the N2/E35. **Speed limits** are 120kph (75mph) on motorways, 80kph (50mph) on main roads, 50kph (30mph) in urban areas, and 30kph (18mph) on speed-bumped residential streets. There are dozens of cameras, radars and laser traps around the country to catch speeders, with spot fines levied.

At junctions, yellow diamonds painted on the road show who has **priority**; if in doubt, always let trams and buses go first, and give way to traffic coming from your right. On gradients, vehicles heading **uphill** have priority over those coming down; some narrow mountain tracks have controlled times for ascent and descent. If you hear an outrageously loud horn or klaxon sounding on country lanes or twisting mountain roads, it means that a **postbus** is approaching: it always has priority, up or down, so get out of the way. In cities, it's forbidden to overtake **trams** when they're at their stops. In the winter, signs indicate where **snow-chains** are necessary (it's a good idea to practise fitting and removing them beforehand).

You can find **fuel** in just about every village in the country. **Unleaded** fuel (*Bleifrei, sans plomb, senza piombo*; green pumps) is the standard. Unstaffed 24-hour automatic filling stations – where you feed cash or a credit card into a machine – are cheapest of all. Super-plus unleaded is widely available (also green pumps), as is diesel (black pumps). Leaded fuel (red pumps) is less common.

You might have unexpected problems with **navigation**, since motorway signs often show the names of distant Alpine passes as general indicators of direction, rather than naming the next major town: if you want to drive on the *autoroute* from Geneva to Montreux, for instance, you'll have to follow signs to "Simplon" and "Grand-St-Bernard", since these are the passes that lie at the end of the road, hundreds of kilometres beyond Montreux (there are no signs to Montreux until you're almost upon it). Similarly, as far away as Zürich and Luzern, the main motorway heading south is simply signed "Gotthard", rather than naming wayside towns like Schwyz or regions such as Uri. However, signs to specific towns are always in the language of that town: Geneva is always "Genève", never "Genf" or "Ginevra". As for crossing the language border, there'll just come a point speeding between Fribourg and Bern when you'll notice that the exits, previously marked "Sortie", suddenly become "Ausfahrt".

For **breakdown assistance**, call ☎140.

Parking

Parking in Switzerland is hellish, and can be very limited and prohibitively expensive. In cities across the country, full car parks will quite often harbour queues of cars, their engines off, drivers waiting – sometimes for over an hour – for the next person to finish their shopping and so liberate a space.

Unlimited-stay covered **parking garages** are signposted in all cities. Prices can be outrageous: Fr.30/day or more in central Geneva and Zürich, an average Fr.15/day around the country, and rarely less than Fr.1/hour anywhere. Out-of-town car parks, often located near motorway exits and tagged **P+R** (Park and Ride), are sometimes free or discounted; they're always served by a bus or tram heading into the town centre, for which you must pay.

Onstreet parking and open **car parks** are colour-coded, as in much of the rest of Europe. Spaces delineated with white lines – the **White Zone** – are most common, controlled either by individual meters or, more usually, a prominently marked central pay-point or *Zentrale Parkuhr, Parcomètre collectif, Parchimetro collettivo*. These take coins only; costs can vary from Fr.0.50/hour in small towns to Fr.4/hour in cities. In most cases, White Zone spaces are time-limited. If your space is numbered, press the corresponding button on the machine (or key the number in), then pay. Sometimes that's enough; other times, you must press another button to get a ticket to display in your car. If your space isn't numbered, then just pay and display your ticket. Outside the hours posted on the pay-point, and where there isn't a machine at all (in a small village, say), White Zone spaces are free, unless there's a sign reserving them – as in *nur für Kunden*, "only for customers" of a particular shop nearby.

You can park in **Blue Zone** spaces if you have a special parking disc, supplied in the glove-box of all rental cars (also available for free from tourist offices, car rental agencies, police stations and banks). Spin the wheel round to show your time of arrival and leave it on your dashboard: this gives you 90 minutes' free parking if you arrive between 8 and 11.30am or between 1.30 and 6pm. If you arrive between 11.30am and 1.30pm, you're safe until 2.30pm; if you arrive after 6pm, you're OK until 9am next day. Rarer **Red Zone** spaces are free for up to 15 hours, as long as you display the disc.

Spaces marked in **yellow** indicate private parking for, say, staff of a nearby company or perhaps guests of a local hotel; the only way to know is to ask.

Illegal parking of any kind is much less tolerated in Switzerland than in its neighbours, and fines of Fr.50–100 for minor transgressions are common.

Accommodation

As a general rule, it's no problem to turn up in any Swiss town at any time of the year and find a room. With the popularity of the bigger cities and resorts, though, booking ahead – especially in the summer and winter high seasons – is strongly advised. This saves you the effort of searching once you arrive, and means you won't be forced into spending over budget. Despite the fact that Geneva and Zürich suffer from high hotel prices, Fr.90–120 will buy you some kind of double room in any town in the country.

Swiss accommodation is relatively expensive but it is nearly always of excellent quality, conscientiously run and hospitable.

Tourist offices always have lists of hotels, hostels, campsites and apartments in their area, and outside office hours they normally have a display board on the street with details of the local hotels, often with a courtesy phone. In many cases you'll find these boards at train stations as well. All towns

and cities, and many villages, display distinctive **yellow-and-brown signposts** directing drivers to named hotels; you're allowed to drive to the door to load and unload, even in a pedestrian-only zone.

Swiss hoteliers, campsite managers and hostel staff almost always speak English, but in the unlikely event that you can't make yourself understood, the local tourist office will make a booking for you, either for free

Accommodation price codes

All the hostels and hotels in this book have been graded according to the following **price codes**, which indicate the price for the cheapest double room available during high season. For dormitories in hostels or mountain inns, the price per bed in Swiss francs has been quoted. Single rooms generally cost between sixty and eighty percent of the double-room rate. Bear in mind that an establishment graded, for example, as a ❸ may also have more comfortable rooms at ❹ prices, and/or may have different rates for the summer and winter peak seasons, reflected by a range (eg ❸–❺).

❶ under Fr.100	❹ Fr.200–250	❼ Fr.350–400
❷ Fr.100–150	❺ Fr.250–300	❽ Fr.400–500
❸ Fr.150–200	❻ Fr.300–350	❾ over Fr.500

or for a small fee. It's rare to be able to negotiate **multi-night bargain rates** over the counter, but many tourist offices run deals throughout the year that can save plenty if you book three or seven nights in a row. Wherever you check in, you should always ask for a free **guest card** (*Gästekarte, carte des visiteurs, tessera di soggiorno*), as this perk for overnight visitors can give substantial discounts for local attractions and transport.

Bear in mind the fluctuating **high and low seasons** between lowland and highland resorts, described in detail on p.27.

Some towns quote accommodation prices **per person**, while others quote prices **per room**. Our code system (see box) standardizes them across the board, but you'd do well to ascertain what the terms are if you ask for prices direct from a hotel or tourist office. Most establishments post prices in both **CHF** (Swiss francs) and **EUR** (an equivalent euro rate): make sure you don't mix the two up.

Hotels

Swiss **hotels** are among the best in the world, with very high standards of service. Value-for-money is the motive force behind the hotel industry, rather than cost-cutting, so you'll find that even the cheapest hotels offer rooms that are perfectly comfortable, clean and respectable, if a little pricey compared to dingier bottom-end establishments in other countries.

At the least expensive level, what makes a difference in price is whether a room contains a shower or an **ensuite bathroom**, since these can add Fr.20 or more to the rate as compared with rooms where the shared shower and toilet are down the corridor.

Breakfast is included in the room price at virtually all hotels apart from the very cheapest and the most expensive; what you get varies with the hotel's classification. One thing to watch out for is that in many mountain resorts, hotel prices quoted for the summer season are **bed and breakfast**, while those quoted for the winter season tend to be **half-board** (ie bed plus two meals – normally breakfast and an evening meal); we've marked this differentiation clearly in the guide text where relevant, but to be certain you should check what you're paying for at the time of reservation.

A hotel advertising itself as **"garni"** has no restaurant, and serves only breakfast to its overnight guests.

Hotel groups

Aside from international brands such as Best Western or The Leading Hotels Of The World, there are a number of Swiss **hotel groups** which, if you can fight your way through their marketing blurb, can be useful for seeking out establishments with particular features that appeal to you, whether they be top-notch five-star quality (Swiss Deluxe), historic buildings and locations (Romantik), complete quiet (Silence), or just plain, good-value inexpensive accommodation (Swiss Budget).

Idyll Hotels ✆ www.idyll.ch. Peaceful country hotels, two- and three-star, run on ecologically sound lines.

Kidshotels ⓦ www.kidshotels.ch. Small group of family-friendly hotels, most in mountain resorts, featuring babysitting and childminding, children's menus, entertainment and more.

Minotel Suisse ⓦ www.minotel.ch. Wide-ranging group of small, family-run, two- to four-star hotels in locations from city centres to rural villages. Useful central booking facility online.

Romantik ⓦ www.romantikhotels.com. High-quality grouping of personally run and managed three- and four-star hotels (none of them chain- or corporate-owned). All are historic properties in their own right, often architecturally unique, placing a focus squarely on pamperment amidst characterful surroundings.

Silence Hotels ⓦ www.silence.ch. Local arm of the international Relais du Silence chain (ⓦ www .relais-du-silence.com), concentrating on providing tranquillity, leisure and relaxation in its hotels, all in countryside locations far from traffic and towns.

Swiss Budget Hotels ⓦ www.rooms.ch. Zero- to three-star places (200 of them) off the beaten track, most with character, ranging from small city hotels to dorms and mountain lodges.

Swiss Deluxe Hotels ⓦ www.swissdeluxehotels .com. Exclusive group of uncompromisingly luxurious hotels, all of them five-star and most of them internationally famous names.

Hostels and "backpackers"

If you're travelling on a budget, a **hostel** or a "**backpacker**" is likely to be your accommodation of choice, whether you're youthful or not. They can often be extremely good value, and offer clean and comfortable dorms as well as a choice of rooms (doubles and sometimes singles) that can often undercut normal hotel prices. City and country locations can get very full between June and September, when you should book in advance.

There are two main hostel associations in Switzerland. The 70-odd properties of **Swiss Youth Hostels** (ⓦ www.youthhostel .ch) are the only ones to use the specific term "youth hostel" (*Jugendherberge*, *auberge de jeunesse*, *albergo/ostello della gioventù*), and are listed on the annually updated map entitled "Know-How", widely available at tourist offices. They're all affiliated to the Hostelling International network (aka IYHF, International Youth Hostel Federation) and are referred to throughout this guide as "**HI**

hostels". They're of a universally high standard, although they tend to be better choices in countryside and mountain locations than in cities, where they are quite often located awkwardly far from town centres and can suffer from an atmosphere of institutionality. Most are closed for cleaning between roughly 10am and 6pm, and lock their doors sometime between 10pm and midnight (although checked-in guests can use entry systems to get in later at many hostels). Most close down in the low seasons: spring and autumn in the mountains, winter in the cities. Prices vary, covering the range Fr.21–35 (average Fr.29) for a dorm bed including breakfast and bedding. Extras such as kitchens for guest use and TV rooms are common, and evening meals, where available, cost a bargain Fr.12.50 or so. If you're not already an HI member (see below for contacts), you pay Fr.6 extra per night, or you can get annual membership while in Switzerland at any affiliated hostel for Fr.33, or Fr.22 for under-18s (membership is also automatic after any six nights of paying the supplement). All accept online reservations.

A rival grouping of independent hostels goes under the name **Swiss Backpackers** (ⓦ www.backpacker.ch). These lively places – referred to throughout this guide as "**SB hostels**" – are less institutional than HI hostels, often in prime locations in the centres of cities and resorts, and priced competitively (average about Fr.28). Most are busy, sociable, resourceful, laid-back places in the mould of backpacker joints everywhere, with kitchen and/or cheap restaurant attached and no curfew. No membership is required. They're all listed – along with a load of spot-on practical information for getting around Switzerland on the cheap – in the useful *Swiss Backpacker* newspaper, published two or three times a year and available for free in all SB hostels, most tourist offices and other prominent touristed places around the country, and on the website.

Otherwise, all ski resorts have places offering **dormitory** accommodation. Such a dorm (*Touristenlager*, *Massenlager* or *Matratzenlager*, *dortoir*, *dormitorio*) may simply comprise one room with as many mattresses as possible squeezed into it side by side, each "bed" sold at bargain-basement prices. This is also the style of dorm accommodation in the 150 or so **Alpine huts** (see below) located at high altitudes on or close to hiking trails, although bed prices tend to rise according to how remote the place is.

Hostelling International ⓦ www.hihostels.com.
Swiss Backpackers (SB) ☎ 062 892 26 76, ⓦ www.backpacker.ch.
Swiss Youth Hostels (HI) ☎ 044 360 14 14, ⓦ www.youthhostel.ch.

Mountain inns

Whole books have been written about the joys of staying in a Swiss **mountain inn** (*Berghaus*, *Berggasthaus*, *Berggasthof* or *Berghotel*, *auberge de montagne*). The term is a tricky one to pin down, since it can refer to varying styles of simple rustic accommodation in a mountain setting. All, though, possess unique character, by dint both of their often spectacular isolated location (generally accessible only by foot, and then often involving long, hard hikes) and of their history – many are old Alpine farmhouses converted more than a century ago to meet the needs of the first holidaying British gentlemen and ladies on their summer tours of the Swiss Alps. Most have undergone some renovation over the intervening decades, but often not much: in general, you can expect an all-wood building in the local architectural style, with rustic decor throughout (window boxes, antiques on the sideboard, ticking grandfather clocks) and a uniquely relaxed, informal atmosphere of cosy communality. Hikers are the main clientele, and Swiss families may return season after season to hike their favourite paths, stay at their favourite *Berghaus*, and catch up on news from the family who owns and runs the place.

Nature, not amenities, is the focus: most *Berghäuser* maintain charmingly old-style bedrooms, with chunky old beds smothered under plump duvets, but very few offer private bathrooms, some may not have showers, and a handful have no hot water, or must generate their own electricity. Most have plenty of **dorm** places (*Massenlager* or *Matratzenlager*). Food is universally good: a *Berghaus* that skimps on sustenance is a

contradiction in terms. Prices are not that much higher than elsewhere – an average Fr.130 for a double, or Fr.45 for a dorm place, both including dinner and breakfast – but you invariably have to pay in cash. It's customary to settle your bill the night before you depart.

Peaceful **Naturfreunde** hotels (ⓦ www .naturfreunde.ch) fall midway between mountain inns and countryside hostels. Often not as remote as *Berghäuser*, they are mostly nonetheless historic buildings well away from beaten tracks, lovingly restored and maintained, and run by individuals with a passion for nature and the environment. About a hundred are scattered around the country.

Farm-stays, B&Bs and private rooms

Schlaf im Stroh, *Aventure sur la paille* or **Sleeping in the Straw** (ⓦ www.abenteuer -stroh.ch) is a great way to get a feel for countryside life while guaranteeing accommodation at a fixed price wherever you are. Hundreds of farming families from all over the country have collaborated in the scheme, which runs from May to October only, each offering 10–15 places to sleep on straw in a barn (but as fresh and pristine a barn as you could wish for), sometimes also offering a handful of bed spaces within the farmhouse, and occasionally a place to pitch a tent or two. An overnight stay costs Fr.20–30 including breakfast at all farms (less for children). You must bring your own sleeping bag if you want to sleep on straw. Your host family can also offer a range of services for modest fees, including putting together a picnic, serving a home-cooked dinner, providing horses, renting bikes and offering guided tours of the countryside around and about.

A slightly less raw option for farm-stays are the 250 **Swiss Holiday Farms** (ⓦ www .bauernhof-ferien.ch), which offer full-blown apartments and rooms for daily or weekly rent on the farm, year-round.

Bed and breakfasts, where you lodge in a room in someone's private house or farmhouse, are something of an innovation in Switzerland, but are becoming steadily more popular. Many tourist offices can give you details of B&Bs in their area, or consult

@www.bnb.ch. Prices can vary quite a bit, depending on the house and the location, but a rough average is a bargain Fr.30–40 per person. You may also come across signs in rural and Alpine resort areas offering **rooms** in private houses (*Zimmer frei*, *chambres à louer*, *affitasi camere*).

Chalets and apartments

Self-catering accommodation in holiday **chalets**, bungalows and apartments tends to be booked solid for entire summer and winter seasons. For chalets in places like Zermatt, Verbier, Gstaad and so on, you may have to book six months or more ahead. Most are let only for a week at a time. Interhome (@www.interhome.ch) is one of the largest and most efficient **international agencies**, dealing with more than 5000 chalets and apartments all over Switzerland, sleeping from two to twelve people. Prices vary tremendously depending on the property and the season, but start from a bargain Fr.17–19 per person per night. High-season bookings are for a minimum of seven nights, Saturday to Saturday, but in the low season you may be able to find properties available for three or four nights only. Booking months in advance ensures you get a full choice of places to stay, but if you leave things to a week before departure, some chalet owners will knock up to a third off their usual prices.

Camping

The typical Swiss **campsite** is clean, well equipped and well maintained. The higher the altitude the more limited the opening times: many close altogether outside the summer season (May or June until Sept or Oct). Just about every town and village in the country has a site or two, classified according to facilities from one to five stars. Average **charges** are Fr.6–8 per person, plus Fr.5–8 for a tent, and Fr.4–5 for a car. Booking ahead is recommended at all times of the year. The motoring organization **TCS** (Swiss Touring Club; @www.tcs.ch) runs a network of sites and is a useful source of information, publishing a national map stocked by larger tourist offices that locates every campsite in the country (theirs and others), as well as the detailed *Camping Guidebook* (*Campingführer*, *Guide Camping*, *Guida dei Campeggi*), available in Swiss bookshops.

An inexpensive **international camping carnet** gives discounts at member sites, serves as identification and covers you for third-party insurance when camping. It's available in the UK from the AA, RAC and Camping & Caravanning Club (℡024/7669 4995, @www.campingandcaravanningclub .co.uk), and in North America from Family Campers and RVers (℡1-800/245-9755, @www.fcrv.org).

Camping rough, outside authorized sites, is formally prohibited by Swiss law, and you may well find yourself with a fine or worse if you try it in populated or cultivated areas, but in the mountain wilds – as long as you take care to clean up properly after yourself – it's hard to envisage how anyone could complain. Discretion and environmental respect are everything.

(*Tagesmenu*, *Tagesteller* or *Tageshit*, *plat/ assiette du jour*, *piatto del giorno*) – often comprising two or even three courses of substantial, quality nosh, whether in a café or a proper restaurant, for around Fr.15. The English term can be confusing: note that in all eating-places the **menu** is the particular dish or dishes on offer that day, while the house list from which you select individual courses is called the *Karte* or *Speisekarte*, *carte*, *carta*. Lunch *menus* are by far the least expensive way to sample the best of Swiss cuisine, and even Michelin-starred gourmet restaurants will offer exquisite multi-course lunches for Fr.30–45 (not including wine). The same meal in the evening, or choosing à la carte anytime, can easily cost double, although beerhalls in the German-speaking cities often serve hearty inexpensive evening meals, and – depending on where you are – pizza-pasta joints and simple informal eateries can fill your stomach for Fr.15–20.

Fondue

These days, you'll find **cheese fondue** everywhere in Switzerland, but it's really a speciality of Suisse-Romande. The word "fondue" refers to the broad, shallow earthenware or cast-iron pot used to heat the cheese… but that's where agreement runs

out. Myriad varieties are served across the country.

The classic style, mainstay of eateries in the fondue heartland of Fribourg and the Vaud countryside, is a **moitié-moitié**, or half-and-half, using either **Gruyère** and **Vacherin Fribourgeois**, or Gruyère and **Emmental**. Others may use several grades of Gruyère, or mix in some local Alpine cheese, Valaisian raclette cheese or Appenzeller. Whichever, it's a winter dish designed to be sampled with friends: a restaurant offering it in the summer is a restaurant to be avoided. Also, since they're never eaten alone, fondues are generally priced as a two-person (or more) deal, or as "fondue à discrétion" or "fondue à gogo" (both of which mean "all you can eat").

There's a whole ritual surrounding fondue consumption, which most Swiss take rather seriously. The cheeses are melted together behind the scenes, generally with a shot of some kind of alcohol (cider in the orchard-rich east, Kirsch in the cherry-growing central regions, white wine in Neuchâtel and Vaud), after which the aromatic pot is brought steaming to your table and set over a small paraffin burner. You use a special long fork to spear a small cube of bread from a separate dish (some places also serve little chunks of boiled potato and/or vegetables), swirl it through the cheese, twirl off the trailing ends, and pop it in. Don't be shy to give it a good vigorous swirl through the pot, since this helps stop the cheese mixture from separating; lose your bread in the fondue, though, and traditionally the drinks are on you. The trick, as the pot gets emptier, is to regularly adjust the heat: have it high enough to keep the cheese from solidifying, but not so high that the mixture boils or burns to the base of the pot.

With roughly 250g of molten cheese consumed per person, a fondue can be quite a heavy load on your system: the Swiss-German remedy is to gulp plenty of hot herbal tea throughout, thus making sure the cheese doesn't solidify in your innards, but the fearless Romands go the other way and favour plenty of chilled white wine. Their *coup de milieu* of a shot of Kirsch (or some other spirit) halfway through supposedly helps things settle – or at least helps mask the stomachache.

On menus nationwide, you'll also see **fondue chinoise**, an entirely different thing where you dip slivers of meat into spicy bouillon; **fondue bourguignonne**, only for the stoutest of constitutions since it involves dousing lumps of red meat in hot spitting oil; **fish** fondues; Valaisian **fondue Bacchus** using mulled wine; and even novelty **chocolate** fondues.

Swiss regional specialities

All across German Switzerland you'll find plentiful variations of **Rösti** or *Röschti*, grated potato formed into a large patty and fried golden-brown on both sides. This can either be an accompaniment to a main course, or, with the embellishment of ham, melted cheese, a fried egg and/or bacon bits, be a comfortably affordable main course itself.

An Alpine stomach-liner that has made its way into the lowlands is **Älper Magrone**, essentially macaroni cheese with extra onion, bacon, potatoes and cream, often served with puréed apples with cinnamon. **Käseschnitten**, in different forms, is Welsh rarebit (toasted cheese), while *Spätzli* and *Knöpfli* are tiny buttons of boiled dough served drizzled with butter.

In and around Bern, you'll find **Bernerteller** or *Bernerplatte*, a hefty pile of cold and hot meats including pork sausage, bacon, various hams, smoked pork, knuckles and beef tongue served with beans and plenty of *Sauerkraut*.

Zürich has **Züri Gschnetzlets**, diced veal in a creamy mushroom sauce, served with *Rösti*, while St Gallen is known for its own pale, milky veal sausages. In Basel, winter menus offer **Basler Mehlsuppe**, a heavy brown brew of onions, pork lard and cream, thickened with flour and topped with grated Sbrinz cheese.

Graubünden is best known for **Bündnerfleisch**, prime beef air-dried in an attic and served paper-thin as part of an aromatic plate of mixed meats known as a *Bündnerteller*, or as prime ingredient in **Bündner Gerstensuppe** (barley cream soup with vegetables). With hunting still very popular in Graubünden, you'll also see plenty of **game** on autumn menus, such as stews (*Pfeffer*, *fratem*) of chamois (*Gemse*, *chamutsch*) or deer (*Hirsch*, *tschierv*).

Zug and Luzern are famous for their black **cherries**, while Basel has its own dark-red variety. **Meringue** was invented in or near Meiringen, and most Emmental and Bernese Oberland villages offer their own spectacular super-rich, cream-laden meringue creations.

The prime speciality of French Switzerland is **fondue**, but there's a host of other cheesy dishes claiming their roots in the region. **Raclette** is known countrywide but born and best savoured in the Valais: a large half-round of special raclette cheese is held in front of a fire, and as it melts it's scraped (*raclé*) onto a plate, and served with boiled potatoes, pearl onions and pickles, often "à gogo".

The **saucisson vaudois**, or pork and beef Vaud sausage, is famous for its delicately smoked flavour, served boiled or steamed, and accompanied by *papet vaudois*, a puree of potatoes and leeks. Lakeside resorts prepare fresh fish in a hundred different ways, most deliciously as **truite meunière**, fresh trout floured and sautéed in butter.

Autumn across Romandie (and across Ticino too) sees **wild mushrooms** (*Pilzen*, *champignons*, *funghi*) making an appearance on the menu, from simple *croûtes aux champignons* (creamy mushrooms on toast) up to flavourful game and mushroom casseroles. In high summer, Valais overflows with golden apricots and peaches, while apples and plums thrive in the lowlands from Lake Geneva to Basel and across to the Bodensee.

Ticino (Italian Switzerland) has its own cuisine, entirely different from what's on offer in the rest of the country and more akin to the flavours and methods of neighbouring Piedmont and Lombardy. **Polenta** (cornmeal) and **risotto** are staples; leafy salads abound, dressed lightly with olive oil instead of the mayonnaise-based concoctions favoured further north; and fresh home-made pastas and **gnocchi** (bite-sized potato dumplings), with the familiar tomato- or pesto-based sauces, are delectable. **Pollo alla cacciatora** is a spicy chicken-and-tomato stew with mushrooms and white wine, served with polenta or boiled potatoes.

The Ticinesi also love their sausages, with Mardi Gras in Lugano serving as an excuse for a public pig-out on risotto with **luganega**, an extra-rich pork sausage. Spicy *mortadella*

Communications

Communications to, from and within Switzerland are as efficient as you'd expect: new-generation public phones have a touch screen from which you can send an email, a text message or a fax, surf the Web, search the complete Swiss phone directory, book a train journey, find somewhere to eat... or even make a call, with everything onscreen in English.

Post

Post offices (☏0800 888 777, ⓦwww .post.ch) – identified by a yellow logo and *Die Post*, *La Poste* or *La Posta* – generally open Monday to Friday 7.30am–noon and 1.30–6pm, and Saturday 8–11am, although watch out for slight regional variations and restricted hours in smaller branches. Some main offices stay open over the lunch break.

For both domestic and international post, there's a two-tier system. **A–Priority post** is delivered next day in Switzerland, within five days to Europe, and within ten days worldwide; **B–Economy post** takes three days domestic, up to ten days to Europe, and up to eight weeks by surface delivery worldwide. Sending a postcard or a 20g letter by A/B post costs Fr.1.30/1.20 to Europe, Fr.1.80/1.40 worldwide. Liechtenstein has stamps which look different but cost the same. For all Priority post, you should write a prominent "A" with a box around it above the address, or ask for one of the blue stickers.

Poste restante is available at any post office: all you need to know is the local four-figure postal code (plus any suffixed digits identifying a particular office in a large city district). They're displayed outside each post office; ⓦwww.post.ch lists the lot. If you want to receive mail at a smaller countryside office in the German-speaking part of the country, where the term "Poste Restante" may be less understood, you should get your correspondents to add the German equivalent – *Postlagernde Briefe*. You need your passport to pick up your mail, and the service is always free. Uncollected mail is returned to sender after 30 days.

Phones

There are always one or two public **phones** (sometimes ranks of them) outside post offices and at train stations, and invariably you'll find that the most remote mountain refuge or country cottage has a phone or two. The former public utility **Swisscom** (☏0800 800 800, ⓦwww.swisscom.com) currently still owns and operates all the public phones.

Useful numbers

Emergencies
Police ☏117
Fire, accidents and life-threatening situations ☏118
Ambulance ☏144
Helicopter rescue
– Rega ☏1414; Air Glaciers ☏1415

Information
Domestic operator ☏111
Directory enquiries
– for Switzerland ☏111
– for Austria ☏1151
– for Germany ☏1152
– for France ☏1153
– for Italy ☏1154
– for all other countries ☏1159
International operator ☏1141

Public services
Breakdown service ☏140
Traffic information ☏163
*Speaking clock ☏161
*Weather forecast ☏162
*Avalanche bulletin ☏187
*in local languages only

A few older phones still accept coins (both Swiss francs and euros, which you can put in together), but the majority take cards only. The easiest, if priciest, option is to insert a Swisscom phonecard (known as a "**taxcard**"), available from post offices, many hotels, newsagents, kiosks, train station ticket counters, and some vending machines in Fr.5, Fr.10 and Fr.20 denominations. You can also swipe a credit/charge card (Visa, MasterCard, Diners, Amex and others); unusually, this doesn't attract any supplementary charges above the cost of the call itself. Pressing button L on the phone switches the display to English.

Most phones have a keyboard and "**Teleguide**" screen attached, from which you can send an email, a fax or a text message, or search the Swiss phone directory (the charge is deducted from your taxcard or credit/charge card as normal). Full onscreen instructions are given in English. You may also spot the new breed of Webpayphones, featuring a touch screen, keyboard and built-in printer, from which you can – in addition to all the above – also access the web, all using a taxcard or a credit/charge card to pay.

For calls **within Switzerland**, you must **dial all ten digits**, even if you're in the same area. Numbers beginning ☎0800 are free; ☎0900 are more expensive than normal; ☎0842 and 0848 are charged as local calls. Domestic rates are highest on weekdays between 8am and 5pm.

Liechtenstein has its own phone company – Telecom FL – although the public phones look and work the same as those in Switzerland, and they accept Swisscom taxcards. Local calls are straightforward (dial all digits), but calling between Liechtenstein and Switzerland counts as international (see "Calling from abroad" below). Some pre-paid discount taxcards may not work from Liechtenstein.

Phoning home

To call **internationally**, there's a wide choice of carriers. It's easiest to use a Swisscom taxcard to dial internationally direct from public phones, but this ties you to Swisscom's prices, which are high. You can save money by asking for an international taxcard

at kiosks (don't get fobbed off with a mobile-phone top-up card instead). Generally, you call a toll-free number to access their lines and type in the PIN number printed beneath a scratch-off layer on the card. You can also use **credit cards** in public phones (Visa, MasterCard, Amex, etc), with no surcharges – you're charged only for the call cost.

To the UK ☎0044
To Ireland ☎00353
To the US or Canada ☎001
To Australia ☎0061
To New Zealand ☎0064

Calling from abroad

First dial your **international access code** (00 from the UK, Ireland and New Zealand; 011 from the US and Canada; 0011 from Australia), followed by **41** for Switzerland, followed by the local number **excluding the initial zero**.

To call **Liechtenstein**, dial your international access code (from Switzerland it's 00), followed by **423**, followed by the seven-digit local number.

Mobile phones

To use your **mobile phone**, check with your provider whether it will work in Switzerland and what the charges will be; technology is GSM (⊛www.gsmworld.com), and coverage – even in the mountains – is generally good. Alternatively, you can **rent** a Swiss mobile from Rentaphone (⊛www.rentaphone.ch), located in Zürich and Geneva airport arrivals.

Email

Access to the **Internet** is everywhere, with cybercafés or public-access terminals (such as in tourist offices or hotel lobbies) either free or costing a few francs. If you're travelling with a **laptop** or palmtop and just need a phoneline, some Swiss phones use the US-style RJ-11, but most of them – and the majority in non-luxury hotel rooms – use either a non-standard chunky square jack or (rarely) an ancient four-pin plug. None uses the British-style design. Many business hotels keep a supply of adaptors and leads for lending to guests. Check out ⊛www.kropla.com for invaluable advice.

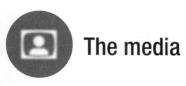

The media

In general, the Swiss have a healthy disregard for the mass media, and watch much less TV than the European average: the German Swiss have the distinction of watching the least TV in Europe. To make up for it they read more, and more locally oriented, newspapers than anyone else on the continent.

Swiss TV and radio

Switzerland has at least seven terrestrial **TV stations** available everywhere, three channels from Schweizer Fernsehen (SF) plus two each from Télévision Suisse Romande (TSR) and Televisione Svizzera Italiana (TSI), plus a handful of national channels from mostly German-speaking private operators, and plenty of local stations for each area. None is what you might call glittering, offering an undemanding diet of chat shows, game shows, made-for-TV movies (dubbed) and lots of local programming. Full details at ⓦwww.srg.ch.

Each language area of the country has at least three broad-coverage regional **radio stations**, one channel devoted to each of news, classical music and popular music (see ⓦwww.srg.ch), as well as a fistful of local city or community stations and networks from neighbouring countries leaking across the border. The Swiss-German **DRS-1** quite often broadcasts concerts of traditional Alpine music and alphorn recitals. The French-language station **Couleur-Trois** plays consistently good cutting-edge rock, pop, world and dance music, though the German-language national equivalent, **DRS-3**, is much less adventurous, sticking with blander chart and mainstream club sounds. Both are around 104–107FM. Italian-language music stations are euroworld in the extreme. English-language **World Radio Geneva** (88.4FM in Geneva only; ⓦwww.wrgfm.com) broadcasts BBC world news, analysis and music shows in amongst its own curiously parochial programming. **Swissinfo** has a daily news service, with audio and video options, at ⓦwww.swissinfo.org.

The Swiss press

Switzerland has a ton of **newspapers** – more than 200 nationwide – but almost without exception they're parochial local news-sheets, reporting cantonal and municipal affairs in some detail, but relegating the rest of Switzerland, let alone the world, to a few inside columns. It's a mark of differing attitudes within the country that whereas French-speaking Swiss regularly turn to Paris's *Le Monde* or *Libération* for opinion from beyond their own borders, and the Ticinesi devour Milan's *Corriere della Sera*, newspapers from Germany have barely any readers at all amongst the proudly Swiss folk south of the border.

Zürich's **Neue Zürcher Zeitung**, or *NZZ* (ⓦwww.nzz.ch), is the best known of Swiss newspapers. Conservative and highbrow in the extreme it nonetheless has gained its reputation by reporting Swiss and world events with scrupulously high journalistic standards. Its francophone equivalent is the more dynamic **Le Temps** (ⓦwww.letemps.ch), published in Geneva, fiercely pro-EU and with consistently progressive stances on social and political issues; it's the only Swiss newspaper that makes it onto Paris newsstands each morning. Otherwise, the field is thin, though Zürich's quality *Tages Anzeiger* offers a lively alternative. Switzerland's biggest-selling paper is *Blick*, a blaring, reactionary rag that regularly espouses anti-immigration and anti-asylum causes.

Of the **weeklies**, *Die Weltwoche* offers quality, left-leaning world news analysis, while the *Wochen Zeitung*, or *WOZ*, has a radical alternative agenda, pushing green issues particularly strongly and packaging once a month the German translation of the highly respected journal of world affairs *Le*

Monde Diplomatique. Lausanne's *L'Hebdo* leads the field of francophone weeklies, but lacks any kind of newsy bite.

The Arts Council of Switzerland *Pro Helvetia* (🌐 www.prohelvetia.ch) twice a year – on paper and online – publishes *Passages*, a heavily intellectual magazine in English of musings on Swiss culture and society, interviews with Swiss artists and short fiction. Subscriptions are free if you live outside Switzerland.

Foreign media

You'll find most British **newspapers** on sale the same day in main train stations and some city kiosks in Geneva, Lausanne, Zürich, Basel and Bern, as well as in well-touristed resorts such as Zermatt, Saas-Fee, Gstaad and Interlaken, and a day late in some other towns. Prices for the normal papers are extraordinary – Fr.5.50 or more for the broadsheets – but most outlets stock *The Guardian*'s condensed European edition, the *Financial Times*, *International Herald Tribune* and *USA Today* for less.

If a hotel room has a **TV** it's very likely to be hooked up to cable or satellite, giving you the dubious pleasure of 30 or 40 channels in a variety of European languages, plus Turkish or Arabic. CNN news is the only English-language certainty wherever you are, although many places have BBC Prime, showing British soaps, drama and comedy, and some also have BBC World, with rolling news and features.

As for **radio**, you might pick up the BBC World Service on 648kHz medium wave, but you may have to resort to short wave instead (17.640, 15.565, 15.485, 12.095, 9.410, 7.130, 6.195 or 5.975MHz). In many Swiss cities you can get the BBC on FM, but only via cable: some hotels offer cable radio; many don't. World Radio Geneva (88.4FM in Geneva) broadcasts the BBC news on the hour. Thousands of stations, including the BBC (🌐 www.bbc.co.uk), Voice of America (🌐 www.voa.gov), Radio Canada (🌐 www.rcinet.ca) and Radio Australia (🌐 www.abc.net.au), broadcast online.

Opening hours and public holidays

Switzerland's reputation for calmness and domesticity is borne out by its down-to-earth attitude to the consumer revolution: in contrast to most of the rest of the Western world, Swiss laws on strictly limited opening times reflect universal public concern to uphold the rights of serving staff at the expense of consumers.

You'll find that banks, post offices, shops, supermarkets, tourist offices – just about everything – in most Swiss towns and villages still shut between noon and 2pm, to allow staff to go home for lunch. This is slowly being eroded in favour of consumer-friendly all-day opening, especially in the big towns and cities, but old habits are dying hard.

Shop opening hours are customarily Monday to Friday 9am–noon and 2–6.30pm, Saturday 8.30am–noon, although it's becoming more common to stay open over the lunch break and also stay open on Saturdays until 5pm; the flipside is that some places then take Monday morning off. Quiet Sundays are sacrosanct. Most towns operate universal late opening until 9pm for one day a week, generally Thursday (Friday in Graubünden). The main exceptions to all this are shops and cafés within the subterranean malls at train stations, where everything stays open daily, and also close later in the evening.

Fairy-tale castles

Château d'Aigle p.317.
Castelgrande, Bellinzona p.531.
Château de Chillon p.158.
Château de Gruyères p.138.
Schloss Thun p.297.

Bank opening hours vary, but in the cities are generally Mon–Fri 8.30am–4.30pm, sometimes with a break for lunch; town and village branches have shorter hours. Some city and tourist-resort banks also open on Saturday, often 9am–4pm.

Cafés fall into two broad categories. Those that open in the morning for coffee and breakfasts might then close when the shops shut, at about 6 or 6.30pm. Some, though, open at noon for lunch or in mid-afternoon (say 4 or 5pm), and then metamorphose into **bars** until midnight or so. Those that serve full meals (which is most of them) will only do so at the customary mealtimes: roughly noon to 2pm and 6 to 10pm. Outside those hours, you'll generally be able to find only snacks. Formal **restaurants** keep to the same mealtimes, closing altogether in between times.

Many **museums** and public attractions are open on Sundays and **closed on Mondays**; a few also take Tuesdays off.

Public holidays

National **public holidays** – when almost everything is closed – are listed below, but they're only part of the story. Most cantons supplement these with a handful of often religious holidays of their own, which can tie in with local festivals: various Catholic cantons, for instance, observe various saints' days (Ticino manages to authorize 17 annual holidays for itself). Common **cantonal holidays** include January 2 (St Bertold's Day, *Berchtoldstag*), January 6 (Epiphany, *Dreikönigstag*, *Epiphanie*, *Epifania*), May 1 (Labour Day, *Tag der Arbeit*, *Fête du Travail*, *Festa del Lavoro*), late May's Corpus Christi,

Top art galleries

Major museums
Fondation Beyeler, Basel p.216. Twentieth-century.
Kunstmuseum, Basel p.214. Holbein, moderns.
Zentrum Paul Klee, Bern p.244. Klee.
Musée d'Art et d'Histoire, Geneva p.97. Rodin, Rembrandt, Hodler.
Sammlung Rosengart, Luzern p.372. Picasso, Klee.
Fondation Pierre Gianadda, Martigny p.325. Temporary shows.
Oskar Reinhart, Winterthur p.450. Holbein, Delacroix, Impressionists.
Kunsthaus, Zürich p.422. Flemish, Baroque, Giacometti, Munch…

Outstanding smaller museums
Collections Baur, Geneva p.98. East Asian ceramics.
Collection de l'Art Brut, Lausanne p.128. Outsider art.
Musée Jenisch, Vevey p.151. Modernists, Rembrandt, Dürer.
Villa Flora, Winterthur p.451. Impressionists.
Museum Rietberg, Zürich p.429. Asian art.

Contemporary art and photography
Kunsthalle, Basel p.214. Contemporary art.
Museum Jean Tinguely, Basel p.216. Tinguely.
MAMCO, Geneva p.98. Contemporary art.
Musée de l'Elysée, Lausanne p.133. Photography.
Fotomuseum, Winterthur p.451. Photography.
Museum für Gestaltung, Zürich p.431. Contemporary design.

August 15 (Assumption, *Mariä Himmelfahrt, Assomption, Assunzione*) and November 1 (All Saints' Day, *Allerheiligen, Toussaint, Ognissanti*). Look out also for the seasonal pageants centred in various cities, and the often tumultuous celebrations of **carnival** on and around Mardi Gras in mid-February, which – amidst raucous partying in Luzern and Basel in particular – can often affect shop opening hours.

Liechtenstein has all the same Swiss public holidays except August 1: the national holiday is on August 15 instead. It also celebrates May 1 (*Tag der Arbeit*).

January 1 New Year's Day, *Neujahr, Nouvel An, Capodanno*

March/April Good Friday, *Karfreitag, Vendredi saint, Venerdì Santo*

March/April Easter Monday, *Ostermontag, lundi de Pâques, Lunedì di Pasqua*

May Ascension Day, *Auffahrt/Christi Himmelfahrt, Ascension, Ascensione*

May/June Whit Monday, *Pfingstmontag, lundi de Pentecôte, Lunedì di Pentecoste*

August 1 Swiss National Day, *Nationalfeiertag, Fête nationale, Festa nazionale* (public institutions and some shops and banks closed)

December 25 Christmas Day, *Weihnachten, Noël, Natale*

December 26 Boxing Day, *Stefanstag, St-Etienne, Santo Stefano*

Festivals and annual events

Running counter to the dour national stereotype, Switzerland has masses of festivals (*Feiertage, jours féries, festività*), held in towns and villages all over the country for the slightest excuse, from celebrating onions up to St Moritz's inimitable horseracing-on-ice extravaganza.

Listing them all would be impossible, and anyway would ruin the experience – well within the bounds of possibility – of stumbling by chance onto some small Swiss village's unadvertised annual knees-up of folk-dancing, street-barbecuing and general merriment. Switzerland Tourism maintains an encyclopedic events calendar at Ⓦwww.myswitzerland.com, detailing hundreds of pageants big and small.

In **music**, the biggest show is July's **Montreux Jazz Festival**, these days featuring as much rock, dance and world music as jazz and blues. Massive open-air weekends in July at Bern, Nyon and St Gallen are regular stopoffs on the European festival circuit, and Bern's own orthodox jazz festival pulls in top artists year after year. Zürich's August **Street Parade** attracts a million techno revellers from all over Europe. In classical music, the **Lucerne Festival** – comprising separate events in March, August and November – is one of the premier events of its kind, with

opera at Avenches and summer performance cycles at Verbier, Gstaad and Sion no less stellar. The **Locarno International Film Festival** is one of the top five in the world.

Of the more **traditional festivals**, carnival, in mid-February, features huge street parties in Luzern, Basel and Bern in particular, with Zürich, Lugano and smaller towns also mounting parades. Spring festivals in Zürich and Lausanne, and autumn harvest festivals all round the country, keep alive traditions of costume and cuisine stretching back to the Middle Ages.

Some of the moveable events worth looking out for include **Schwingen**, traditional Swiss wrestling that's hugely popular in rural areas and is generally accompanied by traditional markets, beer-quaffing and hearty sausage-feasting. Weekends devoted to *Schwingen* championships take place all over the centre and east of the country at various dates between April and September; ask at tourist offices for details.

There are also many **yodelling** events through the springtime, culminating in the annual Swiss Alpine Yodelling Championships, held in early July in a different town each year.

Aside from the large international events, which are primarily moneyspinners, you'll find the dozens of local festivals celebrating **food** or **wine** to be heartfelt community experiences, staged for pleasure. Similarly, in Catholic areas – French-, German-, Italian- and Romansh-speaking – each town or region keeps one day a year to honour the local **patron saint**; these are jovial local events, by, with and for the townspeople, with not a thought of tourism in mind.

Events calendar

January

early Basel – Vogel Gryff: traditional costumed dance and drum festival ⓦ www.vogel-gryff.ch.
mid Wengen – World Cup downhill ski-racing on the Lauberhorn ⓦ www.lauberhorn.ch.
late Mürren – Inferno giant-slalom ski race ⓦ www .inferno-muerren.ch.
late Château d'Oex – international hot-air ballooning week ⓦ www.chateau-doex.ch.

February

early Lötschental VS – Roitschäggättä: elaborate masked parades ⓦ www.loetschental.ch.
early St Moritz – horse-racing on the frozen lake ⓦ www.stmoritz.ch.
mid St Moritz – toboggan competitions on the Cresta Run ⓦ www.cresta-run.com.
mid Around Switzerland – Carnival: the biggest events, which run contiguously, are in Luzern (six days, from the Thursday before Mardi Gras up to Mardi Gras night; ⓦ www.luzerner-fasnacht.ch), Bern (two days, beginning on the Thursday evening after Mardi Gras; ⓦ www.baernerfasnacht.ch), and Basel (three days, beginning at 4am on the Monday after Mardi Gras; ⓦ www.fasnacht.ch). Many towns and villages celebrate Carnival at various times from mid-February until early March.

March

early Geneva – International Motor Show ⓦ www .palexpo.ch.
mid Lucerne Festival – Easter programme of classical music ⓦ www.lucernefestival.ch.
mid St Moritz and around – Engadin Ski Marathon ⓦ www.engadin-skimarathon.ch.

mid St Moritz – Snow and Symphony classical music festival ⓦ www.snowandsymphony.ch.
late Verbier – Xtreme snowboarding championship ⓦ www.xtremeverbier.com.

April

mid Visp – traditional Valaisian cow fights ⓦ www .valaistourism.ch.
mid Zürich – Sechseläuten: traditional spring festival, with parades and fireworks ⓦ www.sechselaeuten.ch.
late Appenzell – Landsgemeinde: annual session of public voting on local issues ⓦ www.ai.ch.
late Lausanne – Fête du Soleil: live bands, open-air restaurants and markets ⓦ www.carnavalausanne.ch.

May

early Glarus – Landsgemeinde: annual session of public voting on local issues ⓦ www.gl.ch.
early Bern International Jazz Festival ⓦ www .jazzfestivalbern.ch.
mid Aproz, near Sion – the cantonal cow-fighting champions' meeting ⓦ www.valaistourism.ch.

June

early Appenzell, Gruyères and many villages in central and eastern Switzerland – celebration of the cattle's ascent to Alpine pastures
until Sept Interlaken – open-air performances of Schiller's play *William Tell* ⓦ www.tellspiele.ch.
until July Zürich Festival: theatre, opera, music and art ⓦ www.zuercher-festspiele.ch.
mid Tour de Suisse cycle race ⓦ www.cycling.ch.
mid Basel – Art Basel, international contemporary art fair ⓦ www.artbasel.com.
late Zürich – inline skating marathon ⓦ www .swiss-inline-cup.ch.
late St Moritz – inline skating marathon ⓦ www .swiss-inline-cup.ch.
late Bellinzona – Piazza Blues festival ⓦ www .piazzablues.ch.
late Winterthur – Albanifest: music festival ⓦ www .stadtfest.ch.
late St Gallen – open-air rock festival ⓦ www .openairsg.ch.
late Ascona Jazz Festival – New Orleans-style ⓦ www.jazzascona.ch.

July

4 Geneva – US Independence Day celebrations: the biggest outside the US ⓦ www.genevatourism.ch.
all month Avenches Opera Festival: open-air performances in the Roman amphitheatre ⓦ www .avenches.ch.
early Montreux Jazz Festival: everyone from Alannis Morrisette to Femi Kuti ⓦ www.montreuxjazz.com.

early Lausanne – Festival de la Cité: free open-air performances and music ⓦ www.festivaldelacite.ch.
early Gstaad – Swiss Open international tennis tournament ⓦ www.swissopengstaad.com.
mid Lugano – Estival Jazz ⓦ www.estivaljazz.ch.
mid Bern – Gurten Festival: mass hilltop rock festival ⓦ www.gurtenfestival.ch.
late Nyon – Paléo Festival: huge rock and dance happening ⓦ www.paleo.ch.
late Verbier Festival and Academy: world-renowned classical soloists and conductors ⓦ www .verbierfestival.com.
until Sept Gstaad – Menuhin Festival: top classical performances ⓦ www.menuhinfestivalgstaad.ch.

August

1st Swiss National Day: fireworks, folkloric shows, parades and more, in every corner of the country.
early Geneva – Fêtes de Genève: fireworks, parades and concerts ⓦ www.fetes-de-geneve.ch.
early Locarno International Film Festival ⓦ www .pardo.ch.
early Saignelégier – Marché Concours: national horse festival ⓦ www.marcheconcours.ch.
early Winterthur – Kyburgiade chamber music festival ⓦ www.kyburgiade.ch.
mid St Gallen – One-Eleven 111km inline skating race ⓦ www.one-eleven.ch.
mid Zürich – Street Parade: immense techno/dance gathering ⓦ www.streetparade.ch.
mid Zürich – Weltklasse: international athletics meeting ⓦ www.weltklasse.ch.
15 Liechtenstein National Day ⓦ www.tourismus.li.
late Willisau Jazz Festival: experimental and modern jazz groups from around the world, performing in the Luzern countryside ⓦ www.jazzwillisau.ch.
late Montreux & Vevey – classical music and lyric poetry ⓦ www.montreux-festival.com.
until mid-Sept Lucerne Festival: one of Europe's leading classical music events, with soloists and orchestras of world renown ⓦ www.lucernefestival .ch.

September

early Zürich – Theater Spektakel: international open-air drama festival ⓦ www.theaterspektakel.ch.
early Bern – Old Town Festival ⓦ www.bern.ch.
early Fribourg – La Bénichon: traditional Thanksgiving festival ⓦ www.fribourgtourism.ch.
mid/late Around Switzerland – winegrowers' festivals: dozens of local village and town celebrations of the grape harvest, especially in cantons Vaud, Valais, Neuchâtel, Bern, Schaffhausen and Ticino.

October

early Charmey, Appenzell and many villages in central and eastern Switzerland – celebration of the cattle's descent from Alpine pastures, often tied in with cheese markets.
late Basel Autumn Fair: traditional food fair held since 1470 ⓦ www.basel.ch.

November

early Vevey and Porrentruy – St Martin's market: festivals devoted to sausages, ham and pork.
early Aarau – Rüeblimärt: festival devoted to carrots ⓦ www.aarau.ch.
late Bern – Zibelemärit: festival devoted to onions ⓦ www.markt-bern.ch.
late Lucerne International Piano Festival ⓦ www .lucernefestival.ch.

December

early Around Switzerland – celebrations either side of Dec 6 for the arrival of St Nicholas (Santa Claus).
10–12 Geneva – Fête de l'Escalade: celebrating Geneva's independence ⓦ www.compagniede1602 .ch.
mid Zürich – Lichterschwimmen: candles floated down the River Limmat ⓦ www.zurichtourism.ch.
late Davos – Spengler Cup international ice-hockey tournament ⓦ www.spenglercup.ch.
31 Urnäsch and other Appenzell villages – masked parades for St Sylvester ⓦ www.appenzell.ch.

Sports and outdoor pursuits

Switzerland is heaven for indulging in sports and outdoorsiness of all kinds. Facilities abound in all areas of sport and exercise for literally all ages and abilities: kids start skiing as young as 2 or 3, while plenty of Swiss grandparents spend their retirement years hiking or cycling around the Alps. Safety is taken very seriously and standards are very high.

Walking

Swiss mountains are among the most dramatic and challenging of all the Alpine ranges, but you don't have to be a skilled mountaineer or climber to enjoy an active holiday among them. Switzerland contains some of Europe's finest **walking** terrain, with enough variety to suit every taste. In the northwest, for example, the rolling Jura hills are heavily wooded, but with open meadows that provide long views across the lowlands to Alpine giants. The Bernese Alps, with notoriously savage peaks such as the Eiger, Schreckhorn and Finsteraarhorn, harbour a glacial heartland but they also feature gentle valleys, pastoral ridges and charming alp hamlets with well-marked trails weaving through. On the south side of the Rhône Valley the Pennine Alps are burdened with snow and glaciers, yet walkers' paths lead along their moraines to give a taste of adventure without overtly courting danger. By contrast the mountains of Canton Ticino projecting south into Italy are almost completely snow- and ice-free in summer, and you'll find a wonderland of trails among their modest, lake-jewelled peaks.

In major tourist areas walkers can use chairlifts, gondolas and cable cars in summer and autumn to reach high and otherwise remote trails, while rustic inns and a network of **Alpine or mountain huts** (*Hütte, refuge, rifugio* or *cabane* or *capanna*) provide rudimentary dormitory accommodation, and often meals too, for those who plan to make multi-day walking tours.

For more information, and general guidance about walking, contact the **Swiss Hiking Federation** (@www.swisshiking.ch). Switzerland Tourism publishes a brochure

"Ways to Switzerland", introducing and mapping six major long-distance hiking routes of particular cultural interest, including the network of Roman roads in Switzerland, the "Chemins de St Jacques", followed for centuries by pilgrims heading from Germany to Santiago de Compostela in Spain, and trans-Alpine mule-tracks used by traders in former ages.

Paths and signposts

Paths are well maintained, and clearly marked with regular yellow signposts displaying the names of major landmark destinations, often with an estimate of the time it takes to walk to them. Most signposts also have a white plate giving the name and altitude of the spot you're standing on. There are three major types of path.

A **Wanderweg**, *chemin de randonnée pédestre* or *sentiero escursionistico* remains either in the valley or travels the hillsides at a modest altitude, is sometimes surfaced and will be graded at a relatively gentle angle. **Yellow** diamonds or pointers show the continuation of the route. (You may also spot some cultural trails – old pilgrims' roads and the like – signposted in **brown**.)

A **Bergweg**, *chemin de montagne* or *sentiero di montagna* is a mountain path which runs higher or steeper and can be quite demanding, often rough, narrow and sometimes fading if not in regular use. They're marked with the same yellow signposts, but with a **red-and-white** pointer instead of yellow. Waymarks along a mountain path are marked with similar white-red-white bars, and you may occasionally come across cairns directing the way across boulder slopes, or where poor visibility could create difficulties.

Best hikes

Best half- or full-day walks

Davos Testing, little-used trail from the Weissfluh over to Arosa. p.499.

Grindelwald Of dozens of possibilities, the walk up through rolling pastures from Grund to Männlichen is stunning. p.293.

Kleine Scheidegg A classic high-country strolling path along the ridge to Männlichen. p.295.

Lake Geneva Plenty of paths weave in and around the Lavaux vineyards above the lake. p.147.

St Moritz Among many superb full-day trails is a panoramic route from Murtèl to Fuorcla Surlej, then over the pass to Pontresina. p.515.

Val Bavona One of the most beautiful valleys of Alto Ticino, with easy routes down to Bignasco. p.535.

Zermatt Routes around the Schwarzsee offer photogenic views of the Matterhorn. p.350.

Best multi-day walks

Interlaken Schynige Platte–Faulhorn–First–Grindelwald; one of the most scenic high-level walks in the Bernese Oberland, best done over two easy days. p.281.

Jura Höhenweg Long, often isolated trail along the length of the Swiss Jura from Zürich to Geneva. p.222.

Kandersteg Outstanding back-country trail into the Gasterntal, over the Lötschen Pass and down into the tranquil Lötschental. p.306.

Parc Naziunal Svizzer Superb walk from Zernez through the pristine park country-side, overnighting at Cluozza. p.507.

Swiss Path Easy route around the romantic, cliff-girt Urnersee, walkable in two days or dividable into sections. p.383.

Walker's Haute Route Demanding two-week trek from Chamonix, traversing a series of craggy valleys to Zermatt. p.329.

Higher, extremely hard-going Alpine trails, marked in **blue**, are only for those accompanied by a mountain guide and carrying specialist equipment.

Planning your walk

No one should venture among the mountains, whatever level of walking is proposed, without consulting a good **map**. Local shops and tourist offices usually have a selection on offer, and the latter sometimes also publish their own walkers' maps with suggested routes and times given on the reverse. On occasion **guided walks** are arranged by tourist offices in mountain areas, which may be free of charge for guests staying in local hotels. A series of excellent English-language **guidebooks** for walkers covering the Bernese Alps, Central Switzerland, Engadine, Ticino, and the Valais, plus several long-distance Alpine walks, are published by Cicerone Press in the UK, most written by Kev Reynolds.

Always check the **weather** forecast before setting out. The local tourist office or mountain guides' bureau invariably displays a two- or three-day forecast. Needless to say, do not venture to high altitudes if bad weather is expected. In any case, though, it's sensible to take a pullover or fleece and a waterproof jacket as minimum protection even if you simply plan to take a cable-car ride followed by a short stroll. On more ambitious outings it is essential to be properly equipped with wind- and waterproof clothing and good footwear. Trainers may be adequate for short valley walks, but for tackling steep hillsides and mountain paths, walking boots with ankle support and hard-wearing soles are indispensable.

Avalanche warnings, published morning and evening 365 days a year by the Federal Institute for Snow and Avalanche Research (⊛www.slf.ch), are posted online and publicized widely in mountain areas.

One-day walks

Never embark on a walk that under normal conditions cannot be completed **well before dark**. Reasonably fit walkers carrying a light rucksack should be able to manage 4.5kph (2mph) on the flat, plus an additional hour for every 350m of ascent. Carry food for the day, including emergency rations, and at least one litre of water per person. Take extra care when crossing snow patches, exposed rocks and mountain streams. On some *Bergweg* routes, fixed ropes are provided as safeguards. Elsewhere there may be sections of metal ladder fitted to enable walkers to overcome a short stretch of rock. Always check these first before committing your weight to them. Do not stray onto glaciers and snowfields unless accompanied by a mountaineer experienced in glacier travel and with the necessary equipment to deal with crevasse rescue. Above all, don't be too proud to turn back should the weather deteriorate or the route become difficult or dangerous.

Multi-day walks

When tackling **hut-to-hut walks** the list of what to take with you increases. It is prudent to carry a map and compass – and to know how to use them. You should also take a first-aid kit. Don't rely on a mobile phone, since mountain coverage may be patchy; always carry a whistle and torch/flashlight in case of emergencies. Leave a note of your planned itinerary and expected time of return with a responsible person who's staying behind in a fixed location, and when staying in mountain huts enter your route details in the book provided. If for some reason you can't reach the destination where you're expected, try to send a message ahead to prevent the mountain rescue team being called out. In an emergency, give the **International Distress Signal**: six short blasts on a whistle (or flashes with a torch), followed by a minute's pause. Repeat until you receive an answer; the response is three signals followed by a minute's silence.

Switzerland has no free mountain rescue service, and the cost of an accident can be extremely high. Standard travel **insurance** policies do not cover such emergencies, so if you are devoting all or most of your holiday to serious walking in the mountains, it's sensible to choose a policy which specifically covers mountain activity and includes emergency rescue.

Mountain huts

Mountain huts provide simple accommodation for climbers and walkers, are invariably situated in remote and scenically spectacular locations and are owned either by local groups of the **Swiss Alpine Club** (⊛www.sac-cas.ch), other clubs, or private companies or individuals. Many are staffed by a guardian during the summer months – usually from mid-June to mid-September – who will prepare simple meals and drinks. Mixed-sex dormitories with large, side-by-side sleeping platforms are the norm. Blankets and pillows, but not sheets, are supplied, so it's a good idea to take a sleeping bag liner (sheet sleeping bag) with you if you plan to use huts. Prices vary, but

---

Favourite views

Cardada p.541. Panoramas over Ascona and Lago Maggiore.
Monte Brè p.554. Eyrie above Lugano and its sugarloaf mountains.
Muottas Muragl p.518. The glittering Engadine lakes.
Schynige Platte p.281. Classic Berner Oberland panoramas.
Vue des Alpes p.175. Jura belvedere with an uninterrupted 100km view.
Wengen p.288. Perched between the Lauterbrunnen valley and the mighty Jungfrau.
Zermatt p.344. Jaw-dropping views up to the Matterhorn.

are around Fr.25–30 for a bed, plus about the same again if you include dinner and breakfast.

Most huts have a phone and as a matter of courtesy you should phone ahead to book a place; we've listed numbers of the more popular and accessible huts throughout the book, but local tourist offices will have details of all of them, and they're also listed in a very useful book, *Schweizer Hüttenverzeichnis*, available throughout bookshops in Switzerland, as well as at ⓦ www.bergtourismus.ch.

Membership of an Alpine club in your home country may entitle you to reduced overnight charges in SAC huts.

Skiing and winter sports

It goes without saying that Switzerland is one of the best **winter sports** destinations in the world. The country managed to escape the worst of the 1960s boom in resort construction which afflicted many parts of the Alps, and benefits today from resorts which are generally small in scale and retain a good deal of **character** compared to the concrete monstrosities in France and Italy. These days you can often get better **value for money** skiing in Switzerland than in its neighbours (even Austria, traditionally bargain-priced), and the general tenor of Swiss ski resorts is much more cosy and village-based than elsewhere. Its resorts benefit from peaceful, mostly entirely natural Alpine runs – many of them starting well above the treeline and set against some of the greatest mountain vistas to be seen anywhere. In addition, Swiss resorts are higher than most, and thus have guaranteed snow cover; lower resorts in neighbouring countries are beginning to feel the pinch from global warming, with snow patchy or non-existent, even in midwinter.

The **winter season** runs from mid-December to mid-April – though at altitudes above about 2500m the season extends from November to May. The busiest times, when you'll pay most for ski passes and accommodation, are clustered together in early January and mid-February. Late April is the best time to take advantage of late snow and snap up cheap deals.

Skiing, snowboarding and beyond

Skiing is generally split into two varieties. Alpine or **downhill skiing** (*Skifahren*, *ski alpin*, *sci*) is the more popular, and involves swooshing down the mountain on **blue** (easy), **red** (intermediate) or **black** (difficult) runs, according to your ability, or – if you're entirely confident of your skills and take all necessary precautions – venturing off-piste. Downhill gets all the glamour and attention, while Nordic or **cross-country skiing** (*Ski Langlauf* or *Ski Wandern*, *ski de fond* or *ski nordique*, *sci di fondo*) is seen as much harder work for much less thrill. However, cross-country eliminates any queues for lifts up the mountain, most of the expensive equipment associated with downhill and all the hassle. It allows you to get way out into the tranquil countryside, is much less punishing for your body and, in fact, gives a much better workout: not for nothing do enthusiasts claim alliteratively that *Langläufer leben länger* ("Cross-country skiers live longer"). Prepared cross-country trails, known as *Loipen* or *loipes*, are laid on sign-posted routes fanning out from most resorts, the cream of the crop being in the Engadine Valley around St Moritz.

Snowboarding is massively popular throughout the country, with all major resorts – and plenty of minor ones too – encouraging the sport with well-maintained half-pipes, lessons for all abilities and boarding tournaments all winter long.

There's any number of more or less crazed minor sports which tag along on the heels of skiing and snowboarding. **Mono-skiing**, like head-on snowboarding, uses a single extra-wide ski into which both feet are strapped side by side. **Ski-joring**, where you're pulled along by galloping horses, is one of the more exhilarating thrills in the snow, as is **snow-biking** or **snow-bobbing** – essentially cycling on snow. **Tobogganing** or sledding is hugely popular, and many places have pistes reserved for it; **bobsleighing** (for instance at St Moritz's death-defying Cresta Run), is the pro's version, while **luge** is a one-person tea-tray, on which you shoot feet-first down a bob-run.

If you're getting bored with all those simple black runs, try **heli-skiing**, where you pay a helicopter pilot to dump you in an inaccessible spot at 4000m amidst virgin powder, or **ski hang-gliding**, where you float to earth out of an aeroplane, and then ski back to the pub. **Zorbing**, which counts as a winter or a summer "sport", has gained new devotees in the classier thrill-seeking resorts of the Valais in particular; it involves being strapped immobile inside a giant plastic sphere, arms and legs spread, and then rolled down a mountainside.

Destinations

The **classic destinations**, a selection (or all) of which are offered by most package operators, include Davos, Klosters, Saas-Fee, Zermatt, St Moritz, Verbier, Crans-Montana, Wengen, Mürren and Grindelwald. Flims-Laax-Falera is also rapidly making a name for itself.

However, it's quite possible that slightly less famous resorts will turn out to be more rewarding, especially for first-timers or relative novices; they'll be cheaper and less crowded to start with, but also with a greater emphasis on the personal touch, and with less of a daunting competitive edge on the slopes. A sample of these might include Arosa, Engelberg, Kandersteg, Villars-Gryon-Les Diablerets, Leysin, Champéry/Portes du Soleil, Lenzerheide, Savognin, Adelboden-Lenk, the Aletsch region, or Airolo and Alto Ticino. **Beginners** are perhaps best served at Arosa, Kandersteg, Saas-Fee or Mürren. Dedicated **family** resorts – major names like Villars-Gryon or Meiringen, and smaller, tucked-away places such as Malbun or Braunwald – are great for **kids** finding their feet. Sporty thrills and spills on the slopes followed by buzzing après-ski **nightlife** is best sampled at Davos, Verbier or St Moritz. The major names of Zermatt, Wengen and Klosters offer top-notch skiing amidst relatively quiet village-style surroundings. Some big-name resorts – most notably Gstaad – tend to deliver more designer-label shopping than on-piste satisfaction.

Year-round **summer skiing** is possible in a few resorts with access to glacier pistes above 3000m; these include Verbier, Zermatt, Les Diablerets (also with access from Gstaad), Engelberg, Crans Montana and Saas-Fee.

Passes and equipment

Passes for the ski lifts and cable cars in and around each resort vary hugely in price: a rough average is Fr.40–50 per day, decreasing for longer periods; the big names charge upwards of Fr.60, smaller or harder-to-reach places as little as Fr.20. You can always get half-day passes, and most resorts offer an array of multi-day passes, non-consecutive day passes, weekday discounts, early- and late-season offers, and more. Many places offer discounted online booking, and you can often get a bargain if you buy your pass before the season starts (by, say, November). Use of buses and other valley transport in and around resorts is invariably included.

You can always **rent** any amount of equipment after you arrive: one day's downhill gear is approximately Fr.45–50, cross-country gear around Fr.20–25. InterSport (ⓦwww.intersport.ch) and SwissRent (ⓦwww.swissrent.com) have outlets in virtually every resort in the country, and both also allow you to reserve equipment online. All Swiss resorts have **ski schools** attached, where you can, in most cases, just turn up and pay for a day's or a week's tuition in a group or one-to-one. Prices vary dramatically, roughly Fr.150–200 for five mornings' tuition; for more information, check with Swiss Ski & Snowboard Schools (ⓦwww.snowsports.ch).

Joining a **ski club** at home gives you access to information and impartial recommendations for resorts around Switzerland. Most can also provide details of tour operators which concentrate on ski- or winter-packages (or occasionally may offer such packages themselves). The Ski Club of Great Britain (ⓦwww.skiclub.co.uk) has particularly good information.

Cycling and mountain biking

Given the nature of the landscape, **cycling** (ⓦwww.cycling-in-switzerland.ch) is not the easiest way of exploring Switzerland, but the scenery more than compensates for the extra effort required. It's a very popular Swiss pursuit, and the locals don't restrict themselves to flat lakeside or valley-floor routes: summer weekends see plenty of sinewy, lycra-clad characters pumping their way slowly up the long 12 or 14 percent gradients of the high Alpine passes. Cycle routes – in the cities too – are plentiful. If you're arriving in Switzerland with **your own bike**, you have to buy a **vignette** from post offices for around Fr.5, which covers road tax and third-party insurance for a year. The Swiss Cycling Federation is at Ⓦwww.cycling.ch.

Under the banner of *Veloland Schweiz*, *La Suisse à vélo*, *La Svizzera in bici*, nine long-distance **cycle routes** crisscross the country on 3300km of dedicated signposted paths, mostly well away from traffic. Tourist offices can give you a map of all nine routes, and information in English on each one, as well as maps showing other cycle routes within their region or city; Ⓦwww.cycling-in -switzerland.ch has full details. **Mountain biking** is very popular at loads of Swiss resorts, many of which produce their own local guides to bike routes in their area.

A day-pass to let you **transport a bike** by train anywhere in Switzerland costs Fr.15; you have to load and unload it yourself using the special carriage marked with a bicycle pictogram, and you must have a ticket or pass for the same destination. Some EC trains and the Bern and Zürich S-Bahn are prohibited during rush hours: yellow train timetables mark those trains on which bikes cannot be transported with a crossed-out pictogram. Station staff have full details, as does Ⓦwww.rail.ch.

Bike rental

You can **rent** a new seven-gear country bike or a quality 21-gear mountain bike from Rent-A-Bike (Ⓦwww.rentabike.ch), located at most Swiss train stations (look for *Mietvelos, location de vélos*, *bici da noleggiare*). If there's no dedicated bike office, you normally rent from left-luggage counters. **Prices** are Fr.23 for a half-day (the cut-off time is 12.30pm) or Fr.31 for a full day. The popular option of one-way rental (for a full day or more) attracts a Fr.7 surcharge; you must let staff know where and when you intend to drop the bike off when you rent. Note that if you hold any kind of Swiss travel pass, all these prices are discounted by about 20 percent. Kids' bikes and seats for children which you can attach to an adult's bike are also available.

Station bike rental is massively popular, especially throughout the summer months, and if you're planning to rent you should always **reserve** as far as possible in advance (normally, a day or two is OK). Look for the bike-train leaflet at stations, which has a list of stations, phone numbers and the number of rental bikes at each one. Even so, on summer weekends, stations like Bern and Zürich that hold dozens of bikes for rent can be completely cleaned out: in these cases, you may have to take a train (or call ahead) to a smaller town and try there.

As a way to teach local unemployed people new skills and get them back to work, Zürich, Bern, Geneva and a handful of other cities run **free bike-rental** schemes year-round, invariably from depots beside or opposite the train station. All you do is pay a Fr.20 deposit and leave some ID, and you're free to cycle off for as long as you like.

Other sports and activities

To complement the many cycle routes, there are currently three long-distance **inline skating** routes of around 200km each, from Geneva to Brig, Zürich to Yverdon, and haffhausen. Inline skating and roller-skating are popular all round the country, from the lakeside promenade at Lausanne to the runway of Samedan airfield, in the mountains near St Moritz. Ⓦwww .swiss-skate-map.ch shows skating routes nationwide.

Swimming and **watersports** have big followings at all the lakeside resorts, and almost everywhere is clean enough (signs are posted otherwise). Boats and equipment for windsurfing are available for rent or almost all lakes, and wakeboarding and kitesurfing are also attracting attention, not least at Silvaplana, near St Moritz. **Rowing** and **canoeing** are also popular, especially on the Rotsee near Luzern, which regularly stages the rowing world championships.

The boom in **adventure sports** has arrived in Switzerland with a vengeance, and places like Interlaken and the Ticino have dozens of companies offering canyoning and bungee jumping, as well as **aerial sports** such as paragliding, hang-gliding and a host of others; we've outlined the options throughout

Spectator sports

Switzerland hosts a fair spread of world-class annual sporting events. In **tennis**, the leading events are the Swiss Open, held at Gstaad in early July (Ⓦwww.swissopengstaad.com), and the Swiss Indoors, at Basel in October (Ⓦwww.swissindoors.ch). Zürich's Weltklasse **athletics** meeting every August (Ⓦwww.weltklasse.ch) is a highlight of the IAAF Golden League. The European Masters **golf** tournament takes place in early September at the stunning Alpine course at Crans Montana (Ⓦwww.omegaeuropeanmasters.com). The **cycling** Tour de Suisse (Ⓦwww.tds.ch) happens in June. **Football** has never been Switzerland's strong point (Ⓦwww.football.ch), but it does boast the oldest club in continental Europe, FC St Gallen, founded in 1879. The most prestigious of dozens of winter sports events is the World Cup **downhill skiing** at Wengen in January (Ⓦwww.lauberhorn.ch), although the Spengler Cup **ice hockey** tournament (Ⓦwww.spenglercup.ch) in Davos in late December can match it for thrills and spills.

the guide. **Hot-air ballooning** is headquartered in Château d'Oex, nerve centre of the 1998 record-breaking balloon flight around the world.

Swiss sports

On a more pedestrian level, the Swiss have a number of sports of their own, most of them rooted in celebrations of Alpine brawn. They tend to be indulged in by local communities – often in traditional dress – on open field sites during spring and summer months, along with much festivity and carousing. **Schwingen** (Ⓦwww.esv.ch) is an idiosyncratic kind of sumo-wrestling, in which both participants wear leather or canvas over-shorts; you've got to keep at least one hand on your opponent's shorts at all times,

and still manage to heave him onto his back within a laid-out circle of sawdust. It's taken very seriously, and champs become rural folk heroes. **Steintossen**, a much less refined activity, involves flinging a massive rock as far as possible.

The classic Swiss sport – completely unlike anything else, and so cherished as an expression of true Swissness – is **Hornussen** (Ⓦwww.ehv.ch): one person launches the *hornuss*, a puck, into the air by hitting it along a curved track with a long cane; the other players, standing well back, try to knock it aside with large wooden bats before it falls to the ground. Tournaments last for some time, with much discussion of the finer points of skill; foreign onlookers rarely make any sense of it all.

Crime and personal safety

Compared to most Europeans, the Swiss are law-abiding to a fault, rendering even the minimal police presence superfluous. There's only a small force of plain-clothes federal police (Polizei, police, polizia), since most police duties are managed by the cantonal authorities, all of which maintain uniformed, armed police. Towns and cities also have their own armed police, operating in conjunction with the cantonal force.

It's very rare you'll even see a police officer in Switzerland. Nonetheless, Swiss police are nothing of a soft touch, and draw continuing approbation from Amnesty International for their heavy-handed approach to foreigners, asylum seekers and Swiss citizens of non-European descent in particular, with random street searches and "unjustified use of violence" cited.

You're obliged to carry your **passport** at all times. Ordinary traffic offences will be dealt with swiftly and courteously – as long as you pay the fine – although police officers, especially outside the cities, may not speak any English; they may insist you accompany them to the nearest police station to have all the necessaries explained. Urban Switzerland has a serious **hard-drug** problem. All drugs are illegal: possession of more than a joint or two's worth of cannabis, or of any other drug at all, will likely lead to either prison or deportation plus a criminal record. Expect no sympathy from your embassy.

If you're unfortunate enough to be **robbed**, you should always go to the nearest police station to get a report filled out (you'll need it for your insurance if nothing else). It may take hours to complete all the paperwork required.

> **Police emergency** ☏ 117

Travellers with disabilities

Switzerland is one of the most enlightened European countries with regard to travellers with disabilities. There's a wealth of information available in advance to help in planning your trip, and once you arrive you'll find most tourist facilities have been designed with everybody, not just the able-bodied, in mind.

There are many organized **tours** and **holidays** specifically put together for people with disabilities; the contacts below will be able to put you in touch with specialists. Switzerland Tourism (see p.35 for worldwide contacts) publishes a useful **hotel guide** specifically for visitors with disabilities, listing and assessing hotels around the country according to their access for people with limited mobility or in wheelchairs. Mobility International Switzerland has its own list, and also publishes **city guides** for 26 localities around the country for around Fr.5 each, written for tourists with disabilities. Procap also sells a **map** and **brochure** in four languages covering travel in Switzerland.

Swiss Federal Railways posts good information online at Ⓦwww.rail.ch and also publishes a brochure covering **train travel** around the country, which includes a table of stations detailing accessible facilities, such as ramps or lifts, waiting rooms and toilets, and a full table of all bus and taxi companies able to accommodate wheelchairs. If you contact their "**Call Center Handicap**" team at least two hours before you want to travel, giving them your name, phone number, date of travel, desired departure and arrival times, and the nature of your disability, they can arrange for people to help you on and off the train and access the "Mobilifts" at most stations; this is a free service. All fast trains (single- and double-decker), and most regional trains have spaces within second-class carriages to park wheelchairs, identified by a wheelchair pictogram. Station facilities are being upgraded nationwide: city **trams** and **buses** around the country are increasingly wheelchair-accessible; **boats** are generally easy to board and often have facilities such as disabled toilets; and private narrow-gauge train companies including MOB (between Montreux, Gstaad and the Bernese Oberland) and FART (the Centovalli line from Locarno) are converting carriages for passengers with disabilities. The Call Center Handicap office has full details.

Contacts in Switzerland for travellers with disabilities

Active Motion Ⓦwww.activemotion.ch. Snow sports school for disabled people.
BöV Ⓦwww.boev.ch. The Swiss Office for People with Disabilities and Public Transport.
Mobility International Switzerland (MIS) Ⓦwww.mis-ch.ch. Useful information and links.
SBB Call Center Handicap ☎0800 007 102, ✉mobil@sbb.ch, Ⓦwww.rail.ch (click on "Sitemap" and look for "Passengers with a handicap"). Part of the Passenger Division of SBB. Gives full details of accessibility on all forms of public transport, and makes arrangements for travel anywhere in Switzerland.

Directory

Electricity 220v, 50Hz (the same as in the rest of continental Europe). Plug sockets are generally of the round or flat two-pin type. British appliances will need a plug adaptor, while North American appliances will also need a 220-to-110v transformer.

Gay and lesbian travellers You'll find Switzerland to be generally very tolerant towards gay (*schwul*, *gai*, *gay*) and lesbian (*lesbisch*, *lesbien*, *lesbico*) lifestyles. The age of consent has been unified at 16 and equality of treatment under the law is guaranteed. All major urban areas have organizations lobbying local and cantonal governments on gay issues which serve as a focus for the local scene, while the national mouthpieces are the Pink Cross (Ⓦwww.pinkcross.ch) for men, and the Swiss Lesbian Organization (Ⓦwww.los.ch). Nightlife is varied and welcoming; we've listed some bars and contacts in the major town accounts. There's tons of information online, starting with Ⓦwww.myswitzerland.com/gay.

Racism Racism is perhaps the biggest current social issue in Switzerland, with ongoing, none-too-civil debates raging about the absorption of foreigners into Swiss society, and the high levels of asylum seekers arriving from conflict-torn parts of Europe and the world. Small-town Switzerland is hopping from foot to foot, forced to address the issue but unable to reconcile traditional Swiss hospitality and respect for others with the equally traditional mistrust and rejection of outsiders. While society is in flux, the fact remains that outside certain parts of Geneva,

Lausanne, Basel, Bern and Zürich, non-white faces are a rare sight on the street. Across the country there's some antagonism directed towards both refugees from the former Yugoslavia, who are commonly perceived as gangsters, and tourists from East Asia, who are often seen as an irritant. Luzern is infamous as the major recruiting ground for Switzerland's expanding extreme right-wing political parties. Despite all this, you're very unlikely actually to encounter any trouble, but some neanderthal attitudes – stares or condescension – may persist in out-of-the-way corners.

Time Switzerland is on Central European Time (CET), 1hr ahead of London, 6hr ahead of New York, and 8hr behind Sydney.

Tipping All bar, restaurant and hotel bills are calculated with fifteen percent service included: tipping is officially abolished. Nonetheless, unless service was truly diabolical, everyone rounds things up at least to the nearest franc; in restaurants, it's common to add a few francs.

Work Chalet-rental companies need staff to cook in and clean their hundreds of chalets. Qualified ski/snowboard instructors and unqualified guides for foreign tour operators are always in demand, as are technicians for maintaining ski equipment and fitting skis and boots in resort shops, large hotels and for tour companies. To find out more, consult *Working in Ski Resorts* by Victoria Pybus.

Guide

Guide

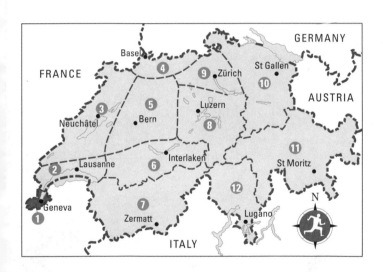

1

Geneva

GERMANY

FRANCE

Basel

St Gallen

Zürich

AUSTRIA

Neuchâtel

Bern

Luzern

Lausanne

Interlaken

St Moritz

Geneva

Zermatt

Lugano

ITALY

N

CHAPTER 1 # Highlights

* **Jet d'Eau** Giant fountain, symbol of the city. **See p.93**

* **Cathédrale St-Pierre** The seat of Calvin's Reformation, at the heart of Geneva's Old Town. **See p.96**

* **Collections Baur** Museum of exquisite Chinese and Japanese art and ceramics. **See p.98**

* **Carouge** Easy-going suburb with Italianate architecture, good shopping and lively bars. **See p.99**

* **Les Pâquis** Gritty, multiethnic district with diverse restaurants and engaging streetlife. **See p.100**

* **Musée de la Croix-Rouge** Superb museum-with-a-conscience, devoted to the history of the Red Cross. **See p.102**

* **The UN tour** Stand in the footsteps of history. **See p.104**

△ Sculpture, the UN

to be organized methodically, with numbered verses, and the city's printing presses turned out hundreds of radical texts, unprintable elsewhere.

In 1602, forces of the Duke of Savoy tried to retake Geneva, but were repulsed in an event that is still commemorated today, in a celebration of the city's independent, patriotic spirit, as **L'Escalade** (see p.87). Wave after wave of refugees flowed into the city. Commerce, banking and watchmaking all flourished, and in 1792 the aristocracy was overthrown and a **Republic** declared with political equality for all. Geneva was annexed by France in 1798, and following the defeat of Napoleon in 1813, threw in its lot with the Swiss Confederation in 1815. A Genevan businessman, Henri Dunant, shaped the **Geneva Convention** of 1864, setting down for the first time rules for soldiers' conduct in war. This led to the creation of the **Red Cross**, designed to help soldiers or civilians caught up in war or natural disasters (see p.103).

After World War I, Geneva was chosen as the seat of the League of Nations and, in 1945, as the European headquarters of the **United Nations**. Since then, the city has looked outwards for inspiration, away from the rest of Switzerland and towards the international community, many of whose conflicts have been negotiated away in the halls and chambers of Geneva's Palais des Nations.

Arrival and information

Geneva's **airport** (Ⓦ www.gva.ch) is 5km northwest at Cointrin. The **tourist information** desk (daily 6am–midnight) is in plain view, offering free maps and hotel reservations boards (with complimentary phone). To the left is a revolving door giving access into the adjacent train station ("Gare CFF").

The simplest onward transport is city **bus** #10, which departs from the top of the escalators just inside the train station's revolving door, and can drop you fifteen minutes later in the centre of town on the Rue du Mont-Blanc (for the Rive Droite) or Place Bel-Air (for the Rive Gauche). If you don't already have a transport pass, you'll need coins to buy a ticket from the machine before you board, valid for unlimited changes either within one hour (Fr.3) or from 9am until midnight (Fr.7) or for 24 hours (Fr.10). The Unireso transport counter in airport arrivals can sell you a **carte touristique**, giving unlimited travel and other discounts (48/72hr for Fr.20/30). All trains from the airport **train** station stop at Geneva's main station (6min) before going on direct to towns all over the country, cutting out the need to change in Geneva. **Taxis** charge around Fr.35 into the city.

By train

Geneva's main **train** station – the **Gare de Cornavin** – couldn't be more central, barely 300m north of the lake. It's also a terminus of the French SNCF rail network: if you're arriving on an intercity train (TGV or not) from Paris, Lyon or Grenoble you'll pass through customs and passport control before joining the throng within the station proper. The station has the usual array of facilities, including a TPG (**Transports publics genevois**) office (Mon–Sat 7am–7pm, Sun 10am–6pm), giving out city tram and bus maps and selling tickets. French SNCF local trains from Evian, Chamonix and Annecy, connecting at Annemasse and La Roche, arrive at the tiny **Gare des Eaux-Vives**, well to the east of the centre; opposite is a terrace of houses, to the right of which is the Rue de Savoie heading 50m up to the main road, from where trams #12 and #16 head right into the centre.

By car, bus and boat

Geneva is surrounded on all sides by France: the only Swiss **autoroute** into the city is the N1 from Lausanne. **Parking** is a nightmare: you'd do well to arrange matters with your hotel or get rid of your vehicle on the city limits. Parking garages citywide are listed at Ⓦ www.geneve.ch /parkings/parkings.html. On-street parking in the centre (see p.50 for details) is very hard to find; garages are fine for short periods (roughly Fr.2/hr), but tend to charge a stiff Fr.35/day. Parking de Cornavin (Ⓣ 022 827 44 90), under the train station square, is cheapest on the lowest levels, and is also discounted for train users (Fr.19/day).

All international **buses** arrive at the Gare Routière, on Place Dorcière (Ⓣ 022 732 02 30, Ⓦ www.coach-station .com), just off Rue du Mont-Blanc in the city centre.

The most romantic way to arrive is by **boat**, on one of the many CGN services (Ⓣ 0848 811 848, Ⓦ www .cgn.ch) that village-hop their way along both shores of the lake from Lausanne, Evian and Nyon. Boats drop off at one or more of the four CGN jetties within Geneva: **Eaux-Vives**, east of the Jet d'Eau; **Les Pâquis**, near the Casino; and **Jardin Anglais** and **Mont-Blanc**, at either end of the Pont du Mont-Blanc.

Information

Geneva's **tourist office** is a mine of information on everything to do with the city and canton. The main branch is in the central post office at

Geneva's festivals

Geneva's biggest celebration is **L'Escalade** (ⓦ www.compagniede1602.ch), commemorating the failed attempt by the Duke of Savoy to seize the town on the night of December 11–12, 1602. Locals dress up in costume and parade by torchlight with drums and fifes, groups of kids sing in city-centre cafés, and confectioners sell the *Marmite d'Escalade*, a small pot made of chocolate and filled with marzipan "vegetables" to commemorate a Genevan housewife who dispatched a Savoyard soldier by tipping her boiling soup over his head from a high window.

Geneva's **Fourth-of-July** celebrations for US Independence Day are the biggest in the world outside the States, and its **Swiss National Day** festivities, every August 1, are equally spectacular. The **Fêtes de Genève** (Geneva Festival; ⓦ www.fetes-de -geneve.ch) is held in early August on the waterfront, with music of all kinds, techno floats on the lake, theatre, funfairs, street entertainers, stalls selling food from around the world and an enormous lakeside musical fireworks display. During the last week of August and early September, **La Bâtie Festival de Genève** features live music and theatrical performances. Finally, Geneva's **Motor Show** (ⓦ www.palexpo.ch), held every March in the Palexpo arena, is the largest and most prestigious in Europe.

18 Rue du Mont-Blanc (Mon–Sat 9am–6pm, July & Aug also Sun 9am–6pm; ☎ 022 909 70 00, ⓦ www.genevatourism.ch), and there's also a desk within the information office of the Municipality of Geneva, situated on the Pont de la Machine (Mon noon–6pm, Tues–Fri 9am–6pm, Sat 10am–5pm; ☎ 022 311 99 70, ⓦ www.ville-ge.ch). Both have stacks of material in English and maintain detailed websites. During the summer, a bus parked at the station end of the Rue du Mont-Blanc houses the "CAR" info-centre; they can help with accommodation and transport information (mid-June to early Sept daily 9am–11pm; ☎ 022 731 46 47).

The weekly **Genève Agenda**, available free from the tourist office and most hotels, is a useful source of information on sightseeing and the latest exhibitions. The municipality's monthly **Genève: Le Guide** (ⓦ www.le-guide.ch), which costs a few francs, also has good information.

City transport and tours

Walking is feasible enough for the heart of Geneva, and even getting to further-flung attractions such as Carouge or the UN takes only twenty or thirty minutes on foot, but you'll probably resort to **city transport** once or twice. Trams and buses form the core of the transport network, and renting a bike (see p.111) can make sense.

Taxis are only for the rich and famous. You can hail them in the street, take them from ranks at the station and elsewhere, or order them (☎ 022 331 41 33, ⓦ www.taxi-phone.ch) – but with a Fr.6.30 flagfall, Fr.3.20 per kilometre (more on Sundays and at night), plus Fr.1.50 per piece of luggage, they're only a ski-mask short of daylight robbery.

Trams, buses and boats

Geneva's **trams and buses** (ⓦ www.tpg.ch) are fast, clean, efficient, safe, affordable and go everywhere. Those running within the city are identified with numbers; those running into the suburbs, or across into France, are marked with letters. A Swiss Pass lets you travel free.

Tickets are valid on all trains, boats and buses within the relevant zones, and you must buy them before you board – but the Unireso machines at every stop accept **coins only** (Swiss francs and euros). The central Zone 11 covers the city, from Place des Nations in the north to the borders of Carouge in the south and from Jonction east to Eaux-Vives; the outer Zone 12 includes Carouge and the airport; and there are further numbered zones beyond. Unless you're travelling in from France or looking to take in a journey well outside the city, such as to Coppet (for which you'll need a "Régional" fare), stick to the **"Tout-Genève"** fare tariff, which is applicable in the area marked in orange on transport maps (covering zones 11 and 12). This includes a short-hop fare, for three stops only (Fr.2); a ticket for unlimited travel within one hour (Fr.3); the **carte dès 9 heures**, valid for unlimited journeys from 9am to midnight (Fr.7); and the **carte 24 heures** (Fr.10) – which, on Saturdays and Sundays, is valid for two people travelling together. TPG transport information offices (within the train station and at the large Rive interchange below the old town; both Mon–Sat 7am–7pm, Sun 10am–6pm) can help, and also give out a map of the network and sell weekly and monthly passes.

Little **mouettes** run by SMGN (Ⓦwww.swissboat.com) ferry passengers across the mouth of the lake on four routes (all Mon–Sat 7.30am–7.30pm, Sun 10am–5pm; June–Aug Sun until 7pm), covered by normal city transport tickets. Route M1 shuttles between the Pâquis jetty ("Port des Mouettes" on Quai du Mont-Blanc) and Place du Molard; M2 between Pâquis and Eaux-Vives (both every 10min). The longer route M3 shuttles between Pâquis and Genève-Plage; M4 between Genève-Plage and the Perle du Lac park (both every 30min).

City tours and walks

There are literally dozens of **tours** around the city and its environs. For **self-guided walks**, simplest is to pick up a Walkman and headphones from the tourist office for an informative 24-point walk in the Old Town at your own pace (Fr.10 plus Fr.50 deposit; max. 4hr). Alternatively, you could choose one of the tourist office's excellent "Geneva On Foot" brochure-led walks through the various parks and neighbourhoods. Official **guided walks** depart from the tourist office (Sat 10am; June–Sept also Mon–Fri 10am plus Tues &

Easy day-trips from Geneva by train

Château de Chillon p.158. Fairy-tale lakeside castle. Change at Vevey, onto bus #1. 1hr 30min.

Château d'Oex p.309. Stunning scenery on the Golden Pass line (p.160) to this quiet Alpine resort. Change at Montreux. 2hr.

Fribourg p.258. Wander the medieval lanes of this relaxed, bilingual university town. Direct. 1hr 20min.

Lausanne p.118. Lively, colourful city with outstanding galleries and a hip waterfront promenade. Direct. 35min.

Les Diablerets p.320. Tiny mountain village on a scenic train line, offering year-round glacier skiing at 3000m. Change at Aigle. 2hr 10min.

Mont Salève p.112. Cable-car ride near Geneva for views and walks. Passport needed. City bus #8 to Veyrier-Douane. 50min.

St-Cergue p.145. Away from the city and the lowlands, refresh yourself with mountain air and tranquil views from 1047m. Change at Nyon. 50min.

St-Saphorin p.148. Beautiful old wine village set amidst the Lavaux vineyards. Change at Lausanne. 1hr.

Thurs 6.30pm; 2hr; Fr.15). Ask about other walks, for instance a stroll through Carouge or a tour focused on Geneva's history of watchmaking.

There are dozens of boat tours. The CGN (ⓦwww.cgn.ch) has plenty of cruises, starting from the Mont-Blanc jetty, including **Les Belles Rives Genevoises** – a circular tour of both lakeshores (April–Oct daily 11am & hourly 1–4pm; mid-May to mid-Sept also 5pm & 6pm; 55min; Fr.12) – and dozens of eat-aboard brunch, lunch and evening cruises for Fr.20–30. Smaller companies ranged along both lakefronts tend to offer more regular departures; just wander along until you see a trip you fancy. The **Croisière Les Rives du Rhône** starts from the Quai des Moulins on the Pont de l'Ile in the city centre and heads downriver to Verbois dam near the French border, and back (April–Oct once or twice daily, except Mon; Fr.22; 2hr 45min). Reservations are essential (☎022 732 29 44).

Accommodation

Geneva has a good selection of budget and mid-range **accommodation**, adding to the swathe of palace hotels catering to diplomats and the international glitterati. Booking ahead is essential, since all affordable rooms can easily get snapped up by delegates to the continuous round of conferences and international events that are the lifeblood of the city. Check ⓦwww.genevatourism.ch for weekend or off-peak deals.

Hotels

Plenty of **inexpensive** hotels pack the centre of town – although bear in mind that parts of the Pâquis district in particular can get sleazy. There's a wealth of choice in **mid-range** rooms, with some bargains available from hotels which haven't yet updated to the slick, generic style that tends to prevail. The Geneva-only chain Manotel has six classy hotels (3 three-star, 3 four-star) located within five minutes of each other in the Pâquis offering unusually good value for money. As you'd expect, there's no shortage of stratospherically **expensive** hotels.

Inexpensive hotels

Station area and Les Pâquis

At Home 16 Rue de Fribourg ☎022 906 19 00, ⓦwww.hotel-at-home.ch. Clean, modern, sound-proofed Pâquis rooms, convenient for the location, but small, soulless and, despite the name, not very homely. Discounts for students. ❸

Balzac 14 Rue de l'Ancien-Port ☎022 731 01 60, ⓦwww.hotel-balzac.ch. Quiet and very spacious rooms – unrenovated but still comfortable – just off the Place de la Navigation. Good value. Parking Fr.10/day. ❸–❹

🏃 **De la Cloche** 6 Rue de la Cloche ☎022 732 94 81, ⓦwww.geneva-hotel.ch/cloche. Eight spotless, characterful, high-ceilinged rooms in what was formerly a private apartment in a quiet area of the Pâquis 50m from the lake. The pleasant atmosphere is enhanced by period fittings such as original fireplaces and wood floors. Regularly full. ❶–❷

Ibis 10 Rue Voltaire ☎022 338 20 20, ⓦwww.ibishotel.com. Generic, functional chain hotel in the city centre, characterless but low-priced. ❷

International & Terminus 20 Rue des Alpes ☎022 732 80 95, ⓦwww.international-terminus.ch. Clean and comfortable, a stone's throw from the station but off the main traffic street. Ask for an upper floor. ❸

Des Quatre-Nations 43 Rue de Zurich ☎022 732 02 24. Divey little Pâquis den above a lowlife Portuguese bar, with blithely unhelpful staff (if you can find them) and dead-cheap shower-free rooms. ❶

Rivoli 6 Rue des Pâquis ☎022 731 85 50, ⓦwww.geneva-hotel.ch/rivoli. Good, quiet central location, but a little gloomy inside: rooms are nothing to write home about, studios are slightly better value. ❸

Windsor 31 Rue de Berne ☎ 022 715 16 00, ⓦ www.hotel-windsor.ch. Simple, unadorned rooms, adequate and not without character. Higher floors avoid the Pâquis street-noise. Formal, friendly staff. ❸–❹

Old Town and Plainpalais

🏃 **Bel'Espérance** 1 Rue de la Vallée ☎ 022 818 37 37, ⓦ www.hotel-bel-esperance.ch. Owned by the Salvation Army, and now completely

renovated into an excellent, modern, family-run hotel on a steep Old Town alley. Exceptionally quiet rooms are bright and simple, with free use of kitchen and great views. A renowned dentist nearby attracts toothache sufferers from all over Europe, making for quirky, cosmopolitan breakfast-times. Completely non-smoking. ❸

Central 2 Rue de la Rôtisserie ☎ 022 818 81 00, ⓦ www.hotelcentral.ch. Quiet, comfortable, reno-vated top-floor rooms just below the Old Town, all with balcony. Prices depend on the room size, but are all good value. ❷–❸

Mid-range hotels

Auberge d'Hermance 12 Rue du Midi, Hermance ☎ 022 751 13 68, ⓦ www.hotel-hermance.ch. Charming inn set amidst the medieval lakeshore village of Hermance 15km northeast of Geneva, with five cosy and attractive rooms. The restaurant is celebrated for its excellent French cuisine. ❹

Edelweiss Manotel 2 Place de la Navigation ☎ 022 544 51 51, ⓦ www.manotel.com. Comfort-able three-star, entirely done-up with Swiss kitsch – carved light pine, images of St Bernard dogs and Alpine flowers and, to top it all, folkloric dinner-shows nightly in the basement restaurant. Ignore it all: beneath the veneer, this remains an excellent city-centre small hotel, with courteous, switched-on staff and good facilities (all rooms have air con). Ask for a top-floor room, facing back over a quiet rooftop panorama. ❹–❺

🏃 **Kipling Manotel** 27 Rue de la Navigation ☎ 022 544 40 40, ⓦ www.manotel.com. A touch of airy, exotic class in the heart of the Pâquis, with this sophisticated three-star hotel, air-conditioned throughout. Rooms are styled with some care: fabrics are rich, woods are dark and highly polished, and artefacts attempt to evoke the colonial era of the Raj. Parking available. ❺

Montbrillant 2 Rue du Montbrillant ☎ 022 733 77 84, ⓦ www.montbrillant.ch. Award-winning

family-run hotel overlooking the station, with some style, plus quiet and atmospheric modern rooms – those under the sloping roof are particularly good. Soundproofing throughout. ❹–❺

Royal Manotel 41 Rue de Lausanne ☎ 022 906 14 14, ⓦ www.manotel.com. Flagship Manotel property on eight floors (one non-smoking), offer-ing outstanding value. Rooms are large, with an air of elegance and air con; superb top-floor suites feature effortless, modern luxury styling – canopied bed, parquet floor, Jacuzzi – at four-star prices. All guests have access to the sauna, hammam and small gym, and there's secure underground parking. ❺–❼

Strasbourg 10 Rue Pradier ☎ 022 906 58 00, ⓦ www.strasbourg-geneva.ch. Best Western chain hotel on a quiet backstreet very near the station, renovated in classic style, with good service and cosy, if generic, rooms. ❺

Tiffany 1 Rue des Marbriers ☎ 022 708 16 16, ⓦ www.hotel-tiffany.ch. Highly successful, attractive and charming Belle Epoque hotel near Plainpalais, with efficient, helpful staff and classic Art Deco styling throughout – from stained glass to swirly bathroom tiles and a stunning painted ceiling. ❻–❼

Expensive hotels

🏃 **Les Armures** 1 Rue du Puits St-Pierre ☎ 022 310 91 72, ⓦ www.hotel-les -armures.ch. Quiet seventeenth-century building in the heart of the cobbled Old Town, with uniquely characterful rooms featuring wood beams and frescoed decor. The height of tasteful, understated luxury. ❽–❾

Beau Rivage 13 Quai du Mont-Blanc ☎ 022 716 66 66, ⓦ www.beau-rivage.ch. Dreamy classical-style palace, centred on a huge atrium with tinkling

fountain and characterized by luxury redolent of its 1865 foundation. The same family tends to the hotel's guests now as then, and a farther cry from international business-class anonymity you couldn't find. Its tragic claim to fame is that Empress Elisa-beth ("Sissi") of Austria died in one of the drawing rooms in 1898, stabbed by an Italian anarchist. ❾

Des Bergues 33 Quai des Bergues ☎ 022 908 70 00, ⓦ www.fourseasons.com. The oldest of Geneva's palace-style hotels, this much-loved

1834 landmark, renovated to glittering international standards, is now part of the Four Seasons chain, yet retains its atmosphere of discreet and unassailable opulence. ❾
Bristol 10 Rue du Mont-Blanc ☎ 022 716 57 00, ⓦ www.bristol.ch. A venerable city-centre institution, dating from 1896, with subtle modern decor and calm, efficient service. ❽–❾
Intercontinental 7 Chemin du Petit-Saconnex ☎ 022 919 39 39, ⓦ www.interconti.com. A vast Sixties high-rise out near the UN, some rooms boasting spectacular lake views, that is the favoured choice of politicos and visiting international delegations. Cosy decor softens the generic interior, but sombre, world-affairs formality is the tone. The visitors' book reads like a roll call of history, running through the last half-dozen US presidents, the late King Hussein of Jordan, Fidel Castro and Nelson Mandela, to name a few. ❼–❾
President Wilson 47 Quai Wilson ☎ 022 906 66 66, ⓦ www.hotelpwilson.com. Outstanding five-star palace on the Rive Droite, with a vast lobby and public areas done up in a subtle Art Deco style – lots of dark wood and armchairs. Rooms are spacious, airy, light and modern, and – with the hotel's location, facing away from the city centre – benefit from uncluttered lake views. ❾

Camping and hostels

Of Geneva's **campsites**, **Camping d'Hermance** is a pleasant site 14km northeast by the French border, at 44 Rue du Nord (☎ 022 751 14 83; April–Sept), reachable on bus E and with free access to the lake. The two **hostels** aside, check with the tourist office for details of the many student dorms which provide budget accommodation to visitors out of term-time.

Auberge de Jeunesse (HI hostel) 30 Rue Rothschild ☎ 022 732 62 60, ⓦ www.youthhostel .ch & www.yh-geneva.ch. 330 beds in a good, central location in the Pâquis, open year-round. Big, bustling and well maintained, with cheap meals and good services. Dorm beds from Fr.26. Bus #1 to Wilson. ❶

City Hostel (SB hostel) 2 Rue Ferrier ☎ 022 901 15 00, ⓦ www.cityhostel.ch. Excellent no-smoking backpacker place a short walk from the HI hostel in the Pâquis, with plenty of services (including laundry facilities), inexpensive rooms and dorm beds from Fr.28. Bus #4 to Prieuré. ❶

The City

Genevans orient the city centre around the Rhône, which flows west into France from the **Rade**, the narrow lake harbour flanked by grand facades. The **Rive Gauche**, on the south bank, takes in a grid of waterfront streets which comprise the main shopping district (Les Rues-Basses) and the adjacent high ground of the Old Town. Just south is the university, spilling over into the Plainpalais district, and a little northeast is the populous working neighbourhood of Eaux-Vives. South, just beyond the city limits, lies the community of **Carouge**, characterized by artisans' shops, picturesque Italianate architecture and a lively, independent spirit.

Six bridges, including the main Pont du Mont-Blanc, link the Rive Gauche to the **Rive Droite** waterfront, where most of Geneva's grand hotels sit. Behind them lies the main train station, alongside the cosmopolitan and occasionally rough Les Pâquis district. The **international area**, centred on Place des Nations 1.5km north, is home to the European headquarters of the UN, set amidst the grand offices of a clutch of major world organizations – not least the International Committee of the Red Cross, which has, as a sideline, one of Switzerland's best museums.

The Rive Gauche

Geneva's **Rive Gauche** (Left Bank, or southern bank) is lined with the blank facades of dozens of bank buildings, behind which the arrow-straight **Rue**

ACCOMMODATION
Tiffany   A

GENEVA: RIVE GAUCHE

Jonction ▲

▼ Carouge

▼ Jet d'Eau

Lake Geneva

EATING & DRINKING
Café des Forces Motrices   3
Café Gallay   9
Moloko   2
Cave Valaisanne/
Chalet Suisse   8
Le 2e (Deuxième) Bureau   6
L'Esquisse   4
Hang Zhou   5
L'Opera de Huissoud   1
Le Pain Quotidien   10
Vesuvio   7

Liquid asset

The **Jet d'Eau** fountain (May to mid-Sept daily 9am–11.15pm; March, April & mid-Sept to Oct Mon–Fri 10am–sunset, Sat & Sun 10am–10.30pm; Nov–Feb daily 10am–4pm), the icon of Geneva, is inescapable, emblazoned on every piece of tourist literature and every book about the city and even illuminated after dark.

Its predecessor dated from 1886, when the new hydraulic turbines on the Rhône built up excessive water pressure every evening after the city's craftsmen had closed the valves in their workshops and gone home. While a reservoir system was being developed to get around the problem, an engineer created a temporary outlet which spurted a 30m fountain to release the pressure – but by the time the reservoir was in operation and the fountain had thus become unnecessary, a few wily Genevois had caught on to its power as a tourist attraction. By then purely decorative, it was moved from the river to an exposed lakeside location, and furnished with more and more powerful pumps. Today, the height of the jet is an incredible 140m, with 500 litres of water forced out of the nozzle every second at about 200kph. Each drop takes sixteen seconds to complete the round-trip from nozzle to lake and, on windy days, the plume can rapidly drench the surroundings (they tend to turn it off if the wind picks up). It's worth risking a dousing by walking out onto the jetty to appreciate the force and noise of the thing close up.

du Rhône – principal thoroughfare of Les Rues-Basses, once a dockside slum and now Geneva's fanciest shopping district – stretches a kilometre or more east, crammed with jewellers, department stores and designer boutiques. Traffic streams over the **Pont du Mont-Blanc** beneath the spectacular view of Europe's highest mountain (4807m), which stands some 80km distant. At the foot of the bridge is the charming lakeside **Jardin Anglais**, focused around a double statue celebrating Geneva's joining the Confederation in 1815, a fountain, bandstand and famous Flower Clock. The **Jet d'Eau** spouts 400m along the lakeshore (see box above), while **Parc La Grange**, 1km further east along the lakeshore, is a fragrant expanse holding some forty thousand rose bushes.

West of the Pont du Mont-Blanc, past the bustling Place du Molard with its medieval tower, is the pedestrianized **Pont des Bergues**, with a footpath midway along it linking to a tiny island, the **Île Rousseau**, formerly a bastion and now a minuscule public garden graced with a statue of the Genevan philosopher. With such controversy surrounding Rousseau, even half a century after his death the city authorities were grudging in honouring him, and the statue, behind its sheltering camouflage of trees, originally faced the empty lake – to all intents and purposes cut off from view until the Pont du Mont-Blanc was built alongside in 1861.

Place Neuve and around

At its western end, the Rue du Rhône feeds into hectic Place Bel-Air, sliced across by tramlines and bus-wires. The Pont de l'Île spans the river here across an island, which boasts the diminutive **Tour de l'Île**, last remaining tower of a thirteenth-century château. Grandiose Rue de la Corraterie heads south to yet more grandiose **Place Neuve**, dominated by the high retaining wall of the Old Town and a host of Neoclassical buildings. The street joins the square beside the **Musée Rath**, Geneva's first art museum, opened in 1826, and still holding a changing series of world-class art shows (Tues & Thurs–Sun 10am–5pm, Wed noon–9pm; admission varies; SMP; ⓦ www.ville-ge.ch/musinfo).

△ Mur de la Réformation

Adjacent is the **Grand-Théâtre**, Geneva's opera house and principal theatre stage, which only just clung onto its facade after the devastating fire of 1951, when a rehearsal of the last act of Wagner's *Walkyrie*, in which Brunhilde is encircled by flames, got out of hand. Further round the square is the equally ornate Conservatoire de Musique.

Heading south from Place Neuve through the enormous gates brings you into the **Parc des Bastions**, a tranquil patch of green below the Old Town ramparts that's much beloved of students (the university buildings are all around). At the east edge of the park, in a dramatic location propping up the Old Town, is the **Mur de la Réformation**, a 100m-long wall erected in 1917 and dominated by forbidding, 5m-high statues of the four major Genevan reformers: Guillaume Farel, first to preach the Reformation in Geneva; Jean Calvin, leader of the Reform movement and spiritual father of the city; Théodore de Bèze, successor to Calvin; and John Knox, friend of Calvin and founder of Scottish Presbyterianism. Behind runs the motto of the city and the Reformation, *Post Tenebras Lux* ("After the Darkness, Light"). Various figures and bas-reliefs show scenes from Protestant history: just to the right of the main statues is Roger Williams, a Calvinist Puritan who sailed on the *Mayflower* and founded the city of Providence, Rhode Island. The English Parliament's 1689 Bill of Rights – which established a constitutional monarchy under the Protestant king William of Orange, and barred Catholics from the throne – is also depicted, but Luther and Zwingli, with whom Calvin came to disagree, are relegated to plain blocks flanking the wall, carved only with their surnames.

The Old Town

A gate at the back of the Parc des Bastions brings you up to a small junction and Rue St-Léger, which winds further up into the atmospheric **Old Town**, characterized by quiet, cobbled streets and tall, shuttered, grey-stone houses that give nothing away. Rue St-Léger arrives at the oddly split-level **Place du Bourg-de-Four**, a marketplace since medieval times that was probably built over the Roman forum, these days adorned with a fountain and lined with relaxed terrace cafés. From here, Rue Fontaine descends to the north to Temple de la Madeleine, a picturesque Gothic church that has clung on to its Romanesque tower, but if you head up the other way on Rue de l'Hôtel-de-Ville, you'll come to **Place de la Taconnerie**, dominated by the cathedral. Tucked on your right is the **Auditoire de Calvin**, a thirteenth-century chapel built over a fifth-century predecessor. Following Geneva's acceptance of the Reformation, refugees flooded into the city from all over Europe and, in the knowledge that most of them spoke no French, Calvin gave this chapel over for the refugees

GENEVA: OLD TOWN

ACCOMMODATION
Les Armures   C
Bel'Espérance B
Central   A

EATING & DRINKING
Alhambar   3
Chocolaterie du Rhône   1
Flanagan's   6
Café du Centre   2
La Favola   5
Le Pied de Cochon   7
Taverne de la Madeleine   4

Russian Church

▲ Plaine de Plainpalais

to worship in their own languages – Geneva's first international building. John Knox preached here in the 1550s (there's still a Church of Scotland service every Sunday, slotted between Dutch and Italian), and the austere building also doubled as Calvin's lecture hall.

Cathédrale St-Pierre

Geneva's **Cathédrale St-Pierre** (June–Sept Mon–Sat 9.30am–6.30pm, Sun noon–6.30pm; Oct–May Mon–Sat 10am–5.30pm, Sun noon–5.30pm) is a mishmash of architectural elements. Begun in 1160, the original building has had a multitude of bits and pieces stuck on over the centuries. A small side-chapel, the Chapelle des Macchabées, was added in 1397; a Neoclassical portico – more reminiscent of a museum than a church – was tacked onto the west front in 1752, facing onto Cour St-Pierre; the two square towers above the east end are totally dissimilar; and between them rises a curious greenish steeple added in the late nineteenth century.

As you enter, though, confusion is stripped away and you're left with the clean lines of dour, severely austere stonework. In 1535, spurred on by Bern, the people of Geneva accepted the Reformation and embarked on an iconoclastic rampage: all the altars in the cathedral, as well as every statue and icon, were destroyed, the organs were smashed and the painted decoration on the interior walls was whitewashed. Only the great **pulpit** and, by chance, the stained glass of the chancel, survived. As you wander through the soaring interior, the architecture, and the austerity, draw your gaze upwards; almost the only decoration to survive is on the capitals of the nave's clustered pillars, grotesque monsters and a bare-breasted double-tailed mermaid. What is purportedly **Calvin's chair** sits at the back of the church on the left, near the door to the North Tower, which is climbable for the spectacular views (Fr.3). You shouldn't leave without spending time in the delightful **Chapelle des Macchabées**, last on the left before you leave. Used as a warehouse and later as a lecture hall, it was rededicated as a place of worship in 1878 and is filled with lavish and beautiful decoration dating from then. Copies of the only fifteenth-century frescoes to survive the Reformation – angels playing musical instruments – are on the ornamented vaults of the chancel within the chapel.

The cathedral is built on the remains of occupation going back to around 350 AD. From then on, the hill on which the cathedral stands saw almost continuous building and rebuilding. Since 1976, archeologists have been working to expose walls, rooms and mosaic floors beneath the cathedral, and the huge **archeological site** is open to the public (Tues–Sun 10am–5pm; Fr.8), pretty rarefied stuff but exceptionally well presented, subterranean catwalks weaving around and over the crumbling remains. With more than 200 levels of building work so far discovered in eleven zones, it's necessarily difficult to tweeze out exactly what's going on, but the free audioguide helps.

On the north side of the cathedral, at 4 Rue du Cloître, the eighteenth-century Maison Mallet houses the airy **Musée International de la Réforme** (Tues–Sun 10am–5pm; Fr.10; SMP; ⓦ www.musee-reforme.ch), dedicated to exploring the ideas behind the Reformation in lively, engaging displays of images and text, from polemics and theological debates to music, the trades practised by Huguenot refugees and the rights of women in Protestantism.

Maison Tavel

From the cathedral portico, an alley leads you on to the Rue du Puits-St-Pierre. A few metres left, at no. 6, is the distinctive grey-blue sandstone facade – etched with *trompe l'oeil* mortar-lines – of Geneva's oldest house, now the **Maison**

Tavel museum (Tues–Sun 10am–5pm; free; ⓦ www.ville-ge.ch/musinfo). Built by the Tavel family in the twelfth century, the house was renovated after a fire in 1334 and maintained, after the Tavel line died out, by various noble families until it was bought by the city in 1963 to display items from the history and urban life of Geneva. The cellars are the oldest part of the house, and they and the three upper floors are filled with diverting items – massive carved doors, painted inn-signs and a complete twelve-room apartment showing everyday life in the seventeenth century. The highlight of the museum is in the attic, a giant **relief map of Geneva** dating from 1850, showing the city complete with its fortifications, before the Pont du Mont-Blanc or the railway had been built.

Around the Old Town

It's a few steps west from the Maison Tavel to a cobbled crossroads. To the right is Grand-Rue, birthplace of Rousseau, and parallel to it **Rue des Granges**, named "Street of Barns" in response to the huge mansions built in the eighteenth century to house Geneva's wealthiest residents. Looming over the junction is the **Hôtel-de-Ville**, ranged around an internal arcaded courtyard from where it's easy to spot the different styles of the building – going counterclockwise, the sixteenth, seventeenth and eighteenth centuries. Ahead is the Alabama Room, where the Geneva Convention on the humanitarian rules of war was signed by sixteen countries in 1864, and where, in 1872, conflict between two states was solved in a neutral state for the first time, when Britain and the US settled their differences over British support for the Confederacy during the Civil War. The League of Nations also gathered here for the first time in 1920. You can work your way up the internal ramp to the top – feeling like an Escher drawing come to life – but all the doors are firmly locked. Behind the building is the lovely **Promenade de la Treille**, with a view over the city framed by chestnut trees and the longest wooden bench in the world, at 126m. The last tree on the left, bent forward, is the official tree of Geneva: tradition has it that the chief city councillor must record the day its first bud blossoms as being the first day of spring. A board of dates has been kept in the Town Hall since 1818 and is added to annually.

Back along the Rue du Puits-St-Pierre, you'll come to a set of stairs leading down towards the Rues-Basses. Off to the left is Rue Calvin, with, at no. 10, the **Musée Barbier-Müller** (daily 11am–5pm; Fr.5; SMP; ⓦ www.barbier -mueller.ch), housing a beautifully displayed collection of non-European sculpture and artwork. Notes are copious, guiding you from a room filled with antique African gold to huge carved masks from Oceania, and more.

Musée d'Art et d'Histoire

A few metres east of the Old Town is the **Musée d'Art et d'Histoire**, 2 Rue Charles-Galland (Tues–Sun 10am–5pm; free; ⓦ www.ville-ge.ch/musinfo), Geneva's most important museum and Switzerland's unofficial national collection. It's a gigantic place, that covers in encyclopedic fashion the whole sweep of Western culture from antiquity to the present; to do it justice would take days, but you could spend a worthwhile few hours absorbing the different areas.

For the marvellous **fine-art** collection, head up the grand staircase. What confronts you at the top is perhaps the highlight of the museum, a heart-stoppingly romantic sculpture in marble of Venus and Adonis, standing alone and lit by a skylight; Antonio Canova, the pre-eminent Neoclassical sculptor, has given Venus the fingers of a pianist. Also at the head of the stairs are two Rodins, *The Thinker* and *The Tragic Muse*. The collection begins in Hall 401 to the right of *Venus and Adonis* and, although it more or less keeps a chronological thread, don't be surprised if you come across photography, concrete installations or even video art scattered in amongst the painting. In room 402 you'll find Konrad Witz's famous altarpiece, made for the cathedral in 1444, which shows Christ and the fisherman transposed onto Lake Geneva. As you work your way around the perimeter rooms, Rembrandt and other Dutch and Flemish artists are in room 406, nineteenth-century Swiss in 408–9, while the inner ring of smaller rooms features work by the eighteenth-century Genevois painter Liotard in 419–20. Perimeter rooms 412–14 are devoted to Vallotton, Pissarro, Cézanne, Renoir and Modigliani, with some striking Hodlers on the inner ring, including a mystical *Lac de Thoune* (1909) in room 425.

Back downstairs, the **applied arts** collection is on the mezzanine gallery and the ground floor, a wealth of silverware, pewter, armour and costume. The Cartigny room, with 1805 wood panelling by the Genevois craftsman Jean Jaquet, shows elegant Louis XV and XVI furniture. The ground floor also often features temporary exhibits (admission charged).

The lower floor is given over to the massive **archeological** collection. Turn right for the Egyptian rooms, including sections from the Book of the Dead, a complete ninth-century BC mummy, and a beautiful granite statue of the goddess Sekhmet, with the body of a woman and the head of a lioness, from the fourteenth century BC. There's also an excellent display on hieroglyphics. The halls devoted to Ancient Greece and Rome are no less impressive, filled with statuary, glassware and good historical notes. Also down here are a **gift shop** and small **café**.

South and west of the Old Town

Within sight of the Musée d'Art, on the high ground opposite, rise the gilded onion domes of the **Russian Church** (Cathédrale de l'Exaltation de la Sainte Croix; open sporadically), built in 1863 on the remains of a sixteenth-century Benedictine priory with money donated by Grand Duchess Anna Feodorovna Constancia, aunt of Queen Victoria and a longtime Geneva resident. A grid-like neighbourhood of long, straight boulevards lined with solid town houses grew up around the church at the end of the nineteenth century, and the area, known as Les Tranchées, is still grand and quiet today. Five minutes from the church, at 8 Rue Munier-Romilly, is the **Collections Baur** (Tues–Sun 2–6pm; Fr.5; Ⓦ www.collections-baur.ch), the country's premier collection of East Asian art. Start at the top floor, with a brightly lit display of nineteenth-century Japanese ceramics. One floor down is the Chinese collection, with delicately luminescent yellow Yongzhang ceramics in room 8. The ground floor has older Chinese work, including simple white bowls from the ninth century, a little interior garden and fountain in room 3 surrounded by Ming porcelain, and other rooms with spectacular Qing jade. Five minutes' walk northwest, at 2 Terrasse St-Victor, the grand **Petit Palais**, formerly an art museum devoted to French modernism, is currently closed indefinitely.

Plainpalais

The broad Boulevard des Philosophes traces a path around the Parc des Bastions and the university district to the Rond-Point de Plainpalais, on the eastern tip of a diamond of open space known as the **Plaine de Plainpalais**. If Geneva still has a village green or a marketplace, this is it. Most days see a market of one kind or another, whether fruit and veg or the famous Wednesday and Saturday flea markets, and the space is always bustling with dog-walkers, bookworms or skateboarders.

Just off the western angle of the diamond is **MAMCO**, the Musée d'Art Moderne et Contemporain, housed in an old industrial space at 10 Rue des

Vieux-Grenadiers (Tues–Fri noon–6pm, Sat & Sun 11am–6pm; Fr.8; SMP; free on 1st Sun of month; Ⓦ www.mamco.ch). The museum has kept the former factory's concrete floors and overhead strip lighting to display its often stark but high-quality collection, covering installations, video art, photographs, sculptures and painting produced since the 1960s. Next door, the **Centre d'Art Contemporain** (Tues–Sun 11am–6pm; Fr.4; SMP; Ⓦ www.centre.ch) also stages temporary shows of young Swiss artists, while down the road at no. 7 is the **Patek Philippe Museum** (Tues–Fri 2–5pm, Sat 10am–5pm; Fr.10; SMP; Ⓦ www.patekmuseum.com), a fine horological collection. Two other museums nearby are the **Musée Jean Tua**, 28 Rue des Bains (Wed–Sun 2–6pm; Fr.8), showcasing vintage cars, and the **Musée d'Ethnographie**, 65 Bd Carl-Vogt (Tues–Sun 10am–5pm; free), with a vast collection especially strong on weapons and art from Edo-period Japan.

From the Place du Cirque at Plainpalais' northern tip, Boulevard de St-Georges heads due west through one of Geneva's most engaging young neighbourhoods. A short way along, a brick wall conceals the **Cimitière de Plainpalais**, permanent home to, among others, Sir Humphry Davy, who invented the miners' lamp. Gravestone #707, close to the wall and the object of much recent care, is marked only with a faint "J.C.": this is presumed to be the last resting place of Calvin. Behind, Rue de la Coulouvrenière feeds into the atmospheric **Place des Volontaires**, with a scattering of cafés and the L'Usine squat, Geneva's biggest alternative arts venue, with galleries, a theatre space, music venue, café and more. The riverfront Quai des Forces Motrices, also with cafés and clubs, is dominated by the arched windows of the **Bâtiments des Forces Motrices**, which once housed gigantic hydraulic turbines supplying the city with water and which has now been converted into a massive space for opera and drama. Further along Boulevard de St-Georges is the rundown district of **Jonction**, at the point where the Arve meets the Rhône; residents have a tradition, in the torrid days of summer, of flinging themselves off the Pont de Sous-Terre for a refreshing float downstream in the cool water.

Carouge

Some 2km south of the city centre, the suburb of **Carouge** (Ⓦ www .carouge.ch) is a quite different experience from Geneva proper. Practically deserted until 1754, the township – then, as now, beyond the city limits – was granted to Victor Amideus, King of Sardinia (ruling from Turin). The king envisioned Carouge as a trading competitor to Geneva and turned it into a refuge for Catholics, Protestants unable to stomach Geneva's puritanical ways and, uniquely in Europe for the time, even Jews. Turinese architects developed a chessboard design of crisscrossing streets planted with trees, and low houses with wooden, Mediterranean-style galleries looking into internal gardens. Between 1774

△ Window shopping, Carouge

and 1792, this hamlet of a hundred people grew to a bustling town of four thousand and, although Carouge never overtook Geneva, it's still something of a refuge from the city, its quiet, attractive streets packed with artists' workshops, old-style cafés and some of the city's best small-scale nightlife.

Trams #12 or #13 from the city centre can drop you at the **Place du Marché** in the heart of Carouge, still used as a marketplace and starting point for exploration of the quarter. **Rue St-Joseph** is shoulder-to-shoulder artisans, from carpenters to milliners – check out the elegant exposed-mechanism clocks of Jean Kazes at no. 21, Anne-Claude Virchaux's linen-cotton clothes at no. 13, and the delicate artworks of the florist Les Cinq Sens round the corner on **Place du Temple**. A major feature of Carouge are the delightful internal galleried gardens which lurk behind almost every gate: most are open, so feel free to explore.

The Rive Droite

Geneva's **Rive Droite** (Right Bank), on the north side of the Rhône, features only a couple of moderately interesting neighbourhoods – the Pâquis for café life, and Les Grottes for architecture. **Rue du Mont-Blanc** is Geneva's landmark street, a broad boulevard lined with airline offices and souvenir shops that slopes down the hill from the train station. As with most such streets, though, it's what happens either side that's of greatest interest. The **St Gervais** quarter, just west, was formerly the preserve of watchmakers, jewellers, engravers and goldsmiths. These days it has lost virtually all its character to traffic and modern commerce, although its old Gothic church survives on Rue du Temple, on the same street as the **Centre pour l'Image Contemporaine**, at no. 5 (Tues–Sun noon–6pm; Ⓦ www.centreimage.ch), with temporary shows often devoted to contemporary video art.

Les Pâquis and around

Spreading east of Rue du Mont-Blanc is the cosmopolitan, rough-edged district of **Les Pâquis**, centred on the long Rue de Berne – not a pretty place but crammed with restaurants and cafés devoted to every conceivable cuisine from

---

EATING & DRINKING

Bar du Nord	**10**	Le Chat Noir	**5**
La Bourse	**3**	La Cuccagna	**2**
Café des Amis	**9**	La Marchand de Sable	**7**
Café de la Plage	**4**	Martel Tea Room	**6**
Cave a Bière	**8**	Sawasdee	**1**

GENEVA: RIVE DROITE

0   300 m

▲ UN, **A** & **1**   ▲ Lausanne

N

LES GROTTES

Gare de
Cornavin

LES PÂQUIS

Bains
des Pâquis

Gare
Routière

Centre pour
l'Image
Contemporaine

Rhône

Île
Rousseau

Lake
Geneva

Jet d'Eau

Jardin
Anglais

▼ Plainpalais   ▼ Old Town   ▼ Eaux-Vives

ACCOMMODATION

At Home	**K**
Auberge de Jeunesse	**C**
Balzac	**F**
Beau Rivage	**Q**
Des Bergues	**T**
Bristol	**S**
City Hostel	**B**
De la Cloche	**L**
Edelweiss Manotel	**I**
Ibis	**R**
Intercontinental	**A**
International &	
Terminus	**N**
Kipling Manotel	**G**
Montbrillant	**J**
President Wilson	**D**
Des Quatre-Nations	**H**
Rivoli	**O**
Royal Manotel	**E**
Strasbourg	**P**
Windsor	**M**

EATING & DRINKING

Al-Amir	**11**	Buvette Cropettes	**3**	Le Dodo	**6**	Manora	**18**	Teranga	**4**
Bains des Pâquis	**12**	Café Arts	**10**	Domaine Châteauvieux	**9**	Miyako	**17**	Vieux-Bois	**1**
Bookworm	**14**	Café de Paris	**13**	El Mektoub	**16**	Mr Pickwick	**2**	Zara	**5**
La Bretelle	**19**	Le Diwane	**7**	Jeck's Place	**8**	Au Petit Chalet	**15**		

Senegalese to Filipino. Equally visible are the numerous sex shops and street
prostitutes of Geneva's flourishing red-light trade. The further north you go,
the quieter it gets; conversely, you could head out to the lakeside Quai du
Mont-Blanc for a tree-shaded stroll north, past the **Bains des Pâquis** artificial
beach, the marina and ranks of luxury hotels on Quai Wilson, to the beautiful
Parc Mon-Repos, first of several adjoining lakefront parks on the edge of the
international area.

Immediately behind the train station is a small residential area known as
Les Grottes, a web of twisting lanes and mostly unrenovated nineteenth-
century houses. In sharp contrast, on Rue Louis-Favre, just off the main Rue
de la Servette, you couldn't fail to spot the public-housing estate which looks

△ Bains des Pâquis

as though it's been thrown together from plasticine. This is **Les Schtroumpfs** ("The Smurfs"), a whimsical exercise in Gaudi-esque architectural fantasy by Robert Frei, Christian Hunziker and Georges Berthoud, designed in 1982 for the municipality. All the buildings have lumps and blobs everywhere, giant mushrooms holding up balconies with cobweb railings, fairy-tale spiral staircases and twisted-liquorice columns, everything in a riot of primary colours. By all accounts the residents, who inevitably have come to be called Smurfs themselves, love it.

Just west of the city centre is the **Musée Voltaire**, 25 Rue des Délices (Mon–Fri 2–5pm; free), occupying the eighteenth-century villa and estate where Voltaire lived before his exile to France. A library of books and manuscripts is filled out with paintings and mementoes.

The international area

A little over 1km north of the train station, at the heart of the so-called **international area**, is the open square of the **Place des Nations**, surrounded by offices of the dozens of international organizations headquartered in Geneva – everything from the World Council of Churches to Eurovision. Gates on the square open to the **Palais des Nations**, now occupied by UNOG, the United Nations Office at Geneva; the huge monolith just off the square to the west (like a bent playing card on its edge) is WIPO, the World Intellectual Property Organization; the high-rise to the south is ITU, the International Telecommunications Union; just to the east is UNHCR, United Nations High Commission for Refugees… and so the alphabet soup continues. Most of these are just ordinary office buildings filled with working people; only the ICRC (International Committee of the Red Cross) and the UN are open to visitors.

The square itself is an obvious gathering place for those who wish to make a point: demonstrators often march here. The giant **Broken Chair** which looms over it was installed in 1997 for the international conference at Ottawa banning the use of land mines, a graphic symbol of the victims of such weapons. The Place des Nations is an easy walk from the station, or you can take any of an array of buses – #8, #28, #F, #V or #Z – all of which go past the square to Appia, the best stop for the museums.

Musée International de la Croix-Rouge

Housed within the headquarters of the International Committee of the Red Cross (ICRC), the **Musée International de la Croix–Rouge et du Crois-sant–Rouge**, 17 Avenue de la Paix (Mon & Wed–Sun 10am–5pm; Fr.10; SMP; Ⓦ www.micr.org) is acclaimed as one of the best museums in Europe. Using video displays and interactive technology (always with an English-language option), it chronicles in detail the history of modern conflict, and the role the Red Cross has played in providing aid to combatants and civilians caught up in war and natural disasters. The displays are strikingly affecting, always using clear single images to tell a story instead of swamping you with facts and figures, and always avoiding judgement or ideological point-scoring.

The Geneva Conventions and the ICRC

The creation of modern humanitarian law, as expressed in the 1949 Geneva Conventions, is closely tied to the history of the **International Committee of the Red Cross** (ⓦwww.icrc.org).

On a single day – June 24, 1859 – during the war of Italian Unification, over 40,000 people were killed or wounded at a battle near the northern Italian town of **Solferino**. Genevan businessman **Henri Dunant**, who happened to be travelling in the area, was shocked at the sight of thousands of wounded soldiers left to fend for themselves with little or no medical provision. Thousands perished where they fell, despite Dunant's efforts to rally local people to give aid. On his return to Geneva, Dunant wrote *A Memory of Solferino*, an eyewitness account of the horror, which ended with appeals for the formation of an internationally protected nursing corps, ready to care for the wounded during times of war. The book was a runaway success, read in translation all over Europe. The Geneva Public Welfare Society, a local charity, set up a committee in 1863 to look at Dunant's proposals; this committee, which took a reversed red-on-white Swiss flag as the emblem to identify its workers in the field, later became known as the **International Committee of the Red Cross**.

In 1864, a conference of sixteen states – chaired by Dunant – signed the "Geneva Convention for the Amelioration of the Condition of the Wounded in Armies in the Field", the first instrument of international humanitarian law. As the ICRC expanded its work during a succession of conflicts, more treaties were agreed by states around the world – banning poison gas and bacteriological warfare, defining combatants and non-combatants, and more. These culminated in the four **1949 Geneva Conventions**, which still provide the legal foundation for humanitarian law and are among the most widely ratified of all treaties. The first and second conventions cover protection of members of armed forces in the field and at sea, the third is concerned with the rights of prisoners of war, and the fourth concentrates on protection of civilians in wartime. **Protocols** adopted in 1977 extend the conventions to cover victims of civil wars.

These Geneva Conventions laid down rules of war which are taken for granted today – for instance, that **prisoners of war** are entitled to withhold all information from their captors except their name, rank, serial number and birth date. Certain definitions have also changed: under the 1949 conventions, **journalists** – who, at the time, often covered conflicts while armed and uniformed – were regarded as combatants, but, with the developing independence of the media, the 1977 Protocols explicitly recognized them to be non-combatant civilians as long as they identify themselves as such, which is why war correspondents now emblazon their flak-jackets with the word "PRESS".

Governments are responsible for enforcing the Geneva Conventions, but the ICRC remains the only organization recognized to carry out relief activities for the victims of armed conflicts. It publicizes the rules of war to all sides involved in hostilities and, through national Red Cross and Red Crescent societies around the world, serves as a global network to help trace prisoners of war and civilians displaced by conflict and provide aid to civilians during and after wars, as well as monitoring conflict conditions. Four-fifths of its budget of about **Fr.1 billion** (US$700m) is spent on relief work. Its **red cross** emblem is now one of the world's best-known symbols, almost universally recognizable as indicating an impartial source of medical care; the **red crescent**, which has enjoyed equal status since 1876, is widely used in the Muslim world. Between them, these are used in more than 190 countries. In 2005, a new, deliberately non-religious, non-partisan emblem – the **red crystal** – was approved in order to allow countries where neither the cross nor the crescent are seen as neutral (such as Israel, which has, since 1930, used its own, unofficial red Star of David emblem) to join the ICRC federation.

You enter through a trench in the hillside opposite the UN, emerging into an enclosed glass courtyard, surrounded by reflected images of yourself beside a group of stone figures, bound and blindfolded, representing the continual worldwide violation of human rights. Inside, above the ticket desk, is a quotation in French from Dostoevsky: "Everyone is responsible to everyone else for everything." The museum's audioguide (Fr.5) takes you through the eleven undemarcated sections, all packed into a small floor area, which piece together in chronological order the history of kindness, from the Good Samaritan and Saladin to the experiences of nineteenth-century Genevan businessman **Henri Dunant** which prompted him to found the Red Cross (see box p.103). In one area of the museum are ranged aisle after aisle of **record cards** from World War I – an astonishing seven million of them – detailing prisoners' particulars in order that they could be traced and reunited with their families. In another is a **reconstructed cell**, 3m by 2m, which an ICRC delegate reported housed seventeen prisoners: 34 footprints on the cell floor only go some way towards helping imagine the conditions. Also memorable is the eye-opening **Wall of Time**, an ingenious representation of those wars and natural disasters which have killed more than 100,000 people, year by year since the Red Cross's foundation: as you reach the second half of the last century, the dizzyingly long lists of wars around the world tell their own, sombre story.

A final note of achievement: despite its skill and artistry, the museum's construction didn't use a penny of Red Cross funds, relying solely on outside donors.

Palais des Nations

The **Palais des Nations** was built from 1929 to 1936 to serve as the world headquarters of the League of Nations, an organization set up to prevent a recurrence of war on the scale of World War I but stymied soon after its birth by the outbreak of World War II. When the organization was re-founded in 1945 as the **United Nations** (*l'Organisation des Nations Unies* in French, abbreviated to ONU), with its headquarters at New York, this complex became European HQ and was retitled UNOG ("the UN office at Geneva"). Since then it has burgeoned, and now encompasses offices administering a vast array of economic and social development work, as well as bodies dealing with the negotiation and signing of treaties and conventions of all kinds. It's also the hub of UN operations to deliver humanitarian aid and uphold human rights around the world.

The UN tour

Some areas of the Palais des Nations are open to the public for **guided tours** (July & Aug daily 10am–5pm; April–June, Sept & Oct daily 10am–noon & 2–4pm; rest of year Mon–Fri 10am–noon & 2–4pm; Fr.10; takes 1hr; Ⓦwww .unog.ch). The tours – in any of the UN's fifteen official languages – are only moderately interesting in themselves, but are packed with star quality for those who want to hobnob with history. This is the world's single largest conference centre for multilateral diplomacy and top-level international politicking: when the news has reports of "negotiations taking place in Geneva", they mean here. If this impresses, then you'll enjoy the visit; if it signals only the dreary prospect of traipsing along corridors and standing in empty conference halls, you should probably take your francs elsewhere.

The main entrance of the Palais des Nations, facing onto Place des Nations, is for UN staff only; the **public entrance** is up Avenue de la Paix opposite the

Red Cross Museum. To enter, you'll have to hand in your **passport** and go through airport-style security procedures (you're effectively leaving Switzerland and entering international territory). You should then walk down the hill to the left, towards **Porte 39** in the new wing, from where tours depart. Note that you may have to wait a little for the next tour in English (there's a bookshop for browsing) and you have to carry your bags with you.

Once you get going, you're regaled with a potted history of the UN and its philosophy, and odd factoids such as when the US denied Yasser Arafat a visa to address the UN in New York in 1988, the entire General Assembly had to fly to Geneva to hear him speak in the great **Assembly Hall**, visitable today in more or less the same condition as when it was inaugurated in 1937. The **Council Chamber**, which hosted the negotiations to end the 1991 Gulf War, is decorated with gold-and-sepia murals painted in 1934 by the Catalan artist José Maria Sert, depicting the progress of humankind through health, technology, freedom and peace; all very heroic. Indeed, the whole style of the main wing – granted to a consortium after Le Corbusier's visionary modernist design had been rejected because he hadn't used Indian ink for his drawings as instructed – is, rather ironically, a prime example of 1930s Fascist architecture, complete with cold marble floors, gigantic bronze doors and the hard lines of Neoclassicist Art Deco. That the building's rear extension, built in the late 1960s, today resembles the worst of London or Paris's inner-city office blocks, merely adds insult to injury.

Musée Ariana

Just down the hill from the Palais des Nations, in a distinctive 1880s Neo-Baroque mansion set in the same park, is the **Musée Ariana** (Mon & Wed–Sun 10am–5pm; free; Ⓦ www.ville-ge.ch/musinfo), devoted to seven centuries of glass and ceramics from Europe and the East. Unless you're a fan, though, the building – semicircular galleries overlooking an internal atrium – is likely to be at least as inspiring as its contents. Highlights of the lavish collection include European faïence and porcelain from the sixteenth to eighteenth centuries, the earth tones of Spanish ware contrasting with deep creamy French colours and light Italian pastels. There are plenty of English notes to mug up on as you go around.

Eating and drinking

With more than a thousand restaurants in the city, you could **eat and drink** your way around the world in Geneva – at a price. The most visible establishments might give you the impression that you could afford nothing more adventurous than a filled baguette, but Genevois café culture is alive and well, and inexpensive diners do exist. If you're prepared to splash, you could dine as grandly as in Paris, London or New York.

Cafés and café-bars

Almost every corner has its **café**, and the following list is highly selective, serving as much to give pointers as to what to expect in each neighbourhood as to recommend these particular establishments over others. The Old Town's Place du Bourg-de-Four, for instance, is lined with busy terrace cafés offering coffees, *apéros* and snacks to fuel hours of reading and people-watching, and there's little point picking one out to recommend. Wherever you end up, you'll have no trouble finding somewhere congenial to rest your feet and sample a little something.

Station area and Les Pâquis

Bains des Pâquis 30 Quai du Mont-Blanc. Excellent and very popular café-bar attached to the lakefront swimming areas, renowned for some of the best people-watching in the city – atmospheric, colourful and cool. Summer only.

Bookworm 5 Rue Sismondi. Mini teashop within a crammed second-hand English bookshop, with tootling Thirties music and a faultless "pot of tea for two with biscuits". Closed Mon & Tues.

La Bretelle 15 Rue des Etuves. Tiny kitsch tavern just off the Rive Droite, a glitz-drenched haven from the mean streets outside, that pulls in plenty of camp, alternative young-at-hearts, especially for the live accordion and/or drag cabaret (Thurs–Sat nights).

Buvette des Cropettes Place Gruet, off Rue de Montbrillant. Tiny atmospheric six-table wood-floor café-bar tucked behind the station, opposite the sunny Cropettes park. Closed Sun & Mon.

Café Arts 17 Rue des Pâquis. Bright café-bar with a young, excited clientele. A pleasant slice of sleaze-free Pâquis. Daily 5pm–midnight.

Café de Paris 26 Rue du Mont-Blanc, @www .cafe-de-paris.ch. Very central café that does one meal only, but does it spectacularly well – entrecôte steak in a special herb-and-butter sauce with golden chips and salad, for Fr.37. Otherwise, it's a perfect place for down-time, seconds from the station.

Mr Pickwick 80 Rue de Lausanne @www .mrpickwick.ch. Generic, rather down-at-heel English pub – a bit expensive, but nonetheless with the right kind of atmosphere and live football on the telly.

Old Town area and Plainpalais

Alhambar 10 Rue Rôtisserie @www.alhambar .com. Relaxed glittery bar behind a Rues-Basses cinema, with a yuppish tone, plenty of tapas and evening DJs. Sunday's laid-back piano-brunch is worth checking out.

Café des Forces Motrices Place des Volontaires. Directly opposite the *L'Usine* (see below), this is one of the best options in a buzzing area, not grand or trendy, but just calm, friendly, attractive and welcoming.

Café Gallay 42 Boulevard St-Georges. Friendly neighbourhood café-bar opposite Plainpalais cemetery, attracting an arty young crowd of students and theatre people. Good, inexpensive food and shared tables add to the appeal. Closed Sun.

Chocolaterie du Rhône 3 Rue de la Confédération. Outlet for fine handmade chocolates, with a small tearoom in the back serving heavenly cakes and confections to accompany tea and coffee. Closed Sun.

Le 2e (Deuxième) Bureau 9 Rue du Stand. Sleek postmodern bar, with sleek postmodern people draped over the sofas as deep beats rattle the glasses. Occasionally features live music or readings.

Flanagan's Rue du Cheval-Blanc. Top-rated Irish pub, hidden on an Old Town alley and generally packed with expats and Genevois alike.

L'Opera de Huissoud 51 Rue du Stand. Charming little nook dedicated to the delights of French pop music over five decades, with photos and record sleeves adorning the walls and Charles Aznavour crackling over the speakers.

Le Pain Quotidien 21 Boulevard Helvétique. No-nonsense café ("Daily Bread") with a well-deserved reputation for superb breakfasts (Fr.8–13) and, especially, weekend brunches of smoked salmon, salads, pastries, eggs, warm bread and fresh-squeezed juices (Fr.30). Seating is on benches at long wooden tables. Closed Tues eve.

Moloko In L'Usine squat, Place des Volontaires. Graffitied upstairs bar-café that once sported a rough-edged clientele puffing clouds of sweet smoke to a background of heavy noise. These days, it's been cleaned up a bit, but is still a good place to access the city's underground. Solid meals for Fr.13 or so.

Carouge

Bar du Nord 66 Rue Ancienne. Dark, plasticky and filled with young designerish Carougeois carousing beneath murals by a local cartoonist.

Cave à Bière 19 Rue Ancienne. Bar with almost 400 beers from around the world that attracts connoisseurs and serious drinkers in equal measure. Closed Sun & Mon.

Café de la Plage 10 Rue Vautier. Trendy alternative hangout, with long carved wooden benches and a pleasant, talkative ambience, regularly spilling drinkers out onto the street. It's a long way from any kind of *plage*, though.

Café des Amis 23 Rue Ancienne. Oldest of the traditional cafés on Ancienne, full of atmosphere from an age now past. Join the locals for a trip down memory lane.

La Marchand de Sable 4 Rue Vautier. Loud, graffitied little nook with a rough edge and student clientele, packed most nights.

Martel Tea Room 4 Rue du Marché. Perfect spot to punctuate an afternoon walk around Carouge, founded in 1818 and still offering exquisite chocolates and pastries as well as good, inexpensive meals. Closed Mon.

Restaurants

Geneva's excellent Swiss **restaurants** are boosted by a plethora of French places, chiefly drawing on influences from *haute-cuisine* Lyon. The **Old Town** in particular (around the Place du Bourg-de-Four) has a host of atmospheric Swiss eateries. **Carouge** is a foodie's paradise, with plenty of sometimes pricey choices. **Eaux-Vives** is much more down-to-earth, with some quality inexpensive Italian joints. Cosmopolitan – and occasionally sleazy – **Les Pâquis** has dozens of low-priced, authentic Arabic, East Asian, South American and African cafés and restaurants.

There's almost limitless choice in **inexpensive and mid-range** dining, with good-value, characterful places just off the main streets in all corners of the city. As you might expect, Geneva has dozens of top-drawer **expensive** restaurants, where you can find cuisine to match the best in the world.

Inexpensive and mid-range restaurants

Station area and Les Pâquis

Al-Amir 12 Rue des Alpes. Excellent Lebanese place, its stool-and-counter area favoured by falafel-munching locals over the sit-down table section. Quality range of *mezze* (Fr.8–14 each), plus chicken or lamb *shwarmas* (Fr.10) as good as they should be. Top choice of the many Pâquis kebab dens.

Le Diwane 6 Rue de Zurich ☎ 022 732 73 91. Excellent, authentically prepared Arabic cuisine. A meal of classy *mezze* is about Fr.25, or you can blowout and order the entire menu for Fr.170 – either way, don't miss the delicious *maamoul* rose-scented cookies afterwards. July–Sept daily; rest of year closed Sat lunch & Sun.

Le Dodo 20 Rue de Montbrillant ☎ 022 734 39 57, ⓦ www.ledodo.ch. Much-loved Mauritian restaurant, with a dodo on the bar and an intriguing menu full of dishes that blend seafood and Indian-style spicing to perfection. Under Fr.20 for lunch; double that in the evenings. Closed Sun.

El Mektoub 5 Rue Chaponnière ☎ 022 738 70 31, ⓦ www.elmektoub.com. Discreet central hideaway for quality North African cooking in a pleasant ambience. Excellent couscous and a wealth of *tajines* are Fr.30–35, with a handful of veggie options too. Closed Sun.

Jeck's Place 14 Rue de Neuchâtel ☎ 022 731 33 03, ⓦ www.jecksplace.ch. Excellent Thai restaurant, with nice wood-and-rattan decor and superb, authentic food that is surprisingly affordable (around Fr.30, or half that at lunch). House speciality is a range of Singaporean dishes, mixing influences from Malaysia, China and India. Closed Sat lunch.

Manora 4 Rue de Cornavin. Excellent, down-to-earth self-service nosh at this huge outlet of the Swiss chain (see p.56). With such a fast customer turnover, its food is very fresh as well as rock-bottom cheap: you can easily stuff yourself for Fr.13.

Au Petit Chalet 6 Rue Chaponnière. Unpretentious city-centre Swiss place for fondues, *rösti* and pizza (Fr.20–25) in a refreshingly untouristic dark-wood setting. Closed Mon.

Teranga 38bis Rue de Zurich ☎ 022 731 15 22. Tiny backstreet Senegalese place, attractively decorated, with good service and great food, including plantains, *yassa* (braised chicken in onion sauce) and fresh ginger juice. Around Fr.25. Closed Sat lunch & Sun.

Zara 25 Rue de Lausanne. Simple little Eritrean/Ethiopian café-restaurant near the station, with uncomplicated menus (meat and vegetarian) for Fr.20–25 and, unusually, weekend breakfasts from 5am.

Old Town area and Plainpalais

Les Armures 1 Rue du Puits-St-Pierre ☎ 022 310 34 42, ⓦ www.hotel-les-armures.ch. Traditional stone-floored Old Town institution on three storeys, refreshingly kitsch-free and once graced by Bill

△ Place du Bourg-de-Four

Clinton and family (with a plaque by the door to prove it). A full range of perfectly prepared Swiss dishes cost from Fr.30.

Café du Centre 5 Place du Molard ☎022 311 85 86, ⓦwww.cafeducentre.ch. A very handy Rues-Basses pitstop with terrace seating in summer. The smell of the sea hits you as you push the door and that's really what this plain, very popular café-restaurant is all about, offering everything from 100g of periwinkles up to a dozen fresh oysters, aided by a huge wine list. Not cheap for dining, at Fr.30–50, but worth a coffee just to sample the old-style atmosphere.

Cave Valaisanne/Chalet Suisse Place du Cirque ⓦwww.chaletswiss.ch. Touristically minded place for those seeking that authentic fondue experience. The chalet side is all dim lights, dark wood-beamed interior and endless Swiss kitsch; the *cave* side less contrived and so slightly less grating. The food is fine at both, and affordable (Fr.20 or so), but neither is what you might call heart-warming.

La Favola 15 Rue Jean Calvin ☎022 311 74 37, ⓦwww.lafavola.com. Charming little family-run restaurant on a cobbled Old Town alley, with a small menu of choice Ticinese specialities to dally over in an atmospheric setting. A romantic evening tête-à-tête could touch Fr.45 each; lunches much less. Closed Sat & Sun.

Hang Zhou 19 Rue de la Coulouvrenière ☎022 781 41 47. Excellent inexpensive Chinese, with a full vegetarian menu and *dim sum* galore (Fr.15–25). Closed Sun.

Le Pied de Cochon 4 Place du Bourg-de-Four ☎022 310 47 97, ⓦwww.pied-de-cochon.ch. Bow-tied waiters bustle their way between the tinkling cutlery of one of Geneva's best-loved bistros, serving meaty Genevois and Lyonnais gutliners

(Fr.35), including the namesake grilled pigs' trotters, to a clientele not short of a *centime* or two.

Taverne de la Madeleine 20 Rue Toutes-Âmes. Quite possibly the oldest restaurant in the city, now an alcohol-free café-bistro, serving only lunches – unreconstructed home-made fare (Fr.15) – in a tiny old dining room below the Old Town. Closed Sun.

Eaux-Vives

Vesuvio 7 Rue Cherbuliez ☎022 736 30 40. Eaux-Vives has many Italian restaurants, but this is one of the best (also known as *Da Gabriele*), boasting fresh-made pasta, a wood-fired pizza oven, relaxed open decor and friendly service. Meals are not expensive, mostly under Fr.20. Closed Sat lunch, Sun & Mon.

Carouge

La Bourse 7 Place du Marché, Carouge ☎022 342 04 66. Celebrated nineteenth-century café-brasserie in the heart of Carouge, with a wide, heavily fishy menu, taking in *moules* and *huitres* as well as a protein-packed *marmite du pêcheur* (Fisherman's Pot). Fondue, salads and steak help out less briny diners, and a quality lunch *menu* can be had for around Fr.15. The cellar doubles as a pizzeria. Closed Sun & Mon.

La Cuccagna Place du Temple. Quality among Carouge's high-class cuisine that won't break the bank, with simple, delicious pizza and pasta dishes for Fr.25 or so.

Sawasdee 24 Avenue Cardinal Mermillod ☎022 300 08 42. Best Thai in Geneva, with calm, attentive service, simply exquisite food and a bill at the end of it to lighten your spirits: a mere Fr.15–18 for lunch, twice that in the evening. Definitely worth the tram ride.

Expensive restaurants

Le Chat Botté In *Hôtel Beau-Rivage*, 13 Quai du Mont-Blanc ☎ 022 716 66 66. Classic French fine dining – with fish dishes celebrated above all – in this most traditional of hotels, with a choice between the somewhat stuffy formal dining room and, in summer, the lighter, easier-going terrace overlooking the lake. Expect Fr.130 at least. Open daily.

Domaine de Châteauvieux 16 Rue Châteauvieux, Peney-Dessus, Satigny ☎ 022 753 15 11, ⓦ www .chateauvieux.ch. An atmospheric château a short drive west of the city, in the heart of Geneva's wine region, complete with a cobbled approach, ancient beams, old stones and a giant open fireplace dominating the dining room (or, in summer, views from the terrace over the vineyards). The fine, traditional cuisine with some innovative modern touches, emphasizing simplicity and seasonal, local ingredients, is highly acclaimed – not least by Michelin, who give the place two stars. Closed Sun & Mon.

L'Esquisse 7 Rue du Lac ☎ 022 786 50 44. Gourmet French cuisine – priced lower than elsewhere – in the unlikely surroundings of an Eaux-Vives backstreet. The place is also a gallery for local artists, and pleasant decor and respectful service aids peaceful digestion of the *foie gras* and *filet mignon* etc. Lunch is Fr.40, evening *menus* around Fr.85. Closed Sat lunch & Sun.

Miyako 11 Rue de Chantepoulet ☎ 022 738 01 20, ⓦ www.miyako.ch. Superb Japanese restaurant, calm, modern and attractive, with three separate areas. The sushi and sashimi bar is first as you walk in, downstairs is a quiet dining room, with low tables and traditional seating, but the best location is the lively main *teppan yaki* area in the rear, ranged at counters around several open hotplates, where chefs expertly slice, dice, toss and sauté your meal in front of you. Quality is outstanding, with everything melt-in-the-mouth fresh. Servers will talk you through the long menu, which includes several options of set meals ("Menu Sushi", "Menu Sashimi" etc) for around Fr.50. Leave space for the exquisite *glace au thé vert* (green-tea ice cream). Expect around Fr.75 a head. Closed Sun.

Vieux-Bois 12 Avenue de la Paix ☎ 022 919 24 26, ⓦ www.vieux-bois.ch. High-quality showcase of the world-famous catering school L'École Hôtelière de Genève: all the chefs and waiting staff are students, which means you'll get sharp, attentive service and an *haute cuisine* lunch – French, with light, inventive touches and veggie options – for a fraction of prices elsewhere. Scoff a four-course meal for as little as Fr.47, or choose from the daily specials for half that, and then retire to the garden for coffee. Mon–Sat noon–2.30pm only; garden May–Sept Mon–Sat noon–6pm. Closed Easter, mid-July to mid-Aug, Christmas & New Year.

Nightlife and entertainment

Geneva's **nightlife** is unlikely to set your pulse racing. Many venues cater to visiting businesspeople and wealthy locals – formal dinner-dance, yawnworthy cabaret, strip-shows and hostess bars – but aside from checking out the handful of alternative arts venues, it's not easy to find what young Genevois get up to… often because they've vanished up the road to the cutting-edge **clubs** in and around Lausanne instead. **Classical music** and **opera** is top-notch, with a world-famous orchestra dividing its time between Geneva and Lausanne. The **Fêtes de Genève** is the city's premier annual arts festival, held in early August on the waterfront, with music of all kinds, theatre, funfairs and street entertainers. What's-on **listings** are published weekly in **Genève-Agenda**, the free city guide available from the tourist office and hotels.

Clubs and live music

Geneva has a handful of worthwhile dance **clubs**, but nothing to compete with Lausanne or Zürich. Often you'll find that places billing themselves as **discothèques** turn out to be deeply depressing floorshows (occasionally nude dancing girls) and/or a Top 40 disco. There are a few venues around town for **live music**; Friday and Saturday nights are when the bars and clubs lining Rue Vautier in Carouge come into their own. There's a festival of rock, jazz and folk in July and August at Parc La Grange in Eaux-Vives, but if you're around in the summer you should aim for the big Paleo festival at Nyon just around the lake (see p.144).

Le Chat Noir 13 Rue Vautier, Carouge ⓦwww .chatnoir.ch. Bar and cellar venue dedicated to live performance, with three or four concerts a week, everything from *chansons* to drum'n'bass, acid jazz and acoustic blues. DJs follow on. Mon–Thurs 6pm–4am, Fri 6pm–5am, Sat & Sun 9pm–5am.
La Pirogue 4 Ruelle des Templiers ⓦwww .pirogue.ch. Reggae and African beats.
Sud des Alpes 10 Rue des Alpes ⓦwww .amr-geneve.ch. Jazz buffs' mecca, with live music that sometimes pushes the boat out a fraction. Generally Thurs–Sat at 9.30pm.

L'Usine Place des Volontaires ⓦwww.usine.ch. Alternative arts squat venue, featuring live bands at the Salle PTR ("Post Tenebras Rock"), experimental dance and drama at the Théâtre de l'Usine and non-commercial movies at the Cinéma Spoutnik.
Weetamix 114 Route de Vernier ⓦwww .weetamix.com. House and techno weekend all-nighters, with international DJs.
XS 21 Grand-Rue. Easy dancing to reggae, disco and popular tunes. Tues–Sat 10pm–5am.

Classical music

There's plenty of **classical music** in Geneva. The Orchestre de la Suisse Romande (ⓦwww.osr.ch), which shuttles between Geneva and Lausanne, is one of Europe's best, and often performs – in amongst big-name visiting orchestras and soloists – at the glittering Victoria Hall, 14 Rue Général-Dufour. The Grand Théâtre (ⓦwww.geneveopera.ch), on Place Neuve, has a continuous programme of classical concerts, chamber music and **opera**, and the Conservatoire de Musique, also on Place Neuve, hosts a prestigious annual international competition for young soloists in late September as well as recitals all year round. Many of the most innovative opera productions, as well as concerts and some dance events, take place at the lofty Bâtiments des Forces-Motrices (ⓦwww.bfm.ch), 2 Place des Volontaires, formerly home to hydroelectric turbines on the Rhône. There are also free classical concerts in many of Geneva's churches year-round, and open-air concerts at the Hôtel-de-Ville in July and August.

Gay and lesbian Geneva

Geneva's **gay** scene is centred around Dialogai, 11 Rue de la Navigation (☎022 906 40 40, ⓦwww.dialogai.org), which, as well as being a library and resource centre for the whole of Romandie, has news about one-offs around the city as well as a regular programme of events. Every week, they put on a mass candlelit dinner in a back room, guys crowding at long tables for the home-made food (Wed 7–10pm; Fr.15; maximum 70 – arrive early). *La Bretelle* (see p.106), *Nathan*, 6 Rue Baudit, and *L'Evidence*, 13 Rue des Grottes, are gay- or gay-friendly café-bars. You'll find no shortage of cruising possibilities among the Pâquis sex-shops.

Dialogai can help out with **lesbian**-oriented information, or you can contact Lestime (☎022 797 27 14, ⓦwww.lestime.ch), or La Clef, 3bis Rue du Stand (☎022 781 71 30), both of which have bars. L'Inédite is a bookshop and resource centre for women – lesbian and not – at 15 Rue St Joseph, Carouge.

Listings

Bike rental The station has the usual bike-rental facilities or you could take advantage of the *Genèv'Roule* scheme, 17 Place de Montbrillant (May–Oct daily 7.30am–9.30pm; ⓦwww .geneveroule.ch), with rental bikes for free (deposit Fr.50).

Boat rental You can rent boats from a handful of quayside operators, including Les Corsaires, 33 Quai Gustave-Ador (ⓦwww.lescorsaires.ch), and Marti Marine, 31 Quai du Mont-Blanc: roughly, a pedalo is Fr.18/hr, a small motorboat Fr.40–50/hr.

Books The best place for English-language books is Payot, 5 Rue Chantepoulet. L'Inédite, 15 Rue St-Joseph in Carouge, has a quirky selection of English and French books by, for and about women. Bookworm (see p.106) is piled high with second-hand English books.

Consulates Australia, 2 Chemin des Fins ⓣ022 799 91 00; Canada, 5 Ave de l'Ariana ⓣ022 919 92 00; New Zealand, 2 Chemin des Fins ⓣ022 929 03 50; UK, 37 Rue de Vermont ⓣ022 918 24 00; USA, 7 Rue Versonnex ⓣ022 840 51 60. Embassies are listed on p.251.

Flights Flight enquiries from Geneva-Cointrin ⓣ0900 57 15 00, ⓦwww.gva.ch.

Laundry Lavseul, 29 Rue de Monthoux (daily 7am–midnight).

Lost property If you lost something on a plane, call ⓣ022 799 33 35; if you lost it in the airport, call ⓣ022 427 92 31; if you lost it in a train station or on a train, call ⓣ051 225 14 33. The main CFF lost property office is on platform 1B of Gare Cornavin (Mon–Fri 6am–9pm, Sat & Sun 9am–7.45pm), and the city's lost property office is at 7 Glacis-de-Rive (Mon–Fri 7.30am–4pm; ⓣ022 327 41 11).

Markets The best markets in the city are the flea market on the Plaine de Plainpalais (Wed & Sat 8am–5pm); the general market on Place de la Madeleine (Mon–Sat 8am–6pm); and crafts (Thurs 8am–6pm) and books (April–Oct Fri 8am–5pm), both on Place de la Fusterie. Plainpalais also has big fruit & veg markets (Tues, Fri & Sun).

Medical facilities The Cantonal Hospital, 24 Rue Micheli-du-Crest (ⓣ022 372 33 11), has a 24-hour emergency room.

Post office 18 Rue du Mont-Blanc (Mon–Fri 7.30am–6pm, Sat 8am–noon).

Radio World Radio Geneva, 88.4FM (ⓦwww .wrgfm.com), is an oddly parochial English-language expat station, with BBC news plus music and phone-ins.

Around Geneva

If you're on an unhurried visit, there's plenty of opportunity to get out into the beautiful countryside of **Canton Geneva**, Switzerland's smallest. The tourist office brochure *Sites naturels et cours d'eau de la campagne genevoise* features eight two- or three-hour **countryside walks** that are easily manageable from the city itself, but it's also simple to strike out alone and discover bucolic villages, châteaux, views of the mountains or the lake for yourself. Many vineyards offer **free wine-tastings** on Saturday mornings; the tourist office brochure *Viticulteurs genevois* lists them all, with opening hours and what's on offer.

Spots to aim for include **Mont Salève**, the nearest high mountain to Geneva – a perfect place for sunshine when the lake is foggy – as well as the atmospheric and easy-to-reach Rive Gauche village of **Cologny**.

Rafting and paragliding

Rafting Genève (ⓣ079 301 41 40, ⓦwww.rafting.ch) runs canoeing, rafting and kayaking trips daily on the Arve's 7km of rapids, as well as whitewater trips on the Dranse and elsewhere, from about Fr.75 per person. They also rent canoes and kayaks and make tandem paragliding jumps off Mont Salève (Fr.150). Their info-shack is on Quai des Vernets south of Plainpalais (May–Oct only).

Mont Salève

First ridge of the Alps rising southeast of Geneva is **Mont Salève** (1380m), the city-dwellers' principal retreat into nature, with wide-open countryside for walking or skiing, and views over the city, the whole canton and the Jura hills opposite. There are footpaths galore on top (which become cross-country skiing trails in winter), both through woodland and, higher up, across expansive green meadows dotted with wildflowers in season. In contrast to the sheer face presented to Geneva, the other, southern side of the mountain is a gentle slope, looking out onto Mont Blanc and the Savoy Alps.

Bear in mind that Salève is across the French border, so if you're going to need a visa (either to get into France, or to get back into Switzerland), you should give it a miss. Bus #8 terminates on the border at Veyrier, from where it's a short walk through customs to the **cable car**, which rises to a crest of the ridge (May–Sept daily; April & Oct closed Mon; check at other times). TPG offices at Gare de Cornavin and Rive, and the Place Dorcière coach station, sell a day pass that includes the cable-car round-trip for Fr.19. There's a panoramic restaurant on top. You can do the trip to the summit and back in a couple of easy hours.

Cologny and Hermance

The Rive Gauche lakeside slopes are dotted with peaceful, attractive villages that can offer beautiful walks. **COLOGNY**, 6km northeast of the city (bus A), has long been known as an exclusive and somewhat refined suburb, and the difference from Geneva is striking, with country lanes weaving between fields and open woods, and many large detached houses set back behind walls. **Byron** wrote the third canto of **Childe Harold** in 1816 while staying at the Villa Deodati, at 9 Chemin de Ruth in Cologny, and waxed lyrical about the rarity of seeing Mont Blanc reflected in the lake from up here. **Milton**, too, came visiting in 1639. If you follow Chemin de Ruth north, you'll come to the district of Montalègre, and the Maison Chapuis, where **Shelley** and Clairmont stayed in 1816 with **Mary Godwin**, who began writing **Frankenstein** here. The association with fame has stayed rock-solid over the centuries, and Cologny still has its fair share of resident big-names. True to form, the tourist office has obligingly dubbed the place the "Beverly Hills of Geneva". Cologny also has an esoteric museum attraction, the **Bibliotheca Bodmeriana**, 19 Route de Guignard next to the bus stop (Tues–Sun 2–6pm; Fr.8; SMP; ⓦwww .fondationbodmer.org). One of the greatest private libraries ever assembled, it takes in 160,000 works of literature, including illuminated medieval manuscripts, one of the few copies of the Gutenberg Bible and the oldest surviving text of the Gospel of St John.

Some 10km further along the lakeshore on a minor road, the tiny village of **HERMANCE**, last before you cross into France and reachable on bus E (or summertime boats), is even more tranquil, with remnants of its thirteenth-century walls and many medieval houses.

Travel details

Full timetables for all trains, buses, trams, boats and cable cars in Switzerland – as well as international connections – are searchable at ⓦ www .rail.ch.

Trains

Geneva to: Basel (every 30min; 2hr 40min); Bern (every 30min; 1hr 45min); Biel/Bienne (hourly; 1hr 30min); Brig (twice hourly; 2hr 20min); Delémont (hourly; 2hr 5min); Fribourg (twice hourly; 1hr 20min); Geneva airport (every 10min; 6min); Lausanne (every 15min; 35min); Martigny (twice hourly; 1hr 35min); Montreux (twice hourly; 1hr 5min); Neuchâtel (hourly; 1hr 10min); Nyon (every 15min; 15min); Sierre (twice hourly; 1hr 50min);

Sion (twice hourly; 1hr 45min); Vevey (twice hourly; 1hr); Yverdon (hourly; 50min); Zürich (every 30min; 2hr 45min).

Boats

Following is a summary of May–Sept summer services; fewer boats run in other months, generally Sat & Sun only, if at all. Full details are at ⓦ *www.cgn.ch.*
Geneva (Quai du Mont-Blanc or Jardin Anglais) to: Evian, France (2 daily; 2hr 45min); Hermance (1 or 2 daily; 45min); Lausanne (3 daily; 3hr 30min); Montreux (3 daily; 5hr); Nyon (4–7 daily; 1hr–1hr 30min); Vevey (3 daily; 4hr 30min).

2

Lausanne and Lake Geneva

CHAPTER 2 # Highlights

✳ **Collection de l'Art Brut**
Moving and highly memorable
gallery of "outsider" art.
See p.128

✳ **Cathédrale Notre-Dame**
Lausanne's elegant Gothic
centrepiece. See p.130

✳ **Ouchy waterfront** Lakeside
catwalk for hip bladers and
old-fashioned promenaders
taking the air. See p.131

✳ **Gruyères** Medieval hilltop
castle-village in the heart of
cheese country. See p.138

✳ **Vevey** The most refined and
alluring of lakeside towns.
See p.148

✳ **Montreux** Lake Geneva's
most upmarket destination
– beautiful, expensive and
exclusive. See p.154

✳ **Château de Chillon** One of
the best-preserved medieval
castles in Europe, perched
over deep water. See p.158

✳ **Golden Pass** Superbly scenic
train journey from Montreux
into the mountains. See p.160

△ Château de Chillon

2

Lausanne and Lake Geneva

Y ou can find the whole of Switzerland on the shores of **Lake Geneva**: snowy mountains, bucolic wine-villages, city nightlife, the sound of cow-bells in rolling pastureland, castles, cathedrals and the beautiful blue lake itself (Lac Léman in French). The southern shore of the lake is in France, taking in the Savoy Alps as well as Mont Blanc a little further south. The northern shore forms the economic and cultural focus of French Switzerland, centred around **Lausanne**, an energetic, endearing city that's too often skimmed over in favour of Geneva's more fastidious pleasures.

Aside from Geneva in the southwest and fragments of Valais in the southeast and Fribourg in the northeast, this is all **Canton Vaud** (pronounced *voh*; Ⓦ www.lake-geneva-region.ch), economically and politically the strongest of the French-speaking cantons, with a turbulent past. A 1798 revolution backed by France returned control to the Vaudois after two centuries of rule by Bernese bailiffs, a struggle commemorated by Napoleon, who formally created a new canton out of the territory. Vaud duly joined the Swiss Confederation in 1803 under a green-and-white flag which still flies in towns and villages to this day bearing the words "Liberté et Patrie". The ambience of the region is thoroughly Gallic: historical animosity towards Catholic France has given way to a yearning on the part of most urban francophone Swiss to abandon their heel-dragging compatriots in the more stolid east and embrace the EU. The short train ride from the Swiss-German cities of the **Mittelland** crosses more than just a linguistic boundary: it seems to span a whole continent of attitude.

Lausanne

[From] the terrace of the cathedral, I saw the lake above the roofs, the mountains above the lake, the clouds above the mountains, and the stars above the clouds. It was like a staircase where my thoughts climbed up step by step and broadened at each new height.

Victor Hugo

Exploring Lake Geneva

Trains and boats

Mainline CFF **trains** describe an arc around the northern lakeshore, from Geneva to Nyon, Lausanne, Vevey, Montreux and on into the Valais. Smaller lines branch off at various points into the hills which cup the lake on both sides – the Jura foothills in the west and the Prealps in the east. However, you shouldn't miss the chance to take a **boat trip** on the lake: CGN boats (ⓦwww.cgn.ch) link all points on the Swiss and French shores. Tourist offices stock their timetable brochures, which are also posted at every *débarcadère* (landing-stage). The lake is divided into three: the **Petit-Lac** in the southwest, between Geneva and Nyon; the **Grand-Lac** between Nyon and Lausanne; and the **Haut-Lac** in the east around Vevey and Montreux. Boats run on short and long tours within and between all three areas, as well as hopping along the shoreline villages. Some also cross the lake, from Nyon and Rolle to Yvoire (France); from Lausanne to Evian (France); and from Vevey to St-Gingolph (a divided village on the French–Swiss border) – for all of which you need your **passport**. Eurail and Swiss Pass holders travel free on CGN boats, but InterRailers get no discounts.

Regional Pass

The excellent **regional pass** is publicized through the GoldenPass train line (ⓦwww.mob.ch): it's available online, at train stations and tourist offices. Coverage is wide, taking in buses, trains and boats across the whole lake from Geneva airport to Montreux (including the French shore), as well as routes into the Vaud Alps and to Gruyères and Gstaad. For Fr.89, you get five consecutive days of validity: any two days of free travel, plus three days at a discount of 25 to 50 percent. The seven-day pass – including three days' free travel – costs Fr.107. Pay more to travel first class; pay less if you hold any sort of Swiss Pass. Children under 16 go half-price.

LAUSANNE tends to inspire hyperbole. In a country of spectacular natural beauty it is the most beautiful of cities, Switzerland's San Francisco – a city of incredibly steep hills that has developed tiered above the lake on a succession of compact, south-facing terraces. Vistas of blue water, glittering sunlight and the purple and grey of the white-capped Savoy Alps peep through between gaps in buildings or at the ends of steeply dropping alleys. Much of the city is still wooded, there are plenty of parks, and the tree-lined lakefront promenades spill over with beds of vibrantly colourful flowers. Attractive, interesting, worldly, and well aware of how to have a good time, it's simply Switzerland's sexiest city.

The comparisons with San Francisco don't stop at the gorgeous setting. If Switzerland has a counterculture, it lives in the clubs and cafés of Lausanne, a fact which lies broadly within the city's long tradition of fostering intellectual and cultural innovation. From medieval times, Lausanne has stood at the Swiss cultural avant-garde. Back then, the **cathedral** crowned the city the most influential of the region; it still sits resplendent on an Old Town hill, Switzerland's most impressive Gothic monument. After the Reformation, students flocked to Lausanne's pioneering university, and in the eighteenth and nineteenth centuries, restless Romantics sought and found inspiration in the setting and the life of Lausanne. It remains a grand-looking city (population 300,000), full of shuttered foursquare mansions and ritzy shopping streets, and with its own glamorous lakeside resort of **Ouchy**; there are few cities in Europe that so

LAUSANNE &
LAKE GENEVA

actively value and support the pleasure principle. For decades, the municipality has subsidized art and culture of all shades, resulting in a range of festivals, live music, clubs, theatre, opera and dance to rival a more sluggish metropolis ten times bigger.

Aiding the dynamism, a defining feature of the city is its international population of **students**, attracted to the prestigious University of Lausanne, Switzerland's biggest, and the French-language arm of the Federal Institute of Technology. Hundreds of language schools and private academies enhance the city's reputation for learning, along with the world-famous École Hotelière, training ground for top chefs and hotel staff. This youthful, outgoing spirit, and the city's hilly aspect, have also given Lausanne a new role as European **blading and skateboarding** capital: when the sun shines, every public space hisses with the spinning of tiny wheels, and the Ouchy waterfront in summer echoes to the clack of skateboards. Bladers have been clocked doing 90kph on the city's hills.

The International Olympic Committee has been headquartered in Lausanne since 1915, and has attracted to the city an array of world governing bodies in sports ranging from chess to volleyball. This has lent the city its marketing tag of "**Olympic Capital**" – a meaningless title which you'll see used everywhere to plug the city's rather vapid Olympic Museum.

Some history

Vidy, on the waterfront immediately west of Ouchy, was a focus of settlement from **Neolithic** times onwards, and was where the **Romans** founded the small town of Lousonna in 15 BC. Lousonna flourished, but during troubled times in the fourth century, the lakefront site was abandoned for a better-defended spot on the heights above, today the site of the Old Town. In 590, Bishop Marius transferred his bishopric from Avenches to Lausanne, confirming the city's rising influence. Succeeding bishops gathered power, even becoming imperial princes in 1125, until by the thirteenth century they were overseeing one of the largest cities in the region, with some nine thousand inhabitants. Both Pope Gregory X and Emperor Rudolf of Habsburg considered the consecration of Lausanne's fabulous **cathedral** in 1275 important enough to grace the ceremony with their presence.

During the fourteenth and fifteenth centuries, Lausanne was buffeted by a series of fires and plague epidemics, as well as increasing social disorder stemming from the division between the opulent lifestyle of the bishops in their lofty palace and the poverty of the people in the **Ville Basse**, or lower town. In 1525, the Lausannois made a pact of mutual military assistance with Bern and Fribourg; eleven years later when the **Bernese** army, fired with the zeal of the **Reformation**, swept down towards Lake Geneva, the Lausannois were finally able to eject the bishops. Their independence was short-lived, though, since no sooner had the bishops departed (founding a new see in Catholic Fribourg) than the Bernese installed bailiffs of their own and reduced Lausanne to the status of a subject city.

Lausanne's university was founded in 1540 as the first French-language centre of Protestant theology, but the city remained a Bernese-run backwater until, in 1803, **Napoleon** hived Canton Vaud away from Bern and granted Lausanne the status of Vaudois capital. Shortly after, the municipality filled in the rivers Flon and Louve, which wound between the city's summits, and threw grand arching bridges over the ditches to link disparate neighbourhoods for the first time. Artists, romantics and adventurers soon flocked to Lausanne and the adjacent *commune libre et indépendante* of Ouchy, turning the place into a rather genteel stop on the Grand Tour of Europe. By the turn of the century, Lausanne was hosting a thriving community of expats – including forty retired British colonels – and boasted English churches, English boarding schools, a cricket pitch, a football field and an English library serving afternoon tea. Lausanne had a quiet twentieth century, flourishing commercially, socially and culturally while content to remain in the shadow of its over-illustrious, sober and considerably less desirable neighbour, Geneva.

Orientation, arrival and information

Lausanne's topography looks confusing on a map, but isn't too hard to grasp. At the top is the Old Town, in the middle are the train station and commercial districts, and at the bottom is the one-time fishing village of **Ouchy**, now prime territory for waterfront strolling and café-lounging. But the gradients between them all are no joke: Mont Jorat, only 10km northeast of the city, rises to 927m; just north of the Old Town is a viewpoint at 643m; the central districts are ranged around 475m; while residential neighbourhoods slide on down for another kilometre to the lakeshore at 372m.

Focus of the city centre is **Place St-François**, hub of bus routes and heart of the shopping district. Gilt-edged **Rue de Bourg** entices shoppers uphill from St-François, while beside it Rue St-François drops down north into the valley and up the other side to the cobbled **Place de la Palud**, an ancient, fountained square plum in the heart of the Old Town and flanked by the arcades of the Renaissance town hall. The elegant Gothic turrets of the **cathedral**

Lausanne's festivals

It can seem like there's always some celebration or other happening in Lausanne. All summer long, the **Ouchy waterfront** hosts informal music events – from techno to chamber music to African dance – just about every weekend, and always free. **Entrée libre pour un été** (ⓦ www.lausanne.ch/entreelibre) is a summer-long programme of free music, dance and culture at various locations around the city, taking in such diversities as organ concerts in the cathedral and hip-hop/DJ spectaculars.

Lausanne's biggest party is the **Festival de la Cité** (ⓦ www.festivaldelacite.ch) held in early July – more spontaneous and cutting-edge than the Montreux Jazz Festival happening at the same time just down the road, not least because everything is free and out in the streets: the whole of the Old Town is given over to live performance of all kinds – music, dance, drama, mime and more. Performances start at dusk and run continuously until the small hours on more than half a dozen open-air stages, with stalls selling beer and food to the crowds.

If you're in town at the wrong time for that, try and coincide with the **Cully-Lavaux Jazz Festival**, held in the wine cellars and medieval alleys of Cully village, 8km east of Lausanne, in late March; or the **Carnaval de Lausanne** in April/May; or the **Fête de la Musique**, impromptu music in the streets and bars in mid-June; or the **Fête de Lausanne**, a weekend of fairground attractions in late June; or the **Paleo Rock Festival**, a mammoth event held every July in a field outside Nyon (see p.144), which draws top-name artists and a crowd of a quarter of a million; or any number of other events. Finally, chilly January hosts the acclaimed **Prix de Lausanne** competition and workshop for young dancers, an annual fixture since 1970, inspired by world-famous choreographer Maurice Béjart and his resident company, the Béjart Ballet Lausanne.

LAUSANNE AND LAKE GENEVA

122

LAUSANNE

Fondation de l'Hermitage

Bois de Sauvabelin

Musée de la Main

Château St-Maire

Cathédrale Notre-Dame

Musée Historique

Hôtel de Ville

Église St-François

Musée Cantonal des Beaux-Arts

Tour de l'Ale

FLON

Collection de l'Art Brut

Théâtre de Beaulieu

Cinémathèque

Montbenon

Opéra

Parc Mon-Repos

Métro Flon

Station

Echallens

Renens

Geneva

A & 6

250 m

0

Parc du
Denantou

Musée
Olympique

Musée de
l'Elysée

Parc
Olympique

Lake Geneva

OUCHY

▶ Vevey

▶ Evian

Crêt de
Montriond

Métro
Montriond

Métro
Jordils

EATING & DRINKING

L'Age d'Or	15
Bleu Lézard	19
La Bossette	1
Buffet de la Gare	23
Café Bel-Air	8
Café de l'Evêché	13
Café du Grütli	14
Café de l'Hôtel de Ville	12
Café Romand	20
Captain Cook	22
Au Château	4
Au Couscous	22
DI	16
La Grappe d'Or	17
Hôtel de Ville	2
Kerrigan's	6
Laxmi	10
Lecaféthéâtre	9
Le Loft	7
MAD	11
Ma Jong	18
Manora	21
MGM	3
Sidewalk	24
La 13ème Siècle	5

N

▼ Vidy, campsite & ⓘ

▼ Nyon

rise loftily above, while the foursquare **château** stands even further up, at the highest and most northerly tip of the Old Town. Beyond rise forests and open parkland.

Northwest of St-François, the Grand-Pont soars over the warehouse district of **Le Flon**, hotbed of Lausanne's burgeoning club culture, to **Place Bel-Air** and on to Place Chauderon at the head of the Pont Chauderon, which also rises above Le Flon. The steep slope south of St-François ends at the main **train station**, south of which a succession of opulent residential districts trickle down to **Place de la Navigation** on the **Ouchy** waterfront. Lakeside promenades lead in both directions from Ouchy, east to the villages of **Pully** and **Lutry**, west to the parkland of **Vidy** and the lakeside campuses of the **university** and adjacent Federal Institute of Technology at Dorigny.

Arrival

Lausanne's imposing **train station** is served by trains from all corners of Switzerland as well as TGVs from Paris. **Boats** dock at the CGN jetty in Ouchy, more or less opposite which is a metro station, with regular shuttles on line M2 climbing the steep hill to the train station ("Gare CFF"), and further up to Flon. Alternatively, bus #2 (direction Désert) snakes up from the Ouchy waterfront to Place St-François, then heads northwest over the Grand-Pont to Bel-Air, and on to Rue Neuve beside Place de la Riponne.

By **car**, the *autoroutes* describe an awkward jink through the outskirts, and it's easy to go wrong. Following *autoroute* signs for "Lausanne-Centre" can get you snarled in suburban traffic; instead, aim for "Lausanne-Sud" – this brings you directly to the Maladière roundabout, a scant kilometre west of the city centre and Ouchy. If you're approaching from Vevey or Montreux, don't bother with the *autoroute* at all, but follow blue signs for Lausanne along the lakeshore road.

Parking is expensive or awkward, or both. Street parking in the centre is a dead loss, but it's worth cruising around south of the train station in search of a blue-zone space. The largest car park is under Place du Riponne (Ⓦwww .parking-riponne.ch), but it's more expensive than the easy-to-find one on the Ouchy lakefront, which has buses and metro nearby. Otherwise, aim for the signed **P+R** (Park and Ride) car parks (in Ouchy and on other approach roads), where you pay Fr.11 or so, depending on the number of people, for a Carte Journalière, which includes your parking space for the day and free public transport.

From **Geneva airport**, trains run direct to Lausanne (every 10min; 45min). Alternatively, an Airport Shuttle Express minivan (Ⓣ021 311 66 66, Ⓦwww .airportshuttleexpress.ch) will bring you and your luggage to anywhere in Lausanne for Fr.49 per person. They run at set times (every 2hr: daily 5.30am–9.30pm; takes 45min) and must be booked at least an hour in advance. The same conditions apply for the return leg (every 2hr: daily 4.45am–8.45pm).

Information

Lausanne has two **tourist offices**, one in the train station (daily 9am–7pm; Ⓣ021 613 73 73, Ⓦwww.lausanne-tourisme.ch), and the other beside Ouchy metro station (daily 9am–8pm; Oct–March closes 6pm). Both have stacks of information on the whole lake region. For more focused information on cultural happenings and the life of the city, drop into the municipality's **information office**, in the Hôtel de Ville (Mon–Fri 7.45am–noon & 1.15–5pm; Ⓣ021 315 25 55, Ⓦwww.lausanne.ch).

Geneva's *Le Temps* newspaper is the best source of **listings** and reviews of film openings, performances and cultural events throughout Romandie (although all in French). Lausanne's own *24 Heures* tabloid has cinema reviews but only a handful of other events listed. The tourist office puts out its own bimonthly offering.

City transport and tours

Although the Old Town is compact, and flying-crow distances don't look too bad, maps can only give half the story: you'll soon find that negotiating Lausanne's mountainous gradients and cat's cradle of valleys and bridges can get wearying. The excellent **public transport** is run by TL (℡0900 564 900, Ⓦwww.t-l.ch); Zone 11 covers the whole city. A short journey of up to three stops costs Fr.1.80; a longer journey inside Zone 11 costs Fr.2.40 (valid 1hr). A *Carte journalière* is Fr.7.

You'll mostly be using the **buses**, many of them electric. Most lines skirt the Old Town from St-François to Bel-Air to Riponne: only bus #16 winds through it. There's also a **metro**: the steep M2 line (known fondly as *la Ficelle*, the String) links the Ouchy waterfront with Flon in the city centre, via the train station (Gare CFF); the Métro-Gare shuttles continuously to and fro between Flon and the train station; and M1 runs from Flon west to the university. For details of the **boat** services on the lake, see p.118.

The station has **bikes** for rent as normal (daily 6.40am–7.40pm), but even the locals have to get off and wheel them up and down the city's hills. Where bikes score is if you fancy a leisurely day cycling through the lakeshore vineyards either side of Lausanne, dropping your bike off in Nyon or Vevey and getting the train back to the city in the evening. You could also take a bike up into the hilly forests above Lausanne and then freewheel down again. To blend in imperceptibly with the locals, rent some **blades** or a **skateboard** from the kiosk at 6 Place de la Navigation in Ouchy (June–Sept daily 11am–10pm, April, May & Oct Sat & Sun 11am–7pm; Ⓦwww.delacombaz.ch); they also rent good bikes, including 21-speed tandems. For a **taxi**, call ℡0800 810 810.

Walking tours

The tourist office sponsors two-hour multilingual **walking tours** of the Old Town, which start from the Place de la Palud (May–Sept Mon–Sat 10am & 3pm; Fr.10). You can request tours at other times, and on a multitude of specialist subjects, from ℡021 321 77 66. During the *Entrée libre pour un été* season of summer cultural activities, there are some literary and historical walking tours of Lausanne guided in English; check with the tourist office for details. Otherwise, the tourist office has booklets detailing excellent self-guided walks with maps.

Metro expansion

From 2006 until 2008, major expansion works on the M2 **metro** line mean that buses (line MB) are replacing the metro between Ouchy and Lausanne's city-centre stations (Gare CFF and Flon). Once complete, the M2 line will extend northwards from Flon to Riponne, Bessières and beyond, creating an easy link between the train station and the old town. Full information is at Ⓦwww.t-l.ch/m2.

Accommodation

Lausanne has **accommodation** to suit all budgets and aspirations. There's only a couple of **hotels** within the Old Town, plus a few more in the heart of the city centre; those on the Ouchy lakefront have an entirely different, more gracious ambience, although the lakefront road sees plenty of traffic. Any number of **luxury** establishments capitalize on Lausanne's topography to offer romantic lake views with a more or less tasteful line in opulence, but the best-value deals come at the array of business hotels, where you'll find cut-price rates at weekends and some special offers to draw in holidaymakers. Lausanne's **hostels** are very good.

Hotels

Inexpensive

Formule 1 67 Rue de l'Industrie, Bussigny ☎021 701 02 02, ⓦwww.hotelformule1.com. Chain motel, offering 73 generic rooms priced unbeatably low: less than Fr.65 for single, twin or triple occupancy. Located 6km northwest of the centre, close to the Crissier/Bussigny *autoroute* exit, with free parking. Bus #35 (not Sun) stops nearby on a route between Renens station (which is linked to Lausanne by trains, bus #7 and metro M1) and Crissier. Bussigny train station is a 500m walk away. ❶

Pension Bienvenue 2 Rue du Simplon ☎021 616 29 86, ⓦwww.pension-bienvenue.ch. Decent and respectable women-only guesthouse a few yards behind the station, with 25 rooms. Breakfast included. ❶

Du Raisin 19 Place de la Palud ☎021 312 27 56. A handful of rooms above an old café in the heart of the Old Town, with character and atmosphere but not much else. ❷

Mid-range

AlaGare 14 Rue du Simplon ☎021 617 92 52, ⓦwww.alagare.com. Decent, serviceable, mid-sized hotel in a quiet pedestrian zone just below the station, part of the Minotel group. ❸–❹

Aulac 4 Place de la Navigation, Ouchy ☎021 613 15 00, ⓦwww.aulac.ch. Large Belle-Epoque building looming over the Ouchy waterfront beside the metro station. Rooms are comfortable, balconied ones at the front with lake views (but more expensive, and exposed to street noise), those at the back cheaper and perfectly quiet. ❸–❹

Château d'Ouchy 2 Place du Port, Ouchy ☎021 616 74 51, ⓦwww.chateaudouchy.ch. Grandiose Neo-Gothic pile put up in the 1890s on the ruins of a twelfth-century bishop's palace (of which the tower survives). This is the one hotel situated on the lake side of the main road, separated from the water only by lush gardens. Stout, woody decor, open fireplaces and some surprisingly affordable rooms add to the charm; the distinctly faded grandeur suits its three-star rating. Romantics will relish the lofty tower room, its Romanesque windows framing dreamy lake views. ❹–❻

Elite 1 Avenue St-Luce ☎021 320 23 61, ⓦwww.elite-lausanne.ch. Extremely pleasant, very quiet and well-run hotel, surrounded by greenery and centrally located between the train station and St-François. Top-floor balconied rooms perch you above the roofs for views over the lake. Best value in this bracket. ❸–❺

Du Port 5 Place du Port, Ouchy ☎021 612 04 44, ⓦwww.hotel-du-port.ch. Quality little three-star lakefront hotel, in the same family for forty years and now fully upgraded, with excellent facilities and no-smoking rooms. Road noise can be a problem, though: ask for a room on an upper floor. Closed Jan. ❸–❹

Regina 18 Rue Grand St-Jean ☎021 320 24 41, ⓦwww.hotel-regina.ch. Friendly little place owned by an English-speaking couple, steps from the central Place de la Palud, offering quality renovated rooms in modern style, with marvellous top-floor views. ❸–❹

Expensive

Alpha Palmiers 34 Rue du Petit-Chêne ☎021 555 59 99, ⓦwww.fhotels.ch. A swanky business hotel, very well located on a busy, central pedestrian street just up from the station, boasting interior palm gardens and ultra-modern rooms – the antithesis of the grand palace hotels that prevail in Lausanne. ❺–❽

Angleterre & Residence 11 Place du Port, Ouchy ☎021 613 34 34, ⓦwww.angleterre-residence .ch. Classy hotel occupying four eighteenth-century mansions on the Ouchy waterfront, including the one where Lord Byron is reputed to have written

The Prisoner of Chillon. Historic features remain, and the tone is one of refined, tasteful comforts, with a range of rooms in both traditional and contemporary styles, and top personal service. Guests can use all facilities of the *Beau-Rivage Palace* alongside. ⑥–⑧

Beau-Rivage Palace 17 Place du Port, Ouchy ☎021 613 33 33, ⓦwww.brp.ch. Lausanne's top hotel and one of Switzerland's finest, set in ten-acre waterside gardens and sparklingly restored to its original 1861 grandeur. Sumptuous decor and fittings, huge, balconied rooms and stylish, contemporary touches raise it well above the standards of the many Swiss five-star palace hotels, while sharp service adds to the allure. ⑨

Hostels and camping

Hostels

Jeunotel (HI hostel) 36 Chemin du Bois-de-Vaux ☎021 626 02 22, ⓦwww.youthhostel.ch. Huge place right beside the *Vidy* campsite. A night in its good four-bed dorms, including breakfast, costs Fr.33. It also has a range of private rooms. ①

Lausanne Guest House (SB hostel) 4 Chemin des Epinettes ☎021 601 80 00, ⓦwww.lausanne-guesthouse.ch. Quality hostel occupying a fine old nineteenth-century town house a couple of minutes' walk behind the train station. All rooms face the lake views, with doubles (ensuite and not) and four-bedded dorms (beds Fr.35, less without sheets). Smoking is banned, except in the gardens. Also has bikes for rent. ①

Campsite

Vidy ☎021 622 50 00, ⓦwww .campinglausannevidy.ch. A five-star site sandwiched between the Roman ruins and the International Olympic Committee's château. From St-François take bus #2 (direction Bourdonette) to Bois de Vaux, or from the station take bus #1 to Maladière and walk for five minutes.

The City

Lausanne's **city centre** spans several hilltops, linked by bridges spanning deep, riverless gorges. **Place St-François** dominates the hilltop district known as the **Bourg**, formerly the wealthiest part of the city and still known for its upmarket shops and boutiques. To the north, the hill of the **Old Town**, crowned by the **cathedral**, dominates the city, while more heights to the west and east were roped in during expansion in the nineteenth century. The whole of Lausanne's explorable centre lies north of and above the train station, with Place St-François at the edge of a pedestrian-only zone covering virtually the entire Old Town. Walking is the best, and often the only, way to explore.

St-François and the Bourg

From the train station, a gap between buildings directly ahead marks the steep **Rue du Petit-Chêne** which winds up to **Place St-François** on the terrace above. Bedecked with bus-wires, buskers and shoppers, with traffic surging through, St-François – given the adenoidal nickname *Sainf* by the locals – is Lausanne's commercial centre, dominated by the bulk of

△ Shopping on the Rue de Bourg

the post office and, opposite, the considerably more attractive **Église St-François**. The Franciscans completed their new church in 1272; it then stood at the centre of a monastic complex against the southern city walls. In 1536 the monastery was dissolved and the building cleared of religious imagery to become the parish church of Lausanne's *Ville Basse* (lower town). Later renovations, not all in especially good taste, disfigured the interior, and although the church remains an atmospheric retreat from the bustle outside, today not a great deal is left of its illustrious past.

The quarter in which St-François stands, the **Bourg**, spreads over a narrow ridge between two gorges, and once stood alone: the **Rue de Bourg**, today a fashionable shopping street rising steeply from behind the church, had much the same style in the past too, lined then with restaurants, inns and luxury shops. In the 1780s, the English historian Edward Gibbon lived in a house on the site of the St-François post office, right at the heart of the high society of the day.

Massive urban expansion in the early nineteenth century included the razing of many slums, the filling in of the Flon river – which followed the course of the present Rue Centrale – and the construction of grand bridges unifying the disparate neighbourhoods of the city. Most dramatic of these is the **Pont Bessières**, spanning the Flon gorge from the eastern (top) end of the Rue de Bourg over to the Old Town. In recent years this has become the favoured spot for suicidal Lausannois to shuffle off this mortal coil, so much so that every New Year's Eve the city posts guardians halfway along the bridge to make sure no melodramatic revellers decide to test out their theories of flight. A walk over the **Grand-Pont**, first of the bridges to be built (in 1844), from Place St-François northwest to **Place Bel-Air**, can highlight Lausanne's extraordinary topography – stairs and alleys running off at odd angles, traffic surging along the valley road way beneath, the lake glittering below on one side and the cathedral crowning the hill above on the other. Below the Grand-Pont, and also accessed by stairs leading down from beside the distinctive Bel-Air tower (Switzerland's modest first skyscraper, dating from the 1930s), is the **Flon** district. Once full of merchants and traders, today its warehouses have been converted into dance clubs, alternative cafés, galleries and theatre spaces.

Collection de l'Art Brut

A fifteen-minute walk northwest of Bel-Air (or bus #2 from St-François or Bel-Air to Beaulieu) brings you to one of the most original art galleries in the country, the **Collection de l'Art Brut**, 11 Avenue des Bergières (Tues–Sun 11am–6pm; Fr.8; SMP; free on 1st Sat of month; ⓦ www.artbrut.ch). This unique collection, founded by Jean Dubuffet, is devoted to what's been called "outsider art", the creative output of ordinary people with no artistic training at all – often loners, psychotics or the criminally insane – who for some reason suddenly began making their own art, on many occasions in middle or old age. What results is art entirely free from any conception of formal artistic rules or conventions, which challenges both how we tend to view such "outsiders" in our own communities, and our expectations of what art should be about.

The gallery and its collection forces you to be open-minded about the artists and their lives, even though short biographies alongside each piece tell some heart-rendingly sad or disturbing stories. One highlight is the work of Henry Darger, a hospital porter in Chicago, who died alone, an old man unknown by his neighbours; it was only after his death that his 19,000-page novel, illustrated with dozens of detailed watercolours up to three metres long, came to light. Scottie Wilson, an illiterate Glaswegian junk dealer, began at the age of 40 to produce whimsical and intricate Escheresque drawings; while a London art gallery was selling his drawings for hundreds of pounds, Wilson was found outside in the street hawking others to passers-by for a pound or two. There's art on show from a factory worker whose talent was only discovered because he pinned his drawings up in his workshop, from a medium imprisoned in the 1930s for her interest in spirituality, from a postman who believed his hand was being directed by an external force, and so on.

As well as its permanent collection, the gallery has regular temporary exhibitions of *art brut* from artists around the world. Whatever is showing, it's worth going some distance out of your way to see.

The Old Town

Located in the tranquil core of Lausanne's **Old Town**, the cobbled **Place de la Palud** is a perfect spot for people-watching: with shopping streets cascading through the square from all sides, plenty of pavement cafés and the handy **Fontaine de la Justice** usually ringed with promenaders perching on its wide rim, it's a tempting place to take a break for a reviving *café renversée*, especially if the Wednesday and Saturday morning markets are in full swing. On the hour, mechanical figures emerge on the wall behind the fountain for a little chiming display. Dominating the south side of the square is the arcaded **Hôtel de Ville** (Town Hall), built in 1675 on the site of a covered marketplace dating back to the fourteenth century.

Place de la Riponne and around

From the Place de la Palud, Rue Madeleine leads up to the huge **Place de la Riponne**, a plain of concrete usually dotted with students sitting on the steps of the overbearing **Palais de Rumine** on the far side – an absurdly grandiose late nineteenth-century neo-Renaissance structure adorned with lions, angels and pink marble, named after a local philanthropist and designed by a Parisian architect who hadn't actually bothered to visit Lausanne beforehand. The palace is now home to a clutch of museums, most interesting of which is the **Musée cantonal des Beaux-Arts** (Tues & Wed 11am–6pm, Thurs 11am–8pm, Fri & Sat 11am–5pm; Fr.10; free on 1st Sun of month; Ⓦ www.beaux-arts .vd.ch). A huge percentage of its works, including those from the medieval and Baroque periods, and all its Renoirs, are currently in storage in the basement; instead it displays three rooms of Swiss art from the eighteenth to twentieth centuries (including many Vaudois artists), and devotes most of its time and energy to high-quality exhibitions of contemporary art hung in the brighter, less fussy rooms at the back. The museum is due to move, at some point before 2010, to a new site on the waterfront at Bellerive; check the website for the current situation.

From Riponne, Rue Haldimand heads down to the church of **St Laurent**, in the heart of the old quarter also known as St-Laurent. The Rue de l'Ale and Rue de la Tour bring you further west – past the crooked **Pinte Besson**, the city's oldest tavern, to the stout, circular **Tour de l'Ale** atop the hill, built in 1340 during a reorganization of the city's defences. The traffic hub of Place Chauderon is a few metres south and downhill, at the head of the **Pont Chauderon**, third of the major bridges spanning the Flon valley. On the south side of the bridge is the Montbenon park with, tucked into the trees, the Swiss film archives, housed in the *fin-de-siècle* casino building now transformed into the Cinématheque.

Cathédrale Notre-Dame

Stairs lead up from both Place de la Palud and Place de la Riponne to the higher points of the Old Town. The atmospheric **Escaliers du Marché**, covered wooden stairs heading up from Palud, deliver you to Rue Viret, circling around the pinnacle of the hill, from where more stairs bring you up to the **Cathédrale Notre-Dame** (Mon–Fri 7am–7pm (Oct–March until 5.30pm), Sat & Sun 8am–7pm; free; ⓦ www.grandesorgues.ch), generally acclaimed as Switzerland's finest Gothic building, on a par with the greatest of French Gothic architecture. Elegant and proportioned towers, turrets and spires claw their way up stage by stage into the sky; the south facade is studded with a spectacular giant Gothic rose window of stained glass, and flying buttresses encircle the exterior of the choir and ambulatory. The foundations of the current building were probably laid in the mid-twelfth century, with construction continuing from 1190 through to the cathedral's consecration in 1275. Despite extensive renovations and alterations just before the Reformation, and the loss of the altars, screens, and most of the statuary, paintings and glass during and after it, the cathedral has lost none of its grace and poise.

You enter through the west portal, bedecked with figures and dubbed the **Montfalcon portal** after a sixteenth-century bishop. The interior **Great Porch**, an unusual lofty open arcade with its recessed doorway and two tiers of columns, echoes similar setups in English cathedrals such as Lincoln and Canterbury, and it's been suggested that Notre-Dame's main architect, Jean de Cotereel, may have been Norman or part English himself. Just beyond, a squarish vestibule gives into the vast, broad **Great Bay** which, prior to 1504, was actually an open thoroughfare which connected the Rue Cité-Devant (to your left) with the Rue St-Étienne (to your right) under a vaulted gallery and beneath arches which seem extra-large now that they have been enclosed within the building.

The interior of the cathedral is stunning, every line and detail drawing your eye dizzily up to the lofty vaulted heights. On the south wall of the nave is the impressive **Painted Portal**, dating from 1215–30; its exterior is still encrusted with original statues, but has suffered badly from weathering in recent years, and may still be covered for protection. The crossing and transept, a few steps up from the nave and filled with light, are endowed on the south side with the glowing thirteenth-century **rose window**. Opposite is the doorway to the former cloister, above which columns in front of the rectangular windows have been snapped off to allow more light to enter the building. A few steps up again is the **choir**, housing some exceptionally beautiful thirteenth-century carved choir stalls; on the left is the tomb of Otto of Grandson, a rather diminutive figure for such a celebrated medieval knight (see p.180). You'll find more extremely worn tombs ranged around the **ambulatory** running under the walls, and also in the **crypt** beneath the choir. With a truly spectacular view over the whole of the city and most of Lake Geneva too, climbing the southwest **tower** (Mon–Sat 8.30–11.30am & 1.30–5.30pm, Sun 2–5.30pm; Fr.2) is one of the highlights of visiting Lausanne.

Beside the cathedral is the Ancien Évêché, the old Bishop's Palace, which has been converted into the **Musée Historique** (July & Aug daily 11am–6pm, rest of year Tues–Thurs 11am–6pm, Fri–Sun 11am–5pm; Fr.8; SMP; free on 1st Sat of month; ⓦ www.lausanne.ch/mhl). Crammed with all kinds of displays illustrating the history of Lausanne, its highlight is the giant scale model of the city in the basement, with an excellent accompanying commentary (in English), detailing the history of the various neighbourhoods since medieval times; the least of it is that you can finally get a clear, bird's-eye view of how the city's hills and valleys lie in relation to each other.

The nightwatch

Lausanne suffered from many devastating medieval fires, and is the last city in Europe to keep alive the tradition of the **nightwatch** (*le guet*). If you install yourself on the cathedral terrace, every night between 10pm and 2am, after the bells have struck the hour, you'll hear – and possibly spot – a sonorous-voiced civil servant calling out from all sides of the cathedral's 75-metre tower *"C'est le guet; il a sonné l'heure"* ("This is the nightwatch; the hour has struck"), assuring the lovers and assorted drunks sprawled under the trees that all is well. Having fulfilled his civic duty, he then retreats to a comfortable little room within the tower for the next 59 minutes. In 2002 Philippe Becquelin, a cartoonist on Lausanne's weekly *L'Hebdo*, who spent the four hours nightly drawing his strips, handed over the job – which involves traipsing up and down the tower's 160 steps – to his former deputy, sports teacher Renato Häusler, himself replaced in 2006 by Polish student Marek Ekrewicz.

North of the cathedral

Two parallel streets, Rue Cité-Devant and Rue Cité-Derrière, lead up from the cathedral to the top of the Old Town. Old-timers bemoan the fact that the **Ancienne Académie** at 7 Rue Cité-Devant, built in the 1580s as Lausanne's first university, formerly lay at the heart of a bustling student quarter, but that the students have all departed since the new out-of-town campus opened. It's true that the alleyways are now quiet, but they're also atmospheric, the blank old facades giving away little of their long history. A number of cellar theatres, as well as mouthwatering smells wafting from the dark interiors of small bistros, hint that the quarter is far from dead. At the top of the Old Town sits the unshakeable **Château St-Maire**, begun in the fourteenth century and completed in brick by northern Italian masons a century later. The structure symbolizes political power; in former times it was the residence of the Bernese bailiffs, and today it is the seat of the Vaud cantonal government.

Rue de la Barre continues north, rising over the workaday district known as **Tunnel**, busy with traffic and home to many students, accessed by stairs down to the left (west) of the street. Place du Tunnel is ringed by bars, cafés and music venues, while the eponymous tunnel itself – a major traffic route – cuts beneath Rue de la Barre and the whole Old Town hill through to the eastern districts of the city.

The open **Bois de Sauvabelin**, the beginnings of the Jorat forests, flanks Rue de la Barre northwards. Set into the park some way up (and this is no mean hill; take bus #16) is an expansive, beautifully preserved nineteenth-century villa housing the **Fondation de l'Hermitage** art gallery, 2 Route du Signal (Tues–Sun 10am–6pm, Thurs until 9pm; Fr.15; SMP; ⓦ www.fondation-hermitage.ch). The foundation owns a permanent collection taking in Degas, Sisley and Magritte, but displays only portions of it to complement the two or three world-class shows it mounts each year.

Ouchy and the lakefront

As if Lausanne weren't relaxed enough already, it has **Ouchy** as a lakeside terrace on which to stroll, chill out and enjoy the mountain views and fresh breezes. Officially – and proudly – a separate commune from Lausanne, Ouchy for years survived as a fishing port, but these days, although some fishing continues, it's become one of the more chic of the Swiss lakeside resorts, with classy hotels and waterfront cafés abounding.

△ Rollerbladers, Ouchy waterfront

Musée Olympique

Some 500m west of Ouchy's neo-Gothic château – now a hotel – and beyond the majestically opulent **Beau-Rivage Palace**, set in its own grounds, you'll come to the Parc Olympique, home of Lausanne's much-touted flagship **Musée Olympique** (daily 9am–6pm; Oct–April closed Mon; Fr.15; SMP; ⓦ www.olympic.org). It's a very grand affair, with formal gardens and fountains preluding the sweeping pomp of the interior design, but rather unsatisfying, a showcase more for the IOC administrators (International Olympic Committee, headquartered in Lausanne) than for the achievements of the athletes.

Displays on the Olympics of ancient Greece and the restoration of the games in modern times are moderately engaging, but the main focus of the museum – banks of video screens replaying events from past summer and winter games, to the accompaniment of suitably stirring music – ends up as little more than glorified TV. Rows of medals, sheets of Olympic postage stamps, and cases of objects from athletes past (signed swimming trunks, basketballs and Carl Lewis's old running shoes) do nothing to help tell any special stories, flung together here in a rather self-congratulatory manner.

In the basement, the computerized **video library**, which lets you select and view any of several hundred past events from the Olympics, the soccer World Cup, European championships, the NBA, Wimbledon or the Tour de France, **would** make the museum unmissable but for the fact that you're only allowed to choose two events, and they tend to comprise, for instance, a few minutes of goal action, or one single track event. Even for sports fans, it's a washout.

Across the lake to Evian

One of the best excursions from Lausanne is the short but scenic voyage across the lake to the venerable French spa town of **EVIAN**, almost directly opposite Ouchy. The best of the trip is on the water: little Evian (population 7500) has been gentrified almost to stupefaction, and there's not much to do other than stroll the boulevards, poke around the backstreets and gawp at the modern spa complex that exploits the famous mineral springs. One of the grand nineteenth-century edifices, the **Hall d'Exposition** on Rue Nationale, has an exhibition on the town's watery past (May–Sept daily; free), and can take bookings for a visit to Evian's giant bottling plant, 5km out of town (mid-June to mid-Sept; €1.60, includes transport). The **tourist office** is on Place d'Allinges (ⓦ www.eviantourism.com). Take your pick of the cafés and restaurants that line every street: all of them are shameless about flogging the local product.

In high summer, **boats** shuttle across from Lausanne-Ouchy almost hourly, the last one heading back at 10pm (Fri & Sat 11.20pm); service is reduced in other seasons, but this is one of the few Lake Geneva routes that runs daily, all year round. You can **change money** at the customs desk on arrival, or withdraw some euros from any of the plentiful bank ATMs. Don't forget your **passport**.

Musée de l'Elysée

On an upper level in the same park, set back from the Olympic Museum, you'll find the much more worthwhile **Musée de l'Elysée** (daily 11am–6pm; Fr.8; SMP; free on 1st Sat of month; ⓦwww.elysee.ch), dedicated to photography from the earliest daguerrotypes up to contemporary photojournalism. Its continuous cycle of exhibitions are generally outstanding, and there are often a range of shows on different subject matter running concurrently, so even if Czech avant-garde photography from the 1920s isn't your thing, a retrospective of David Hockney's photos might be.

Vidy

A kilometre or so west of Ouchy is the district of **VIDY**, marked by a boxy building on stilts in a lakeside park: this is the Théâtre de Vidy, home of Switzerland's leading contemporary drama company. The parkland just beyond the theatre was the location of the first settlements in the Lausanne area, in Neolithic times, and then later under the Romans. Approaching through the park, you'll discover remnants and ruins of the Roman town of Lousonna, an assembly of low walls and tumbled stones with an explanatory board nearby. A short distance beyond, at 24 Chemin du Bois-de-Vaux, is the modern and well-laid-out **Musée Romain** (Tues–Sun 11am–6pm, Thurs until 8pm; Fr.8; SMP; ⓦwww.lausanne.ch/mrv). Finds include particularly impressive glassware, some mosaic work and interesting displays of Roman artefacts.

Eating and drinking

If all you want is a reviving drink and somewhere to take the weight off your feet, the city centre and the Old Town can offer dozens of **cafés and café-bars**: almost every corner of every quarter has its local haunt, most of which offer food as well. Ouchy is a little less straightforward, since the cafés lining the waterfront are universally overpriced and under-quality, and although there's no shortage of **restaurants** offering fresh lake fish, none stands out as particularly noteworthy.

Aside from the city's reasonable choice of ethnic eateries, there are plenty of places offering Vaudois specialities. A **tomme** is a round soft cheese baked to melting point within its white Brie-like rind, and often served on a bed of leafy salad. A local speciality of the La Côte region just west of Lausanne is a **malakoff**, a hot, fried round of cheese served on a bread or pastry base; the nearby villages of Vinzel and Luins (see p.146) compete for whose *malakoff* is the best, but you can also find Lausannois versions. The mighty **saucisson vaudois**, a smoked pork and beef sausage, is served hot accompanied by **papet vaudois**, a puree of leek and potato, and graded according to quality, with the best labelled reverentially with the green cantonal flag.

Cafés and café-bars

Bleu Lézard 10 Rue Enning. Fashionable and lively café-bar on a busy corner, with a windowful of gnomes and a comfy colourful interior. The mood mutates into restaurant territory in the evenings, when food (including veggie options) is pricey – but you don't have to eat and the atmosphere is free.

La Bossette 4 Place du Nord, east of Tunnel. Comfortable and uniquely friendly local café on a patch of green beneath the château, serving a range of speciality beers along with excellent food.

Buffet de la Gare In the train station. Wonderfully atmospheric station buffet, with high ceilings, wood-panelled walls, white-aproned waiters and more than a hint of the age of steam. If your eye's on the minute hand, ask for the *assiette express*.

Café Bel-Air Place Bel-Air. The place to be seen, with the gentle tinkle of teaspoons accompanying the most discreet of gossip behind plate-glass windows.

Café de l'Évêché 4 Rue Curtat. Atmospheric little haunt of talkative students and local old-timers just below the cathedral – perfect for morning coffee, authentic fondue or beer and dominoes.

Café de l'Hôtel de Ville 10 Place de la Palud. Wonderful little intimate wood-floor café, with excellent Vaudois specialities – including hot and cold goats' cheeses with salad – quality service and especially fancy desserts. The cellar features small-scale shows of *chansons*, jazz and comedians.

Café Romand Place St-François. Unmissable and much-loved city-centre retreat, a bustling, heartwarming place with parquet floor and cosy alcoves for beer, coffee or heavy Swiss fare. Closed Sun.

Lecaféthéâtre 10 Rue de Genève. Appealing café-bar in the Flon, with a cellar atmosphere, fantasy art on the walls and nightly live sessions of piano, guitar or French *chansons* for entertainment. Food is excellent, home-cooked style, and not expensive. Closed Sun & Mon.

MGM 14 Rue du Lac. Café-bar in Ouchy, the best of the bunch, with tunes and rather tacky decor which aim for Miami Beach and miss.

Du Raisin 19 Place de la Palud. Prime people-watching terrace café in the Old Town.

Sidewalk 7 Place du Tunnel. Popular local joint in a little-visited area.

△ *Café de l'Hôtel de Ville*, Place de la Palud

Restaurants

Inexpensive and mid-range

L'Age d'Or 3 Pont Bessières ☎021 323 73 14. The city's top vegetarian restaurant, with a spectacular terrace tucked beneath the bridge. *Menus* range from Fr.30 to Fr.100 or more, with mains on their own hovering around Fr.22. Exquisite fresh fish is a highlight. Closed Mon eve & Sun.

Café du Grütli 4 Rue de la Mercerie. Venerable old tile-and-dark-wood brasserie in the heart of the Old Town, with very affordable *menus* (Fr.16 or so), or idiosyncratic options like a dozen snails. Head past the pavement tables and make for the hum of conversation within. Closed Sun.

Au Couscous 2 Rue Enning ☎021 321 38 40. Long-standing Arabic restaurant in a lively part of town, lacking some atmosphere but making up for it with excellent couscous and tajine (Fr.22+) and *mezze* (Fr.25), with veggie and macrobiotic dishes too. *Menus* from Fr.17. Closed Sat & Sun lunchtimes.

Laxmi 5 Escaliers du Marché ⓦwww.laxmi-suisse .com. Excellent authentic Indian/veggie food, well prepared and cooked. Budget all-you-can-eat buffet lunches are Fr.15, or Fr.11 for veggies, or Fr.10 for cold dishes; evening *menus* cost no more. Students get a ten percent discount. Closed Mon lunch & Sun.

Ma Jong 3 Escaliers du Grand-Pont. Just down from *Manora*, with excellent-value freshly wok-fried meals, piled high for Fr.15. Sushi too. Closed Sun.

Manora 17 Place St-François. Self-service place with a wide range of excellent cheap food. Daily 9am–10.30pm.

Expensive

La Grappe d'Or 3 Cheneau-de-Bourg ☎021 323 07 60, ⓦwww.lagrappedor.grandestables.ch. Top gourmet temple for classic and modern French cuisine, benefiting from attentive service and a warm ambience. Expect little change from Fr.200. Closed Sat lunch & Sun.

Hôtel de Ville 1 Rue d'Yverdon, Crissier ☎021 634 05 05. Formerly the domain of the legendary Frédy Girardet, said to be the greatest chef in the world in his day, and now taken over by Philippe Rochat, an underling for some seventeen years. Many consider this Switzerland's best restaurant – Michelin give it three stars. The style is classic, the presentation and service are impeccable. Reserve two months ahead for dinner, two weeks ahead for lunch. Located 7km west of the city. Closed Sun & Mon, and early Aug.

Nightlife and entertainment

Lausanne's **nightlife** and cultural offerings are second to none in Switzerland, with a vast range of music and performance to check out, aside from the swathe of festivals listed in the box on p.121.

Bars, clubs and live music

Bars and clubby nightlife abound. First place to look is Le Flon, a low-lying warehouse district bounded by Bel-Air, Grand-Pont and the metro station, where following your ears after dark will bring you to the happening joints of the moment. Otherwise, good areas for concentrations of bars and night-people are Rue Enning; Le Tunnel, around Place du Tunnel; and, on a more sedate note, the streets immediately behind the château. The bars listed here all close at 1–2am, the clubs at 4–5am.

Bleu Lézard 10 Rue Enning ⓦwww.bleu-lezard .ch. Hip and exciting cellar venue, beneath a lively bar/restaurant (see above), staging DJ nights, live music, jam sessions, dance nights and more.

Café Freeport Train station. Quite a pleasant, if tackily neon, bar, with an intriguingly random clientele and the longest opening hours in town (Sun–Thurs 5am–1am, Fri & Sat 5am–2am).

Café de l'Hôtel de Ville 10 Place de la Palud. Wonderful little wood-floor café with *chansons* and jazz quartets in the cellar.

Captain Cook 2 Rue Enning. Crammed and smoky pub in the heart of the action, offering English TV football.

Au Château 1 Place du Tunnel. Funky music bar serving flavourful home-brewed beers – pale, dark and red – to an excited, talkative crowd.

D! Place Centrale ⓦwww.dclub.ch. Highly respected Flon basement club, close and sweaty, playing house some nights, jungle other nights, and able to pull in some international DJs. Entry Fri & Sat Fr.15. Closed Mon–Wed.

Kerrigan's 8 Rue de la Barre. Hilltop Irish pub in a peaceful spot behind the château. Closed Sun.
Lecaféthéâtre 10 Rue de Genève. Flon café-bar with live entertainments most nights. Closed Sun & Mon.
Le Loft 1 Escaliers Bel-Air ⓦ www.loftclub.ch. A techno club on the stairs up from the Flon, which has a rather tougher reputation than its near neighbours, but has free Friday night admission (Sat Fr.15). Occasional live acts. Closed Mon & Tues.

MAD (Moulin à Danse) 23 Rue de Genève. Infamous and hugely popular Flon dance club with adjoining theatre, galleries and alternative-style café. The club is open from 11pm, and comprises a basement "parlour", dancefloor, bar and chill-out room. Entry Fri & Sat Fr.20. Gay night Sun. Closed Mon & Tues.
Le 13ème Siècle Rue Cité-Devant. Atmospheric cellar DJ-bar in an Old Town street above the cathedral.

Classical music, opera, dance and film

The Théâtre de Beaulieu, 10 Avenue des Bergières (ⓦ www.beaulieu.org), is the main venue for full-scale **classical music** productions – the Orchestre de la Suisse Romande (ⓦ www.osr.ch) performs here regularly when not in Geneva – and is also famous as the place where the highly acclaimed **Béjart Ballet** (ⓦ www.bejart.ch) presents new material every June and November. The **Opéra de Lausanne** performs at Beaulieu too, as well as at its home at 12 Avenue du Théâtre (ⓦ www.opera-lausanne.ch), while the **Orchestre de Chambre de Lausanne** (ⓦ www.ocl.ch) stages concerts at the stunning Salle Métropole (ⓦ www.sallemetropole.ch), also the venue for many Béjart productions. The arts centre at Rue Sevelin 36 is the home of **contemporary dance**, with continuous seasons of productions year-round. Don't miss the cycle of free Friday evening concerts in the **cathedral** (June–Oct, plus Easter, Whitsun and Christmas; ⓦ www.grandesorgues.ch) – mostly, but not exclusively, organ recitals. Some 3km west of Lausanne in the ancient lakefront village of **St–Sulpice** (ⓦ www.st-sulpice.ch), a triple-apsed Romanesque church built by Cluniac monks in the eleventh century also stages classical concerts.

Plenty of **cinemas** show latest releases, often with afternoon shows in the original language (v.o., or *version originale*) and evening shows dubbed into French. The **Cinématheque Suisse**, in Montbenon park (ⓦ www.cinematheque .ch), has a programme of non-commercial movies from around the world, occasionally with English subtitles.

Listings

Boat rental Rowing boats and pedalos are available to rent from opposite the *Hôtel d'Angleterre* for around Fr.20/hr, motorboats for about Fr.45/hr.
Books Librairie Payot, 4 Place Pépinet.
Changing money In the station (daily 6.20am–7.30pm).
Gay and lesbian life VoGay, 10 Chemin des Epinettes (☎ 021 601 46 15, ⓦ www.vogay.ch), is the local gay association. *Le Saxo*, Rue de la Grotte 3 (ⓦ www.lesaxo.com), is a central bar-restaurant; *Tramway*, 6b Rue de la Pontaise (closed Sun & Mon), is a bit further out. There's an array of gay club nights; check the latest with VoGay or the tourist office.
Laundry At the top of town, 24 Rue de l'Université (Mon & Wed–Sun 9am–9pm, Tues noon–9pm);

and behind the station, 15 Rue Simplon (daily 8am–9pm).
Lost property The city office is at 7 Place Chauderon (Mon–Fri 8am–noon & 1.45–5.45pm, Sat 8–11.30am; ☎ 021 315 33 85), or try in the train station (Mon–Fri 8am–noon & 2–6pm; ☎ 051 224 27 07).
Markets The Place de la Palud hosts a regular lively food market (Wed & Sat 6am–2.30pm) as does the Petit-Chêne (Fri 6am–1pm). Palud also has a crafts market (March–Dec 1st Fri of month 6am–7pm), and Place Chauderon's weekly flea market is renowned (Thurs 6am–7pm). During December, Riponne hosts a Christmas market, with mulled wine stalls and roasting chestnuts.

Medical facilities The Centre hospitalier universi-
taire vaudois (CHUV) is at 46 Rue du Bugnon
☎ 021 314 11 11. The train station has a pharmacy
(daily 6am–9pm).

Post office Main office is beside the station
(Mon–Fri 7.30am–noon & 1.30–6.30pm, Sat
8am–noon), but the most convenient large office
is at Place St-François (Mon–Fri 7.30am–6.30pm,
Sat 8am–noon).

Sport Prime arena for Lausanne's passion, blading
and skateboarding, is the giant indoor La Fièvre
skatepark, also called HS36 (36 Avenue Sévelin;
Ⓦ www.fievre.ch), open daily – you'll also find
dance companies, artists' ateliers and music
rehearsal rooms in the same complex. For summer
swimming, the beach is free at Vidy.

North of Lausanne

Past the hills **northeast of Lausanne** you leave the tourist trails behind and enter the classic scenery of Switzerland's rural heartland – rolling emerald-green hills backed by distant peaks and tinkling with the neck-bells of happily munching cows. Vaud's cantonal boundary is only about 20km northeast of Lausanne, and most of the sights in this region fall inside Canton Fribourg; however, unless you have your own transport, Fribourg's famous cheese-making centre of **Gruyères** is most easily accessible by train from Lausanne. **Romont**'s Gothic church and thirteenth-century town centre make a beautiful detour on the journey to or from Fribourg itself (see p.258), while the untouristed **Gros de Vaud** region north of Lausanne is perfect for countryside cycling.

The northern stretches of Canton Vaud – Yverdon, Payerne and Avenches, as well as the Vallée de Joux – are covered in Chapter 3.

La Gruyère region

The walls and turrets of **Gruyères**'s fairy-tale castle, 50km northeast of Lausanne, bristle atop a single crag rising above the rolling lowlands of Canton Fribourg. The whole region – of which Gruyères village is the best-known attraction – is known as **LA GRUYÈRE** (Ⓦ www.la-gruyere.ch), taking in the long Lac de la Gruyère and the Sarine valley south of Fribourg, the market town and regional transport hub of **Bulle**, and a handful of resorts clinging to the slopes of the Prealpine peaks which prelude the Pays d'Enhaut (see p.309) further south. Dominating the landscape is the great towering wedge of the **Moléson**, a jutting chunk of mountain rising to 2000m with plenty of hiking possibilities and some gentle skiing in winter. This is dairy country, the most famous product being Gruyère cheese, run a close second by the local butterfat-rich double cream, served with forest fruits in Gruyères's heavenly, artery-clogging version of afternoon tea.

The chocolate factory at Broc

Some 30km northeast of Lausanne, **BULLE** isn't lacking in charm, but there's little reason to visit other than to switch transport. On the road to Gruyères, you'll pass through **La Tour de Trême**, its eponymous thirteenth-century tower plum in the middle of the village.

On the edge of the village of **BROC**, which lies 4km east of La Trême astride the route leading up through the tiny resort of Charmey to the Jaun Pass, you'll detect luscious scents emanating from the Cailler **chocolate factory** (May–Oct: Mon 1.30–4pm, Tues–Fri 9–11am & 1.30–4pm; Fr.4; reservations essential on ☎ 026 921 51 51, Ⓦ www.cailler.ch). This factory, founded in 1898, is the sole production facility for Nestlé's Cailler brand, named after one of

The Swiss Chocolate Train

One of the region's top excursions is a full-day package on the first-class **Swiss Chocolate Train**. Classic luxury Pullman carriages, built in 1915, and modern panoramic carriages run **from Montreux** (June–Oct Mon, Wed & Thurs) on the spectacular climb above Lake Geneva to **Gruyères**, where there's a stop to visit a cheese factory as well as two hours free in the village to visit the château and have lunch. In the afternoon, you move on to **Broc** for a visit to the Nestlé-Cailler **chocolate factory**, and then, around 4pm, settle back for the scenic return journey from Broc to Montreux. The full return fare is Fr.83, which includes your seat reservation, coffee and croissants on the morning train, bus transfers and all admission fees, but if you already hold a first-class pass or ticket, you only pay a reservation fee of around Fr.25. You must buy your own lunch in Gruyères (or carry a picnic). You can reserve at any station in Switzerland, or with the GoldenPass train company (℗0900 245 245, Ⓦwww.goldenpass.ch).

the nineteenth-century pioneers of chocolate-making. On arrival, you're led through to watch a super-schmaltzy costume-drama movie about life, love and chocolate in a small Swiss town, after which a guide leads you on an explanatory tour of part of the factory. The climax comes in the Tasting Room, where you're let loose on tables piled with bite-sized chunks of every Cailler product, in unlimited quantities; placards outline how a professional chocolate taster measures quality, but most people are far too busy scoffing to notice. Just beyond lies a shop where you can buy discounted Nestlé chocolate.

The factory, signposted on all approach roads, is a short walk from Broc-Fabrique **train station**, which is served by local scheduled trains from Bulle and La Tour and also by the **Swiss Chocolate Train**, a packaged excursion from Montreux (see box).

Gruyères

A perfectly preserved old castle-village, isolated on its crag but within easy reach of Lake Geneva, **GRUYÈRES** is one of Switzerland's most photogenic sights and attracts hordes of day-trippers throughout the summer season, come to stroll on the village's only street and explore the impressive château. By 10am in season, the village can get uncomfortably crowded and can stay so until late afternoon. Cars are banned, but you'll find several large parking areas on the hillside just below.

At the foot of Gruyères village in **Pringy** (the location of Gruyères train station) is the **Maison du Gruyère**, a working dairy (daily 9am–7pm; Oct–May closes 6pm; Fr.5; Ⓦwww.lamaisondugruyere.ch) where you can watch the cheesemaking process close up (production runs 9–11am & 12.30–2.30pm). There's also a restaurant and shop, both concentrating on local produce.

Up on the hill, the **Château de Gruyères** (daily: April–Oct 9am–6pm; Nov–March 10am–4.30pm; Fr.6.50; joint ticket with Giger Museum Fr.14; SMP; Ⓦwww.chateau-gruyeres.ch) was occupied from 1080 to 1554 by the nineteen counts of Gruyères, but was decimated by a fire in 1493 which destroyed virtually everything but the dungeons. Michel, the last count, ran up huge debts reconstructing the living quarters in Savoyard style and then fled, leaving his creditors – the governments of Fribourg and Bern – to divide up his lands between them. A rich Geneva dynasty, the Bovy and Balland families, bought the castle in 1848 and supported a number of artists in residence, including the French landscape painter Corot, before the cantonal government of Fribourg assumed control in 1938. To approach, you must walk the length of Gruyères's dipping, picturesque main street with its central fountain and quaint old houses on either side bedecked with hanging signs. A huge **gate** affords entry to the castle grounds. Highlights include Flemish **tapestries** decorating the count's bedchamber, Corot's room with landscapes painted by him, and other rooms with grand fireplaces, heraldic stained glass, often featuring the dynastic symbol of a crane (*grue* in French), and booty from the Battle of Murten (see p.187) where Louis II of Gruyère fought. The wood-panelled Knights' Hall is impressive, as is the small formal garden at the very back, on the tip of the hill. Beside the castle, Gruyères's **church** is in an exceptionally beautiful location, backed by valley vistas.

In a couple of odd counterpoints to the grandeur of the castle, you'll find at the gate of the castle (and covered by the same entrance fee and opening hours), the **Centre International de l'Art Fantastique**, a small gallery devoted to modern fantasy art – which is fine if you like that kind of thing but has no connection with the cobbled quaintness all around. This, though, is as nothing compared with the truly nasty **H.R. Giger Museum** adjacent (April–Oct daily 10am–6pm; Nov–March Tues–Fri 11am–5pm, Sat & Sun 10am–6pm; Fr.11; joint ticket with château Fr.14; SMP; Ⓦwww.hrgiger.com). Giger is a Swiss graphic artist, most famous for designing the special effects for the movie *Alien* – for which he won an Oscar – as well as *Poltergeist II*, *Alien 3* and others. He has turned one of Gruyères's old houses into a dark and unpleasant showcase for his unique brand of grotesque art – sexualized surrealist visions of machine-like humanoids, nightmarish cityscapes and fantasy porn. "Giger," enthused Timothy Leary, 1960s acid guru, "you give us courage to say hello to our insectoid selves." The latest innovation is an *Alien*-style bar alongside.

Practicalities

Trains from Lausanne to Fribourg pass through **Palézieux**, where you must change for the local GFM trains that trundle through the countryside to **Bulle**, and then on to **Gruyères-gare** at the foot of the village; it's a short but stiff walk from the station up the hill to Gruyères, or you could time your arrival to coincide with one of the half-dozen buses a day shuttling between Gruyères-gare and Gruyères-ville. The Palézieux–Gruyères trains terminate at **Montbovon**, on the MOB line between Montreux and Gstaad. If you're approaching from Fribourg, take an express bus to Bulle and switch onto a train there. Occasional buses go direct to Gruyères-ville from Bulle station.

Everything in Gruyères is on the village's single street. The **tourist office** is at the car park end (May–Oct daily 9am–noon & 1.30–5.45pm; rest of year Mon–Fri 10am–noon & 1.30–5pm; ☎026 921 10 30, Ⓦwww.gruyeres.ch). There are only a few **hotels**, most of which take one or two days a week off in the winter. Whichever side of the street you're on, getting a room at the back gives you a view over the valley. The pinewood *Fleur de Lys* (☎026 921 82 82, Ⓦwww.hotelfleurdelys.ch; ❸) is a sound choice; the grand *Hôtel de Ville* (☎026 921 24 24, Ⓦwww.hoteldeville.ch; ❸–❹) takes a step up in comfort and cuisine; and nicest of the lot is the *Hostellerie des Chevaliers* (☎026 921 19 33, Ⓦwww .gruyeres-hotels.ch/chevaliers; ❸–❹), just outside the village.

Finding a place to **eat** isn't difficult: everywhere offers terraces on both the village side and the valley side at which to nosh cheesy delights or bowls of berries slathered in silky *crème-double*. The *Auberge de la Halle* is one of the least pretentious places to get a proper meal, with Fr.17 *menus*. All the hotels offer quality traditional Gruyères and French cuisine, with the *Hostellerie St-Georges* (☎026 921 83 00) top choice within the village.

Moléson

Ten minutes on the bus past Gruyères-gare is **MOLÉSON** village (Ⓦwww
.moleson.ch), a small resort giving access to the heights of **Le Moléson** mountain (2002m), via a funicular and gondola; panoramic views from the summit
take in Lake Geneva, the Prealps and even Mont Blanc. There are plenty of
ridge-top walks and, in winter, easy-to-medium ski runs.

Romont and the Gros de Vaud

Train tracks and minor roads between Lausanne and Fribourg pass by
ROMONT, a medieval town perched atop an isolated round hill, with lofty
360-degree views. From the train station, it's a steep ten-minute walk up to the
thirteenth-century ramparts. Romont consists of little more than two broad
streets with a distinctive round tower at each end. The **castle** dominates, with
one tower converted into the **Musée du Vitrail** (Stained Glass; April–Oct
Tues–Sun 10am–1pm & 2–6pm; Nov–March Thurs–Sun 10am–1pm & 2–5pm;
Fr.7; SMP), holding mostly modern examples. Nearby is the beautiful Gothic
collegiate **church**, replete with original woodcarving from a rebuilding in
1434. The **tourist office** is at 112 Rue du Château (Mon–Fri 10am–noon &
2–4pm, April–Oct also Sat 10am–noon; Ⓣ026 652 31 52, Ⓦwww.romont.ch).

To the west, the peaceful country between Lausanne and Yverdon is known
as the **Gros de Vaud** (Ⓦwww.gros-de-vaud.ch), rural heart of the canton and
Switzerland's breadbasket. **ECHALLENS** (Ⓦwww.echallens.ch), 15km north
of Lausanne, is the main centre, formerly an important market town but now
metamorphosed into a popular retreat for young families. Despite its sometimes
twee touches, it's still a picturesque place, with a thirteenth-century château and
many eighteenth-century buildings. The LEB narrow-gauge **railway** (Ⓦwww
.leb.ch) – Switzerland's oldest, opened in 1873 – runs here from Lausanne; in
summer especially, this is a lovely, scenic ride.

Lake Geneva

The croissant-shaped **LAKE GENEVA** (Lac Léman in French), bluest of the
Swiss lakes, is ringed with villages, castles and gorgeous walks that demand
attention. This is wine country, with vineyards spread around the full sweep

---

Facts and figures

Lake Geneva is the largest freshwater lake in Western Europe, holding some 89
trillion litres. It's really just a big bulge in the course of the River Rhône, which rises at
the Furkapass and flows westwards between the mountains of Canton Valais to enter
the lake near Villeneuve. Its water takes an estimated seventeen years to cover the
73km to Geneva before flowing on through France to an outlet into the Mediterranean
near Marseille. Although the lake is only 14km wide at its broadest point, it plunges
to 310m maximum depth and is subject to heavy winds which rip across the surface,
causing stormy conditions not unlike an inland sea.

of the lakeshore and carpeting the first slopes of the hills which rise behind. Genteel small towns such as **Nyon** and **Vevey**, either side of Lausanne, have made a living recharging the batteries of frazzled urbanites for generations. Over the decades, the lake has also attracted the world's wealthiest people, and the shores around the jet-set playground of **Montreux** in particular are lined with opulent villas – although a lakeside stroll can still let you taste the unspoilt beauty which drew Byron and the Romantic poets in a former age. Relaxing on one of the boats which crisscross the lake beneath the looming presence of the Savoy Alps and the Dents-du-Midi mountains on the French side helps bring home the full grandeur of the setting.

The Lake Geneva hall of fame

Hundreds of notable writers, artists, musicians and poets have visited Lake Geneva over the centuries. For cultured nineteenth-century sophisticates, the lakeside was as important a stop on the Grand Tour of Europe as Paris, Florence or Vienna, and where one artist settled others inevitably followed, drawn – depending on individual circumstance – by the fresh air, the romance of the Château de Chillon, political neutrality, or the numbered bank accounts.

Edward Gibbon spent long periods in Lausanne, meeting **Voltaire** there in the 1750s, and completing his monumental *Decline and Fall of the Roman Empire* during an eleven-year stay between 1783 and 1793. Jean-Jacques **Rousseau**, a native of Geneva, set his *La Nouvelle Héloïse*, completed in 1761, in Clarens near Montreux. **Wordsworth** came through Lausanne in 1790 and 1820. The English artist **Turner** first visited the area in 1802, painting watercolours of the landscape around Chillon. In 1816, while **Mary Shelley** stayed in Geneva to write *Frankenstein*, **Lord Byron** and **Percy Bysshe Shelley** set off on an eight-day boat tour of the lake; they both almost drowned off St-Gingolph, then toured the Château de Chillon, which inspired Byron to dash off *The Prisoner of Chillon* in his Ouchy hotel room. **Robert Southey** waxed lyrical about Lausanne following a visit in 1817, as did **Victor Hugo** in 1839. The famous English actor **John Kemble** died and was buried in Lausanne in 1823. **Alexandre Dumas**, on one of his many Swiss journeys, wrote of a visit to Chillon in 1832. **Tennyson**, **Thackeray** and others dropped in to visit **Charles Dickens**, who began *Dombey and Son* while staying in Lausanne in 1846; Thackeray himself worked on *The Newcomes* in Vevey in 1853. **George Eliot** spent nine months writing in Geneva over the winter of 1849–50. In 1861, **Hans Christian Andersen** wrote *The Ice Maiden* in Montreux. **Tolstoy** and **Dostoevsky** both passed through Lausanne, the latter spending two years in Geneva writing *The Idiot*, followed by a summer writing *The Gambler* in Vevey; **Gogol** began *Dead Souls* in Vevey, which was the setting for **Henry James**'s *Daisy Miller* and which was also where **Arnold Bennett** spent 1908–09 writing *The Card*. **Tchaikovsky** composed his Violin Concerto in F major (Op.35), and also began *Eugène Onegin* while in Clarens in 1877–78. **Stravinsky** spent 1911–14 in the same town, where he composed his revolutionary *The Rite of Spring*; he spent the World War I years working in Lausanne. **T.S. Eliot** convalesced in Lausanne in 1921 and 1922 while writing his equally revolutionary *The Waste Land*. In 1952, at the age of 63, **Charlie Chaplin** moved to Vevey to escape Hollywood's McCarthyism, and died there 25 years later. **Noël Coward** lived in Les Avants, above Montreux, from 1958, while **Audrey Hepburn** lived in Tolochenaz, near Morges, from 1963. **Vladimir Nabokov** spent the last sixteen years of his life in Montreux (after 1961); and **Graham Greene** died in Vevey in 1991. Of the dozens of pop musicians who've dabbled with second, third or fourth houses on the lake, **Freddie Mercury** had a particularly soft spot for Montreux, and returned many times during the last ten years of his life.

La Côte

The gently curving northwestern shore of the lake from Geneva to Lausanne (some 65km) is known as **La Côte** (ⓦwww.lacote.ch), characterized by a succession of hamlets and small villages, almost without exception pretty, well kept and pristinely picturesque. Those along the minor shoreline road, the *Route Suisse*, are less numerous and more visited than those placed back behind the main *autoroute* on the first slopes of the Jura foothills, amongst vineyards tilted towards the sun which produce some of the highest-prized **wine** in Vaud.

Things are much less developed here for **wine-tasting tours** than in the Lavaux region east of Lausanne (see p.147). However, if you rent a bike from larger train stations for a day's gentle exploration along the narrow **Route des Vignerons**, which winds from vineyard to vineyard along the slope, you'll find plenty of *caveaux* (wine cellars) offering *dégustations* (tastings) of local products. You have to pay for the tasting – which generally comprises a few choices of wine, in 1dl glasses – but can then turn up a bargain if you choose to buy a bottle. Countless *auberges* and *pintes* (country taverns) along the way offer local home-cooked specialities.

You'll also pass dozens of **châteaux**, evidence both of the region's key strategic significance in medieval times, and its attraction to Europe's nobility in more recent centuries. Some are now museums, but most remain in private hands. Major stopoffs include the historic **Château de Coppet**, close to Geneva, the attractive little harbour-town of **Nyon** with its own château and Roman museum, and the nearby **Château de Prangins**, housing an excellent museum devoted to Swiss history.

Coppet and Céligny

From the landing-stage at **COPPET**, 2km inside Vaud, it's easy to make out Geneva's Jet d'Eau fountain, only 12km away. The bulge of low hills opposite is French territory, culminating in the wooded headland of Yvoire. Coppet sits astride the lakeshore *Route Suisse* and has an attractive arcaded main street, but is unremarkable but for the lavish **Château de Coppet** (ⓦwww.swisscastles.ch). Entry is only on the multilingual **guided tours** (Easter–Oct daily 2–6pm; July & Aug also 10am–noon; Fr.8) given by the knowledgeable staff: these run every half-hour or so, according to demand.

The house was built by **Jacques Necker**, Minister of Finance to the French king Louis XVI from 1776 until the Revolution in 1789. Necker seems to have been rather disgusted by the excesses of the regime he was publicly responsible for, and built up a dossier documenting the extent of financial corruption which, it's said, helped to initiate the Revolution.

During the 1780s, his daughter **Germaine** gained a reputation in the Paris *salons* for her intellect and vivacity. Necker retired to Coppet in 1790, from when Germaine's (now **Madame de Staël**'s) literary and philosophical *salon* began to attract the leading intellects of the day, gaining the nickname "the Parliament of European Opinion". The Swiss author Benjamin Constant was a regular visitor, as were the philosopher Schlegel, Chateaubriand, Lord Byron and others. Life at the château was organized around the constant flow of guests: lunch, it is said, was served at 5pm, dinner at 11pm, with musical *soirées* and playlets in the library in between, and debates and discussions afterwards which continued late into the night.

Madame de Staël died a celebrated writer and commentator in 1817, at the age of 51, and the château is still in her family to this day. The renowned portraitist Ingres painted de Staël's granddaughter Louise de Broglie, Countess of Haussonville, and proceeds from the recent sale of this masterpiece to a gallery in New York enabled the current Count to retain ownership of the château. The Haussonvilles stay in Coppet for a couple of weeks each summer, and maintain the house in its original style; part is now given over to a research centre attached to the University of Geneva.

The approach to the château – grand, but no Versailles – is beneath a vaulted arch into a peaceful interior courtyard, open on one side to the gardens behind a wrought-iron gate surmounted with the elaborate initials "N.C.", demonstrating the partnership between Jacques Necker and his wife Suzanne Curchod. Nine rooms are open to the public, including the library, formerly the main reception room, filled with Empire and Directoire furniture; Madame de Staël's bedroom, with her Louis XVI bed draped in Lyon silk; Juliette Récamier's bedroom next door, hung with exquisite eighteenth-century Chinese wallpaper; and, upstairs, a drawing room and a gallery of family portraits.

Coppet also boasts the splendid **hotel** *Du Lac*, 51 Grand'Rue (☎022 776 15 21, ⓦ www.hoteldulac.ch; ❺–❻). This wood-beamed inn was classified as a *grand logis* in 1628: after ducking in off the busy road, you trail through grand dining rooms and antique-laden drawing rooms until you reach the shady, perfectly calm lakeside terrace at the back. It's a fine, atmospheric retreat.

Céligny

Tucked in a tiny enclave of Canton Geneva, surrounded by Vaud, gentle **CÉLIGNY** is about as endearing a rural gem as you could hope to find, enjoying waterside lawns, vineyards all around and, through the village, an atmospheric church and château (not open to the public). The air of undisturbed tranquillity hanging over the fountained village square proved particularly balming for the actor Richard Burton, who spent the last few years of his life here. If you walk up into the village from the train station, across the square and then head left, cutting around a parking area, you'll find the Vieux Cimitière, a mossy grove by a stream (the other bank is Vaudois territory) that is Burton's final resting place.

Nyon

NYON – a major town under the Romans which has mellowed into a laconic and attractive little port, 9km north of Coppet – is a perfect stopover on a leisurely tour of the area. The town, on a flattish plain sandwiched between the Jura and the lake, is spread out among fields and lawns which reach down to the water, and is backed by acres of vineyards on the slopes behind. There's a château and an excellent Roman museum, and the nearby **Château de Prangins** houses the regional branch of the National Museum. And if museums aren't your thing, there's the option of riding a mountain railway up to the little Jura resort of **St-Cergue**.

After Julius Caesar conquered Gallia Comata (Long-Haired Gaul) in 52 BC, he retired his cavalry veterans to the **Colonia Julia Equestris**, built over the old Helvetian settlement of Noviodunum. For two centuries, the colony flourished, becoming a town of 3000 people (the population didn't reach such heights again until the mid-nineteenth century). The third century saw attacks from Alemans and Franks, and by the mid-fifth century the colony was virtually deserted. Only its Roman name survived, the Latin word "Colonia" compressed into the single nasal syllable "Nyon". The region became part of **Burgundy** after 443, then was passed from lord to lord until the Bernese conquered Vaud in

Paleo Rock Festival

Nyon's biggest party is also one of Europe's biggest – the giant **Paleo Rock Festival** (ⓦwww.paleo.ch), which takes place over a week in late July in a field outside town, with a consistently excellent line-up of musicians attracting hundreds of thousands of revellers. Acts in past years have been as diverse as Franz Ferdinand and Ruben Gonzalez, the Fun Lovin' Criminals and Jamie Cullum, George Clinton and Blur. If you buy early, you can snap up a day ticket for as little as Fr.40, or a full six-day pass for around Fr.200; transport between Nyon and the festival site is free. The tourist office has festival-plus-hotel packages, which rise in price the later you book.

1536. In 1781 a French entrepreneur Jacques Dortu opened a **porcelain** workshop in the town, staffed by local artisans who produced work of exceptionally high quality, rapidly establishing Nyon as a centre of the craft: museums around Europe now display Nyon porcelain alongside the best of Limoges china as some of the highest-prized ceramic art of the period. These days, Nyon's claim to fame is as the location of football cup draws: the European governing body **UEFA** is headquartered in the town.

The Town

Heading southeast from the train station towards the lake will bring you in a couple of minutes into the compact Old Town, centred on **Place du Château**, a charming, shaded square with terrace cafés that is backed by the **château** itself, a twelfth-century turreted fortress looking out over the lake. The town's **Musée Historique**, its displays of silver, fine art, photographs and a comprehensive collection of Nyon porcelain closed at the time of writing, reopened in mid-2006. Opposite, at 4 Place du Château, is the headquarters of Focale (ⓦwww.focale.ch), a leading association of Swiss photographers; their cramped **bookshop** is excellent, as is the gallery downstairs. Rue du Vieux Marché leading west off the square brings you past a statue of Julius Caesar to the impressive **Musée Romain** on Rue Maupertuis (Tues–Sun 10am–noon & 2–6pm; July & Aug also Mon; Nov–March closed mornings; joint ticket with Musée du Leman Fr.6; SMP; ⓦwww.mrn.ch). The museum is housed in a Roman basilica, originally part of Nyon's forum; a trompe l'oeil fresco of the basilica's interior on the wall outside, as well as a model in the museum, give an idea of the size of Nyon's public buildings in its Roman heyday. The museum's extensive collection is well laid out; you pass first into the central area (the nave of the basilica) which houses inscriptions, statues and architectural details, and from there move around the walls of the room through zones devoted to daily life, crafts and religion.

The street ends at the small **Église Notre–Dame**, dating from 1110 and of unusual asymmetrical design, endowed with new stained glass. The arched Porte Ste-Marie round the corner gives onto the **Esplanade des Marronniers** (Chestnut Trees), exposed to fresh lake breezes and dominated by two and a half Roman columns, sited impressively against the blue. Walking along the city walls east and down some steps to the lakefront delivers you to the little **Musée du Léman**, 8 Quai Louis-Bonnard (Tues–Sun: April–Oct 10am–5pm, Sept–March 2–5pm; same ticket as Musée Romain; SMP; ⓦwww.museeduleman .ch). The ground floor has informative displays on the lake's fauna, with large aquariums, while upstairs are paintings, models of ships and disquisitions (in French) on how to protect the lake. From the **Place de Savoie**, 150m east, atmospheric Rue de Rive heads slightly uphill, lined with antique shops and odd cartoonish murals. At the end, Rue de la Colombière continues uphill, and where it meets Rue de la Porcelaine you should spot Nyon's **Roman amphitheatre** half hidden in the grass, virtually the same size as the one at Avenches (see p.186) but much more ruined and unfortunately now hemmed in by modern housing.

Practicalities

Plenty of **trains** serve Nyon, although note that not all those heading east go to Lausanne: some branch off at Morges on their way to Yverdon. Regular **boats** arrive from Geneva and Lausanne. The **tourist office** is one minute's walk from the station, at 8 Avenue Viollier (Mon–Fri: mid-May to mid-Sept 8.30am–noon & 2–5.30pm, closed Wed pm; rest of year 8.30am–12.30pm & 1.30–5.30pm; ☎022 365 66 00, ⓦwww.nyon.ch), with a summer office by the landing-stage (mid-May to mid-Sept daily 9.30am–4pm, July & Aug until 6pm). A **guided walk** starts from the landing-stage (May–Sept Wed 2.30pm & Sat 11am; 1hr 30min; Fr.10).

Nyon's top **hotel** is the *Beau-Rivage*, 49 Rue de Rive (☎022 365 41 41, ⓦwww.hotel-beau-rivage-nyon.ch; ❺–❼), a grandiose pile that's been in business since 1481 and boasts large, traditionally furnished rooms, most looking lakewards. The charming *Hostellerie du XVIe Siècle*, 2 Place du Marché (☎022 994 88 00, ⓦwww.16eme.com; ❷–❸), occupies an arcaded building in the cobbled Old Town; some rooms are ensuite, others not. Rue de Rive has any number of places to **eat** fresh fish, but the fillet of perch (Fr.30) served at *Du Cheval Blanc* at no. 62 must rank with the best. More affordable pizzas and pasta *menus* (Fr.17–19) can be munched at *Le Léman*, 28 Rue de Rive.

Château de Prangins

A kilometre or two east of Nyon is the village of **PRANGINS**, in the midst of which, set in its own formal English gardens, is the **Château de Prangins** (Tues–Sun 11am–5pm; Fr.7; SMP; ⓦwww.musee-suisse.com), built in the 1730s in the French style and now an arm of the Swiss National Museum devoted to the history of Switzerland in the eighteenth and nineteenth centuries. It's a huge place holding an imaginative collection that's well worth a couple of hours; all the rooms are numbered sequentially, but the layout can be very confusing and you may find yourself backtracking more than once.

Above Nyon – St-Cergue

Rising above Nyon are the final stretches of the Jura range within Switzerland, known as the **Pied du Jura**, sliced across by the international border separating the French Pays de Gex from the Swiss mountain resort of **ST-CERGUE**. This unassuming town is set in some wild countryside, with hiking trails that see few ramblers; the tourist office on Place Sy-Vieuxville (closed Mon; ☎022 360 13 14, ⓦwww.st-cergue.ch) has details. In winter, St-Cergue concentrates on providing easy downhill **skiing** for families, and plenty of excellent cross-country routes. The *desalpe*, or annual descent of cattle from the high pastures to winter quarters in the valley, accompanied by much floral decoration and folkloric celebrations, is a highlight of St-Cergue's calendar, taking place on a Saturday in late September. Riding on the little red narrow-gauge NStCM **trains** (InterRail not valid) which depart from the forecourt of Nyon station on a winding route up into the hills is worth an afternoon in itself, whether you get off at St-Cergue or continue over the **Col de la Givrine** (1228m) to the hamlet of **La Cure** on the border.

Exhibits on the ground floor, outlining the ideals of aristocrats and the bourgeoisie around 1800, and in the cellars, detailing Switzerland's pre-industrial rural economy, are less engaging than those on the two upper floors, which are devoted to Swiss cultural history from 1750 into the twentieth century. Each room ("From Birth to Death", "The Display of Power", "Travellers and Tourists") has good English notes, with items from everyday life displayed next to historically significant objects. Numerous multimedia stations enhance wanderings by letting you play period music while you're examining the cases. Reconstructed interiors, such as that of a late nineteenth-century schoolroom, display uncanny attention to detail. Outside, an extensive kitchen garden has been planted with fruit and vegetables according to eighteenth-century accounts of horticulture.

Bus #5 runs hourly from Nyon's train station on a circular route through Prangins, stopping either at the village post office three minutes from the château (Mon–Sat) or at the château itself (Sun).

Luins and Vinzel

Some 10km northeast of Nyon on the **Route des Vignerons** are the neighbouring wine villages of **LUINS** and **VINZEL**, both famous for their *malakoffs*. These little gastronomic curiosities – a rich, fried cheese-and-egg mixture served hot on a round bread base – are a local speciality, renamed to celebrate the triumphant return of a band of Vaudois mercenaries under the Russian general Malakoff from the 1855 siege of Sebastopol. The two villages, which are ten minutes' walk apart, have competed since then for whose *malakoff* is better. Take the taste test at the *Auberge Communale* in Luins (☎021 824 11 59), then wander down the road past the vineyards to *Au Coeur de la Côte* in Vinzel (☎021 824 11 41) – both are open daily, serving *malakoffs* for around Fr.6 each; while you're at it, take the chance to compare and contrast the excellent village wines. A good hike reaches above Luins to a tiny church-with-a-view, dating from 1393, and on up past the vineyards into woods of beech, oak and chestnut, eventually emerging into open pasture on the plateau above.

Rolle and Morges

ROLLE lies at the heart of the La Côte wine country, roughly midway between Nyon and Lausanne. Its lakeside château dates from 1270 but is not open to the public. Just offshore is the tiny **Île de la Harpe**, built up in 1835 from earth dumped during construction of the town's harbour. These works

---

A shaggy dog story

The château of **St-Saphorin-sur-Morges** (not to be confused with St-Saphorin near Vevey) has long been the ancestral home of the de Mestral family. **Georges de Mestral** (1907–90), an engineer, was on a shooting trip one day in 1948 in the Jura foothills when, as usual, he found himself spending ages extracting burrs that had got caught in his dog's soft furry ears. The legend goes that it was here, on his knees in the forest, that de Mestral had the idea to copy nature and invent a fabric using sharp little burr-like hooks to stick to soft furry material. Thus, he thought, could rackety, unreliable zips be consigned to history. He patented his idea and started production in nearby Aubonne; although zips have survived, de Mestral's **Velcro** – a conflation of the words "velour" (velvet) and "crochet" (hook) – is now a household name, manufactured under licence around the world. Regrettably, though, St-Saphorin-sur-Morges has forgotten its most famous son.

tragically destroyed remnants of prehistoric offshore stilt dwellings – where-upon, shortly afterwards, the railway arrived, instantly rendering the harbour uneconomical and leaving Rolle doubly bereft. The island, named after a local statesman, is now the focus for Rolle's yachties. Some 5km east stands the **Château d'Allaman** – built in the twelfth century, torched in 1530, rebuilt in 1723 and sold off in 2005 to be split up into luxury apartments; time will tell whether the wine-tastings and sales formerly held in the splendid cellars will continue.

The lakeside road winds on to Lausanne through **MORGES**, another peaceful little harbour town famed for its kilometre-long Quais du Dahlia and the Fête de la Tulipe in April and May. Its château holds a military museum. Formerly, the main reason to come was to visit the outlying village of **Tolochenaz**, home to the actress Audrey Hepburn from 1963 until her death in 1993: the commune and local volunteers had set up an excellent little museum – complete with Oscars and the black dress worn in *Breakfast at Tiffany's* – that channelled funds to the Audrey Hepburn Foundation for Children, supporting UNICEF. However, in 2002, Hepburn's two sons effectively closed the museum by taking back all the exhibits, claiming over-commercialization of their mother's memory. Bar Hepburn's grave in the village cemetery, nothing remains.

The Lavaux wine villages

The compact stretch of Lake Geneva shore east from Lausanne to Vevey – known as the **Lavaux** (Ⓦ www.lavaux.com) – is one of the most alluring of all Swiss regions, its floral waterside promenades flanked on one side by wide expanses of vines and on the other by vistas across to the Savoy Alps rising behind the Dents-du-Midi on the far shore. Trains heading to Montreux and beyond hug the shoreline, seeming to whisk you along inches above the glittering lake. Some of the country's best **wines** come from the dozens of vineyards clustered cheek by jowl along the steep Lavaux slopes: this is perfect country for gentle walks and bike rides punctuated by samplings of the local nectar. Cafés and *pintes* abound, set in the cobbled streets of picturesque villages.

Tourist offices have information to guide you through the Lavaux's **wine villages**, a line of hamlets strung along the slopes between Lausanne and Vevey devoted to the art of viticulture. Between May and October, most reliably on weekends (Thurs–Sun), you'll find *caveaux* (cellars) and *carnotzets* (cellars with rough benches and tables for extended wine- and food-sampling sessions) open in every village, some of them belonging to that commune's *vignerons* association, others attached to private châteaux or independent *vignobles*. The Lavaux website and Vevey tourist office have full details.

Cully

The shuttered village of **CULLY** (pronounced "kwee"), 8km east of Lausanne, is full of *caveaux* and *carnotzets* offering the forest-fruity wines of nearby Epesses, Calamin, Riex, Villette and Lutry. The village also boasts the *Auberge du Raisin*, 1 Place de l'Hôtel de Ville (℡ 021 799 21 31, Ⓦ www.relaischateaux.ch/raisin; ❼), the old thirteenth-century town hall, which has been converted into a uniquely characterful hotel, filled with period furniture, original Old Masters and individually decorated rooms which vary greatly in price. Its restaurant is outstanding, acclaimed by Michelin, Gault & Millau and others, but not cheap

(*menus* from Fr.50). The last Friday in November is Cully's **Nuit du vin cuit**,
a masked musical parade accompanied by quaffing of mulled must (new unfer-
mented wine).

St-Saphorin and east to Vevey

About 3km east of Cully are the vineyards of **Dézaley**, producing some of
the highest-rated *grand cru* wines in Switzerland. From the landing-stage at
nearby **Rivaz**, it's just 1km east to **ST-SAPHORIN** – about as romantic and
photogenic a waterside hamlet as you could ever hope for, piled up on steep
slopes above the lake, with an old church, skinny cobbled alleys that crook their
way up between crumbling old cottages, and superb flinty, smoke-perfumed
wines best sampled at the village's central ✚ *Auberge de l'Onde* (☎021 925 49
00, ⓦwww.aubergedelonde.ch; closed Tues, Wed lunch). This atmospheric old
inn, once a halt for stagecoaches plying between Geneva and Italy, is simply
bewitching: you could easily find its languorous combination of wood-beamed
quaintness, day-fresh perch sautéed delectably in herb-butter and a heady carafe
or three of the village wine charming you into abandoning whatever plans you
had for the rest of the day.

If your legs haven't already turned to spaghetti, you could try strolling 2km up
the hill from St-Saphorin to picturesque **Chexbres**, which clings to a terrace
with great views and a choice of hotels and restaurants, and then 4km further
east to **Chardonne** on the slopes of towering Mont Pèlerin, home of the excellent **Cure d'Attalens** wine. An amble under the funicular tracks and through
uninspiring **Jongny** brings you down to Corsier, on the western edges of Vevey.

Vevey

At the little town of Vevey, there is a particularly comfortable hotel... The entertainment of tourists is the business of the place, which, as many travellers will remember, is seated upon the edge of a remarkably blue lake – a lake that it behoves
every tourist to visit.

Henry James, from *Daisy Miller* (1878)

Whereas brassy Montreux, a few kilometres down the road, has over the years
freely embraced all that glisters – gold, paper or otherwise – its old-fashioned

neighbour **VEVEY** is more discriminating. Vevey quietly cleans its streets, tends its flowerbeds, makes sure it has enough, but not too many, hotels and then waits for visitors of a certain style to find the town for themselves, become enchanted, and stay. It's a hard place to quantify, neither prim, nor stuffy, nor sophisticated, nor especially graceful... yet it somehow manages to incorporate strands of all of them in an ambience of tasteful, restrained gentility. It *is* enchanting, a world apart (or a remnant of a world now past), and you may well find yourself lulled into staying.

Henry James set his *Daisy Miller* – the story of a headstrong young woman on the Grand Tour who broke the rules of propriety by visiting the Château de Chillon unchaperoned, and so got her comeuppance – in Vevey, specifically at the *Hôtel des Trois Couronnes*, which is much the same now as it seems it must have been in James's day. In a similar

△ Back street, Vevey

vein, **Anita Brookner** set her Booker Prize-winning novel *Hotel du Lac* in a taciturn but anonymous lakeside town opposite the Dent d'Oche (the huge 2222m mountain on the French shore facing Vevey). Generations of tourists return to Vevey to stroll the flowered promenades, muse on the Dent d'Oche, venture across the water on the Belle-Epoque ships of the Lake Geneva fleet, and take high tea in grand hotels. Yet there's plenty more to do than this suggests: the shops, museums and local life are far more engaging than in Montreux, and if big cities such as Lausanne or Geneva don't appeal, you could easily use smalltown Vevey as a comfortable base from which to explore the whole lake region.

Arrival, information and accommodation

Vevey's **train station** is 300m north of the lakeshore on a busy east–west main road: cross over and head towards the lake on the Rue de Lausanne, and within a minute or two you'll come to the huge central square of Grande-Place, also

Vevey–Montreux transport

If you're shuttling between Vevey and Montreux, it's worth abandoning the trains in favour of the much more useful electric **city bus #1** (Ⓦ www.vmcv.ch). This runs on a straight lakeside route from Vevey's funicular station (west of the centre), past Vevey train station, through La Tour-de-Peilz and Clarens into Montreux town centre, on through Territet (stopping outside the Château de Chillon), and terminating in Ville-neuve. Buses run every ten minutes, and journey time between Vevey and Montreux is twenty minutes. Vevey and La Tour are in Zone 1; Montreux is in Zone 2; Chillon and Villeneuve are in Zone 3. A journey across two zones is Fr.3, across three is Fr.3.70, and a pass valid for 24 hours is Fr.7. All Swiss passes are valid for free travel. Ticket machines in buses dispense one-way fares only.

known as Place du Marché, which fronts directly onto the lake. The Old Town alleys are clustered to the east. The town has three **ferry stops**: Vevey-Plan is to the west, behind the Nestlé building; Vevey-Marché is metres from Place du Marché in the town centre; and Vevey-La Tour is east, close to La Tour-de-Peilz.

The **tourist offices** of Vevey and Montreux have joined forces: you can get exactly the same information from both. Vevey's office is in the pillared Grenette building on Grande-Place (mid-May to mid-Sept Mon–Fri 9am–6pm, Sat 8.30am–noon; rest of year Mon–Fri 8.30am–noon & 1–5.30pm, Sat 9am–noon; ☎0848 868 484, ⓦwww.montreux-vevey.com). Vevey's most colourful annual event is August's **Street Artists' Festival** (ⓦww.artistesderue.ch), when the town is taken over by jugglers, acrobats, mime artists, puppeteers and more.

Accommodation

Vevey has a limited, but high-quality, range of accommodation options. ☆ *Riviera Lodge SB hostel*, 5 Place du Marché (☎021 923 80 40, ⓦwww.rivieralodge.ch; ❶), has excellent dorms in the centre of town for Fr.32, while you can **camp** on the lakeside 2km west at *La Pichette* (☎021 921 09 97).

Of the **hotels**, ☆ *Les Négociants*, 27 Rue du Conseil (☎021 922 70 11, ⓦwww.hotelnegociants.ch; ❸), and *Hostellerie de Genève*, 11 Place du Marché

(☎021 921 45 77, ⓦwww.hotelgeneve.ch; ❸), are both good, family-run places in the centre. At the top end of the scale, lapping up the lakeside panoramas, the *Hôtel du Lac*, 1 Rue d'Italie (☎021 921 10 41, ⓦwww.bestwestern.ch; ❻–❽), offers small-scale, understated grandeur, with inevitable associations with Anita Brookner; while ✒ *Des Trois Couronnes*, 49 Rue d'Italie (☎021 923 32 00, ⓦwww.hoteltroiscouronnes.ch; ❾) – the original setting for Henry James's *Daisy Miller* – retains all its period style, stuffy but utterly charming. It has been named as Swiss Historic Hotel of the Year, in honour of its superb restoration work and minute attention to original detailing.

The Town

The best way to get the flavour of Vevey is simply to wander: its narrow Old Town alleys, enclosing the huge **Grande-Place** – or **Place du Marché** – in a cat's cradle of arcades and shuttered facades, are alive with people, shops and activity. Arrive on a Tuesday or Saturday and you'll find the marketplace packed with stalls: food, crafts, wine or all three. The pillared building dominating the square is the Grenette, or town granary, dating from 1808 and now housing the tourist office.

Vevey's excellent fine-art museum is the **Musée Jenisch**, 2 Rue de la Gare (Tues–Sun 11am–5.30pm; Fr.8–15, depending on the exhibition; SMP; ⓦwww.museejenisch.ch), built in 1897 with a donation from a Hamburg émigré family named Jenisch; despite the tide of Swiss who apparently make the long journey from Graubünden expecting exhibits on the Jenisch gypsy people (see p.488), there's no connection. The museum, now about ten times too small for its collection, stages changing exhibitions of Swiss art, while its Cabinet cantonal des Estampes (Cantonal Museum of Prints) holds the largest collection of Rembrandt lithographs in Europe, as well as graphic works by Dürer, Corot, Le Corbusier and others. The museum is also the repository of the Oskar Kokoschka Foundation, displaying work from this Austrian expressionist who spent the last 26 years of his life in Villeneuve.

About 500m west of the centre, the giant green building on the waterfront is Nestlé's world HQ. A little uphill on the Chemin de Meruz is the village of **CORSIER**; on the right of the road you'll find a small cemetery, location of

---

Walks around Vevey

Vevey's tourist office runs a two-hour **guided walk** around the town (April–Sept Wed–Fri 10am; Fr.10), starting from their office, but you should check in advance about the availability of an English-speaking guide. Their excellent brochure *On The Trail of Hemingway* pinpoints a welter of sites in the area with famous-name associations.

One of the most pleasant long walks in the area is the three-hour **Chemin Fleuri** (Flowered Path), covering the sumptuous 9km lakefront promenade between Vevey and Villeneuve (aside from a short stretch east of La Tour-de-Peilz, where private lakefront properties force you back into the town). The tourist office has a brochure describing the walk and its various highlights.

The tourist office has a **"Poets' Ramble"** brochure for the **Talking Benches** walk (Fr.2), which outlines a long route from bench to bench through Vevey and the surrounding hillside villages; each bench is dedicated to a particular writer or philosopher with some connection either to Vevey or to that particular location. At each one, you can press a button to hear a short extract of their writings while enjoying the view. It's a great idea that works very well; the map is good enough to follow easily and the walk takes around 3 or 4 hours.

Nestlé

Henri Nestlé was born in Frankfurt in 1814, and moved to Vevey in his 20s, a merchant and small-scale inventor. He began experimenting with recipes for baby-food to help mothers unable to breastfeed. In 1867, he fed his *"farine lactée"* to a premature baby boy whose mother was dangerously ill; the boy survived, and Nestlé's reputation skyrocketed. The following year he opened an office in London to cope with the quantity of orders, and within five years was exporting to South America and Australia. In 1874 he sold his company for a million francs. In 1929, Nestlé bought out Peter, Cailler and Kohler – pioneers in making milk chocolate – and started to diversify, launching the world's first instant coffee, Nescafé, in 1938. More takeovers followed, and by the 1960s, Nestlé was Switzerland's biggest company. Today, still based in Vevey and having swallowed up cosmetic firm L'Oréal in 1974 and British confectioner Rowntree's in 1991, Nestlé employs almost a quarter of a million people, and buys up more than ten percent of the world's entire crop of coffee and cacao beans.

Nestlé's most controversial product is its original one: baby formula. The company has been riding a storm of anger in recent years from parents' organizations and health watchdogs, concerned at a marketing policy in developing-world countries that many see as aggressively profit-driven. Many of these groups lobby for boycotts of Nestlé products unless the company takes a role in helping educate mothers in the developing world to breastfeed whenever possible, and to buy formula only as a last resort. The company maintains its ads don't dissuade mothers from breastfeeding, and are merely offering them a choice. The dispute shows few signs of resolution.

the graves of Oona and Charlie Chaplin, who moved to Corsier in the 1950s as an escape from McCarthyite America and never left. Their house, the Manoir de Ban, is – at the time of writing – in the process of becoming the lavish **Charlie Chaplin Heritage Site** (🌐 www.chaplinmuseum.com).

Back on the main lakefront Route de Lavaux, some 200m west of the Nestlé building you'll find **Villa Le Lac**, an elegant low white bungalow designed by modernist architect Le Corbusier for his parents in 1924 (guided tours March–Oct Wed 1.30–5pm; Fr.5), which also features much original Corbusier furniture.

To the east, Vevey merges imperceptibly with its neighbour, the colourful port village of La Tour-de-Peilz. Along the way, you'll pass a photogenic statue of a bowler-hatted Chaplin twirling his cane amidst the roses on the Quai Perdon-net, followed shortly after by the **Alimentarium** (Tues–Sun 10am–6pm; Fr.10; SMP; 🌐 www.alimentarium.ch), a rather dull Nestlé-sponsored exhibition on food and nutrition. Another 200m brings you to the **Musée Historique**, 2 Rue du Château (Tues–Sat 10.30am–noon & 2–5.30pm, Sun 11am–5pm; Nov–Feb Tues–Sun 2–5.30pm; Fr.5; SMP; 🌐 www.museehistoriquevevey.ch), with a large section devoted to Vevey's Fête des Vignerons (Wine-Growers' Festival), a mammoth celebration in music, costume and dance of the region's viticulture traditionally held about every 25 years – most recently in 1999. The Quai d'Entre Deux Villes leads you on into **LA TOUR-DE-PEILZ**, 1km east of Vevey and dominated by its white château (the towers of which were once roofed with animal pelts – hence the odd name). Inside is the **Musée Suisse du Jeu** (Tues–Sun: March–Oct 11am–5.30pm; Nov–Feb 2–5pm; Fr.6; SMP; 🌐 www.museedujeu.com), an absorbing museum of games, from ancient Egyptian dice to the latest handheld devices; you're encouraged to tinker as much as you like.

Eating and drinking

Vevey has plenty of pavement **cafés and restaurants**. The excitable *Wall Street Café*, 6 Rue du Torrent, is spacious and friendly, with quality nosh for under Fr.15; *La Clef*, 1 Rue du Théâtre, is an atmospheric little corner bistro serving up steaming Vaudois specialities; while the cafés all around Place du Marché, including *Du Raisin* and *Le Cep d'Or* on the east side of the square, offer terraces for people-watching and simple *menus* for under Fr.20. The boss of *Hôtel Les Négociants* rolls up his sleeves of an evening and cooks solid, unpretentious fare in the hotel brasserie. There's also a self-service *Manora* in the St Antoine mall opposite the station.

Above Vevey

Aside from the little Train des Vignes (see box p.148), there are two routes for excursions by train into the hills above Vevey.

From Vevey-Funi station opposite the Nestlé building (at the terminus of bus #1), a **funicular** (every 20min; April–Oct only) rises through the wine village of Chardonne to a terrace on the slope of **MONT-PÈLERIN** at 800m, where you'll find plenty of places to appreciate the views over a little something to whet the whistle – not least at *Le Mirador Kempinski* (☎021 925 11 11, ⓦwww.mirador.ch; ❾), a huge luxury spa hotel. A stiff hike (at least 1hr) up to the summit brings you to the TV tower, with its high-speed **Plein-Ciel** glass lift whisking you up to the even better views at 1100m (lift Fr.5; funicular & lift Fr.16).

More dramatic is the curving train line from Vevey station up to the vantage point of **LES PLÉIADES**, perched in the hills way above the lake at 1364m.

Taking to the water

The section of Lake Geneva around Vevey and Montreux – the **Haut-Lac Supérieur** – dominated by the Dent d'Oche on one side, the heights above Montreux on the other, and glimpses of the snowy Pennine Alps further south, is utterly spectacular, and the best way to take it all in is **by boat**. Daily in summer (mid-May to mid-Sept), CGN (ⓦwww.cgn.ch) operates a ferry continuously from 10am to 6pm on a circuit between Vevey, Montreux, Château de Chillon, Le Bouveret, St-Gingolph and Vevey: you can get on anywhere and be taken round for two hours back to your starting point (Fr.28; free to Swiss Pass and Eurail holders, full price to InterRailers). Boats follow similar, direct routings between the same points all year round.

A few kilometres round the lakeshore from Chillon, across the Rhône (which marks the Vaud–Valais cantonal border), **LE BOUVERET** is a holiday village heavily touted for its family-friendly attractions. First up is the **Swiss Vapeur Parc** (May–Sept daily 10am–6pm; March, April, Sept & Oct Mon–Fri 1.30–6pm, Sat & Sun 10am–6pm; Fr.13; ⓦwww.swissvapeur.ch), a miniature railway complex featuring replica locos pulling passengers around 1.5km of track. A stroll away is the giant **Aquaparc** (April–Oct daily 10.30am–8.30pm, mid-July to mid-Aug until 9.30pm; Nov–March Sun–Thurs 10.30am–7.30pm, Fri & Sat 10.30am–9pm; ⓦwww.aquaparc.ch), a heated, indoor waterpark complete with multiple flumes, slides, rides and eateries; a half/full-day adult ticket costs Fr.40/44; kids and families get discounts.

About 5km west is the divided village of **ST-GINGOLPH** (ⓦwww.st-gingolph.ch), half in Switzerland and half in France. Apart from the busy border crossing, it's a soporific place that lives a quite different life from its lake neighbours: trains run not to Montreux but to the Valais villages south along the Rhône. Down by the water on the Swiss side are cafés and restaurants; on the French side is a supervised beach, with pedalos for rent. **Evian** (see p.132) is about 20km west.

The section beyond **Blonay** village – a junction for the line down to Montreux as well as the old steam railway to **Chamby** (see p.160) – is rack-and-pinion to cope with the gradient. Beside the penultimate station, **Lally**, is the cosy old-world *Hôtel Les Sapins* (☎021 943 1395, ⓦwww.les-sapins.ch; ❸), with great food and a little spa. From here, it's a quarter-hour climb (or the last six minutes of the train ride) to the summit, face to face with the mighty Dent de Jaman peak, only 1875m but prominent and pyramidal enough to earn the nickname of the Vaudois Matterhorn. Views yawn out in all directions, as do hiking trails – a leg-stretching one leads east across the hilltops to Les Avants (see p.160).

Montreux and around

If you want your soul to find peace, go to Montreux.

Freddie Mercury

MONTREUX can be a snooty place, full of money and not particularly exciting. It's spectacularly located, bathed in afternoon sunshine streaming across the lake and protected from chill northerlies by a wall of giant mountains, but once you've had your fill of window-shopping and strolling beneath the palm trees, it can be a bit dull.

From the early nineteenth century, Montreux was one of the centres for pan-European – and particularly British – tourism to Switzerland, following on from the importance of the medieval **Château de Chillon** 3km away as a controlling presence on the transalpine road: an edict dated 1689 authorized the building of inns in the area to accommodate travellers making their way to and from the Grand-St-Bernard pass, and since then travel and tourism have been mainstays of the local economy. Up until the 1960s, the name Montreux referred to just one village in a loose affiliation of some 24 vineyard-communes spread around the neighbouring hills, including picturesque **Clarens** to the west, and **Territet** to the east. Both of these are now super-plush suburbs, their long and venerable visitors' books taking in the great and the good, crowned heads of Europe and Russia, and literary and artistic personages galore. The main reasons to

Montreux's festivals

The star-studded **Montreux Jazz Festival** (ⓦwww.montreuxjazz.com) – featuring world-famous artists from REM to B.B. King – takes place over two weeks in early July, mainly at the two stages (Auditorium Stravinski and Miles Davis Hall) within the Congress Centre, plus at the Casino; it covers the gamut of music from around the world, these days only very loosely committed to formal jazz. Check online for tickets (Fr.40–130); otherwise, just join the street parties and free entertainment which spring up on the lakefront. Montreux is turned upside down during festival-time, with only the mornings left relatively normal: from mid-afternoon onwards, the main roads are blocked off, with huge car parks set up on the outskirts served by free buses. Bars and restaurants do a roaring trade until the early hours as thousands pour into town, and there's a constant thrumming of music from buskers and live stages on the lakefront. All accommodation is booked solid, and special post-event trains and buses run every night from about 1am onwards, returning revellers to towns as far afield as Sion and Bern.

Montreux's other big events include April's **Choral Festival** (ⓦwww.choralfestival .ch) and the classical **Festival de Musique "Septembre Musical"** (ⓦwww.septmus .ch), which runs in August and September at venues in Montreux and Vevey.

visit are to absorb the spectacular panorama of the Dents-du-Midi peaks across the lake, to visit the unmissable Château de Chillon, and to catch the stellar annual **Montreux Jazz Festival**.

In a gleeful case of truth being stranger than fiction, a century ago Montreux's hoteliers were casting about for a logo they could attach to the advertisements they placed in the English press each season. On a walk in the nearby hills they came across the perfect answer, growing in lush abundance all around; and so since 1897 the symbolic flower of Montreux has been, with ever-increasing aptness, a **narcissus**.

Arrival, information and accommodation

Montreux occupies a bulge of land jutting out into the lake, with the landmark Casino on the tip of the bulge. The large **train station** is set on a terrace above and slightly west of the town centre; stairs and escalators within the station raise you up to the Old Town on the slopes above, while Avenue des Alpes, the street outside the station's ticket office, has stairs and a lift which shuttle you down to the main central boulevard, Grand-Rue. A patch of park sandwiched between Grand-Rue and the lakefront prom-enade has at its western end the **ferry** *débarcadère*, and at its eastern end the covered market, Place du Marché. East of here, Grand-Rue becomes the Avenue du Casino

Brent & ❶ ▲

Centre de Congrès (Auditorium Stravinski & Miles Davis Hall)

Clarens, Vevey, A & B

ACCOMMODATION	
Auberge de Jeun.	F
Elite	E
L'Ermitage	A
Montreux Palace	C
La Rouvenaz	D
Villa Germaine	G
Villa Toscane	B

EATING	
Brasserie d. Alpes	2
Caveau d. Vignerons	3
Confiserie Zürcher	6
La Corsaz	4
Migros	7
Palais Oriental	5
Le Pont de Brent	1

Station

Vevey

Débarcadère

Lake Geneva

Château de Chillon

Freddie Mercury statue

PLACE DU MARCHÉ

Musée de Vieux-Montreux

RUE DU MARCHÉ

Territet & Chillon, F & G

Casino

0   75 m

MONTREUX

which heads out of town as Avenue de Chillon on its way along the lakefront to the château. **Bus #1** (see p.149) from Vevey runs along Grand-Rue, stopping below the train station, at the *débarcadère*, the covered market and the Casino, before heading on to Chillon.

The **tourist office** is next to the *débarcadère* on the lakefront (mid-May to mid-Sept Mon–Fri 9am–6pm, Sat & Sun 10am–5pm; rest of year Mon–Fri 9am–noon & 1–5.30pm, Sat & Sun 10am–2pm; ☏0848 868 484, ⓦwww .montreux-vevey.com).

When it comes to **accommodation** Montreux favours its high-rollers more than its backpackers – and prices rise across the board in summer. If you're arriving in early July (when the Jazz Festival is on) you're likely to find the town booked solid.

Hotels

Elite 25 Avenue du Casino ℡021 966 03 03, ⓦwww.montreux.ch/elite. Small, generic place – well located slap in the heart of town. ❷–❸

L'Ermitage 75 Rue du Lac, Clarens ℡021 964 44 11, ⓦwww.ermitage-montreux.com. A waterside villa set in its own grounds, with only seven rooms, all fresh and attractive, accompanied by spectacular gastronomic delights from the resident chef. ❻

Le Montreux Palace 100 Grand-Rue ℡021 962 12 12, ⓦwww.montreux-palace.com. Legendary luxury palace hotel, dominating the Montreux lakefront. This giant Belle-Epoque folly, one of the most famous hotels in the world, was opened in 1906 and later expanded both along the main street and across the road to the *Petit Palais* restaurant and teahouse, set in its own gardens on the lake. Newer wing or original wing, rooms are spacious, superbly well equipped and retain a good deal of character; plump for one of the lakeside balconies with sweeping panoramic views over the water. The public areas are effortlessly grand, and the associations with Vladimir Nabokov (he occupied the older wing's penthouse apartment for his last sixteen years) still resonate. ❾

La Rouvenaz 1 Rue du Marché ℡021 963 27 36, ⓦwww.montreux.ch/rouvenaz-hotel. Six comfy enough rooms in a central but quiet family-run place with Italian restaurant. ❸

Villa Germaine 3 Avenue Collonge, Territet ℡021 963 15 28, ⓔcecileparisi@gve.ch. Attractive, fin-de-siècle villa, considerably more characterful than in-town options, and well out of the hubbub to boot. ❷

Villa Toscane 2 Rue du Lac ℡021 966 88 88, ⓦwww.villatoscane.ch. A fabulous white, Art Nouveau creation on the Montreux waterfront, with balconies, meticulous service and a good deal of style; it's a "garni" place (without restaurant), so prices are lower than they might otherwise be. ❺

Hostel

Auberge de Jeunesse (HI hostel) Passage de l'Auberge 8, Territet ℡021 963 49 34, ⓦwww.youthhostel.ch. Good hostel located 1.5km east of Montreux centre, beside Territet train station (slow trains only) and near the L'Eaudine stop on bus #1. Dorm bed Fr.31.50. Mid-Feb to mid-Nov. ❶

The Town

Aside from rubbing shoulders with the hoi polloi of international tourism on thronging Grand-Rue and Avenue de Casino – everyone looking at everyone else wondering where all the rich people are – there's actually precious little to do in Montreux. Backing onto the Place du Marché, with impressive views across the water to the Dents-du-Midi, stands the town's most popular photo-op: a flamboyant bronze statue of long-time local resident **Freddie Mercury**. His group Queen first recorded an album in Montreux in 1978 and

Walks around Montreux

There's a two-hour **walking tour** of the town, which leaves from the tourist office (April–Sept Wed–Sat 10am; Fr.10); check in advance about the availability of an English-speaking guide, and beware too that the walk heads up the steep slopes into the Old Town and down again.

Alternatively, the other side of the tourist office's "**Poets' Ramble**" brochure on the **Talking Benches** of Vevey (see p.151; Fr.2) has a similar map outlining a long route from bench to bench all across hilly Montreux; each bench is dedicated to a particular writer or philosopher with some connection either to Montreux or to that particular location, and at each one, you can press a button to hear a short extract of their writings while enjoying the view. The walk takes 3 or 4 hours.

returned many times afterwards, Freddie eventually buying an apartment on the Territet waterfront (now private property), where he spent his last few months in 1991.

Associations with rock music continue when you reach the **Casino**, on Rue du Théâtre: this dour modern building replaced the grand original, which opened in 1883 and was burned to the ground on December 4, 1971, during a concert by Frank Zappa and the Mothers of Invention. During the show, someone in the audience let off a rocket-flare, which set the ceiling on fire; everyone got out without injury, but the building continued to burn all night. Ian Gillan, lead singer of the band Deep Purple, who were holed up in a hotel nearby, watched the flames leaping into the sky and was thus inspired to write his seminal rock classic "Smoke On The Water".

△ The immortal Freddie Mercury

The zigzagging streets and hillside terraces of the steep Old Town above the train station provide marginally more interest. A group of eighteenth-century buildings houses the modest **Musée de Vieux-Montreux**, 40 Rue de la Gare (April–Oct daily 10am–noon & 2–5pm; Fr.6; SMP; ⓦ www.museemontreux .ch), illustrating the town's history.

Eating and drinking

There are plenty of inexpensive places to **eat and drink** around the station on Avenue des Alpes offering meals for Fr.13–15, including some with lakeview terraces: *Brasserie des Alpes*, at no. 23, has pasta staples, while *Migros* on Place du Marché is self-service. In the Old Town, check out the fondue and Swiss dishes at *Caveau des Vignerons*, 30 Rue Industrielle (closed Sun); or take a chance with the home-style fare – tripe, sauerkraut and all – at the local diner variously entitled *La Corsaz*, *La Petite Brasserie Alsacienne* or *Le Flamm's* at Rue de la Corsaz 24 (closed Sun & Mon). *Confiserie Zürcher*, 45 Avenue du Casino (☎021 963 59 63; closed Mon), is Montreux's most venerable old tearoom (since 1894), perfectly situated with plate-glass windows for crowd-watching, a patisserie for exquisite cakey creations and a restaurant section with mid-priced *menus*.

The most appealing place to eat is the ⚒ *Palais Oriental*, 14 Quai du Casino (☎021 963 12 71, ⓦ www.palaisoriental.ch), done up inside with Persian carpets, beautiful inlaid furniture and works of calligraphy on the walls. Arabic/ Persian meals start from Fr.25, with plenty for veggies, or you could just savour the lakeside views over a Moroccan mint tea. If you've got a spare Fr.150, take a taxi to the unassuming *Le Pont de Brent*, in the nearby suburb of Brent (☎021 964 52 30), which has three Michelin stars for the excellence of its *haute-cuisine* (closed Sun & Mon, late July, Christmas and New Year).

Château de Chillon

There are seven pillars of Gothic mould,
In Chillon's dungeons deep and old,
There are seven columns massy and grey,
Dim with a dull imprison'd ray,
A sunbeam which hath lost its way...

Lord Byron, *The Prisoner of Chillon*

The climax of a journey around Lake Geneva is the thirteenth-century **CHÂTEAU DE CHILLON** (daily: April–Sept 9am–6pm; March & Oct 9.30am–5pm; Nov–Feb 10am–4pm; Fr.10; SMP; ⓦwww.chillon.ch). This impressive specimen, among the best-preserved medieval castles in Europe, is in Veytaux, about 3km south of Montreux; whether you opt for the 45-minute shoreline walk, bus #1 from Vevey or Montreux, a bike, or best of all a boat (which run year-round), your first glimpse of the castle is unforgettable – an elegant, turreted pile jutting out into the water, framed by trees and the craggy mountains. You could easily spend a half-day soaking up the atmosphere.

Some history

Although the scenery all around the castle is impressive enough, the **location** of the building is more impressive still – and is the key to its history. The mountains in front of the castle fall directly into the lake, with only the narrowest of through-routes between the sheer rock wall and the water. Directly opposite the defile, a razor-edge, sheer-sided islet rises from the water, of which only the very top is visible. This is where Chillon sits: if you were to drain the lake, the castle would teeter above an incredible drop of over 300m, as high as the Eiffel Tower. Such depths are cold and the lake's weather is capricious, making attack from open water extremely unlikely. Equally, the road is narrow, the heights are virtually unscaleable, and there's no other way to pass, making it impossible to avoid the castle. Whoever controlled the castle could control the traffic.

In **Bronze Age** times, there was no path around the lake: travellers had to climb the steep, 200m slopes at Chillon to a village on the heights above, then drop back down to rejoin the path. The **Romans** cut a narrow ledge along the lakeshore, and also opened up the Grand-St-Bernard Pass over the Alps further south, turning the road past the unfortified islet into the only route connecting northern and southern Europe through the mountains. By the **Middle Ages**, the quantity of traffic meant the road had to be widened and also that a form of toll could be set up. The village above was abandoned in favour of a new town (*ville neuve*, today's Villeneuve) built on open, accessible land a little way south on the valley floor. First surviving mention of a "guardian of the stronghold of Chillun" dates from 1150.

The Counts of **Savoy**, particularly Pierre (1203–68), made Chillon a princely residence, also developing Villeneuve into a major trading centre which poured tolls and customs duties into Chillon's coffers; in 1283, on average, one horse rider and perhaps a dozen foot travellers were crossing the Grand-St-Bernard Pass every hour of daylight, on every day of the year. Pierre's architects and engineers transformed Chillon, rebuilding the half facing the shore as a fortress with three strong towers and a keep, and filling the half facing the water with grand halls and royal apartments.

As the Savoyards began to threaten the Habsburgs, Chillon became their military and naval headquarters. The castle was both the centre of court life and a much-feared prison: when **plague** broke out in Villeneuve in 1348, the town's Jews were accused of plotting with Christian accomplices to poison the water supply, and large numbers of both were tortured in Chillon's dungeons. By this time, the Gotthard Pass further east was in use, and the transfer of traffic away from Chillon and the Grand-St-Bernard led to the castle's terminal decline as a military fortress, although it remained handy as a secure jail. In 1530, the Savoyards imprisoned a scholar, **François Bonivard**, at Chillon for inciting the Genevois people to form an alliance with the Swiss against Savoy. They left him shackled to a pillar in the dungeons for six years, until his release in 1536, when the **Bernese** army took control.

Fortunately for posterity, Chillon became a quiet backwater. In 1816, after Vaud had won independence from Bern, **Byron** (aged 28) and **Shelley** (24) visited the castle on their tour of the lake. A guide took them into the dungeons where Bonivard had been shackled and wove enough of a tale around him, and around the castle's history, to catch the poets' imagination. In his Ouchy hotel, Byron scribbled out his *Prisoner of Chillon*, a long narrative poem supposedly spoken by Bonivard (but entirely fictitious throughout), which celebrates the cause of individual liberty, and which brought Chillon to the attention of the wealthy tourists who were starting to explore the Alps. Archeologists and historians launched renovations of the crumbling infrastructure in the late nineteenth century, which restored a great deal of the castle's original grandeur. Work to maintain the castle continues today.

Visiting the Château de Chillon

As throughout history, the **road** passes outside the castle walls – these days, it's the Montreux–Villeneuve highway, served by bus #1 (the *autoroute* clings to the hillside high above). The eighteenth-century **gatehouse** is supported on stilts, replacing the original drawbridge. At the ticket window you'll get a follow-the-numbers pamphlet, which plunges you straight down into the vaulted and atmospheric **dungeons** (rooms 4–7) where the dukes of Savoy imprisoned François Bonivard: he was manacled to the fifth pillar along, which still bears a ring and a length of chain. Bonivard wrote that the dungeon was excavated to below the water-line, and Byron also wrote about the damp, but the room is in fact above the water and quite airy. The Irish novelist Maria Edgeworth, visiting in 1820, perhaps missed the point when she brightly chipped in: "If I were to take lodgings in a dungeon I should prefer this to any I have ever seen because it is high and dry with beautiful groined arches and no bad smells." She also noted that Byron's name was cut into the third pillar of the dungeon, as it still is, and that the guide remembered his visit four years previously. A grille in the external wall gives onto the lake, facilitating a rapid exit by rowing boat should things have ever got nasty up above.

The real wonder of the castle lies in the rooms upstairs, gloriously grand knights' halls, secret twisting passages between lavish bedchambers, gothic windows with dreamy views, a frescoed chapel, and more. The **Grand Kitchen** (room 8) still has its original wooden ceiling and two massive oak pillars, installed around 1260. The **Bernese Bedchamber** (room 10) has original bird and ribbon decorations dating from the 1580s, while the expansive **Hall of Arms** (room 12), complete with fireplace and windows over the lake, is covered with escutcheons of the Bernese bailiffs. The **Lord's Chamber** adjacent (room 13) retains its original thirteenth- and fourteenth-century wall paintings, rustic scenes of animals in an orchard with St George slaying the dragon on the chimneypiece. The **chapel** (room 18) features an impression of the full glory of the fourteenth-century decoration, with slides projected onto the partly decorated walls. Next door, the breathtaking **Great Hall of the Count** (room 19) has slender black marble pillars, shimmering chequered wall decoration, a coffered ceiling dating from the fifteenth century, and four windows over the lake topped by a beautiful four-leafed clover design.

Above Montreux

Montreux's train station is served by three different gauges of track. As well as the mainline CFF trains running west along the lake and south into the Valais, there are two different narrow-gauge lines operated by **MOB** (Montreux-Oberland-Bernois; ⓦwww.mob.ch) climbing up into the hills above Montreux that offer spectacular viewpoints, excellent hill walking, and panoramic rides through the countryside towards the high Alps of the Bernese Oberland.

The smaller line has creaking trains winding their laborious way northeast up to the giant Rochers-de-Naye summit (Eurail not valid, InterRail gets half-price, and the Swiss Pass is free to Caux, with a 25 percent discount from there to Rochers). Emerging from a series of corkscrew tunnels you come to **GLION**, an eyrie of a village perched amidst fields of narcissi directly above Montreux, with jaw-dropping views over the lake and the Rhône. There are a couple of luxury old-world hotels up here, but the more affordable *Hôtel des Alpes Vaudoises*, on Rue du Bugnon and with its own train station (ⓣ021 963 20 76, ⓦwww.hotel-alps.ch; ❸), is just as characterful and tranquil a place to unwind. A steep **funicular** also serves Glion from Territet on the lakeside below.

Further up on the train line is **CAUX**, home to the Conference Centre for Moral Re-Armament, the dramatically turreted headquarters of a rather odd collective which seeks to ease global political and economic strife through personal religious reconciliation. After another half-hour, trains reach the rugged vantage point of **ROCHERS-DE-NAYE** (2045m), with incredible views over the lake and plenty of hiking trails over the grassy hilltops.

The Golden Pass line: Montreux-Gstaad-Interlaken

The more important MOB narrow-gauge line above Montreux climbs northwest through the steep hills into Canton Bern (Eurail, InterRail and Swiss Pass all qualify for free travel). This is the route of the **Golden Pass** (ⓦwww.goldenpass.ch), one of the showcase journeys of Swiss railways (see p.42) – you must pay a small supplement on the special panoramic trains, but not on the ordinary ones. A little above Montreux is **CHAMBY**, one end of the Chemin de Fer-Musée (Museum Railway; May–Oct Sat & Sun 10am–6pm; Fr.16; SMP; ⓦwww.blonay-chamby.ch), which has steam trains running on a 3km stretch of track to and from **Blonay**, on the Vevey–Les Pléiades line (see p.153), as well as a depot full of old rolling stock.

The trains from Montreux continue up on a spectacular route, coiling through the village of **LES AVANTS** – starting point of a number of beautiful walks – to **Montbovon**, junction point for trains north into the countryside around **Gruyères** (see p.138). The Golden Pass line continues east to **Château d'Oex** and **Gstaad** (see p.306), but runs out at **Zweisimmen**, where you must change for connections to Interlaken and Lucerne.

Travel details

Full timetables for all trains, buses, trams, boats and cable cars in Switzerland – as well as international connections – are searchable at ⓦwww .rail.ch.

Trains

Coppet to: Geneva (every 30min; 20min); Nyon (hourly; 5min).

Gruyères to: Bulle (for Fribourg; hourly; 10min); Montbovon (for Montreux or Gstaad; hourly; 20min); Palézieux (for Lausanne; hourly; 55min).

Lausanne to: Basel (twice hourly; 2hr 10min); Bern (twice hourly; 1hr 10min); Biel/Bienne (hourly; 1hr); Brig (twice hourly; 1hr 40min); Echallens (every 30min; 25min); Fribourg (twice hourly; 45min); Geneva (every 15min; 35min); Interlaken Ost (twice hourly; 2hr 15min); Martigny (twice hourly; 50min); Montreux (every 15min; 20min); Neuchâtel (hourly; 40min); Nyon (3 hourly; 25min); Palézieux (for Gruyères; every 20min; 20min); Sion (twice hourly; 1hr 5min); Vallorbe (hourly; 45min); Vevey (every 15min; 15min); Yverdon (every 20min; 25min); Zürich (twice hourly; 2hr 10min).

Montreux to: Caux (hourly; 25min); Geneva (twice hourly; 1hr 5min); Gstaad (hourly; 1hr 20min); Lausanne (every 15min; 20min); Martigny (every 30min; 30min); Montbovon (for Gruyères; hourly; 45min); Vevey (4 hourly; 7min); Zürich (twice hourly; 2hr 35min).

Nyon to: Coppet (hourly; 5min); Geneva (every 15min; 15min); Lausanne (3 hourly; 25min); Neuchâtel (hourly; 55min); St-Cergue (every 30min; 35min); Yverdon (hourly; 35min).

Vevey to: Geneva (twice hourly; 1hr); Lausanne (every 15min; 15min); Martigny (every 30min; 35min); Montreux (4 hourly; 7min); Zürich (twice hourly; 2hr 30min).

Buses

Bulle to: Fribourg (twice hourly; 35min); Gruyères-ville (3 daily; 20min).

Gruyères to: Bulle (3 daily; 20min); Moléson (every 2hr; 15min).

Montreux to: Chillon (every 10min; 10min); Vevey (every 10min; 20min).

Vevey to: Chillon (every 10min; 30min); Montreux (every 10min; 20min).

Boats

Following is a summary of May–Sept summer services; fewer boats run in other months, generally Sat & Sun only, if at all. Full details at ⓦwww .cgn.ch.

Chillon (Château) to: Lausanne (3 daily; 1hr 45min); Montreux (4–5 daily; 20min); Vevey (3 daily; 35min).

Coppet to: Geneva (2–3 daily; 45min); Lausanne (2–3 daily; 2hr 45min).

Lausanne (Ouchy) to: Chillon (3 daily; 1hr 45min); Coppet (2–3 daily; 2hr 45min); Evian, France (10–15 daily; 40min); Geneva (3 daily; 3hr 30min); Montreux (5–6 daily; 1hr 20min); Nyon (3–4 daily; 2hr 10min); Vevey (5–6 daily; 1hr).

Montreux to: Chillon (4–5 daily; 20min); Geneva (3 daily; 5hr); Lausanne (5–6 daily; 1hr 20min); St-Gingolph (3–4 daily; 50min); Vevey (5–6 daily; 20min).

Nyon to: Geneva (4–7 daily; 1hr–1hr 30min); Lausanne (3–4 daily; 2hr 10min).

Vevey to: Chillon (3 daily; 35min); Geneva (3 daily; 4hr 30min); Lausanne (5–6 daily; 1hr); Montreux (5–6 daily; 20min); St-Gingolph (6–7 daily; 1hr 20min).

3

The Arc Jurassien

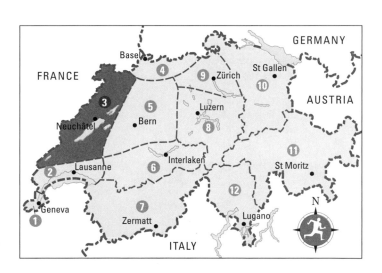

CHAPTER 3 # Highlights

✳ **The three lakes** Ferries criss-cross their way between the scenic lakes of Neuchâtel, Murten and Biel/Bienne. See p.168

✳ **Neuchâtel** Attractive, graceful city with a fine old quarter. See p.169

✳ **Yverdon** Sci-fi fans will love the outlandish "House of Elsewhere" museum. See p.178

✳ **Château de Grandson** Perhaps Switzerland's grandest castle. See p.180

✳ **Vallée de Joux** High, remote Jura valley, perfect for lonely hikes and cross-country skiing. See p.183

✳ **Payerne** A superb Romanesque abbey dominates this quiet country town. See p.185

✳ **Avenches** Former Roman capital, whose amphitheatre is still used for opera and shows. See p.186

✳ **Saignelégier** Gateway to exploring the far-flung Canton Jura on foot or by bike. See p.194

△ The Collégiale Church, Neuchâtel

The Arc Jurassien

The northwest frontier dividing Switzerland from France is the **Jura** mountain range – line after line of long, northeast-southwest ridges that trap between them a succession of sausage-shaped lakes. The Jura are nothing like the Alps: much lower to start with (rarely more than 1500m), with none of the majesty but all of the ruggedness. Scrubby hilltops and deep, parallel valleys are dotted by windswept, privately minded villages nursing a weatherbeaten Gallic culture cut off for centuries from both France and Switzerland. The whole **Arc Jurassien**, which takes in the highlands of the Jura Vaudois, the region's three largest lakes – the Lac de Neuchâtel, Murtensee/Lac de Morat and Bielersee/Lac de Bienne – Canton Neuchâtel, and Canton Jura in the far northwest, is well off the beaten track of most visitors to Switzerland. Guidebooks and brochures tend to skimp on detail, since it doesn't easily fit into the usual Swiss pigeonholes. If you choose to venture out here, you'll find a minimum of tourist hype and few actual sights other than the main towns of **Neuchâtel** and **Biel/Bienne**, but what exists in abundance is virtually untouched nature – and this is why the Swiss know and love the place. The recent brainwave to call the region "**Watch Valley**" (Ⓦwww.watchvalley.ch) in order to market it abroad – despite the fact that it isn't a valley, and only some areas have a tradition of watchmaking – rather misses the point of its charm.

Once you leave the lakes and the lowlands, public transport isn't easy, and even main roads are a relatively recent innovation. If you don't have a car, the best way to get around is by bike or on foot. Tourist offices can direct you onto any number of cycling trails or footpaths that reach all scenic spots. On p.222, we've outlined a long, multi-day walk through the area, which starts near Zürich, winds through the whole Jura region and ends up at Lake Geneva.

Language issues: Crossing the Röstigraben

The majority of the area covered by this chapter is francophone, and yet it straddles the linguistic divide, the *Röstigraben*, between French- and German-speaking Switzerland (see p.612). Many places or regions have two names, making travel to and fro across the language border a confusing business. Glossy publicity material may use the German word *Seeland* ("Lake District") or *Drei-Seen-Land* alongside *La Région des Trois-Lacs* to refer to the area, but since local tourist offices and bus and boat timetables tend to stick to either French or German, it's useful to be aware of dual naming.

Neuchâtel, the main town of the region, is entirely French-speaking, but German speakers call it Neuenburg and expect you to understand; the Lac de Neuchâtel is one and the same as the Neuenburgersee. Nearby is the small

FRANCE

Besançon

N

Dijon & Paris

Les Brenets

Pontarlier

Frasne

1275m

1242m   1277m

NEUCHÂTEL
VAUD   1419m

Fleurier   1369m

1476m   Mont Aubert
1339m

Le Chasseron   Concise
1607m

Sainte-Croix

L'Auberson

Grandson

Le Suchet
1588m   Yverdon-les-
Bains

Mont d'Or
1380m

Montcherand   Orbe

VAUDOIS

Vallorbe   Bercher

Dent de
Vaulion   Romainmôtier
1483m   JURA   Moudon

1409m   L'Abbaye

1384m   Châtel
1369m   Le Sentier   1432m   Echallens

MONT RISOUX   JOUX   Mont Tendre
DE   1679m   Cossonay

Le Brassus

1264m   VALLÉE   1389m

Lausanne

Lake Geneva

Nyon   Vevey

Belfort

Boncourt

AJOIE

Porrentruy

Basel

St Ursanne

Delémont

Doubs

Glovelier

JURA
BERN

Moutier

Montfaucon

Solothurn

Goumois

Saignelégier

Le Noirmont

Tramelan

Le Montoz
1328m

Grenchen

Olten

a Chaux-
e-Fonds

Les Prés d'Orvin
1340m

St-Imier

Le Chasseral
1607m

Mont Sujet
1382m

Magglingen

Biel/
Bienne

Büren

Mont d'Amin
1417m

BERN
NEUCHÂTEL

Bielersee/
Lac de Bienne

Nidau

Vue des Alpes
1283m

La Neuveville

Lyss

e de Ran
1422m

St Petersinsel

Mt. Racine
1439m

Erlach

Neuchâtel

Ins

Kerzers

Cortaillod

Mt. Vully
653m

Vully

BERN

Lac de
Neuchâtel

Portalban

Murtensee

Murten/
Morat

Bümpliz

BROYE

Avenches

Bümpliz

tavayer-
e-Lac

H E

Misery

Schwarzenburg

Payerne

Fribourg

BERN
FRIBOURG

Romont

0   10 km

Bulle

Gruyères

167

Montreux

Château d'Oex

majority-German-speaking lake resort of Murten, known to French speakers as Morat, sitting alongside the Murtensee/Lac de Morat. Just south of here the language border weaves between communities, and you'll find, for instance, the German village of Münchenwiler (Canton Bern) a kilometre or so from the francophone village of Cressier (Canton Fribourg). Tiny enclaves of Bern, Fribourg and Vaud jostle for position in this impossibly fragmented region. The lake to the north, almost surrounded by Canton Bern, is called both the Bielersee and Lac de Bienne, with the town at its head known as Biel/Bienne – the only officially bilingual town in Switzerland.

Further north is German-speaking Solothurn, known as Soleure in French. Beyond the Jura Bernois, the only French-speaking area of Canton Bern, lies francophile Canton Jura, founded in 1979 on a wave of anti-Bern separatist feeling. For Canton Jura, taking pride in French language and culture is a political, almost nationalistic, matter, and little quarter is given to German-ness of any kind – even though strongly Germanic Basel lies next door.

Ferries around the region

The lakes of Neuchâtel, Murten/Morat and Biel/Bienne are connected by canals, and one of the scenic highlights of the area is taking a long **ferry cruise** (3–4hr one-way) between them all. Point-to-point routings link the major towns of Neuchâtel, Estavayer, Yverdon, Murten and Biel/Bienne, along with a host of smaller lakeside villages. It's also possible to take a peaceful **river journey** (2hr 40min) up the River Aare from Biel/Bienne to Solothurn. As ever, there's only a handful of boats running outside the summer season (June–Sept), and then only on local routings: none of the long cruises operates in winter.

Two companies provide service: the LNM (ⓦwww.navig.ch) on the Lacs de Neuchâtel et Morat, and the BSG (ⓦwww.bielersee.ch) for Biel/Bienne and Solothurn. There's some overlap between them, but not much. Both advertise each other's routings and connections, and you can pick up timetables for both at all tourist offices. Eurail and Swiss Pass holders go free on both, while Inter-Railers pay half-price on BSG boats and full price on LNM.

"Hoppy" – Switzerland's first GPS audioguide

A great innovation for car drivers looking to explore the Arc Jurassien is **"Hoppy"**, a small electronic box which provides an in-car commentary to guide you around the region. You connect it to your car and it then links in to a GPS system: as you drive around, it offers little briefings (in English) through your car's loudspeakers on towns and villages, as well as history, gastronomy, sports, leisure and more, each triggered automatically by satellite as you approach a point of interest. So far, 960km of routes in the territory between Geneva, Bern and Basel have been covered, and if you cross the French border, "Hoppy" becomes "Navidoo", guiding you through the *département* of Doubs, which abuts the frontier here. The narrative style is a bit forced, but it's a great little toy.

"Hoppy" costs Fr.15 for one day, Fr.25 for two days, Fr.30 for three days, then Fr.4/day thereafter. You can pick one up at any tourist office in the region (as well as Geneva, Basel, Bern and Solothurn) – but you must **reserve in advance**, either directly with the relevant tourist office, or online at ⓦwww.watchvalley.ch. You can drop it off at any of the partner tourist offices.

Neuchâtel

Beam yourself down into **NEUCHÂTEL**, and you might think you've landed up in France. The Neuchâtelois people are the most French-oriented in Switzerland, speaking a dialect of Swiss-French that is celebrated – by those for whom such a thing is significant – as the "purest" in Romandie (that's to say, the closest to the "true" French spoken over the border). The town's air of dignity and easy grace is fuelled by a profusion of French-influenced architecture: many of the seventeenth- and eighteenth-century buildings are made from local yellow sandstone, a fact which led Alexandre Dumas to describe Neuchâtel as looking "like a toytown carved out of butter". And the modern and disarmingly Gallic street life of pavement cafés and studenty night bars, upscale street markets and hip designer boutiques, has the slightly unreal flavour of a town actively seeking influences from beyond its own borders – a rare thing indeed in Switzerland.

The Neuchâtelois, for whom the issue of joining the EU is a matter of the plainest common sense, are perhaps the epitome of the Swiss mystery; they are about as far removed in attitude, values, style and language from the people of Luzern – with whom their future is inextricably linked – to the east, as they are closely related to the people of Dijon – the supposed foreigners – to the west. You get the feeling while in Neuchâtel that the locals have thrown up their hands in disbelief at such injustice, and, ensconced between their broad lake and the mountain border, have sought solace in a life of fine wines, rich foods and French TV while waiting for their compatriots to see sense.

The town's main attractions are its café-lounging Gallic atmosphere and its location, with boats weaving to and fro across the lake and the first ridges of the high Jura range standing poised over the town. However, the Musée d'Art is worth going out of your way to experience, both for its innovative fine-art collection, and for its set of charming eighteenth-century mechanical figurines which demonstrate the exceptional skills of the Neuchâtel watchmakers of the era.

Some history

In 1011, Rudolf III of Burgundy presented a new castle (*neu-châtel*) on the lakeshore to his wife Irmengarde. The first Counts of Neuchâtel were named shortly afterwards, and in 1214 their domain was officially dubbed a city. In 1530, the people of Neuchâtel accepted the **Reformation**; future rulers were required to seek investiture from the citizens.

With increasing power and prestige, Neuchâtel was raised to the level of a principality. On the death in 1707 of Mary of Orléans, Duchess of Nemours and Princess of Neuchâtel, the people had to choose her successor from among fifteen claimants. They wanted their new prince to be a Protestant, and also to be strong enough to protect their territory but based far enough away to leave them in peace. Louis XIV actively promoted the many French pretenders to the title, but the Neuchâtelois people passed them over in favour of Frederick I, King of Prussia. With the requisite stability assured, Neuchâtel entered its golden age, with commerce, banking and industry (including watchmaking and lace) undergoing steady expansion.

At the turn of the nineteenth century, the Prussian king was defeated by Napoleon and forced to surrender Neuchâtel in order to keep Hanover. After the fall of Napoleon, Frederick III of Prussia reasserted his rights by proposing that Neuchâtel be linked with the other Swiss cantons (the better to exert influence over the lot of them). On September 12, 1814, Neuchâtel became the 21st

NEUCHÂTEL

ACCOMMODATION
Beau-Rivage   F
De l'Ecluse   C
Maison du Prussien   A
Du Marché   D
Touring au Lac   E

EATING & DRINKING
L'Atlas   8
Du Banneret   4
Chauffage Compris   1
Corsaire   7
Café du Cerf   6
Case à Chocs   5
Crêperie Elysée   2
Gelateria Fiorentina 3
Le Lotus   6
Maison des Halles   9

canton, but confusingly also remained a Prussian principality. It took a bloodless revolution for the region to shake off its princely past and declare itself, in 1848, a republic within the Swiss Confederation.

Arrival, information and accommodation

Neuchâtel's **train station** is perched above the town; it's a walk of about ten minutes, or a short hop by bus, down to the compact lakefront town centre focused around Place Pury, at the foot of the Old Town. The Fun'Ambule **funicular** runs from the station down to the university on Avenue du Premier-Mars. Pury is 100m west of Place du Port, which backs onto the harbour and the *débarcadère*: **boats** arrive at Neuchâtel from all points around the three lakes, including Yverdon, Estavayer, Murten/Morat and Biel/Bienne.

The tourist office, which has information on the city and the canton, is in the Hôtel des Postes building (main post office) on Place du Port (July & Aug Mon–Fri 9am–6.30pm, Sat 9am–4pm, Sun 10am–4pm; rest of year Mon–Fri 9am–noon & 1.30–5.30pm, Sat 9am–noon; ☎ 032 889 68 90, 🌐 www .paysdeneuchatel.ch). Neuchâtel is not a grandiose city, and the accommodation on offer is serviceable but not spectacular. Campsites either side of town are pretty good: 7km west is *Paradis Plage* in Colombier (☎ 032 841 24 46; March–Oct), while 5km east in Marin-Epagnier is *La Tène* (☎ 032 753 73 40; April–Sept).

Hotels

Beau-Rivage 1 Esplanade du Mont-Blanc ☎ 032 723 15 15, 🌐 www.beau-rivage-hotel.ch. Top of the range lakefront palace, with double-swanky rooms and views to match. ❽

De L'Ecluse 24 Rue de l'Ecluse ☎ 032 729 93 10, 🌐 www.hoteldelecluse.ch. Simple, beautiful rooms, characterized by ochre tones, tasteful wrought-iron furniture and stone floors, in this fine small hotel above the town centre. ❸

🏃 **Maison du Prussien** Gor du Vauseyon ☎ 032 730 54 54, 🌐 www.hotel-prussien .ch. One of Neuchâtel's most characterful choices:

a restored sixteenth-century mill beside a stream 2km west of town, with seven comfortable, well-appointed wood-beamed rooms and three expensive suites. ❸–❹

Du Marché 4 Place des Halles ☎ 032 723 23 30. The only hotel in the Old Town, with ten pleasant and spacious rooms (none ensuite) overlooking a bustling café-lined square. ❷

Touring au Lac Place Numa-Droz 1 ☎ 032 725 55 01, 🌐 www.touring-au-lac.ch. Not a tranquil location beside both the harbour and the main road, but with some nice views. Its boxy rooms (some ensuite) are nothing to write home about. ❷–❸

Above Neuchâtel – Chaumont

From the suburb of **La Coudre**, some 4km east of the town centre and reached on bus #7, a panoramic funicular (🌐 www.tnneuchatel.ch) rises through thick forests to the village of **CHAUMONT** (1087m). Set on a balcony above Neuchâtel, on the first of the Jura ridges, the viewpoint of Le Signal (1171m), a short walk from the funicular station, offers a vista over the three lakes of Neuchâtel, Murten and Biel/Bienne, with the plateau of Mont Vully rising opposite Murten and a patchwork of fields and forests stretching clear across the Swiss flatlands to the distant snowy fringe of the Bernese Alps. On the clearest of days, with such an unobstructed view across the whole country, it's claimed that you can even make out Mont Blanc and the Matterhorn.

The Town

Neuchâtel's **Old Town** is extremely attractive, and random wanderings through its steep alleys are as good a way as any to appreciate the golden beauty of the architecture, as well as the 140-odd street fountains, a handful of which date from the sixteenth century. From the rather anonymous **Place Pury** – hub of buses and shoppers alike – with the main artery of Rue du Seyon leading northwards, alleys to the west bring you to **Place des Halles**, perpetually filled with talkers and drinkers spilling out of a handful of cafés. The square itself is overlooked by fine Louis XIV architecture: shuttered facades and the turreted orioles of the sixteenth-century **Maison des Halles**. You'll find informal lunchtime *boules* sessions on the nearby Rue du Coq d'Inde, a tranquil court-yard away from the bustle. A two-minute walk east, on Rue de l'Hôpital, is the grand 1790 **Hôtel de Ville** (Town Hall), designed by Louis XVI's chief architect Pierre-Adrien Paris.

The highlights of the Old Town are poised on the very top of the hill, accessed by the steeply winding Rue du Château. The **Collégiale church** (daily 8am–6pm), begun in 1185 and consecrated in 1276, is a graceful example of early Gothic. Stairs from Rue du Château bring you up to the east end of the church, with its three Norman apses. The main entrance, to the west, is crowned by a giant rose window of stained glass. Within the vaulted interior, the nave draws you along to the glowing transept, lit by a lantern tower, and the unique Ceno-taph of the Counts of Neuchâtel on the north wall of the choir. Begun in 1372, and the only artwork of its kind to survive north of the Alps, the monument comprises fifteen near-life-size painted statues of various knights and ladies from Neuchâtel's past, framed by fifteenth-century arches and gables.

Beside the church is the imposing **château**, begun in the twelfth century and still in use as the offices of the cantonal government: entry is only on 45-minute guided tours, which start from the signposted Door no. 1 (on the hour: April–Sept Tues–Fri 10am–noon & 2–4pm, Sat 10am, 11am & 2–4pm, Sun

△ Place des Halles

& Mon 2–4pm; free). The nearby turreted Tour des Prisons (April–Sept daily 8am–6pm; Fr.1), the remains of a medieval bastion, has panoramic views along with interesting models of Neuchâtel in different eras.

Musée d'Art et d'Histoire
The **Musée d'Art et d'Histoire**, Esplanade Léopold-Robert (Tues–Sun 11am–6pm; Fr.8, free on Wed; SMP; Ⓦwww.mahn.ch), and its star attractions, the astonishing Automates Jaquet-Droz (Jaquet-Droz Mechanical Figurines), is unmissable. Renovations, completed in 2006, have changed much of the museum's interior. The historical collections, examining the urban development of Neuchâtel, have been moved to the separate Galeries de l'Histoire, a few minutes away, at 7 Avenue du Peyrou (Tues–Sun 1–5pm; free). In the main building, the galleries of fine and applied art keep a focus on interdisciplinary themed exhibits – painting sharing a space with crafts or coins or historical documents, inducing you to make dynamic connections between diverse works.

But the most extraordinary exhibits are the Automates Jaquet-Droz, three mechanical figurines built to the most exacting technical standards by a Neuchâtelois watchmaker in the 1770s (see box) and still in perfect working order today. The three – the Draughtsman, the Writer and the Musician – are displayed static behind glass, with a fascinating accompanying slide-show in English by way of explanation, but if you can you should really time your visit for one of their regular demonstrations (1st Sun of month at 2pm, 3pm & 4pm). The Draughtsman is a child sitting at a mahogany desk and holding a piece of paper with his left hand; his right hand, holding a pencil, performs extraordinarily complex motions to produce intricate little pictures of a dog, the god Eros in a chariot pulled by a butterfly, or a noble profile of Louis XV. The Writer, a

---

The celebrated Monsieur Jaquet-Droz

Pierre Jaquet-Droz (1721–90) was born in La Chaux-de-Fonds into a wealthy local family. In Neuchâtel he worked to combine his interest in mathematics with the skills of applied mechanics used by the artisans of the watch industry. He quickly gained a reputation for technical brilliance, and in 1758 travelled to Madrid to show off the skill of Neuchâtelois clockmakers at the Spanish court; his "Shepherd's Clock" is still on display in one of the king of Spain's palace museums.

Wealthy enough to retire, Jaquet-Droz withdrew to concentrate on problems of applied mathematics, exemplified in his construction of incredibly complex mechanical figurines designed to do particular tasks – the earliest of computers. He trained his son, Henri-Louis, and a colleague, Jean-Frédéric Leschot, to work with him; together, they produced **the Writer, the Draughtsman** and **the Musician**, and presented all three for the first time to the public in La Chaux-de-Fonds in 1774. Writers of the day reported that people flocked to see such extraordinary works of whimsy and technical skill. The same year, the three craftsmen showed their figurines in drawing rooms and royal palaces all across Europe, receiving high acclaim wherever they went.

Perhaps aware of impending revolutionary violence in France and Switzerland, Jaquet-Droz sold the figurines to a collector in Spain in 1778. After the conflicts, in 1812, they reappeared in Paris and began touring again. Some twenty years later, they became the centrepiece of Martin and Bourquin's "Museum of Illusions", which toured Central Europe until the turn of the century. In 1906, helped by a grant from the Swiss government, Neuchâtel bought the figurines back, and they have been on display in the town's museum ever since, in virtually the same condition as when they were first made, 230 years ago.

chubby-cheeked little boy, also sits at a mahogany desk, with a goose quill in his right hand and a tiny pot of ink nearby for dipping. He writes in a florid and chunky style, and can be programmed to produce any text of up to forty characters: watching him write, for instance, "*electricité*" lifts the hairs on the back of your neck. While he writes, his eyes follow the words across the page. The most charming of the three is the Musician, a gracious young girl with slender and dexterous fingers who plays a small organ – a real instrument, not a disguised musical-box. As her fingers strike the keys to produce the notes and her eyes, head and body move subtly from side to side in time, her chest rises and falls delicately in an imitation of rhythmic breathing. Her melodies were composed in the early 1770s by Henri-Louis Jaquet-Droz – a fleeting and unique auditory time capsule from pre-Revolutionary Europe.

Centre Dürrenmatt

On the hillside above Neuchâtel, reached on bus #9, is the **Centre Dürrenmatt**, 74 Chemin du Pertuis-du-Sault (Wed–Sun 11am–5pm; Fr.8; SMP; ⓦwww .cdn.ch). This is a museum and research centre devoted to the Swiss writer and artist Friedrich Dürrenmatt (1921–90), who was born in the German-speaking Emmental, but came to Neuchâtel in 1952 and spent the last 38 years of his life here. Dürrenmatt's papers, and his Expressionist-style paintings, aside, the chief reason to visit is the superb architecture: the Ticinese architect Mario Botta has designed a sleek, curving gallery partly buried in the hillside below Dürrenmatt's former home to display the art works. Botta's achievement here is eye-popping: enjoy it, along with spectacular lake views, from the terrace café.

Eating and drinking

Neuchâtel takes **eating and drinking** seriously, with dozens of pavement cafés and relaxed bistros all over the centre. Local specialities, best sampled at places like the *Hôtel du Marché* (see below) include tripe in wine, *tomme panée* (baked cheese) and fresh lake fish. A *fondue neuchâteloise* takes full advantage of the nearby vineyards, with local whites splashed liberally into the bubbling pot for an especially heady cheese-dipping experience. In a quiet Old Town courtyard off the main street is *Gelateria Fiorentina*, 31 Rue des Moulins, a perfect place to relax with an ice cream.

Restaurants

L'Atlas 14 Rue Fleury ☎032 724 11 98. Tiny Moroccan restaurant tucked away on an Old Town alley, with Fr.13–15 menus, authentic couscous and tajine, Moroccan wine, and sweet mint tea as it should be.

Du Banneret 1 Rue Fleury ☎032 725 28 61. Peaceful little spot in a crook of the Old Town's steep alleys, opposite a fountain at the foot of Rue du Château. The food is consistently good – regional specialities, lightly prepared, with fresh fish a staple. *Menus* around Fr.23. Closed Sun.

Crêperie Elysée 26 Rue des Moulins. Old Town joint for crêpes with dozens of fillings to choose from, from a Fr.4 snack up to a Fr.13 meal. Closed Sun.

Hôtel du Marché Place des Halles ☎032 723 23 30. Central Old Town landmark, serving hearty Swiss and French cuisine for Fr.20 or so. Closed Sun & Mon lunch.

Hôtel Touring au Lac Place Numa-Droz. Overlooking the harbour and the open lake, one of the best terraces for croissant-and-*renversée* breakfasts, mellow salad lunches and long sundowner *apéros*. Excellent fresh fish is an added attraction.

Le Lotus 4 Rue de l'Ancien Hôtel-de-Ville ☎032 724 27 44. Upper-floor Cambodian restaurant, with high-quality Asian cuisine for Fr.20-odd (*menus*) or Fr.30 (à la carte). Closed Sun.

Maison des Halles Place des Halles ☎032 724 31 41. Not to be confused with the *Hôtel du Marché*, this is in the fairy-tale turreted building next door – an excellent wood-fired pizzeria down below (from Fr.13), and perhaps the town's most refined *haute cuisine* restaurant (closed Mon, Sat lunch & Sun) up above.

Maison du Prussien Gor du Vauseyon ☎ 032 730
54 54; see "Hotels". One of Neuchâtel's gourmet
highlights, with characterful French-oriented *menus*
for as little as Fr.30 or so. Closed Sun.

Bars and clubs

Café du Cerf 4 Rue de l'Ancien Hôtel-de-Ville.
Lively central watering hole, serving beers from
around the world.

Case à Chocs 16 Quai Godet. Top club in town,
with innovative DJ nights of everything from ska
to acid jazz and drum'n'bass, plus occasional live
bands. Thurs–Sat only.

Chauffage Compris 37 Rue des Moulins. Friendly,
sociable Old Town bar attached to the CAN arts
centre.

Corsaire 16 Faubourg de l'Hôpital. Popular DJ bar
and hangout.

Around Canton Neuchâtel

Above Neuchâtel, roads and train tracks rise steeply into the Jura – known
within the canton as the **Montagnes Neuchâteloises**. This is wild and hilly
country, characterized by remote, windswept settlements and deep, rugged
valleys. It is also the heartland of the celebrated Swiss watchmaking industry,
centred on the once-famous towns of **La Chaux-de-Fonds** and **Le Locle**.
The Doubs river marks the border with France, set down in a gorge and forming along its path an impressive waterfall, the **Saut du Doubs**, and lake, the
Lac des Brenets, which together make a pleasant day out.

La Chaux-de-Fonds

LA CHAUX-DE-FONDS is an oddity. More people live there than in
Neuchâtel, although you'd never guess it from the sparsity of street life.
Strangest of all, however, is the fact that this rather unprepossessing place
was once a household name across Europe, the humming centre of the Swiss
watchmaking industry, which in its heyday of the late eighteenth and
nineteenth centuries was largely responsible for establishing Switzerland's
reputation – which survives today – for producing refined luxury goods of
the highest quality. The town was burned to the ground in 1794 and rebuilt
on a grid system, characterized by enormously long, very broad parallel boulevards. This feature, combined with the municipality's taste for postmodern
glass towers, has given La Chaux-de-Fonds the rather unfortunate air – very
odd for Switzerland, and frankly bizarre for such an historic place – of a new
town transported from somewhere in anonymous Middle America. It's rather
an exhausting place to walk around, though its museums merit a visit.

If you have your own transport and are approaching from Neuchâtel (whether
on the winding minor road or through the climbing motorway tunnels), make
sure you stop for a while at the **Vue des Alpes** (1283m), a magnificent viewpoint just short of La Chaux-de-Fonds, giving a broad panorama of the Swiss
plateau backed by the snowy Bernese Alps.

Arrival, information and accommodation

The **train station** is reasonably central, set back 100m from the main Avenue
Robert, which cuts a straight northeast–southwest groove through the centre
of town. In the tall Espacité cylindrical glass tower on the north side of Avenue
Robert some 500m east of the station you'll find the **tourist office** (July &
Aug Mon–Fri 9am–6.30pm, Sat 10am–4pm; rest of year Mon–Fri 9am–noon
& 1.30–5.30pm, Sat 9am–noon; ☎ 032 919 68 95, ⓦ www.paysdeneuchatel
.ch). In front of the tower is a monumental nineteenth-century fountain, central
landmark of the town.

The town's buses (@www.trn.ch) run on circular routes, and all pass in front of the train station. A day ticket is Fr.5.80. Note that after 7pm on weekdays, and all day at weekends, routes combine under different numbers. Alternatively, you could book at the tourist office for a tour of town by horse-drawn carriage (May–Oct daily; 1hr 15min; Fr.15 per person).

The hotel *De France* is next to the station (☎032 913 11 16; ❷), a "garni" place with reasonable rooms both ensuite and not. The *Fleur-de-Lys*, 13 Avenue Robert by the fountain (☎032 913 37 31, @www.fleur-de-lys.ch; ❹), is a pleasant business hotel. On the approach to town is *Motel du Jura*, 50 Rue de l'Hôtel de Ville (☎032 968 28 22; ❷), with free parking.

The Town

La Chaux-de-Fonds' main draw is the award-winning **Musée international d'horlogerie**, 29 Rue des Musées (Tues–Sun 10am–5pm; Fr.15; SMP; @www .mih.ch), about 500m east of the station, set back 150m from Avenue Robert. There are hundreds of items tracing the art of keeping time, with a concentration of beautiful pieces from La Chaux's heyday in the eighteenth and nineteenth centuries as well as ultra-modern atomic and electronic clocks. In one corner local watchmaking firms (which are also the world market leaders) put their latest bejewelled creations on display – but without price tags. In the park outside is a giant tubular-steel **carillon** with digital readout – all the rage when it was built in 1980 – that chimes every quarter-hour.

Immediately adjacent is the **Musée des Beaux-Arts**, 33 Rue des Musées (Tues–Sun 10am–5pm; Fr.6; SMP), housed in an impressive Neoclassical building with an airy annexe for temporary exhibits. The permanent collection takes in a Modigliani, a couple of Van Goghs, Delacroix and Renoir among a selection of mostly little-known early modern works. The troubled face of local artist Léopold Robert, in a portrait by his son Aurèle, hints at his disturbing fate: he cut his own throat in 1835 at the age of 41 after the failure of an unhappy relationship with Charlotte Bonaparte. Plenty of Robert's own romantic images of Venetian sailors, exotic peasant women and rogueish mountain bandits – as well as mawkish works on death and impending mortality – cover the walls.

La Chaux's most famous son was the modernist architect Charles-Edouard Jeanneret, known as **Le Corbusier** (his face adorns the Swiss ten-franc note). He was born in 1887 at 38 Rue de la Serre; dotted around town are several examples of his work, including the Villa Blanche, 12 Chemin de Pouillerel (Fri–Sun 10am–5pm; Fr.10; @www.villa-blanche.ch), built for his parents in white following a journey aged 25 to the East, and the Mediterranean-style Villa Schwob or Villa Turque, 167 Rue du Doubs (1st & 3rd Sat of month 11am–4pm; free), which now houses the public relations arm of the Ebel watchmaking firm. The tourist office has a brochure outlining an eleven-point Le Corbusier itinerary through the town.

Eating, drinking and nightlife

For **eating and drinking**, a few pavement cafés are dotted along Avenue Robert offering standard brasserie fare – the *Trattoria Toscana* at no. 13 is typical. *Il Caminetto*, 15 Rue de la Balance, has wood-fired pizzas for Fr.15 and good fish for under Fr.20. There's a reliably good *Manora* at 20 Boulevard des Eplatures, and traditional fare such as fondue and tripe at the *Pinte Neuchâteloise*, 8 Rue Grenier (closed Sun). The best view in town is from the *Citérama* café, on the 14th floor of the Espacité tower; aside from ice cream, coffee and light meals, they have an outside terrace with bird's-eye views along the arrow-straight length of Avenue Robert – best after dark, when with a beer or two inside you, you might just imagine yourself in LA for a brief second. The vaulted *P'tit Paris*, 4 Rue du Progrès (closed Sun; Ⓦwww.petit-paris.ch), as well as serving good inexpensive food, has some **live music** downstairs, while the town's best music venue is the *Bikini Test*, 3 Rue Joux-Perret (Ⓦwww.bikinitest .ch), hosting everything from death metal to dancehall to world jazz.

Le Locle and around

About 8km west of La Chaux is the small town of **LE LOCLE**, where Swiss watchmaking was born. Daniel Jeanrichard, a native of Neuchâtel (where he made his first watch in 1681, aged 16) settled in Le Locle in 1705 and taught the trade to his family and a small group of apprentices, who then took the skill on to La Chaux and elsewhere in the Jura. The **Musée d'horlogerie** in the Château de Monts above the town (Tues–Sun: May–Oct 10am–5pm; Nov–April 2–5pm; Fr.7; SMP; Ⓦwww.mhl-monts.ch), features eighteenth-century rooms crammed with ticking timepieces of all kinds. To reach Le Locle from La Chaux, it's easiest to get the regular **buses** #60 or #61, which stop at the central Place du Marché.

Postbuses from Le Locle to La Brévine stop at the Col-des-Roches **underground mills** (May–Oct daily 10am–5pm; Nov–April Tues–Sun 2–5pm; Fr.12.50; SMP; Ⓦwww.lesmoulins.ch), 2km west of Le Locle. These dank chambers were chiselled out in the seventeenth century in order to take advantage of the water flowing down to the Doubs: there are various mills and other bits of heavy machinery down there. The obligatory hour-long guided tour is in spoken French and German, with English notes.

A side road branches 3km north from the Col-des-Roches down to the riverside village of **LES BRENETS**, where the Doubs broadens into the Lac des Brenets (known to the French on the other bank as the Lac de Chaillexon), which freezes over in winter to form the largest natural ice rink in Europe. Narrow-gauge trains from Le Locle pull into Les Brenets train station; walk left down through the village for twenty minutes to the riverbank to reach the landing stage, which is also served by direct buses from Le Locle. From here, you can take a fine boat trip (takes 20min; Ⓦwww.nlb.ch) east through a craggy gorge to the 27m-high **Saut du Doubs** waterfall.

Yverdon-les-Bains and around

A market town on the southern tip of Lac de Neuchâtel, **YVERDON-LES-BAINS** is best known for its thermal springs – celebrated at least since Roman times – and is handy as a jumping-off point both for the terrific old castle at nearby **Grandson**, and for trips into the Vaudois hinterland around **Vallorbe** (see p.182) and into the **Vallée de Joux** (see p.183).

Yverdon was founded in 1260 when Pierre of Savoy built a castle on what was then the lakefront to defend against attack from the east (the lake has since silted up so that the fortress is now the best part of a kilometre inland). However, prehistoric standing stones and Roman remains show that the Savoyards were not the first to see the strategic importance of Yverdon's location on one of Europe's most significant ancient crossroads. The shortest routes from central France to Italy, and from southern France to Germany, not to mention the vital water route linking the Rhône and the Rhine, all passed through Yverdon, whose name derives from the Gallo-Roman Eburodunum ("Fortress of the Yew Tree").

These days, Yverdon lies second in Vaud to Lausanne. Visit for its castle, compact Old Town with many Baroque and Neoclassical facades, spa complex, 5km of sandy beaches, and the Champ-Pittet marshland nature reserve (ⓦwww.pronatura.ch/champ-pittet) stretching along the lakeshore 2km north-east of town.

③ The Town

Yverdon's central **Place Pestalozzi** is dominated by the broad-fronted Louis XV-style Hôtel de Ville and, next to it, the foursquare turreted **château**, built after 1260 by Pierre II of Savoy, occupied by the Bernese in 1536, and seized during the Vaudois revolution in 1798. From 1805 to 1825 the château housed an educational institute set up by the visionary reformer Heinrich Pestalozzi (see box); Yverdon's schoolchildren continued to be taught within the castle walls right up until 1974. Today it's the home of the **Musée d'Yverdon** (Tues–Sun 11am–5pm; Oct–May 2–5pm; Fr.8; joint ticket with Maison d'Ailleurs Fr.12; SMP), which includes a couple of Gallo-Roman dugout canoes, a rather homesick Egyptian mummy in the Jew's Tower and a costume collection.

Far more engaging is the Maison d'Ailleurs opposite the château ("House of Elsewhere"; Wed–Fri 2–6pm, Sat & Sun noon–6pm; Fr.7, joint ticket with Musée d'Yverdon Fr.12; SMP; ⓦwww.ailleurs.ch). This self-billed "museum of science fiction, utopia and amazing journeys", housed in the old prison, holds a massive collection of some 80,000 items, featuring antiquarian books from as early as the fifteenth century (notably a 1631 Amsterdam edition of Thomas More's *Utopia* in Latin), and sci-fi paperbacks galore, including an array of Asimovs in what seems like all the languages of the world. Changing exhibits might cover fantasy art, posters, old sci-fi magazines, unpublished drawings from Hollywood movie designers, and samples from an amazing collection of toys

Johann Heinrich Pestalozzi

Johann Heinrich (Henri) Pestalozzi, born in Zürich in 1746, was an educationalist, who devoted his life's work – twenty years of it in Yverdon – to giving poor and under-privileged children the chance to have a decent education. Pestalozzi first lived with his wife Anna Schulthess in Birr (Canton Aargau), where they tried to organize help for local abandoned children. After four years in Bern as a schoolteacher, Pestalozzi was invited in 1804 by the Yverdon municipality to establish an educational institute. He took in up to 150 boys aged 7 to 15 who would otherwise have been begging on the streets, fed and clothed them, and organized a flexible school curriculum suited to each child's abilities, covering mathematics, languages, music, gymnastics, biology and more, thus gaining worldwide attention from social scientists of the day. Two years later, he set up a similar school for girls, followed in 1813 by Switzerland's – and one of the world's – first schools for children with hearing and/or speech disabilities.

Pestalozzi died in Birr in 1827, but to this day there remains a great deal of interest in his methodology, documented in sheaves of letters and articles. His vision of education for all was seized upon by Victorian reformers in Britain and elsewhere as a cornerstone of the development of welfare policy. Indeed, Pestalozzi's legacy is only beginning to be fully realized today, with the UN acknowledging education to be a human right.

When Pestalozzi wrote, "Development of a child's mind should be made continuously relevant to that child's personality and everyday life," such an idea was laughable. Today it seems obvious, largely due to his example.

(1950s ray-guns, original Superman dolls, Star Trek and Star Wars figures, and more). You're welcome to browse through their English library, and kick back in their "Giger Cell" – a room kitted out by *Alien* designer H.R. Giger (see p.139) – for a spot of solo literary journeying during the afternoon.

Yverdon is suffixed "-les-Bains" for its spa waters, 14,000-year-old mineral springs bubbling up from 500m below ground and rich with all kinds of curative properties. The water emerges at between 28 and 34°C, and is these days corralled into various indoor and outdoor pools about 1km southeast of the Old Town at the Centre Thermal, a state-of-the-art complex off Avenue des Bains (Mon–Sat 8am–10pm, Sun 8am–8pm; Fr.17; ⓦ www.cty.ch). Over a thousand people come here every day to take the waters. Extras include saunas, massages and any amount of physiotherapy and inhalation courses. You can even drink the stuff, which is bottled and sold around Switzerland as "Arkina".

Practicalities

Yverdon's **train station** is 100m northeast of the Old Town, and about 600m southwest of the lakeshore. **Boats** dock at the *débarcadère* on Quai de Nogent near the racecourse; it's a fifteen-minute walk south along the River Thièle and under the train tracks (or take bus #2) to reach the Old Town. The focus of the Old Town is Place Pestalozzi, in front of the castle walls. The **tourist office** is by the station, 1 Avenue de la Gare (Mon–Fri 9am–noon & 1.30–6pm; April–Oct also Sat 9am–noon; ⓣ 024 423 61 01, ⓦ www.yverdon-les-bains.ch).

Accommodation includes *Du Théâtre*, 5 Avenue Haldimand (ⓣ 024 424 60 00, ⓦ www.hotelyverdon.ch; ❸), a characterful, modern hotel very near the tourist office, with king-size beds and a fresh, uncluttered feel. Nearby, *L'Ecusson Vaudois*, 29 Rue de la Plaine (ⓣ 024 425 40 15, ⓦ www.ecussonvaudois.ch; ❷), is a pretty good option featuring rooms ensuite and not, and pleasant staff. A handful of hotels cluster around the Centre Thermal on Avenue des Bains, 1km southeast of the centre, including the four-star *Grand Hôtel des Bains* (ⓣ 024 424 64 64, ⓦ www.grandhotelyverdon.ch; ❻). *Des Iris* campsite is on the lakefront northeast of the station (ⓣ 024 425 10 89; April–Sept).

All the hotels above have good restaurants. Alternatively, *Crêperie l'Ange Bleu*, 11 Rue du Collège (closed Mon), has salads, crêpes and light *menus* for around Fr.10; *Don Camillo*, 10 Rue du Pré (closed Sun), has excellent pizza/pasta dishes; and *La*

The Clendy stones

About 1.5km northeast of Yverdon, between the suburb of **Clendy** and the lakeshore, are **standing stones**, or menhirs, some five thousand years old. Take bus #1 to Clendy, walk left (north) under the railway bridge, and then head straight along a footpath beside a wood for about 50m. Cut right on paths through the trees, and you'll emerge into a neatly mown clearing set with the stones.

The Clendy stones were reset in their original positions in 1986, just one of many significant clusters of **Neolithic** stone circles and dolmens on the north shore of Lac de Neuchâtel, the greatest concentration of them in Switzerland (more are on Lake Geneva and around Sion). These pitted and blotchy stones – big, but no Stonehenge – form a rough rhomboid shape, with a line extending out from one corner; their purpose is unknown, but may have been connected with worship and/or ley-lines, since Yverdon sits at a conjunction of ancient roads. The atmosphere of the place is tangible, but the stones now stand beside a main road, shielded by trees from all but the sound of modern traffic.

Fourchette, 8 Rue du Casino, offers simple but well-prepared French and Italian favourites. *Intemporel*, 8 Rue du Lac, is an upstairs café-bar popular with young people and open late nightly, with ten kinds of coffees and teas plus salad meals.

Grandson

A lakeshore village 4km north of Yverdon, **GRANDSON** resonates in the mind of every Swiss schoolchild as the location of one of the three greatest victories ever won by a Swiss army, against Charles of Burgundy in 1476. Its castle, the focus of the battle, now houses one of the best **castle museums** in the country.

Although a tower was built by Adalbert of Grandson as early as 1050, the main buildings date from 1281, when Otto I of Grandson returned from the Eighth Crusade wealthy enough to build a new castle, a Franciscan cloister in the village (of which the beautiful Romanesque St-Jean-Baptiste survives, five minutes' walk southwest from the castle up Rue Haute) and a Carthusian monastery further along the lake near Concise. Otto's tomb is prominent within Lausanne cathedral.

In 1475, during clashes as Charles the Bold, duke of Burgundy, expanded his territory and influence, the Swiss confederate army besieged the fortress at Grandson for the first time; after less than a month, the Burgundian garrison surrendered and was allowed to escape. Early the following year, on February 26th, the Burgundian army under Charles retook the town of Grandson and, on the 28th, the castle. Treacherously, the Swiss garrison of 412 men were hanged from the apple trees in the castle orchard. Two days later, the Swiss army marched against Charles, and met him in battle north of Grandson, lining up rank after rank of their feared fusiliers, pikemen and halberdiers. "The sun was opposite them," reports an eyewitness, "and their weapons sparkled like mirrors. The raised bugles of Uri and the Luzerner battalion were bellowing, and the din was such that the Duke's men took fright and began to retreat." The Swiss had no cavalry to give chase, and so they let most of the Burgundians run away unscathed, only to discover that the Bold Duke had abandoned his vast riches on the battlefield: 400 decorated tents and precious tapestries, countless items of gold and silver, 400 cannon, 10,000 horses, 600 flags, 300 tons of powder... booty totalling several hundred million francs at today's value, much of which remains on display in Grandson and other Swiss museums.

Soon afterwards, the Swiss defeated Charles again at Murten and conclusively at Nancy, thus eliminating the principal threat to the French throne and, in at least a small way, permitting France instead of Burgundy to grow as a united imperial force in the centuries following.

The castle

Grandson's **train station**, 700m west of the castle along Rue Basse, has only one or two slow trains on the line between Lausanne and Neuchâtel (via Yverdon). It's better to get the regular **postbus** from Yverdon to Gorgier-St-Aubin, which can drop you in Grandson's Place du Château (takes 10min), or the **boat**.

At the castle ticket desk (Mon–Sat 8.30–11am & 2–5pm, Sun 8.30am–5pm; Fr.12; SMP) – which doubles as the tourist office (same hours; ☏024 445 29 26, ⓦ www.grandson.ch) – you're given a follow-the-numbers leaflet. It's worth pausing awhile at the foot of the walls to look out over the lake and up at the massive fortress above; Grandson sees a fraction of the visitors who cram into the Château de Chillon on Lake Geneva, and its past lingers more tangibly in the old stones. (Bear in mind, though, that Wednesday tends to be school-trip day.)

Highlights inside include the Torture Chamber (room 3), with original wheel and executioners' axe; an informative English-language slide-show on the history of Grandson and the Burgundian Wars in room 7; vast quantities of booty from 1476, as well as a life-size mock-up of Charles the Bold's war tent (room 12); the claustrophobic Prison (room 16); and a ramparts walk leading through the various towers and watch-rooms. Accessed by stairs leading down from a corner of the Banqueting Hall (room 15) is an incongruous Vintage Car Museum (rooms 17–19), whose dream machines include Greta Garbo's white 1927 Rolls-Royce Phantom.

The Jura Vaudois

West of Yverdon is a stretch of hilly countryside known as the **Jura Vaudois** (Ⓦ www.juravaudois.ch), characterized by rushing streams (and the remnants of iron-working industries which exploited their power), hidden valleys and ancient cobbled villages. The area lies wholly within Canton Vaud hard up against the French frontier – one of Europe's oldest borders, unchanged since 1186.

Main town of the region is Vallorbe, positioned at the southern end of a pass through the Jura mountains that has been used since antiquity as a route from France southeast to the Grand-St-Bernard pass, and thus into Italy. Railway engineers followed the old roads when they carved a tunnel beneath the Jura early in the twentieth century, forming the last link in a chain of railways that allowed the launch of the classic Orient-Express train journey from Paris to Venice and on to Istanbul. The same route through Vallorbe is used by high-speed trains to this day.

The Jura Vaudois was also a stopoff for medieval pilgrims following the Chemin de St-Jacques from Germany southwest to Santiago de Compostela in Spain: Romanesque and Gothic churches at Orbe and Montcherand and the huge priory at Romainmôtier fulfilled both spiritual and material needs on the journey. Behind parallel bands of hills, and guarded by high peaks at either end, the secluded Vallée de Joux has only a couple of roads, a handful of villages, and some great walking and cross-country skiing routes.

Sainte-Croix

A small village up in the Jura, 19km northwest of Yverdon on a steep and tortuous road, **SAINTE-CROIX**'s claim to fame is its 200-year history of making musical boxes, on show at the absorbing **Musée du CIMA** (Centre International de la Méchanique d'Art), 2 Rue de l'Industrie (guided tours Tues–Sun 2pm, 3.30pm & 5pm; June–Aug also Mon 3pm & Tues–Sun 10.30am; hours limited in winter; Fr.12; SMP; Ⓦ www.musees.ch). The tours, which are in French with English notes available, last an hour and a quarter, and take in the full history, design and development of the art, with demonstrations. Some 6km west of Sainte-Croix is the village of **L'AUBERSON**, with – on much the same lines – the **Musée Baud**, 23 Grand-Rue (July–Sept daily 2–5pm; rest of year Sat 2–5pm, Sun 10am–noon & 2–6pm; Fr.8; SMP; Ⓦ www.museebaud.ch), displaying a Parisian fair-organ from 1900 and other musical figurines. Northeast of Sainte-Croix, a sharp-edged ridge culminates in **Mont Chasseron** (1607m), one of the highest of Jura peaks, commanding a majestic panorama across the whole sweep of the distant Alps.

Hourly narrow-gauge trains climb from Yverdon to Sainte-Croix, terminating at the lower end of Rue de l'Industrie, 200m from the Musée du CIMA, which also houses the **tourist office** (Mon–Fri 8.30am–noon & 1.30–4.30pm; ☎024 455 41 42, ⓦwww.ste-croix.ch). Buses shuttle to L'Auberson. Within Sainte-Croix, there's a good HI hostel, 18 Rue Centrale (☎024 454 18 10, ⓦwww.youthhostel.ch; ❶; May–Oct), with small dorms from Fr.29 and bikes for rent. Of the hotels, *Les Fleurettes*, 3 Chemin des Fleurettes (☎024 454 22 94, ⓦwww.fleurettes.ch; ❶) has plain rooms and some dorm beds, while the pine-shaded *Grand Hôtel des Rasses* in nearby Les Rasses (☎024 454 19 61, ⓦwww.grandhotelrasses.ch; ❸–❹) has spacious balconied rooms facing south to drink in the sunshiny views.

Vallorbe and around

VALLORBE, right on the Franco-Swiss frontier, is these days just a stop on the TGV line between Paris and Lausanne, but in times past this small, rather austere town, loomed over from the southwest by the 700m-high Dent de Vaulion, was the centre of a thriving iron industry. This is commemorated in the riverside Grandes-Forges building, dating from 1495 and now housing the **Musée du Fer et du Chemin de Fer** (Iron and Railway Museum; April–Oct daily 9.30am–noon & 1.30–6pm (closed Mon am); rest of year Tues–Fri same hours; Fr.10; SMP). The main draw is the working smithy, powered by waterwheels on the River Orbe outside. Upstairs is the railway section, where memorabilia from the Venice-Simplon Orient Express do well to resurrect the exoticism of early twentieth-century train travel. There's also a lengthy – and rather good – slide-show (in French only, but you can still enjoy the pictures) detailing the construction of the tunnel from Vallorbe through the Jura.

From Yverdon, several fast buses a day run to Vallorbe, beating the train. Vallorbe's train station is perched on a terrace high above the town; it's a ten-minute walk down to the **tourist office** (☎021 843 25 83, ⓦwww.vallorbe.ch), in the same building as the museum. Their Fr.30 Carte Trèfle covers entry to the Musée du Fer, the Grottes and the Prè-Giroud fort (see below). **Accommodation** is basic: go for the *Auberge Pour Tous* hostel, 11 Rue du Simplon (☎021 843 13 49, ⓦwww.aubergepourtous.ch; ❶), with good dorms from Fr.25. The main street, Grand-Rue, has plenty of inexpensive eating and drinking options, including the pleasant *Le France* brasserie/pizzeria at no. 20, and cosy *Café de la Poste* on parallel Rue de l'Ancienne Poste.

Around Vallorbe

More rewarding than Vallorbe itself is the wild and largely unvisited countryside around and about. Local trains and buses go everywhere but they're rather less convenient than your own transport.

Just over 2km southwest of Vallorbe are some caves, **Les Grottes de Vallorbe** (April–Oct daily 9.30am–4.30pm, June–Aug until 5.30pm; Fr.14), replete with stalactites and stalagmites and an exhibition of minerals dubbed Le Trésor des Fées (Fairy Treasure). Some forty minutes' walk from Le Day train station just outside Vallorbe is the Fort de Pré-Giroud (July & Aug daily noon–5.30pm; May, June, Sept & Oct Sat & Sun same times; Fr.11; SMP), an extensive military complex dug into a hillside in 1937 to defend against possible incursion by enemy forces over the nearby Col de Jougne from France. An innocuous chalet on the surface hides vertical shafts giving access to a subterranean bunker complete with kitchen, dorms and a hospital, capable of supporting 130 people.

ROMAINMÔTIER, a small village in a secluded valley about 14km east of Vallorbe near Croy, has managed to preserve in near-mint condition its fine Romanesque priory church. Switzerland's oldest monastery was founded on the same site in about 450, and the current building was constructed by Cluniac monks in 990–1028. The church (daily 7am–6pm) is approached from the picturesque village street beneath an even more picturesque fourteenth-century clock-tower. As you enter, you pass into the harmonious nave, with its massive piers and a vividly painted thirteenth-century vault. On the left of the choir and chancel, with fourteenth-century frescoes, is the separate Chapel of the Holy Virgin, with a beautiful medieval statue of Mary. The remains of the cloister run along the outside of the south wall.

Continuing the ecclesiastical theme, **MONTCHERAND**, a tranquil village 8km northeast of Romainmôtier with a view over the Orbe valley, shelters a small but notable tenth-century church (daily 8.30am–8.30pm; Oct–April closes 6.30pm). Its most striking feature is a set of twelfth-century frescoes in the apse, depicting the saints Paulus, Ithos, Andreas, Jacobus, Matias and Filipus standing shoulder to shoulder in brilliantly restored colours.

ORBE, halfway between Vallorbe and Yverdon on the bus or train, is a picturesque old town up on a rock, with steep cobbled streets and another atmospheric church, a five-naved effort dating from the fifteenth century. Orbe was known to the Romans as *Urba*, and 2km north of the town, at Boscéaz near the junction of the *autoroute* and highway, are some of the best Roman mosaics to be seen in Switzerland (Easter–Oct Mon–Fri 9am–noon & 1.30–5pm, Sat & Sun 1.30–5.30pm; Fr.4; ⓦ www.orbe.ch). Nearest to the ticket hut is Pavillon IV, sheltering hexagonal mosaics of gods and goddesses, with the central medallions showing the deities of the seven days of the week. Further on, Pavillon III has a countryside procession, led by a trumpeter; and Pavillon II displays an intriguingly complex mosaic maze. Excavations are ongoing.

The Vallée de Joux

About 5km southwest of Vallorbe, the sharp Dent de Vaulion rises to 1483m, standing guard over the secluded **Vallée de Joux**, a long thin valley sandwiched at 1000m between the Grand Risoud pine forest, which conceals it from France, and the parallel Mont Tendre range, which cuts it off from Lake Geneva. This is perfect summer walking country, with many routes along the valley floor beside the **Lac de Joux**, while the thickly wooded valley sides turn into cross-country skiing heaven in winter. The valley has its own, bracing microclimate, reminiscent of Alpine areas 400m higher in altitude: temperatures of -20°C on the valley floor are not unknown in winter, and precipitation tops 1800mm a year. High winds can also rip their way along the valley. It's no surprise that the first people to consider settling in the valley were ascetic monks: even by 1700 there were still just 173 inhabitants, plus 22 bears.

Between the small Lac Brenet and Lac de Joux is **LE PONT** village. In front of the train station is what's left of a colossal hangar, used between 1880 and 1936 to store ice, which was hacked from the lakes and then transported by fast train to Paris, Lyon and Geneva. (In 1927, the hangar was somehow gutted by fire.) Roads run west from Le Pont along both shores of the Lac de Joux; the south road passes through L'Abbaye with ruins of a medieval abbey. Both roads meet at the end of the lake at **LE SENTIER**, chief town of the valley and a one-time watchmaking centre to rival those in the Neuchâtel mountains (such prestigious names as Audemars Piguet, Blancpain and Breguet still make watches in this valley). The Espace Horloger, 2 Grand-Rue (Tues–Sun

2–6pm; Fr.9; SMP; ⓦ www.espacehorloger.ch), has a fine collection of historic timepieces. **LE BRASSUS**, 4km southwest, is pretty, quiet and boasts nothing at all to divert you from the wilds of nature all around. From here all the way southwest to the Col de la Givrine above Nyon is the Parc Jurassien Vaudois (ⓦ www.parc-jurassien.ch), Switzerland's second-largest protected natural environment.

Practicalities

Trains from Vallorbe (connecting with services from Lausanne at Le Day) run along the north shore of the Lac de Joux, terminating at Le Brassus. One **boat** a day in summer does a circular cruise of the lake, to and from Le Pont. A **road** from Le Brassus (open summer only) surfs over the mountains at Marchairuz before dropping down to Lake Geneva.

The tourist office for the valley is in the sports centre at the southern end of Le Sentier (daily 9am–noon & 1–6pm; ℡ 021 845 17 77, ⓦ www.valleedejoux .ch). They have plenty of maps and information for walkers. You can rent ice skates here (Fr.5) for either the indoor ice stadium (admission Fr.6) or, when everyone is skating on it, the lake itself. They also have mountain bikes (Fr.40/ day), kayaks (Fr.10/half-day), a climbing wall, tennis courts and even plain dorms (Fr.15). For hotels, *La Lande* (℡ 021 845 44 41, ⓦ www.hotellalande .com; ❷–❸), in Le Brassus, is fresh and pleasant, as is *Hôtel de Ville de L'Abbaye* (℡ 021 841 13 93, ⓦ www.hotelabbaye.ch; ❷) in L'Abbaye. Camp year-round at *Le Rocheray* in Le Sentier (℡ 021 845 51 74). Eating and drinking is a hotel experience, but for a few brasseries in Le Pont and Le Brassus.

The Broye

The mellow countryside between Yverdon and Bern is named after the River **Broye** which flows gently through the area. Not a great deal happens here, and it's perfect cycling country: reasonably flat, with plenty of small villages and the shores of both the Lac de Neuchâtel and the Murtensee (Lac de Morat) to explore. **Estavayer-le-Lac** is a lakeside resort town with peace and quiet as its main attributes; nearby **Payerne** is home to a splendid Romanesque abbey, while **Avenches** was once the capital of Roman Switzerland and has plenty for ruin-hunters to enjoy. **Murten/Morat**, on the line where French-speaking Western Europe meets German-speaking Central Europe, is a variation on the theme of attractive but staid lakeside resorts with well-preserved medieval centres.

Estavayer-le-Lac

ESTAVAYER-LE-LAC is a picturesque little yachties' town on the Lac de Neuchâtel 19km northeast of Yverdon, with plenty of medieval architecture: the town centre has remained largely unchanged since 1599. Today it occupies a little enclave of Canton Fribourg, surrounded on three sides by Vaud. It trades on two features: the town museum, which has a collection of stuffed frogs, and the climbing roses which cover its ancient stones throughout the summer, giving the place its nickname of the City of the Rose.

It's a ten-minute walk from the station northwest along Route de la Gare to Place du Midi on the edge of the Old Town. Heading east from here takes you past the Hôtel de Ville to the Gothic Église St-Laurent, from where turn left (north) to reach Place de Moudon, the medieval marketplace which formerly looked over the lakeshore. Over to the east is the solid Château de Chenaux, built and added to over 450 years, with towers and turrets sprouting all over; you can wander through its courtyards. South of the church, Grand-Rue heads out of town via the Porte des Religieuses. Partway down, Rue du Musée branches off to the medieval Maison de la Dîme, which houses a diverting museum (March–Oct Tues–Sun 10am–noon & 2–5pm; July & Aug also Mon; rest of year Sat & Sun 2–5pm; Fr.5; SMP; Ⓦ www.museedesgrenouilles.ch). A random collection of bits and bobs – ivory Chinese chesspieces from the eighteenth century, some old playing cards, assorted railway memorabilia – is overshadowed by 108 small frogs, stuffed in the 1860s by François Perrier, a retired captain of the Vatican's Swiss Guard, and posed in glass cases to mimic the social life of the period. It's all utterly pointless, and

△ Yachts at Estavayer-le-Lac

more than a bit macabre; the frogs don't look impressed in the least.

The train station – on the slow Yverdon–Fribourg line – is 600m southwest of Place du Midi, where you'll find the tourist office (April–Sept Mon–Fri 8.30am–noon & 1.30–5.45pm, Sat 10am–noon & 2–4pm; July & Aug also Sun 10am–noon; rest of year Mon–Fri 10am–noon & 1.30–5.30pm; Ⓣ026 663 12 37, Ⓦ www.estavayer-le-lac.ch). Boats arrive from Yverdon and Neuchâtel. The most appealing hotel is 🌂 *My Lady's Manor*, 7 Route St-Pierre (Ⓣ026 663 23 16, Ⓦ www.myladysmanor.org; ❷), a romantic manor house set in its own gardens, with large, characterful rooms (none ensuite). Otherwise, try the pleasant *Hôtel de Ville* in the centre (Ⓣ026 663 92 92, Ⓦ www.hotel-de-ville.info; ❷–❹), with a fine restaurant and terrace.

Payerne

Some 8km inland from Estavayer is the market town of **PAYERNE**, highlight of which is the **Abbatiale** (Tues–Sun 10am–noon & 2–6pm; Oct–March closes 5pm; Fr.3 or more, depending on exhibition; SMP; Ⓦ www.payerne.ch), one of the most impressive examples of Romanesque architecture in the country. There's a wealth of detail in the five-naved church, which dates from the eleventh and twelfth centuries and which stands amidst the buildings of an abbey; its square, turreted **tower**, with a slender **twisted spire**, dominates the town. Within the lofty barrel-vaulted interior, natural light reflects off the variegated sandstone pillars of the nave to set the whole space glowing. Carved **capitals** the transept and detailed **frescoes** from around 1200 on the vaultings of porch and in the narthex are gorgeous. However, the church has not been as a house of worship since 1562, and it's unfortunate that you may well modern art exhibitions filling the space with distractions and the hum of ation.

Avenches

About 10km northeast of Payerne, **AVENCHES** was the capital of Roman Switzerland, at one time supporting a population of 20,000. These days, life in the town is more smugly suburban, but it's well worth visiting, both for the medieval town centre and the extensive Roman remains.

After defeat at the hands of Julius Caesar, the Helvetians founded their new capital of Aventicum in the early first century BC (Aventia was the name of the local Celtic goddess of water). Emperor Vespasian granted it the status of colony in 72 AD, and during the second and third centuries the city wall boasted 73 watchtowers; many of the public buildings of that period – a baths, temples, the amphitheatre, and more – have been excavated. Aleman tribes raided the town around 277, and by 450 Aventicum's glory days were over.

Climbing the hill from the train station, the first thing you come to is the large amphitheatre crowning the eastern edge of the Old Town, well restored and now the scene of an annual summer opera festival (see box). The tower at the rear of the arena houses the excellent **Musée Romain** (Tues–Sun: April–Sept 10am–noon & 1–5pm; Oct–March 2–5pm; Fr.4; SMP). The ground floor is filled with statuary and mosaics, while upstairs are very impressive collections of Roman bits and bobs, sensibly organized and with English notes available. Fascinating details of ordinary life – such as the fact that a glass of wine cost a quarter of a sesterce, while commissioning a statue of the goddess Aventia with an inscription would set you back 5200 sesterces – are filled out with maps and figurines, including a copy of a spectacular gold bust of Emperor Marcus Aurelius (the original is in Lausanne). Dotted around town are seven other (free) Roman sites – the tourist office has a brochure – all of which are well signposted; aim for the Tour de la Cigogne, a gnarled old column standing tall in a field, once part of a temple sanctuary and now almost swamped by suburbia.

Avenches' train station is on the Murten–Payerne line. There are also plenty of buses: the ride from Fribourg is especially picturesque and, as a bonus, passes through Misery – a rather self-satisfied-looking village. Avenches' tourist office

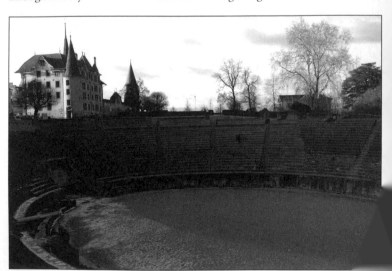

△ The amphitheatre,

is at 3 Place de l'Église (Mon–Fri 8am–noon & 1.30–5pm, Sat 9am–noon; ☎026 676 99 22, Ⓦwww.avenches.ch). An HI hostel is five minutes' walk south, at 5 Rue du Lavoir (☎026 675 26 66, Ⓦwww.youthhostel.ch; ❶; April–Oct), with dorms from Fr.29. The grandest hotel is the *Couronne*, 20 Rue Centrale (☎026 675 54 14, Ⓦwww.lacouronne.ch; ❸–❹), which also has the poshest brasserie around (*menus* Fr.25). There are pavement cafés along Rue Centrale, or you could try inexpensive pizza/pasta in *Tearoom du Musée*, opposite the amphitheatre.

Murten/Morat

Belying its historical resonance for the Swiss, **MURTEN**, 6km northeast of Avenches, has the air of a holiday town, its neat suburban streets and low-key waterfront promenade reminiscent of the English south coast. It's bang on the *Röstigraben* (linguistic divide), though among its 5000 inhabitants, German speakers outnumber French (who call the place **MORAT**). It's also one of the best preserved of Switzerland's medieval towns, and is still encircled by its fifteenth-century walls. These days, offering nothing much to do other than strolling on cobbled lanes, sipping drinks at lakeview terrace cafés and taking the odd ferry, it's the perfect place for a romantic getaway. The Old Town's hotels oblige with a range of "honeymoon" suites.

The town's name is derived from the Celtic word *moriduno*, meaning "lakeside fortress". Fire in 1416 led to rebuilding in stone, a useful move since, in 1476, Murten allied itself with Bern and Fribourg against the Burgundians and found itself facing down a siege from Charles the Bold. The town hung on for thirteen days until a Bernese force arrived to slaughter the Burgundians: 10,000 died, and local legend tells of bones being washed up eighteen years later. A runner took news of the victory 17km to Fribourg, but expired after recounting his tale; his exploit is commemorated by thousands who take part in a fun run between the two towns on the first Sunday in October.

Murten's **Old Town** is a simple three-street affair, full of picturesque medieval architecture. From the castle (closed to the public) – which has a peaceful courtyard with lake views – Rathausgasse leads east, packed with hotels whose rear terraces afford prime views across the lake to the Vully vineyards. Parallel to the south are Hauptgasse, crammed with bars and eateries; and tranquil Schulgasse/Deutsche Kirchgasse. One of the best ways to see Murten is from the ramparts, accessible at a number of points along Deutsche Kirchgasse. The main eastern gate is the Berntor, or Porte de Berne, with a distinctive clock face. Five minutes west of the harbour, just below the castle, an old mill houses **Museum Murten** (April–Oct Tues–Sat 2–5pm,

Arrival, information and accommodation

The **train station** is between the town and the lakeshore, with the **post office** alongside: it's a 500m walk northeast along Bahnhofstrasse/Rue de la Gare to Zentralplatz/Place Central, heart of the modern shopping districts, from where the Old Town is the same distance again northwards. **Boats** dock at the *Schiffländte/débarcadère*, some 500m southwest of the station. The **tourist office** is directly opposite the station (Mon–Fri 8am–12.30pm (Thurs until 8pm), Sat 9am–3pm; ☎032 329 84 84, ⓦ www.biel-seeland.ch). Most **accommodation** is geared towards businesspeople: character tends to take a back seat.

Hotels

Bären-en-ville Nidaugasse/Rue de Nidau 22 ☎032 322 45 73. A creaky, rather shabby place in the town centre. ❷

Elite Bahnhofstrasse/Rue de la Gare 14 ☎032 328 77 77, ⓦ www.hotelelite.ch. Four-star business hotel built in 1930, now renovated in Art Deco style throughout – chic, classy and rather elegant. Two no-smoking floors and cut-price weekend deals add to the appeal. ❹–❺

Goya Neuengasse/Rue Neuve 6 ☎032 323 02 36. Slightly more going for it than the *Bären* in terms of service and decor. ❷

Pension Ring Ring 16 ☎032 322 81 08. A few airy but frill-free rooms above a café on the Old Town's central square. ❶

🏃 **Villa Lindenegg** Lindenegg 5 ☎032 322 94 66, ⓦ www.lindenegg.ch. The nicest choice in town, a dreamy mansion built in 1831 in its own little park in the Old Town, bought by the city in 1985, renovated by three local women and reopened in 1996 as a bistro and hotel. All seven rooms are different, each of them fresh, light and wood-floored, the best (room 4) with a balcony over the garden. ❸

Hostel

Lago Lodge (SB hostel) Uferweg 5, Nidau ☎032 331 37 32, ⓦ www.lagolodge.ch. Pleasant, attractive spot just south of the centre, with its own micro-brewery; bus #4 to Schloss Nidau. Dorms Fr.26. ❶

Campsite

Lindenhof Sutz-Lattrigen ☎032 397 10 77. Decent campsite in this lakeside village, 4km southwest by narrow-gauge train. April–Oct.

△ Bilingual signs, Biel/Bienne

Above Biel/Bienne

A favourite local getaway is to ride the **funicular** from Seevorstadt/Faubourg du Lac, west of the station, up through the forested slopes to the village of **MAGGLINGEN/ MACOLIN** on the ridge 400m above. Even when the town is swathed in autumn lake mist, the funicular can lift you into sunshine. Once you're up there, there's not an awful lot to do, other than to head further up for some hiking trails: you'll be in fit company, since Magglingen is famous as home of the Federal Institute of Sport. With strong legs, you can get 16km west to **Le Chasseral** (1607m), one of the highest summits in the Jura, where you'll find a simple hotel and mountain restaurant, *Chasseral* (☎032 751 24 51), along with great views. Buses run from the hotel down the other side of the ridge to **St-Imier**, which is on the Biel/Bienne–La Chaux-de-Fonds train line.

The Town

Heading from the station along the main shopping streets of Bahnhofstrasse/ Rue de la Gare and then Nidaugasse/Rue de Nidau, the bustle and high-street brand names suddenly fade painlessly away as you cross the line into the cobbled **Old Town**. Burggasse climbs past the old Zeughaus (arsenal), rejuvenated as the city's theatre, and the impressive 1676 step-gabled Rathaus (Town Hall), now police headquarters, into the open **Burgplatz/Place de Bourg**. Quaint old shuttered houses line the square, which centres on the Fountain of Justice, dating from 1714. Continue uphill, and head right to the **Ring**, core of the Old Town and named for the circle of head shakers who would sit here to deliberate on the fate of criminals brought for trial. Head east along arcaded Obergasse/Rue Haute, and then double back onto Untergasse/Rue Basse to stroll past the town's oldest houses.

A couple of the town's museums are worth a look. Museum Neuhaus, Schüss-promenade/Promenade de la Suze 26 (Tues–Sun 11am–5pm, Wed until 7pm; Fr.7; SMP; Ⓦwww.mn-biel.ch), covers local art and history in a jumble of paintings and costumes, while Centre PasquArt, Seevorstadt/Faubourg du Lac 71 (Wed–Fri 2–6pm, Sat & Sun 11am–6pm; Fr.10; SMP; Ⓦwww.pasquart.ch), is devoted to contemporary art and photography.

One of the best boat trips in the region is the Aarefahrt/Croisière sur l'Aar (2hr 30min; Ⓦwww.bielersee.ch), a trip up the River Aare from Biel/Bienne to Solothurn, passing the stork colony at Altreu on the way.

Eating and drinking

The best place for **restaurants** is in the Old Town. Biel/Bienne's sizeable student population ensures plenty of **bars** around the centre, including the grungy *Rock Café* on Zentralstrasse/Rue Centrale. Also check out the DJ nights at the *Gaskessel/Coupole* (Ⓦwww.chessu.ch), an alternative arts centre under a dome in a car park off Zentralstrasse.

Cafés and restaurants

Le Citron In *Hôtel Elite* ☎032 328 77 77. Fresh, attractive restaurant in this Art Deco hotel, serving Mediterranean-style cuisine from a surf-and-turf menu. Expect around Fr.50 for lunch, Fr.75 or more in the evenings. Closed Sat lunch & Sun.

Café Hasard Bahnhofstrasse/Rue de la Gare 4. A small and attractive little meeting-place with juices, coffee, beers, light meals and a genial ambience.

Kreuz Hauptstrasse/Rue Principale 23 in Nidau ☎032 331 93 03, Ⓦwww.kreuz -nidau.ch. Wonderfully relaxed co-operative-run café and restaurant in this pleasant little town contiguous with Biel/Bienne to the south (a short walk, or bus #4). Old wood floors inside, and a garden terrace out back – the food is excellent, organic and veggie (*menus* from Fr.15). Closed Wed.

St Gervais Untergasse/Rue Basse 21 Ⓦwww .stgervais.ch. Lively, friendly, alternative-style joint in the Old Town with quality inexpensive nosh; not the only choice on this street. Closed Tues eve.

Caffè Spettacolo Opposite the station, with coffees and focaccia-style snacks.

Villa Lindenegg Lindenegg 5 ☎032 322 94 66. This hotel restaurant has gourmet evening *menus* (Fr.20) with or without meat, using market-fresh produce inventively and attractively.

Around Biel/Bienne

Walking or cycling through the **vineyards** and wine villages on the northern shore of the Bielersee/Lac de Bienne can be a peaceful way to spend an afternoon; ask for information at the Biel/Bienne tourist office.

From Erlach/Cerlier, opposite Biel/Bienne at the southwestern end of the lake and served by plenty of boats, a footpath leads out for an hour-and-a-half's stroll along a causeway to the **St Petersinsel/Île de St-Pierre**. No longer an island (the level of the lake dropped in the late nineteenth century during engineering work to control water flow throughout the Jura), this little dot of car-free, sun-dappled forest was first populated by Cluniac monks, who built a monastery here in 1127. Its most famous resident was the Genevois philosopher Jean-Jacques Rousseau, who spent two months here in 1765, later calling it the happiest time of his life. The renovated monastery buildings, idyllically set amidst vineyards, now house a gourmet restaurant (*menus* from Fr.20) and hotel (☎032 338 11 14, Ⓦwww.st-petersinsel.ch; ❸–❹; March–Oct), with thirteen characterful and tranquil rooms.

Northeast of Biel/Bienne is the **Taubenloch Gorge**, accessible on bus #1 or on foot from Magglingen above. There's a well-engineered path running through the defile above the fast-flowing River Schüss/Suze for about 2km, and entry is free. Check with the Biel/Bienne tourist office for details of local adventure operators running canyoning trips in the gorge.

Canton Jura

Ignored by most travellers, but well loved by the Swiss themselves, **Canton Jura**, in the far northwest corner of Switzerland, is a rural gem, perfect if all you want from your holiday is to walk or cycle your way through gentle, rolling countryside and dark, fragrant forests, with only the smallest of villages and simplest of hotels (or campsites) to provide material comforts. This little bulge of land has over the centuries been shunted from pillar to post: from the dukes of Burgundy to the bishops of Basel, seized by the Swiss, ruled by the French,

Exploring Canton Jura

Chemins de fer du Jura (Ⓦwww.les-cj.ch) run many of the local trains and buses in the region; their website has full details. The *Carte journalière Regio CJ* (Fr.18) gives a day's travel on CJ's network; the *Railevasion* pass (Fr.46) is valid for any three days' travel in 14. The *Carte journalière Arc jurassien* (Fr.27) has a wider validity, including some mainline CFF trains, extending to La Chaux-de-Fonds and Les Brenets. All are buyable from train stations in the region.

handed to the Bernese, and finally in the 1970s – after decades of political turmoil that briefly threatened to ignite violent conflict (see box on p.194) – granted independence to form its own government. Graffiti throughout the region showing the cantonal flag and the pro-separatist slogan "Jura libre" speak of a turbulent and politically active recent past. There's only a handful of towns, but most, including the cantonal capital **Delémont**, have spent the last centuries sidelined, well away from heavy industry and the major currents of European history, and so have retained a graceful, historic, Gallic air.

More than forty churches and chapels around the canton are decorated with stained glass by modern and contemporary artists, including Fernand Léger; the tourist office has put together an itinerary, with notes, at ⓦwww.jura .ch/vitraux.

Delémont

An ancient town first mentioned in 737, **DELÉMONT** retains much of its medieval centre, and is an atmospheric place to stop over for an afternoon or a day. Its main historical claim to fame was as the summer residence of the prince-bishops of nearby Basel from the Middle Ages through to the Revolution. Last century, the stirrings for Jurassien independence (see box) led to Delémont being named in 1976 as capital of the new canton, but it retains a small-town charm – only around 12,000 people live here – and has good access into the rolling Jura countryside for walks and rides.

It takes five minutes to cross the river and stroll northwest from the station into the Old Town. The main street is Rue du 23-Juin, longer and more impressive than you might expect for a little town, and home to the eighteenth-century **Hôtel de Ville**, set skewed to the road and shaded by a huge tree. This ornate building was the scene, in 1947, of a historic demonstration which sparked the subsequent liberation movement. A few steps west is the **Église St-Marcel**, built in the 1770s in a mixture of the lavish decoration of Rococo and the formal lines of Neoclassical, and with some lovely dark oak-wood stalls. Beside the church is the **château**, built in 1721.

At the western end of the road is the Porte de Porrentruy, one of the old city gates, with the Fontaine du Sauvage and, adjacent, the modest **Musée Jurassien d'Art et d'Histoire** (Tues–Sun 2–5pm; Fr.6; SMP; ⓦwww.mjah .ch). This interesting museum houses the treasures from the St-Marcel church: the star exhibit, prominent and proudly spotlit, is the beautiful golden mitre of St Germain, first abbot of Moutier in the seventh century. It's a shame that his twisted old leather sandals, which are far more evocative, get rather shorter shrift.

Practicalities

Delémont's tiny **tourist office**, 12 Place de la Gare (Mon–Fri 9am–noon & 2–5.30pm, Sat 9am–noon; ☎032 420 47 71, ⓦwww.juratourisme.ch), can help with local odds and ends, but the main office is in Saignelégier (see below). A kilometre east of the centre is an excellent HI **hostel**, 185 Route de Bâle (☎032 422 20 54, ⓦwww.youthhostel.ch; ❶; April–Oct), with good facilities for families, quality food and dorms from Fr.27. *Hôtel du Boeuf*, 17 Rue de la Préfecture (☎032 422 16 91; ❷), is a clean, well-run **hotel** within the Old Town. On the same street you'll find places to **eat**, including *La Cigogne* at no. 7 (closed Tues) serving home-made pasta and wood-fired pizzas. Place Roland-Béguelin, one street west, has plenty of shaded pavement cafés, and is also the scene of the town **market** (Wed & Sat morning).

Discontent and secession

From the 1940s to the 1970s, Switzerland underwent serious political crisis, as a group of disaffected, historically marginalized people from the Jura pushed the flexibility of Swiss democracy to its limits. The origins of the conflict can be dated back to the 1815 Congress of Vienna which handed the area to Canton Bern. Bern welcomed the **Protestants** who lived in Biel/Bienne and the southern districts of the Jura around Moutier, but were powerful enough to ignore the destitute French-speaking **Catholic** peasants of the northern districts around Delémont and Porrentruy. Bernese moved into the region, bringing a new language and culture with them. Economic boom in the nineteenth century brought prosperity to Biel/Bienne yet largely passed Porrentruy by – but any rumblings of discontent in the north were quelled by the extreme hardship suffered by the whole region in the depression of the 1930s.

On September 20, 1947, a Jurassien member of Bern's parliament was refused election to the cantonal government because he spoke French. The outrage that followed led to the formation of a hardline anti-Bern grouping, which commanded popular support throughout the northern districts, and which got enough backing to force an extremely controversial **cantonal referendum** on splitting the Jura away from Bern. The voters of Canton Bern unsurprisingly rejected the proposal. However, it surprised the separatists that Jura too had voted against it: Porrentruy, Delémont and Saignelégier had supported separation two-to-one, but Moutier and its neighbours had rejected it by three-to-one. The francophone, separatist Catholics of the north, a minority within Protestant, German-speaking Bern as a whole, and also a minority within the Jura itself, decided to resort to direct action.

The late 1960s were taken up with obscure and complex attempts by Canton Bern to solve the problem, none of which garnered any support in the Jura. Hardliners became more entrenched in their demands for out-and-out secession, and **paramilitaries** – with their slogan "Jura libre" – stepped up their campaigns, seizing a police station in Delémont and the Swiss Embassy in Paris, sabotaging Bern's trams, and,

Saignelégier and Franches-Montagnes

The stretch of the Jura range within Canton Jura itself is called **Franches-Montagnes**. Following wars between local lords in the twelfth and thirteenth centuries, Bishop Imier de Ramstein granted tax exemptions (*franchises* in French) to the whole area as a way to encourage repopulation, thus giving the area its name. It's a beautiful landscape of rolling green hills and wide meadows flanked by fir trees, and is fiercely loved by the locals: one writer commented, "A Franc-Montagnard who sells off the land for profit is considered a traitor." In the 1960s, when the Swiss army proposed creating military installations in these beloved hills, the locals got together and ensured (by voting) that such philistinism didn't get off the drawing board.

SAIGNELÉGIER is the main – indeed only – town in the region, just a shop or two larger than a village. Opposite the train station is the cantonal tourist office (Mon–Fri 9am–noon & 2–6pm, Sat 10am–4pm; ☎032 420 47 70, ⓦwww.juratourisme.ch), with an array of information, as well as local crafts and bottles of the delectable local firewater – a plum-based *eau-de-vie* called Damassine – for sale. On the second weekend in August, the Marché-Concours National de Chevaux rolls into town (ⓦwww.marcheconcours.ch), a horse market and show occupying an arena south of town with parades, races and celebrations.

There are limitless possibilities for hikes and cycle routes through the countryside around and about: aim southeast to the idyllic Étang de la Gruère lake, in a show of support for Walloon separatists, simultaneously storming the Belgian Embassy in Bern and the Swiss Embassy in Brussels. In 1973, Bern's cantonal government accepted terms for a **referendum on separation**, and on June 23, 1974, over ninety percent of eligible voters turned out, with a majority backing separation.

This shocked the Protestant southern districts of the Jura to the core, and precipitated the formation of a pro-Bern, **anti-separatist bloc**, which threatened violence against the Catholics of the north and demanded another referendum to allow the south to detach itself from the Jurassien independence movement and thereby remain part of Bern. On March 16, 1975, this proposal was carried, but with a majority in Moutier of just 286 votes. Amidst the accusations of manipulation that followed, a pro-Jura demonstration turned into a full-scale riot, with 800 militants involved in an all-night running battle with police. Discontent simmered throughout the year, bursting into violence again in September.

Nonetheless, after a series of commune-by-commune referenda, popular opinion was shown to favour both the formation of a new canton in the north, and the adherence of the south to Bern. The split became inevitable. Moutier remained in Bern, and a new **Canton Jura** came into existence on January 1, 1979. Individual communes continued to shift over the next two decades: in 1989, the residents of Laufenthal voted to leave Bern and join Canton Basel-Land, and in 1995, Vellerat (population 70) voted to leave Bern and join Canton Jura.

As Jonathan Steinberg notes in his excellent book *Why Switzerland?* (see "Books", p.588), it was this minute concentration on opinion within the tiniest linguistic, cultural or ethnic units, as well as a political structure able to take such micro-referenda into account, that meant that the Swiss could address Jurassien discontent, allow it to be expressed (with a minimum of violence and no casualties) and then have the flexibility to incorporate it into a new national order. Most countries facing similar discontent have neither the political structures nor the flexibility to effect similar solutions.

or southwest along the ridge to the ancient village of **LE NOIRMONT**, or north, down into the Doubs valley for the riverside forest trails around the border hamlet of **GOUMOIS** – also known for its canoeing and kayaking.

You can camp at *Sous La Neuvevie* (☎032 951 10 82; May–Oct), 2km south beyond the arena, or at the municipal site in Goumois (☎079 314 19 38; April–Oct). Hotels and pensions abound, in every hamlet and scenic spot. The friendly ☙ *Café-Hôtel du Soleil*, two minutes south of the station in Saignelégier (☎032 951 16 88, Ⓦwww.cafe-du-soleil.ch; ❷), has several **rooms** and a dorm (Fr.25), and doubles as a local arts centre, with concerts and exhibitions as well as good veggie food in their restaurant. *Hôtel du Doubs*, just by the riverside border crossing in Goumois (☎032 951 13 23; ❷; closed Jan & Feb), offers comfortable, rustic rooms as well as excellent cuisine.

With your own transport, you can get to a couple of excellent **restaurants**. ☙ *Le Theusseret* (☎032 951 14 51; closed Wed & Dec–Feb), just uphill from Goumois, is an outstanding restaurant in an idyllic old mill beside a weir, specializing in fresh local produce and melt-in-the-mouth fish (*menus* from Fr.20). The pricier *Restaurant Georges Wenger* in Le Noirmont (☎032 957 66 33, Ⓦwww.georges-wenger.ch; ❺–❻; closed Jan; restaurant closed Mon, Nov–April also Tues) has won national acclaim; the fresh, locally inspired cuisine has a Michelin star, while the hotel embraces a handful of classic, individually styled guest rooms.

Porrentruy

In the heart of the **Ajoie** region – the bulge of Canton Jura that sticks out into France – is the graceful town of **PORRENTRUY**, filled with eighteenth-century buildings; the presence of several schools and colleges lends the cobbled streets a vivacity lacking in towns twice the size. Walking 500m west from the train station brings you onto the main Grand-Rue, dotted with medieval fountains and lined with ornate facades, including the **tourist office** housed in the old hospital at no. 5 (Mon–Fri 9am–noon & 2–5.30pm, Sat 9am–noon; ☎032 420 47 72). Following the street down to the river leaves you a few metres west of the fourteenth-century **Porte de France** and at the foot of the impressive **château** towering above. Its mighty Tour Refouss (daily 9–11.45am & 1.30–6pm; free) gives an expansive view.

Hôtel de la Poste, 15 Rue Malvoisins (☎032 466 18 27; ❷), is a tidy little hotel in the Old Town with pleasant, quiet rooms. The same street has many pavement cafés, including jolly *Aux Deux Clefs* at no. 7 and the *Monkey Bar* opposite, which serves inexpensive crêpes (Fr.5–10). *Au Faucon*, 15 Rue des Annonciades, is a lively student bar, with DJs and bands in the cellar. Don't miss *Guillaume Tell*, 36 Grand-Rue, a combination bistro (serving fondues) and patisserie: they make fresh cheesecake every Friday morning, which is as good a reason as any for spending Thursday night in Porrentruy. In November, the huge Marché de St-Martin is an excuse for scoffing vast quantities of the local pork *saucisse d'Ajoie* at stand-up stalls, along with plenty of local Tête-de-Moine cheese and Damassine to wash it down.

St-Ursanne

South of Porrentruy, the River Doubs loops into Swiss territory for the only time, enclosing a neck of land known as the **Clos de Doubs**: the scenic road from Saignelégier running alongside the valley is dubbed, romantically, the Corniche du Jura. **ST-URSANNE** is a picturesque old walled village on the river, 10km from Porrentruy, blessed with both a twelfth-century church and several hotels. The 1km walk down from the station is lovely, and you approach the village through its eastern, sixteenth-century Porte de St-Pierre. The same road passes through to the Porte de St-Paul at the village's western end, while midway along, an alley branches south through the Porte de St-Jean to an ancient, narrow bridge over the river. The beautiful **collégiale** church in the heart of the village, with its sculptured and painted south doorway, has a Romanesque choir filled with Baroque ornament. Above the nave, which has fifteenth-century frescoes, the vaulting is crowned with carved keystones giving the date 1301, and you'll find fewer more peaceful corners to spend a sunny hour or two than the Gothic cloister alongside.

The **tourist office** is on Place Roger Schaffter (Mon–Fri 10am–noon & 2–5pm, Sat 10am–noon; ☎032 420 47 73). Of the hotels, the *Demi-Lune* (☎032 461 35 31, ⓦwww.demi-lune.ch; ❷–❸; closed Nov–Feb) and *Hotel du Boeuf* (☎032 461 31 49; ❷–❸) are fine choices. St-Ursanne's **Fête Médiévale** in early July sees everyone in costume, with medieval foods and beers on offer, minstrels and musicians, dancers, acrobats, jugglers and fire-eaters, and, to top it all, Gregorian mass on Sunday morning.

Travel details

Full timetables for all trains, buses, trams, boats and cable cars in Switzerland – as well as international connections – are searchable at ⊕ www .rail.ch.

Trains

Avenches to: Kerzers (for Bern; hourly; 30min); Murten (hourly; 5min); Payerne (hourly; 15min).
Biel/Bienne to: Basel (twice hourly; 1hr 5min); Bern (3 hourly; 30min); La Chaux-de-Fonds (hourly; 40min); Delémont (hourly; 30min); Lausanne (hourly; 1hr); Neuchâtel (3 hourly; 15min); Solothurn (3 hourly; 20min); Yverdon (twice hourly; 35min).
La Chaux-de-Fonds to: Bern (twice hourly; 1hr 20min); Biel/Bienne (hourly; 40min); Delémont (hourly; 1hr 15min); Lausanne (hourly; 1hr 15min); Le Locle (twice hourly; 7min); Neuchâtel (twice hourly; 30min); Saignelégier (hourly; 35min); Yverdon (hourly; 50min).
Delémont to: Basel (twice hourly; 30min); Bern (hourly; 1hr 5min); Biel/Bienne (hourly; 30min); Neuchâtel (hourly; 50min); Porrentruy (twice hourly; 25min); St-Ursanne (twice hourly; 20min).
Estavayer-le-Lac to: Fribourg (hourly; 40min); Payerne (hourly; 10min); Yverdon (hourly; 15min).
Murten/Morat to: Avenches (hourly; 5min); Fribourg (hourly; 25min); Ins (for Neuchâtel; hourly; 10min); Kerzers (for Bern; hourly; 10min); Payerne (hourly; 20min).
Neuchâtel to: Basel (twice hourly; 1hr 25min); Bern (3 hourly; 35min); Biel/Bienne (3 hourly; 15min); La Chaux-de-Fonds (twice hourly; 30min); Delémont (hourly; 50min); Geneva (hourly; 1hr 10min); Lausanne (hourly; 40min); Porrentruy (twice hourly; 1hr 25min); Solothurn (twice hourly; 40min); Yverdon (twice hourly; 20min); Zürich (3 hourly; 1hr 35min).
Saignelégier to: La Chaux-de-Fonds (hourly; 35min).
Vallorbe to: Le Brassus (hourly; 40min); Lausanne (hourly; 45min).

Yverdon to: Bern (hourly; 1hr 10min); Biel/Bienne (twice hourly; 35min); La Chaux-de-Fonds (hourly; 50min); Estavayer (hourly; 15min); Fribourg (hourly; 55min); Geneva (hourly; 50min); Lausanne (3 hourly; 25min); Neuchâtel (twice hourly; 20min); Payerne (hourly; 25min); Sainte-Croix (hourly; 35min).

Buses

Avenches to: Estavayer (4 daily; 45min); Fribourg (8 daily; 25min).
La Chaux-de-Fonds to: Le Locle (every 30min; 25min).
Orbe to: Croy-Romainmôtier (3 daily; 10min).
Yverdon to: Orbe (hourly; 25min); Vallorbe (11 daily; 30min).

Boats

Following is a summary of June–Sept summer services; fewer boats run in other months, generally Sat & Sun only, if at all. Full details at ⊕ www .navig.ch & www.bielersee.ch.
Biel/Bienne to: Erlach & St Petersinsel (at least 3 daily; 45min–1hr); Neuchâtel (2 daily except Mon; 2hr 20min); Murten/Morat (1 daily; 2hr 50min); Solothurn/Soleure (at least 4 daily except Mon; 2hr 30min).
Estavayer-le-Lac to: Neuchâtel (at least 3 daily except Mon; 1hr 30min); Yverdon (at least 3 daily except Mon; 1hr 25min).
Murten/Morat to: Biel/Bienne (1 daily; 3hr 45min); Neuchâtel (at least 4 daily; 1hr 40min).
Neuchâtel to: Biel/Bienne (at least 1 daily; 2hr 20min); Erlach & St Petersinsel (at least 1 daily; 1hr–1hr 30min); Estavayer (at least 3 daily except Mon; 1hr 35min); Murten/Morat at least 4 daily; 1hr 45min).
Yverdon to: Estavayer (at least 3 daily except Mon; 1hr 25min).

Basel and around

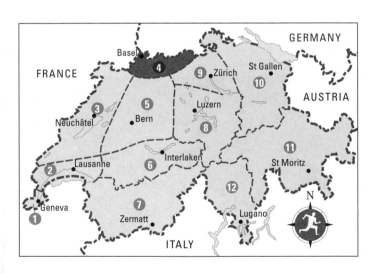

CHAPTER 4 # Highlights

* **Fasnacht** Basel's carnival, an exultant three days of music, parades and merry-making. **See p.210**

* **The Münster** Highlight of a cathedral visit is a peaceful stroll around the adjoining cloisters. **See p.213**

* **Basler Papiermühle** Delightful little riverside museum devoted to printing and papermaking. **See p.216**

* **Museum Tinguely** A stunning home for the mechanical sculptures of Switzerland's best-loved artist. **See p.216**

* **Fondation Beyeler** The city's best gallery, where the architecture sets off the modernist art within to serene effect. **See p.216**

* **Baden** Genteel provincial spa town partway between Basel and Zürich. **See p.221**

△ Museum Tinguely

4

Basel and around

Y ou might expect **BASEL** (**Bâle** in French, and often anglicized to **Basle**), situated on the Rhine exactly where Switzerland, Germany and France touch noses, to be the focal point of the continent, humming with pan-European energy. Basel's voters are the most fervently pro-European of all Switzerland's German speakers but, somehow, the close proximity of foreign languages and cultures has introverted the city rather than energized it: Basel is a curiously measured place, where equilibrium is everything. You won't find anyone shouting about the new Europe here; in fact, you're unlikely to find anyone shouting about anything at all. Even the city's massive carnival is a rigorously organized set piece.

With both a gigantic river port – Switzerland's only outlet to the sea – and the research headquarters of several pharmaceutical multinationals, Basel nurtures its reputation as Switzerland's wealthiest and most discreet city. Its historic centre, dominated by the awe-inspiring Münster, is definitely worth seeing, and the city's long-standing patronage of the arts has resulted in dozens of first-rate museums and galleries, including the stunning Fondation Beyeler. And yet, bequeathed a glittering medieval past endowed with some of the greatest minds of European history (Erasmus, Holbein and Nietzsche, to name just three) and centuries-long access to the best of three neighbouring worlds, it's almost as if Baslers lost the plot when it came to defining their city for today. Most seem to back the standard Swiss default option of gathering wealth in a discreet and orderly fashion, saving money shopping in France and having a better time partying in Germany. Which is all very well, but it tends to leave their own city rather bereft in the process; no town in Switzerland is harder for outsiders to penetrate.

Another fly in the ointment was the "Nazi gold" controversy of recent years (see Contexts, p.574), in which it was indicated that Basel – and, more specifically, the little-known but extremely powerful Bank for International Settlements headquartered in the city – spent the 1930s and 1940s quietly laundering the Nazis' ill-gotten gains under a cloak of neutrality. Evidence of such murky banking practice was received with shock, anger and disbelief in Basel and around the country, and has yet to be fully accepted. Unaccustomed to being faced with pointing fingers, Baslers may take some decades to assess and absorb the accusations.

Some history

A **Celtic** town stood on the hill now occupied by Basel's cathedral in the first century BC, but the city is traditionally dated to 44 BC, when the nearby Roman city of Augusta Raurica (see p.220) was also founded. By 374 AD,

201

It was a Friday afternoon, April 16, 1943, in the laboratories of one of Basel's major pharmaceutical companies, Sandoz. The 37-year-old **Dr Albert Hofmann**, who had worked for Sandoz for fourteen years, was doing research into the various properties of rye fungus, in a search for a cure for migraine. During the afternoon he began to feel peculiar, and went home to lie down. "With eyes closed," he wrote, "I perceived an uninterrupted stream of fantastic pictures, extraordinary shapes with intense, kaleidoscopic play of colours." Unwittingly, Dr Hofmann had taken the first-ever acid trip: he had synthesized lysergic acid diethylamide, or **LSD**, from the fungus and had absorbed the drug through his fingertips.

After the weekend, he decided to experiment on himself with more scientific precision, and so dosed himself with some more LSD. This time, though, his apprehension at exploring an untested area of pharmacology led to unforeseen paranoias. While cycling home, "a demon had invaded me," he later wrote. Thinking that milk would act as an antidote to the drug, he knocked on his neighbour's door to ask for some, only to discover that "she was no longer Mrs R., but rather a malevolent, insidious witch with a coloured mask." He took to his bed. Next morning, though, he wrote, "breakfast tasted delicious and gave me extraordinary pleasure. When I later walked out into the garden, in which the sun shone after a spring rain, everything glistened and sparkled in a fresh light."

Dr Hofmann continued his quiet work into the psychoactive properties of both LSD and other **hallucinogens**, such as magic mushrooms, in Basel, while the drug itself – his so-called "problem child" – escaped the confines of the laboratory. A small band of writers were attracted to LSD as a way of unlocking the secrets of the mind: Aldous Huxley's *Doors of Perception* (1954) is probably the most famous creative work to stem from experiments with mescalin, an LSD derivative. Underground tests on volunteers by the British and American military were so dramatic that subsequent top-secret reports suggested that if LSD could be deployed in a missile fired at the Soviet Union, it could at a stroke put the entire Red Army out of action.

The drug hit the headlines through its role at the core of the 1960s hippy counter-culture: the turmoil it appeared to be causing to US society, with teenagers dropping out of college and discovering alternative lifestyles, unnerved the establishment to such an extent that the US Congress passed a bill criminalizing LSD in 1966. World-wide governments followed suit shortly afterwards. In the late 1980s and 1990s, illegality notwithstanding, a whole new generation of partygoers rediscovered LSD, on a wave which popularized a variant hallucinogen, Ecstasy, and gave rise to club culture.

Massive controversy persists as to the medical uses of LSD and hallucinogens in general (such as cannabis). Dr Hofmann himself, in an interview given in 1993 at the age of 87 to the British *Independent* newspaper, said: "LSD is not addictive, it is not toxic. The danger with LSD is this very deep change in consciousness: it can be beautiful, it can be terrifying. We have integrated alcohol and tobacco, but we've not integrated the hallucinogens. The next step is that it should be put into the hands of the psychiatrists. Fifty years' experience is nothing. For a substance which exhibits such new and extraordinary properties you must have much longer. It should be possible to study this substance properly."

Dr Hofmann's hopes might yet be realized. In 2005, the British Journal of Psychiatry called for a reassessment of psychedelics "based upon scientific reasoning and not influenced by social or political pressure". And to celebrate Dr Hofmann's 100th birthday in 2006, Basel staged an international symposium on LSD, as a prelude to the restart of clinical studies in the US under the auspices of the Multidisciplinary Association for Psychedelic Study (⑩ www.maps.org).

Basilia was a fort, and seat of a bishopric. In 917, the **Huns** sacked the town, but by the thirteenth century Basel had recovered to become a prominent settlement. In 1225, Bishop Heinrich II of Thun built the first **bridge** across the Rhine – ancestor of today's Mittlere Brücke – which coincided with the opening of a road over the Gotthard Pass into Italy, thus ensuring Basel's continuing growth as a natural focus for trade. Plague in 1349 killed some 14,000 people, and just seven years later an earthquake and fire razed much of the city. Shortly after, the two communities on either side of the Rhine – Grossbasel and Kleinbasel – united as a single city.

For almost twenty years (1431–49), the ecumenical **Council of Basel** pushed the city into the European limelight, as the Church set about reforming itself; Pope Felix V was crowned in Basel during the council's deliberations in 1440, and merchants, philosophers, emperors, princes and bishops flocked in, spurring the growth of papermaking, printing, and the development of ideas and trade. Responding to the impetus of the Renaissance, in 1460 Pope Pius II founded Basel's **university**, Switzerland's oldest and a major centre for humanism – home to the philosopher **Erasmus of Rotterdam** in the 1520s and 1530s.

During the sixteenth and seventeenth centuries, Protestant refugees from France, Flanders and Italy expanded Basel's industries but, since the city remained under the thumb of both noble families and the Church, most were not accepted as citizens. In 1831, disaffected residents in the rural communities around Basel launched a **rebellion** against the city oligarchs and after a brief civil war managed to secede, forming their own half-canton of Basel-Land (countryside), separate to this day from Basel-Stadt (city).

Throughout the nineteenth century, a massive growth in industry led to the construction of the huge **port** facilities on the Rhine at the turn of the twentieth century, which still handle a large proportion of Swiss import/export trade. But Basel is best known these days as a centre of both banking and chemical industry: the companies which started out dyeing silk ribbons woven by Huguenot refugees centuries ago are now the world's largest **pharmaceutical** companies, with their headquarters and laboratory facilities still in Basel.

Arrival, information and city transport

Basel has two **train stations** straddling three countries. **Basel SBB** is the main one; most of it is in Switzerland, although platforms 30–36 at the far end, used by trains to and from France, form an area known as **Bâle SNCF** which is in French territory, divided from the main concourse by passport control. Lots of trams pass through Centralbahnplatz outside the main doors; trams #1 and #8 run to Barfüsserplatz and the city centre. Many fast trains from Germany serve Basel SBB, but plenty – including local trains from Freiburg-im-Breisgau – stop short at Basel Badischer Bahnhof (**Basel Bad.** for short), run by Deutsche Bahn (DB) and located within an enclave of German territory in Kleinbasel; passport control separates the platforms from the ticket hall. Tram #6 from outside runs to Barfüsserplatz.

The **airport** (Ⓦwww.euroairport.com) is 5km north in France, shared between Basel (Switzerland), Mulhouse (France) and Freiburg (Germany). A special customs-free fenced road links the Swiss terminal with Switzerland proper, along which express postbus #50 runs to and from Basel SBB station (daily every 15min 5am–midnight; Fr.6.80; Swiss passes valid; takes 15min). Several buses a day link the airport directly to Zürich's Sihlquai bus terminal

– but they must be booked in advance (€12; takes 1hr 15min; ☎0848 660 660, ⓦ www.transferbus.net). A taxi into the centre costs about Fr.40.

By car, the Basel-City *autobahn* exit delivers you directly to parking at SBB station, but car parks in Basel-Nord at the Messe and beneath Basel Bad. station are less outrageously priced. The most convenient cheap deal is at short-term car park S5 at the airport (Fr.15 for 24hrs; max. 5 days).

Information

The main **tourist office** is in the city centre, in the Stadtcasino on Barfüsserplatz (Mon–Fri 8.30am–6.30pm, Sat 10am–5pm, Sun 10am–4pm; ☎061 268 68 68, ⓦ www.baseltourismus.ch), with a branch office inside the main SBB train station (Mon–Fri 8.30am–6.30pm, Sat & Sun 9am–2pm). They both have tons of information, maps and brochures. Best buy is the **BaselCard** (Fr.20/27/35 for 24/48/72 hours), which covers free entry to all the city's museums, plus Augusta Raurica and the Vitra museum, free guided walking tours of Basel and Augusta Raurica, free ferry rides, discounts at a clutch of restaurants, bars and clubs, and more. Ask about the tourist office's good-value **weekend-break** deal (valid Fri–Mon): a double room from about Fr.150 per night, including B&B and free city transport.

You'll find listings and cultural information in the *Basler Zeitung* newspaper, and also in the tourist office's free *Basel Live*, published fortnightly.

City transport and tours

Stay overnight in Basel and you're automatically entitled to a **Mobility Ticket**, giving free tram and bus travel throughout the city for the duration of your stay. Pick up the card when you check in to your hotel.

Basel's public transport – run by BVB (ⓦ www.bvb-basel.ch), part of the TNW Tarifverbund Nordwestschweiz (ⓦ www.tnw.ch) – focuses on **trams**, virtually all of which pass through Barfüsserplatz; buses serve outlying neighbourhoods only. The whole of the city centre is in Zone 10; the airport is in neighbouring Zone 13. Swiss Pass holders travel free. Tickets for a four-stop

Basel's festivals

Basel's huge **carnival** (see p.210), held over three days from the Monday following Mardi Gras, attracts attention from all over Switzerland, as does January's **Vogel Gryff** festival, centred specifically on Kleinbasel (see p.215).

The most prestigious of the city's many events is **Art Basel** (ⓦ www.artbasel .com), the largest contemporary art fair in the world, held at the Messe in mid-June. Although more trade- than public-oriented, it's fascinating to attend (tickets are around Fr.30/day), with major galleries and artists from around the world exhibiting a range of work, inspiring many associated arty happenings throughout the city.

The night before the Swiss National Day – **July 31** – sees a festival of folk music on the Rhine, with stalls, traditional foods and a huge fireworks display, and the last Saturday in October marks the start of Basel's two-week **Autumn Fair**, Europe's longest-running traditional fair, held without a break since 1471 and now metamorphosed into sub-carnival festivities centred on funfairs and street jollity.

Several major events – of little general interest in themselves – tend to book the city's hotels solid: the Swiss Trade Fair, or MUBA, in March; the annual World Clock, Watch and Jewellery Fair in April; and the International Art and Antiques Show in early autumn.

journey (press button "K") cost Fr.1.90, for a longer journey within one zone Fr.3, across two zones (valid for the Vitra museum in Germany) Fr.3.80. A day pass, valid for Zones 10, 11 and 13, costs Fr.8. All these are valid for unlimited changes between trams, buses and local trains within the zonal boundaries. Ticket machines take Swiss coins and euros, but rarely notes. BVB kiosks in the station (daily 5.30am–10pm) and on Barfüsserplatz (Mon–Fri 8am–6pm, Thurs until 7pm, Sat 9am–5pm) provide information and sell tickets.

Ferries

There are three bridges linking the city centre with Kleinbasel, but a more fun way to cross the Rhine – and a method used by many locals – is on one of the **cable-ferries** (Ⓦwww.faehri.ch) that have plied to and fro for centuries (although the boats themselves are newer than that). The most useful, from north to south, are the *Vogel Gryff*, or Klingentalfähre; the *Leu*, or Münsterfähre; and the *Wild Maa*, or St Alban-Fähre. All three run continuously during the day, with restricted hours in winter. Fares are in the order of Fr.1.

The **ferry** company Basler Personenschifffahrt (☎061 639 95 00, Ⓦwww .bpg.ch) runs a host of eat-aboard cruises as well as a couple of scheduled boats to nearby points on the Rhine (May–Oct only), including a round trip to the German border at Dreiländereck (Fr.14.20), and longer journeys east to Kaiseraugst (Fr.42) and Rheinfelden (Fr.48). You can even take a ferry from the city centre to the Museum Tinguely (see p.216; Fr.10 return). Boats depart from Schifflände in the city centre, where there's a BPG ticket booth (April–Oct Mon–Fri 9am–6.30pm, Sat 9.30am–4pm, Sun 9am–2.30pm; rest of year Mon–Fri 11am–6pm).

Taxis, such as those from 33er (☎061 333 33 33, Ⓦwww.33ertaxi.ch), are a great way to get around if you think a Fr.5.60 flagfall plus Fr.3.20/km is a fair and reasonable price.

Tours

Guided **walking tours** of the Old Town start from the tourist office (May to mid-Oct Mon–Sat 2.30pm; rest of year Sat 2.30pm; Fr.15; takes 2hr). Otherwise, you can follow any of five **self-guided** historical wanders around the Old Town, all starting from Marktplatz (corner of Sattelgasse) and marked by small blue information signs: the Erasmus Walk (red on blue; 30min); Burckhardt Walk (light blue on blue; 45min); Platter Walk (yellow on blue; 45min); Paracelsus Walk (grey on blue; 1hr); or Holbein Walk (green on blue; 1hr 30min). All of them are described in a free leaflet, or you can enhance your wanderings with the **iGuide**, a handheld personal computer which brings up pictures and sound (via headphones) for each walk – you can follow one walk all the way through, pausing when you like, or you can dot around between points of interest. The tourist office has iGuides to rent (Fr.15 for 4hr; Fr.22/day), as well as a brochure showing two self-guided **bike tours**. Another option is to roll through the city for an hour on a restored **vintage tram**, with a commentary (in English) describing highlights; the ride starts in front of the SBB train station (Sun 10.30 & 11.30am; Fr.20; reserve ahead with the tourist office).

Accommodation

Basel thrives on the conference and convention trade: the Messe in Kleinbasel is Switzerland's largest exhibition centre, and attendees to major events

△ Streets around the Münster

often fill all **accommodation** in the city (and most in neighbouring cities too). Reserving ahead is strongly advised. As a way to service the tide of expense-account travellers, Basel's hoteliers tend to focus more on providing comforting extras, such as minibars and big-screen cable TV, than on character. You'll also find prices hiked during the week and/or while a big trade fair is on. Modest, inexpensive hotels are rarer than sharks in the Rhine, although the **B&B Agency Basel** (☎061 702 21 51, ⓦwww .bbbasel.ch) controls 150 inexpensive private rooms and furnished apartments in and around the city. All hotels, hostels and guesthouses offer overnight guests a **free Mobility Ticket**, covering city transport (see p.206).

Hotels

Inexpensive

🏃 **Au Violon** Im Lohnhof 4 ☎061 269 87 11, ⓦwww.au-violon.com. Once a convent, then a women's prison, now beautifully renovated to offer comfortable, stylish rooms above a quiet Old Town courtyard. Service is faultless, and they offer discounts for entry to the nearby *Bird's Eye Jazz Club*. ❸

Casa O Sole Mio Gatternweg 41, Riehen ☎061 641 54 16, ⓦwww.basel-bed-breakfast.ch. Fine B&B on the outskirts (tram #6 to Pfaffenloh), decorated in Laura Ashley style, with three separate two-room apartments, a studio apartment, and five B&B rooms, all demonstrating the kind of personal touch no hotel can manage. Keen prices, large breakfasts and free use of bikes make this an excellent choice. ❷

easyHotel Riehenring 109 (no phone) ⓦwww .easyhotel.com. Central, budget-priced hotel, in the same family of companies as the no-frills airline easyJet. What you get for your money is a tiny room with a double bed, a shower, toilet and washbasin, and one towel per person; everything else, including food, drinks, TV and housekeeping, costs extra. Most rooms have windows; some don't (they have air-conditioning instead). Check-out time 10am. Prices start around Fr.70. Tram #2 to Messeplatz. ❶

Hecht am Rhein Rheingasse 8 ☎061 691 22 20. Plain, unfussy "garni" place, with some pricier rooms overlooking the river and both ensuite and shared-bath options. ❸

Rochat Petersgraben 23 ☎061 261 81 40, ⓦwww.hotelrochat.ch. Centrally placed two-star option beside the Peterskirche, with pleasant, if generic, rooms and a modestly cosy atmosphere. ❸–❹

Stadthof Gerbergasse 84 ☎061 261 87 11, ⓦwww.stadthof.ch. Plain and simple little hotel, bang on the main shopping drag. No ensuite rooms. ❷

Mid-range and expensive

Krafft Rheingasse 12 ☎061 690 91 30, ⓦwww .hotelkrafft.ch. Atmospheric old pile on the Kleinbasel waterfront which has had a complete makeover: rooms are now swish and elegant, with contemporary, minimalist styling. Riverside rooms are pricier. ❹–❺

Merian Rheingasse 2 ☎061 685 11 11, ⓦwww .hotel-merian.ch. Affordable quality above the renowned waterfront *Café Spitz*, with spacious rooms furnished in a pleasant, non-traditional style. ❺

Novotel Schönaustrasse 10 ☎061 695 70 00, ⓦwww.novotel.com. Excellent business hotel in Kleinbasel's Messe district: the surrounding streets are dull, but the comfortable rooms compensate with superb facilities, including multi-channel TV and hi-tech bathrooms. Onsite parking is an added bonus. Heavy discounts for early booking and/or weekend stays. ❹–❻

🏃 **Teufelhof** Leonhardsgraben 47 ☎061 261 10 10, ⓦwww.teufelhof.com. Outstanding and highly acclaimed boutique hotel in the heart of the city centre. The prestigious "Kunsthotel" section has eight rooms, redecorated every two or three years by a different artist; if you're prepared to do without minibars or TVs, you get the opportunity to live inside a work of art. The "Galeriehotel" bit, with 25 rooms, is less lavishly done up, and so less expensive, but still reworked annually by a local artist. A breath of fresh air compared with Basel's standard business hotels. ❺–❼

Trois Rois/Drei Könige Blumenrain 8 ☎061 260 50 50, ⓦwww.lestroisrois.com. The oldest hotel in Europe, which began life as a small inn in 1026; that year it hosted Emperor Conrad II, his son Heinrich (later Heinrich III) and Rudolf III of Burgundy – the three kings of the title – who met to thrash out the details of Switzerland's absorption into the German Empire. These days, having received most of the crowned heads of Europe over the past millennium, it's still the haunt of presidents and royalty – who of course occupy the beautiful Rhineside suites. Reopened in 2006 after top-to-bottom renovations. ❾

Hostels

Basel Backpack (SB hostel) Dornacherstrasse 192 ☎061 333 00 37, ⓦwww.baselbackpack .ch. Friendly, independent hostel about ten minutes' walk behind the main SBB train station. Dorms Fr.31. ❶

Jugendherberge Basel City (HI hostel) Pfeffingerstrasse 8 ☎061 365 99 60, ⓦwww .youthhostel.ch. Fresh, modern hostel with single

and double rooms only (all without ensuite bathrooms), located two minutes' walk behind the SBB train station. March–Oct. ❶

Jugendherberge Basel St Alban (HI hostel) St Alban-Kirchrain 10 ☎061 272 05 72, ⓦwww .youthhostel.ch. Pleasant riverside hostel – quiet, spotless and well run. Dorms Fr.31. ❶

The City

The River **Rhine** describes an elegant right-angled curve through the centre of Basel, flowing from east to north and dividing the city in two. On the south/west bank is **Grossbasel** (Greater Basel), focused on the historic Old Town. Glitzy shopping streets connect **Barfüsserplatz** and **Marktplatz**, the two main Old Town squares, while medieval charm is retained in the steep lanes leading off to either side, where you'll find peaceful leafy courtyards surrounded by sixteenth-century town houses, a host of medieval churches, and the majestic steepled **Münster** dominating the skyline from its lofty Rhineside terrace. The Old Town and surrounding districts comprise the main business, shopping and nightlife areas of the city. The university, off Petersgraben, overlooks the Old Town from the west, while the main Swiss and French train stations are about a kilometre south.

On the north/east bank of the Rhine is down-to-earth **Kleinbasel** (Lesser Basel), more residential and less weightily historical than its neighbour, with some laid-back nightlife and the German train station near the giant Messe conference centre some 500m east of Kleinbasel's central Claraplatz.

The **international border** with France is on the west bank of the Rhine, about 2km north of the city centre. The border with Germany is on the east bank, about 3km north of the centre.

Barfüsserplatz and around

The focus of the Old Town is **Barfüsserplatz**, crisscrossed by trams and surrounded by terrace cafés. Rubbing shoulders with the fast-food joints and raucous pubs, on the corner with Steinenvorstadt, is the **Yellow House**, designed by Roger Diener, a yellowish concrete building adored by architects but ignored by the general public. Across the way is the **Puppenhausmuseum** (Doll's House Museum; daily 10am–6pm; Fr.7; Ⓦ www.puppenhausmuseum .ch), with rather fun displays telling the story of the teddy – including plenty of venerable old bears – as well as glass-case displays of doll's houses.

Historisches Museum

Overlooking Barfüsserplatz are the soaring, pointed-arch windows of the **Barfüsserkirche**. This elegant white church, built by and named after the bare-footed Franciscans, dates from the fourteenth century, was deconsecrated in the eighteenth, and is now home to the impressive **Historisches Museum** (Mon & Wed–Sun 10am–5pm; Fr.7; SMP; Ⓦ www.historischesmuseumbasel .ch), devoted to documenting Basel's cultural pre-eminence during the Middle Ages. Once you've absorbed the detail of the monumental **choir stall** (1598)

Basel Fasnacht

Basel is famous around Switzerland and Europe for its ancient masked carnival, or **Fasnacht** (Ⓦ www.fasnacht.ch), a three-day affair starting on the Monday after Mardi Gras.

Some history

The earliest documented record of the carnival is from 1376, although celebrations undoubtedly date back to well before that (earlier city records were destroyed in a fire in 1356): it's said that *Fasnacht* is related to an old word *faseln*, meaning fruitfulness. In the fourteenth century, carnival took the form of **knightly tournaments** held on Münsterplatz, events which may have had an origin in pagan ancestor worship since noble families had been buried in and around the Münster for generations. Through the **Middle Ages**, theologians railed against both excessive drinking at carnival time and the use of devilish masks and disguises: it's no coincidence that the iconoclasm which marked the beginning of Basel's Reformation broke out on Mardi Gras, 1529. For some unexplained reason, over time celebrations were shifted one week later to after the beginning of Lent (Basel still celebrated carnival despite its embrace of Protestantism after the Reformation), and were transformed into a series of **processions** organized by the city's guilds and associations. Drum-and-pipe bands accompanied the display of weaponry, dancing and fancy-dress revelry. Greater organization throughout the nineteenth and early twentieth century resulted in the carnival of today, where some 12,000 people take part under the auspices of several hundred **Cliques**, groups or musical bands, all of which must apply in advance to the Fasnachts-Comité for permission to march.

The night before

On the Sunday after Mardi Gras, thousands of *Fasnächtler* kick off their celebrations at the town of **Liestal**, 17km south of Basel, where, after dark, the **Chienbesen** parade begins, giant bonfires dragged through the medieval town on floats with onlookers brandishing flaming torches of pine branches above their heads in a dramatic, ancient spectacle. The tradition is a long-standing one, described as far back as the sixteenth century, but it's been dogged by controversy, at one time from the Church, which regarded it as diabolic in origin, and in more recent times from the fire service. Despite the raging inferno dragged through Liestal's narrow streets each year, flames as high as the houses and people crammed shoulder to shoulder throughout the Old Town amidst the flying cinders and scorching heat, no harm facing into the church, the highlight of the ground floor is the collection of sumptuous fifteenth-century **tapestries** (press the button to raise the protective blind shielding each one); these vivid, wall-sized pieces were woven to decorate private houses and churches, specifically in Basel and Strasbourg, and are exceptionally rare, both for their artistic quality and their excellent condition. Their imagery frequently concentrates on woodsmen, fabulous animals and courtly lovers – only three of the sixteen pieces show religious imagery – and one of the best is no. 235 (from 1490), the allegorical *Garden of Love*, showing two lovers playing cards inside a summer pavilion. The man has just slapped down a card with the words, "That last play of yours was a good one," while the woman nods in anticipatory triumph: "And it's won me the game!"

Downstairs you'll find an excellent detailed survey of Basel's history, including a board locating ancient buildings, maps and globes galore, the original 1640 **Lällekeenig** (see p.212), and bedchambers and elaborate wood-panelled rooms from the seventeenth century. Head to the back, and you'll come across a side

has yet been done. Neighbouring **Sissach** has similar fiery revels, with the torching of a 10m-high effigy, the Chluris, while in **Biel-Benken** to the west, locals fling burning wooden discs into the night sky in an equally mesmeric fire-orgy termed the Reedlischigge.

Morgestraich, Schnitzelbängg and Guggemuusige

Well after midnight, everyone decamps back to Basel in preparation for the **Morgestraich**, a magical parade of huge illuminated lanterns through the city centre which begins in invariably freezing darkness at 4am on the Monday morning. From lunch time, the various masked *Cliques* parade through the city in a **Cortège**, with much music, dancing and jollity, followed in the evening by masked bands and small groups with fifes and drums roving through the Old Town. The ornately decorated Morgestraich lanterns are left on display in Münsterplatz from Monday evening through to Wednesday morning.

Baslers take their costumes seriously (half-masks and face paint are taboo), and many people spend weeks in advance making huge, cartoonish papier-mâché heads and sewing lavish jester-like costumes. However, it's a feature of Basel's carnival that unless you're part of a performing *Clique*, you have to stay as an **observer** – unlike, for instance, in Luzern, where carnival is an all-in street party. You're encouraged to contribute to the *Cliques'* expenses by buying a **Blaggedde**, a metal badge produced by the Fasnachts-Comité each year in copper (Fr.7), silver (Fr.14) and gold (Fr.45) versions; get them on the street, from kiosks and hotels, or the tourist office.

During the Monday and Wednesday evenings, it's a tradition for locals to recite **Schnitzelbängg**, satirical verses directed at local bigwigs, in the city's taverns and restaurants. Tuesday night sees **Guggemuusige** concerts of comical oompah, played on old and dented brass instruments by bands gathered in Barfüsser-, Clara- and Marktplatz, and musical groups and masked *Cliques* continue to prowl through the Old Town during Wednesday afternoon until nightfall – whereupon everybody turns in for some restorative sleep. Throughout the celebrations, you'll come across places selling *Fasnachtsküchli*, a light, thin round cake covered in icing sugar, and *Fastenwähe*, a kind of caraway-seed pretzel.

If you're serious about attending Basel *Fasnacht*, get hold of Peter Habicht's excellent book *Lifting The Mask* (see p.587), the most evocative description in English of the topsy-turvy few days, replete with personal anecdotes, explanations of otherwise incomprehensible carnival behaviour and, most importantly, plenty of dos and don'ts.

room displaying the **treasury** of Basel cathedral, including two stunning silver-and-copper busts dating from 1270–1325, of St Pantalus (no. 251) and, with an even, almond-eyed gaze, a Buddhic St Ursula (no. 253). Another highlight is a series of paintings showing the **Dance of Death**. The sequence originally formed part of a sixty-metre-long mural, which covered the inside of the cemetery wall of Basel's Dominican convent until its demolition in 1805. The mural depicts, in a graphic reminder of human mortality, an array of people of all different ages and professions on a macabre procession, which leads, eventually, to the cemetery's charnel house.

Marktplatz and around

Shop-lined Gerbergasse and Freiestrasse, as well as a dense network of narrow, sloping medieval alleys such as Schneidergasse (Tailor Street), Sattelgasse (Saddle Street) and Imbergässlein (Ginger Alley), run north from Barfüsserplatz to **Marktplatz**, the Old Town's other main square, crowded every morning with fruit-and-veg stalls. Lighting up the broad rectangular space with a splash of eye-catching colour is the elaborate scarlet facade of the **Rathaus** (Town Hall), the central arcaded section sixteenth-century, the tower and side annexe both late nineteenth-century. Feel free to wander into the frescoed interior courtyard.

At the northern end of Marktplatz is the small Fischmarkt, with its central fountain, just beyond which is Schifflände at the southern end of the Mittlere Brücke, a modern construction at the site of what was for centuries the only bridge over the Rhine between the Bodensee (Lake Constance) and the North Sea. On a facade looking along the bridge, you'll spot an odd little bust of a bearded man: this is the **Lällekeenig**, or Tongue King. The original Lällekeenig adorned the gate of the bridge from the mid-seventeenth century,

greeting all arrivals to the city until the gate's demolition in 1839, and had a clockwork motor so that he rolled his eyes and stuck out his tongue in time with the ticking. He was probably made to demonstrate what Grossbaslers thought of their down-at-heel Kleinbasel neighbours, but these days the city is united, the clockwork original is in the Historisches Museum, and the Lällekeenig still staring along the bridge is a static copy.

From Marktplatz and Fischmarkt, quiet old lanes climb steeply west towards the former city walls; up here are the Gothic **Peterskirche** (Tues–Sun 10am–5pm) on Petersgraben, the plain exterior of which harbours late-medieval frescoes, and more or less opposite, Basel's **university** campus. Among many famous names connected with the university, Nietzsche taught classical philosophy here

△ Rathaus courtyard

from 1869 to 1879. The narrow Spalenvorstadt leads west to the **Spalentor**, most elaborate of the surviving city gates, with massive wooden doors and a huge portcullis. Nietzsche lived round the corner, at Schützengraben 47. The small **Jüdisches Museum der Schweiz**, Kornhausgasse 8 (Jewish Museum; Mon & Wed 2–5pm, Sun 11am–5pm; free; ⓦwww.igb .ch), displays gravestone fragments with Hebrew inscriptions which date back to 1222, as well as interesting historical items from religious and everyday Jewish life. Their short video (in English) on the history of the Jews in Basel is excellent.

Both Leonhardsgraben and the lovely Heuberg trickle on through an old residential quarter to the beautiful **Leonhardskirche**, a Gothic construction built after the great 1356 earthquake with portholed windows and an elaborate

△ Cloister of the Münster

cat's cradle of vaulting within. The gallery is accessible, but only up the tightest, narrowest spiral staircase imaginable. Barfüsserplatz is just down the hill.

The Münster

Sixteenth-century lanes lead up behind Barfüsserplatz to Basel's cathedral, the impressive **Münster** (Easter–Oct Mon–Fri 10am–5pm, Sat 10am–4pm, Sun 1–5pm; rest of year Mon–Sat 11am–4pm, Sun 2–4pm), built in the thirteenth century of red sandstone with a patterned roof and rebuilt following an earthquake in 1356. The tower of St George, on the left of the main frontage, has some white stonework dating from the original church (consecrated in 1019), as well as a thirteenth-century statue of the saint impaling a dragon. Stone carving from 1280 above the main portal shows the cathedral's founder, Emperor Heinrich II, holding a model of the church, with his wife Kunigunde to the left. To the right is a Foolish Virgin, with her Satanic seducer.

Inside, the north aisle holds the tomb of the Renaissance humanist Erasmus. Close by is the **St Vincent panel**, a Romanesque relief from around 1100 telling the story of the martyr who was killed in 312 AD: on the top left, Vincent speaks up for his bishop and is flogged for it; to the right he is tortured and led into a furnace; below, angels carry his soul to heaven while ravens protect his body before it is dumped at sea, retrieved and buried in a proper tomb. The lacy **pulpit** was carved – incredibly – from a single block of stone in 1486. On the north side of the choir, which has some intricate capitals, is the **tomb of Queen Anna**, wife of Rudolf of Habsburg, who chose to be buried in Basel alongside her three-year-old son Karl, in an attempt to make up for her husband's cruelty whilst ruling the town during the 1270s. In the crypt you'll find ninth-century remains of an earlier cathedral along with some late-Romanesque frescoes.

One of the highlights of Basel is a wander through the memorably atmospheric **cloisters** adjoining the cathedral to the south, filled to bursting point with timeworn tombs and memorial stones. You emerge onto the **Pfalz**, an open, tree-lined terraced bastion behind the cathedral choir which overlooks the Rhine and gives views as far as the Black Forest. Carved elephants and grotesque creatures support the external arches of the choir, and round the corner, on the north side of the church, is the **St Gallus Doorway**, a rich piece of Romanesque carving, with Christ at top centre.

Tranquil alleys run northwest from Münsterplatz, amongst them Augustinergasse, with, at no. 2, the **Museum der Kulturen** (Tues–Sun 10am–5pm; Fr.7; SMP; ⓦwww.mkb.ch) housing a massive anthropological collection, and, separately in the same building, the equally daunting **Naturhistorisches Museum** (same hours and ticket; SMP; ⓦwww.nmb.ch).

The narrow lane Rheinsprung leads on to the **St Martinskirche** with, beside it, the little Elftausendjungfern-Gasse, or Alley of the Eleven Thousand Virgins. Its curious name commemorates the martyrdom in Cologne of St Ursula and her legendary company of female supporters. The tiny lane feeds down to the Mittlere Brücke.

East of Barfüsserplatz

From Barfüsserplatz, Steinenberg climbs east. A short way up, past the sputtering Tinguely fountain in the grounds of the theatre, is the **Kunsthalle** (Tues, Weds & Fri 11am–6pm, Thurs 11am–8.30pm, Sat & Sun 11am–5pm; Fr.10, ⓦwww .kunsthallebasel.ch), its big white rooms staging a continual flow of cutting-edge contemporary art shows. The same building houses the **Architekturmuseum** (same hours & ticket; ⓦwww.architekturmuseum.ch), showcasing the achievements of Swiss and international contemporary architects. One of Basel's most impressive recent buildings is the Zentralstellwerk, a giant signal-box sitting beside the train tracks alongside the Münchensteinerbrücke (take tram #10 or #11 from the junction outside the museum a couple of stops past SBB station). Designed by award-winning Swiss architects Herzog and de Meuron, it is a mesmerizing structure encased in shimmering twisted copper sheets.

At the top of Steinenberg, St Alban-Graben heads northeast to the river. The venerable **Antikenmuseum** is at no. 5 (Tues–Sun 10am–5pm; Fr.7; SMP; ⓦwww.antikenmuseumbasel.ch). Chronological displays begin on the top floor and work downwards, with superb Greek and Etruscan pottery standing out on every floor. The upper-floor vestibule of House B has a set of fourth-century BC floor-standing funerary vases from Apulia in southern Italy, one of which is painted with an entertaining scene of three men stealing honey and being chased by a swarm of bees. The basement holds temporary exhibitions, often of Egyptian or Middle Eastern antiquities.

The Kunstmuseum

Basel's world-famous **Kunstmuseum** is at St Alban-Graben 16 (Tues–Sun 10am–5pm; Fr.10, also gives entry to Museum für Gegenwartskunst; free on 1st Sun of month; SMP; ⓦwww.kunstmuseumbasel.ch). It's a rather stern Neoclassical building – all marble floors, high ceilings and grand staircases – which tends to do the art down a bit, but don't let yourself be put off. There's a dazzling array of **twentieth-century art**, including Dali's nightmarish *Perspectives*, roomfuls of paintings by Arp, Klee, Léger, Munch, Braque and the Impressionists, a fantastically attenuated cat by Giacometti, and fluid sculptures in wood by Kirchner and Scherer. In 1967, the Basel electorate voted to use

Vogel Gryff

Dating back to the thirteenth century or so, Kleinbasel's strange **Vogel Gryff** festival (ⓦwww.vogel-gryff.ch) incorporates pagan rituals and customs in the guise of fêting the head of one of the three guild associations of Kleinbasel. It takes place on January 13, 20 or 27, depending on which association holds the baton that year. At 11am, a raft carries the **Wild Maa** (a hairy figure symbolizing fertility) down the Rhine to the Mittlere Brücke; he holds an uprooted pine sapling and dances – with his back always turned to Grossbasel – to an ancient drum march. The **Leu** (lion) and **Vogel Gryff** (griffon) meet him on the bank to the accompaniment of booming cannon, and at noon the three of them stand at the midpoint of the Mittlere Brücke and dance a traditional, highly ritualized dance to the sound of a drum. This is as close as the party gets to Grossbasel, since everyone then heads back to Kleinbasel for the **Gryffemähli**, a luncheon for the members of the three guilds (where the symbolic dance is repeated), and a procession through the streets accompanied by four jingling jesters who collect money for Kleinbasel's poor. During the evening, the party enters full swing, with much drinking and merrymaking, while the three figures continue to dance their odd and mysterious dance in the older Kleinbasel restaurants.

Fr.6 million of public funds to buy two Picassos for the museum, *Arlequin assis* and *Les deux frères* – and then stumped up another Fr.2.4 million to guarantee the purchase. The artist was so impressed by this popular enthusiasm that he personally donated four more works.

The gallery's modern art, and its large collection of nineteenth-century German, French and Swiss painting, is, however, overshadowed by its vast and absorbing **medieval** collection. Dozens of rooms are devoted to works by the prolific Holbein family in particular, including the extraordinary two-metre-long *Body of the Dead Christ in the Tomb* (1521), a painting which obsessed Dostoevsky when he visited the museum on August 23, 1867. He climbed on a chair to get a better view of it, and then started to yell "Holbein was a great painter and a poet!" His wife, who thought he was about to have a fit, had to usher him from the room. The work subsequently popped up in Dostoevsky's novel *The Idiot*, when a character's recollections of it lead him to question the existence of God.

Down to the river

St Alban-Vorstadt continues east to the **St Alban-Tor**, one of the city's thirteenth-century gates. Nearby, down by the river, is the **Museum für Gegenwartskunst**, St Alban-Rheinweg 60 (Contemporary Art; Tues–Sun 11am–5pm; joint admission with Kunstmuseum; SMP), its installations by Frank Stella, Joseph Beuys and others sharing space with recent German painting.

△ Cycling along the river, Basel

215

An annexe, the **Schaulager** (Ⓦwww.schaulager.org) – a vast concrete box, designed by Herzog and de Meuron, located south of the centre at Ruchfeld-strasse 19 (tram #11) – holds part of the collection in storage, accessible only for researchers and during occasional public shows.

A stroll away, in a restored medieval waterfront mill at St Alban-Tal 37, is the **Basler Papiermühle** (Basel Papermill), housing the wonderful Schweizerisches Papiermuseum und Museum für Schrift und Druck (Swiss Museum of Paper, Writing and Printing; Tues–Sun 2–5pm; Fr.12; SMP; Ⓦwww.papiermuseum .ch). The waterwheel alongside, remnant of the growth of the industry in the fifteenth century, still functions, and, in amongst exhibits of paper and typography, the museum stages demonstrations of typecasting, typesetting, bookbinding and – most engagingly – papermaking, where you can work through the whole process yourself, from pulp to final product.

A landing-stage across from the mill marks the St Alban ferry *Wild Maa*, which can scoot you across the Rhine to the north bank for the leisurely stroll east along Solitude Promenade to the Tinguely Museum.

Museum Tinguely

On the north bank of the Rhine, in Solitude Park under the Wettsteinbrücke – and also reached by ferry from Schifflände in the city centre – is the outstanding **Museum Tinguely** (Tues–Sun 11am–7pm; Fr.10; Ⓦwww.tinguely.ch), occupying a building designed by the celebrated Swiss architect Mario Botta that is a work of art on its own terms. Jean Tinguely, who was born in Fribourg in 1925 and died in Bern in 1991, is perhaps Switzerland's best-loved artist, a maverick postmodernist who broadened the confines of static sculpture to incorporate mechanical motion. Living for years on a farm in the Swiss countryside with his long-time partner and fellow artist Niki de St-Phalle, Tinguely used scrap metal, plastic and bits of everyday junk to create room-sized Monty-Pythonesque machines that – with the touch of a foot-button – judder into life, squeaking, clanking and scraping in entertaining parody of the slickness of our modern performance-driven world. Most are imbued with an irreverent sense of humour (*Klamauk*, or Din, is a moving tractor complete with banging bells and cymbals, smoke, smells and fireworks), but some, such as *Mengele Dance of Death*, are darkly apocalyptic. Elsewhere in the city, a Tinguely fountain spits and burbles outside the Kunsthalle.

Fondation Beyeler

If you had to pick just one of Basel's many top-rated museums to visit, go for the gallery run by **Fondation Beyeler**, at Baselstrasse 101 in the northeastern suburb of Riehen (daily 10am–6pm, Wed until 8pm; Fr.21; reduced fee Fr.12 applies all day Mon and after 5pm on Wed; tram #6 to Riehen Dorf; Ⓦwww .beyeler.com). A masterfully elegant building, designed by Renzo Piano, houses a small but exceptionally high-quality art collection featuring some of the best works by some of the twentieth century's best artists – Picasso, Giacometti, Warhol, Rothko, Rodin, Klee, Kandinsky, Bacon, Miró and more. Both Matisse's paper cutouts (*Nu bleu* and others) and Mondrian's geometric abstractions – familiar from innumerable posters and T-shirts – still have the power to startle as full-size originals, as do Mark Tobey's crazed *White Journey* and *Oncoming White*.

For some gentle relief, sink into a huge white sofa opposite a giant Monet to indulge in dreamy contemplation both of the waterlilies in front of you and, through the floor-to-ceiling window, the watery gardens outside.

Swiss
cheese and chocolate

Cheese is an institution in Switzerland, with individual varieties savoured like ales in Britain or wines in France. Some are still made in the traditional way – by hand on summer mountain pastures – and so represent the essence of Swissness, with many being exported. Chocolate, meanwhile, is also a way of life: the Swiss eat a world-beating 11.6kg per person each year, compared with 9.2kg in the UK and 5.4kg in the US. Swiss chocolate is held to be the best in the world, rich with cocoa butter, super-smooth and above all, creamy. Like cheese, chocolate stands as one of the iconic Swiss exports.

Origins

Cheese has been around in Switzerland at least since the Romans. For centuries cheesemaking was a skill of mountain farmers, isolated for the summer months with their herds, but these days some twelve hundred village dairies are in daily operation processing fresh milk from local cows. Pasteurization is frowned upon by most cheesemakers, who claim it undermines the body and aroma of the cheese; all Swiss cheese is made from **raw milk** unless otherwise stated (and is thus not a good idea for pregnant women).

Pastureland, Affoltern

For years, Switzerland had no system controlling use of the names of its cheeses. In 2001 an AOC mark (Appellation d'Origine Contrôlée) was established – too late, in many cases. Swiss Emmental now comprises only 2.5 percent of world Emmental production, and must rely on the wording "Emmentaler Switzerland" to identify it in the marketplace.

Alpine cheeses

Most cheese is now produced in the valleys, but the tradition of making **Alpine cheese** (*Bergkäse* or *Alpkäse*, *fromage des alpes*, *formaggio alpe*) continues over the short summer on high pastures.

Emmental dairy

Only cheese which has been made on the alp from raw milk processed from cows fed on fresh grass, wildflowers and clover can qualify for the Bergkäse name. Such cheeses are produced by hand, allowed to ripen for a few months and then handed out to local farmers at the end of the summer proportionately according to how many head of cattle they own. Many are sold to specialist cheese shops and market stalls around the country, where they are much in demand for their richness and individual nuances of flavour. Check out ⓦwww .switzerland-cheese.com for the full story.

Top 10 Swiss cheeses

- **Appenzeller** ⓦwww.appenzeller.ch. Family name for some of the world's smelliest cheeses. The most pungent, known as Räss, gains its odour from being brushed with a herb-and-brine marinade throughout the ripening process. Hugely popular within Switzerland but little known outside.
- **Emmental** ⓦwww.emmentaler.ch. The holey mousetrap classic, known simply as "swiss" in the US. King of Swiss cheeses, with a massive 55,000 tonnes produced annually in Emmental and across the German-speaking lowlands. Although it comes in various grades, it tends to be mild, and has a subtle, nutty flavour.
- **Gruyère** ⓦwww.gruyere.com. Smooth, rich and creamy-tasting hard cheese, with a distinctive salty-dry sharpness that makes it the favourite of the Swiss themselves. A prime ingredient in fondue, and exported worldwide.
- **Raclette** ⓦwww.raclette-suisse.ch. Spicy, easily meltable cheese produced throughout Switzerland for the popular Alpine winter dish raclette: melted cheese served with boiled baby potatoes and silverskin onions.
- **Sbrinz** ⓦwww.sbrinz.ch. Originating in Brienz, but now produced around Luzern, this is Switzerland's Parmesan, matured over three years – crumbly, grainy and powerful.
- **Schabziger** (Sapsago) ⓦwww.schabziger.ch. Distinctive green conical cheese made in Glarus for centuries according to the same recipe, using a herb known as melilot that was originally imported from the Middle East by returning Crusaders.
- **Tête de Moine** ⓦwww.tetedemoine.ch. First made at Bellelay monastery in the Jura in the twelfth century, but gleefully renamed "Monk's Head" following widespread guillotining during the French Revolution. Today, it's still made only in the Jura, at just nine dairies. The small cylinders of aromatic, spicy cheese are spiked and then shaved by hand into tissuey rosettes at the table with a special revolving blade called a Girolle.
- **Tilsiter** ⓦwww.tilsiter.ch. Creamy, full-flavoured semi-hard cheese developed by Swiss emigrés in Tilsit in eastern Prussia in the late nineteenth century, and brought to Switzerland shortly after. Produced in the eastern cantons bordering the Bodensee.
- **Vacherin Fribourgeois** ⓦwww.vacherin.ch. A recipe reputed to have been brought back from Catalonia by a Swiss monk in the thirteenth century, and produced only in Canton Fribourg since then. The fondue cheese par excellence.
- **Vacherin Mont d'Or** ⓦwww.vacherin-montdor.ch. A mild, creamy soft cheese made only in winter at fifteen dairies in the Jura Vaudois.

Taking a dip: fondue

Confectioner's counter, Zürich

Swiss chocolate

Many of the pioneers of chocolate-making were Swiss. In 1819, François-Louis Cailler started production at Vevey, soon followed by Philippe Suchard in Neuchâtel. Until the 1870s, all chocolate was dark and bitter; in 1875, Vevey-based Daniel Peter (aided by his neighbour Henri Nestlé) invented milk chocolate, and then, in 1879, Rodolphe Lindt of Bern invented "conching", a process which created the smooth, melting chocolate familiar today. Jean Tobler, also of Bern, was another pioneer.

Their names live on. The Swiss food giant Nestlé today incorporates the Cailler marque, Kraft/Philip Morris controls brands such as Toblerone, Suchard and Milka, while Lindt remains an independent concern.

As well as robust daily consumption – the chocolate aisle in Swiss supermarkets is quite a sight – Switzerland has a long tradition of confectioners producing hand-filled luxury chocolates for special occasions. Aside from chocolate bunnies at Easter, you'll see chocolate chestnuts in autumn and chocolate flowers in spring. *Chocolatiers* in the Jura make chocolate watches, while chocolate bears are a Bernese favourite.

Chocolate factories

Several Swiss chocolate factories are open for public visits, including:
- **Alprose** in Caslano, near Lugano (p.558)
- **Maestrani** in Flawil, near St Gallen (p.465)
- **Nestlé** in Broc, near Gruyères (p.137)

Don't miss the "**Swiss Chocolate Train**" – see p.138.

Sumptuous Swiss chocolate

Three Countries' Corner

One of Basel's curiosities is its location at the meeting-point of France, Germany and Switzerland. If you take tram #8 to its terminus amongst the warehouses and shipping cranes at Kleinhüningen, cross to the north bank of the River Wiese, head left 200m to the Rhine, then right (north) along a spit of land beside more warehouses and train sidings for 300m, you'll come to **Dreiländereck** (Three Countries' Corner), marked by a futuristic rounded steel-and-glass building. This is the *Restaurant Dreiländereck* (☎061 639 95 40, ⓦwww.dreilaendereck.ch), a pricey and rather soulless place for a meal, but not bad for a riverside coffee and bun. Just beyond, on the very nose of the spit of land, is a tall, slender sculpture pointing the way west to the French bank of the Rhine, north to the German customs shed 50m away, and south into Switzerland. Unfortunately, as you might have predicted, everything looks more or less the same on all shores. Boats depart from beside the restaurant to take you back to Basel Schifflände.

Vitra Design Museum

Across the border in Germany, 10km north of Basel, is the small town of **WEIL-AM-RHEIN**, unremarkable but for being the location of Vitra, a famous design company which collaborates with top international designers to produce office and home furniture, and whose premises – on an out-of-town greenfield site – are the work of some of the world's leading contemporary architects. If you're halfway interested in design, you'll love the **Vitra Design Museum** (Charles Eames Strasse 2; Tues–Sun 11am–6pm; €7.50; ⓦwww.design-museum.de). Bus #55 from Basel Bad. station takes twenty minutes to drop you outside the museum (passport needed); a Fr.3.80 two-zone transport ticket is valid, but Swiss passes and the free mobility ticket you get from your hotel are not.

The building is engaging enough to start with, a teetering, almost Cubist concoction by US architect Frank O. Gehry, while inside are temporary exhibitions on various themes of design, anything from furniture – with original chairs by Frank Lloyd Wright, Charles and Ray Eames, Philippe Starck and others – to lighting or industrial design. It's also possible to join a two-hour guided **architectural tour** of the array of avant-garde buildings comprising the Vitra site (Tues–Sun noon & 2pm; €9, joint ticket with museum €13), which includes two factory units by Nicholas Grimshaw, an elegant, award-winning fire station by Zaha Hadid (now used as an extension to the museum), Tadao Ando's serene conference centre and Alvaro Siza's assembly hall.

Eating and drinking

Drawing influences from the cuisines of France and Germany into its native Swiss culinary tradition, Basel manages deftly to sit on the fence as far as **eating and drinking** go. Beer and sausages is the snack of choice, but it's equally possible to find venues to savour classic French cuisine and, if the city could be said to have a local speciality, it's salmon (originally plucked from the Rhine but these days more likely to be imported) marinaded in the fruity local white wine and topped with fried onions.

Cafés and café-bars

There are plenty of **cafés** and *Bierstuben* around Marktplatz and Barfüsserplatz, with nearby Steinenvorstadt also core snacking territory. Perfect accompaniment to a Basel teatime is the local speciality *Leckerli*, a melt-in-the-mouth ginger biscuit made with honey, spices, almonds and candied orange- and lemon-peel: buy over-the-counter at the Läckerli-huus patisserie at Gerbergasse 57 or in *Café Spitz* (see "Restaurants").

Grossbasel

Fumare non fumare Gerbergasse 38 ⓦ www .mitte.ch. Cool, high-ceilinged espresso bar on a people-watching junction, also with its own beer – one side is smoking, one non-smoking (hence the name). Open late.

Paddy Reilly's Steinentorstrasse 45. Standard Irish pub, Guinness and all, also serving up fish and chips and shepherd's pie for around Fr.16.

Pfalz Münsterberg 11 ⓦ www.salat-laden.ch. Tiny, bright nook, with excellent fresh juices, sandwiches, quiches and a salad buffet. Closed Sat & Sun.

Teufelhof Leonhardsgraben 47 ⓦ www.teufelhof .ch. Supremely trendy wine bar attached to the art-hotel of the same name, with a wide range of bottles to sample and a clientele that knows it's living at the city's artistic cutting edge.

Zum Isaak Münsterplatz 16 ⓦ www .zum-isaak.ch. A tranquil, much-loved tea-drinkers' café and cellar-theatre that knows its Darjeeling from its Lapsang Souchong, and also offers lovingly prepared snacks and full meals. Also with a courtyard terrace. Closed Mon.

Zum Roten Engel Andreasplatz 15. Cosy den on a secluded Old Town courtyard, with trestle tables outside and amiable, alternatively minded regulars scoffing veggie snacks, fresh juices and full meals (Fr.16).

Kleinbasel

El Platanero Webergasse 21 ⓦ www.platanero.ch. Incongruously exuberant little corner deli-café, with two or three tables for *chorizo picante con arroz* and fried bananas, with red-hot salsa bottled on the tables and playing on the stereo.

Fischerstube Rheingasse 45 ⓦ www .uelibier.ch. Excellent backstreet beerhall, full of atmosphere, that brews its own beers as a snub to the big-name breweries and so attracts dedicated, single-minded drinkers. Salted pretzels hanging from wooden stands on every table, a dark, smoky interior, rich, powerful beer plus a uniquely hearty clientele make for a memorably convivial evening.

Grenzwert Rheingasse 3. Cool, jazzy, spotlit little bar, attracting black-clad Kleinbaslers by the score.

Hirscheneck Lindenberg 23 ⓦ www.hirscheneck .ch. Graffitied budget café-bar-restaurant, co-op owned and popular with a rough-edged crowd, with loud music and simple food in generous portions (Fr.15).

Kaserne Klybeckstrasse 1b ⓦ www .restaurantkaserne.ch. An alternative-style hangout, with shady outdoor trestle tables and benches, offering veggie *menus* from Fr.16 and a very popular weekend brunch buffet that exemplifies the difference between laid-back Kleinbaslers and their more traditional neighbours across the river. The evening bar section retains much the same atmosphere, on Tuesdays becoming Basel's premier gay and lesbian meeting place. Closed Mon.

Zum Goldenen Fass Hammerstrasse 108. Small but very popular bar attached to a restaurant (see below), regularly packed.

Restaurants

The host of international visitors to Basel with access to high-end expense accounts pushes up **restaurant** costs, but it's also not hard to uncover cosy local eateries for home-cooked fare in all corners of the city centre. Aside from these listed, you'll find straightforward places to nosh on all the main squares, including a *Mövenpick* brasserie on Marktplatz, although we've bypassed the clutch of rather stiff restaurants within all the big business hotels around the Messe.

Inexpensive

Café Damas Steinenberg 23. Small Arabic eatery on one side of Barfüsserplatz, offering takeaway falafel and kebabs, as well as sit-down dishes like *magloubah* (chicken with rice).

Country Life Sattelgasse 3 ⓦ www.countrylife.ch. Small veggie and wholefood diner off Marktplatz for weekday lunches only (*menus* Fr.17–20). Closed Sat & Sun.

Manora Greifengasse. Self-service restaurant in this department store chain (see p.56).

Mr Wong Steinenvorstadt 3 ⓦ www.mister-wong .ch. Popular fast-food joint just off Barfüsserplatz that piles your dish high with fresh-cooked Asian fare for Fr.12 or so. There's another branch by the SBB train station.

Pinar Herbergsgasse 1 ⓦ www.restaurant-pinar .ch. Simple Turkish neighbourhood diner, with inexpensive *pide* (Turkish pizza). Closed Sun.

Mid-priced and expensive

🏃 **Au Violon** Im Lohnhof 4 ⓣ 061 269 87 11, ⓦ www.au-violon.com. Very pleasant brasserie in a renovated old building near the Leonhardskirche, offering seasonal specialities prepared with care. *Menus* from Fr.20. Closed Sun & Mon.

Bruderholz-Stucki Bruderholzallee 42 ⓣ 061 361 82 22, ⓦ www.stucki-bruderholz.ch. One of Switzerland's best-known restaurants, awarded a Michelin star for its classic style and inventive touches. Expect *menus* starting from Fr.85 – if you can book far enough ahead to secure a table. Closed Sun & Mon.

Café Spitz In *Hotel Merian*, Rheingasse 2 ⓣ 061 685 11 11, ⓦ www.hotel-merian.ch. Historic building in the Kleinbasel district, with a fine riverside terrace and the best fish in Basel, if not Switzerland. Fr.30 upwards. No closing day.

🏃 **Gifthüttli** Schneidergasse 11 ⓣ 061 261 16 56, ⓦ www.gifthuettli.ch. The best place for traditional local cooking (even the menu is in Basel dialect), whether in the standard *Stube* downstairs or the more formal restaurant upstairs. They specialize in *cordon bleus* – slabs of cheese-slathered meat – with thirteen choices (around Fr.33), as well as plenty of other Swiss beltbulgers. Closed Sun.

Gleich Steinenvorstadt 23 ⓣ 061 261 48 83, ⓦ www.vegetarisches-restaurant.ch. Upscale, very genteel vegetarian restaurant, with nothing but the tinkling of cutlery to disturb the low hum of discreet chat. Closed Sat & Sun.

Kunsthalle Steinenberg 7 ⓣ 061 272 42 33, ⓦ www.restaurant-kunsthalle.ch. Contemporary art gallery with a leafy terrace café favoured by Basel's sizeable crowd of arty literati. The restaurant section is a reliable city-centre choice, open daily with 600 covers and a range of *menus* from Fr.20 upwards.

Teufelhof Leonhardsgraben 47 ⓣ 061 261 10 10, ⓦ www.teufelhof.ch. Gourmet restaurant ("Bel Etage") attached to a super-trendy design hotel. The food is of impeccable quality, although the cuisine is like the art: avant-garde. No classics here, with a constantly changing menu marrying diverse flavours and styles, with panache. A broad array of wines by the glass and bottle complete the picture. Expect to pay well over Fr.100 a head. Closed Sat lunch, Sun & Mon.

Wilhelm Tell Spalenvorstadt 38 ⓣ 061 261 15 38. Cosy, quiet den for solid Swiss fare – *rösti*, sausages and all, from Fr.15. Closed Sun.

Zum Goldenen Fass Hammerstrasse 108 ⓣ 061 693 11 11. Quality formal restaurant with an informal air, in a Kleinbasel residential neighbourhood. Excellent, top-quality organic food, lightly prepared (plus veggie options), with lunchtime *menus* around Fr.20, evening ones double that.

Zum Goldenen Sternen St Alban-Rheinweg 70 ⓣ 061 272 16 66, ⓦ www.sternen-basel.ch. Gracious old riverside wood-beamed inn, restored perfectly, serving upmarket, old-fashioned French cuisine in the banqueting room and the waterfront garden terrace, with a number of highly regarded fish dishes. Expect to pay Fr.25 and up. No closing day.

Nightlife and entertainment

You wouldn't really come to Basel for the **nightlife**: even the locals tend quite often to prefer skipping across the border to nearby towns in Germany or France to let their hair down.

The Basel Symphony (ⓦ www.sinfonieorchesterbasel.ch) and Chamber (ⓦ www.kammerorchesterbasel.com) orchestras both perform at the central Stadtcasino, along with a host of guest performers. The Musik–Akademie, Leonhardsstrasse 6 (ⓦ www.musakabas.ch), has an international reputation, often presenting concerts and recitals from students and visiting soloists. Basel's main draw is its burgeoning theatre scene – universally in German; the celebrated Baseldytschi Bihni, Im Lohnhof 4 (ⓦ www.baseldytschibihni.ch), offers a truly incomprehensible evening of drama in the local dialect.

Clubs and music venues

Atlantis Klosterberg 13 ⓦ www.atlan-tis.ch. Universally known as "Tis", and the most popular venue in Basel, hosting live bands and dance nights, generally with a Fr.15 entrance. Closed Sun & Mon.

Babalabar Gerbergasse 4. City-centre club, with plenty of variation in dance styles (nightly), and famed all-nighters (Sat). Undergoing rebuilding at the time of writing.

Bird's Eye Kohlenberg 20 ⓦ www.birdseye.ch. Live jazz every weekend (Thurs–Sun), jazz DJ-ing

the rest of the week – very popular, very lively. Around Fr.15.

Hirscheneck Lindenberg 23 ⓦ www.hirscheneck .ch. Grungy hardcore, metal and ska acts in this café-bar venue, generally on weekends.

Kaserne Klybeckstrasse 1b ⓦ www.kaserne-basel .ch. Focus of Kleinbasel nightlife, a café-bar with adjacent venue for live bands, DJs, readings and happenings. Fr.10–15.

Kuppel Binningerstrasse 14 ⓦ www.kuppel.ch. Lively club for a range of music, plus salsa nights.

Listings

Bike rental At the station (daily 7am–9pm).

Books Bergli Bookshop, Rümelinsplatz 19 ⓦ www .bergli.ch, near Marktplatz, is the hub of Basel's sizeable English-speaking community, with a broad range of books in English plus community information and regular events. Bider & Tanner, Aeschenvorstadt 2, is the city's top bookshop, a multi-department outlet with a diverse English-language section.

Flights Flight enquiries from Basel-Mulhouse ☎ 061 325 31 11, ⓦ www.euroairport.com.

Gay and lesbian life You'll generally find livelier scenes in nearby Freiburg and Mulhouse. The local support group HABS (ⓦ www.habs.ch) has information and links, but *Kaserne*, Klybeckstrasse 1, is the place to start, with its popular Tuesday evening gathering named *Zisch*.

Lost property SBB station ☎ 051 229 24 67; Bad. station ☎ 061 690 12 51; on a tram, bus or on the street ☎ 061 267 70 34.

Markets Basel's main fruit and veg market is in Marktplatz (Mon–Sat mornings; also Mon, Wed & Fri afternoons); otherwise, check out the flea markets in Barfüsserplatz (2nd & 4th Wed in month) and Petersplatz near the university (Sat).

Medical facilities 24-hour emergency room at Kantonsspital Basel Universitätsklinik, Hebelstrasse 30 ☎ 061 265 25 25.

Post office The most central office is on Rüdengasse, with another near the station.

Train information Swiss: Basel SBB ☎ 0900 300 300, ⓦ www.rail.ch. French: Bâle SNCF ☎ 0900 571 056, ⓦ www.sncf.com. German: Basel Bad. ☎ 061 690 11 11, ⓦ www.bahn.de.

Around Basel

There's little to stop for in the countryside around Basel, known as the Baselbiet, although on a journey south you may find yourself having to change trains at **Olten**, beyond the Hauenstein range in Canton Solothurn, which has a quiet, attractive old quarter. An impressive set of Roman ruins stands on the Rhine a short boat-ride east of Basel at **Augusta Raurica**, while further east, just fifteen minutes from the outskirts of Zürich, is the comfortable spa town of **Baden**.

Augusta Raurica

In its heyday, **AUGUSTA RAURICA** – a Roman Rhineside provincial capital 20km east of Basel near the modern village of **Kaiseraugst** – was home to some twenty thousand people. These days it comprises the largest set of Roman ruins in Switzerland, and is an easy day-trip from Basel.

Augusta was founded at the same time as Basel, 44 BC, in the territory of the Gallic Raurici tribe. During the first and second centuries AD it was a prosperous city, but was virtually destroyed by an invasion of the Alemanni tribes around 260 AD. Many of its stones were pilfered during the Middle Ages. Exploration of the site has been continuous for more than a century, and has uncovered the best-preserved classical theatre north of the Alps, temples, a forum, taverns, many public buildings and more.

Focus of the site, well signposted from all over the village, is the **Römermuseum** (Roman Museum; Glebenacherstrasse 17; Mon 1–5pm, Tues–Sun 10am–5pm; Nov–Feb closed noon–1.30pm; Fr.7; SMP; Ⓦ www.augusta -raurica.ch). If you can fight your way through the stream of school parties, you'll find a well-laid-out display of finds from the site, including a full reconstruction of a Roman house. The ticket desk can give you a leaflet showing a map of the whole site and recommended walks through the ruins (which are open and **free**), spreading out around the museum and down to the river. The impressive 10,000-seat **theatre** is opposite the museum, still under excavation and renovation, with a small sculpture garden to one side. Schönbuhl Hill in front of the theatre is topped by a **temple**. Some 200m south of the theatre is a large **amphitheatre**, with to the east of the theatre the **forum** and an exhibition of mosaics in the basement of the **curia** (Town Hall). Further east are taverns, potteries and houses in varying states of crumble. Down on the riverbank beside the boat jetty, 500m north, is an enclosed **fortress**, housing an extensive baths complex. Excellent display panels all over the site ensure that you're never short of information.

Two or three slow **boats** a day (May–Oct only) from Basel to Rheinfelden stop at the jetty at Kaiseraugst, about fifteen minutes' walk below the Roman Museum. Otherwise, regular local **trains** take about ten minutes to Kaiseraugst, or **bus** #70 (every 30min) from Basel's Aeschenplatz goes to Augst village, ten minutes' walk from the museum.

Baden

A pleasant, relaxing spa town on the River Limmat, 24km downstream from Zürich in Canton Aargau, **BADEN** makes for a good stopover on a journey across the north of the country. There's not an awful lot to do, other than enjoy the ancient Old Town, take in a fine collection of Impressionist art, and enjoy a soothing dip in the warm, sulphurous spring waters… but that's the point. People have been coming to Baden for centuries to sit around doing absolutely nothing, and there are few more genteel and stately towns in the country in which to follow suit.

The town is divided into two, with the station in the middle. South of the station is the centre, focused around the **Old Town** with the ruined castle above. North of the station, in a bend of the Limmat, is the low-lying **spa area** (signed as *ThermalBaden*). The main Badstrasse, which becomes Bäderstrasse, connects the two neighbourhoods, running along a terrace above the Limmat valley.

The Town

At Schlossbergplatz at the southern end of Badstrasse is the turreted fifteenth-century **Stadtturm**, gateway into the Old Town. On a hill above to the west, and visible from all over town, is the **Stein castle**, partially destroyed in 1712 by the Protestant forces of Bern, Basel and Zürich during a battle against the Catholic cantons. Rathausgasse runs east from the Stadtturm just inside the walls, and partway along you'll find the **Stadthaus** (Town Hall): take a look inside at the whimsical modern ceiling murals of clouds and sky, and then head two floors up to the **Tagsatzungssaal** (Meeting Hall), for three centuries the meeting-place of the Confederate Diet (Switzerland's parliament of the day), with a restored

The **Jura Höhenweg** (or High Route; ⓦ www.jura-hoehenwege.ch) makes for a multi-day hiking tour through a region unlike any other in Switzerland, stretching 299km along the length of the Swiss Jura from Dielsdorf, 12km east of Baden, to Borex near Geneva. End to end it takes about fourteen days to complete, past small villages and isolated farms: you can often find yourself walking for long distances without signs of habitation. In this limestone country there's a rich flora in summer, and long views across the *Mittelland* from open ridge crests show either the abrupt wall of the Bernese Alps or the snowy Mont Blanc range.

The notes below are meant as a guideline only: you shouldn't set off without a good **map** (those covering the route are LS 5005, 5019, 5016, 241, 242, 5020 and 260 – all at 1:50,000). The essential accompaniment to any part of the walk is *The Jura* by Kev Reynolds and R. Brian Evans (see p.587), which gives details of accommodation to be had along the route in modest inns or mountain farms with outhouse dormitories, and also includes winter ski traverses. Local tourist offices can also supply information on hiking short stretches. See p.69 for the basics.

Reached by S-Bahn train from Zürich, **Dielsdorf** slumbers in a countryside of farms and market gardens, but within an hour of setting out the way goes through **Regensberg** which, with its thirteenth-century castle turret, stone-walled houses and cobbled square, is the finest village of the whole route. You'll also pass through **Baden** and **Brugg** on the first day, but thereafter the true nature of the Jura becomes evident, with the well-marked trail undulating to the horizon through steep green hills and charming farmland basins. From Brugg the route takes to high ground north of the River Aare, and beyond **Staffelegg** it almost reaches 1000m on the wooded summit of the Geissflue with views between the trees to the Black Forest. Edging above **Olten**, on day four the route joins a track engineered by Swiss soldiers during World War I across the flank of the 1098m Belchenflue, adorned with large regimental insignia carved and painted on the steep rock walls. Later the same day hundreds of reinforced timber steps take the path up towards the Roggenflue to emerge on a prominent limestone cliff with more expansive views before descending to **Balsthal**. Day five ends on the Weissenstein (1284m), whose panorama was immortalized in *The Path to Rome* by Hilaire Belloc: "One saw the sky beyond the edge of the world getting purer as the vault rose. But right up… ran peak and field and needle of intense ice, remote from the world."

On reaching **Frinvillier** on day six the Höhenweg passes suddenly from German to French Switzerland, to become known instead as the **Chemin des Crêtes**. Architectural styles change too, as though you've crossed an international frontier. Above Frinvillier you'll gain the 1607m **Chasseral** (see p.191); ribs of limestone project through the turf, and a hotel just below (☎032 751 24 51) gazes out to Lac de Neuchâtel with the Eiger, Mönch and Jungfrau floating on the horizon. On day nine the trail edges a huge limestone cauldron, the Creux du Van, the most dramatic feature on the long walk. A farm nearby offers a mattress in an outhouse for the simplest of overnight lodgings, and next day the path leads down to **Sainte-Croix**, home of the Swiss musical-box industry (see p.181). A steady climb then gains an open plateau close to the French border with military defences in evidence, before a sharp pull culminates on the summit of Le Suchet at 1588m. Passing through **Vallorbe** on day twelve (see p.182), the route investigates the Source de l'Orbe in a woodland whose glades are soggy with newborn streams. Mont Tendre, crossed on the same day, marks the highest point of the Jura at 1679m. From it, you can absorb a panorama of Lake Geneva and the snowcapped Alps. The last two days are spent mostly along the ridge among flowers – from the final high point of La Dôle, walkers can share Rousseau's pleasure: "The moment when from the very top of the Jura mountains I discovered Lake Geneva, was a moment of ecstasy and delight." From there, 1200m of descent through woodland, meadows and an open plain of wheatfields, brings the wanderer at last to **Borex** above Lake Geneva itself.

interior dating from 1497, complete with wood panelling and original stained glass showing the Swiss cantonal flags. You'll have to ask in one of the offices on the same floor for the key, since the door to the hall is kept locked.

An alley from Rathausgasse leads through to Kirchplatz, with its atmospheric **church**, built in 1420 (and retaining its Gothic arches) but later renovated in a surprisingly frill-free Baroque style. Stairways and steep alleys head down to a covered **wooden bridge** of 1813, leading to the bailiff's castle on the other bank. If the rock nearby looks oddly flat, it's because after the rainy night of June 25, 1899, the whole top of the crag sheared off and crashed into the river – a momentous event that is still talked about today.

It's a short walk north along the banks of the Limmat, on a footpath fragrant with wild garlic, to the **spa area**. Kurplatz, a peaceful little square, is surrounded on all sides by dignified Belle Epoque hotel architecture. Baden's nineteen **springs** were well known to the Romans, who called the place *Aquae Helveticae* and built a lavish baths complex to exploit the hot water, a million litres of which emerges every day at a toasty 47°C, having spent the last 30,000 years rising from 3km down. All the Kurhotels are built over their own springs which serve their own thermal pools; the **public pools**, dubbed *ThermalBaden* (Mon–Fri 7.30am–9pm, Sat & Sun 7.30am–8pm; Fr.16; Ⓦ www.thermalbaden .ch), are on Kurplatz, with a drinking fountain outside – although you may have trouble keeping the warm, smelly water down long enough for it to do any internal good. A wide range of massages and other treatments is offered.

The Langmatt Foundation

At Römerstrasse 30, 150m west of the spa area, is the **Langmatt Foundation** (April–Oct Tues–Fri 2–5pm, Sat & Sun 11am–5pm; Fr.10; SMP; Ⓦ www.langmatt.ch), housing a small but excellent collection of French Impressionist art. The charming house, dating from 1900–05 and resplendent in its own gardens, belonged to one Sidney Brown, a founder of the engineering multinational ABB, which is still headquartered in Baden. Off the reception area, the **Venetian salon** (room 3), with Louis XV and XVI furniture, is hung with views of the city painted by an unknown artist around 1745; next door you'll find work by Cézanne, Renoir and Pissarro. A wonderful Degas nude, and several small Renoir portraits, are curiously hung in a corridor (room 7) opposite the toilets. The atmospheric **library** (room 8) has landscapes by Corot and Degas, while the purpose-built **gallery** (room 9) is hung with, among other works, the beautiful *Portrait of Suzanne Valadon plaiting her hair* by Renoir. Upstairs rooms are mostly devoted to the history of the family.

Practicalities

The friendly and helpful **tourist office** is opposite the station (platform 1 exit), at Bahnhofplatz 1 (Mon noon–7pm, Tues–Fri 9.30am–7pm, Sat 9.30am–4pm; ☎056 210 91 91, Ⓦ www.baden.ch). On the east side of the Limmat, about 200m south of the wooden bridge, is the fine HI **hostel** *Jugendherberge*, Kanalstrasse 7 (☎056 221 67 36, Ⓦ www.youthhostel.ch; ❶; March–Dec; dorms Fr.29). Baden's **hotels** are good value, but they're geared towards monied longstayers taking the waters. Top choice is the *Blume*, Kurplatz 4 (☎056 222 55 69, Ⓦ www.blume-baden.ch; ❹), a fine Belle Epoque building in the spa district, built around an eye-popping interior atrium space, with classically grand public areas and a range of elegant rooms; it's been on this site since 1421. The modern Best Western *Du Parc*, nearby at Römerstrasse 24 (☎056 203 15 15, Ⓦ www .duparc.ch; ❺), is a fallback option.

For **eating**, there are plenty of pavement cafés and restaurants along Badstrasse and in the Old Town. The *Schwyzerhüsli*, Badstrasse 38 (☎056 222 62 63; closed Sun), is a popular place to sit and watch the world go by, and has plenty of healthy salads as well as substantial Swiss fare, with *menus* from Fr.17. *Rose*, Weitegasse 23, is a bright, modern, friendly little place with good food (Fri & Sat until 1.30am). Up on the east bank of the Limmat is the *Schloss Schartenfels* (☎056 426 19 27, ⓦwww.schartenfels.ch; closed Tues), an 1894 folly now housing a gourmet restaurant with a terrace overlooking the town.

Lengnau and Endingen

The Aargauer countryside around Baden holds a succession of quiet farming communities which include **LENGNAU**, 8km north of Baden, and **ENDINGEN**, 3km further. These two villages, for centuries up to about 100 years ago, were almost exclusively Jewish. Since the early thirteenth century Jews had lived in Basel and Zürich: Jewish financing, for instance, made it possible for Basel's bishops to buy Kleinbasel outright in the 1220s and to build the first Rhine bridge shortly afterwards. On January 16, 1349, the Basel government decided to pack the town's Jews into a wooden house on an island in the Rhine and burn it to the ground; those who escaped were expelled six months later when plague arrived, accused of poisoning the city's water supply. Jews were allowed back to the city after the 1356 earthquake in order to finance rebuilding work, but in 1397 they were again expelled, this time for good. They took refuge in the Baden countryside, settling at Lengnau and Endingen, where Jewish life in Switzerland was concentrated for more than four centuries. In 1805, a Jewish community was refounded in Basel, but it was only in 1874, after extreme pressure was brought to bear by the US and France, that Switzerland finally guaranteed full religious and civil rights to all religious denominations in its constitution, one of the last European states to do so.

Today, Lengnau and Endingen – despite being largely depopulated of their Jews – still bear many traces of the past. Lengnau's little village square is overlooked not by a church, but by a large **synagogue**, and the village has many characteristic old double-doored houses, not seen elsewhere in the country. The great **domed synagogue** in the middle of Endingen has been extensively renovated. Between the two villages, in a quiet location off the road, is an overgrown **Israelitischer Friedhof** (Jewish Cemetery), with graves dating back to 1750.

All these sites are kept locked, but staff at the Jüdisches Museum in Basel (see p.213), or at the Lengnau municipality (☎056 266 50 10, ⓦwww.lengnau-ag .ch), can – with notice – put you in touch with a guide from the local Jewish community, who will take you round and explain more.

Travel details

Trains

Baden to: Basel (twice hourly; 50min); Bern (twice hourly; 1hr 10min); Zürich (every 15min; 15min).
Basel SBB to: Baden (twice hourly; 50min); Bern

(every 30min; 1hr); Biel/Bienne (hourly; 1hr 5min); Brig (hourly; 2hr 50min); Chur (hourly; 2hr 30min); Geneva (every 30min; 2hr 40min); Interlaken Ost (twice hourly; 2hr 10min); Kaiseraugst (twice hourly; 10min); Lausanne (twice hourly; 2hr 10min); Lugano (hourly; 3hr 40min); Luzern (hourly; 1hr 10min); Neuchâtel (twice hourly; 1hr 25min); Olten (every 15min; 25min); Zürich (every 15min; 55min).

Buses

Baden to: Endingen (every 20min; 25min); Lengnau AG (every 20min; 20min).

Boats

Basel (Schifflände) to: Kaiseraugst (May–Oct 1–3 daily; 2hr 10min); Dreiländereck (May–Oct Mon–Sat 1 daily; 1hr 45min).

Bern and around

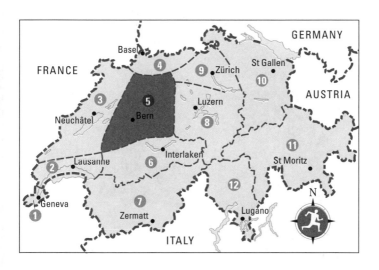

CHAPTER 5 **Highlights**

❋ **Old Town, Bern** Wander the atmospheric cobbled streets, dipping in and out of the arcades on a street plan unchanged since medieval times. **See p.237**

❋ **Münster, Bern** Switzerland's tallest steeple adorns this mighty cathedral. **See p.241**

❋ **Zentrum Paul Klee, Bern** The world's largest Klee collection, housed in a spectacular modern gallery. **See p.244**

❋ **The Emmental** Home region of the best-known Swiss

cheese, featuring classic scenery of velvety green hills. **See p.252**

❋ **Kemmeriboden** Tiny trailhead village in the upper Emmental that makes meringues to die for. **See p.255**

❋ **Solothurn** The finest Baroque city in the country, a day-trip from Bern, Basel or Zürich. **See p.256**

❋ **Fribourg** Switzerland's best-kept secret, a genial, bilingual university town with a fine tradition of fondues. **See p.258**

△ Old Town, Bern

5

Bern and around

The giant Canton Bern is one of the country's largest, taking in a swathe of diverse countryside from snowy Alpine peaks to gently rolling farmland. The north of the canton is focused around the city of **Bern** itself, Switzerland's low-key and attractive federal capital. With a glorious history at the fulcrum of Swiss history, Bern has often dominated the economic and political fortunes of the populated west-central heartland – or **Mittelland** – of the country. This arc of territory stretching from Lake Geneva to Zürich holds, and has always held, Switzerland's most fertile country, densest population and greatest wealth. The Reformation may have begun in Zürich, and flourished in Geneva, but it was the Bernese army that seized hearts and minds in the countryside between the two. For centuries after the Burgundian wars, the patrician nobility of Bern controlled a wealthy city-state covering the entire Mittelland; it was a French-backed revolution in 1798 that saw Bern stripped both of its Lake Geneva breadbasket (carved out to form Canton Vaud) and the rolling farmland of the north (Canton Aargau). Nonetheless, Bern was a natural choice for Swiss federal capital under the 1848 constitution, and with overwhelming economic and political clout, Bern still calls the shots in its home region.

Every Swiss values his or her home canton above all the others, but the Bernese draw on a particularly deep wellspring of nationalistic pride in celebrating their own identity, culture and language. They're famous for their slow, deliberate manner, and you'll pick up a sing-song tone in the lethargic Bernese dialect of Swiss German that sparks inevitable associations with Welsh or Texan accents of English. Parallels don't stop at language: like Wales and Texas, Bern – once an independent state – is now bound into a larger polity but has a relatively static, self-assured population who tend to feel little affinity with the people over the border. Luzerners and Fribourgeois are strangers, with whom the Bernese share a nationality but neither a cultural nor a religious identity. The slow-talking Bernese traditionally decry Zürichers for being big-city hotheads, and Baslers and Genfers for being snobs – and the compliment is returned, with the Bernese dismissed as hair-splitting dullards.

Around Bern, the lush hills and tidy, picturesque farming communities of the **Berner Mittelland** hold plenty of rustic charm, not least in the **Emmental** region to the east. (The Berner Oberland, or Bernese Alps, in the south of the canton, has its own chapter, beginning on p.269.) Two cities near Bern worth making time for are **Solothurn** to the north, and the much-overlooked town of **Fribourg** to the southwest.

Bern

Of all Swiss cities, **BERN** (**Berne** in French) is perhaps the most immediately charming. Crammed onto a steep-sided peninsula in a crook of the fast-flowing River Aare, its quiet, cobbled lanes, lined with sandstone arcaded buildings straddling the pavement, have changed barely at all in over five hundred years but for the adornment of modern shop signs and the odd car or tram rattling past. The hills all around, and the steep banks of the river, are still liberally wooded. Views, both of the Old Town's clustered roofs and of the majestic Alps on the horizon, are breathtaking. Coming from Zürich or Geneva, it's hard to remember that Bern – once voted Europe's most floral city – is the nation's capital, home of the Swiss parliament and wielder of final federal authority.

For all its political status, Bern is a tiny city of under 130,000 people and retains a small town's easy approach to life. The attraction of the place is its ambience; traffic is kept out of the Old Town and you could spend days just wandering the streets and alleys, café-hopping and – if it's warm – joining the locals for a plunge into the river. The perfectly preserved medieval street plan, with its arcades, street fountains and doughty towers, persuaded UNESCO to deem Bern a World Heritage Site, placing it in the company of such legendary sites as Florence, Petra and the Taj Mahal. In a competition for the world's most beautiful and relaxing capital city, it's hard to think what could knock Bern into second place.

Some history

A castle probably stood at **Nydegg**, on the eastern tip of Bern's peninsula, from the eleventh century, before Berchtold V, Duke of Zähringen, chose the strategically ideal spot to found a new city in 1191. He had the oak forests covering the peninsula felled, using the timber for the first houses, and then – legend has it – went hunting nearby and named the new city after his first kill, a **bear** (*Bär* in German). Bern's coat of arms, sporting a bear, first appeared in 1224, and to this day bears remain indelibly associated with the city.

The Aare encircles Bern's Old Town on three sides; Berchtold's fourth defence was a wall, which initially ran through the Zytglogge tower. Under the Zähringens, and by virtue too of being in close proximity to the wealthy and powerful kingdom of **Burgundy**, Bern expanded rapidly. By 1256 it had a new wall at the present Käfigturm, and a century later the city reached as far as the Christoffelturm (at the present-day train station). In 1339, at the Battle of Laupen, Bern defeated the united nobility of Burgundy, and asserted its new-found independence by joining the Swiss Confederation in 1353.

Shortly before 5pm on May 14, 1405, **fire** broke out in Brunngasse and tore through the timber-built city, killing one hundred and razing most of the town. The subsequent programme of rebuilding (this time in the local sandstone) gave the city much of its present character, including the street arcades, the surviving town plan, and monumental public buildings such as the Rathaus and the Münster. In 1528, Bern enthusiastically accepted the **Reformation**, and the sixteenth and seventeenth centuries saw a programme of upgrading the city's streets and arcades. Meanwhile Bern's nobility gathered greater and greater power, successfully putting down a series of citizens' revolts before finally falling prey to **French invaders**, who ransacked the city's treasury in 1798. The Congress of Vienna in 1814 forced Bern to surrender its eastern and western territories, thus creating Cantons Aargau and Vaud, and donated parts of the Jura to Bern as a consolation prize; the Bernese complained that they'd lost their cellar and their granary, and been given an attic instead. Nonetheless, the city retained its old prestige enough to be a popular choice for **federal capital** in 1848.

In 1864, after six years of fierce controversy, the communal authorities voted by 415 to 411 to demolish the medieval Christoffelturm to make way for construction of Bern's new railway station (the tower's foundations survive on display in the train station's lower level). **Einstein** published his Special Theory of Relativity in Bern in 1905, and **Hermann Hesse** spent the World War I years in Bern, when the city was already known as a hub of politically progressive ideas, hosting the anarchists Kropotkin and Bakunin.

During the twentieth century Bern continued to expand, its new, arching bridges linking to suburbs over the Aare such as **Kirchenfeld**, a planned district to the south characterized by grand 1920s–30s mansions. To the west, **Bümpliz** has mushroomed to accommodate most of the city's rapid new growth, its low-income housing and high proportion of Arab, South Asian and Slavic immigrants contrasting dramatically with the settled affluence and ethnic homogeneity of the city centre.

The new century has brought a number of prestigious **architectural** commissions to the city. Top of the list is Renzo Piano's **Zentrum Paul Klee** gallery (see p.244). Daniel Libeskind has designed the stunning **Westside** shopping and entertainment complex (Ⓦ www.westside.ch), located west of the city to act as a bridge between German- and French-speaking communities, and the old Wankdorf stadium, in the northeast suburbs, has been rejuvenated as the glittering 32,000-seat **Stade de Suisse** (Ⓦ www.stadedesuisse.ch), a venue for the 2008 European football championships.

Bern's festivals

The famous **Zibelemärit** (Onion Market) – held on the fourth Monday in November, preceded by a very chilly mass swim in the Aare the day before – is Bern's major annual festival, an excuse, despite the food stalls and the rustic-sounding name, for people to run around Spitalgasse throwing confetti, spraying silly-string and brandishing blow-up bananas. It is claimed that the spectacle originated after the fire of 1405, when people from nearby Fribourg helped Bern clean up the mess and, in gratitude, the Bernese granted the Fribourgeois the right to sell their onions every autumn in the city (down the centuries, the onions developing into blow-up bananas). In fact, Bern's Zibelemärit began – much more mundanely – in the mid-nineteenth century, when rural women, selling onions and other vegetables, began to turn up in Bern on the first day of the city's Martinmas Fairs, which had been celebrated since the Middle Ages to mark the transition to winter. The quality of the produce, and the engaging demeanour of the vendors, meant that news of the women's market spread rapidly, until the newspapers got hold of the story in 1860 and proclaimed the Onion Market to be the "traditional" start of Martinmas. The tale quickly wove its way into popular thinking, somehow getting muddled with the 1405 fire and the Fribourgeois along the way.

Zibelemärlt aside, Bern's biggest party is probably its **Fasnacht/carnival** (ⓦwww .baernerfasnacht.ch), spread over a weekend slotted in between the massive celebrations in Luzern (before) and Basel (after). Spring and summer see a host of cultural events, including an international **jazz festival** in May (ⓦwww.jazzfestivalbern.ch) – Bern is home to one of Switzerland's best jazz schools – a **modern dance festival** (ⓦwww.tanztage.ch) in June, and the **Gurten festival** (ⓦwww.gurtenfestival.ch) of rock, dance and folk in July.

Arrival and information

Bern's huge **train station** is centrally situated at the western edge of the Old Town, within a few minutes' walk of practically all the hotels and sights. Trains arrive at the lower level, postbuses on the uppermost level. The **Old Town** stretches to the east, occupying the central high ground of a thin, finger-like peninsula: three long, parallel cobbled streets (which all change their names along their length) define the Old Town area: Aarbergergasse-Zeughausgasse -Rathausgasse-Postgasse is the northernmost; Spitalgasse-Marktgasse-Kramgasse-Gerechtigkeitsgasse is in the centre; Schauplatzgasse-Amthausgasse-Münstergasse-Junkerngasse is to the south. The Zytglogge clock-tower is bang in the centre of the Old Town; the Bärengraben (Bear Pits) are to the east; and the main museums are clustered around Helvetiaplatz to the south.

Bern's tiny **airport** (ⓦwww.flughafenbern.ch) is 9km southeast of the city in Belp. A minibus (misleadingly named "Airport Taxi") meets all arrivals, shuttling to Bern train station (20min; Fr.14), or you can take a taxi (around Fr.35). The "Tangento" bus only goes to Belp station (Fr.3), from where ordinary trains head to Bern (3 hourly; 20min). Flying out, a minibus heads to the airport from outside Bern station about an hour before every flight departure.

Most of the centre is off-limits to traffic. Unless you can find a blue-zone space (see p.50; max. 1hr 30min with parking disc, or Fr.15/day with machine-issued permit), **parking** (ⓦwww.parkingbern.ch) is expensive; the large car park at the station (ⓦwww.bahnhofparking.ch) charges Fr.4 per hour (Fr.30/day). Others are at Waisenhausplatz, Casinoplatz and behind the Rathaus.

BERN

ACCOMMODATION
Allegro C
Bären and Bristol G
Bellevue Palace J
Bern Backpackers/
Hotel Glocke F
City H
Goldener Schlüssel E
Innere Enge A
Jugendherberge K
Landhaus D
Marthahaus B
National I

EATING & DRINKING
Altes Tramdepot 17
Anker 12
Art Café 21
Brasserie Lorraine 1
Café Litteraire 6
Café des Pyrénées 10
China Imperial 14
Cinématte 22
Della Casa 15
Dragon d'Or 5
Govinda 13
Kornhauscafé 8
Lorenzini 16
Manora 20
Markthalle 18
Menuetto 19
Du Nord 3
Postgasse 4
Reitschule 7
Ringgenberg 9
Tibits 11
Zum Blauen Engel 2

0   200 m

▲ Rosengarten

▲ Unitobler building

Bern's friendly and efficient **tourist office** is on the upper level of the train station (June–Sept daily 9am–8.30pm; Oct–May Mon–Sat 9am–6.30pm, Sun 10am–5pm; ☎031 328 12 12, ⓦwww.berninfo.com). There's a smaller tourist information desk at the Bärengraben (June–Sept Mon–Sat 9am–6pm; March–May & Oct Mon–Sat 10am–4pm; Nov–Feb Fri–Sun 11am–4pm).

City transport and tours

Bern's city centre is small enough that you can easily **walk** everywhere: the stroll from the train station to the Bärengraben is only around twenty minutes and takes in the length of the Old Town on the way. Walking is the only way you're going to be able to get a sense of the atmosphere of the arcades – and it's the principal delight of Bern – but a close second-best comes in the form of **horse-drawn carriages**, which ply for trade in the central squares during the summer months.

Bern's network of **buses and trams** (ⓦwww.bernmobil.ch) is comprehensive. Pretty much all lines run through Bahnhofplatz, which is bedecked with directional signs. Swiss Pass holders travel free; otherwise a **fare** for up to six stops is Fr.1.90 (valid 30min), for seven or more stops Fr.3.20 (valid 1hr), while a Tageskarte (Fr.12) is valid all day, all buyable from the machines at every stop. The **BernCard**, buyable from the tourist office and all hotels, gives unlimited travel and free admission to all museums for Fr.17 (24hr), Fr.27 (48hr) or Fr.33 (72hr). Make sure you have a ticket before you start your journey: the fine for travelling without one is Fr.60.

Bern's **taxis** are vying to be the most expensive in Europe: with a Fr.6.80 flagfall, plus Fr.3.40 per kilometre (more at nights and Sundays), they're about twice as pricey as London's. There are public ranks at the train station, Casinoplatz and Waisenhausplatz; two companies are Bären (☎031 371 11 11) and Nova (☎031 331 33 13).

Tours

The tourist office has several **tours**, including a **guided walk** through the Old Town, starting from the office in the train station (Jan–March Sat 11am; Fr.15; April–Oct daily 11am; Fr.16; lasts 1hr 30min). One of the more interesting ways to see the city is from a **river dinghy** – ask at the tourist office for details of where to meet. Otherwise, there are plenty of **bus tours** of the city and various **boat trips** on the river (Fr.23–30), as well as day-trips to the Thunersee and into the mountains. Most of the tours run in the summer season only.

Sightseeing by bus

Bern's most useful bus line is the electric **bus 12** (every 6min). Aside from trams along Marktgasse, this is also the only public transport running through the Old Town. From the train station (direction Schosshalde/Zentrum Paul Klee), the bus heads to the Zytglogge, then on down picturesque Kramgasse and Gerechtigkeitsgasse, and across the Nydeggbrücke to the Bärengraben, terminating beyond Schosshalde in the eastern suburbs at the Zentrum Paul Klee gallery. In the other direction (signed Länggasse), bus 12 climbs the hill from the train station west to the university.

Other useful routes are tram 9 (direction Wabern), which heads south to the Gurtenbahn station, and bus 20 (direction Wyler) for the Lorraine district.

Accommodation

Bern's **accommodation** is good value: it's easy to choose an inexpensive hotel and still find yourself in a tasteful, tranquil room overlooking historic cobbled streets, with only voices and church bells as background. Standards, even within historic buildings, are high – the only drawback is the need always to book ahead. None of these places is more than ten minutes' walk from the train station, or a few stops on a tram or bus.

Inexpensive

City Bahnhofplatz ☎031 311 53 77, ⓦwww .fhotels.ch. Geared towards a business clientele, with slick designer interiors renovated in 2005. Seconds from the train station and not at all bad; a sound choice for facilities and location. Street-side rooms are marginally noisier. ❸–❹

Goldener Schlüssel Rathausgasse 72 ☎031 311 02 16, ⓦwww.goldener-schluessel.ch. Comfortable place on a quiet Old Town street, with efficient, pleasant service. Simple, spacious rooms are clean and mostly ensuite, with some cheaper shared-bath rooms up under the eaves. ❷–❸

🏃 **Landhaus** Altenbergstrasse 4 ☎031 331 41 66, ⓦwww.landhausbern.ch. The most attractive budget rooms in town, in an historic, renovated building (with spiralling wooden stairs but no lift) overlooking a curve in the river. Spacious, modern design prevails throughout, with ensuite or shared facilities, and some rooms have floor-to-ceiling windows and balcony. Bus #12 to Bärengraben (direction Schosshalde). ❷–❸

Marthahaus Wyttenbachstrasse 22a ☎031 332 41 35, ⓦwww.marthahaus.ch. Excellent value. A characterful hotel-pension on a quiet cul-de-sac a few minutes out of the Old Town, friendly, well run and cosy. Most rooms are ensuite, and are spotless, fresh and airy. Bus #20 to Gewerbeschule (direction Wyler). ❷

National Hirschengraben 24 ☎031 381 19 88, ⓦwww.nationalbern.ch. Something of an institution, with a restaurant, theatre and – up above – a hotel occupying a lovely old building on an atmospheric tree- and tram-lined street. The ancient wooden lift rattles you up to characterful, renovated rooms with big windows and wood floors; some are ensuite, all have modern facilities. ❷–❸

Mid-range and expensive

Allegro In the Kursaal, Kornhausstrasse 3 ☎031 339 55 00, ⓦwww.allegro-hotel.ch. Innovative business hotel set in the ultra-modern renovated Kursaal building (which also boasts a large casino). Super-slick postmodern design swishes you into stylish rooms – go for the Warhol ones – featuring widescreen TVs, video games, Internet and more.

Top-floor balconies with Alpine vistas cost more. Weekend discounts can make this the best-value, and least traditional, top-end accommodation in the city. Tram #9 (direction Guisanplatz). ❺

Bären and **Bristol** Within 50m of each other at Schauplatzgasse 4 & 10 ☎031 311 33 67, ⓦwww.baerenbern.ch & www.bristolbern.ch. Two identical hotels seconds from the Bundeshaus, with different owners but shared Best Western management. Rooms are modern, well designed and comfortable, though rather soulless. ❺–❻

Bellevue Palace Kochergasse 3 ☎031 320 45 45, ⓦwww.bellevue-palace.ch. Top hotel in the city, right beside the Bundeshaus. This is the haunt of presidents, diplomats and billionaires, with as much palatial grandeur as you'd expect plus the added bonus of views of the river winding far below the hotel walls and, in the distance, the snow-capped Alps. Rooms are spacious, sumptuous, traditionally styled and horribly expensive. ❽–❾

🏃 **Innere Enge** Engestrasse 54 ☎031 309 61 11, ⓦwww.zghotels.ch. Lovely choice, well out of the city on the edge of open parkland but only five minutes by bus from the centre. This fine old building, which hosted Empress Josephine in 1810, features superb Art Nouveau styling throughout; the 26 rooms are characterful and quiet, many with expansive views of the Alps. Breakfast – which is optional – is served in the octagonal Park Pavilion, while the intimate Marian's Jazzroom in the basement (closed July & Aug) hosts top international jazz performers. Free parking. Bus #21 (direction Bremgarten). ❺

Hostels

Bern Backpackers/Hotel Glocke (SB hostel) Rathausgasse 75 ☎031 311 37 71, ⓦwww .bernbackpackers.com. Old Town fixture benefiting from a perfect central location and excellent dorms and facilities, with some pleasant, bargain-priced singles and doubles too. Dorm beds are Fr.31. ❷

Jugendherberge (HI hostel) Weihergasse 4 ☎031 311 63 16, ⓦwww.youthhostel.ch & www .jugibern.ch. Well-run place, with good facilities and a nice riverside location in Marzili – it's regularly chock-full. Dorm beds are Fr.31, and they do good solid lunches and evening meals for around Fr.12. Walk down from the Bundesterrace, or take the funicular and then the lowest of three left-hand streets when you emerge. ❶

Landhaus (SB hostel) Altenbergstrasse 4 ☎031 331 41 66, ⓦwww.landhausbern.ch. Attractive building in an old part of town by the river, with beds in quiet, super-clean partitioned dorms for Fr.30; you can use the kitchen for free, and there's a café downstairs. Bus #12 to Bärengraben (direction Schosshalde). ❷

Campsite

Eichholz Strandweg 49 ☎031 961 26 02, ⓦwww.campingeichholz.ch. Decent site on the riverbank in Wabern, a few minutes south of the city by tram #9 (to Gurten). Mid-April to Sept.

The City

Wandering through Bern's UNESCO-protected **Old Town** can be a magical experience: few cities in Europe are so visibly wedded to their distant past, with architecture and a street plan essentially unchanged since medieval times. The most hectic shopping goes on in the **western half** of the Old Town, on Marktgasse and Spitalgasse in particular; the older, **eastern half** is slower-paced. However, not for nothing does the tourist office tout the famous arcades, lining both sides of every street in the Old Town, as being "the longest covered shopping promenade in the world". In a strange turnaround of expectations, it's when you walk under the crowded arcades that you get a full-on blast of modern consumerism, with music, shop windows and advertising vying for your attention. Step a few metres to the side to walk in the open air and – with a little imagination – it's easy to picture yourself in the Bern of the sixteenth century.

The Zytglogge

An imposing presence at the centre of the Old Town, the **Zytglogge** (*tseet-klok-uh*), Zeitglockenturm or Clock Tower, is as much the symbol of Bern as the bear. The focal point of public transport and walking routes within the Old Town – and both the benchmark of official Bern time and the point from which all distances in the canton are measured – its squat shape, oversized spired roof and giant, gilded clock face will imprint themselves on your memory of the city.

The tower was originally constructed partly in wood as the westernmost city gate in 1218–20, but by 1256 the city walls had moved west to the Käfigturm; the tower was then converted into a prison for those prostitutes who made a living servicing the clergy. After the devastating fire of 1405, the tower was rebuilt in stone with a new, squat design, a turreted staircase to one side (still used today) and a clock mechanism. The clock soon broke and stayed broken for 122 years until one Caspar Brunner designed an elegant new mechanism which has functioned since he installed it in 1530, and which is still complete with nearly all its original parts. Below the main east face of the clock is an intricate astronomical and astrological device, which, in one small diameter, displays a 24-hour clock, the twelve hours of daylight, the position of the sun in the zodiac, the day of the week, the date and the month, the phases of the moon and the elevation of the sun above the horizon, everything kept accurate by linkage to the main clock mechanism. The external appearance of the Zytglogge dates from Baroque embellishments of 1770–71.

The main draw of the thing is generally touted to be a rather underwhelming little **display** of mechanical figures – a crowing cock, a parade of bears, Chronos with his hourglass and a dancing jester – which is set into motion four minutes before every hour on the clock's east face. What's far more interesting is to see close-up (and have explained) the actual inner workings of the mechanism as the pendulum swings and linked cogs turn gracefully: check with the tourist office for details of their fascinating **guided tour** of the tower.

On Kornhausplatz, below the west face of the Zytglogge, stands the **Kindlifresserbrunnen**, or Ogre Fountain (1544), topped by a statue of a man devouring a struggling baby. The Bernese authorities would have you believe this is a light-hearted carnival scene, but the nightmarish statue was once painted yellow (the colour used to stigmatize Jews) and may possibly be an unusually graphic representation of the suspicion held throughout medieval Europe that Jewish religious ritual involved the murder of children. Whichever, Bern's happy shoppers of today seem unfazed by images of cannibalistic infanticide in their midst.

△ Kindlifresserbrunnen, the Ogre Fountain

The eastern Old Town

From the Zytglogge, the atmospheric lanes of the Old Town branch out in all directions. The meandering walking tour outlined below covers notable sights, but what's just as appealing is to follow your nose and explore unremarkable alleys and passageways that cut through and around the main routes.

The impressively wide main cobbled thoroughfare of the Old Town stretches away on both sides of the Zytglogge: the **western Old Town** is covered on p.242, while elegant **Kramgasse** runs east, featuring many Baroque facades which were added to the medieval arcaded buildings early in the eighteenth century. At no. 49 is the **Einstein-Haus** (March–Sept daily 10am–6pm; rest of year Tues–Fri 10am–5pm, Sat 10am–4pm; closed late-Dec; Fr.6; Ⓦ www .einstein-bern.ch), the apartment and workplace of the famous scientist, who develo ped his Theory of Relativity in 1905 while working in the Bern Patent Office, having graduated from the Zürich Institute of Technology a few years before.

On Kramgasse are more of Bern's many ornamented **fountains**. First is an armoured bear holding the standard of the city's founder, Berchtold von Zähringen (dating from 1535). Halfway along the street is another, with a copy of a 1545 statue of Samson, and just before the Kreuzgasse junction is a statue-less fountain dating from 1779. At this eastern end of Kramgasse, and above head height, you'll also spot several eighteenth-century oversized figures mounted on pedestals, which indicated the location of Bern's various craft guilds: the Moor represented the clothworkers, the ape stonemasons and bricklayers, and the axe-wielding carpenter graphically demonstrates his own trade.

While the main street continues ahead, changing its name to **Gerechtig-keitsgasse**, the small Kreuzgasse heads left (north), past a quaint little shop which has been a pharmacy since 1571, to **Rathausplatz**, dominated by the double-staircased **Rathaus**. Although the building dates from 1406–17, it's been much altered over the centuries. Opposite is a 1542 fountain sporting a Bernese standard-bearer in full armour. Next to the Rathaus is the **St Peter & St Paul-Kirche**, built in 1858 as the first Catholic parish church to go up in the city since the Reformation. It's a cool, musty place in a mock-Gothic style which since 1875 has belonged to the heterodox Christ Catholic church (see box). This is one of the most peaceful and atmospheric corners in the Old Town. **Rathausgasse** to the west retains its facades, though many of the old upper floors have been converted into luxury apartments, while to the east, tiny **Postgasse**, with a handful of cafés and antiquarian booksellers, trickles its way down the slope towards the oldest part of the city around Nydegg.

An alternative route heads the other way on Kreuzgasse, right (south) onto tranquil **Junkerngasse**. The apse of the Münster (see p.241) is opposite, but if you head east (left), down the street, you'll pass a succession of fine town houses on the route to Nydegg. First, set back from the street on the right at no. 59, is the Beatrice von Wattenwyl-Haus, its frontage and arcades dating from the 1440s, the south wing and upper floors from a major expansion in 1705. At no. 51 is the sixteenth-century Zeerlederhaus, with neo-Gothic heraldic exterior murals done in 1897. The main draw, at no. 47, is the **Erlacherhof**, the grandest patrician mansion in the city, designed in 1746 around its own courtyard; it's been the seat of the municipal government since 1832 and for a decade after 1848 housed the federal government. A short stroll past the Louis-XVI Lerber-haus at no. 43 and Morlothaus at no. 32 leads on down to Nydegg.

Nydegg

The three most characterful streets in the Old Town – Postgasse, Gerechtigkeits-gasse and Junkerngasse – meet at the **Nydeggbrücke** (*nee-dek*), the easternmost

---

The Old (Christ) Catholic Church

In 1870, the **First Vatican Council** confirmed the rule of the Pope over the whole of the Catholic Church and asserted the doctrine of papal infallibility. At the same time, political unification in Italy, and Bismarck's *Kulturkampf*, or Culture Struggle, in Germany – a thinly veiled assault on church authority – drew Switzerland into conflicts between church and state. Swiss liberals in particular saw the Vatican's dogmatism as challenging the basic principles of the church and the right to individual freedoms. In a meeting in Olten in 1872, they were troubled enough to form a separate church hierarchy. When the Bishop of Basel began to excommunicate priests who refused to accept the notion of papal infallibility, cantonal authorities in the north of Switzerland deposed him, and the dissenting priests formed a new church.

Known in Germany, Austria and the Netherlands as "Old Catholic" but generally in Switzerland as **"Christ Catholic"**, the church flourishes today in northern areas influenced by political liberalism, principally cantons Bern, Basel, Aargau and Solothurn, with scattered communities as far apart as Geneva and St Gallen. About 140,000 Swiss consider themselves Christ Catholics, as opposed to Roman Catholics (of which there are 3.2m); they follow a church which holds that there is a priesthood of all believers, that priests are allowed to marry, that women can be ordained as deacons, and that services should always be performed in the language of the congregation. This has brought it closer in spirit to Anglicanism than to Roman Catholicism, with which relations have often been bitter and strained.

point of Bern's peninsula and the location of Nydegg Castle, built probably before the 1191 founding of Bern and the spur to the city's construction. It was destroyed in the mid-thirteenth century and its location is now marked by the **Nydeggkirche**, although parts of its massive stone foundations survive here and there. The church is a mishmash of elements added to an original 1341 building, and it's worth stopping to savour the tranquil atmosphere of the courtyard outside, with a well which originally stood within the precincts of the twelfth-century castle and a picturesque view of the medieval houses clustering on the slopes all around. The covered Burgtreppe steps lead down from the courtyard to **Gerberngasse**; at the bottom, if you cross the street and walk 20m or so left, you'll find more steps leading down to the riverside, through a thirteenth-century arch which originally belonged to the **Ländtetor**, landing stage for the first ferry across the river. The wall fresco beneath the arch depicts the neighbourhood in the early nineteenth century.

Matte and Marzili

Emerging back onto Gerberngasse, to the right (northeast) is **Läuferplatz**, its fountain-statue of the city herald standing at the head of the low **Untertor-brücke**, one of the oldest bridges in Switzerland (1468). To the left (southwest), Gerberngasse follows the bend of the river down into one of the most appealing districts of the Old Town, **Matte** (Ⓦ www.matte.ch). For many centuries this was a self-contained district of craftspeople and dockworkers which long retained its own dialect, related to the Jenisch language of the Swiss gypsies (see p.488) and dubbed *Mattenenglisch* by the other Bernese, to whom it was an incomprehensible language (as obscure as *Englisch*) spoken in a meadow (*Matte*). Gentrification of the neighbourhood in the 1970s brought sweeping social changes. The river is still channelled into an open canal along the main street, and there are plenty of crooked half-timbered houses all around, but a look at wall plaques will turn up more software companies and design partnerships than you could shake a stick at. You'll find a great deal of graffiti down here too, a legacy of the presence of the *Wasserwerk*, one of Bern's leading dance clubs. During the disastrous floods of 1999 and 2005, Matte spent several weeks underwater: you may still see evidence of high-water marks.

From Matte, the least energetic way to get back to the Old Town is to continue southwest along the riverside Schifflaube until Badgasse, where there is a **lift** (Mon–Sat 6am–8.30pm, Sun 7am–8.30pm; Fr.1) to whisk you up to the Münsterplattform overhead. Many flights of steps wend their way up the hillside all around too. Otherwise, you could continue a riverside stroll under the Kirchenfeldbrücke into **Marzili**, a peaceful residential district with a handful of old industrial buildings on the riverbank now converted into music venues and arts centres. The Aare is particularly fast at Bern; summer sees hordes crowding the riverbank lawns, and many people leave their possessions at the pool complexes at Marzili or Lorraine and walk or take public transport south to a convenient jumping-in point to let the strong current float them back north again. Cheapskates wrap their clothes up in a plastic bag and tie it to their wrist as they float along.

Across the Nydeggbrücke

There are few attractions on the eastern bank of the Aare. At the bridgehead across the river is the **Bärengraben** (Bear Pits; freely accessible), two large, sunken dens in the open air which have housed a collection of shaggy brown bears – the symbol of Bern – since the early sixteenth century. Plans are under way to revamp this whole area as a Bear Park, with large enclosures so the bears can roam more widely and even swim in the river.

The tourist complex adjacent, housed in a century-old converted tram depot, has a restaurant-bar and tourist information desk, as well as the much-touted **Bern Show** (every 20min: June–Sept daily 9am–6pm; March–May & Oct daily 10am–4pm; Nov–Feb Fri–Sun 11am–4pm; free), where – having waited for the English version to come round – you sit on benches to watch a potted history of Bern, evoked by a large model of the city and clever use of lights and pictures. It's a valiant attempt to bring history to life, but is just too cheesy for its own good.

Heading left up the steep hill next to the Bärengraben will bring you to the **Rosengarten** (Rose Garden), which has a lovely collection of flora (220 varieties of rose, 200 of iris, and more) and spectacular morning views over the Old Town.

The Münster

Bern's late-Gothic **Münster** (Easter–Oct Tues–Sat 10am–5pm, Sun 11.30am–5pm; Nov–Easter Tues–Fri 10am–noon & 2–4pm, Sat until 5pm, Sun 11.30am–2pm; Ⓦwww.bernermuenster.ch) is unmistakeable, its feathery spire – the highest in Switzerland – towering over the Old Town and its sonorous bells dominating the quiet city. It's a reverential place, both for its lofty, gloomy interior and the terrific views from its tower.

The first chapel on the site – recorded in 1224 – probably dated from the founding of the city. On March 11, 1421, when just five thousand people lived in Bern, Matthäus Ensinger, a master builder from Strasbourg who already had three cathedrals under his belt, started construction on the new minster using the greenish local sandstone. Work continued according to his original plans until the mid-sixteenth century and, after a gap of three centuries or so, was finally completed in 1893 with the addition of the spire. Bern was a rapid convert to the Reformation and most of the church's treasures were destroyed in or soon after 1528, although some notable pieces such as the portal sculpture, choir stalls and stained-glass windows survived.

Outside the cathedral, cobbled **Münsterplatz** features the imposing Baroque facades of, among other buildings, the chapterhouse, and a 1790 fountain showing Moses, fired with the zeal of the Reformation, pointing to the Second Commandment (the one forbidding idolatry). It's worth stopping at the **central portal** of the cathedral before heading inside – this spectacular depiction of the **Last Judgement** is one of the only remaining unified examples of such late-Gothic sculpture in Europe. The 170 smaller figures are the fifteenth-century originals (the 47 larger freestanding pieces were replaced by copies in 1964, the originals now sitting in the Bernisches Historisches Museum). The left half of the portal depicts the saved, the right half the damned: you can imagine that the graphic, didactic counterpoint between the beatific smiles of one side and the naked, screaming torment of the other would have appealed even to the iconoclastic Reformers, who chose to spare it from destruction. In the centre is Justice, flanked by angels, the Wise and Foolish Virgins and, above, the Archangel Michael wielding a sword and scales.

Entry is through the right-hand gate, and the hushed **interior** is immediately impressive. The immense roof span is laced around with vaulting (1572–3), the aisles are flanked by rows of porches and small chapels, and the nave, with square pillars placed diagonally and a pulpit dating from 1470, channels attention towards the stained glass of the choir. Keystone busts of saints, Mary, Christ and others were left untouched by the Reformers, possibly because they were too high to reach. The 1520s **choir stalls** are marvellous, carved with faces of

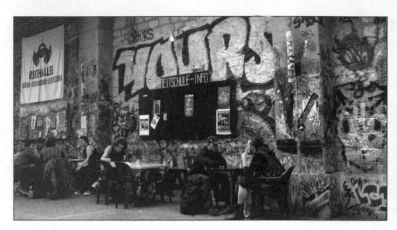

△ Alternative Bern: the graffitied Reitschule

the prophets and much intricate detail of ordinary life. The gorgeous **stained-glass windows** of the choir date from 1441–50, although a hailstorm in 1520 damaged the right-hand windows (two replacements were installed in 1868).

You can also climb the **tower**, the tallest in Switzerland. The way up is just inside the church door (closes 30min early; Fr.4), but be warned: this is a 100m climb up a narrow spiral of 254 stone stairs. (You might want to ask in the church when the bells will be rung and make your ascent to coincide, since the experience of standing beside a gigantic, tolling ten-and-a-half-ton bell – the largest in the country, cast in 1611 – is one you and your ribcage will remember.) The 360-degree vistas over the whole city, most of the surrounding countryside, and out towards the Alps, are dreamy.

On the south side of the church is the **Münsterplattform**, a buttressed terrace above the Aare which took about a hundred years from 1334 to build. Abandoned icons were dumped here during the Reformation, but later it was planted with lime and chestnut trees and given elegant Baroque corner pavilions in order to serve as an open promenade, which is how it has remained. The views of the Aare and of silhouetted trams creeping along the soaring Kirchenfeldbrücke are spectacular. The net below the parapet was added a few years ago as a disincentive to desperate Bernese who chose this rather dramatic and beautiful spot to end it all.

The western Old Town

Some 100m west of the Münster is Casinoplatz – the Casino itself is a concert venue – from where trams head south to the Helvetiaplatz museums (see p.245). A few steps north on Kornhausplatz is the Zytglogge; just beyond, past the Kindlifresserbrunnen (see p.238), stands the **Kornhaus** (Granary; ⓦwww.kornhaus.org), now occupied by offices, a chic bar and the attractive **Kornhausforum** exhibition space, used for shows of design and media (ⓦwww.kornhausforum.ch). Behind is the **Französische Kirche** (French Church; ⓦwww.paroisse.gkgbe.ch), the city's oldest, which originally formed part of a thirteenth-century Dominican monastery. The compact but beautiful interior (Mon–Fri 9–11am & 2–5pm, Sat 10am–3pm) has been much renovated, but retains its stalls (1302) and a rare frescoed rood screen (1495).

Nasty, brutish and short?

There was much social unrest in Switzerland in 1980, most noticeably among radical leftists. Zürich's Autonomous Youth Centre (AJZ) – intended as a police-no-go building where young people could run their own entertainment free from mainstream commercial and social pressures – was violently suppressed, and a similar AJZ movement in Bern which took over the **Reitschule** (an abandoned city-owned former riding school, also known as the **Reithalle**; ⓦ www.reithalle.ch) was also evicted by the police. The situation simmered until late 1987 when, following the eviction of the riverside Zaffaraya community, thousands demonstrated in the city centre, a large group re-squatted the Reitschule and, perhaps most significantly, retailers reported a ten-percent loss in profits over the Christmas shopping season. In the face of such a groundswell of discontent, the police and city council adopted a damage-limitation policy, and left the Reitschule squatters to their own devices.

Despite problems with violent anarchist gangs in the early 1990s, the Reitschule – now an arts centre and activist collective – has come to be highly valued by alternatively minded Bernese, and has even gained a certain official legitimacy while remaining in a curious legal grey area. Its cinema, for instance, is licensed with the council but the bar next to it is illegal; the concert venue pays its taxes, while the adjacent café is packed with dope-smokers. Unlike the similar *Rote Fabrik* movement in Zürich (see p.407), the Reitschule cooperative has consistently rejected proposals to accept funding from the city council, sticking tight to its counter-cultural principles ("No violence, no sexism, no commercial exploitation") by raising its own money through ticket sales, bar profits and a popular annual fundraising party. Through effective word-of-mouth networking, it's been able to stage gigs by British, European and American bands and DJs, raising its profile still further, yet to this day the police don't venture into the complex, turning a deliberate blind eye to such a self-contained concentration of – mostly very innocuous – lawbreaking. It's a run-down, heavily lived-in place and an obvious honeypot for drug dealers (who are barred from entry, but nonetheless gather outside), yet these days is quite safe. More to the point, it's become an icon of opposition to the city council, which has been trying for years to turn it into a multistorey car park and supermarket. A huge graffito as you approach reads *Reitschule bleibt autonom* ("Reitschule still rules itself"). In a remarkably effective and purposeful demonstration of communal self-government, virtually unknown in other European countries and running entirely counter to the Swiss stereotype, it's true.

From the main **Kornhausplatz**, trams weave their way west along Marktgasse, heart of the city-centre shopping district, neatly avoiding the fountain statues of a musketeer in full armour and Anna Seiler, founder of Bern's first hospital, who's been set up to serve as an allegory of moderation. Just beyond the Seilerbrunnen is the **Käfigturm**, an early city gate (1256–1344) which was used as a prison from 1642 until 1897. The broad, sunny **Bärenplatz** opens beyond, and a little further west along hectic Spitalgasse, with its bagpiper fountain, stands the late-1720s **Heiliggeistkirche** (Holy Spirit Church; Tues–Fri 11am–6.30pm; ⓦ www.heiliggeistkirche.ch), acclaimed as Switzerland's finest example of Protestant church building, boasting a fine Baroque pillared-and-galleried interior.

The train station – metres away – marks the limit of the medieval city: several sections of excavated city wall are exposed on the lower shopping concourse.

The Bundeshaus

Immediately south of Bärenplatz is **Bundesplatz** (ⓦ www.bundesplatz.ch), with a display of 26 fountains – one for each canton of Switzerland – spouting in front of the **Bundeshaus**, or Federal Assembly building, built in Renaissance style in 1902 and inscribed *Curia Confoederationis Helveticae* (Assembly Building of the Swiss Confederation). When the parliamentarians are not in session, you can join a free 45-minute guided tour (on the hour Mon–Fri 9–11am & 2–4pm; arrive 25min early at the security entrance on the east side), which takes you through the various chambers, decorated with coats of arms, statues and paintings commemorating events in Swiss history. When the assembly is sitting (the flag overhead will be flying), you can watch proceedings from the public gallery. The building sits on a cliff-edge above the Aare, and the **Bundesterrasse** behind rests on a massive retaining wall. On one side, a quirky little **funicular** runs down to the riverside district of Marzili (daily 6.30am–9pm; Fr.1).

The Kunstmuseum

Bern's **Kunstmuseum** is five minutes' walk northeast of the train station, in an impressive building at Hodlerstrasse 8–12 (Tues 10am–9pm, Wed–Sun 10am–5pm; Fr.6; temporary shows Fr.8–18; SMP; ⓦ www.kunstmuseumbern .ch). Aside from often excellent changing exhibits, the permanent collection comprises large numbers of works by Kandinsky, Modigliani, Giacometti, Rothko, Miró, Pollock and more, including some by Paul Klee (although most now reside at the Zentrum Paul Klee). Cézanne's *Self-portrait with Black Felt Hat* (1879) stands out, as does a depressing, dark Picasso drinker from 1902 and the accomplished, late *Blue Blouse* by Matisse (1936). The finest work in a small group of Old Masters is a luminous gold *Maestá* by Duccio (1290) – rather out of place amidst the rest. Elsewhere, you'll find a range of works by contemporary artists, a wide selection from **Swiss artists** such as Anker and Hodler, as well as the curious naïve art of Adolf Wölfli (1864–1930), a paedophile farmworker who spent most of his life confined to a Bernese asylum creating thousands of pages of writing, musical scores and drawings (his work is also displayed at the Collection de l'Art Brut in Lausanne; see p.128).

Nearby, on Waisenhausplatz, an old school building is earmarked for conversion into the **Museum für Kunst der Gegenwart** (Contemporary Art; ⓦ www.gegenwart.com), to free up space in the main Kunstmuseum gallery.

Zentrum Paul Klee

Alongside the A6 *autobahn* in the eastern suburbs, linked to the city centre by bus #12, rises the glittering **Zentrum Paul Klee** (Tues–Sun 10am–5pm, Thurs until 9pm; Fr.14; temporary exhibits extra; ⓦ www.zpk.org), built to showcase the artist's creative output and reason enough, by itself, to visit Bern. This magnificent building, opened in 2005, was designed by the architect Renzo Piano with a steel roof that undulates in three fluid, graceful waves, or "hills". The northern "hill" is dedicated to Klee the teacher and musician; below this part of the roof is a children's museum, Creaviva, and a subterranean concert hall staging works inspired by Klee's art. The southern "hill" focuses on Klee the researcher and mathematician, housing a research centre and archive relating to the artist.

However, the main draw is the superb **gallery** occupying the central section of the building. This holds over four thousand works by Klee, the largest such collection in the world, comprising almost half of his total output. The permanent exhibition on the ground floor displays two hundred works at a time, changed twice a year, while the basement level stages four annual shows focusing on Klee's contemporaries or highlighting cultural/historical themes. This means that you can't be certain which works will be on display when you

Paul Klee

Born in Münchenbuchsee, just north of Bern, on December 18, 1879, **Paul Klee** is perhaps the best known of all Swiss artists, his attractive, dream-like works filled with allusions to music and poetry and suffused with an endearing humour and humanity. Art historians have difficulty classifying his work, since his unique style takes in elements of primitive art, cubism, surrealism, naïve art and expressionism. Klee was a major influence on the abstract expressionist movement and on non-figurative painting of all kinds in the second half of the century.

His family was very musical, and it was only after a great deal of hesitation that Klee gave up developing his early proficiency on the violin to enrol in the Munich Academy of Art in 1900. There he met the pianist Lily Stumpf, playing duets on violin and piano with her. Shortly afterwards Klee toured Italy, finding inspiration in Byzantine and early Christian art. He made many idiosyncratic sketches, ink drawings and etchings during this period, two of the most famous of which, from 1903, are *Virgin in a Tree* and *Two Men Meet, Each Believing the Other to Be of Higher Rank*.

In 1906 Klee and Stumpf married and settled in Munich, at that time a dynamic centre for avant-garde art. There, Klee met the painter Wassily Kandinsky, starting a lasting friendship; on Kandinsky's urging, Klee joined the expressionist circle Der Blaue Reiter (The Blue Rider), and in 1914 journeyed to Tunisia on a trip which was to change his life. "Colour has taken possession of me," he wrote. "No longer do I have to chase after it, I know that it has hold of me for ever. Colour and I are one. I am a painter." The same year, the Sturm gallery in Berlin staged a joint exhibition of Klee and Chagall.

After the Great War, Klee taught at the famous Bauhaus school in Germany, alongside Kandinsky and the architect Walter Gropius. In 1931 he moved to the Düsseldorf Academy, but after Hitler's rise to power, the Nazis condemned Klee's art – which by now was using delicate, ethereal colour harmonies in subtle, semi-abstract figurative compositions – as "degenerate". Klee fled back to Bern just before Christmas 1933, continuing both his painting and his elaborate ink drawings based on fantasy imagery. He soon, however, developed a crippling disease of the skin and muscles, which affected his ability to work and would eventually kill him. After 1935, his style changed to incorporate thick, crayonish lines and blocks of muted colour in a set of increasingly gloomy musings on war and death. Picasso visited the sick artist late in 1937, as did Braque. Following a giant retrospective of 213 later works at the Zürich Kunsthaus early in 1940, Klee died on June 29, in hospital in Locarno.

visit – but the experience of viewing any of Klee's art in such a breathtaking space is well worth the visit. Check the website for details of the occasional gallery tours in English (free) and the regular programme of music events. Onsite are a shop, café and restaurant.

The Helvetiaplatz museums

Most of Bern's museums are clustered together around **Helvetiaplatz**, on the south side of the Kirchenfeldbrücke. Some, like the Bernisches Historisches Museum, shouldn't be missed; others have less going for them. Trams #3 (direction Saali) and #5 (direction Ostring) shuttle from the train station and the Zytglogge to Helvetiaplatz.

Bernisches Historisches Museum

The fascinating **Bernisches Historisches Museum** (Tues–Sun 10am–5pm; SMP; ⓦ www.bhm.ch), was undergoing major renovation work at the time of writing, due for completion in 2008. Access to its collections was disrupted and you may find only a limited amount on display until the museum's reopening.

Highlights include a series of macabre paintings showing "**The Dance of Death**"; these are 1649 copies of originals (now lost) that were painted in 1516–17 on the wall of Bern's Dominican monastery. The sequence of 24 vivid images, showing a hideously grinning and fooling skeleton leading kings, prostitutes, nuns and lawyers alike to their inevitable fate, sends a chill down your spine – as, no doubt, it was intended to. Also formerly on view were the original sandstone figures from the **Last Judgement** portal of the Münster, fascinating for the chance to view their details up close. There is a spectacular **Islamic collection**, with daggers galore, a mounted Turkestan warrior in full armour, jewellery, ceramics and a reconstructed Persian sitting room, as well as some impressive wall-sized medieval **Flemish tapestries**, including the "**Thousand Flowers Tapestry**", the only one surviving of a set of eight made in Brussels in 1466, which was looted by Bern during the Burgundian wars of 1474–77.

Schweizerisches Alpines Museum

Beside the Historical Museum, the **Schweizerisches Alpines Museum** (Mon 2–9pm, Tues–Sun 10am–5pm; Fr.9; SMP; Ⓦ www.alpinesmuseum.ch) is surprisingly good, taking an intelligent, sensitive look at all aspects of life in the mountains, from tourism, the history of mountaineering and the social identity of mountain dwellers to surveys of Alpine flora and fauna and the impact of industry on the mountain environment. There's plenty to play with and read up on (in English). Crowded all over the museum are dozens of examples of relief mapmaking gone berserk, with mountains, whole valley systems and complete Swiss ranges rendered in perfect scale detail, almost rock by rock, by enthusiasts whose energy and patience can only be imagined.

Other museums

On or very close to Helvetiaplatz are plenty of other museums, as well as the Swiss national library and federal archives. Worth aiming for are the porticoed **Kunsthalle**, Helvetiaplatz 1 (Tues 10am–7pm, Wed–Sun 10am–5pm; Fr.8; Ⓦ www.kunsthallebern.ch), with changing exhibits of contemporary art, usually of high quality, and the **Museum für Kommunikation**, Helvetiastrasse 16 (Tues–Sun 10am–5pm; Fr.9; SMP; Ⓦ www.mfk.ch), which surveys media and communication from postage stamps to the web and beyond.

Outer districts

If you're on an extended visit to Bern, or if you just fancy something a bit different from medieval history at every turn, more modern districts can provide a little urban realism. Easiest to reach – just a short walk north of the train station across the river – is **Lorraine** (Ⓦ www.lorraine.ch). Once a dyed-in-the-wool working-class district, in the last decades Lorraine has attracted a growing population of students and young people. They have created a funky, relaxed community atmosphere, which nonetheless doesn't exclude the many old-timers still in the neighbourhood. Lorrainestrasse and the streets around still retain much charm. On the way, you pass the **Botanischer Garten**, Altenbergrain 21 (daily 8am–5pm; free; Ⓦ www.boga.unibe.ch), a fixture since 1858 with Alpine flora as well as hothouses to explore.

If you follow Schanzenstrasse up behind the train station, a short climb will bring you to Länggassstrasse, heart of the bustling university district of **Länggasse**. The **Unitobler** building, at no. 49a, 300m along on the left (bus #12

A favourite Bernese getaway – if one were needed from such a gentle, slow-paced capital – is to the hill of **Gurten** (Ⓦ www.gurtenpark.ch), which towers over the city from the south. Take tram #9 to Gurtenbahn, in the neat suburb of Wabern, and walk 100m along Dorfstrasse to the **funicular** (every 10–20min; Fr.9 return; passes valid; Ⓦ www.gurtenbahn.ch). The whole journey from the train station to the summit only takes about half an hour. On top you'll find a kids' play area, a lavish folly of a castle (housing the gourmet restaurant *Bel Etage* and the more down-to-earth eatery *Tapis Rouge*) and wide expanses of countryside laced with hiking trails that give views over Bern, out towards the Jura, and across the peaks of the Bernese Oberland. In winter the hill and snowy slopes are crowded with sledding families; in summer, you might have difficulty escaping the hikers and picnickers. Every year, for a weekend in mid-July, Gurten plays host to a very popular **rock festival** (Ⓦ www.gurtenfestival .ch); ask for details at the tourist office.

5

stops outside), was formerly the factory where, for most of the twentieth century, the famous Toblerone chocolate was produced. In the 1980s, production moved to a more modern site outside Bern, and the building was renovated for use by the university (hence the Unitobler name), subsequently receiving numerous architectural awards for sensitivity of renovation. You're basically free to explore: the student café spills onto a sunny plaza behind the building, and the library occupies an extraordinary site between two wings of the building that has been converted into an impressive three-storey atrium space. Just behind Unitobler, on Freiestrasse, is the elegant **Pauluskirche**, dating from 1905 and one of the best examples of Art Nouveau in the country.

Eating and drinking

Bern's compact Old Town groans with **eating and drinking** possibilities, and you'll have no trouble finding something to suit your palate and your budget. The broad Bärenplatz, always busy with people, performers and market stalls, is shoulder to shoulder with cafés – *Gfeller* is a Bernese institution – and is top choice for cappuccinos in the sunshine, but there's a host of places all through the cobbled lanes offering *al fresco* consumption during the summer and firelit warmth in winter.

Cafés and café-bars

Altes Tramdepot Beside the Bärengraben Ⓦ www.altestramdepot.ch. Weave your way past the tourist crowds and into this fine old high-ceilinged place, formerly a tram depot and now a microbrewery, offering three house beers and a speciality monthly brew. The food is solid Bernese, Viennese and Bavarian fare, heavy on game, sausages and rich desserts. It's a sociable place, with good panoramic views from the garden terrace. Daily until 12.30am.

Art Café Gurtengasse 3 Ⓦ www.artcafe.ch. Bright, trendy café just off the main shopping streets that

discovers a new line in studied urban dissipation after the shops shut.

Brasserie Lorraine Quartiergasse 17. Just about the last café in Bern still owned by a cooperative, with excellent, inexpensive food, wood floors and a summer terrace. Games galore fill the cupboards for free use, and the Sunday brunch is the best in Bern. A cosy, calm meeting-place for alternative types and politicos. Take bus #20 to Lorraine (direction Wyler); Quartiergasse is a little ahead on the left. Closed Mon.

Café Litteraire In Stauffacher bookshop, Neuengasse 25. Cosy espresso bar in Bern's largest bookshop, with snacks and newspapers. Closed Sun.

Café des Pyrénées Kornhausplatz 17. Jovial and unpretentious meeting-place for artists, alcoholics and others with loud voices. Equal quantities of twenty- and forty-somethings crowd the place out nightly, with the *Ringgenberg* next door catching the overflow. Closed Sun.

Kornhauscafé In the Kornhaus. The vaulted and renovated interior of the city's former granary is now home to a starkly postmodern-style café, with coiffed customers and pricey desserts and sandwiches. A cool contrast to the raucous *Pyrénées* opposite.

Du Nord Lorrainestrasse 2 ☎ 031 332 23 38. A quality Lorraine café-bar and eatery, offering a nice mixture between heavy meat-and-potatoes dishes and lighter veggie options. A meal might only come to Fr.23 in the evening, or as little as Fr.13 at lunchtime. All the food is organic and comes from small local producers ensuring freshness, and monthly dance events and occasional concerts add to the allure. Bus #20 to Gewerbeschule (direction Wyler). Closed Wed.

Reitschule (aka Reithalle), graffitied buildings next to the railway bridge 5min north of the station ⓦ www.reithalle.ch. See also box p.243. Cooperative-run bastion of Bernese counterculture. The hash-smoky café-bar (named *Sous Le Pont*) is uniquely amiable; however, if sharing a scratched-up table with a green-haired character in a holey sweater rolling a joint isn't your idea of fun, you should head elsewhere. A red traffic light means table service, green means bar service. Open Tues–Thurs 11.30am–12.30am, Fri 11.30am–2.30am, Sat 7pm–2.30am, Sun 10am–4pm; food generally noon–2pm & 6–10pm, during which dope-smoking is discouraged.

Zum Blauen Engel Seidenweg 9b. Cosy student café near the university, with objets trouvés, worn gilt mirrors, hosts of candles and a crowd of young, arty regulars creating a pleasantly seductive atmosphere in which to while away the evening. Eat before you come, though, since the food is disappointing. Bus #12 to Mittelstrasse (direction Länggasse) – Seidenweg is first right. Closed Mon.

Restaurants

Anker Kornhausplatz 16 ⓦ www.roeschti.ch. Cosy, smoky pub, with a restaurant section in the back where you can scoff Swiss stomach-liners such as fondue, *Röschti* and a meat-laden Berner-Teller (around Fr.20).

China Imperial Bärenplatz 21 ⓦ www .baerenplatz.be. Moderately good Chinese, worth mentioning for its unique "Tellerservice": for around Fr.20, choose from a large buffet of uncooked ingredients and marinades, and present the lot to the chef who will wok-fry it all on the spot for piling over rice. They also have à-la-carte options, but at a premium. Tellerservice Mon–Fri 11am–2.30pm & 10–11.30pm only.

Cinématte Wasserwerkgasse 7 ☎ 031 312 21 22. Pleasant riverside nook attached to Bern's premier arthouse cinema. *Menus* (meat or veggie) and the à-la-carte choice are varied and not expensive. It's a small place, though, so booking is advised. Closed at lunch, and all day Tues.

Della Casa Schauplatzgasse 16 ☎ 031 311 21 42, ⓦ www.della-casa.ch. An unprepossessing exterior preludes a fine old Bernese institution serving high-quality Swiss fare. The Bernerplatte – a plateful of half-a-dozen varieties of meats with potatoes and sauerkraut – is a house speciality, but doesn't come cheap: you'd be lucky to walk out with change from Fr.50. Closed Sat eve & Sun.

Dragon d'Or Bollwerk 41. Small Thai/Chinese restaurant, on an unromantic, trafficky corner by the Lorrainebrücke, but nonetheless with a long, inventive menu and well-prepared fare.

Govinda Marktgasse 7, 3rd floor. Tiny Krishna-run diner, serving vegetarian food in an unlikely

---

Cheap eats

It's not hard to find good, filling food in Bern for Fr.10–15, and the best way to cut costs is to take advantage of lunchtime specials and daily *menus*. *Sous Le Pont* in the Reitschule has consistently appealing fare, and a feature of their social policy is to offer one square meal a day for a rock-bottom Fr.5 or so. Bern's branch of the **self-service** *Manora* chain (see p.56), opposite the station at Bubenbergplatz 5a (Mon–Sat 7am–10.30pm, Sun 9am–10.30pm), is a good one, while the station itself has the usual array of low-priced diners in the underground shopping level.

Embassies Australia: embassy in Berlin ☎004930/880 0880, consulate in Geneva. Canada: Kirchenfeldstrasse 88 ☎031 357 32 00. Ireland: Kirchenfeldstrasse 68 ☎031 352 14 42. New Zealand: embassy in Berlin ☎004930/20 6210, consulate in Geneva. UK, Thunstrasse 50 ☎031 359 77 70, ⓦwww.britain-in-switzerland.ch. USA, Jubiläumstrasse 93 ☎031 357 70 11, ⓦbern .usembassy.gov.

Flights Flight enquiries from Bern-Belp ☎031 960 21 11, ⓦwww.flughafenbern.ch.

Gay and lesbian life *Anderland*, Mühleplatz 11, is a popular gay café-bar, also home to HAB, the Homosexuelle Arbeitsgruppen Bern (☎031 311 63 53, ⓦwww.gay-bern.ch). The Reithalle (see p.243) has regular gay and lesbian club nights and its café is gay- and lesbian-friendly at all times.

Lost property City Fundbüro, Predigergasse 5 (Mon–Fri 10am–4pm, Thurs until 6pm; ☎031 321 50 50). Train station Fundbüro (Mon–Fri 8am–noon & 2–6pm; ☎0512 202 262).

Markets Bern has a wealth of markets (ⓦwww .markt-bern.ch), both year-round and annual one-off events. There are general markets on Tuesdays and Saturdays all year on Waisenhausplatz,

Bundesplatz and Bärenplatz, with extra late-opening markets on Thursdays in summer. The Münster hosts a handicrafts market on the first Saturday of every month, and there's a wonderful riverside flea market on Mühleplatz in Matte on the third Saturday of the month (May–Oct only). In December Münsterplatz and Waisenhausplatz host Christmas markets (ⓦwww.weihnachtsmarktbern.ch).

Medical facilities The Inselspital university hospital on Freiburgstrasse (☎031 632 21 11) has a 24-hour emergency room. Bahnhof Apotheke Hörning, on the upper level of the train station, is open daily 6.30am to 10pm.

Police Headquarters is at Waisenhausplatz 32 (☎031 321 21 21).

Post office Main office is the Schanzenpost (Mon–Fri 7.30am–9pm, Sat 8am–4pm, Sun 4–9pm), on Schanzenstrasse just behind the train station. You can collect poste restante mail from counter 16 with your passport.

Radio Radio Bern (known as RaBe; ⓦwww.rabe .ch), at 95.6FM, has diverse, multicultural programming by everyone from Brazilian expats spinning salsa to Reithalle activists condemning the city council over deep ambient beats.

Around Bern

To the east of Bern, a bucolic region of farmhouses and dairies, undulating hills and peaceful villages, spreads through and around the **Emmental**, the valley (*tal*) of the River Emme. Despite the presence of a show dairy and the region's prominent place in the hearts of the rurally minded, cheese-loving Swiss, the Emmental has managed to escape heavy tourist development. It's a wonderful place for long country walks or bike rides. To the north, generic suburban prosperity quietly covers the land as far as the dignified old city of **Solothurn**, capital of its own canton, and now included, along with the Bernese Mittelland, under the rather awkward tourist-office rubric of the "Schweizer Mittelland".

To the west and south, the Mittelland merges into the lakeside country of Canton Fribourg and the Broye (see p.184), with the extremely attractive and

Exploring the Mittelland

You can get information on the whole Mittelland region from the **Schweizer Mittelland tourist office** (☎031 328 12 28, ⓦwww.smit.ch), which is based, along with Bern tourist office, in Bern's main train station. They have plenty of contacts with companies running multi-day adventure packages in the area, and can put together any kind of itinerary covering hikes or long-distance cycling or inline skating on the hundreds of trails through the Mittelland, often throwing in extras such as canoeing on the Aare or panning for gold in the Emmental hills. Pro Emmental (ⓦwww.emmental .ch) also has details of deals in the area.

much overlooked city of **Fribourg** set in lovely countryside southwest of Bern on the French–German language border.

The Emmental

Just outside the eastern city limits of Bern rises the Bantiger mountain (947m); behind it stretches the **EMMENTAL**, a quintessentially Swiss landscape of peaceful, vibrantly green hills dotted with happily munching brown cows, sleepy rustic hamlets and isolated timber-built dairies. This is where Emmental **cheese** (the one with the holes) originates. A local nineteenth-century clergyman-writer celebrated the sturdiness and moral rectitude of Emmentaler dairy farmers in a series of famous novels under the pseudonym Jeremias Gotthelf; since then the place has gathered to itself an atmosphere of earnest rural stability and honesty. The salt-of-the-earth locals have the reputation of being the most reliable, the most sensible, the most Swiss of all the Swiss – a reputation which, in a distasteful modern turnaround, has been exploited by politicians: the extreme right-wing SVP (Swiss People's Party) has expanded

Customs and festivals in the Mittelland

The Mittelland is one of the more traditional areas of the country, and has hundreds of **folk customs and festivals** surviving in various forms, many of them dating back to the pre-Christian pagan religions of the Celts. "Chilbi" is the generic name given to the summer highland festivals of the Emmental, raucous events taking in folk singers and dancers, yodellers, flag-throwers, alphorn blowers and more. The **Lüderenchilbi** is one of the most famous, held on the Lüderenalp meadow every second Sunday in August and centred on a Schwingfest, a traditional Swiss wrestling contest held in a sawdust ring. The winner gets to take home a heifer decked out in garlands. The **Schafsheid**, or sheep-sorting, held in Riffenmatt, 20km south of Bern, on the first Thursday in September, is a colourful event, when the sheep, after spending the summer on the alp, are sorted out by owner, amidst market stalls and celebrations. The **Sichlete** is a communal autumn meal, where in years gone by everyone who'd worked to bring in the harvest would sit down to gorge on stew, sausages, hams and fresh garden produce, helped down by huge meringues and local apple Schnapps; these days, with increasing farm mechanization (and so fewer seasonal farmhands taken on), the Sichlete has become an excuse for two or three villages to get together for a feast and a knees-up. In Burgdorf, the last Monday in June sees the **Solennität**, a 250-year-old festival for children, featuring contests, games and traditional costumes.

Many pagan New Year's Eve rituals survive in the villages of the Mittelland. Laupen's **Achetringele** stems from a Celtic exorcizing of evil spirits and demons on the winter solstice; now shifted to December 31, it involves all the boys in the village chasing away the old year either as one of the masked *Bäsemänner* (broom-sweepers) or as a noisy, cowbell-swinging *Tringeler* (bell-ringer). One of the most bizarre customs survives in Schwarzenburg, 8km north of Riffenmatt, where the **Altjahresesel** (Old-Year Donkey) – these days a man dressed in a donkey suit – is whipped and beaten before being led away by a grim figure representing death. Other characters take part in the ritual, including a bride and groom, representing joy in the year to come, the devil, a priest, and, most chillingly of all, a two-faced woman, the *Hinnefürfraueli*, whose beautiful front face looks forward to the new year, while her hideous rear face despatches the old year to memory.

out of its traditional base in Luzern to make significant gains in the Emmental countryside on a tide of anti-immigration, anti-foreigner, anti-EU rhetoric.

Emmentaler **architecture** is distinctive, the local timber-built inns and dairies crowned by huge roofs with overarching eaves, ringed by wooden balconies, and encrusted with rows of tiny windows, each with its window box and neatly tied-back set of net curtains.

Emmentaler **cooking**, featuring cheese or cream with everything, is renowned around the country (this is where you can find some of Switzerland's finest meringue creations) and protected by the **Ämmitaler Ruschtig** mark (ⓦ www.aemmitaler-ruschtig.ch), which guarantees quality local ingredients and methods. Many inns and restaurants offer – among other dishes – the Ämmitaler Ruschtig *menu*, a gut-busting four-course blowout for around Fr.50: starting with *Beeri Schämpis* (sparkling berry wine) and a cheese salad served with the local *Züpfe* plaited bread, it takes in soup with whipped cream and *Chlepfer Ännis Schwynsschnitzu* (pork escalope in cream sauce, with creamy mashed potatoes and vegetables), then moves on to *Meielis Merängge Gschlaber* (fresh meringue with whipped cream, ice cream and caramelized cream), before rounding it (and you) off with Schnapps-laced coffee. Local tourist offices and the website have the full list of *Ämmitaler Ruschtig* establishments.

Burgdorf and the northern Emmental

On a pleasant road 19km northeast of Bern through Krauchthal village, the picturesque old town of **BURGDORF** is built on a prominence above the Emme. From the train station, follow Bahnhofstrasse south and then head east on Oberstadtweg to meander up into the Old Town, an atmospheric quarter characterized by steep cobbled streets. At the top is the mighty **Schloss Burgdorf**, the Zähringens' largest castle, begun in the seventh century and expanded in the twelfth. Several rooms grouped around an attractive courtyard comprise the **Schlossmuseum** (April–Oct Mon–Sat 2–5pm, Sun 11am–5pm; Nov–March Sun 11am–5pm; Fr.5; SMP; ⓦ www.schloss-burgdorf.ch), outlining local history; the ticket also lets you into the adjacent **Goldmuseum** (same hours), tribute to the history of gold-panning in these hills. Below, the late-Gothic **Stadtkirche** features an elaborate choir screen that looks rather too grand for the church housing it. Every Thursday, the Old Town hosts Burgdorf's weekly **market**.

Roads climb northeast from Burgdorf to a viewpoint at **Lueg** (887m), offering classic panoramas over the rolling countryside. Nearby is **AFFOLTERN**, a pleasant village that's home to the Emmental's flagship **Schaukäserei** (Show Dairy; daily 8.30am–6.30pm; free; ⓦ www.showdairy.ch), a rather hectic place that seems to always be full of busloads of excitable Swiss-German old ladies. As well as being able to watch the various cheesemaking processes – the dairy gets through some seven billion litres of milk a year – you can take in plenty of English-language videos on the cheese industry. A noisy and rather pricey café-restaurant adjacent serves the *Ämmitaler Ruschtig Menü*. Plus, of course, you can buy any amount of cheese, ranging from a bag of "Schnouserli" (bite-sized cubes of different strengths of Emmental) up to a full 9kg round of Emmental shipped direct to your door.

Hasle-Rüegsau and Lützelflüh

Roads drop back down from Affoltern into the Emme valley at **HASLE-RÜEGSAU**, two small villages which, over the years, have grown to hate each other like only next-door neighbours can. Pressured by economic hardship a century or so ago, the farmers of Rüegsau were forced to move down from their original hillside village (tiny Rüegsbach) through an intermediate settlement (Rüegsau itself) to a village down on the Emme (Rüegsauschachen), alongside the settled folk of Hasle; spurred on by displacement, they've since developed a strong community and prosperous commercial base. Static, conservative Hasle has been left behind, and is now struggling with old-fashioned, unrenovated buildings and a stagnating economy. To this day, the two merely tolerate each other: Rüegsauschachen has carefully kept gardens, modern houses and an air of suburban pride, and tends to regard its neighbour as backward, while in Hasle resentment and bitterness run high. This stretch of the river has become known locally as the Jordan, symbolizing the depth of feeling on both banks.

The two were formerly linked across the river by the largest arched wooden bridge in Europe, **Holzbrücke**, a mightily impressive 69m-long construction built in 1839. Unfortunately, it was damaged by cars in 1955 and – another nail in the coffin of neighbourly relations – was shifted 800m downstream to its current position, a five-minute walk west in a hard-to-spot woodsy location behind the train tracks. Hasle and Rüegsau now have an undistinguished modern bridge that seems to divide them as much as join them.

Along the valley floor 8km is a turning for **LÜTZELFLÜH**, a captivatingly charming village at the heart of the Emmental that was home to the local novelist Gotthelf from 1831 to 1854. On the outskirts of the village you'll pass the **Kulturmühle**, an old mill from 1821 that has been turned into a cultural centre (Ⓦ www.luetzelflueh.ch/kulturmuehle), staging everything from the Emmentaler Cock-Crowing Contest to monthly classical music concerts which attract the Bern cognoscenti out into the sticks. The small garden nearby, laid out in French Baroque style, isn't out of place: you can find similar examples outside farmhouses throughout the Emmental – a legacy of French influence over Bern following the 1798 revolution – though today the formal squares and circle patterns are just as likely to be planted with carrots and lettuces. From Lützelflüh, back roads climb to Affoltern, while the main valley road runs on south beside the Emme.

Langnau and the southern Emmental

Some 17km southeast of Bern, the tranquil town of **Konolfingen** marks the start of a scenic road along the Kiese valley through Zäziwil to **LANGNAU**, the main town of the Emmental, but a singularly sleepy place nonetheless, with not much traffic and less than 10,000 people. A small **tourist office** in a travel agent off the main square at Dorfmühle 22 (Mon–Fri 8am–noon & 1–6pm, Fri until 9pm, Sat 9am–4pm; ☎034 409 95 95, Ⓦ www.langnau-tourismus.ch), has information on the region, including details of local walking routes, as does Pro Emmental, Schlossstrasse 3 (Mon–Fri 8am–noon & 2–5pm; ☎034 402 42 52, Ⓦ www.emmental.ch).

East of Langnau, the main road passes through the picturesque village of **Trubschachen**, with big old wooden Emmentaler houses lining the street and a demonstration **pottery** turning out examples of the pretty local ornamental ware. To the north rises the **Napf** (1408m), the most famous of the Emmental's hills and a mecca for hikers and Sunday hill walkers. East of Trubschachen, the road crosses briefly into Canton Luzern and an area known as the **ENTLE-BUCH** (Ⓦ www.entlebuch.ch), with its small countryside resort of **Marbach** boasting a couple of ski lifts serving the Marbachegg (1483m). The Entlebuch recently became a UNESCO-affiliated Biosphere Reserve, in a move to protect this rural area and kickstart sustainable development.

Less than 5km southwest, and back in Canton Bern again, is **Schangnau** village, at the upper end of the Emme valley. A minor road southeast from here winds dramatically between the cliffs, which rise to 2000m on both sides, through tiny **Bumbach** (with lifts up to the wedge-shaped Hohgant, towering overhead at 2197m) and on to **KEMMERIBODEN** (976m). This end-of-the-road hamlet, sliced through by the rushing, tumbling Emme – a mountain torrent at this stage – is the place to get the single best **meringue** in Switzerland (see below), and is also the trailhead for many wilderness hikes, principally the tough path through the mountains to the 2350m Brienzer Rothorn (7hr), from where a rack railway can take you down to Brienz (see p.300).

From Schangnau, the main road crosses the Emme and heads north through **Eggiwil** to Langnau, crossing nine picturesque wooden covered bridges that are typical of the area. From Eggiwil, you can also reach Langnau by a parallel road further west over the crest of **Chuderhüsi** (1103m), which offers spectacular views over the Emmental hills and valleys backed by the snowy Alps.

Emmental practicalities

The best way to get around in the Emmental is **by bike** or **on foot**, both of which allow you to set your own itinerary and pace; stations at Bern, Langnau and Burgdorf have bikes for rent. A scenic **train** line between Bern and Luzern passes through Konolfingen and Langnau, while a branch line runs north from Langnau through Hasle to Burgdorf, shadowing the Emme through verdant countryside. **Postbuses** from Marbach run through Schangnau to Kemmeriboden.

Tourist offices in Bern and Langnau heavily tout **hiking**, with maps and route suggestions galore. Walking through hillside pastureland from Burgdorf to Affoltern, for instance, takes about three hours; from Burgdorf along the riverbank to Hasle, or from Walkringen (above Konolfingen) to Lützelflüh, a little less. For a ramble down the Emme from Langnau to Burgdorf, or a stiffer hike from Langnau up to the Napf, reckon on a leisurely six hours or more. Pro Emmental also has details of companies that can inexpensively transport your bags around the region, enabling you to spend the day walking unencumbered.

Accommodation and restaurants

There are **campsites** around the area: modest *Mettlen* at Gohl, 2km north of Langnau (℡034 402 36 58), and *Sternen* at Marbach (℡041 493 41 05); or the high-quality *Waldegg* at Burgdorf (℡034 422 79 43; April–Sept). The spartan HI **hostel** *Jugendherberge*, Mooseggstrasse 32 in Langnau (℡034 402 45 26, ❷www .youthhostel.ch; closed Oct), has dorm beds (Fr.25), as do the Berghotels on the summits of the Napf (℡034 495 54 08) and the Marbachegg (℡034 493 32 66).

Otherwise, every hamlet has its choice of small-scale country inns which double as **hotel** and **restaurant**, virtually all of which, big and small, use farm-fresh produce and ingredients brought straight into the kitchen from that morning's market – bad Emmentaler cooking is a contradiction in terms. Affoltern, for instance, has the *Sonne* (℡034 435 80 00, ❷www.sonne-affoltern.ch; ❷), with a few pleasantly renovated rooms above a good local restaurant; while dominating the centre of Langnau is the excellent *Hirschen* (℡034 402 15 17, ❷www.hirschen-langnau.ch; ❸), a huge inn in typical Emmentaler style. In far-flung Kemmeriboden is the wonderful ✴ *Kemmeriboden-Bad* (℡034 493 77 77, ❷www.kemmeriboden.ch; ❸), with comfortable rooms, superb local cooking and delectable home-made meringues.

Solothurn

SOLOTHURN (Soleure in French), some 35km north of Bern at the confluence of the Emme and the Aare, is touted as the most beautiful Baroque city
in Switzerland – with justification. Its compact but characterful Old Town is
crammed with an odd architectural mix of Swiss-German sturdiness and Italianate excess dating from the town's heyday in the seventeenth and eighteenth
centuries. It's an easy day-trip from points all over the Mittelland, with a couple
of fine Baroque churches, a worthwhile art gallery and a high viewpoint nearby
for breezy walks.

In Celtic times, Salodurum was a fortified town; after Roman domination
and Alemannic invasion, it was only in the tenth century that Solothurn rediscovered some stability. With the demise of the Zähringen dynasty in 1218,
the city expanded its territory to form a buffer zone between Bern and Basel,
and joined the Swiss Confederation in 1481. In the decades following, despite
the turmoil of the Reformation all around, Solothurn remained Catholic and
so, in 1530, was chosen by the Catholic ambassadors of the king of France as
their place of residence. For more than 250 years, these **French ambassadors**
oversaw Solothurn's redevelopment in the contemporary **Baroque** style. Some
destruction followed the 1798 revolution, but much of Solothurn's graceful Old
Town has survived. These days it's a lively, cosmopolitan place, with thriving
industry (watchmaking and precision manufacturing figure large) and a varied
mixture of ethnicities on its streets.

Arrival, information and accommodation

Solothurn is on the main SBB **train** line between Biel/Bienne and the big rail
junction at Olten. It's also served by regular mini-trains from Bern operated
by RBS (ⓦ www.rbs.ch); these don't appear on the big departures board in
Bern station – aim instead for platforms U1–4. Solothurn's **train station** is a
few minutes' walk south of the river: Rötistrasse is the highway heading north
from in front of the station, but quieter Hauptbahnhofstrasse, one street to the
left, will deliver you to the pedestrian-only Kreuzackerbrücke, which leads into
the Old Town. **River boats** on the *Aarefahrt* route to and from Biel/Bienne
(May–Oct; see p.266; ⓦ www.bielersee.ch) dock at the Romandie jetty beside
the railway bridge, two bridges west (upstream) of the Kreuzackerbrücke.

The **tourist office** is in the Old Town, at the foot of the cathedral steps,
Hauptgasse 69 (Mon–Fri 8.30am–noon & 1.30–6pm, Sat 9am–noon; ☎032
626 46 46, ⓦ www.solothurn-city.ch & ⓦ www.mysolothurn.com), and runs
excellent ninety-minute **walking tours** of the town beginning from the
Baseltor (May–Sept Sat 2.30pm; Fr.5).

Hotels

Baseltor Hauptgasse 79 ☎ 032 622 34 22,
ⓦ www.baseltor.ch. Popular and friendly
brasserie with just six ensuite rooms, all appealingly simple and fresh, and so generally snapped
up well in advance. Worth booking for. ❸
Kreuz Kreuzgasse 4 ☎ 032 622 20 20, ⓦ www
.kreuzkultur.ch. Rough-and-ready cooperative,
offering shared-bath rooms – spartan and wood-floor
creaky (newer rooms are upstairs) – plus discounts
for stays beyond one night and free kitchen use. ❶

Krone Hauptgasse 64 ☎ 032 626 44 44,
ⓦ www.hotelkrone-solothurn.ch. Top choice in
town, its Baroque decor preluding solidly comfortable traditional rooms in either Biedermeier or
Louis XV style, with stout, tasteful furnishings
and rooms at the back looking over the cathedral
steps. ❹–❺
Zunfthaus zu Wirthen Hauptgasse 41 ☎ 032 626
28 48, ⓦ www.wirthen.ch. An all-wood guildhouse
with plasticky but spacious rooms, some ensuite,
some not. ❷

Hostel

Jugendherberge (HI hostel) Landhausquai 23 ☎032 623 17 06, ⓦwww.youthhostel.ch. One of the country's best hostels, modern steel-and-glass decor insinuated into a seventeenth-century building on the Old Town riverbank just west of the Kreuzackerbrücke. There's a wide choice of dorms (from Fr.29) and rooms with and without river views, and as well as all the usual services, including bike rental, they'll put together an inexpensive packed lunch for you. March–Nov. ❶

The Town

Centrepiece of the town is the massive **St-Ursen-Kathedrale** (daily 8am–noon & 2–7pm; Oct–Easter closes 6pm), an Italianate vision in local grey-white stone that seems to float above the main Hauptgasse. It's crowned by a greenish tower which rises to 62m. (Incongruously, the steps leading up to the entrance are a favourite smoking spot for the local kids; not all the fragrant odours drifting about are ecclesiastical incense.) Overhead, the Latin inscription in gold running around the building refers to Solothurn's patron saints, Ursus and Victor, who refused to worship Roman gods and were martyred. The bright, soaring wedding-cake interior has a riot of intricate stucco covering the white stone walls that is typical of the lavish late-Baroque era in which the church was built (1762–73).

Sandwiched between shopfronts barely 100m along Hauptgasse is the atmospheric **Jesuit church**: push the unremarkable door to gain entry to the extremely remarkable interior, dating from the 1680s and encrusted with a dizzying amount of lacy stuccowork. Halfway along Hauptgasse, overlooking the central Marktplatz, is the **Zytglogge**, Solothurn's oldest building, the lower part dating from the twelfth century, the upper part from 1467, and the astronomical device in the centre from 1545. The hour hand on the giant clock face is longer than the minute hand.

A few steps north of the cathedral is the doughty **Altes Zeughaus** (Old Arsenal), housing a moderately interesting museum of militaria (May–Oct Tues–Sun 10am–noon & 2–5pm; Nov–April Tues–Fri 2–5pm, Sat & Sun 10am–noon & 2–5pm; Fr.6; SMP). This massive collection documents Solothurn's history of battles and booty, most impressively with a hall full of swords and suits of armour. Some 50m east is the **Baseltor**, a city gate dating from 1508. Hug the walls north to the corner bastion of the Old Town and you'll come to the circular **Riedholz** tower, now the location of a summer cycle of prestigious classical concerts.

Across the lawns to the north lies the **Kunstmuseum** (Tues–Fri 10am–noon & 2–5pm, Sat & Sun 10am–5pm; free; ⓦwww.kunstmuseum-so.ch). Highlights of this surprisingly good collection are Holbein's *Solothurner Madonna* (1522), on a panel backed by the *Madonna in the Strawberries* (1425), painted by the anonymous Master of the Garden of Paradise. Some spectacular Alpine canvases are led by Ferdinand Hodler's much-reproduced portrait of a Herculean William Tell emerging from a break in the clouds. One of Hodler's famous sequences of larger-than-life moving bodies decorates the stairs, while Klimt's luscious *Goldfish* is another highlight.

Last but not least, way on the other side of town, on the southern bank near the river-boat landing stage, is the highly odd **Krummer Turm**, or Twisted Tower, a fortification of the town dating from the 1460s. Looked at from any point other than its axis of symmetry, it appears to be hopelessly lopsided; in fact, though, its base is an irregular pentagon (due to the tower's original location at the sharp corner of a bastion of entrenchments). The spire, although it seems about to topple off any minute, has been safe and secure these past five

Above Solothurn – the Weissenstein

One of the best viewpoints in the Swiss Jura is the **Weissenstein**, a ridge rising to 1284m with a breathtaking panorama towards the Bernese Alps. Local **trains** from Solothurn to Moutier stop at Oberdorf, from where you can either hike up or take the **chairlift** – which is closed on Mondays – to the summit (Fr.19 return; ⓦwww .seilbahnweissenstein.ch). On top is the slick *Weissenstein Hotel* (℡032 628 61 61, ⓦwww.weissenstein.ch; ❸), complete with gourmet restaurant, modern conference facilities and, alongside, a lovely garden planted with Jura flowers and plants, best in June and July. Plenty of walks branch out from the hotel, mostly along the crest of the ridge; you could also do a chunk of the long-distance Jura Höhenweg walk from here (see box p.222).

centuries. From the tower, you can cross to the northern bank and hike the riverside road for two hours west to the stork colony at **Altreu**.

Eating and drinking

Of the many Old Town terrace **cafés**, *Rust* on Marktplatz (ⓦwww.rust -restaurant.ch) has the edge, overlooked by the Zytglogge and facing the cathedral along the length of Hauptgasse. Look out for the local delicacy *Solothurner Kuchen*, a tart of nut fondant and whipped cream piled on a biscuit base, supplied by the slice in cafés and whole – in many sizes – by any of the *confiseries* in the centre.

Manora, the self-service **restaurant** in the Manor department store just off Marktplatz, has a rooftop terrace and a range of fresh-cooked dishes at rock-bottom prices (Mon–Fri 9am–6.30pm, Thurs until 9pm, Sat 8am–5pm). Both *Kreuz* and *Baseltor* hotels have cooperative café-bar-restaurants serving up delectable organic food in gargantuan portions; *Kreuz* is less expensive (*menus* from Fr.12, day and night), while *Baseltor* has the slight edge on quality (both closed Sun lunch). Otherwise, *Taverna Amphora*, Hauptgasse 51, offers Greek specialities for well under Fr.20.

Fribourg

Some 34km southwest of Bern, **FRIBOURG** (Freiburg in German) is one of Switzerland's best-kept secrets. Its winningly attractive medieval Old Town, almost perfectly preserved, is set on a forested peninsula in a meander of the River Sarine. Steep, cobbled streets, bedecked with wrought-iron lamp standards and ornate inn signs, are picturesque and characterful. Six bridges, from medieval wooden fords to lofty modern valley spans, provide woodcut-pretty views across the town of the old houses piled up together on the slopes.

But the views only scratch the surface. For, behind its visual charm, Fribourg is perhaps Switzerland's most amiable and easy-going town, thoroughly modern at heart despite the medieval appearance of some quarters. It's small enough to have kept most of its city centre residential, but large enough to have attracted a lively, cosmopolitan mix of people to fuel the community atmosphere. One of the country's most prestigious universities – and its sole Catholic one – attracts students from all over the country (and especially from Italian-speaking Ticino), generating a social dynamism that is tangible on the streets.

The River Sarine (Saane in German), which carves a path through the town, is the local defining line of the *Röstigraben*: Fribourg is split roughly 70:30 between French Swiss, who call their town *free-boor* and are a majority on the western bank, and German Swiss, to whom the place is *fry-berg* and who form a majority on the eastern bank. The town's radio station has two separate channels, many streets have two names, and almost everyone is instinctively bilingual. Some of Fribourg's older folk even cling on to the ancient Bolze dialect, a mixture, unsurprisingly, of French and German which you might be able to catch in the taverns and public squares of the Basse-Ville (Lower Town).

Within easy reach of both Bern and Lausanne, Fribourg is an understated town. For the time-pressed must-see visitor, it merits barely an hour or two – which is all the better for those on a long, slow journey of familiarity around Switzerland, who could spend a week in the place and not see it all.

Some history

Bertold IV of Zähringen founded Fribourg in 1157 as part of his consolidation of regional power, which also saw the establishment of Bern, Burgdorf, Thun and Murten, as well as Freiburg-im-Breisgau in Germany. After 1218, the Zähringens were succeeded by the Counts of Kyburg, who were themselves bought out by the Austrian Habsburgs in 1277, Fribourg passing from hand to hand each time. In 1452, Savoy took over, although in the Burgundian wars shortly afterwards Fribourg backed the victorious Swiss against Savoy, and so became a free city. In 1481, it joined the Swiss Confederation.

For reasons which haven't been fully explained, Fribourg remained Catholic throughout the Reformation (and is still determinedly Catholic today): virtually surrounded by Protestant Bern, it became a place of refuge for the exiled bishops of Geneva and Lausanne. The ruling families retained their grip on power even throughout the 1798 upheavals, and in 1846 Fribourg joined the reactionary Sonderbund, fighting against Protestant liberalism all around. It lost, and suffered expulsion of its Jesuits as revenge. Intolerance was short-lived,

---

Fribourg's festivals

In February, Fribourg's **carnival** is focused on the ritual mass torching of the Grand Rababou effigy, bearer of the winter and of all evil. However, the event to watch out for is **Bénichon** (Kilbi in German), a kind of harvest feast held in the first half of September similar to the Emmental's Sichlete (see p.252). In former years, this would take the form of large communal meals: lamb stews and hams and meringues and all kinds of seasonal specialities, such as a special mild mustard spread on oven-hot bread, *poires à botzi* (a sweet pear compote), and paper-thin *beignets de Bénichon* (pastry leaves sprinkled with icing sugar). These days, the celebrations have lost their communal, seasonal edge, and tend to be more public affairs, with food stalls and tastings in the street.

Every July, Fribourg stages the prestigious **Festival de Musiques Sacrées** (ⓦwww.fms-fribourg.ch), featuring concerts of ancient and modern sacred music by performers from around the world. In early September, the Auge district hosts a **Semaine Médiévale**, featuring markets, events, costumed processions, concerts and food stalls designed to evoke the fifteenth century. In the first week of October, there's a **fun run** over the 17km between Murten/Morat and Fribourg, to commemorate the messenger who brought news to the town of victory at the Battle of Murten in 1476 (see p.187). **St Nicholas Day**, in the first week of December, sees an evening parade headed by a jolly old man with a long white beard, who rides in on a donkey distributing *biscômes* (spicy cake squares) to the children of the town amid much revelry.

FRIBOURG

Gottéron gorge

Bern

Lausanne

ACCOMMODATION
Auberge de Jeunesse   C
Auberge de Zaehringen   E
Elite   D
Musée   A
De la Rose   B
Sauvage   F

EATING & DRINKING
Aigle Noir   8
Belvédère   6
Bindella   3
Buffet de la Gare   12
Café Populaire   2
La Cigogne   10
Fleur-de-Lys   7
Gothard   1
Manora   9
Midi   5
Pans' Ami   4
La Spirale   11

0   250 m

Chapelle de St Beat

Musée de la Marionnette

Église des Augustins

AUGE

BOURG

Chapelle de Lorette

Granary

Cathédrale St-Nicolas

Musée Gutenberg
Espace Jean Tinguely
Basilique Notre-Dame

Église des Cordeliers

Musée d'Art et d'Histoire

Hôtel de Ville

NEUVEVILLE

Fri-Art

Funicular

Collège St-Michel

Église St-Michel

University

Tinguely Fountain

Station

though: Jews were allowed to return to Fribourg in 1866 after almost 400 years of banishment, and a local entrepreneur, Georges Python, founded the Catholic university in 1889. The boom of the last few decades has brought new wealth and energy to Fribourg.

Arrival, information and city transport

Fribourg's **train station** is high on the hill overlooking the Old Town from the northwest, with the **bus** terminal beneath. As you emerge from the station, Avenue de la Gare heads at an angled left down to the central Place Python (pronouced *pee-tohh*). From here, the Old Town covers the hill in front of you. Rue de Lausanne is the main thoroughfare, heading east and down to the **Bourg** district, centred on Place Notre-Dame (aka Place Tilleul) and the cathedral. From the Bourg, steep lanes cascade south down the hillside into **Neuveville**, while Grand'Rue heads east down to **Auge**, the oldest part of the Old Town at the tip of Fribourg's peninsula. It's a walk of about 1.5km – downhill all the way – from the station to Auge.

The **tourist office** is beside the station – turn right as you come out (Mon–Fri 9am–6pm, Sat 9am–3pm; Oct–April Sat closes 12.30pm; ☏026 350 11 11, ⓦwww.fribourgtourism.ch & www.pays-de-fribourg.ch). Cheery staff can provide information on the city and the whole canton, which extends as far south as Gruyères (covered in Chapter 2) and also takes in Murten/Morat and Estavayer-le-Lac (in Chapter 3). Ask for details on the many easy **countryside walks** which start from the city centre.

Vegetable and flower **markets** occupy Place Python (Wed morning) and the area around the Hôtel de Ville (Sat morning) all year round. The Place du Petit-St-Jean features a traditional flea market on the first Saturday of the month (April–Nov), while there's a crafts market on Rue de Lausanne on the last Saturday of the month (March–Dec).

City transport

Fribourg is definitely a **walking** city, but the hills are steep enough that you may want to take advantage of at least one **bus** line (ⓦwww.tpf.ch): bus #4 runs every fifteen minutes on a handy route between Auge and the station, running via Place du Petit-St-Jean, Planche-Supérieure and Neuveville. This is the only bus to serve the lowest reaches of the peninsula. Individual **tickets** are Fr.2.20, or you could get a general **city pass** for one/three days (Fr.6/11). **Bike rental** is available from the station (Mon–Sat 6am–8.45pm, Sun 7am–8.45pm).

Accommodation

Business **hotels** aside, Fribourg has some characterful accommodation options, all well located in or next to the Old Town, and covering a range of budgets.

Hotels

Auberge de Zaehringen 13 Rue de Zaehringen ☏026 322 42 36, ⓦwww.auberge-de-zaehringen.ch. Fribourg's oldest patrician mansion is now a venerable and beautiful gourmet restaurant with just a couple of guest rooms – spacious, luxurious and characterful like five-star hotels can never be. ❹

Elite 7 Rue du Criblet ☏026 350 22 60, ⓦwww.elitefribourg.ch. Plain but perfectly adequate rooms within a couple of minutes' walk of the station. Discounts apply for weekend stays. Cheaper attic rooms. ❷–❸

Musée 11 Rue Pierre-Aeby ☏026 322 32 09. Large-ish, spartan rooms seconds from the cathedral and the Musée d'Art, with both ensuite and shared-bath options. Reception closed Sun. ❷

De la Rose 1 Rue de Morat ☏026 351 01 01, ⓦwww.hotelrose.com. Cosy and very central

Minotel hotel, with efficient and friendly staff. Good value, but some rooms can be a little gloomy. ❹

Sauvage 12 Planche-Supérieure ☎026 347 30 60, ⓦ www.hotel-sauvage.ch. Stylish renovated rooms in an old Neuveville house, spacious and individually decorated. Free parking, and bus #4 stops outside. ❹–❺

Hostel

Auberge de Jeunesse (HI hostel) 2 Rue de l'Hôpital ☎026 323 19 16, ⓦ www.youthhostel.ch. Good-quality hostel occupying part of the old city hospital a few minutes' walk north of the station, with clean dorms (Fr.29) that are a tad institutional. Closed Nov–Feb. ❶

Campsite

La Follaz ☎026 436 24 95. Basic riverside site in Marly, 5km south. April–Sept.

The Town

Just south of the train station, the grassy, open **Grands-Places** marks an entry into the commercial heart of the city, overlooked by department stores and an ugly tower-block hotel – shown to be even uglier by its proximity to a beautiful shuttered medieval house on the square, now a café. The ensemble is mocked by one of Jean Tinguely's famous **fountains**, a spouting, spitting affair installed in 1984 and described by one critic as "a firework in iron and water".

Shopping streets lead east to the busy **Place Python**, at the centre of the modern city. From here, three routes lead you into the Old Town. To the south, the trafficky **Route des Alpes** is supported on pillars above Neuveville; its valley-side railings offer wonderful views of the river and of Fribourg's rustic location. The central **Rue de Lausanne**, a picturesque cobbled thoroughfare of pavement cafés and bookshops, heads directly downhill from Place Python. It's worth, though, cutting north from Python on the narrow, steeply rising **Ruelle de Lycée** up to the atmospheric medieval **Collège St-Michel**, for most of its history a Jesuit seminary and now part of Fribourg University; the shaded grounds of the academy are very peaceful, and there's a terrace from where you can look out over the city. Ancient covered steps, the **Escaliers du Collège**, lead down from the terrace to join the lower end of Rue de Lausanne.

The Bourg

All routes from the new town converge in the Old Town's most historically important district, known as the **Bourg**, home to churches, the cathedral, the town hall and an array of mansions and patrician town houses. The Bourg's central square is a small space with four names. At the foot of Rue de Lausanne is **Place de Nova-Friburgo** with, opposite it, **Place de l'Hôtel de Ville**; next to it is a tree-lined square known either as Place des Ormeaux (Elm Trees) or **Place de Tilleul** (Lime Tree); and next to that is **Place de Notre-Dame**. Just to confuse matters, the indeterminate, 50m-long Rue du Pont-Muré connects them all.

An impressive presence to one side is the late-Gothic **Hôtel de Ville** (Town Hall), a highly photogenic building dating from 1501–22, whose double exterior staircase was added in 1663. St George spears the dragon on a fountain statue dating from 1525 in the square in front of the building. A regular Saturday morning market spills over into the streets around, one of which, Rue des Épouses (Street of Spouses), is spanned by a decorative old sign attesting to the fidelity of the couples who once lived there. The dourly impressive **Grand'Rue** heads off down the hill, a virtually intact example of a seventeenth- to eighteenth-century street, complete with Baroque, Regency, Rococo and Louis-XVI facades jostling for position all the way down.

Fribourg's highlight is the towering, High Gothic **Cathédrale St-Nicolas** (Mon–Sat 7.30am–7pm, Sun 8.30am–9.30pm), just off Place Notre-Dame. Take a moment to view the soaring, buttressed **tower**, exposed to view for its entire 73m height clear to the ring of feathery spires on top. Built over a church dating from the city's foundation in 1157, the present building was begun in 1283, and took two centuries to complete. Traffic swishes past the elaborate main portal, featuring a tympanum with the Last Judgement. The vast interior is immediately impressive, its mustiness and gloominess redolent with old incense. The **pulpit** (1516) and, opposite it, the octagonal **font** (1499) are both particularly ornate, and the tracery **choir screen** (1466) is dazzlingly intricate. Virtually all the stained glass in the cathedral is modern Art Nouveau. Don't miss the tiny **Chapel of the Holy Sepulchre**, to the left of the door as you head out, beside a plaque commemorating the mass celebrated here by Pope John Paul II in 1984: inside you'll find a group of 10 figures, sculpted from sandstone in about 1430. Christ is being laid in the tomb by Nicodemus and Joseph of Arimathea; behind, Mary is supported by John the Baptist, Mary Magdalene, two other women and two angels. Three sleeping soldiers are placed nearby. The life-sized ensemble, drenched in a blueish submarine light from modern stained-glass windows, is extraordinarily moving, every stony figure conveying an intense emotion that effortlessly spans the six centuries it has stood here.

About 50m north of the cathedral is the porticoed **Basilique Notre-Dame**, with white-and-gold stuccowork dating from the late eighteenth century adorning the spacious, airy interior. Samson prises apart the lion's jaws on a fountain statue in front (1547), copied from a design by Dürer. Adjacent on Rue de Morat is the Espace Jean Tinguely museum (see below), with beside it the Franciscan **Église des Cordeliers**. Originally part of a friary founded in 1256, the church was renovated in the eighteenth and nineteenth centuries, but retains its impressive medieval decor, including a vast altar painting (1480) showing the crucifixion and, on the opened wings, the adoration. High Gothic oak choir stalls (1300), the oldest in Switzerland, and a larger-than-life 1438 statue of Christ at the whipping post also stand out. Between the two is the **Musée Gutenberg**, Place Notre-Dame 16 (Wed–Sat 11am–6pm, Thurs until 8pm, Sun 10am–5pm; Fr.10; ⓦwww.gutenbergmuseum.ch), with engaging displays of printing, graphics and bookbinding.

Espace Jean Tinguely and Musée d'Art et d'Histoire

In front of the Musée Gutenberg is the highly recommended **Espace Jean Tinguely–Niki de St-Phalle**, 2 Rue de Morat (Wed–Sun 11am–6pm, Thurs until 8pm; Fr.5; ⓦwww.fr.ch/mahf), devoted to the twentieth-century Swiss kinetic artist, who was born in Fribourg, and his wife. Housed in an old transport depot, this museum complements the more famous one in Basel (see p.216), documenting Tinguely's whimsical but trenchantly purposeful sculptural machines. Old rusty wheels, bits of iron and *objets trouvés* are all recycled in constructions which use a lot of energy and demonstrate great skill and ingenuity – but which go absolutely nowhere. One of the grandest on display is the *Retable de l'Abondance occidentale et du Mercantilisme totalitaire*; press the foot button to set things in eccentric but somehow poetic motion.

About 150m north, within sight of the medieval Porte de Morat, is the **Musée d'Art et d'Histoire**, 12 Rue de Morat (Tues–Sun 11am–6pm, Thurs until 8pm; Fr.6; ⓦwww.fr.ch/mahf), housed in an elegant sixteenth-century patrician mansion and, bizarrely, an adjacent slaughterhouse. Begin on the left in the Ratzé mansion, filled with medieval art and reliquaries with, upstairs, a striking series of fourteen biblical scenes carved in relief from panels of lime wood (1600). Upstairs again is the especially revolting jewel-bedecked skeleton of St Felix, dating from 1755, with glitter for lips and a phial of dried blood resting beside the bones. From the ticket desk, a subterranean tunnel runs through to the old abattoir, whose sombre stones now shelter a line of fourteen saints taken from the cathedral portal alongside a particularly mournful Tinguely sculpture.

Neuveville and Planche-Supérieure

From the Hôtel de Ville, the ancient cobbled Rue de la Grand-Fontaine heads sharply downhill into **Neuveville** – men walking here may find themselves whistled and clicked at by women hanging from the top windows of the old buildings: this street amounts to Fribourg's red-light district. Neuveville is, nonetheless, perhaps the most peaceful and picturesque area of the city, exemplified by the Escaliers du Court-Chemin (Short-Cut Stairs). They clatter down the hill through a triangular open square adorned with the tinkling Fountain of Strength (1550) onto **Rue de la Neuveville**, which boasts whole rows of original Gothic buildings overlooked by the Hôtel de Ville on high. A quirky **funicular** runs down from St-Pierre, beside Place Python, to Place du Pertuis at the western end of Rue de la Neuveville (daily 9.30am–7pm; Fr.1.60, city passes valid): it works by tapping the city's sewers and diverting raw sewage into a chamber beneath the car at the top to make it heavy enough to be able to haul its partner up the slope. It's the smelliest ride in Switzerland.

A back street off Rue de la Neuveville is home to the **Fri-Art** contemporary art centre, Petites-Rames 22 (Tues–Fri 2–6pm, Thurs until 8pm, Sat & Sun 2–5pm; Fr.6; Ⓦ www.fri-art.ch), hosting a challenging array of shows of anything from painting to video art and multimedia.

From Neuveville, the triple-arched Pont de St-Jean crosses the river and leads past a tiny church up into the huge, open **Planche-Supérieure**, overlooked by a fountain statue of John the Baptist (1547) and these days used as a car park. Dominating the square is the old **granary** (1708), in shimmering white with

△ Granary, Fribourg

Trains

Bern to: Baden (twice hourly; 1hr 10min); Basel (every 30min; 1hr); Biel/Bienne (3 hourly; 30min); Brig (hourly; 1hr 35min); Burgdorf (3 hourly; 15min); Fribourg (every 30min; 20min); Geneva (every 30min; 1hr 45min); Interlaken West & Ost (every 30min; 45min); Langnau (4 hourly; 40min); Lausanne (twice hourly; 1hr 10min); Luzern (twice hourly; 1hr 5min); Neuchâtel (3 hourly; 35min); Solothurn (every 30min; 40min); Thun (4 hourly; 20min); Zürich (3 hourly; 1hr).
Burgdorf to: Bern (3 hourly; 15min); Fribourg (every 30min; 45min); Langnau (hourly; 30min).
Fribourg to: Bern (every 30min; 20min); Estavayer (hourly; 40min); Lausanne (twice hourly; 45min); Murten/Morat (hourly; 25min); Yverdon (hourly; 55min).
Langnau to: Bern (every 30min; 40min); Burgdorf (hourly; 30min); Luzern (hourly; 55min).
Solothurn to: Bern (every 30min; 40min); Biel/ Bienne (3 hourly; 20min); Neuchâtel (twice hourly; 40min); Zürich (twice hourly; 55min).

Buses

Fribourg to: Avenches (8 daily; 25min); Bulle (for Gruyères; hourly; 30min).
Kemmeriboden to: Schangnau (every 2hr; 15min).

Boats

Solothurn to: Biel/Bienne (April–Oct 2–3 daily; 2hr 50min).

The Bernese Oberland

CHAPTER 6 # Highlights

✳ **Interlaken** Bustling resort town at the hub of the region's excellent mountain railway network. **See p.275**

✳ **Schynige Platte** One of the finest Alpine viewpoints. **See p.281**

✳ **Lauterbrunnen valley** Breathtaking U-shaped cleft, its high, craggy walls doused by waterfalls such as the Trümmelbach. **See p.284**

✳ **Wengen & Mürren** Car-free mountain resorts with superb skiing and fine hiking. **See p.287**

✳ **Schilthorn** The cable-car ride up to this lofty summit is unforgettably dramatic. **See p.288**

✳ **Grindelwald** Long-acclaimed ski and sports resort at the foot of the mighty Eiger. **See p.290**

✳ **Jungfraujoch** The train ride up to Europe's highest station is easily done in a day from Interlaken. **See p.294**

✳ **Gstaad** Legendary Alpine hideaway of the rich and famous, set amidst lovely countryside on the Golden Pass train line. **See p.306**

△ Chalet, Mürren

6

The Bernese Oberland

South of Bern and Luzern lies the grand Alpine heart of Switzerland, a massively impressive region of classic Swiss scenery – high peaks, sheer valleys and cool lakes – that makes for great hiking and gentle walking, not to mention world-class winter sports. The **BERNESE OBER-LAND** (Ⓦwww.berneseoberland.ch) is the most accessible and touristed area, and also the most spectacular, best known for a triple-peaked ridge of Alpine giants at its core: the Eiger, Mönch and Jungfrau, cresting 4000m. However, the Oberland takes in a vast tract of territory, and the approaches to the high mountains have their own, gentler pleasures: the twin lakes of the **Thunersee** (with the atmospheric old town of **Thun** at its head) and the **Brienzersee** (with **Brienz**) offer Alpine horizons and beauty enough to merit a stop of their own. Between the two, the bustling town of **Interlaken** is the main

Exploring the Bernese Oberland

Rail ticket offices sell the **Bernese Oberland Regional Pass** (Ⓦwww .regiopass-berneroberland.ch), which has a vast area of validity well beyond the borders of Canton Bern. The **core region** extends from Gstaad to Meiringen, and includes boats and trains between Thun, Interlaken and Brienz, as well as trains, buses, funiculars and cable cars serving Schynige Platte, Lauterbrunnen, Mürren, Stechelberg, Wengen, Grindelwald, First, Kleine Scheidegg and Kandersteg. Core-region transport is free on the days you choose, and half-price the rest of the time. **All other transport** in the region is half-price throughout the pass's validity (aside from a few cable cars which offer only a 25 percent discount): this includes the rides up to the Jungfraujoch and the Schilthorn; trains from Bern to Thun, Luzern to Brienz, and Montreux to Gstaad; buses over the Grimsel, Furka and Susten passes; and a network of connections further afield.

There are two passes, both available in the summer season only (May–Oct); they're pricey but very worthwhile if you're keen to explore the Oberland. The **seven-day pass** (Fr.220) covers any three days of free travel in the core region, plus the remaining four days' travel throughout the area at half-price. The **fifteen-day pass** (Fr.265) covers any five days' core-region travel for free, plus the remaining ten days at half-price across the area.

transport hub for the region, but the sheer volume of tourist traffic passing through can make it a less-than-restful place to stay; you'd do better to head straight for the mountains.

On a visit to the region, and stunned by the natural drama all around, the composer Felix Mendelssohn wrote: "Anyone who has not seen the scenery which surrounds Interlaken does not know Switzerland." Once you've seen it, you'll know what he meant. Arguably the single most captivating place in the entire Alps lies just a short way south of Interlaken – the gorgeous **Lauterbrunnen valley**, with the resorts of **Wengen** and **Mürren** perched on plateaux above providing excellent winter skiing and summer hiking. **Grindelwald** is another bustling resort in its own valley slightly to the east. Both offer access to one of Switzerland's top excursions, the rack-railway journey winding up through spectacular mountain scenery to the ice-bound **Jungfraujoch**, a windswept col nestling at 3454m just below the peak of the Jungfrau itself, and the site of the highest train station in Europe. Further west, the Oberland rolls on through less-visited wooded valleys and pastureland, out to the borders of the German-speaking area, where sits probably the most famous name in the region: **Gstaad**.

Tourist offices in virtually every town control the thousands of **chalets and private rooms**, most of which, at higher altitudes anyway, close in the quiet off-season. Tourist offices can also provide details of the region's numerous **mountain huts** (generally open June–Sept), which offer hikers or ski trekkers a bed and simple comforts in the wilds of nature.

Beware that almost everything in the high resorts – shops, hotels, attractions, walking routes, mountain railways and cable cars – may be **closed during off-season** (mid-April to early June & mid-Oct to mid-Dec), or possibly operate with limited service only; see p.27 for more. We've specified months of opening only when they differ from this pattern.

The Jungfrau region

The **JUNGFRAU REGION** (Ⓦ www.jungfrau.ch) lying south of the major gateway resort of **Interlaken** is the rather uninspiring title foisted on what is perhaps the most dramatic, certainly the most memorable, mountain scenery in the whole of Switzerland. The Matterhorn may be more recognizable, Davos and St Moritz may be flashier, but the quantity and sheer scale of the awesome giants on offer here at close quarters takes your breath away.

Sightlines throughout the area are dominated by the mighty triple crest of the **Eiger**, **Mönch and Jungfrau** (Ogre, Monk and Virgin) – three giant peaks rising side by side to 4000m. The Jungfrau is the focus, partly because it's the highest (at 4158m), and partly because the network of mountain trains from Interlaken Ost culminates at the **Jungfraujoch**, a saddle below the peak that claims the honour of hosting the highest train station in Europe. The ride up – dubbed the "Top of Europe" – is touted endlessly in Interlaken and beyond as being the highlight of your holiday; despite the hype, it's not far wrong, although the competing journey up the **Schilthorn**, also accessed from Interlaken Ost, is cheaper, quicker, less crowded and uses cable cars – always more scenic and dramatic than cogwheel trains.

There's plenty of equally stunning scenery to be enjoyed at lower altitudes. The region is centred on two valleys, which divide a few kilometres south of Interlaken. To the west is the **Lauterbrunnen valley**, celebrated with justification as the loveliest mountain valley in Europe, with its alluring car-free resorts of Wengen and Mürren. To the east, the narrow Lütschental widens out on its way to the bustling town of **Grindelwald**, perfectly placed for its many visitors to take advantage of the hiking and skiing possibilities all around. Excellent transport around all these places – mostly trains, but also taking in cable cars, funiculars and the odd bus – means that you can roam to your heart's content, which, with the quality of natural scenery on offer, may take a while.

Interlaken

Don't be ashamed of being a tourist in **INTERLAKEN** – that's what the place exists for. Interlaken is all that many visitors ever see of Switzerland, whisked through the country on a rapid lakes-and-mountains tour. The town is perfectly positioned as the gateway into the Oberland, linked into main train routes to and from Bern and Zürich, with branch lines feeding out in all directions into the high Alps nearby. It's a pleasant enough place, even if overly commercial and packed with Swiss-kitsch souvenir shops, and it's useful for its proximity to the mountains.

The town is situated on the Bödeli, a small alluvial neck of land between the twin **lakes** of the Thunersee and Brienzersee. It's one of the oldest resorts in the country, famed for its superb **views** towards the Jungfrau massif, which lies perfectly framed between two hills to the south of town. And that's pretty much the whole story: history, character and tradition take a back seat to the necessities of providing for the millions of trippers who pass through on their way to more dramatic backdrops. Many of the shops which cram the centre of town have prominent signs in Japanese; of Interlaken's tourists, fully a quarter are from Japan, as many as from around Switzerland.

△ Interlaken souvenirs

INTERLAKEN

Amtshaus

Beatushöhlen

UNTERSEEN

OBERDORF

SCHEIBGASS

HAUPTSTRASSE

SEESTRASSE

UNTERDORF

HELVETIASTRASSE

BAUMGARTENSTRASSE

BAHNHOFSTRASSE

SPIELHÖLZLI

UNTERE GASS

SPIELMATTE

A

NEUGASSE

BLUMENSTR.

2

MARKTGASSE

C

POSTGASSE

HARDERSTRASSE

VIKTORIASTRASSE

Kursaal

i F

HÖHEWEG

E

3

BAHNHOFSTRASSE

West
Station

KANALPROMENADE

Thunersee

AARMÜHLESTRASSE

FLORASTRASSE

NIESENSTRASSE

BAHNHOFPLATZ

7

4

5

6

ROSENSTRASSE

G

ZENTRALSTRASSE

JUNGFRAUSTRASSE

Höhematte

ALPENSTRASSE

GENERAL-GUISAN STRASSE

I

BERNASTRASSE

SULEGGSTRASSE

WALDEGGSTRASSE

JUNGFRAUSTRASSE

PARKSTRASSE

HAUPTSTRASSE

MATTE

Heimwehfluh, Spiez & K

J

RUGENPARKSTRASSE

RUGENAUSTRASSE

ROTHORNSTRASSE

FRIEDWEG

BERNASTRASSE

WYCHELSTRASSE

L

0   200 m

WALDEGGSTRASSE

Rugen
Woods

Open-air
Theatre

Wilderswil, Lauterbrunnen Valley & Grindelwald

Arrival and information

Interlaken clusters around its long main street, **Höheweg**, which has a train station at each end. Mainline trains terminate at **Interlaken Ost** station, 1km east of the centre, but those coming from the Bern/Thun direction pass first through **Interlaken West** station, a more useful place to get off since it's closer to the town centre. (Be aware that branch-line trains into the mountains depart only from Ost station.) Both stations are linked by trains and city buses, which run roughly every ten minutes from one to the other.

For coverage of Interlaken's twin **lakes** of Thun and Brienz, turn to p.296.

THE BERNESE OBERLAND | Interlaken

6

Harderkulm

Funicular

Aare

Sackgut
Campsite

HÖHEWEG

SCHLOSSSTRASSE

Ost
Station

Höhematte

Schloss

KLOSTERSTRASSE

LINDENALLEE

KLOSTERSTRASSE

SPORTWEG

ALPENSTRASSE

FREIESTRASSE

ALLMENDSTRASSE

MITTENGRABENSTR

KLOSTER GASSLI

UNTERDORFSTRASSE

GELESTRASSE

BÖNIGSTRASSE

KESSLERSTRASSE

RUTISTRASSE

BÜHLSTRASSE

Brienzersee

Bönigen & N

ACCOMMODATION
Backpackers Interlaken/
 Alp Lodge | A
Backpackers Villa Sonnenhof | H
Balmer's Herberge | M
City | C
Du Lac | B
Happy Inn | G
Hirschen | L
Jugendherberge | N
Lötschberg | I
Metropole | F
Neuhaus | K
Royal-St-Georges | D
Rugenpark | J
Victoria-Jungfrau | E

EATING & DRINKING
Café Runft | 7
El Azteca | 6
Goldener Anker | 2
PizPaz | 4
Positiv Einfach | 5
Schuh | 3
Spycher | 1

See the box on p.297 for details of the **boats** which run on the lakes flanking Interlaken; those from the Brienzersee dock directly behind Ost station, those from the Thunersee behind West station.

Interlaken is only one of five communities on the neck of land between the two lakes: to the west is **Unterseen**; to the south are **Matten** and, a little further out, **Wilderswil**; to the east is **Bönigen**. Although the built-up area is contiguous from one to another, all five retain their individual identity and postal codes: if you go looking for something on Hauptstrasse, be aware that Unterseen's Hauptstrasse is a long way from Matten's Hauptstrasse.

The **tourist office** is in the town centre, on the ground floor of the *Hotel Metropole*, Interlaken's only skyscraper, at Höheweg 37 (May & June Mon–Fri 8am–6pm, Sat 8am–4pm; July–Sept Mon–Fri 8am–7pm, Sat 8am–5pm, Sun

10am–noon & 5–7pm; Oct–April Mon–Fri 8am–noon & 1.30–6pm, Sat 9am–noon; ☎033 826 53 00, ⓦwww.interlakentourism.ch). Staff remain surprisingly cheerful despite an onslaught of enquiries, and have tons of information to hand, including details of cut-price deals at hotels.

More than half-a-dozen operators have mountain and city **bikes for rent**, including both train stations and several of the hostels.

Accommodation

Interlaken is well geared up for visitors: there are literally dozens of **accommodation** options. The downside of the town's popularity is that breakfasts can be skimpier, corners dusted less assiduously, and personal service less expansive than in quieter towns. Beware that hotels fill up very quickly at the frantic height of the summer season; in winter, when most people stay in the mountains, many places close for a month or two.

Inexpensive hotels

City Marktgasse 6 ☎033 822 10 22, ⓦwww.city -hotel.ch. Slick modern place in the heart of town, spotlessly clean and efficient enough at providing the creature comforts. ❷–❸

Hirschen Hauptstrasse 11, Matten ☎033 822 15 45, ⓦwww.hirschen-interlaken.ch. Atmospheric old inn on a crossroads south of the centre, in the same family for some 300 years, with freshly redone pinewood rooms – comfortable and pleasant – boosted by the dark-beamed *Stübli* and restaurant. Also has plenty of parking. Closed Nov. ❸

Lötschberg General-Guisanstrasse 31 ☎033 822 25 45, ⓦwww.lotschberg.ch. Characterful family-run smoke-free hotel in a residential quarter, with excellent-value attic rooms in particular and a good-value B&B guesthouse attached. Keenly priced apartments also available. Discounts for long stays. Closed Jan. ❷–❸

Rugenpark Rugenparkstrasse 19 ☎033 822 36 61, ⓦwww.rugenpark.ch. Quiet, very friendly family-run little place close to West station, with modest, attractive rooms that are cosily unrenovated – only some are ensuite. Has a non-smoking floor. ❶–❷

Mid-range and expensive

Du Lac Höheweg 225 ☎033 822 29 22, ⓦwww .dulac-interlaken.ch. Comfortable, stylish old house in a perfectly quiet riverside location beside Ost station. In the same family since 1888 (and at one time hosting Field Marshal Montgomery during World War II), it offers bright, light rooms that are a mid-range bargain. Closed Dec–Feb. ❹–❺

Metropole Höheweg 37 ☎033 828 66 66, ⓦwww.metropole-interlaken.ch. The town's major landmark, and its sole high-rise, soaring above

the tourist office. Generic business-class facilities inside, memorable only for the stunning upper-floor views (the fourteenth is top), which are worth paying for. ❺–❼

Neuhaus Seestrasse 121, Neuhaus on the Thunersee ☎033 822 82 82, ⓦwww.hotel -neuhaus.ch. Far and away the most relaxing spot in and around Interlaken, a lone old inn guarding this end of the Thunersee, 4km west of the centre. It styles itself a golf and beach hotel – stretching the definition on both scores – although, with sailing and watersports on offer, it's a popular weekend draw for locals. You can always find a quiet spot on the lakeside lawns to take in the stunning views over to the Niesen. Reception is in the modern annexe to one side, but ask for a room in the main house (which doubles as a fine restaurant): they're neither big nor modern, but are characterful and wonderfully quiet. The welcome is warm – this is a corner few tourists find – and boosts the feeling of being well out of the Interlaken hubbub. Free parking. ❸–❹

Royal-St-Georges Höheweg 139 ☎033 822 75 75, ⓦwww.royal-stgeorges.ch. Wonderfully stuffy town-centre palace hotel, renovated to prime Victorian-era condition throughout. Closed Nov–Jan. ❺–❻

Victoria-Jungfrau Höheweg 41 ☎033 828 28 28, ⓦwww.victoria-jungfrau.ch. One of the grandest hotels in the country, dating from 1864–65, which is located perfectly in the town centre and once hosted Mark Twain on his journey around Switzerland. These days it's been entirely restored (although its front rooms still boast sensational views of the Jungfrau) and now incorporates a beautiful, state-of-the-art luxury spa. Staying here is a really special treat. ❾

Open-air Tell

Interlaken is famous throughout Switzerland for its annual staging of Schiller's play **William Tell**, performed every summer since 1912 in an open-air theatre (with covered seating) in the Rugen woods near Matten. The stage is framed by old wooden houses in thirteenth-century style, and backed by the forest – the perfect backdrop for the cast of 250, all sporting Swiss national dress and authentic medieval uniforms, and the several dozen horses, cattle and farm animals which wander around bringing a festive air to the show. The dialogue is in German only, but it's pretty obvious what the plot is (see p.394).

Evening performances run twice weekly throughout July and August. **Tickets** (Fr.26–50) are available at ⓦ www.tellspiele.ch and from most tourist offices in the region. The Interlaken tourist office has packages comprising one or two nights' accommodation, plus show tickets, from around Fr.175.

Camping and hostels

There are thirteen **campsites** within 4km of town. The closest is the simple *Sackgut* (☎033 822 44 34, ⓦ www.campinginterlaken.ch; May–Oct) behind Ost station. Less than 1km south of the centre is *Jungfraublick* (☎033 822 44 14, ⓦ www.jungfraublick.ch; May–Sept), a more comfortable family choice. Of the sites in Unterseen, lakeside *Manor Farm* (☎033 822 22 64, ⓦ www.manorfarm .ch) is a five-star site open all year.

Hostels

Alp Lodge/Backpackers Interlaken Marktgasse 59 ☎033 822 47 48, ⓦ www.alplodge.com. Modest place, with dorms from Fr.19 and rock-bottom room prices. ❶

🛌 **Backpackers Villa (SB hostel)** Alpenstrasse 16 ☎033 826 71 71, ⓦ www .villa.ch. A quality low-cost option – an attractive chalet with comfortable, spotless rooms, a good shared kitchen, and dorm beds from Fr.33; rooms at the back, with stunning views of the Jungfrau, command a small surcharge. ❶

Balmer's Herberge (SB hostel) Hauptstrasse 23, Matten ☎033 822 19 61, ⓦ www.balmers.com. Located fifteen minutes south of the centre, this is the oldest privately run hostel in the country, with fifty years' experience of catering to backpackers, offering kitchen access, laundry, and spartan comforts in well-tended pinewood dorms (from Fr.24), quads, triples and doubles. The atmosphere

is brash and convivial, a perfect place to hook up with other travellers for trips into the mountains; you can get discounts on extreme sports and activity excursions if you book direct through the hostel. In summer, when the frat-party atmosphere and queues for the shower and for breakfast get too much, they set up a tent village in a field 800m south, with bunks sleeping over a hundred. ❶

Happy Inn (SB hostel) Rosenstrasse 17 ☎033 822 32 25, ⓦ www.happy-inn.com. A backup dorm option (from Fr.22), clean and centrally located but uninspiring. Partying downstairs in the bar can go on until after midnight. ❶

Jugendherberge (HI hostel) Aareweg 21, Bönigen ☎033 822 43 53, ⓦ www.youthhostel .ch. Quiet, pleasant place in this Brienzersee village 2km east of Interlaken town centre, with dorms from Fr.30 and bike rental. Closed mid-Nov to mid-Dec. ❶

In and above the town

The town itself is only of passing interest, with precious little to see or do other than a couple of hours of exploratory wanderings, either on foot or from the back of one of the horse-drawn carriages which ply for business outside West station. The large grassy **Höhematte** in the centre of town was where the monks of Interlaken's ancient Augustinian monastery pastured their cattle; on the east side of the park is the **Schloss**, dating from 1747 but incorporating some of the fifteenth-century monastical buildings. Parts of the Gothic church survive in the renovated **Schlosskirche** adjacent, which has also clung onto its old cloister, each window of which, curiously, is of a different design. Strolling west along the River Aare beneath the looming cliffs brings you into pretty **Unterseen**. This atmospheric district houses some of the area's oldest buildings: the square in front of the Amtshaus off Untere Gasse is particularly picturesque.

Interlaken starts to reveal its secrets when you explore further afield. Before you even venture into the mountains, there are a couple of viewpoints above the town to enjoy, both laced around with hiking trails. A funicular (May–Oct) rises from behind Ost station through the woods to the **Harderkulm** (1310m), offering vistas over the town, both lakes and a panorama of snowy peaks close enough to touch. Friday evening sees folk music and dancing at the summit restaurant, with special late trains laid on; book through the tourist office. On the other side of town, some 500m south of West station, is a station for the vintage red funicular (May–Oct) serving the **Heimwehfluh** (669m), a more touristic venture, with the summit often crowded with parents taking the kids round the model-train exhibition and the miniature bob-run.

Just east of the centre is the **Mystery Park** (daily 10am–6pm; Nov–March closed Mon & Tues; Fr.48, family tickets available; ⊛www.mysterypark.ch), an ambitious theme park devoted to unexplained phenomena. A central sphere is surrounded by seven pavilions dedicated to evoking and exploring various mysteries – the Pyramids of Giza, ancient Indian mysticism, the earth patterns of Nazca in Peru, Stonehenge, and so on. There's plenty of slick multimedia gadgetry, flight simulators and pop-science experiments, as well as shops, cafés and restaurants – good for a rainy day, though even then, whether it's worth the very high admission price is debatable.

Touring the Alpine passes

The configuration of roads over the high Alps means that it's straightforward to put together a looping day-long driving tour of the highest roads in Europe, bringing with it spectacular scenery from every angle. Every one of the passes mentioned below has at least a restaurant on top, and most have some form of inn accommodation as well, making it easy to break your journey.

From Interlaken, roads flank the Brienzersee to Brienz and on to Meiringen (see p.302), just beyond which at Innertkirchen is a split of mountain routes. East lies the Susten Pass (see below), while south is the stunning climb to the **Grimsel Pass** (2165m; see p.355), beyond which, at Gletsch, is another choice of routes. You could head down the valley of the young Rhône and branch off near Oberwald to the **Nufenen Pass** (2478m; see p.354), followed by a scenic drive to Airolo and up over the celebrated **Gotthard Pass** (2108m; see p.398) to the Alpine hub town of Andermatt. Alternatively, from Gletsch another hairpin route leads steeply up on a breathtaking drive over the **Furka Pass** (2431m; see p.399) and on down to Andermatt. From Andermatt, continue north through the Reuss gorges to Wassen, where a road climbs west up over the **Susten Pass** (2224m) and back to Meiringen.

The easiest way to go is with one or other of the excellent summer tours by **postbus** (⊛www.postbus.ch). The **Four Passes tour** from Meiringen follows the route outlined above, taking in the Grimsel, Nufenen, Gotthard and Susten in a full-day loop. Alternatively, the **"Ticino Route Express"** runs from Andermatt over the Gotthard and Nufenen passes to Oberwald, while the **"Romantic Route Express"** runs from Andermatt over the Furka and Grimsel before following the spectacular narrow route from Meiringen over the **Grosse Scheidegg Pass** (1962m; closed to private cars) to Grindelwald. All transport passes are valid, but you must pay a small surcharge and reserve a seat in advance (see the website).

Eating and drinking

Food is not an especially high priority in Interlaken, and much of what's on offer is fairly basic, unadventurous fare. *Migros* restaurant opposite West station has self-service staples (closed Sun).

Cafés and café-bars

Balmer's Herberge See "Hostels". The sociable travellers' bar attached to this busy hostel serves up cheap beer nightly to its backpacking clientele.

Brasserie 17 Rosenstrasse 17. Loud central bar beneath the *Happy Inn* hostel, with cheap food (sandwiches, snacks and veggie fare) and big beers.

Café Runft Bahnhofplatz 51, opposite West station. A cosy tearoom, snackery and bar open daily until 3am.

Goldener Anker Marktgasse 57 Ⓦ www.anker.ch. Local pub crammed most nights with young people hanging out and shooting pool. The food is cheap and simple (*menus* around Fr.14), and occasional live bands fill out the atmosphere.

Positiv Einfach Centralstrasse 11 Ⓦ www .positiv-einfach.ch. Popular and crowded little DJ-bar in the centre of town.

Schuh Höheweg 56 Ⓦ www.schuh-interlaken .ch. A tearoom-cum-*chocolatier*-cum-restaurant on the corner of the Höhematte – refinement in the midst of kitsch-souvenir hell. The supremely elegant interior preludes equally elegant tea and cakes or international cuisine (plus veggie options), helped down by the cocktail pianist tinkling away in the corner.

Top o'Met Top floor of *Hotel Metropole*, Höheweg 37. Fifteenth-floor views out over the town and lakes, with an outdoor terrace.

Restaurants

El Azteca Jungfraustrasse 30 ☎ 033 822 71 31, Ⓦ www.hotel-blume.ch. Attractive little Mexican place on a side street, with *menus* from Fr.15 and live mariachi (Fri & Sat). Closed Wed in winter.

Hirschen Hauptstrasse 11, Matten ☎ 033 822 15 45, Ⓦ www.hirschen-interlaken.ch. Traditional, rustic old wood-beamed inn serving up huge portions of steaming Swiss fare, with *menus* from Fr.25 or so. Closed Tues & Nov.

Matahari In *Hotel Lötschberg*, General-Guisanstrasse 31 ☎ 033 823 80 01. Quality Indonesian cuisine, including *rijsttafel*, a sampler of many Indonesian dishes, plus a range of Indian dishes with plenty for vegetarians. *Menus* around Fr.22. Closed Tues & lunch Wed.

Neuhaus See "Accommodation". Comfortable old inn situated right on the Thunersee shore, with views across the water from the large waterside terrace. Quality of both the cooking and the service is high. The speciality is, of course, freshly caught fish (around Fr.30), and there are some excellent vegetarian dishes (Fr.23 or so).

PizPaz Centralplatz ☎ 033 822 25 33. A pleasant place serving generic pasta, pizza and fish dishes for Fr.16 upwards, on a central crossroads. Closed Mon in off-season.

Spycher In Casino Kursaal, Strandbadstrasse 44 ☎ 033 827 61 00, Ⓦ www.casino-kursaal.ch. Just one part of this entertainment complex, housing a casino, bars, cafés and a formal garden, this restaurant is dedicated to touristic dinner-plus-folklore shows. They run three to six nights a week (May–Oct), and you can just watch the dancing and alphorn blowing for around Fr.16, or choose from five *menus* of typical Swiss fare for Fr.40–60, which include the show.

Schynige Platte

The best short trip from Interlaken – and one of the finest mountain excursions in the country – is the ride up to the breathtaking **SCHYNIGE PLATTE** at 2000m, from where you can survey some of the best panoramic views in the entire Alps.

The rack-railway (June–Oct only) up to Schynige Platte starts from the peaceful village of **Wilderswil**, a few kilometres south of Interlaken, reachable from Ost station by train or from West station by bus #5. It's an attractive little place in its own right, full of traditional wooden houses; the main road bypasses the village centre. From Wilderswil, trains coil their way up for fifty minutes through some spectacular scenery to the top station, from where perfect views of the Eiger, Mönch and Jungfrau, ranged high above the valley opposite, open up. A short walk away is the busy restaurant and *Kulm* **hotel** (☎033 822 34 31, ⓦwww.schynigeplatte.ch; ❷).

One of the kiosks at the top station is a test centre for Lowa hiking boots: you can select any pair you like and try them out for free all day, with no obligation to buy – handy, since marked trails lead out in all directions from here. The **Panoramaweg** is unmissable: an easy trail, it leads you on a two-hour circuit of the summit ridge above the station, with, at the halfway point, an unforgettable panoramic view taking in the full sweep of the Thunersee, Interlaken and the Brienzersee. The return leg continues in a wide arc through meadows to the **Botanischer Alpengarten** (Fr.3), filled with the local flora, and one of the few places where you can be guaranteed to see a genuine living edelweiss.

As a longer alternative, one of the most attractive walks in the whole Oberland region leads from Schynige Platte along the crest up to the Faulhorn

Sports and activities in the Jungfrau region

The Jungfrau region offers a vast array of **sports and activities**. We've outlined the best summer walks throughout this chapter, and highlighted a week-long trail in the box on p.289. You'll also find operators offering adventure sports all summer long (and some year-round).

Winter sports

In winter, resorts like Wengen, Mürren and Grindelwald can offer some of the finest skiing and snowboarding in the Alps: ⓦ**www.jungfrauwinter.ch** has the full rundown. The Jungfrau region is divided into three ski sectors: **Grindelwald-First**, **Kleine Scheidegg-Männlichen** (which includes lifts from both the Grindelwald and Wengen sides) and **Mürren-Schilthorn**. There's skiing and snowboarding for all levels and, with access to very high altitudes, the season is unusually long: from mid-November through to the end of April. Beginners are best served at **Wengen** and **Grindelwald**, both of which have nursery slopes and plenty of blue runs very close to the village centres. Red pistes run beneath the long Männlichen–Grindelwald gondola line, while there are long blue runs from **Kleine Scheidegg** down to Brandegg and Grindelwald-Grund. **First** (2168m), above Grindelwald, also has a host of leg-stretching blue and red runs. **Mürren** offers some wonderfully scenic skiing, with a chairlift accessing more than half-a-dozen routes down from the Schiltgrat (2145m), and the Allmendhubel funicular linking with a draglift to access lots more pistes-with-a-view.

There are thrilling red and black runs from the **Lauberhorn** down to Wengen, following the course of the famous World Cup downhills and slaloms. At 4km, this is the world's longest competition piste; if you're around in mid-January try and catch a glimpse of the professionals. Black runs around the region are satisfyingly testing, most notably those down to Wengen from the **Eigergletscher** (2320m). The incredibly steep "Inferno" piste from the Schilthorn summit (2970m), through difficult mogul fields and the infamous "Gun Barrel" down to Mürren, covers 11km.

The best location for **snowboarding** is the Snowpark at Oberjoch (2501m), above First, where there's an array of rails, bank jumps, waves and kickers, plus a giant superpipe at Schreckfeld. Kleine Scheidegg also has a popular boarder park. Plenty of options for **sledging** include from Alpiglen to Brandegg in the shadow of the Eiger's North Wall, and a huge 15km run from First round to Bussalp and down to Grindelwald.

Passes are good value. For the Mürren-Schilthorn sector, 1/6 days cost Fr.56/244, for the joint First-Kleine Scheidegg-Männlichen sectors, 1/6 days cost Fr.56/259. The

(2681m), and then down past the tranquil Bachalpsee to First and Grindelwald (roughly 6hr). This is worth doing at any time, but if you're around in July and August, grab the unique opportunity to walk the route **by moonlight**: on the two Saturday nights with the fullest moon, trains leave Interlaken Ost at 10.20pm, bringing you to Schynige Platte by 11.40pm, from where a local guide leads you along the six-hour trail. Ask the Interlaken tourist office for more details.

The standard **fare** from Interlaken is Fr.60 return (Swiss Pass half-price), or Fr.30 after 2pm; two kids can travel free with a fare-paying adult. Buying a cheaper ticket to the midway station of Breitlauenen and enjoying the views on the walk to the top (1hr 30min) is no hardship. Every Wednesday in July and August, trains depart Wilderswil at 5.35am to catch the summit **sunrise**, with the optional extra of breakfast (Fr.15) at the *Kulm* hotel.

Jungfrau Region Sportpass, valid in all sectors, costs Fr.120 for 2 days, Fr.288 for 6 days, or Fr.820 for the season. (Note that all these are not valid for lifts descending from the Schilthorn, only those ascending.) There are various **discount** deals for early/late season skiing, as well as skiing/boarding **classes** and more; check online for details.

Adventure sports

Loads of companies in and around Interlaken run all kinds of adventure sports, many of them year-round. A popular choice is **tandem paragliding** (from about Fr.150), with tandem hang-gliding not far behind: top takeoff spots are the Beatenberg, Schynige Platte, the Niederhorn and even the Schilthorn. **Tandem skydiving** from 4000m or 4600m (around Fr.400) gives you up to a minute of freefall at 125mph. **Bungee jumping** is also hugely popular, from various vantage points around the region (Fr.125 or more), and plenty of operators offer **canyoning** on any of several whitewater rivers above the Thunersee, Brienzersee and further afield (half-day about Fr.110, full day Fr.170). **Rafting** on the Lütschine, the Simme, the Saane and elsewhere costs around Fr.100. Summer **ice-climbing** – no experience necessary, and all equipment provided – is about Fr.150 for the day, **rock-climbing** Fr.90 for half a day. More extreme options including **zorbing** (Fr.100), where you're pinned immobile inside a giant plastic sphere and rolled down a mountainside. **Horse-trekking** costs around Fr.75 for 2hr.

The biggest operators include **Alpin Raft**, beside *Balmer's Herberge* (☏033 823 41 00, ⓦ www.alpinraft.ch), **Alpin Center**, opposite *Balmer's* and at Wilderswil station (☏033 823 55 23, ⓦ www.alpincenter.ch), and **Swissraft**, Jungfraustrasse 72 (☏033 823 02 10, ⓦ www.swissraft.ch), but also check out ⓦ www.outdoor-interlaken.ch, ⓦ www.paragliding-grindelwald.ch, ⓦ www.paragliding-interlaken.ch, and ⓦ www .skydiveinterlaken.ch. You can generally book at your hotel too.

Gunten on the Thunersee is a centre for **windsurfing**, **water-skiing** and **wakeboarding** (ⓦ www.wasserskischule.ch), and there are tons of options all around the region for **mountain biking** solo (tourist offices stock maps and route details) or on guided trips (ⓦ www.mtbeer.ch).

Meanwhile ⓦ www.swissalpineguides.ch, ⓦ www.grindelwaldsports.ch and ⓦ www .be-je.ch, among others, run full- or multi-day **guided treks** in the high mountains; these are serious excursions with full equipment on tough terrain – often glaciers – and cost, accordingly, hundreds of francs.

The Lauterbrunnen valley

It's hard to overstate just how stunning the **LAUTERBRUNNEN VALLEY** is – even hardened Alpinists shrug their shoulders and call it the most beautiful valley in Europe, bar none. An immense U-shaped cleft (the world's deepest) with bluffs on either side rising 1000m sheer, doused by some 72 waterfalls, it is utterly spectacular. Staying in Interlaken or Grindelwald comes a poor second to basing yourself in or above Lauterbrunnen for your time in the Oberland: whether you stay two hours or two weeks, you won't want to leave.

Lauterbrunnen village stands on the valley floor, while the slopes above nurture two of Switzerland's most appealing little resorts. **Mürren** to the west is the transfer point for the dramatic cable-car ride up to the **Schilthorn** peak, while **Wengen** to the east is a stop on the train line up to Kleine Scheidegg and the **Jungfraujoch**. Both of them are car-free, perched on narrow shelves of pasture way above the world below, and both offer some of the best hiking and skiing to be had in the Alps.

Lauterbrunnen

The road south from Interlaken shadows the train tracks and the River Lütschine through Wilderswil. Cliffs close in either side as you reach **Zweilütschinen**: the Schwarze Lütschine tumbles in from Grindelwald further east, while the road and railway continue south alongside the rushing Weisse Lütschine (named "white" for its foaminess) through a charming wooded gorge. At the point where the valley opens up, airily broad, sunlit and impossibly picturesque, you enter the busy little village of **LAUTERBRUNNEN** (796m). The train station here is the junction point for journeys up to Wengen and on up to the Jungfraujoch.

Opportunities for sightseeing and exploring around and about are virtually limitless. At the entrance to the village, opposite the train station, a gondola run by BLM ("Mürrenbahn") crests the west wall of the valley to **Grütschalp**, from where a train – one of the most scenic rides in Switzerland – trundles its way along the cliff edge, in full view of the snowy giants across the way, to Mürren (see p.287). You might, instead, fancy the steep path up to Grütschalp (rising 690m in 2hr), in order to take advantage of the panoramic stroll alongside the tracks to Mürren (1hr 10min).

Just before Lauterbrunnen, precipitous roads and footpaths wind up west to **Isenfluh**, an isolated little hamlet on a tiny patch of green alp, from where little-trod hiking trails fan out and a cable car rises to the Sulwald alp, at the foot of the distinctively jagged Lobhörner crag (2566m).

At the southern end of Lauterbrunnen village, the delicate **Staubbach Falls** – at nearly 300m, the highest in Switzerland – gush out of a sheer cliff, like a lacy decoration on the rugged precipice. From Lauterbrunnen it's a scenic half-hour walk, or an hourly postbus, 3km up the valley to the hugely enjoyable **Trümmelbach Falls** (daily: July & Aug 8.30am–6pm; April–June & Sept–Nov 9am–5pm; Fr.11; ⓦwww.truemmelbach.ch). These impressively thunderous waterfalls – the runoff from the high mountains – have carved corkscrew channels through the valley walls: a stepped catwalk leads you over and around the enclosed, boiling cauldrons of rushing water (up to 20,000 litres a second), which throw up plenty of spray and have gradually eroded the rock into weird and wonderful shapes.

From the top, above the falls, trails from Mettlenalp connect to paths leading to Wengen and Wengernalp.

△ The frozen Staubbach Falls

Practicalities

Lauterbrunnen's **train station** is at the northernmost end of the village, directly opposite both the gondola station for Mürren and the **tourist office** (July & Aug Mon–Fri 8am–7pm, Sat 9am–12.30pm & 1.30–5pm, Sun 9am–12.30pm & 1.30–4pm; June & Sept Mon–Fri 8am–12.30pm & 1.30–6pm, Sat & Sun 9am–12.30pm & 1.30–4pm; Oct–May Mon–Fri 8am–12.30pm & 1.30–5pm; ☎033 856 85 68, ⊛www.lauterbrunnen.ch).

Lots of places offer dorm **accommodation**. Down by the tracks is the cosy SB *Valley Hostel* (☎033 855 20 08, ⊛www.valleyhostel.ch; Fr.25), most of its rooms with balconies. There are two **campsites** at the southern end of the village, including *Jungfrau* (☎033 856 20 10, ⊛www.camping-jungfrau.ch) on the west bank – also with dorms (from Fr.26).

Among the **hotels** are jovial, backpacker-ish *Horner* (☎033 855 16 73, ⊛www .hornerpub.ch; ❶), just beyond the tourist office. Beside the station is the *Bahnhof* (☎033 855 17 23, ⊛www.bahnhof-hotel.ch; ❷), with cosy, uncomplicated rooms and cooking to match. ❧*Silberhorn* (☎033 856 22 10, ⊛www.silberhorn.com; ❸)

Long-term parking

Since both Wengen and Mürren are car-free, Lauterbrunnen has built for itself a huge multistorey **car park** directly behind the train station at the northernmost edge of the village. Horrendous though that sounds, the community knows the value of its views, and has ensured both that the car park doesn't disturb the eye, and that it filters most of the traffic away from the village centre. Parking for a 24-hour day costs Fr.13 (July to mid-Sept), Fr.18/24 (mid-Dec to mid-April weekdays/weekends) and Fr.12 at other times; eight-day equivalents are Fr.59, Fr.80 and Fr.57. You should always try and **reserve in advance** online at ⊛www.jungfraubahn.ch – at least two weeks ahead if you intend to park for seven days. Two other small open-air parking areas within the village cost around Fr.8–10 per day. Stechelberg has another large parking area at the foot of the Schilthornbahn cable car (Fr.8/day, Fr.24/week).

is up off the main drag but only a minute from the station, with pristinely quiet rooms. **Eating and drinking** are best done in the various hotels along the main street: the *Horner* has bargain pizza/pasta meals for under Fr.13, while the *Oberland* and *Schützen*, either side of the tourist office, are solid places for solid fare, both also specializing in afternoon tea with fresh apple strudel.

Stechelberg and beyond

The bus from Lauterbrunnen to the Trümmelbach Falls continues to **STECH-ELBERG** (900m), a peaceful hamlet at the end of the road. It has a minuscule **tourist office** (☎033 855 10 32, ⊛www.stechelberg.ch), open limited hours. Stechelberg is the starting point for the **cable-car ride** (see below) up to Gimmelwald, Mürren and the Schilthorn; the huge base station complex is 1km before the hamlet. Buses stop here, and terminate at the end of the road in front of the *Hotel Stechelberg* (☎033 855 29 21, ⓔhotel@stechelberg.ch; ➊), a fine old hikers' inn with creaky rooms upstairs. Round the corner are dorm beds in the friendly *Naturfreundehaus Alpenhof* (☎033 855 12 02, ⊛www .alpenhof-stechelberg.ch; Fr.31).

Beyond Stechelberg, trails continue into the undeveloped and unpopulated upper part of the valley, which forms part of the hiking circuit described in the box on p.289. Only the hardiest folk venture here, but the trails aren't difficult and can offer some of the most rewarding hikes in the region, both for the spectacular views and for the isolation. There are no roads, and a short distance beyond Stechelberg begins a large area of land protected as a **nature reserve**. Three comfortable old **inns** along the main trail, all open May to October only and all requiring advance reservation, might persuade you to stay a night or two. An hour beyond Stechelberg is the *Berghaus Trachsellauenen* (☎033 855 12 35; ➊), a pretty half-timbered house set in the woods; an hour and a quarter further is the atmospheric and characterful *Hotel Tschingelhorn* (☎033 855 13 43; ➊), while twenty minutes on up the trail is the *Obersteinberg* (☎033 855 20 33; ➊), a working farm that relies on candlelight after dark and has no showers.

△ Imposing Mürren chalet

Both the *Tschingelhorn* and the *Obersteinberg* also have dorm places, and both are above the treeline, giving spectacular views.

Mürren

The Schilthorn cable car from Stechelberg leaps the valley's west wall to reach the idyllically quiet hamlet of **GIMMELWALD** (1400m; ⓦwww.gimmelwald -news.ch), a little-visited spot set among meadows ablaze with spring and summer wildflowers. Walking is lovely here, and there's also the attraction of the excellent, self-catering *Mountain Hostel* (☎033 855 17 04, ⓦwww .mountainhostel.com; Fr.23).

You have to switch cable cars at Gimmelwald, rising further to car-free **MÜRREN** (1650m), an eyrie of a village set on an elevated shelf of pasture which has managed to retain its endearing desert-island atmosphere (in the off-season at least). It's worth the journey for the **views**. From Mürren, the valley floor is 800m straight down, and the panorama of snowy peaks filling the sky is dazzling: you gaze across at the blank wall of the Schwarzmönch, with the great Trümmelbach gorge slicing a wedge of light into the dark rock, while the awesome trio of the Eiger, Mönch and Jungfrau are ranged above and behind in picture-perfect formation.

Mürren itself was "discovered" by the British in the 1840s, and has a long tradition both of winter sports (see p.282) and of hospitable gentility: some of the first competition **skiing** in Switzerland was done on the slopes around Mürren. An Englishman, Arnold Lunn, claims to have invented the slalom here in 1922, while the famous "Inferno" amateur downhill race from the Schilthorn peak to Mürren (a descent of 2170m) was held for the first time in 1928, and is still an annual fixture in February.

The Schilthorn cable-car station is at the southern end of the village; at the opposite, northern, end is the Mürrenbahn BLM train station, starting point for the cliff-edge train (see p.284) to Grütschalp. Between the two a vintage funicular rises from between the chalets up to the **Allmendhubel** meadow (1907m), from where hiking trails connect to the Blumental (see opposite) and another trail (3hr 15min) leads up to Marchegg, then down into the rugged Saustal and through the Sprissenwald forest to Grütschalp.

Practicalities

Mürren's sports centre houses the **tourist office** (Mon–Sat 8.30am–7pm, Thurs until 9pm, Sun 8.30am–6pm; shorter hours in spring and autumn; ☎033 856 86 86, ⓦwww.wengen-muerren.ch & www.muerren.ch), with plenty of information and listings of chalets and apartments.

Accommodation is excellent, and service is warm and efficient wherever you go. Almost all places close for April and November. Most hotels will arrange to pick you and your bags up from either the cable car or the train station, if you've reserved in advance. *Eiger* (☎033 856 54 54, ⓦwww.hoteleiger.com; ❺–❻) is opposite the train station, an excellent four-star hotel, with a modern, well-equipped guesthouse annexe, run by a Swiss-Scottish couple (☎033 856 54 60, ⓦwww .eigerguesthouse.com; ❷). The *Regina* (☎033 855 42 42, ⓦwww.regina-muerren .ch; ❷–❸; closed May, June & Sept–Nov) has well-appointed, Art-Deco-style rooms, while the ⚑ *Alpenruh*, beside the Schilthorn cable car (☎033 856 88 00, ⓦwww.alpenruh-muerren.ch; ❹), is tops: simply one of the most appealing little hotels in the whole region – cosy, attractive, friendly and with dreamy views.

Eating, as ever, is a hotel affair, with top billing going to the *Alpenruh*'s excellent fare. *Snacks and Drinks*, on the main street, has – incongruously enough – authentic Japanese and Thai food done to order for around Fr.16. For an early-morning excursion, a few hotels (notably the *Alpenruh*) allow you to defer your breakfast until you reach the Schilthorn summit restaurant – and the food (the cost of which is covered by your hotel deal) is actually not that bad once you get there.

Above Mürren, a short half-hour hike east brings you up to the *Sonnenberg* (℡033 855 11 27, ⓦwww.muerren.ch/sonnenberg; dorms Fr.43), a cosy and atmospheric modern inn in the **Blumental** (so-called for its carpet of wildflowers). A little further on is the *Suppenalp* (℡033 855 17 26, ⓦwww .suppenalp.ch; dorms Fr.55), an older building with simple comforts and simpler rooms.

To the Schilthorn

One of the most dramatic mountain excursions in the region is by a series of cable cars from the valley floor at Stechelberg, via Mürren, on a breathtaking ride up to Birg and then the **Schilthorn** summit (2970m; ⓦwww.schilthorn .ch). The trip's less expensive than that to the Jungfraujoch, and also less of a tourist merry-go-round, but just as memorable. The exposed top terrace is, if anything, even more dramatic than the Jungfraujoch, with a wraparound vista of icy peaks, from the Eiger to the Matterhorn to Mont Blanc, plus a clear view down to Thun and Bern. You can enjoy the exceptional views and sip cocktails in the revolving *Piz Gloria* summit restaurant, which featured in the James Bond film *On Her Majesty's Secret Service*; a touristy Bond-centred audiovisual show plays in the basement.

As with the Jungfraujoch, it's easy – if you're based in Interlaken, say – to go up one way and down another. The train from Interlaken Ost to Lauterbrunnen connects well with the link to Mürren (by gondola to Grütschalp and then clifftop train), from where the cable car rises to the summit. On the way down, you can stay with the cable car to Stechelberg, and then make your way by bus back down the valley floor to Lauterbrunnen (perhaps via the Trümmelbach falls), from where trains return to Interlaken. This whole trip, with an hour on top to enjoy the views, takes four hours, compared with six for the equivalent ride from Interlaken up the Jungfraujoch (the last 40min of which is climbing inside a dark tunnel).

Fares on the Schilthornbahn are steep, but not outrageous. A round-trip from Interlaken to the top is Fr.114, from Stechelberg Fr.96, from Mürren Fr.66. Swiss Pass holders travel free to Mürren and pay half-price from there upwards. There's a 25 percent discount if you travel up from Stechelberg before 8.40am or after 3.10pm.

Wengen

On the opposite side of the valley from Mürren, trains bound for Kleine Scheidegg (see p.294) grind up from Lauterbrunnen to **WENGEN** (1274m), another gorgeous, car-free haven perched on a shelf of tranquil southwest-facing meadow. Wengen is one of Switzerland's best-known ski resorts (see p.282 for winter sports information), most famous for hosting World Cup downhill and slalom races on the Lauberhorn every January. It's slightly bigger and livelier than Mürren but still no more than a chalet-style village, with as long a tradition of hospitality as its competitor. The resort stays bustling with skiers well into April. Once the snows have receded, Wengen sits amidst ideal hiking country, overlooked by the Jungfrau and the distinctive creamy cone of the Silberhorn. Its lofty outlook means it enjoys unrivalled valley sunsets.

Walks of varying degrees of toughness thread through the countryside around and above Wengen. Even simple little excursions such as down to **Wengwald** below the village can reveal flower-strewn meadows, romantic footpaths and stunning views out over the great chasm of the Lauterbrunnen valley. Opposite, the horse's tail of the Staubbach falls is clearly visible, while the jagged Lobhörner peak stands out, silhouetted against the sky. The cliff-edge **Mönchblick** viewpoint beyond Wengwald is less than an hour's stroll (120m down) from Wengen. Longer walks lead up to **Wengernalp** (also with a useful train station) and on up to the rail junction at Kleine Scheidegg (3hr total). The LWM cable car from Wengen crests the bluff overlooking the village to the beautiful plateau of **Männlichen** (see p.295); you can, as an alternative, hike the steep three-hour trail, which rises a testing 1070m.

Walking in the Bernese Alps

Making a loop around the Lauterbrunnen valley, the week-long **Grindelwald Circuit** enjoys magnificent big-mountain scenery without treading glaciers or major screes, and is ideally suited to keen walkers. The paths are mostly good, but with some very long and steep slopes to negotiate – both in ascent and descent – and you'll need to be fit. With an abundance of accommodation along the route, each stage could be shortened or lengthened to suit personal preference, and there's the option of staying either in major resorts or in more peaceful lodgings in idyllic surroundings. The map LS 5004 (1:50,000), and the paperback *The Bernese Alps, a Walking Guide* by Kev Reynolds (see "Books", p.587), are both essential companions.

Start by riding the rack railway from **Wilderswil** outside Interlaken to the tremendous viewpoint of **Schynige Platte** and set out on what many consider to be *the* classic walk of the area, the high route to Grindelwald by way of the Faulhorn and Bachsee. Instead of going all the way to Grindelwald though, it's better to spend the first night at the hotel on the summit of the **Faulhorn** in order to enjoy sunset and sunrise over the mountains. On day two descend past the tranquil Bachsee lake before the crowds gather – there are stunning views directly ahead to the Wetterhorn, Schreckhorn and witch's-peak Finsteraarhorn (4274m) – and from there continue down to **Grindelwald**.

Below Grindelwald head southwest up steep meadows at the foot of the notorious North Face of the Eiger to **Kleine Scheidegg** and one of the nearby inns. Crossing the saddle on day three, a track leads down to Wengernalp and Mettlenalp from whose meadows you can safely watch avalanches pour down the face of the Mönch and Jungfrau. Either take the easy way to **Wengen**, and steeply down from there to **Lauterbrunnen**, or for preference tackle a knee-testingly steep path via the little alp of Preech which descends through the **Trümmelbach Gorge** into the Lauterbrunnen valley. Wherever you reach the valley, wander upstream to **Stechelberg** and continue on into the secluded upper valley where several rustic mountain inns provide peaceful lodging with romantic views from every window.

On day four take the path which climbs steeply above the *Berghotel Obersteinberg* to gain the crown of the **Busengrat** at an astonishing little meadow known as the Tanzbödeli (the dance floor). The pasture plunges dizzyingly to great depths on two sides, but a 360° panorama will hold you in its spell. On the north side of the Busengrat the path descends to the wild Sefinen valley (also with accommodation), then climbs to **Gimmelwald** and **Mürren**. Next day go up into the Blumen valley and follow a gentle trail across pastures to Grütschalp, and then through forest to the Soustal before tackling a final climb that leads to the **Lobhorn Hut** (☏ 033 855 30 85). The hut enjoys a privileged view of the Jungfrau – unforgettable at sunset. Day six is spent climbing to the Ballehochst viewpoint, then descending to **Saxeten** and finally all the way down to **Wilderswil** to complete the circuit.

Practicalities

Heading out of the **train station** and up onto Wengen's main street brings you to the **tourist office** (Mon–Fri 8am–noon & 2–6pm, Sat 8.30–11.30am; July–Sept & Dec–April also Sat & Sun 4–6pm; ☎033 855 14 14, ⊛www .wengen-muerren.ch & ⊛www.wengen.com). Trains from Lauterbrunnen to Wengen are free to Swiss Pass holders, but beware that they can be crowded even in the between-seasons; during the summer and winter peak periods, there's often standing room only.

Accommodation is plentiful, but watch out for between-season closures (as at Mürren) and also for the international skiing in January, which can book the village, and the valley, out. Just downhill from the station is *Old Lodge Backpackers* (☎033 855 15 73, ⊛www.oldlodge.ch; Fr.25), with dorms and rooms. ⅍ Smoke-free *Hotel Edelweiss* (☎033 855 23 88, ⊛www.edelweisswengen.ch; ❷–❸) is a cosy, welcoming choice with fresh, modern rooms overlooking the valley, run by the same couple for 25 years. The *Belvédère* (☎033 856 68 68, ⊛www.belvedere-wengen.ch; ❸–❹) is a beautiful old Jugendstil house from 1912 in a quiet location above the village centre. A handful of grand old palaces, including the superb ⅍ *Regina* (☎033 856 58 58, ⊛www.wengen.com/hotel /regina; ❺–❻), of 1894 vintage, have got the room-with-a-view-plus-all-the-luxury-trimmings package down to perfection.

All these hotels have **restaurants** attached – elsewhere, the popular *Chili's* café-bar on the main street does budget food (*menus* from Fr.14), while *Da Sina's* is a pleasant and similarly priced pizzeria and steakhouse at the end of the main street, also with a pub attached.

Grindelwald and around

At Zweilütschinen south of Wilderswil, the road and the train tracks divide: one branch heads south to Lauterbrunnen, while the other follows the course of the Schwarze Lütschine torrent east through the Lütschental into broad, open uplands and the hugely popular resort of **GRINDELWALD** (1034m). Unlike Wengen and Mürren over the ridge, Grindelwald *is* accessible by car and bus, and thus sees a great deal more tourist traffic than the Lauterbrunnen resorts. Although there are many ways to escape the crush, the village's main drag can come as a jarring blast of commercial reality.

Rural character is to be found out of the village. Nestling under the craggy trio of the Wetterhorn, Mettenberg and Eiger, Grindelwald offers easy access to explore some large glaciers close-to, and has a network of cable cars leading up to numerous short- and long-distance trails throughout the region and beyond. Skiing is excellent (see p.282), but there are also plenty of hiking trails which stay as such all winter, making this a top choice for non-skiers on a winter holiday.

Practicalities

The village is tiered above the valley floor on a series of long terraces. Trains to and from Interlaken Ost and Kleine Scheidegg (see p.294) arrive at the **station**, at the western end of the centre. Most facilities are strung east from here along the 1km-long main street. The base-station for the GGM gondola to Männlichen (see p.295) is alongside **Grindelwald-Grund station** (also a stop for the Kleine Scheidegg trains), way down on the valley floor – it's a stiff hike (or a shuttle-bus ride) up to the village. At the eastern edge of the village, a cable car

GRINDELWALD

ACCOMMODATION	
Bernerhof	F
Eiger	H
Fiescherblick	E
Gletschergarten	D
Gydisdorf	G
Jugendherberge	A
Mountain Hostel	I
Naturfreundehaus	B
Wetterhorn	C
RESTAURANTS	
Hirschen	2
Mercato	4
Onkel Tom's	1
Wee Lee	3
Ye Old Spotted Cat	5

Oberer Gletscher & C

Pfingstegg

N

Firstbahn

Pfingsteggbahn

Gletscherdorf campsite

Sports and Mountaineering Centre

Station

Schwarze Lütschine

TERRASSENWEG

Grund Station

Männlichenbahn

500 m

Interlaken Ost *Männlichen* *Aspen campsite*

Kleine Scheidegg

rises north to **First**; while a little further east, another rises south to **Pfingstegg**. The **road** into Grindelwald from Interlaken continues east through the village, but a few kilometres on (at a car park near the Oberergletscher) the road is barred to private cars; only **postbuses** go on to cross the Grosse Scheidegg pass to Meiringen.

Grindelwald's friendly **tourist office** (May–Oct & Dec–Easter Mon–Sat 8am–noon & 1.30–6pm, Sun 9am–noon & 1.30–5pm; Easter–May Mon–Fri 9am–noon & 1.30–5pm, Sat 9am–noon; closed Nov; ☎033 854 12 12, ⊕www .grindelwald.com) is 200m east of the station, alongside **Grindelwald Sports** (☎033 854 12 80, ⊕www.grindelwaldsports.ch), which offers bungee jumps, canyon leaps and easy guided ascents. The box on p.283 has more on adventure sports.

Accommodation

There's a wider range of **accommodation** – and kitschy souvenir shops – in Grindelwald than in the Lauterbrunnen resorts, but prices aren't any lower. The nearest **campsite** is *Gletscherdorf* (☎033 853 14 29, ⊕www.gletscherdorf.ch) near the Pfingstegg cable car.

Hotels

Bernerhof ☎033 853 10 21, ⊕www .bernerhofhotel.ch. Reliable three-star quality in the village centre, with a range of decent, modern rooms, some with Eiger-view balconies, that are unusually good value. ❸–❹

Eiger ☎033 854 31 31, ⊕www .eiger-grindelwald.ch. In the heart of the bustle, but with rooms well off the street that remain quiet, this is a chic, contemporary place rather reminiscent of a city business hotel – a breath of fresh, modern design amidst the kitschy chalets. ❻

Fiescherblick ☎033 854 53 53, ⊕www .fiescherblick.ch. The road climbing to the east from the village centre brings you to this outstanding upper/mid-range choice, with friendly staff and a superb restaurant. It's worth paying a little extra for the space and pleasant decor of the superior-class rooms. ❸–❺

Gletschergarten ☎033 853 17 21, ⊕www .hotel-gletschergarten.ch. A wonderful old, rustic, window-box-laden pension next door to the *Fiescherblick*, with a loyal clientele who return year after year. ❹

Gydisdorf ☎033 853 13 03. A comfortable, welcoming hotel at the foot of the First cable car that has a reputation for fine service to complement its pleasant rooms. ❷–❸

Wetterhorn ☎033 853 12 18, ⊕www.hotel -wetterhorn.ch. Comfortable old roadside inn an hour's walk east of the village opposite the Oberergletscher, at the point where private cars must park or turn back. It attracts plenty of hikers, not only for its location and its dorms (Fr.40) but also for the hearty portions of Swiss cooking on offer in the restaurant. ❷

Hostels

Jugendherberge (HI hostel) ☎033 853 10 09, ⊕www.youthhostel.ch. A bus from opposite *Hotel Bernerhof* outside the station, or a steep fifteen-minute walk north, will get you to Terrassenweg, a quiet lane running on a terrace 100m above the village proper. Up here is this excellent hostel, with a cosy atmosphere, spotless dorms (Fr.30), good facilities and amazing views. ❶

Mountain Hostel (SB hostel) ☎033 854 38 38, ⊕www.mountainhostel.ch. A lively and well-run hostel on the valley floor beside Grindelwald-Grund station (free shuttle bus from the village on demand). Dorms are Fr.40, less if you bring your own sleeping bag. ❶

Naturfreundehaus ☎033 853 13 33, ⊕www .naturfreunde.ch. Spartan, less studenty dorms (Fr.39) not far from the HI hostel on the same street, Terrassenweg. ❶

Eating and drinking

Eating and drinking, again, is chiefly a hotel-based occupation: for fine dining, the restaurant in the *Fiescherblick* is especially well regarded (*menu* around Fr.42). On the main street, *Mercato* has good pizzas and pasta for around Fr.17, or a little more in the evenings, while the fish at *Hirschen* – plucked fresh from the Thunersee – is rightly celebrated (Fr.20–25). The latter also has good veggie dishes for Fr.15 or so. *Onkel Tom's* is a tiny chalet at the east of town (closed Mon) serving up excellent (and enormous) wood-fired pizzas in a cosy ambience. For authentic, quality Chinese cuisine, try *Wee Lee*, on the main drag beneath *Hotel Spinne* (closed Sun), though it's not cheap (Fr.35 and up); they do equally good Japanese specialities, with veggie options.

There are a couple of obvious **bars** up and down the main street – including the misleadingly titled *Espresso Bar* – but the back terrace of *Ye Old Spotted Cat* in the *Hotel Bellevue* (closed Sun) is the quietest and most atmospheric place to enjoy a tipple as the sunset fades on the Eiger.

First, Pfingstegg and the glaciers

The possibilities for exploring the area are endless. The area around **First** (2168m) has some particularly lovely hiking trails (for skiing, see p.282): the gondola rises in three stages, and from the hotel/restaurant on top relatively easy routes lead off in all directions – to the Schwarzhorn summit (3hr) passing through Schilt, renowned for its population of marmots; or a high-level route over the Grosse Scheidegg pass (2hr or so); or back down to Grindelwald (2hr 30min); or, best of all, on a stunning ridge-top walk to the Bachalpsee lake and on to the **Faulhorn** summit (2hr 30min) with its atmospheric *Berghaus* (☎033 853 27 13; Fr.36); the stunning sunset and sunrise views from here are one of the high points of a walking tour of Switzerland. Schynige Platte (see p.281) is about the same distance again further on.

The cable car (May–Oct) up to **Pfingstegg** (1391m) and the little café at the top station with its giant views, make for a pleasant excursion for non-athletic types; an interesting trail leads for a little over an hour from Pfingstegg through varying geological formations on the slopes of the Mettenberg (the Breitlou-wina terrace is celebrated for its evidence of glacial action), to the Obererglet-scher (see below), from where an easy valley-floor hour's stroll brings you back into Grindelwald.

Grund station is the start for several fine walks, including a two-hour ramble up the sloping pastureland through Brandegg to the *Berghaus des Alpes* at **Alpiglen** (☎033 853 11 30, ◍www.alpiglen.ch; ❷; dorms Fr.35; June–Oct), a stop at 1616m on the Kleine Scheidegg train line. Starting from here cuts the cost of the ride up to the Jungfraujoch, as would continuing up the Eiger-Trail from Alpiglen to the hut alongside Eigergletscher station, a spectacular, but steep, route (3hr) that passes directly beneath the awesome North Face.

The five-hour trail from Grund beneath the gondola line to Männlichen brings you up through meadows and rolling open countryside, also with the towering Eiger a constant presence. From Grund, if you cross the river and head southeast for a few minutes, you'll come to the **Gletscherschlucht** (Glacier gorge; May–Oct daily 9am–6pm; Fr.5), catwalks leading you for 1km or more into a narrow defile above the Lütschine river, with evidence of glacial erosion everywhere, including polished valley walls, corkscrew potholes and lumps of green and pinkish marble in the river bed.

An hourly bus from Grindelwald station (or an hour's walk east) leads you close to the icy caverns of the **Obererletscher** – from the *Hotel Wetterhorn* bus stop, follow the leafy trail down to the river and, on the other side, climb the 890 stairs to the nose of the glacier. There's a missable ice-grotto up there (May–Oct daily 9am–6pm; Fr.5), and, a ten-minute walk further up, a much more dramatic path which runs alongside the glacier itself, giving spectacular views.

To the Jungfraujoch

Switzerland's most popular (and expensive) mountain railway excursion is touted endlessly throughout the Oberland under the shoutline "**Top of Europe**": for once, though, the reality justifies the hype. Trains trundle through lush countryside south from Interlaken before coiling spectacularly up across the high pastures above either Wengen or Grindelwald, breaking the treeline at Kleine Scheidegg and tunnelling clean through the Eiger to emerge at the **JUNGFRAUJOCH**, an icy, windswept col at 3454m, just below the Jungfrau summit. This is the highest train station in Europe, and offers an unforgettable experience of the mountains; you'd be missing out if you decided against shelling out the exorbitant sums necessary to get there.

Trains run all year round, come rain, fog, snow or shine. However, **good weather** is essential for the views: if there's a hint of cloud you'd be wasting your time heading up. Check the pictures from the summit, broadcast live on ⦿www.jungfrau.ch and on cable TV throughout the region, for an idea of the weather conditions, or ask your hotel or nearest tourist office for the latest forecasts. Remember, too, that it takes two and a half hours to reach the summit from Interlaken, and weather conditions can change rapidly on the journey. You should also bring **sunglasses** with you: the snows never melt up here, and if the sky is blue, the sun's glare and glitter can be painful.

There are two **routes** to the top. BOB trains head southwest from Interlaken Ost along the valley floor to Lauterbrunnen, from where you pick up the WAB mountain line which climbs through Wengen to Kleine Scheidegg. Alternatively, different BOB trains head southeast from Interlaken Ost to Grindelwald, where you change for the climb, arriving at Kleine Scheidegg from the other direction. All trains terminate at Kleine Scheidegg, where you must change for the final pull to Jungfraujoch; the popular practice is to go up one way and down the other.

Currently, the adult round-trip **fare** to Jungfraujoch from Interlaken is a budget-crunching Fr.173. One way to cut costs is to take advantage of the discounted **Good Morning ticket** (Fr.149), valid if you travel up on the first train of the day (6.30am from Interlaken), and leave the summit by noon (Nov–April: first or second train plus later departure permitted).

Walking some sections of the journey, up or down, is perfectly feasible in summer, and can also save plenty, with fares from intermediate points along the route considerably lower. The Good Morning ticket from Lauterbrunnen is Fr.130 (6.55am train), from Grindelwald Fr.130 (7.15am), from Wengen Fr.118 (7.15am), from Kleine Scheidegg Fr.80 (7.55am) and from Eigergletscher Fr.68 (8.05am). Excellent transport networks and vista-rich footpaths linking all stations mean that with judicious use of a hiking map and timetable you can see and do a great deal in a day and still get back to Interlaken, or even Bern or Zürich, by bedtime.

Kleine Scheidegg

Trains climbing from Wengen and Grindelwald meet at **KLEINE SCHEIDEGG** (2061m) – four buildings huddled in the most dramatic of locations directly below the soaring Eiger Nordwand, or **North Face of the Eiger**, a sheer wall of rock 2300m high. The settlement (it doesn't even count as a hamlet) throngs with daytime crowds switching trains on their way to or from the Jungfraujoch, but sees virtually nobody staying overnight.

The station building, which doubles as the *Röstizzeria* restaurant and *Mountain Lodge* (☎033 828 78 28,⦿www.bahnhof-scheidegg.ch;❷), has spartan, comfortable

dorms (Fr.50) and rooms, while the grand old *Bellevue des Alpes* (☎033 855 12 12, ⓦwww.scheidegg-hotels.ch; ❻, including half-board) – the two large chalets beside the station, focus of the Clint Eastwood film *The Eiger Sanction* – has historically been the base station for worried relatives scanning the Eiger wall to track the progress of loved ones engaged in what's become known as one of the most difficult mountaineering ascents in the world. The hotel decor, all chintzy pelmets, wood panelling and armchairs by the fire, is from another world – an odd counterpoint to the muddy-boot hiking fraternity who tramp the area. Within view behind the hotel is the *Grindelwaldblick* (☎033 855 13 74, ⓦwww.grindelwaldblick.ch; Fr.38), a serviceable restaurant with dorms.

Kleine Scheidegg is the trailhead for a wealth of **high-country walks**. Hikes down to Wengen (roughly 2hr) or Grindelwald (roughly 4hr), or up the "back" of the nearby Lauberhorn (1hr), are relatively easy-going. There's a tougher one-hour trail up to the **EIGERGLETSCHER** train station (2320m), overlooking the massive sheet of ice sliding down from the high peaks; the station has well-maintained double and triple rooms (☎033 828 78 66, Ⓔguesthouse@jungfrau .ch; ❷) alongside husky kennels. A superb two-hour walking trail from here arcs around directly beneath the looming North Face down to Alpiglen.

Männlichen

North from Kleine Scheidegg, away from the Eiger, a picturesque ninety-minute trail to **MÄNNLICHEN**, perched on a ridge and with one of the best mountain refuges in the region (☎033 853 10 68, ⓦwww.maennlichen.ch; ❷–❸), is particularly lovely and virtually flat the whole way. From Männlichen, the LWM cable car drops down to Wengen in one direction, while in the other, the GGM gondola glides for an amazing half-hour – the longest gondola line in the world – across the pastures to Grindelwald-Grund (both closed May & Nov). All winter long, you can get away from it all to an **igloo camp** up here: ask local tourist offices for details of the overnight package, which includes meals, a polar sleeping-bag in your personal igloo and – free of charge – a magnificent, silent sunrise over the mountains.

The Jungfraujoch

Most people at Kleine Scheidegg don't leave the area of the station buildings, only stopping to switch trains for the final leg up to the "Top of Europe". After the short run to the Eigergletscher station, the train enters a long tunnel carved out of the heart of the Eiger. There are five-minute stops at Eigerwand and Eismeer stations, both with viewing galleries out over the frozen landscape, and after forty minutes in the dark, you pull into the **Jungfraujoch** summit station (3454m).

Inevitably, the place is a tourist circus of ice sculptures, husky sleigh rides, glacier walks, a short ski run, dismal restaurants and a post office, all invariably overflowing with tour groups. Nonetheless, panoramic views from the open-air **Sphinx Terrace**, at 3571m, to Germany's Black Forest, the Vosges in France and across a gleaming wasteland to the Italian Alps are heart-thumping – as is the thin atmosphere up here. Yawning away below the silver-domed weather station on top is the mighty Jungfraufirn glacier, which joins up with several others (including the Aletschgletscher, largest in the Alps) at the resonantly named Konkordiaplatz ice plain 3km southeast.

The best way to avoid being smothered by snap-happy crowds is to travel up on the first train of the day, and on arrival follow the signs quickly straight to the high-speed lift for the Sphinx Terrace – that way, you can snatch five or ten minutes of crisp, undisturbed silence at the loftiest point of all, and be the first of the day to sweep the snow off the railings. At other times, you may have to queue for an hour or more just to get your nose into the fresh air. Once you've finished at the terrace, it's easy to leave the bustling summit station behind and head out across the snows into solitude and silence, although you must stick to the marked trails (crevasses give no warning).

If you've had experience of snow hiking in the mountains, and you have good boots, a map, sunglasses and proper clothing, let the tourist office in Interlaken know that you want to head out on the simple one-hour trail from the Jungfraujoch around the base of the Mönch to the **Mönchsjochhütte** at 3629m (☎033 971 34 72, ⊛www.moenchsjoch.ch; April–May & July–Sept; dorms Fr.26, half-board Fr.56) – you don't need a guide, and the isolation of the hut offers a night to remember. You should walk at half pace, or you may find yourself dizzy and labouring to catch your breath. A handful of other glacier-bound huts are dotted around the area, but you need a mountain guide and all the professional gear to reach them.

The lakes

Flanking Interlaken in the heart of the Bernese Oberland, the two lakes of the **Thunersee** and the **Brienzersee** form the gateway to the region. They are often overlooked by visitors in a hurry to get into the mountains, or returning to the lowlands, but there's something very peaceful about them, poised between the big cities of the north and the high Alps further south. Even the most hurried of Oberland tours should leave a day or two for enjoying the beauty of the lakes, set amidst cliffs and forested hillsides, dotted with quiet villages, and backed by a long chain of dramatic snowy heights.

Both lakes are well served by transport, with mainline **trains** running between Thun, Spiez, Interlaken West & Ost, Brienz and on to Luzern, quite often swishing along within metres of the water, plunging in and out of tunnels cut beneath the mountains which ring the shoreline. Unless speed is of the essence, though, you'd do well to take at least one trip by **boat** (see box).

Around the Thunersee

The **Thunersee** (**Lake Thun**) is one of the prettiest in the country, a tranquil patch of misty blue loomed over by high shoreline mountains. The presence of the snowy Bernese Alps to the south, ranged above the water in a breathtaking panorama, constantly beckons you on. **Thun**, at the northernmost tip of the lake where the Aare flows out towards Bern, is an attractive overnight stop on the way into or out of the mountains – much more relaxing than Interlaken – and small, rather twee little lakeside resorts such as **Spiez** can pleasantly break a slow journey south.

The **BLS** company (named for its main rail route "Bern-Lötschberg-Simplon", between the Swiss capital and Milan; www.bls.ch) runs boats on both lakes, which are free to Swiss Pass holders.

The Thunersee is the more picturesque of the two, overlooked by the pyramidal Niesen and the Stockhorn on the west, the wooded slopes of the Beatenberg on the east, and with the snowy peaks of the Eiger, Mönch and Jungfrau always in view to the south. There are at least half-a-dozen boats a day in summer (June–Sept) between **Thun and Interlaken West** (2hr), stopping at – among other places – Hilterfingen, Oberhofen, Spiez and the Beatushöhlen; one of the boats, the Drachenschiff, is done up to look like the giant green dragon vanquished by St Beatus (see p.299) – quite a sight on the water, huffing smoke from between its huge teeth. Service is just as regular on the bleaker, cliff-girt Brienzersee between **Brienz and Interlaken Ost** (1hr 15min). If you're visiting out of season, note that boats run on both lakes at least once daily from April to October, although in winter, service is drastically reduced and may be cut altogether.

There's also a host of eat-aboard **cruises**, some on vintage steamships, generally running three times a day throughout the summer. Special evening cruises run on Friday and Saturday evenings all summer long departing from Thun, and occasionally from Interlaken Ost. The paddle steamer *Blümlisalp* makes a six-hour meander from Thun to Interlaken West, while its sister ship the *Lötschberg* does a similar three-hour round trip from Interlaken Ost (both daily mid-June to mid-Sept; ordinary tickets valid).

The Thunersee tourist office (☎033 251 00 00, www.thunersee.ch) has devised an easy five-day walking tour around the lake (May–Oct) for Fr.550 per person, including four nights' half-board, luggage transport and documentation.

Thun

Set astride the River Aare on the lake which bears its name, **THUN** (pronounced *toon*) – with its picturesque castle and quaint medieval centre – is well worth a visit. Views of the Eiger, Mönch and Jungfrau and, closer at hand, the giant pyramidal Niesen (2362m) and flat-topped Stockhorn (2190m) are a gentle prelude to the Alpine vistas further south.

The town has an odd secret. After World War II, the authorities decided that in the event of a future invasion, the whole of Switzerland south to Thun was to be abandoned, and the entire population was to assemble here for dispersal into mountain retreats. Switzerland's largest hospital was hollowed out of the Niesen, but despite constant upkeep, has never been used; it remains pristine and fully equipped, and there are probably dozens of other major military and civil emergency installations hidden in the mountains nearby.

Across the river from the station, Thun's low-lying Old Town is renowned for the arcading both of the main street, split-level **Obere Hauptgasse**, and the cobbled **Rathausplatz** at its northwestern end. Steps lead up from various points along the picturesque street to the fairy-tale turreted **castle** which looms above, built in 1190 and occupied by the Bernese in 1386. Its lofty halls now contain a historical **museum** (April–Oct daily 10am–5pm; Feb & March daily 1–4pm; Nov–Jan Sun 1–4pm; Fr.7; SMP; www.schlossthun.ch), with the usual period furniture and militaria. A short walk east is a grand Belle-Epoque lakeside building housing the **Kunstmuseum** (Tues–Sun 10am–5pm, Wed until 9pm; Fr.8; SMP; ⓦwww.kunstmuseumthun.ch), which stages worthwhile exhibitions of modern Swiss and international art.

At the lakeshore but on the station side of the river is the **Schadau Park**, home to perfectly tended flowerbeds, stunning views across the water to the mountains, and a nineteenth-century folly planted majestically on the water-side. Beside it is an odd cylindrical building housing the **Wocher Panorama** (May–Oct Tues–Sun 10am–5pm; Fr.5), a giant painting – the oldest of its kind in the world – running all the way around the interior wall, which depicts the daily life of Thun circa 1810.

Practicalities

The **train station** is five minutes south of the centre; adjacent is the **tourist office** (July & Aug Mon–Fri 8am–7pm, Sat 9am–noon & 1–4pm; rest of year Mon–Fri 8am–noon & 1–6pm, Sat 9am–noon; ☏033 225 90 00, ⓦwww .thuntourismus.ch). **Boats** around the lake, and to Interlaken West, depart from outside the station.

For **accommodation**, walk right from the station for the spotless *Herberge zur Schadau* **hostel**, Seestrasse 22 (☏033 222 52 22, ⓦwww.herberge.ch; ❶), an old house in a quiet location, newly renovated but pricey at Fr.39 for a dorm bed; or you could plump for a bunk in a metal tubular module at the lake-side **campsite** (☏033 336 40 67) at Gwatt, a 3km bus-ride southwest. Of the **hotels**, quiet *Zunfthaus zu Metzgern* on Rathausplatz (☏033 222 21 41, ⓦwww .zumetzgern.ch; ❷) – an inn dating back to 1361 – is most atmospheric, and has exceptionally good-value rooms overlooking the cobbled square. *Emmental*, Bernstrasse 2 (☏033 222 01 20, ⓦwww.essenundtrinken.ch; ❸), is a colourful old guesthouse with a handful of pleasant rooms. *Krone* on Rathausplatz (☏033 227 88 88, ⓦwww.krone-thun.ch; ❹–❺) is a step up in ambience and quality.

The many **restaurants** around Scheibenstrasse are varied and competitively priced, while Bälliz, a central shopping street with a twice-weekly **market** (Wed & Sat), is lined with pavement cafés, most relaxed of which is the *Altes Waisenhaus* at no. 61, perfect for a beer in the sun or a quality Italian meal (*menus* around Fr.25). *Trattoria Rimini*, Bernstrasse 26, has good, inexpensive pasta dishes, while the atmospheric restaurant attached to *Hotel Metzgern* (see above) serves Swiss and Italian *menus* for around Fr.20 (closed Mon). Scheibenstrasse also has numerous **bars**, while *Café-Bar Mokka*, Allmendstrasse 14 (ⓦwww .mokka.ch), is the best club and live music venue (closed Mon).

Along the northern shore

Visitable castles and stately homes are dotted around the shore of the Thunersee. All are served – and best visited – by boats which stop at or very close to the castles themselves.

Schloss Hünegg at Hilterfingen, 2km southeast of Thun (mid-May to mid-Oct Mon–Sat 2–5pm, Sun 11am–5pm; Fr.5; ⓦwww.schlosshuenegg.ch), was built in the 1860s in the style of a Loire château. It houses an interior unchanged since 1900, with bedchambers, boudoirs and halls displaying the wealthiest of lifestyles (the owner was a former officer in the Prussian army).

A couple of kilometres further along the lakeshore is the mighty **Schloss Oberhofen** (mid-May to mid-Oct Mon 2–5pm, Tues–Sun 11am–5pm; Fr.5; SMP), set in its own lush gardens. It dates from the thirteenth century, and houses collections of furnishings from the Bern Historical Museum: a range of restored interiors, a stone-flagged knights' hall, salons furnished in Empire style and even a Turkish *selamlik*, or smoking room, way up under the eaves. The formal waterside **park** (March–Nov daily 10am–dusk; free) is delightful, shaded by trees and planted with all kinds of flowers.

St-Beatus-Höhlen

On the north shore, beyond the funicular at Beatenbucht, are the **ST-BEATUS-HÖHLEN** (St Beatus Caves; ⓦwww.beatushoehlen.ch), an impressive set of drippy subterranean chambers filled with stalactites and stalagmites that were formerly the residence of the early Christian ascetic St Beatus. The caves are tucked into the cliffs 3km northwest of Interlaken; it's a **walk** of about 2hr from Interlaken, or you can take hourly **bus** #21, which runs both ways along the shoreside road between Thun and Interlaken's Ost and West stations. In the summer, about half-a-dozen **boats** a day between Thun and Interlaken West stop at Beatushöhlen-Sundlauenen, ten minutes' walk south of the cave entrance.

Beatus himself reputedly came from Britain. The story goes that having given all his wealth to the poor to follow Christ, he was baptized in Rome by St Peter and sent with a companion, Justus, into the Alps as the first apostle to the heathen Helvetians. (In all probability, though, Beatus was one of the Irish followers of St Columba who brought Christianity to Switzerland in the sixth century.) When Beatus and Justus came to the lake, local people told them of a terrible **dragon** who occupied a cave overlooking the water. Beatus climbed up to the cave alone, and when the dragon emerged, raised his cross and spoke the name of the Holy Trinity, thereby sending the monster over the cliff edge into the water below. Beatus took over its cave, praying and working miracles until his death at the age of 90. A cult of pilgrimage rapidly grew up around him and the cave.

Today, you can visit only on **guided tours**, which depart every half-hour (April–Oct daily 10.30am–5pm; Fr.17; duration 1hr) from the ticket office a short climb above the lakeside road. Note that a visit involves a full 2km walk through the caves (1km each way), which are chilly year-round. You can leave bags at the ticket desk for Fr.1. The guides lead you past the grotto where Beatus reputedly passed his days, and then on into the cool gloom of the cave interior, filled with the noise of rushing underground streams – the best time to visit is springtime, when a wet winter and snowmelt conspire to shoot torrents of water through the corkscrewing channels.

Spiez

On the opposite, southern shore, huddled above and around a small bay 11km south of Thun, **SPIEZ** is a gentle little resort village, dominated by its medieval waterside castle and stunning views over the lake to the high mountains all around. It lies at a major **rail junction**, where the main line from Bern splits: one branch continues to Interlaken, another climbs south into the Kander valley (see p.304) to the Lötschberg Tunnel under the Alps and on to Brig. In addition, trains from Spiez head west to Zweisimmen, Gstaad and Montreux on the celebrated Golden Pass panoramic route (see p.160).

The **train station** is in a modern shopping area high above the Old Town; find your way down on stairs and the descending main Seestrasse. Boats from Thun and Interlaken dock right beside the Old Town. The castle, **Schloss Spiez** (April–Oct Mon 2–5pm, Tues–Sun 10am–5pm; July–Sept closes 6pm; Fr.4; SMP), dating from the fifteenth and sixteenth centuries but with earlier foundations, was the residence of the Stretlingen family before passing to the Bernese noble dynasties of Von Bubenberg and, from 1516 to 1875, Von Erlach. Inside, don't miss the Baroque banqueting hall. The Romanesque **church** adjacent, with its seventeenth-century spire, has original frescoes in the apse and the crypt. Wandering through the tiny lanes around the castle, and around the bay filled with yachts (Spiez is home to a renowned sailing school), is a good way to get a feel for the town.

Spiez's friendly **tourist office** is on platform 1 of the station (July & Aug Mon–Fri 8am–6.30pm, Sat 9am–noon & 2–4pm; rest of year Mon–Fri 8am–noon & 2–6pm; May, June & Sept also Sat 9am–noon; ☎033 655 90 00, ⊛www .spiez.ch). The town's popularity with holidaying German and Swiss-German families leads to some conservatism among the **hotels**. *Bellevue*, Seestrasse 36 (☎033 654 84 64, ⊛www.bellevue-spiez.ch; ❷), is a cosy if uninspiring place, while lakefront *Aqua Welle* (☎033 654 40 44, ⊛www.aquawelle.ch; ❸) has better views but less character. A few kilometres south at Leissigen is an HI **hostel** (☎033 847 12 14, ⊛www.youthhostel.ch; ❶; May–Oct), a peaceful place with only a few dorm beds (Fr.29). Seestrasse holds a clutch of inexpensive tearooms and pizzerias, including the popular *Brasserie 66* at no. 4 (⊛www.brasserie66 .ch), up near the station.

The Brienzersee and beyond

Stretching east of Interlaken, the **Brienzersee** (**Lake Brienz**) is much vaunted as the cleanest lake in Switzerland, beautifully set in an enclosed bowl amidst forested slopes, streams tumbling down from on high, overlooked to the south by the Faulhorn (2681m) and to the northeast by the Brienzer Rothorn (2350m), the latter served by a nostalgic old rack railway from the main town of the lake, **Brienz**. East of Brienz, a tortuous road crosses the Brünig Pass into Canton Obwalden, heading for Luzern, while the main road scoots along the floor of the Haslital, beside the youthful Aare, to **Meiringen**, scene of the "death" of Sherlock Holmes and final staging-post before the major trans-Alpine routes over the Grimsel and Susten passes.

Brienz

At the easternmost tip of the lake, **BRIENZ** has a quiet, community feel; not many people come visiting, and most that do stop for just an hour or two before heading on to Interlaken. The town is known as a centre of **woodcarving**, and has many workshops and souvenir shops hawking everything from mass-produced tat to quality hand-tooled busts, figurines and nativity scenes in limewood. Brienz also boasts the last steam-driven rack railway in Switzerland, with a fine old beast puffing its way up the flower-strewn slopes for an hour, from the lake at 566m to the **Brienz Rothorn** summit station at 2244m (daily June–Oct; ⊛ www.brienz-rothorn-bahn .ch). There are plenty of strolls around and about on the top, as well as a tough trail heading northwest through the mountains to Kemmeriboden (see p.255).

Brienz **tourist office**, Hauptstrasse 143 (July & Aug Mon–Fri 8am–6.30pm, Sat 8am–noon & 4–6pm; rest of year Mon–Fri 8am–noon & 2–6pm; May, June & Sept also Sat 8am–noon; ☎033 952 80

△ Woodcarving, Brienz

80, ⊛ www.alpenregion.ch) is metres from the jetty where **boats** dock from Interlaken Ost and directly opposite the **train station**. A stone's throw away is the Rothornbahn station, departure point of the vintage locos. **Hotels** include some generic options in the ❷–❸ range along the lakefront, while on the Rothorn summit is the *Rothorn Kulm* hotel (☎033 951 12 21, ⊛ www .brienz-rothorn-bahn.ch; ❷) with plain rooms and dorms (Fr.35). Brienz's comfortable HI **hostel** is at Strandweg 10, a fifteen-minute walk east around the head of the lake (☎033 951 11 52, ⊛ www.youthhostel.ch; ❶; dorms Fr.26; April–Oct).

All along the waterfront Hauptstrasse are any number of **restaurants**, all offering fresh lake fish: the best is the *Steinbock* chalet, at no. 123 (☎033 951 40 55; closed Tues), a rather fussy place but with the best fish in town (*menus* from Fr.20).

Just opposite Brienz, reachable by boat or on a scenic lakeside trail from the hamlet of Iseltwald, are the **Giessbach falls**, which tumble over a series of terraces down the cliffside. Above stands the ♣ *Grandhotel Giessbach* (☎033 952 25 25, ⊛ www.giessbach.ch; ❹–❻; April–Oct), saved from redevelopment and now restored to its turn-of-the-century elegance.

Freilichtmuseum Ballenberg

Near Brienz is the **Freilichtmuseum Ballenberg** (Open-Air Museum; April–Oct daily 10am–5pm; ⊛ www.ballenberg.ch; Fr.18; SMP), 3km east of the town, a huge area of rolling parkland which serves as a living showcase for traditional Swiss architecture and crafts. There are two entrances, the West nearest Brienz and, some 4km away, the East entrance near Brienzwiler; regular postbuses from Brienz station serve both. In between are thirteen separate areas, each containing several examples of traditional houses from different parts of Switzerland, transported here piece by piece from their original settings, reassembled and restored. Within each building are held daily demonstrations of traditional crafts, everything from needlework to faggot binding. The whole place is fascinating, but it's really too big to absorb in one go; you'd do well to select a few areas from the museum map (Fr.2) and aim for them alone – or, alternatively, ask for a discounted two-day pass and spread your visit. There are three restaurants on site, as well as groceries where you can buy provisions for a barbecue (free firewood provided).

Meiringen and around

The creation of meringue and the death of Sherlock Holmes are the two claims to fame of the old town of **MEIRINGEN**. From the way visitors approach the place, though, it seems that many have difficulty deciding which story is real and which invented.

Set at the heart of the Hasliberg hiking region, the town has long been a favourite mountain-walking resort of the English. Sir Arthur Conan Doyle, creator of Sherlock Holmes, stayed in genteel Meiringen many times, and the town's sole attraction is the **Sherlock Holmes Museum** in Conan Doyle Place (May–Sept Tues–Sun 1.30–6pm; Oct–April Wed & Sun 4.30–6pm; Fr.4; joint ticket with Reichenbach Falls funicular Fr.11; SMP). This interesting little den is in the cellar of the English Church, and includes a life-size replica of the detective's study at 221b Baker Street, complete with taped commentary. The town **church**, north of the centre on Kirchgasse, has a free-standing Romanesque tower with a wooden spire, some fourteenth-century interior frescoes, and remnants below the crypt of the eleventh-century predecessor. Meiringen was popular enough with English visitors of a bygone age to attract not only Conan Doyle, but also semi-official trinket hunters: ancient bits and pieces from the old church now sit in the vaults of the British Museum in London.

The "death" of Sherlock Holmes

The novelist **Sir Arthur Conan Doyle** chose the Reichenbach falls as the setting for the death of his character Sherlock Holmes. In *The Final Problem* (1891), Conan Doyle wrote of Reichenbach:

It is, indeed, a fearful place. The torrent, swollen by the melting snow, plunges into a tremendous abyss, from which the spray rolls up like the smoke from a burning house. The shaft into which the river hurls itself is an immense chasm, lined by glistening coal-black rock, and narrowing into a creaming, boiling pit of incalculable depth, which brims over and shoots the stream onward over its jagged lip.

The story goes on to tell of the death of Holmes. On May 4, 1891, the detective met his archenemy Professor Moriarty on a ledge above the falls. The two became locked in a titanic hand-to-hand struggle before both tumbled over the precipice, presumably to their deaths. This neat device was Conan Doyle's way to free himself of the burden of constantly churning out pulpy detective stories and was intended to give himself the freedom to write more elevated literature instead. But he didn't reckon on public opinion. The outcry against the death of such a popular character as Holmes was so great that in 1903 Conan Doyle was forced to give in to the pressure of his fan mail. He resurrected his nemesis by claiming that Holmes had managed to grab a tuft of grass during the fall into the "dreadful cauldron" and so had lived to solve another mystery. Conan Doyle – much to his chagrin – was far more celebrated during his lifetime for his detective stories than for his various expeditions and good works; these days his elevated writings have largely been forgotten, while his Holmes tales are world-famous.

Every year on May 4, members of the international Sherlock Holmes Society make a pilgrimage to the falls to commemorate the "death" of their hero.

THE BERNESE OBERLAND | The Brienzersee and beyond

A sticky end

Odd though it seems for such a delicate creation, **meringue** originated in the rural Bernese Oberland. At some unknown time in the pre-Revolutionary eighteenth century, an Italian baker by the name of Gasparini invented a baked concoction of egg whites, sugar and cream, and named it after Meiringen, the scene of his inspiration. Documented names of the rich dessert include *meiring* (plural *meiringe*) and *meirinken* – until Louis XV took a liking to Gasparini's creation, whereupon the French name "meringue" took over.

Unfortunately, the documentary evidence for Meiringen's noble patrimony went up in smoke long ago during two disastrous town fires. Undaunted, researchers in Frankfurt's Culinary Museum early last century turned up further solid evidence. Meiringen's bigwigs thought their claim to fame was secure… but Allied fighter pilots during World War II had other ideas, and bombed Frankfurt – and the museum – into dust. Nonetheless, the locals are sticking to their story, and patisseries in Meiringen still churn out 1500 top-quality meringues a day to fuel the legend.

Meiringen's **train station** is in the town centre, with the **tourist office** opposite (July & Aug Mon–Fri 8am–6pm, Sat 8am–noon & 4–6pm; Sept–June Mon–Fri 8am–noon & 2–6pm, Sat 8am–noon & 2.30–4pm; ☎033 972 50 50, ⊛www.alpenregion.ch). **Hotels** include the modern *Victoria* on Bahnhofplatz (☎033 972 10 40, ⊛www.victoria-meiringen.ch; ❸–❹), which is excellent value. Conan Doyle's old haunt, the *Parkhotel du Sauvage* (☎033 971 41 41, ⊛www.sauvage.ch; ❹–❺), is still around: the management undoubtedly benefits by a few francs from associations with fame, but can still come up with the appropriate atmosphere and comforts. **Eating and drinking** is a case of follow-your-nose: the *Victoria* has a decent-ish restaurant, with some veggie options, as does the *Alpin Sherpa* hotel opposite. The best **meringue** in Meiringen, by all accounts, is served at the low-key *Café Brunner*, Bahnhofstrasse 8 – but on careful analysis you may feel that the ones whipped up over the mountains at Kemmeriboden (see p.255) steal a march.

Around Meiringen

Meiringen itself is much less appealing than the countryside all around. The tourist office can supply details of the many hikes in and around the Hasli valley and Hasliberg region, but the most accessible excursion is to the dramatic **Reichenbach Falls**. A wonderful old funicular (May–Oct; Fr.8; joint ticket with Sherlock Holmes Museum Fr.11; joint ticket with Aareschlucht Fr.12; ⊛www.reichenbachfall.ch) runs from the south of town up to a vantage point below the roaring falls, best visited in spring laden with snowmelt from the glaciers further upstream.

Stepped paths lead up beside the falls through the mossy forests to **Zwirgi** village, at the foot of the dramatic Reichenbach valley. Trails lead on southwest up the valley past the hamlet of Kaltenbrunnen to **Rosenlaui**, where a grand four-storey pile, the atmospheric ⚜ *Rosenlaui Hotel* (☎033 971 29 12, ⊛www .rosenlaui.ch; ❷; dorms Fr.70 incl. half-board; May–Oct), stands overlooking a stream. The hotel was built a hundred years ago; its public rooms are a breath of elegance from a former age. From Rosenlaui, trails head on up to Schwarzwaldalp (beyond which private cars are forbidden) and over the **Grosse Scheidegg** pass to Grindelwald, a route also served by postbuses from Meiringen (June–Sept).

A couple of kilometres east of Meiringen, served by buses to Innertkirchen, is the **Aareschlucht** (Aare Gorge; daily: July & Aug 8am–6pm; April–June, Sept

& Oct 9am–5pm; Fr.7; ⓦ www.aareschlucht.ch), with a path snaking for 1.4km through the sheer-sided gorge, which is floodlit on summer nights (July & Aug Wed & Fri 9–11pm).

The western valleys

The section of the Bernese Oberland west of the Thunersee, which holds the only route through the mountains towards Lake Geneva, stands in sharp contrast to the rock and ice of the Jungfrau region. Broad, leafy valleys reach between the peaks, sheltering a handful of resorts and quiet country towns which see much less tourism than their hectic counterparts around Interlaken. The especially lovely Kander valley runs south from Spiez, climbing to the old-style resort village of **Kandersteg**, while the forested, picture-pretty gorge of the River Simme heads west through a succession of old villages filled with examples of the local heavy-eaved darkwood chalets, some dating from as early as the 1750s. The valley of the **Simmental** curves south into the rural, hilly **Saanenland**, focused around the world-famous ski resort of **Gstaad**. Continuing west, you cross into an outpost of French-speaking Canton Vaud, whereupon the same rolling hills and broad, quiet valleys are re-titled the **Pays d'Enhaut**.

The Kander valley

South of Spiez, the Niesen stands sentinel over the peaceful **Kander valley**, a narrow finger pointing the way south to the wall of high peaks around the mighty Blümlisalp massif (which rises to 3663m). Nestling at the end of the sharply ascending valley, hard up against the mountains in the most idyllic of locations, is the laid-back resort of **Kandersteg**. Further south are the remote and little-visited Üschinen and Gastern valleys, which offer hikers fantastic opportunities to get out in the wild.

Kandersteg

Long a centre for mountaineering, the picturesque, chalet-strewn village of **Kandersteg** (1200m) was for centuries the trailhead for travellers crossing the high mountain passes into Canton Valais. In 1912, it was changed forever by the completion of the **Lötschberg Tunnel** (see box) just south of the village, a crucially important rail link between northern and southern Europe – the only one between Geneva and the Gotthard – which created a through route from Bern to Milan. Although the small valley road into the village can get heavy with trans-Alpine traffic, most vehicles are heading for the car-train terminus, situated on the outskirts; once you arrive in Kandersteg itself, all is tranquil. The new **Lötschberg Base Tunnel** (see box) has its entrance further north at Frutigen, thus ensuring Kandersteg remains quiet.

The main reason to visit is to explore the countryside. Kandersteg is a fine place to learn how to ski: beginners can test out their snowplough techniques

The Lötschberg Tunnel

Kandersteg is the north portal of the long-standing **Lötschberg Tunnel**, a rail-only route beneath the Alps to Goppenstein in the Valais (see p.342) that also runs car-carrying trains. For drivers, this is a very handy connection, since without it you'd be forced to drive over the Grimsel Pass or make a detour to Montreux. Regular shuttle trains through the tunnel run year-round, every half-hour between 5am and midnight; in July only, there are hourly shuttles throughout Friday nights. Both termini have drive-on drive-off facilities, and journey time is only fifteen minutes. You can buy your ticket on the spot – Fr.20 for a car (Fri–Sun Fr.25). For more information, check Ⓦ www.bls.ch.

After 2007, train and road traffic around Kandersteg and along the length of the Kander valley will change, with the opening of the new **Lötschberg Base Tunnel**. This mammoth engineering project comprises a twin-bore rail tunnel 34.5km long, at a depth well below that of the original tunnel. Trains will enter at Frutigen, well north of Kandersteg, running at up to 250kph underground before emerging at Raron in the Rhône valley just west of Visp. Journey times between Bern and Brig will be halved, and a large swathe of trans-Alpine goods traffic will be shifted away from the roads onto rail. It is envisaged that the original tunnel will remain operational for car-carrying trains. See Ⓦ www.loetschberg.ch for details.

on the easiest and least daunting of slopes, with other beginners all around and not a trace of big-resort swagger. The village itself is strung out along the valley floor for several kilometres, loomed over by the Doldenhorn to the southeast and the First massif to the northwest. Prime hiking and recreation spot above the village is the dramatically crag-ringed **Oeschinensee** (Ⓦ www.oeschinensee .ch), a small lake accessed by a chairlift from the eastern edge of the village. From the top station, it's a twenty-minute stroll to the lake itself, warm and glittering in summer and iced over for cross-country skiing in winter. A handful of trails fan out around the area, dotted with mountain refuges (the tourist office in Kandersteg has a complete list, with hiking routes), and the walk back down to Kandersteg is only about an hour. Another lift on the opposite side of the valley accesses the **Allmenalp**.

A ten-minute drive north of Kandersteg, just off the main valley-floor road, is the underwhelming **Blausee** (Fr.4.50; Ⓦ www.blausee.ch), a privately owned area of land surrounding a tiny boating lake. It's pleasant enough but a bit overblown, since once you stroll through the trees to the lakelet itself, there's not much to do other than order a plate of fresh trout on the restaurant terrace, and watch kids boating around the lake. Even the views are hemmed in by thick pine woods.

Practicalities

Kandersteg's **tourist office** is on the main street, just ahead from the train station (July–Sept & Dec–March Mon–Fri 8am–noon & 1.30–6pm, Sat 8am–noon & 1.30–4.30pm; rest of year Mon–Fri 8am–noon & 2–5pm; ☏033 675 80 80, Ⓦ www.kandersteg.ch). Even before the Lötschberg Tunnel put Kandersteg on the map, the village had a tradition of hospitality, and **accommodation** is of universally good quality.

Plenty of places offer **dorms**, including the *Rendezvous*, near the Oeschinen chairlift (☏033 675 13 54; Fr.25), and *Hotel National*, near the turning for the Allmenalp chairlift (☏033 675 10 85, Ⓦ hotelnati.isuisse.com; ❶; Fr.30). There's a good **campsite** (☏033 675 15 34, Ⓦ www.camping-kandersteg.ch) next to the *Rendezvous*.

Standing out among the **hotels** is the fine *Ruedihus* (☎033 675 81 82, ⓦwww .ruedihus.ch; ❹), in a meadow off the road south of the *National*. A beautifully restored chalet from 1753, its nine characterful rooms display minute attention to detail, with original rustic furniture and fittings set off by the most spotless of modern ensuite bathrooms. The *Zur Post* (☎033 675 12 58, ⓦwww.hotel -zur-post.ch; ❷), in the centre, is a quality lower-end choice. There's a welter of luxury pads, best of which is the central ⚘ *Victoria Ritter* (☎033 675 80 00, ⓦwww.hotel-victoria.ch; ❹–❺), a stout old place with a good reputation. The *Waldhotel Doldenhorn* (☎033 675 81 81, ⓦwww.doldenhorn-ruedihus.ch; ❺) is out in the countryside, boasting comfort and quiet.

Eating and drinking covers the gamut from the simple but palatable dishes (some veggie) in the *Bahnhofbuffet* train station diner, up to the gourmet spreads at the luxury hotels. Meals at the *Ruedihus* (see above) are excellent, with a choice between the formal restaurant above and the atmospheric *Stübli* below, serving a range of inexpensive Swiss specialities (from Fr.20). Most of the hotels along the main street serve food, but the *Victoria-Ritter* prides itself on its kitchen – justifiably so, with a changing menu of intricately well-presented international cuisine (from Fr.25).

Beyond Kandersteg

At the end of Kandersteg village, beside the rushing Kander torrent, is a small crossroads. To the southwest a tortuous path climbs into the bleak **Üschinental**, which penetrates for 4 or 5km between the summits, and is the scene for some tough mountain-bike trails and tougher hikes up to the Gemmi Pass above the town of Leukerbad (see p.342).

Southeast from the same crossroads, a private road (Fr.10 per car, pay at tourist office) accesses the wild **Gasterntal**; beware that the road is narrow and rocky, and runs on an alternate one-way system (into the valley between 30 and 50mins past each hour; out of the valley between the hour and 20 past). A private bus follows the road in good weather only (June–Sept 2–7 daily; Fr.20 return; reservations essential ☎033 671 11 72). Nobody comes down here apart from local hikers in the know, but this was formerly the main route by foot into the Valais: about an hour-and-a-half's walk from the crossroads into the forgotten valley – the walls of which are laced with dramatically spouting waterfalls – you'll come to the hamlet of **SELDEN** (1535m) with a couple of inns, including cosy *Gasthaus Selden* (☎033 675 11 63; ❶). From here, a path cuts south four hours up to the **Lötschen Pass** (2690m), passing another inn, the *Gfelalp* (☎033 675 11 61; ❶), on the ascent. From the basic *Lötschenpasshütte* (☎027 939 19 81, ⓦwww.loetschenpass.ch; Fr.56 incl. half-board; June–Sept) on the summit, three more paths lead down to the villages of the Lötschental on the other side (see p.342). A little east of Selden, the Gasterntal is blocked by the huge Kanderfirn glacier. Check with the Kandersteg tourist office before setting out in these remote areas.

Gstaad

GSTAAD – twinned expertly with Cannes – is an odd place. You'd think, from the high profile of its name, that it would be some kind of glittering Geneva-in-the-Alps, a fantastically expensive mountain paradise. Yet although its instant name-recognition may effortlessly attract Europe's royal households, celebrities galore and countless hangers-on, Gstaad is in fact just a one-street

There's plenty of **hiking** in the four main valleys surrounding Gstaad. A cable car, and trails, run up to the nearby **Eggli** (1557m), favoured excursion from the village, with plenty of paths from there across the plateau, and a long high-level route winding past the tranquil Arnensee and down to **Feutersoey**, some 9km further up the Saane. On the opposite, eastern side of Gstaad looms the **Wispile** (1911m), also served by a cable car, with trails of about two and a half hours leading back to Gstaad. It's equally easy to head due east from the village along the **Turbach** valley, through a hamlet or two on the banks of the stream, and then keep heading straight over the low pass at Reulissen to the busy resorts of **Lenk** or **St Stephan**, both on the Simme some 12km east (4hr 30min total) and linked to Zweisimmen by train.

Swissraft (☏033 744 50 80, ⓦwww.swissraft.ch) offers mountain-bike rental (Fr.45/day) and a host of **adventure activities**, including rafting (Fr.105) and canyoning (Fr.110/half-day). Alpinzentrum (☏033 748 41 61, ⓦwww.alpinzentrum.ch) does many of the same things, throwing in extreme winter sports as well.

The **skiing**, however, might be a disappointment. None of the lifts around the village rises above 2200m, which means that snow cover is unreliable, although some lifts within reach beyond Gsteig do serve the Diablerets 'Glacier 3000' (see p.319), at just under 3000m. Roughly half the pistes in the whole area are rated blue or easy red. There's a complicated system of **lift passes**, covering six very widespread sectors. A one-day pass costs Fr.55 for sector 1 (Zweisimmen, Gstaad, Rougemont); Fr.39 for sector 3 (Château d'Oex); Fr.54 for sector 4 (Diablerets, including the glacier); Fr.29 for sector 5 (Gsteig); and Fr.39 for sector 6 (Lauenen). Four-hour passes are available. For longer periods, you must buy an all-inclusive Top-Card for the whole region, which costs Fr.107/266 for two/six days.

village, a rather charming, attractively located place full of restored weathered-wood chalets and an overabundance of jewellery shops and furriers. But its high-roller status makes it a village like no other: if you fancy being snubbed by the world's richest people, come here for Christmas week, scene of a heady round of sparkling soirées and lavish banquet-style dinner parties all but barred to ordinary mortals.

Glossy magazines may advertise the town as some kind of winter wonderland, but Gstaad is really more of a place to spend the odd ten grand renting a hillside chalet and sipping champagne around town than it is somewhere you can get stuck into any serious skiing. Where the area really enters into its own, prosaically enough, is as a centre from which to **hike** the surrounding Saanenland during the summer months.

Gstaad's main pedestrian-only street, running north–south through the village, is dubbed **Promenade** – no more than five minutes' walk end to end. Focus of the village centre is an open area just at the point cars are barred, which in July is the location for the highly prestigious **Swiss Open** tennis tournament, and which becomes an ice rink all winter.

Practicalities

Gstaad is on the MOB narrow-gauge "Golden Pass" **train** line (see p.160) between Montreux and Zweisimmen. Arriving by car, a turning from **Saanen** – the village on the main Simmental road some 45km west of Spiez – heads south for 3km to Gstaad. Cars are diverted away from Gstaad centre, although if you head straight on at the first roundabout – where you can see the main street stretching out ahead of you – just before the barrier is a covered parking

Gstaad events

Gstaad hosts two of Switzerland's most glittering events, in two very different fields. Early July sees the world's sporting media and celebs galore descend on the village for the **Swiss Open** tennis tournament (Ⓦ www.swissopengstaad.com), a principal fixture on the international ATP tour, drawing the best players in the world.

The **Menuhin Festival** (Ⓦ www.menuhinfestivalgstaad.ch) runs from mid-July until early September. Founded by the violinist Yehudi Menuhin to serve as a showcase for young talent, it has developed into a cycle of major classical concerts – with stellar performers – staged at a variety of locations, principally the church at Saanen, but also at venues in Gstaad and the nearby villages of Lauenen, Zweisimmen and Gsteig.

Lesser events, both still with enough pulling power to book the area out, are the Polo Silver Cup in mid-August, and an international country music weekend in mid-September.

garage; otherwise, turn right at that roundabout and head through the Gstaad Tunnel west of the centre for more parking.

The tiny **train station** is just off the main Promenade. Some 100m further south on Promenade, after the railway bridge, is the **tourist office** (July, Aug & Dec–March Mon–Fri 8am–6.30pm, Sat & Sun 9am–5pm; rest of year Mon–Fri 8.30am–noon & 1.30–6pm, Sat 10am–noon & 1.30–5pm; ℡033 748 81 81, Ⓦ www.gstaad.ch).

Accommodation

As you might expect, the sky's the limit if you choose to **stay** in Gstaad. However, it's not impossible to find inexpensive accommodation, either in the village or nearby. Ten minutes' walk northwest of Saanen is a comfortable, rustic HI **hostel** *Jugendherberge* in the old-style Chalet Rüblihorn (℡033 744 13 43, Ⓦ www.youthhostel.ch; ❶; closed Nov), with quality dorms from Fr.33.

Saanen and neighbouring villages also have the least expensive **hotels**, including the *Bahnhof* in Saanenmöser (℡033 744 15 06, Ⓦ www.hotelbahnhoefli .ch; ❸), 3km east of Saanen. Within Gstaad, *Posthotel Rössli* is a cosy lower-end choice (℡033 748 42 42, Ⓦ www.posthotelroessli.ch; ❹–❺), the oldest hotel in the village, with renovated pine-decor rooms, while *Olden* (℡033 744 34 44, Ⓦ www.hotelolden.com; ❻–❼) is a slicker choice but still with plenty of atmosphere. Steps from the station is the *Bernerhof* (℡033 748 88 44, Ⓦ www .bernerhof-gstaad.ch; ❺–❼), a huge place with generous rooms and an indoor pool. Towering over the village and visible from all points is the fantasy *Palace Hotel* (℡033 748 50 00, Ⓦ www.palace.ch; ❾), laughingly calling itself a "family pension" as it asks Fr.1500 for a double room on a weekend night in the skiing peak (and half that in the summer) – but then again, with underwater music in the pool, giant bedrooms and lavish dinners on the south-facing terrace, they know their clientele well.

Eating and drinking

For **eating and drinking**, check out where the champagne set are gathering in any of half-a-dozen terrace cafés and restaurants along Promenade. *Charly's* is perhaps the most famous, followed up by *Rialto* and *Pernet* facing each other near the chapel. The restaurant in *Posthotel Rössli* has good, plain Swiss meals without the fuss (*menus* Fr.22 or so), while *Sporthotel Rütti*, ten minutes' walk south of town, is acclaimed for its tasty Swiss and Italian-ish cooking, from

Fr.15. At the other end of the scale, *Chesery* (☎033 744 24 51, ⊛www.chesery .ch) is the place to see and be seen, a lively late-night gourmet eatery and piano-bar, with the prices as high as the stilettos: not less than Fr.150 for dinner.

The Pays d'Enhaut

Barely 3km west of Saanen you cross the border from Canton Bern into Canton Vaud, and with it the linguistic *Röstigraben*: not 1km further on is the francophone resort of **Rougemont**, a charming little place full of character that is, so far, successfully fending off the encroachment of Gstaad's high rollers. This area is known as the **PAYS D'ENHAUT**, or Highlands, a sliver of mountain territory originally owned by Gruyères, then seized by Bern, before forming part of the new Vaudois territory after the 1798 revolution. The main valley, with its succession of broad, enclosed side valleys set amidst gentle peaks carpeted by lush summer pasture, is separated from Vaud's better-known Alpine resorts such as Leysin and Les Diablerets (see p.320) by the Col des Mosses pass (1445m) further south. West of Rougemont is the largest town of the region, **Château d'Oex**, best known as a centre for hot-air ballooning.

The MOB narrow-gauge **train** line runs along the valley floor from Gstaad through Château d'Oex, shortly afterwards winding its way down alongside the Dent de Jaman to Montreux (see p.154). A branch line from **Montbovon**, some 11km west of Château d'Oex, runs north to Gruyères (see p.138).

Rougemont

About 7km west of Gstaad, **ROUGEMONT** is an attractive, historic village full of the traditional broad-eaved wooden chalets that characterize the region. Its late eleventh-century Romanesque church is especially picturesque, as is the sixteenth-century château behind, although the latter is privately owned. It's a quiet and attractive place to base yourself for hiking or skiing; the village (⊛www.rougemont.ch) is included in the Gstaad ski pass and, as well as hosting its own blue and red runs, it's only a short train ride from access to the pistes above Gstaad. Amidst the village's handful of simple **hotels**, *Valrose* (☎026 925 81 46, ⊛www.valrose.ch; ❷) is a cosy and friendly little place with appealingly home-cooked meals. The **Videmanette cable car** (⊛www.videmanette .ch) runs from the village up to a trailhead for high-country walks at 2186m, where you'll find a restaurant and, round the corner, a mountain inn with dorms (☎026 924 64 65; Fr.28). The pleasant stroll along the valley floor from Rougemont to Saanen takes about an hour and a half.

Château d'Oex

A family ski and sports resort located where the road from the Col des Mosses joins the valley, **CHÂTEAU D'OEX** (pronounced *day*) is a quiet place in a spectacular location. The wide, sloping valley bowl in which it sits generates exactly the right kinds of thermal air currents for perfect **hot-air ballooning**, and the town is acclaimed as one of the world centres for the sport. When Bertrand Piccard, from Lausanne, and the Briton Brian Jones made their record-breaking 45,000km round-the-world balloon flight in 1999, the takeoff point, and nerve centre of the whole operation, was Château d'Oex. Every January, the town hosts perhaps the most beautiful sports event in the Swiss calendar, the annual **Hot-Air Ballooning Week**, when eighty or more colourful giants catch the thermals to float peaceably over the hills and valleys round about. For speedier thrills, the town and its slopes are linked in to the Gstaad ski pass (see p.307): as well as easy and intermediate pistes all around the town, there are a few testing runs down from the La Braye cable car, spanning the valley up to a height of 1630m.

The **station** is in the centre, right opposite the cable-car station. About 100m west is the **tourist office** (Mon–Fri 8am–noon & 2–6pm, Sat 9am–noon & 2–5pm; ☎026 924 25 25, ⓦwww.chateau-doex.ch). They can set you up with a balloon flight, or you should contact Swissraft in Gstaad (☎033 744 50 80, ⓦwww.swissraft.ch), who charge around Fr.370 for an hour's silent floating.

There's an HI **hostel** *Auberge de Jeunesse* a few minutes' walk downhill from the centre (☎026 924 64 04, ⓦwww.youthhostel.ch; ❶; closed Nov & Dec), with dorms from Fr.29. Of the **hotels**, the *Bon Acceuil* (☎026 924 63 20, ⓦwww .lebonacceuil.ch; ❸–❹), set in its own grounds about 1km west of the centre, is the bargain of the region, a small, charming hotel in a restored eighteenth-century light-wood chalet overlooking the valley; attention to detail – and the lightly prepared cuisine in the atmospheric restaurant – mark it out as extra special.

Travel details

Full timetables for all trains, buses, trams, boats and cable cars in Switzerland – as well as international connections – are searchable at ⓦwww.rail .ch. For details of mountain transport in the Jungfrau Region, see ⓦwww.jungfraubahn.ch.

Trains

Brienz to: Interlaken Ost (twice hourly; 15min); Luzern (hourly; 1hr 35min); Meiringen (twice hourly; 10min).
Grindelwald to: Interlaken Ost (hourly; 35min).
Gstaad to: Château d'Oex (twice hourly; 20min); Interlaken West & Ost (hourly; 1hr 20min; change at Zweisimmen); Montreux (hourly; 1hr 20min).
Interlaken Ost to: Bern (every 30min; 50min); Brienz (twice hourly; 15min); Grindelwald (hourly; 35min); Gstaad (hourly; 1hr 25min; change at Zweisimmen); Lauterbrunnen (every 30min; 20min); Luzern (hourly; 1hr 55min); Meiringen (twice hourly; 30min); Thun (every 30min; 35min); Zürich (twice hourly; 2hr 5min).
Interlaken West to: Bern (every 30min; 45min); Gstaad (hourly; 1hr 20min; change at Zweisimmen); Thun (every 30min; 30min); Zürich (twice hourly; 2hr).
Kandersteg to: Bern (hourly; 1hr); Brig (hourly; 35min); Interlaken West & Ost (hourly; 1hr 5min; change at Spiez); Thun (hourly; 40min).
Lauterbrunnen to: Interlaken Ost (every 30min; 20min); Mürren (every 15min; 30min); Wengen (every 20min; 15min).
Meiringen to: Brienz (twice hourly; 10min);

Interlaken Ost (twice hourly; 30min); Luzern (hourly; 1hr 25min).
Mürren to: Lauterbrunnen (every 15min; 30min).
Thun to: Bern (twice hourly; 20min); Interlaken West & Ost (every 30min; 30min); Spiez (3 hourly; 10min).
Wengen to: Lauterbrunnen (every 20min; 15min).

Buses

Château d'Oex to: Leysin (3 daily; 1hr 30min; change at Le Sépey).
Grindelwald to: Meiringen (June–Oct hourly; 1hr 35min; change at Schwarzwaldalp).
Gstaad to: Les Diablerets (5 daily; 50min).
Interlaken Ost & West to: Beatushöhlen (hourly; 25min).
Lauterbrunnen to: Stechelberg (hourly; 20min).
Meiringen to: Grindelwald (June–Oct hourly; 1hr 55min; change at Schwarzwaldalp).

Boats

Following is a summary of June–Sept summer services; fewer boats run in other months, generally Sat & Sun only, if at all. For details, see ⓦ *www.bls.ch.*
Brienz to: Interlaken Ost (hourly; 1hr 20min).
Interlaken Ost to: Brienz (hourly; 1hr 20min).
Interlaken West to: Beatushöhlen (6 daily; 30min); Spiez (hourly; 1hr 20min); Thun (hourly; 2hr 5min).
Thun to: Beatushöhlen (5 daily; 1hr 30min); Interlaken West (hourly; 2hr 5min); Spiez (hourly; 45min).

7

Valais

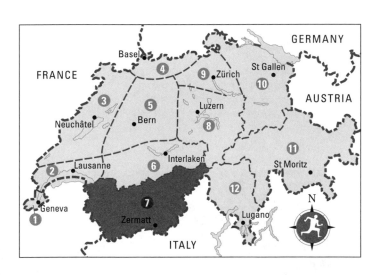

CHAPTER 7 # Highlights

* **Fondation Pierre Gianadda, Martigny** Outstanding art gallery in this little-visited crossroads town. **See p.325**

* **Verbier** One of the Alps' top mountain resorts, offering marvellously scenic skiing and walking. **See p.328**

* **Sion** Characterful valley-floor town, with a fine old quarter and twin castles. **See p.333**

* **Sierre** Lovely wine town on the Rhône, sunny and unpretentious. **See p.337**

* **Crans Montana** High-glitz resort, with shopping and skiing in the limelight. **See p.340**

* **Zermatt** Switzerland's most famous mountain resort offers a vast array of skiing and boarding, plus great summer walks – all watched over by the giant Matterhorn. **See p.344**

* **Saas-Fee** Beautiful village set in an amphitheatre of glaciers, ideal for sunny summer walks and gentle skiing and boarding. **See p.351**

* **The Goms** Unsung, rarely visited high country: remote, tranquil and sublime. **See p.353**

△ Igloo village, Gornergrat

Valais

The Valais is not so much Mediterranean as Iberian in tone: east of Sion, the cicada begins.

John Russell, *Switzerland* (1950)

The **VALAIS** (Wallis in German; Vallese in Italian; ⓦ www.valaistourism .ch) is Switzerland's third-largest canton, a diverse swathe of country occupying the valley – hence the name – of the **River Rhône**, from its source in the glaciers of the central Alps to its inflow to Lake Geneva. Fully twenty percent of the canton is covered by glaciers, and yet the region has the driest climate, with the lowest rainfall and the most sunshine, of the whole country. The artificial irrigation system set in place by the valley dwellers in the Middle Ages – a vast network of channels, called *bisses* in French and *Suonen* in Swiss-German – still weaves a cat's cradle over the foothills of the high mountains, supplemented these days by half-a-dozen of the tallest and highest-altitude dams in the world.

For the Swiss, the Valais somehow represents a piece of common heritage all but lost elsewhere in the country: in the most unlikely corners of Geneva and Zürich, you can find restaurants done up as traditional Valaisian-style darkwood chalets, complete with window boxes full of geraniums and farm tools as decoration on the walls, serving up the local speciality **raclette** (see p.58) under a nameboard "Chalet Valaisanne" or "Walliser Stube". The dryness and sunshine of the valley are ideal vine-growing conditions, and the canton's 22,000 vineyard owners are famous for producing some of the finest **wine** in the country.

The Valais is still a wild and little-known place outside the trio of famous resorts bred by the mountains: **Zermatt**, **Verbier** and **Crans-Montana**. Few outsiders bother to penetrate the deep rural side valleys either side of the single road and rail line that run along the valley floor – though those who do make the effort find plenty of long-distance hiking and adventure sports of all kinds. The only town of any size is the cantonal capital **Sion**, with a low-key, easy-going atmosphere and a handful of sights. In the northernmost extremities of the region, an area of Vaud known as **Haut-Léman** occupies the east bank of the Rhône just before it flows into Lake Geneva, where the resorts of the **Alpes Vaudoises** share the mountainous scenery of Valais Romand.

As well as Canton Valais, this chapter covers parts of Canton Vaud, including towns around **Aigle** and the mountain resorts of the **Alpes Vaudoises** (though not Château d'Oex and Rougemont, which are covered in Chapter 6, p.309). For an account of the tiny stretch of Lake Geneva shoreline that falls within Canton Valais, including St-Gingolph and Le Bouveret, turn to Chapter 2, p.153.

Some history

Cut off on all sides by mountains, the Valais has always been a world apart. On a push to conquer the Celtic peoples of the valley in the first century BC, a Roman army under **Julius Caesar** ventured the crossing of the Grand-St-Bernard Pass from Italy and then spread out through the valley. They got as far as modern-day Sierre, and left behind them a legacy of Latin. Even today, Sierre is the easternmost French-speaking town in the canton, while beyond it the mother tongue is Swiss-German, descended from the language of the Aleman tribes who remained unconquered.

Once the Romans retreated, few outsiders had much success in challenging the peoples of the valley. **Christianity** arrived before the fourth century, with the travel of clerics and merchants over the Grand-St-Bernard Pass, but the

Reformation never made it any further into the valley than Aigle, in neighbouring Canton Vaud, and Valais remains majority Catholic to this day. Even the mighty **Bernese** army was stopped by the mountains and the wildness of the terrain. At times of severe hardship during the Middle Ages and later, however, many **Walsers** have voluntarily chosen to depart, forced to leave their home villages and travel over the mountains to seek a better life elsewhere. Walser communities survive in places as far apart as Argentina and Liechtenstein, still nurturing their distinctive dialect and culture.

The Valais remained independent until 1815, when it joined the Swiss Confederation as a new canton. It's a mark of the social changes taking place over recent years that German speakers in the east of the canton are now starting to worry about the encroachment of **French** up the valley: with the economic power and prestige of the French-speaking lower valley, German speakers are increasingly finding employment in francophone areas, while francophone firms are expanding their bases of operation into German-speaking communities. Locals in Brig in particular shake their head at the quantity of French now being heard in the town, but there seems little they can do about it.

Haut-Léman

Before mainline trains heading south from Montreux enter Valais, they first pass through a diverse area of **Vaud** known as **HAUT-LÉMAN**, extending southeast of Lake Geneva. The Rhône – which here marks the cantonal border between Vaud on the east bank and Valais on the west – meanders between the craggy Dents-du-Midi and the heights of Les Diablerets. The valley floor and west-facing foothills make up the acclaimed wine region of **Chablais**, centred on the fine old town of **Aigle**, with its turreted castle surrounded by vineyards. Above Aigle rise the 3000m-plus peaks of the **Alpes Vaudoises**, centred on a handful of attractive, small-scale resorts such as **Villars** and **Les Diablerets** that offer excellent skiing and a cosy atmosphere well away from the bustle of Verbier and Crans-Montana further south.

The **Lake Geneva Regional Pass** (see box p.118) is valid for transport in the whole of Haut-Léman, including routes to Aigle, Leysin, Les Diablerets, Villars and St-Maurice.

Aigle

Although the main valley highway bypasses **AIGLE**, this alluring little town is well worth the small detour for a lazy afternoon of castle exploration and wine-tasting. Aigle is the main town of the Chablais wine region, and its prime landmark – the fantastical **Château d'Aigle**, a fifteenth-century folly with corner towers and witch's-hat turrets – is home to two excellent **museums** devoted to wine and wine production. Aigle's other claim to fame is five hundred years old: in 1476, the town was integrated into Canton Bern as the first French-speaking territory to join the Swiss Confederation. Shortly after, in 1526, newly converted Bernese Protestants sent Guillaume Farel to preach the Reformation in Aigle, the first time this had ever been done in a francophone region.

Along with its near-neighbour Yvorne, Aigle produces what are acclaimed as the best **wines** of the region, and some of the best in all Switzerland, the gravelly, clay-like soil nurturing especially good, dustily elegant, fruity whites ("It's difficult to find a bad white Aigle," commented wine writer John C. Sloan). *Les Murailles*, from the Badoux winery, is one of the very few Swiss wines to be marketed in North America; it and the *Crosex Grillé* Grand Cru are the two best names to ask for. Further south, the nearby towns of Bex and Ollon produce their own tangy, flowery whites: *Philos* is probably the best of them.

The salt mines of Bex

Some 9km south of Aigle and connected by train is the small town of **Bex** (pronounced *bay*), unremarkable but for the fact that it sits beside Switzerland's only working **salt mine**, named Le Bouillet. All through the Middle Ages Switzerland had to rely on expensive imports of salt, mainly from Franche-Comté. Then, in the fifteenth century, legend has it that a shepherd pasturing his flocks above Bex noticed that the animals preferred drinking from two particular springs. Tasting the water himself, he discovered that it was salty. This led to further investigation and the mines have been worked ever since. Today a labyrinthine network of galleries burrows for some 50km beneath the mountains, still producing salt for domestic consumption.

You can visit some parts of the mines on **guided tours** (July & Aug daily 9.45am, 11am, 2 & 4pm; lasts 2hr; June & Sept daily 9.45am, 11.15am, 2.15 & 3.45pm; lasts 1hr 45min; April, May & Oct Tues–Sun only; Fr.18; reservations essential at ⓦwww .mines.ch or ☎024 463 03 30). Tours (available in English) begin with an audiovisual show and include a long underground narrow-gauge train ride and plenty of subterranean walking. There's no public transport to the mine entrance. Irregular **buses** run from Bex station to the village of Les Dévens, twenty minutes' walk away, or you can walk from Bex in about 45 minutes.

Arrival, information and accommodation

Aigle's **train station** is the focus of the Transports Publics du Chablais network (ⓦwww.tpc.ch): in addition to mainline CFF trains, it's served by AL (Aigle–Leysin) and ASD (Aigle–Sépey–Diablerets), which both climb into the adjacent hills, as well as AOMC (Aigle–Ollon–Monthey–Champéry), which crosses the Rhône. Just up the valley, the BVB line climbs from Bex to Villars and Bretaye.

The station lies west of the centre, at one end of the 300m-long Rue de la Gare; at the other end is the small **tourist office**, 5 Rue Colomb (April–Oct Mon–Fri 8.30am–noon & 2–6pm, Sat 9am–noon; rest of year closed Sat; ☎024 466 30 00, ⓦwww.aigle.ch & www.alp3000.ch). It lies just past turnings to the pedestrianized café-street of **Rue de Bourg** and, parallel to it, the remarkable little cobbled alley **Rue de Jérusalem**, so named because the upper floors of its old wooden houses span the street in a style which reminded one nineteenth-century observer of the shaded residential quarters of Middle Eastern cities. From the central Place du Marché, Avenue du Cloître leads southeast towards the château.

Aigle has only a couple of central **hotels**: *Les Messageries*, 19 Rue du Midi (☎024 466 20 60; ❷), has plain ensuite and shared-bath rooms; *Hôtel du Nord*, 2 Rue Colomb (☎024 468 10 55, ⓦwww.hoteldunord.ch; ❷–❸), is more upmarket.

Château d'Aigle

Ten minutes' stroll southeast of the town centre loom the turrets of **Château d'Aigle**. Ranged beneath is an attractive little quarter of old houses, among which stands the ancient Église St-Maurice or Église du Cloître, founded in 1143 and renovated over the centuries in a mixture of styles.

Atmospheric cobbled lanes wind up from here to the **château** (July & Aug daily 10am–6pm; April–June, Sept & Oct Tues–Sun 10am–12.30pm & 2–6pm; last entry 1hr before closing; ⓦwww.chateauaigle.ch). The main castle building houses the Musée de la Vigne et du Vin (Vine and Wine); opposite the gates, in the stout **Maison de la Dîme**, is the Musée de l'Étiquette (Wine-Labels). Combined admission for both museums is Fr.9 (SMP valid).

The château is an impressive example of medieval castle building, founded and expanded by the advancing Savoyards in the thirteenth century. The Bernese burnt the place to the ground in 1475, rebuilding it to serve both a defensive function on the fringes of Bernese power and as a residence for their bailiffs. Following the Vaudois revolution of 1798, the castle reverted to local hands, and remained the town's prison right up until 1972, when nobody could be found to take on the job of jailer and so all the resident convicts had to be transferred to Vevey. As you enter, you're given a follow-the-numbers pamphlet, which leads you through the rooms around the courtyard that house the **Musée de la Vigne et du Vin**. Look out for the old shop signs in the vestibule of the main dwelling (room 9) and the mighty barrels and winepress in the cellar below (room 10). The ramparts walk is a good one, with frescoes in the various watchtowers and romantic views out over the sea of vines all around. The **Musée de l'Étiquette** is a rather sedate affair, ornate labels from bottles around the world displayed on placards in a wood-beamed attic.

Eating and drinking

Rue de Bourg is lined with pleasant **restaurants** – check out popular *La Croix Blanche*, serving reasonably priced pizzas and simple *menus* (Fr.15); *Des Alpes* at no. 29 (closed Wed) also serves a good range of salads, and has an outdoor terrace. A shady unnamed courtyard-café at the southern end of Rue de Jérusalem offers light meals along with seven kinds of *Rösti* (Fr.15–20). Top choice in town is the *Pinte du Paradis* within the château's Maison de la Dîme (Tues–Sat 10am–11pm, Sun 10am–6pm), for excellent Vaudois cuisine and local Chablais wines. The streets around the château offer plenty of places to buy and sample **wine**, and there are special wine-tasting sessions (July–Sept Sat & Sun 11am & 3pm) in the castle cellars, or, if sunny, in the courtyard.

The Alpes Vaudoises

The huge peaks east of Aigle and the Rhône valley are collectively dubbed the **Alpes Vaudoises**, sheltering a few attractive, isolated little ski villages – all family-oriented – that offer some of the best facilities outside the huge Valaisian resorts further south. Friendly **Villars** leads the bunch, connected by a system of lifts both with its neighbour, Gryon, and with the separate resort of **Les Diablerets**, which is linked to Gstaad's lift pass and is subtitled "Glacier 3000" for its access to year-round glacier skiing and boarding above 3000m. Tiny **Leysin**, tucked away in a valley above Aigle, completes the picture. In summer, all these villages slumber quietly in the sunshine, hosting walkers and those seeking undisturbed Alpine isolation. **Transport** between the three is sporadic; they serve better as places to base yourself for a few days or a couple of weeks rather than as stepping stones around the region.

The twin resorts of **Château d'Oex** and **Rougemont** – formally part of the Alpes Vaudoises, but cut off from their neighbours by the Col des Mosses pass (1445m) and nearer to Gstaad – are covered in Chapter 6, p.309.

The **skiing** in the neighbouring areas of Villars-Gryon, Les Diablerets and Leysin is good. **Diablerets** village has close access to the Col de Pillon gondola serving the "**Glacier 3000**" (Ⓦ www.glacier3000.ch), which slides down from the peaks of Scex Rouge (2970m) and Les Diablerets itself (3209m). Most of the pistes up here are blue and red, even way on top around the Quille du Diable – a jutting natural obelisk up at 3000m. A single hair-raising black run plunges beneath the gondola from **Pierres-Pointes** (2217m) down to the Col du Pillon. From Diablerets village, another gondola serves the slopes of **Isenau** to the north, laced with blue and red runs, while a third rises to **Meilleret**, in the direction of Villars. Les Diablerets also prides itself on its **summer skiing**, with good snow assured even in June and July on the glacier.

From **Villars** village, a gondola rises to the **Roc d'Orsay** (2000m), from where a long blue run delivers you to the hub of the skiing at **Bretaye**, set in a broad bowl and also served by a rack railway from Villars centre. Gentle red pistes abound, and from **Barboleuse** a gondola heads up to Les Chaux (1750m), offering a long and rewarding blue run, as well as a red or two and a long steep black down to Sodoleuvre. It's also easy to work your way over to Les Diablerets – although beware that if the snow at Villars or Gstaad isn't that great, everybody heads up to the glacier, which can sometimes make things a bit overcrowded. From **Leysin** village, lifts and gondolas serve a host of red and blue pistes, as well as a half-pipe for snowboarders below the peak of **La Berneuse** (2048m), where there's a panoramic revolving restaurant.

Lift passes are good value. For a full day, Les Diablerets plus Villars-Gryon (excluding the glacier) is Fr.47, Leysin Fr.43. Otherwise, an all-inclusive pass takes in the above plus the Glacier 3000, Les Mosses and sectors of the Gstaad ski region (see p.307) for Fr.55/261 for one/six days.

Adventure sports are a mainstay of all three resorts. Mountain Evasion (Ⓦ www .mountain-evasion.ch) and Centre Par Adventure (Ⓦ www.swissaventure.ch) are two companies in Les Diablerets organizing canyoning, zorbing, luge, mud biking, rappelling and more.

Villars-Gryon

The neat, unpretentious little resort of **VILLARS** is linked to Bex, down in the valley, by a quaint Edwardian train on the BVB line, and to Aigle by a rather less romantic postbus. It wins no awards for grace or stylishness, but where it does score (and where it *has* won awards) is for its family-oriented service. Winter after winter, Villars and the neighbouring community of **GRYON**, 4km away on the train line, attract scores of families on skiing breaks, while remaining virtually unknown to a wider clientele. The skiing around the town is pretty good (see box), with the added bonuses of direct lift linkage to the Diablerets sector for glacier pistes up to 3000m. Multi-day lift passes are also valid in the Gstaad ski region (see p.307), a bus ride away.

Villars' **station** is in the heart of the village; 50m to the right on the main Avenue Central is the **tourist office** (daily 8am–6.30pm; ☎024 495 32 32, Ⓦ www.villars.ch). For **accommodation**, the large *Eurotel Victoria* (☎024 495 31 31, Ⓦ www.eurotel-victoria.ch; ❺–❻) has spacious, modern rooms, some with a balcony. *Alpe Fleurie* (☎024 495 34 64, Ⓦ www.alpe-fleurie.com; ❸–❹) and *Ecureuil* (☎024 496 37 37, Ⓦ www.hotel-ecureuil.ch; ❸–❹) are old-style chalet-hotels with a long history of catering to families, both conveniently central. A low-end option is the charming *Chalet Martin* **hostel** five minutes' walk above Gryon station (☎024 498 33 21, Ⓦ www.gryon.com; ❶; no credit cards), a cosy, friendly place run by a Swiss-Australian couple, with dorm space for around Fr.25. *Le Vieux-Villars*, on the Route des Hôtels, is a three-storey **restaurant** known for its fondues and raclettes.

Les Diablerets

Snoozing quietly in its peaceful backwater valley, **LES DIABLERETS** really deserves to be left well alone. It's so tranquil that it's almost a shame to mark it on a map – indeed, less than a century ago, it wasn't on any maps, and it was only with the arrival of the railway in 1914 that outsiders noticed the place. These days Les Diablerets has a small but loyal band of guests, who return each year to enjoy the valley's charm.

Regular ASD **trains** run to Les Diablerets from Aigle; **buses** also connect the village with Gstaad via a steep road which winds over the Col du Pillon (1546m), 4km east of Les Diablerets. The tiny switchback road over the Col de la Croix (1778m), 4km south of Les Diablerets, leads to Villars; three buses a day (July–Sept only) shuttle between the two resorts.

The **station** is beside the river, about 100m north of the **tourist office** (July, Aug & Dec–April daily 8.30am–6.30pm; rest of year Mon–Sat 8.30am–12.30pm & 2.30–6pm, Sun 9am–12.30pm; ☎024 492 33 58, ⒲www.diablerets .ch). Every September, Les Diablerets hosts the International Alpine Film Festival (⒲www.fifad.ch).

Most accommodation is in chalets, but of the **hotels**, the *Auberge de la Poste* (☎024 492 31 24, ⒲www.aubergedelaposte.ch; ❷), a 200-year-old inn that claims to have hosted Victor Hugo, Stravinsky and Lenin in years gone by, is pleasantly rustic. Top place in town is the lovely *Hôtel des Diablerets* (☎024 492 09 09, ⒲www.hoteldesdiablerets.ch; ❺–❻). There are two mountain inns with **dorms** above the village, including the *Cabane des Diablerets* (☎024 492 21 02; Fr.31; mid-June to mid-Sept), at 2525m overlooking the glacier. **Eating** is mainly a hotel option, with the inexpensive restaurants at the *Auberge de la Poste* and *Hotel Les Lilas* worth checking out.

The devils of Les Diablerets

The mountain communities of the Alpes Vaudoises are replete with legends and **folk tales**, and Les Diablerets – its name meaning "abode of devils" – is no exception. To the south and east of the village rise the heights of Les Diablerets themselves, with their two glaciers, Diablerets and **Tsanfleuron**. Legend has it that the latter ("Field of Flowers" in the local dialect) was a beautiful sunny meadow until the arrival, long ago, of demons and devils in the mountains. Soon after, the shepherds of Tsanfleuron and the Ormont Valley began to be troubled by boulders bouncing down from on high, as the devils played their games of skill, trying to hit a huge tower of rock, the **Quille du Diable** (Devil's Skittle). The shepherds, fearing for the safety of their flocks and themselves, moved away from the area, which lost its vitality and beauty and turned into the icy wasteland it remains today.

Other tales abound of **lost souls** seen at night, drifting with lanterns alone or in groups through the woods, pastures and rocky defiles of the mountain; local people attested to seeing their lantern lights and hearing their moans just before the two terrible landslides of 1714 and 1740. The meadows and hills are also said to be inhabited by elves, goblins and a local brand of **imp** named a *servan*, one of whom, it is said, once mischievously turned himself into a fox and was seen sitting at night in a hay loft knitting with the hair of his own tail.

Leysin

The road from Aigle up into the mountains divides at Le Sépey: Les Diablerets is east, the Col des Mosses leading to Château d'Oex is north, while buses follow a tiny winding road west to the beautifully located little village of **LEYSIN**, once a high-altitude centre for the treatment of respiratory diseases, but now metamorphosed into a popular and well-maintained Alpine resort. For **accommodation**, the warmest welcome can be found at the excellent SB hostel *Hiking Sheep*, in the Villa La Joux (☎024 494 35 35, ⓦwww.hikingsheep .com; ❶), which has some twin rooms and space in good dorms (Fr.30). Satellite TV, a large cosy lounge, dining rooms with log fires, kitchen use, balconies with perfect views and switched-on multilingual staff add to the attraction (as do reductions for long stays). The beauty of the surroundings, and relative isolation, make Leysin a perfect place for a quiet getaway.

Valais Romand

Tacked seamlessly south of Haut-Léman, **VALAIS ROMAND**, or the French-speaking part of Valais, comprises the westernmost portions of the canton. Occupying the broad Rhône valley floor and the most accessible foothills just above, it's more populated and livelier than the wilder German-speaking east. Mountain passes aside, the road and train line from Montreux is the sole route in and out: the mountains flanking the Rhône are cut through with a handful of dead-end valleys, ideal for long-distance hiking, but only the high pass roads over the **Grand-St-Bernard** to Aosta (Italy) and the Col de la Forclaz to Chamonix (France) give access from outside. These two roads join the valley at **Martigny**, a rather unprepossessing place much overshadowed in both style and appeal by the cantonal capital **Sion** and its neighbour **Sierre**. The vapid resort towns of **Verbier** near Martigny, and **Crans-Montana** above Sierre, are two of the best-known ski resorts in the world, offering the combination of groomed pistes and chic après-ski that Switzerland is famous for.

South to Martigny

Roads and train tracks cross the broad Rhône at Aigle and Bex to a slice of Valais to the west holding the small resort of **Champéry**, where you can ski the vast **Portes du Soleil** region, straddling the French border. Main roads head on south towards Martigny, crossing the Vaud–Valais frontier at the ancient town of **St-Maurice**.

The Portes du Soleil

Spreading across a mountainous region west of the Rhône valley, in the shadow of the Dents du Midi range, is the huge **Portes du Soleil** ski area (ⓦwww .portesdusoleil.com), comprising twelve linked Swiss and French resorts. It's a very popular ski destination, but, in truth, is too low to have consistently good snow cover: its top height is only around 2400m and, if snow is poor lower down, the bottlenecks to reach higher pistes can be terrible. On the French side, the key resort – with some superb facilities for snowboarders and the notorious "Wall" black run – is **Avoriaz**, an ugly collection of 1960s apartment blocks on a cliffside above overcrowded **Morzine**.

On the Swiss side, access is via a couple of small, relatively characterful villages. From the gateway town of **Monthey**, just across from Bex, roads and a train line from Aigle penetrate the narrow, steep Val d'Illiez to **CHAMPÉRY**, an attractive Alpine tourist resort that's been in business since the 1850s and boasts large-capacity cable cars up to Croix de Culet. A tourist office (daily 8am–noon & 2–6pm; ☎024 479 20 20, ⊛www.champery.ch) has information on the whole area. The *Hôtel Suisse* (☎024 479 07 07; ❸–❺) retains much of its old-fashioned character; *Pension Souvenir* (☎024 479 13 40; ❶) is a good downmarket option. From Monthey, an alternative route branches off to the less appealing base of **Morgins**, right on the border. A lift pass for the Portes du Soleil costs Fr.55/263 for one/six days, or Fr.41 for a day on the CLCF sector around Champéry only.

St-Maurice

About 3km south of Bex, at the point where the narrowing of the Rhône prompted the Romans to build a bridge, is **ST-MAURICE**, named after the warrior-saint Maurice who is purported to have been martyred nearby. Maurice was ordered in 287 AD by Emperor Maximian to serve against his fellow Christians on campaigns in Gaul, but refused, according to a later chronicler with the words: "We are your soldiers, O Emperor, but we freely acknowledge that we are also the servants of God... To you is due military obedience, but to God, justice... We cannot take up arms to strike pious men." The Emperor duly had the whole legion slaughtered. Today, of course, mighty Maximian is forgotten, while there are apparently 4 cathedrals, 598 churches and 74 towns around the world named after Maurice, not counting two entire countries (Mauritius and Mauritania).

A shrine grew up around the supposed tomb of the saint, hard up against a rocky cliff on the banks of the Rhône, as early as 390, replaced by a monastery in 515; this is still in existence as the oldest surviving abbey north of the Alps. Pilgrims have come to the **abbey church** for over 1500 years, bringing with them items of gold and silver as homage, and the church **treasury** holds many exquisitely beautiful pieces, including a Roman sardonyx vase, the intricate gold cloisonné Casket of Teuderic, an embossed silver bust of St Candidus and filigreed silver Arm of St Bernard. Although the church is open at any time, you can only visit the treasury on **guided tours** (in English; Tues–Sun: July & Aug 10.30am (not Sun), 2pm, 3.15 & 4.30pm; May, June, Sept & Oct 10.30am (not Sun), 3 & 4.30pm; Nov–April 3pm; Fr.6; ⊛www.abbaye-stmaurice.ch).

Heading straight ahead out of the **train station** along Avenue de la Gare will bring you after 100m to the **tourist office** (July & Aug Mon–Fri 9am–7pm, Sat 9am–5pm; rest of year Mon 3–6pm, Tues–Fri 9am–noon & 3–6pm, Sat 9am–noon; ☎024 485 40 40, ⊛www.st-maurice.ch). The abbey church stands more or less opposite; nearby, the ancient Grand-Rue runs through the centre of town, bedecked with wrought-iron inn signs. The small **hotel** *Dent-du-Midi*, set in gardens at 1 Avenue du Simplon (☎024 485 12 09, ⊛www.torrente.ch; ❷), is comfortable and modern. For **eating**, the *Dent-du-Midi* serves up Valaisian specialities, while the best place for fondue is *La Croix Fédérale*, 45 Grand-Rue (closed Sun).

Martigny

There are few more dramatically sited cities in Switzerland than **MARTIGNY**. Set down on the broad valley floor, with wooded heights soaring on all sides, it's positioned at a natural crossroads. The Rhône, having flowed almost arrow straight along its valley for over 100km, suddenly makes a sharp right-angled turn at Martigny, heading off between the mountains to Lake Geneva; elevated points within the town give yawning views along both valleys, east and north. The major attraction is the **Fondation Pierre Gianadda**, one of the country's most prestigious art galleries. Roman ruins add more interest, and the small, cobbled Old Town, or Bourg, makes for some attractive wandering.

And yet Martigny is a curiously unsatisfying place to spend more than an afternoon. It's not an unpleasant town, but there's just not much going on, and – even worse – not many characterful places to sit and watch life go by. Stay overnight and make the best of it, or cut your losses and look elsewhere: St-Maurice has held onto its history better than Martigny; atmospheric Sion is close by; or plump for a wilder night way up on the Grand-St-Bernard Pass. See p.43 for details of the **Mont Blanc Express** and **St Bernard Express** (ⓦwww.momc.ch), two scenic Alpine train rides that begin from Martigny.

Arrival, information and accommodation

Martigny's **station** is at the northeastern end of Avenue de la Gare, which cuts a broad swathe through the centre. At the other end, 500m away, is the main Place Centrale, with the **tourist office** on one side (July & Aug Mon–Fri 9am–6pm, Sat 9am–noon & 2–6pm, Sun 10am–noon & 4–6pm; rest of year Mon–Fri

ACCOMMODATION
Auberge Poste-Bourg D
City Garni C
Forclaz-Touring A
Poste B

EATING & DRINKING
Les Arcades 6
Café de la Place 3
Casino 2
Kwong-Ming 1
Le Lion d'Or 4
Trois Couronnes 5

Valaisian cowfighting

One of the oddest of the Valais's peculiar local traditions is **cowfighting**. Utterly unlike Spanish bullfighting – an altogether gorier spectacle – bloodless Valaisian cowfighting stems from village get-togethers to see whose cow was best suited to lead the herds up to the summer Alpine pastures. The cattle all come from the local Hérens breed – bright-eyed with short legs and powerful chests – who would naturally pick fights with each other in the open meadows: early on, farmers merely corralled them together to see who would win the squabbles. These days, the contests have become rather more important: breeding means big money for the Valaisian cattle farmers, and the winner of the annual cowfighting championship can be assured a head price in the tens of thousands of francs plus the prestigious title "Queen of the Herd".

Farmers feed up the most bullish of their cows on a special extra-rich diet to improve (or worsen) the temper, occasionally allowing her the odd bucket of wine as a tonic and coaching her in sparring contests amongst the herd. Come the day of battle, farmers tie a huge cowbell around their champion's neck, lead her into the "arena" (generally just a meadow), and introduce her to her opponent. Hérens cows rarely need any encouragement to provoke each other, and they happily lock horns. There's never any bloodiness, and the winner is generally deemed to be the cow who has intimidated her opponent into submission.

Local contests are held on Sundays once or twice a month in various towns from late March through to September, accompanied by much revelry and the consumption of gallons of local wine. Two events stand out: the **cantonal championships** are held in Aproz, a small town just outside Sion, in mid-May, with the winners going on to Martigny for the **Combats des Reines**, a huge show held in the 5000-seater Roman amphitheatre in early October. It's here that the supreme champion is crowned Queen of the Herd.

9am–noon & 1.30–6pm, Sat 9am–noon; May, June, Sept & Oct also Sat 2–5pm; ☎027 721 22 20, ⓦwww.martignytourism.ch). They're well equipped with information and maps for the whole area.

There's a handful of town **hotels**, many unromantically planted on the busy Avenue du Grand-St-Bernard as sleepover motels to catch the traffic heading for the Alpine passes. Least expensive are the spartan shared-bath rooms of the old *Auberge Poste-Bourg*, 81 Avenue du Grand-St-Bernard (☎027 723 17 23; ❶). *City Garni*, 7 Place St-Michel (☎027 723 36 00; ❶), is modern but generic. The bland *Forclaz-Touring*, 15 Rue du Léman (☎027 722 27 01, ⓦwww.hotelforclaztouring .ch; ❷–❸), has comfortable ensuite rooms near the station, whereas the *Poste*, 8 Rue de la Poste (☎027 722 14 44, ⓦwww.ngscan.com/hotelposte; ❷), is in the heart of town but could do with a good spring-clean.

The Town

Just behind Place Centrale and the tourist office is the **Église Notre-Dame-des-Champs**, completed in 1687, with magnificent carved doors but a modest interior. From Place Centrale, if you follow Rue Marc-Morand north, you'll come to an old covered wooden bridge over the Dranse river; this is an 1818 replacement of the 1350 original, and leads to a winding path climbing to the semi-ruined thirteenth-century **Château de la Bâtiaz**, its lofty round tower visible from all parts of the town, and especially dramatic when floodlit at night beside the meandering tail-lights of cars on the tortuous switchback road to Chamonix. The château (July & Aug Mon–Thurs 1–6pm, Fri–Sun 11am–6pm;

May, June, Sept & Oct Thurs 4–6pm, Fri–Sun 11am–6pm; free; ⓦ www.batiaz
.ch) has a display of medieval siege engines and pillories. Below is the small
Chapelle de Notre-Dame-de-Compassion, built in the 1620s with a
Rococo altar added more than a century later.

Fondation Pierre Gianadda

The main reason for coming to Martigny is to visit the galleries of the **Fondation Pierre Gianadda** (daily: June–Nov 9am–7pm; rest of year 10am–6pm;
Fr.15; SMP; ⓦ www.gianadda.ch), well signposted about 500m south of Place
Centrale on a patch of parkland off Rue du Forum. Established in 1978 by a
local philanthropist, Léonard Gianadda, and named after his brother, the complex
takes in several areas within a single museum. Various special deals on admission
are available, such as a twenty-percent discount on your train fare to Martigny
and museum entry if you book the two together at any Swiss station.

The main focus is the changing series of top-flight art exhibitions staged
in the **main gallery** area: recent major shows have focused on such names
as Chagall, Modigliani, Cartier-Bresson, Picasso and Van Gogh. The gallery
space is not huge, but the quality of works brought in from around the world
is always very high. The upper level of the gallery is given over to the **Musée
Archéologique Gallo-Romain**, an interesting collection of statues, coins,
pottery, jewellery and other bits and bobs garnered from digs around Martigny.
Prime exhibit, which serves as the Foundation's mascot, is an impressive bronze
head of a bull, dating from the first or second century AD. The whole building is constructed around the remains of a Gallo-Roman temple dedicated to
Mercury, the inner-sanctum walls of which have been left intact in the middle
of the museum's floor space.

In a back area off the gallery is a small permanent exhibition in the **Salle
Franck** of ten modernist works donated from a private collection, which
includes Picasso's *Nu aux jambes
croisées* (1903), produced during
the artist's blue period. Further
along the corridor, the smell of
motor oil and rubber prelude
the subterranean **Musée de
l'Auto**, displaying fifty-odd
vintage cars including a Model
T Ford (1912), and a dashingly
elegant Lagonda (1936). Outside
is another highlight, the **Parc
des Sculptures**, an open area of
green overlooked by Martigny's
wooded slopes and dotted with
works by – among many others
– Rodin, Moore and Miró, as well
as Brancusi's celebrated *Le Grand
Coq* (1949), a striking zigzag of
gleaming metal, and the **Cour
Chagall**, devoted to a monumental mosaic by the artist (1964).
Alongside the café at the rear of
the park is the **Vieil Arsenal**,
which stages excellent shows of
photography or modern art.

△ The sculpture garden, Fondation Pierre Gianadda

The museum also stages a prestigious cycle of **classical music concerts**, around fifteen a year, which give the unique opportunity to see stellar world-class artists performing at close quarters in the intimate gallery space: Cecilia Bartoli is a regular performer, as are the Beaux Arts Trio and legendary soloists such as Pinchas Zukerman. Tickets (roughly Fr.30–200) are very limited.

Within a few hundred metres of the museum, to the south beyond the train tracks, lies Martigny's Roman **amphitheatre**, dating from the second to fourth centuries AD and now restored to seat 5000 spectators. It comes into its own as the venue for the annual cowfighting championships in early October (see box), but otherwise it's a quiet, grassy corner from which to survey the wooded slopes all around.

Eating and drinking

Place Centrale is where it happens in Martigny – though "it" covers little more than sitting around under the plane trees at pleasant terrace cafés **eating** plates of chips and drinking beer. Ranged along one side are bustling *Café de la Place*, specializing in fondues and raclettes (Fr.15–20), and adjacent *Barock* and *Les Platanes*, all of which get crammed on summer evenings churning out meals, beers and coffees. Down in the Bourg, the *Auberge Poste-Bourg* (see "Accommodation") offers inexpensive Valaisian dishes (Fr.16 or so), while the *Hôtel des Trois Couronnes*, 8 Place du Bourg (℡027 723 21 14; closed Sun & Mon), is an old traditional-style *auberge* from 1609, no longer offering lodging, but still serving up quality French *menus* at Fr.20 and up – go for the house speciality of kidneys in garlic. Near Place Centrale, *Le Lion d'Or*, 1 Avenue du Grand-St-Bernard (closed Sun & Mon), makes its own fresh pasta, and has pizzas and other Italian favourites such as *osso bucco*. The Gault & Millau-recommended *Kwong-Ming*, Place de Rome (℡027 722 45 15; closed June), serves up perfect Chinese dishes in a calm, darkwood interior or *al fresco* beside the interior garden (or takeaway); *menus* can be Fr.20 at lunch, double that in the evening. Reserve ahead to dine medieval-style at the Château de la Batiaz (see above): various menus of local fare (including veggie options) are around Fr.30–35.

Along Avenue de la Gare, the **bar** in the *Casino* cinema, open daily until midnight, is a fairly civilized choice. Alternatively you could head down to *Les Arcades*, in a vaulted cellar at 31 Rue du Bourg, one of a handful of sociable taverns in the area.

Pays du St-Bernard

South of Martigny, the **Pays du St-Bernard** (ⓦ www.saint-bernard.ch) comprises wild valleys hemmed in by the giant Pennine Alps marking the Italian border. Branch-line trains from Martigny station follow the Dranse valley and divide; one branch serves **Le Châble**, tucked beneath the ski resort of Verbier (see p.328), while the other is the gateway to the Val d'Entremont, leading south to the **Grand-St-Bernard Pass**, beyond which is Italy. If you plan to explore in the area, pick up from the Martigny tourist office the excellent 1:40,000 map and English guidebook *Au Pays du Grand-St-Bernard* (Fr.20).

Trains, and the road, from Martigny divide at **SEMBRANCHER**, long a staging post on the route up to the pass. It's an attractive, medieval village, with a Baroque church and street fountains flowing with water that is unusually high in natural fluoride. About 6km south – and up – is **ORSIÈRES** (820m), where

History of the Grand-St-Bernard Pass

The **Grand-St-Bernard Pass** is the oldest of Alpine pass routes, in use at least since the Bronze Age (about 800 BC). Tribes and armies have tramped their way to and fro for millennia – in 390 BC, a Gaulish army crossed to defeat Rome – and from the earliest times ordinary people used the pass to trade goods between northern Europe and Italy. **Hannibal**'s famous crossing of the Alps in 217 BC, reputedly with elephants, is indelibly associated with the Grand-St-Bernard, despite the lack of evidence for the event. In 57 BC, **Julius Caesar** crossed the *Summa Poenina*, as it was known, to conquer the pagan peoples of Martigny who worshipped the Celtic god Poenn (the chain of great peaks on the Swiss–Italian frontier is still called the Pennine Alps). Shortly after, Emperor **Augustus** built a road across the pass. His summit temple to Jupiter was sacked with the fall of Rome, but a refuge may well have remained on the pass. Pope Stephen II crossed in 753 to meet with Pepin the Short, King of France, while in 800 **Charlemagne** crossed back following his coronation in Milan.

In the early 900s, Huns and Saracens swept through the region, raping, pillaging and destroying churches: to keep them quiet, Hugh of Provence, King of Italy, granted them guardianship of the pass, whereupon they began to terrorize travellers and demand payment. Deeply concerned at the disruption caused to merchants and pilgrims Europe-wide, King Canute of Denmark had a quiet word with King Rudolf III of Burgundy, and together they ejected the heathens in short order; the archdeacon of Aosta, one **Bernard of Menthon**, then oversaw the construction of a hospice on the pass. Bernard himself travelled around the area, spreading the word of God, and was beatified shortly after his death in the 1080s. (Pope Pius XI confirmed him as patron saint of the Alps in 1923.)

The hospice became a welcome point of safety on an extremely dangerous route, attracting favours and gifts from royal and noble households. By 1177, a papal bull confirmed that the monks owned some 78 properties in Vaud, Valais, Savoy, Italy, France and England (including Hornchurch in Essex). Throughout the Middle Ages, the hospice provided free shelter and food to pilgrims, clerics and travellers, many crossing to and from Rome. By 1817 some 20,000 people were using the road annually. During the wars of the 1790s, entire armies crossed the pass: in May 1800, **Napoleon** led 40,000 troops over the pass into Italy, on the way consuming 21,724 bottles of wine, a tonne and a half of cheese, 800kg of meat, and more, running up a bill with the hospice of Fr.40,000 before departing with a wave of his hand. Fifty years later, the monks received Fr.18,500 towards payment, and had to wait until 1984 for a token gesture of account-settling from French president François Mitterrand.

First mention of the famous **St Bernard dogs** – product of an unknown cross between a mastiff, Great Dane and/or Newfoundland – was in 1708. Since then, these heavy-set, jowly beasts, with a little flask tied round their collars – supposedly holding brandy, though milk seems to have been more likely – have come to stand as icons of the mountains. The hospice still keeps a kennel for them on the pass. (Some fifteen pure-bred St Bernard puppies are born every year, each worth a cool Fr.1700.)

With the construction of the Simplon Tunnel further east in 1905, train travel rapidly superseded the road journey over the Grand-St-Bernard, and in 1964 a motorway **tunnel** (⊛ www.sitrasb.it) opened beneath the pass in order to safeguard traffic flow year-round. These days the hospice spends the summer crowded with visitors and hikers, and the winter receiving people climbing up from below to spend a few days or weeks on a solitary, snowbound retreat.

trains terminate and buses take over. Orsières is notable for the beautiful Gothic bell-tower alongside its relatively modern church, featuring double- and triple-arched windows and grotesque gargoyles. A branch road from here penetrates the lonesome **Val Ferret**, extending for some 20km between towering peaks and acclaimed as an excellent birdwatching area; as one visitor wrote in 1876, "there are few valleys in the Alps so fearsomely wild."

On a zigzagging road above Orsières lies the little resort of **CHAMPEX** (1470m), ranged around its lakelet and well known as a mountaineering centre and trailhead, including for the famous Circuit of Mont Blanc. Two **hotels** stand out, both country inns in idyllic woodland settings: down-to-earth *Belvédère* (℡027 783 11 14, Ⓦwww.le-belvedere.ch; ❷–❸) is renowned for its organic, home-produced cuisine, while *Au Vieux-Champex* (℡027 783 12 16, Ⓦwww .champex-immobilier.com; ❷–❸) is more upmarket, with a gourmet edge and several comfortable apartments.

The main road from Orsières continues to climb amidst increasingly spectacular scenery up to the village of **Bourg-St-Pierre** (1632m), residence from the eighth century of the guardians of the pass; the old church, rebuilt in 1739, has at its northeastern corner a Roman milestone dating from about 310 AD. Above the village, the main road is roofed over to limit problems with driving snow in winter. Shortly afterwards, traffic shoots into the Grand-St-Bernard tunnel, emerging 5.9km on in Italy, but a tiny winding road to one side continues up the mountainside, past a ski lift serving the small Super-St-Bernard peak (part of the Four Valleys ski area – see p.330 – with a couple of red runs and a wild and lonesome black), before it eventually arrives at the dramatic **Grand-St-Bernard Pass** itself, at 2470m.

Col du Grand-St-Bernard

The **Col du Grand-St-Bernard** is the oldest Alpine pass route (see box), protected for almost a millennium by monks inhabiting the **hospice** on top. The views aren't outstanding, and the souvenir stalls are an eyesore, but the sense of history is what draws you in: for centuries, this was the only road between northern Europe and southern Europe for hundreds of miles on either flank, and countless travellers have arrived to the same view of the little summit lake backed by the same mountain panorama. The interesting **museum** (daily: July & Aug 9am–7pm; June & Sept 9am–noon & 1–6pm; Fr.7) documents the history of the pass, and includes several quaking accounts of fatal or near-fatal crossings. The two buildings which make up the hospice, exposed to winter storms which have been known to bring 25m of snow and temperatures of -30°C, date from 1560 and 1898; the older one contains a Baroque **church**. If you walk down from the hospice, the Italian frontier guards will let you cross the international border to explore the rocky area behind the customs post and Italian hospice; around the **statue** of St Bernard atop its round pillar (1905) you'll find traces of the Roman road cut into the bedrock.

In summer, it's possible to **stay** in the ⚑ hospice (℡027 787 12 36, Ⓦwww .gsbernard.ch; ❶), which is still a functioning religious community, either in plain, cosy rooms, or dorms (Fr.21); the cooking is suitably hearty and the atmosphere jovial. During the winter months (Nov–June) and over Easter, you can arrange an individual retreat, to take advantage of the solitude for personal reflection.

Verbier

It's the skiing that put **VERBIER** on the map: few places in the world offer such breadth of possibilities with such awe-inspiring scenery as a backdrop. Before 1910, the plateau on which Verbier sits was an empty summer pasture;

Walking from Chamonix to Zermatt

The snowy Pennine Alps of Canton Valais drain north to the Rhône through a series of spectacular valleys walled by high and craggy ridges. The **Walker's Haute Route** makes a traverse of these on a west-to-east journey which begins in **Chamonix** (France) below Mont Blanc, and ends in Zermatt at the foot of the Matterhorn, one of the most beautiful and scenically rewarding of Europe's long walks. It's a demanding **two-week trek**, but there are no glaciers or permanent snowfields to cross, and overnight accommodation is plentiful in huts, mountain inns or valley hotels. You can also easily join the route partway along at strategically accessible points for a few days' hiking: the Val de Bagnes, Arolla and Zinal, for instance, are all served by public transport from main Valais towns. Along with the 1:50,000 **maps** LS 5003 Mont Blanc-Grand Combin, and 5006 Matterhorn-Mischabel, take *Chamonix to Zermatt, the Walker's Haute Route* by Kev Reynolds (see "Books", p.587).

With a long climb out of the Chamonix valley, the Haute Route enters Switzerland by way of Col de Balme and descends to **Trient**. On day three there are two routes to choose from: either the formidable but non-technical Fenêtre d'Arpette alongside the Trient Glacier, or the more pedestrian Alp Bovine route to **Champex** – the former is tough but visually exciting, the latter an energetic alternative, also with fine views. From Champex an easy valley walk leads to **Le Châble** in Val de Bagnes, from where the route on day five makes a 1600m climb to the **Cabane du Mont-Fort** (℡ 027 778 13 84), a mountain hut with stunning views across to Mont Blanc. Leaving the hut next day, an airy balcony walk takes you along the Sentier des Chamois, with the Grand Combin (4314m) a mighty presence across the valley, then over Col de Louvie to skirt below the Grand Désert glacier, and across Col de Prafleuri to **Cabane de Prafleuri** (℡ 027 207 30 67). Views from this hut are restricted, but a short climb to Col des Roux reveals the tranquil Lac des Dix below, with Mont Blanc de Cheilon (3870m) at the head of the valley. Beyond the lake, the way traces old moraines alongside a rubble-strewn glacier, then crosses either Col de Riedmatten (2919m) or the neighbouring Pas de Chèvres – the latter by way of two long and very steep ladders. Once you've crossed this ridge, there's a very pleasant descent through pastures to **Arolla**.

Day eight is an easy one, taking you from Arolla down to Les Haudères and up to **La Sage**, while on day nine Col de Torrent (2919m) leads you into the Moiry glen, near the head of which **Cabane de Moiry** (℡ 027 475 45 34) overlooks a cascading icefall and the glacier easing from it. Col de Sorebois is next, with the descent from there to **Zinal** in Val d'Anniviers allowing you to make the acquaintance of the hugely impressive **Weisshorn** (4505m) and its attendant peaks on the far side. On day eleven, you leave Zinal on another balcony path, this time heading north for about four hours to the *Weisshorn* (℡ 027 475 11 06), a Victorian hotel perched high above the valley looking to the sunset from its glass-fronted dining room. Next day you cross the Meidpass (2790m) to **Gruben** in the Turtmanntal, the first German-speaking valley and a truly forgotten little corner. The penultimate stage (day thirteen) is the setting for another high-level crossing – the 2894m **Augstbordpass**. This brings you into the Mattertal, the valley which leads to Zermatt and the Matterhorn; an hour and a half below the pass the trail turns a spur to confront you with the most amazing of panoramas. Across the unseen depths of the Mattertal soars the **Dom** (4545m), the highest mountain entirely in Switzerland; at the head of the valley far away a long crest of snow and ice stretches from Monte Rosa to the Breithorn (the Matterhorn is just hidden from view), while the Weisshorn dominates the right-hand wall. An hour below that viewpoint lies Jungen, a summer alp hamlet clinging to the near-vertical hillside. The path then plunges steeply to **St Niklaus** in the bed of the valley. The last stretch (day fourteen) offers no passes to cross, but a mere wander up the valley to **Zermatt**, in order to make your final pilgrimage to the **Matterhorn**.

the first hotel opened in 1934, and even by 1950 the place was still a tiny village. No more. Following the 1960s ski boom, Verbier now sprawls, characterized by apartment blocks and modern housing. It's not a particularly charming or endearing place, but with this quality of skiing on offer, it doesn't have to be. European high society flocks to the resort in season, and the mood of the place can get tediously brash and trendy, but still the slopes hold sway. Fully half of the million annual visitors are Swiss, many scooting over from Lausanne and Geneva for a weekend in their apartments or chalets; it's a feature of Verbier that chalet accommodation outnumbers hotel beds ten-to-one, making it much more advisable to visit on a ski-chalet package booked from home than to arrive independently without a hotel reservation.

Practicalities

Branch-line **trains** from Martigny split at Sembrancher: one half terminates at Orsières, the other at **Le Châble**, the valley community at the foot of Verbier's hill. From Le Châble, a gondola runs every fifteen minutes up to Verbier, arriving at the huge Médran station at the east end of the resort. Postbuses also do the run from Le Châble, climbing first through "Verbier-Village" (the locals' town) before terminating in "Verbier-Station" (the resort), at the central post office just off Place Centrale.

Orientation around the resort is straightforward. The Rue de Médran climbs southeast from Place Centrale to the **Médran** lift station, arrival point for

---

Sports and activities at Verbier

Winter sports

For years, Verbier suffered from notoriously long queues and poorly planned lift transport, but these days, with the opening of new gondolas or chairlifts almost every season, things are getting better. Verbier is the main resort of the **Four Valleys** ski area (ⓦ www.4vallees.ch), covering some 400km of piste at all levels of difficulty, stretching from Thyon, Veysonnaz and Nendaz in the west, through the central Savoleyres and Mont-Fort areas, out to the Super-St-Bernard. The **Verbier** sector covers lifts to Les Ruinettes, Attelas and Mont-Gelé (but not Mont-Fort); the **Savoleyres** sector is accessed both from Verbier village and La Tzoumaz; and the family-friendly **Bruson** sector faces Verbier across the valley, accessed from La Châble.

Aside from a handful of blues at Bruson, beginners have a dedicated "**Station**" sub-sector, comprising nursery slopes in and just above Verbier village itself. There's a host of red runs from **Savoleyres** (2354m), and the Médran lifts take you up to **Les Ruinettes** (2200m), with its own cat's cradle of reds and a scarily vertiginous black run, in addition to some carving. Large-capacity gondolas connect to **Attelas** (2727m), with blacks and reds, and on either to the **Mont-Gelé** summit (3023m), or by chairlift over to **Tortin** (2050m) from where reds or a fiendishly difficult black connect to the Siviez and Thyon ski areas. From **La Chaux** (2260m) above Ruinettes, one of Switzerland's largest cable cars, the Jumbo, swooshes 150 people at a time up to the glacier slopes of **Mont-Fort** (3330m), also one of the best places in the country for **summer skiing**. This is prime territory for snowboarders, with half-pipes and excellent facilities at Gentianes on Mont-Fort and at "BoarderX" at La Chaux itself (2260–2845m), as well as at Savoleyres.

A **lift pass** for one/six days on the Verbier sector is Fr.54/277, on Savoleyres/Tzoumaz Fr.48/246, on Bruson Fr.35/182, and for the entire Four Valleys region Fr.62/319. Discounted part-day and advance-purchase passes, and other deals, are available (ⓦ www.televerbier.ch).

gondolas up from Le Châble, and departure point for gondolas and a chairlift continuing up to Les Ruinettes, main access point for the pistes. It's along Rue de Médran, and in the surrounding area, that most of the resort's après-ski happens. Verbier's other gondola rises from the **Savoleyres** station, best part of a kilometre north of Place Centrale. West of Place Centrale is the massive Centre Sportif with, below and south of it, workaday Verbier-Village. **Free buses** link all of these throughout the summer and winter seasons (July, Aug & Dec–April daily 8am–7pm).

The highly organized **tourist office** is on Place Centrale (July, Aug & Dec–April Mon–Sat 8.30am–12.30pm & 2–6.30pm, Sun 9am–noon & 4–6.30pm; rest of year Mon–Fri 8.30am–noon & 2–6.30pm, Sat 9am–noon & 4–6pm, Sun 9am–noon; ☏027 775 38 88, ⓦ www.verbier.ch).

Late July sees Verbier staging one of Switzerland's most prestigious classical music events, the **Verbier Festival and Academy** (ⓦ www.verbierfestival .com). For two weeks, the resort plays host to top-flight soloists and conductors, who come to perform and also lead masterclasses and discussions. Tickets for individual concerts are around Fr.35–130.

Accommodation

Verbier is tricky when it comes to **hotels**: there just aren't that many of them, and you may find they won't accept bookings in season for less than seven days. Many places close in the April/May and October/November between-seasons and you're looking at through-the-roof prices for the winter high season;

Adventure sports and extreme events

Verbier is a mecca for **adventure** addicts, with a host of companies competing with each other to come up with the newest and most exciting extreme thrill of the season. The **Maison du Sport** (☏027 775 33 63, ⓦ www.maisondusport.ch) is home to official ski and snowboarding schools and the mountain guides office, and has a huge range of activities, including heli-skiing and heli-boarding, snow-shoeing, ice-climbing, guided high-altitude walking, and more, as well as summer canyoning, rafting and caving. **No Limits** (☏027 395 45 55, ⓦ www.nolimitscanyon.ch) has luge, snow-carting, snow-scooting and plenty more, while **Centre Parapente** (☏027 771 68 18, ⓦ www.flyverbier.ch) offers tandem paragliding. **La Fantastique** (☏027 771 41 41, ⓦ www.lafantastique.com) offers heli-skiing, guides for off-piste (Fr.400/day for one person) and long-distance ski safaris. **Adrenaline** (☏027 771 74 59, ⓦ www .adrenaline-verbier.ch) is a ski and snowboard school.

Xtreme Verbier (ⓦ www.xtremeverbier.com), one of the top international show-cases of freeride snowboarding, is held each March. Bec des Rosses (3222m), way up on the mountainside at Gentianes, is the scene for 25 of the world's best boarders to do their thing, competing by invitation only in the most dramatic of locations, with 55° gradients, broad expanses of powder and plenty of obstacles. **Verbier Ride** (ⓦ www.verbierride.com) is an exhibition showcase of freeskiing, held in early March. The **Patrouille des Glaciers** (ⓦ www.pdg.ch) is a long-distance endurance test across the 53km of glaciers, summits and passes from Zermatt to Verbier. Dubbed "Paris–Dakar on skis", it was halted in 1949 after three deaths, and restarted in 1984 with more than six hundred participants; since then it has taken place every other year. In August, Verbier also hosts the world's longest mountain-bike race, the exceptionally tough **Grand Raid Cristalp** (ⓦ www.grand-raid-cristalp. ch), a one-day race across six valleys (rising at one point to 2792m) on a 131km route to Grimentz.

summer and between–season prices can be up to a third cheaper. Accommodation is least expensive in the handful of private rooms on offer through the tourist office, or in any of the thousands of chalets, which must be booked months in advance.

Bristol ☎ 027 771 65 77, Ⓦ www.bristol-verbier .ch. Friendly, cosy and quiet, and very central, but watch out for that peak-season price hike. ❸–❻

Ermitage ☎ 027 771 64 77, Ⓦ www.ermitage -verbier.ch. Well-run and very convenient place on Place Centrale, delivering unexpected value for money. ❸–❺

Garbo ☎ 027 771 62 72, Ⓦ www.hotelgarbo.com. Central spot, midway between Place Centrale and the Médran lifts. OK value, except around the New Year, when prices shoot up. ❸–❺

Mont-Gelé ☎ 027 771 30 53. The least expensive hotel in the resort open year-round; beside the

Médran lift station, with just fifteen comfortable, balconied rooms. ❷

Rois Mages ☎ 027 771 63 64, Ⓦ www.skiverbier .com. Good modern choice by the church. ❹–❻

🏃 **Les Touristes** ☎ 027 771 21 47, Ⓦ www .hoteltouristes-verbier.ch. One of the best ways to avoid Verbier's high prices and uninspiring anonymity: it's on a street corner in Verbier-Village, linked to the lifts by bus, with spartan, TV-free rooms, most with shared bathrooms. The quiet restaurant and chic-free atmosphere are a breath of fresh air. ❷

Eating and drinking

Eating options aren't very inspiring. Aside from supermarket fare, or burgers from *Harold's* on Place Centrale (Ⓦ www.harolds.ch), food is generally poor value. Wander your way up Rue de Médran from Place Centrale until you see something you fancy: there's a handful of pizzerias – the *Fer à Cheval* is one of the better ones (Ⓦ www.feracheval.ch), with a reasonably lively après-ski scene to boot, or there's the *Garbo* close at hand, which also shakes a leg. *Al Capone* is another friendly pizza joint, west of the centre towards the Savoleyres lift. As you emerge from the Médran station, *Au Vieux Valais* is within view, a cosy traditional-style place for raclette, fondue and other belly-warmers; similar fare can be found at *Les Touristes* (see "Accommodation"), a quiet, pleasant place down in Verbier-Village.

Le Bouchon Gourmand (☎027 771 72 96) makes a change, a relatively good French bistro west of the post office, specializing in rich *foie gras* and duck, but also with fresh pastas and salads (*menus* Fr.24 and up). The gourmet choice is the *Rosalp* (☎027 771 63 23, Ⓦ www.rosalp.ch), a staggeringly expensive place to savour what's been called the best cuisine in the country. The restaurant, and the chef Roland Pierroz, have been showered with awards. Even choosing from the wine list is likely to be quite an event: the cellar runs to 50,000 bottles. *Rosalp's* ground-floor brasserie is slightly more affordable (around Fr.40).

Of a number of places to **drink** around the resort, the one with most colour is the raucous *Pub Mont Fort* (Ⓦ www.pubmontfort.com), near the Médran station. The *Nelson*, off Place Centrale, is another good option, while the snobby *Farm Club* (Ⓦ www.kingsverbier.ch), west of the centre, is the best place for a spot of celeb- and royal-watching.

Val de Bagnes

From **Le Châble**, a peaceful, rural community tucked on the valley floor below Verbier, the long **Val de Bagnes** runs southeast into the high mountains. Le Châble is the capital of the Bagnes commune, Switzerland's largest – at 295 square kilometres, larger than the cantons of Geneva, Schaffhausen or Zug (although about a third of the Bagnes is covered by glaciers). Buses run twice a day (July–Sept only) from Le Châble up to the impressive **Mauvoisin Dam**, a giant 250m-high wall blocking the end of the valley. At 1961m, it's one of the highest-altitude dams in the world. A **hotel** at the base (☎027 778 11 30, ⓦ www.mauvoisin.ch; ❶) has rooms and dorms (Fr.23) – handy for an overnight stay either after a walk up from Fionnay or Lourtier villages in the valley, or before taking a full day to hike back to Le Châble.

Sion

SION (pronounced *see-ohh*), known as Sitten in German, is the capital of Valais, an alluring and attractive town of 27,000 with an exceptionally long history: archeological evidence points to the site having been inhabited during Neolithic times. What attracted settlement, no doubt, was the incongruous presence, on the otherwise flat valley floor, of two jutting rocky hills, visible from afar and now adorned with the medieval castles **Valère** and **Tourbillon**. They're an odd and slightly sinister sight, which matches the common Swiss notion that the locals (named Sédunois, after the town's Latin name Sedunum, meaning Place of Castles) are themselves a bit odd, impenetrably taciturn and clannish. Prejudice aside, Sion enjoys a simply glorious **climate**, dry, mild and consistently clear; afternoons are bathed in bright sunshine, and on mild summer evenings you could imagine yourself in rural Spain – warm, dry breezes blending the aroma of dusty pine needles with the scraping of thousands of cicadas. Sion's **wines** (see p.60) are outstanding.

Throughout the 1990s, the municipality and the people exerted extraordinary efforts to attract the Winter Olympics to Sion, based on the nearby presence of Verbier, Crans-Montana and Zermatt – and yet they were rejected, both for the 2002 and (amidst profound controversy) the 2006 games, the latter awarded obscurely by the IOC to Turin. Switzerland finally secured the 2008 European football championships (with Austria), but Sion gains no benefit from games played in the big cities. For now, the Sédunois have lapsed into a shocked and sulky silence, while the town itself remains refreshingly down-to-earth after the grinding glitz of the big resorts.

Arrival, information and accommodation

Sion's **train station** is at the southern end of the long, straight Avenue de la Gare, with the **postbus station** to one side. Some 500m north along Avenue de la Gare is the concrete **Place de la Planta**, on which stands the well-equipped **tourist office** (July & Aug Mon–Fri 8am–6pm, Sat 9.30am–4pm; rest of year Mon–Fri 8.30am–noon & 2–5.30pm, Sat 9am–noon; ☎027 327 77 27, ⓦwww .siontourism.ch). They offer a good two-hour **walking tour** of the town (July & Aug Tues & Thurs 10.30am; Fr.8, wine-tasting included). Sion's tiny **airport** (☎027 329 06 00, ⓦwww.sionairport.ch) is 5km west of the centre.

Aside from the annual **cowfighting** championship held in May at nearby Aproz (see p.324), Sion plays host to the prestigious **Festival International de Musique** (ⓦwww.sion-festival.ch), which runs from July to September at a number of venues around Valais. Running concurrently in July and August are the **Académie de Musique de Sion** (ⓦwww.amsion.ch), a cycle of masterclasses given by international soloists, and the **Festival International de l'Orgue Ancien**, a season of ancient music centred on the world's oldest organ, still playable in the Château de Valère.

Accommodation

Of Sion's **hotels**, the 🏨 *Elite*, 6 Avenue du Midi (☎027 322 03 27, ⓦwww .hotelelite-sion.ch; ❷–❸), doesn't look like much, but it's been tastefully renovated inside and is a good choice. *La Channe*, 9 Rue Porte-Neuve (☎027 322 32 71; ❷), is a quiet place in the Old Town with a choice of ensuite or shared-bath rooms, while the cinder-block *Du Rhône*, Rue du Scex 10 (☎027 322 82 91, ⓦwww.bestwestern.ch; ❸), a definite step up in quality and service. Sion's best is the "garni" *Europa*, a pleasant business hotel out towards the airfield, at 19 Rue de l'Envoi (☎027 322 24 23, ⓦwwww.zghotels.ch; ❹).

The good HI **hostel** *Auberge de Jeunesse*, 2 Rue de l'Industrie (☎027 323 74 70, ⓦwww.youthhostel.ch; ❶; closed Dec & Jan), is just behind the station – modern, clean and well run, with dorms from Fr.29. The nearest, and best, **campsite** is the five-star *Des Iles* (☎027 346 43 47), 4km west.

The Town

Sion's Old Town is interesting: a slow wander through the cobbled alleys, with their old inns and sixteenth-century shuttered town houses, can fill an atmospheric afternoon. Just northeast of Place de la Planta is the small **Église St-Théodule**, dating from the sixteenth century and with some fine vaulting in the choir. Just beside it is the **Cathédrale Notre-Dame du Glarier** (Our Lady of the Gravel – referring to the ground on which the cathedral was built). The main building is fifteenth century, with elements of earlier Romanesque and Gothic structures incorporated within it, including a fine belfry. Its most noticeable feature, though, is the bells, which strike every quarter-hour in a near-exact copy of the sound of Big Ben in London, although the bass bell's slightly higher pitch gives the ensemble an inescapably mournful tone. Some 100m to the south is Rue Supersaxo, with the **Maison Supersaxo** (Mon–Fri 8am–noon & 2–6pm; free) tucked into an alley off the street. This lavish residence was built in 1505 by the local governor, Georges Supersaxo, to show the town's bishop, Matthias Schinner, who was boss: climb the Gothic staircase inside to a hall on the upper floor with a magnificent carved and painted ceiling. Two minutes north on Rue de la Tour brings you to the witch's-hat **Tour des Sorciers**, part of the town's medieval fortifications.

Beside the imposing **Hôtel de Ville** on Rue du Grand-Pont (visitable only on the tourist office's walking tour), lanes and back alleys cut east to Rue des Châteaux, which climbs steeply towards the twin hills of Tourbillon and Valère. Before you get there, though, after 150m you'll pass on the left the modest **Musée Cantonal des Beaux-Arts**, Place de la Majorie (Tues–Sun 1–6pm; Oct–May closes 5pm; Fr.5; SMP; free on 1st Sun of month), in an attractive fifteenth-century house. There are few outstanding works, although the section on Valaisian identity holds some interesting pieces. Opposite is the **Musée Cantonal d'Archéologie** (same hours; Fr.4; SMP; free on 1st Sun of month), with an impressive collection of mainly Roman bits and pieces, as well as Bronze Age steles and a display of prehistoric dolmens.

Valère and Tourbillon

Rue des Châteaux climbs to a parking area in the groove between the twin castles of Sion. From here, paths divide up the dry, scrubby hillsides – left (north) to Tourbillon, right (south) to Valère.

Château de Valère is the more interesting of the two, and the more complete. The hike up brings you past the tiny Chapelle de Tous-les-Saints (dating from 1310 but unfortunately kept locked) and massive Roman foundation walls to the castle-church. As it stands, the château dates from the thirteenth century, but elements survive of earlier buildings, and the whole thing may well stand on the ruins of a Roman temple. A climb up rickety stairs brings you into the church interior (Mon–Sat 10am–6pm, Sun 2–6pm; Oct–May Tues–Sun only, closes 5pm; Fr.3), where the most notable feature, high on the back wall, is the oldest playable **organ** in the world, dating from 1390.

The **Château de Tourbillon** on the opposite hill dates from 1294, but was ruined by fire in 1788 and today, aside from the external walls, little is left. These days, it's open for scramblings (mid-March to mid-Nov Tues–Sun 10am–6pm; free) and yields excellent views along the valley and over the town.

Eating and drinking

There are a surprising number of good places to **eat and drink** for such a small city as Sion. The basics are taken care of at various **self-service** restaurants, including a *Manora* within the Placette department store on Avenue du Midi, and a huge *Migros* supermarket and diner west of the station on Avenue de France.

Rue du Grand-Pont in the Old Town is lined with attractive, pleasant little corners to sample something nice. *Grotto de la Fontaine*, at no. 21 (closed Tues & Wed), is a Ticinese-style inn serving fresh pastas, pizzas and Ticinese stews and risottos (*menus* Fr.17); *La Croix Fédérale*, at no. 13 (℡027 322 16 95; closed Mon), specializes in mouthwatering fish dishes; while the *Brasserie du Grand-Pont*, at no. 6 (℡027 322 20 96; closed Sun), is a solid, down-to-earth place to have a good square meal and a carafe of local wine.

To the east, and well out of the hubbub on steep, cobbled Rue des Châteaux, there are two excellent places very close to each other: ✻ *L'Enclos de Valère*, at no. 18 (☎027 323 32 30; Oct–April closed Sun & Mon; ◍www.enclosdevalere .ch), has a big shaded terrace on which to enjoy its classic gourmet cuisine (*menus* Fr.25), while just about next door is the ✻ *Cave de Tous Vents* (☎027 322 46 84; May & June closed Mon & Tues; ◍www.cave-tous-vents.ch), an atmospheric vaulted cellar in a thirteenth-century building that opens in the evenings only for quality raclettes, fondues (including an alcoholic "fondue Bacchus") and sampling of local wines; *menus* are Fr.25.

Val d'Hérens

The hills south of Sion are pierced by two long valleys, which are worth a detour to explore the hinterlands of the Valais. To the southwest a minor road winds into the **Val d'Hérémence**, culminating in the giant **Barrage de la Grande Dixence**, the largest and one of the highest-altitude dams in the world.

Of more interest, though, is the valley branching southeast from Sion. This is the **VAL D'HÉRENS**, a world apart from the main valley, dotted with mountain farms and high-altitude hamlets, and giving fascinating glimpses of traditional rural life. Even people from Sion can barely understand the thick valley patois, which rings with odd guttural sounds and strikes city folk as being a little like Arabic. Unsubstantiated supposition brings out the idea that the generally dark-skinned, dark-eyed people of the Val d'Hérens may be descended from the conquering Saracen armies who swept through the area after the Battle of Poitiers in 732. Having planted that idea, Sédunois will then tell you about the people of Isérables, a town west of Sion, who have been called *Les Bedjuis* for as long as anyone can remember – a nickname remarkably close to "Bedouin". The Allalinhorn peak near Saas-Fee is another clue, its name apparently derived from "Allah".

One of the sights of the valley can be found near the village of Euseigne, where the road passes beneath the **Pyramides d'Euseigne**, a bizarre geological outcrop of glacial moraines. Whereas erosion flattened the area all around, these stone jags were protected from smoothing by hard rock caps. Today, they're hard to believe – a wall of unnaturally bare and pointed stalagmites in the open wooded valley, each crag crowned by a dark boulder balanced on a needle point. A stall at the base lets you stop to gawp, and then buy a souvenir postcard.

Some 15km south of Euseigne is the village of **Evolène**, a quaint village now bypassed by the main road, which has preserved along its main street traditional wooden houses and an air of rural tranquillity. The locals have cheerfully capitalized on this by wearing traditional dress – only partly, it seems, in a self-conscious bid for tourist appeal. A handful of cafés and simple inns cater to hikers and day-trippers.

Walking in the Val d'Hérens

Sion tourist office has an all-inclusive deal for a self-guided **walking tour** right around the Val d'Hérens. Starting from Sion, this involves 5–7 hours of walking a day: from Thyon to the Dixence dam; from the Lac des Dix over the passes to Arolla; a valley-floor stroll to Evolène; and finally on a scenic path high up the valley side and down to Nax. Included are five nights' half-board accommodation and five picnic lunches, postbuses to and from Sion, transport of one bag per person from hotel to hotel, documentation and a 1:25,000 map. This all-in deal costs Fr.785 in ensuite hotel rooms, less for shared-bath rooms and mountain huts.

Arolla

South of the hamlet of **Les Haudères** beyond Evolène, you begin to penetrate the wild countryside. One road branches east over the crest to Ferpècle, while another climbs west up and over into the tranquil hidden **Val d'Arolla**, terminating some 12km south after a series of nerve-racking tunnels at the pristine hamlet of **AROLLA** (1998m). This tiny, outdoorsy place is one of the stops on the Walkers' Haute Route between Chamonix and Zermatt (see p.329), and offers a wealth of half- and full-day hikes all around, including a testing one up to the Col de Riedmatten (2919m), three hours away. There's a handful of blue and red ski-pistes served by lifts rising from the village; passes are Fr.32/150 for one/six days. Four or five **hotels** offer quality retreats, including the excellent *Hôtel du Pigne* (☎027 283 71 00, Ⓦ www.hoteldupigne.ch; ❸), entirely renovated inside in an attractively sleek, contemporary style. Half-a-dozen places offer dorms; the **tourist office** (☎027 283 10 83, Ⓦ www.arolla.com) has information.

Amazingly, during January, ski-passes are **half-price** and all hotels slash their rates by a third or more, giving seven nights amidst the deep snow for just Fr.550 half-board in a double room at *Hôtel du Pigne*, as little as Fr.180 in a pension.

St-Léonard

On the road from Sion east to Sierre is the small village of **ST-LÉONARD** with, as its sole draw, one of the largest **underground lakes** in Europe (March–Oct daily 9am–5pm; Fr.10). Regular buses drop off either in the village or at the car park beneath the ticket office, which can get crowded with day-tripping families. Tours of the lake, by large rowing boats with everyone crowded in side by side, take about forty minutes – and it's cold down there, so bring a jumper. The cave entrance is just a gap in the mountainside, but as you launch off onto the inky water, the illuminated, other-worldly cavern stretching out ahead of you is very impressive. The guides, who do the rowing, have a nice line in multilingual patter, regaling you on the voyage with all kinds of stories and details about the lake and its geology.

Sierre

Hardly any foreigners come to **SIERRE** (Siders in German) unless they're catching the funicular up to the ski resorts of Crans and Montana on the hillside above. Which is all to the good, because it leaves this idyllic little valley-floor town quiet, perfect for a day or two of strolling and wine-tasting in the vineyards all around. The German poet Rainer Maria Rilke spent his last six years in Sierre, where he wrote the celebrated *Sonnets to Orpheus*; he suffered from leukaemia, and died in 1926 after pricking his finger on a rose-thorn.

Sierre lies almost exactly on the French–German language border, which is marked by the tiny Raspille stream a couple of kilometres east of the town. The road east from Sierre to the sleepy village of **Salgesch** (Salquenen in French) begins as the Rue de la Gemmi and ends five minutes later as the Gemmistrasse; Sierre sits alongside the Rhône, while in Salgesch the same river is dubbed the Rotten. **Wine** is what fuels both communities, and there are plenty of trails through and between the vineyards, with equally numerous opportunities to stop and sample a glass or two. Sierre is the driest town in Switzerland, and gets an average of almost seven and a half hours of sunshine daily from May

The nomads of Switzerland

The people and history of Sierre are inextricably linked with the culture of the communities in the **Val d'Anniviers**, which opens at a narrow chink in the mountain high up opposite Sierre to the south but broadens out to extend southwards for some 40km, terminating in the hiking trailhead of **Zinal**.

The residents of the Anniviers (the name itself means "seasonal") are the last people left in Switzerland to follow a genuinely **nomadic** lifestyle, although modern ease of transport and economic pressures are making inroads. Up until a few decades ago, people would arrive in Sierre from the Anniviers in March or April: those from the village of **Grimentz** occupied the Villa quarter of Sierre, alongside people from **Vissoie**, while the Viouc quarter was for villagers from **Chandolin**, the Muraz quarter for those from **St Luc**, and so on. Each community had its own slightly distinct dialect, brought with it flocks, a schoolteacher and a priest, and celebrated Sunday mass in its own tiny chapel. For a few months, everyone would stay and work on the vineyards around Sierre, before departing in mid-June to pasture their flocks on the heights above the town. In mid-September, everybody would drift down again to Sierre for the grape harvest, which would continue for a few weeks, before dispersing back to their villages in the Anniviers valley for the winter. This kind of nomadism still carries on today, although these days families don't have to bring bag and baggage with them from their village when they come to work in Sierre, and tend also to keep their children in school in one place or the other.

Curiously, the patois of the Val d'Anniviers is very similar to that of the rural Val d'Aosta on the southern side of the Grand-St-Bernard Pass in Italy – even though the main language of Sierre is French and the main language of Aosta is Italian. Linguists, anthropologists and sociologists between them haven't yet come up with a theory as to why this should be.

The Sierre tourist office has put together a self-guided **Tour pédestre du Val d'Anniviers** – a perfect way to explore this beautiful, isolated landscape. This runs for six nights, with postbus connections, all meals, baggage transport and a map included. Prices start at a bargain Fr.325, staying in B&Bs and mountain huts.

to October (and a total of 330 sunny days a year), helping it to produce excellent Fendant whites; Salgesch, meanwhile, is renowned for its Pinot Noir reds. Not for nothing did the Romans call the place *Sirrum amoenum*, Sierre the agreeable.

The Town

If you turn left (west) from the train station and then aim northwest up Avenue du Marché, you'll come into the little-visited old quarters of Sierre. The Rue de Villa, alongside a vineyard, marks the eponymous quarter of Villa, with, at the very top, the **Château de Villa**, one half of Sierre-Salgesch's modest **Musée Valaisan de la Vigne et du Vin** (April–Nov Tues–Sun 2–5pm; Fr.5 for both museums; SMP; ⓦ www.museevalaisanduvin.ch). The Sierre half focuses on the wine itself, with interesting displays (in French and German) on grape varieties and the history of cultivation and some old presses. In the same building are a restaurant and oenotheque (see below). From here, a six-kilometre *Sentier Viticole/Rebweg* (Wine Path) runs through the quiet, shuttered lanes of old quarters of Sierre, such as Muraz and Veyras, for a couple of hours over to Salgesch and out through the open hillside vineyards to the other half of the wine museum, in the creaky old **Zumofenhaus** in the heart of Salgesch. Displays are yet more scholarly here, on the technical aspects of viticulture, cultivation methods and history, but the enthusiastic guardian will

△ Château de Villa, Sierre

be happy to give you a rundown in English on what's what. Buses (every 2hr) can run you back to Sierre.

An interesting detour from the Wine Path is to the small **Musée Charles-Clos Olsommer**, signposted in Veyras (July–Sept Wed–Sun 2–5pm; Oct–June Sat & Sun 2–5pm; Fr.5; ⓦwww.musee-olsommer.ch). Olsommer, born in Neuchâtel in 1883, studied in Munich at the same time as Klee and Kandinsky, but unlike them became fixated with a Klimt-like style rooted in symbolism. He lived in Veyras from 1912 until his death in 1966, painting moody scenes of women praying in the wilderness or surrounded by psychedelic patterns.

A fifteen-minute walk east of Sierre lie half-a-dozen low rounded hills, the result of alluvial deposits and an ancient landslide. The whole undulating area is one of the last remaining examples of undeveloped valley-floor ecology in the country. It's carpeted by a vast, pristine pine forest, the **Forêt de Finges/Pfyn-wald** (both terms derived from the Latin *fines*, or border; this was the ancient limit of Roman control; ⓦwww.pfyn-finges.ch), and is fringed by swamps and marshland on the Rhône banks. Protected and maintained but not developed, it's perfect for long, shady hikes and peaceful picnics.

Practicalities

Sierre's **station** houses the **tourist office** (mid-July to mid-Sept Mon–Fri 8.30am–6.30pm, Sat 9am–5.30pm, Sun 9am–1pm; rest of year Mon–Fri 8.30am–5.30pm, Sat 9.30am–12.30pm (Dec–April also Sat 1–4.30pm); ☎027 455 85 35, ⓦwww.sierre-anniviers.ch). The longest **funicular** in Switzerland (4.2km) heads up to Montana from the SMC station two minutes' walk away, left onto the main Avenue Général-Guisan outside the station.

Of the **hotels**, 🍴 *Le Terminus* opposite the station (☎027 455 13 51, ⓦwww.hotel-terminus.ch; ❸–❹) has been entirely renovated in a chic, modern style, and has an excellent **restaurant** and bistro attached. The restaurant in the Château de Villa (see above; ☎027 455 18 96) is one of the more prestigious places to sample Valaisian specialities, and its oenotheque (daily 10.30am–1pm

& 4.30–8.30pm) stocks more than 500 of the region's wines. If you head behind the station and down to the small Lac de Géronde, on the way you'll pass a handful of basic *auberges*, including the *Promenade* (℡027 456 34 04, ⓦwww .hotelpromenade.ch; ❷), with rooms ensuite and not. On the lake itself is the pleasant ✻ *La Grotte* (℡027 455 46 46), a terrace restaurant known only to the locals, serving very good fish (*menus* Fr.25), with a handful of comfortable, characterful rooms upstairs (❶–❷).

Crans Montana

CRANS MONTANA is another of Switzerland's big, world-famous ski resorts, occupying what is claimed to be the sunniest plateau in the Alps, facing south over the Rhône valley with a spectacular panorama of peaks yawning beyond. Along with Verbier and St Moritz, it's also one of the glitziest (Roger Moore is a long-time resident), with what the tourist office likes to call the finest shopping in the Alps.

The resort actually comprises three villages, **Crans-sur-Sierre** (pronounced *crawh*), **Montana** and, out on a limb, **Aminona**; the agglomeration sprawls for more than 2km between Crans, to the west, and Montana, to the east, with nothing to mark the shift from one to another. There's no restriction on cars at all and traffic is permanently heavy: in high season, village-to-village gridlock is not unknown. The **skiing**, rather unfairly dubbed "irretrievably intermediate" by some sports writers, takes second place to the round of wining and dining embarked upon by aficionados of Crans Montana's affluent social life – although the resort does have the advantage of access to year-round skiing on the Plaine Morte glacier, way up above 3000m.

Skiing aside, the place is best known for hosting the **European Masters golf** tournament every September (ⓦwww.omegaeuropeanmasters.com), second only to the British Open for prestige and top names. Crans's scenic course – "the most spectacular tournament site in the world" according to Greg Norman – was redesigned by Seve Ballesteros, and now boasts fiendishly complex upturned-saucer greens, which led one frustrated player to describe playing a round as "having eighteen teeth pulled one by one".

Practicalities

The SMC **funicular** from Sierre arrives at **Vermala station** at the eastern end of Montana. **Buses** (ⓦwww.cie-smc.ch) also run up from Sierre on two

---

Winter sports at Crans Montana

Access to the pistes (ⓦwww.mycma.ch), almost all of which are relatively straightforward blues and reds – if beautifully scenic – is via five gondolas ranged along the base of the mountain. From west to east, these are **Chetseron** and **Crans** (both within Crans village), **Grand Signal** in Montana, **Violettes** near the Montana funicular station, and **Aminona**. The woods above Montana are crisscrossed by red runs winding between the trees, while **Cry d'Err** above Crans has a host of lifts serving blues galore down to the village. Violettes gives access to the **Plaine Morte** top station (3000m), with some exciting blues, and the start of a long meandering red back to the village. **Lift passes** valid in all four sectors (Crans, Montana, Violettes and Aminona) for one/six days cost Fr.56/274.

different routes. The first (via Chermignon) passes through Crans, then Montana, then on to Aminona; the second (via Mollens) passes through Montana before terminating in Crans. In addition, a bus runs up to Crans from Sion. All SMC buses shuttling to and fro on circular routes within the resort boundaries are free.

Montana tourist office (June to mid-Sept & Dec–Easter Mon–Sat 8.30am–6.30pm, Sun 10am–noon & 4–6pm; rest of year Mon–Fri 8.30am–noon & 2–6pm, Sat 8.30am–noon; ☎027 485 04 04, ⓦwww.crans-montana.ch) is 100m west (left) of the Vermala funicular station, in the post office. The village centre is another 200m west, focused around the Ycoor ice-skating rink. Just beyond is the small **Lac Grenon**; running along its northern shore is the Route de Rawyl – always busy with cars – which, some 800m west, feeds into Rue Centrale in Crans, site of the **Crans tourist office** (same hours; ☎027 485 08 00). More or less opposite is the **Étang Long** lakelet, which backs onto the championship golf course.

Accommodation

A host of basic **hotels** offer inexpensive rooms, normally with a choice of ensuite or not: *Central* in Crans (☎027 481 37 67, ⓦwww.3963.ch/central; ❷–❸) and *Olympic* in Montana (☎027 481 29 85, ⓦwww.amadays.ch; ❷) are two examples, both in the centre of their villages, and both tidy and well kept. The *Beau-Site* (☎027 481 33 12, ⓦwww.beau-site-crans.com; ❸–❹) is a cosy, family-run hotel in a quiet location within easy reach of the lifts. *Robinson* (☎027 481 13 53, ⓦwww.valaisonline.com/robinson; ❸) is an uncomplicated "garni" place beside the two Crans gondolas. The *Lac Moubra* **campsite** in Montana (☎027 481 28 51; closed mid-Oct to Dec) also has basic **dorms** (Fr.22).

Eating and drinking

Eating wins no prizes for invention or quality. Body and soul are kept together by simple diners such as *Crêperie Ma Bretagne* opposite Parking Victoria in Montana or *Café du Centre* beside the church. The *Auberge de la Diligence* (☎027 485 99 85), 500m east of Montana's Vermala station, is Lebanese-run, and serves up quality Middle Eastern food (*menus* Fr.22); it also has affordable rooms (❷). Next door, the *Hôtel de la Forêt* (☎027 480 21 31; ⓦwww.delaforet.ch) caters specifically for vegetarians. *Café-Bar 1900* is the place to hang out in the centre of Crans, just round the corner from the Rue du Prado with all the big, glitzy designer names – Vuitton, Gucci, Hermès and all.

Oberwallis

East of Sierre stretches the German-speaking portion of Valais – or **Wallis**, as it officially becomes. To mark it out from the Lower Valais to the west, this is known as Upper Valais, or **Oberwallis**. The main town of the region, **Brig**, is an important road and rail junction, but is otherwise of limited interest; the concealed **Lötschen valley** is a more worthwhile detour. The reason that everybody passes through the area is to make a pilgrimage to the little mountain village of **Zermatt**, in order to lay eyes upon the **Matterhorn**, the most famous (if not actually the highest) of all Switzerland's mountains. In a side valley nearby sits the equally alluring resort of **Saas-Fee**, while east of Brig, the remote **Goms** region follows the Rhône to its glacial source.

East of Sierre

Heading **east of Sierre**, traffic on the valley-floor road starts to build up as you approach the Lötschberg Tunnel, the turnoffs to Zermatt and Saas-Fee and the Simplon Pass route into Italy. A couple of diversions bring you out of the crush. Just beyond the French–German language border is a turning to the ancient village of **Leuk**, with the spa resort of **Leukerbad** further up; while beyond the Lötschberg Tunnel terminus at Goppenstein, a minor road penetrates between the high rocky walls into the lovely **Lötschental**.

Leuk and Leukerbad
Perched above the valley floor, **LEUK** (Loèche in French; ⓦ www.leuk.ch) is remarkably good-looking, with an array of photogenic ancient buildings, including a fine Rathaus and medieval Bischofsschloss. Beyond, the road winds up to **LEUKERBAD** (Loèche-les-Bains), Europe's highest spa, at 1411m. Above the village, amidst some good winter skiing, is the pedestrian-only Gemmi Pass, one end of a tough hiking trail from Kandersteg (see p.304), from where cable cars bring you down to the village. Soothe your tired muscles at either of the main public spa complexes. The Burgerbad (Sun–Thurs 8am–8pm, Fri & Sat 8am–9pm; May, June & Nov closes 1hr earlier; Fr.22; ⓦ www.burgerbad .ch) has outdoor and indoor thermal pools as well as steam baths, plunge pools and exercise rooms; the Lindner Alpentherme (same hours; Fr.27; ⓦ www .alpentherme.ch) is a more refined affair – indulge in the works at the Roman-Irish bath. The **tourist office** (☎027 472 71 71, ⓦ www.leukerbad.ch) has details of the many discount deals and all-in packages offered by spa hotels.

The Lötschental
A short distance east, above the villages of Steg and Gampel, is the valley of the River Lonza. A narrow road switchbacks in tight curves up from the valley floor; traffic remains heavy until the tiny village of **Goppenstein**, at the southern exit of the Lötschberg Tunnel from Kandersteg (see box p.305), used by car-carrying trains that shuttle continuously beneath the Alps. Ignore the bustle of this most incongruous rail station, towered over by rocky crags, and head on. You emerge into the stunningly beautiful **LÖTSCHENTAL**, comprising half-a-dozen tranquil communities strung along 10km of the valley floor and overlooked on both sides by Alpine ridges topping 3300m. The huge glaciers sliding down from the Konkordiaplatz (see p.295) are a constant presence at the head of the valley. There are few more impressive scenes in the Alps.

Trails from Kandersteg via the **Lötschen Pass** (see p.306) drop down to the valley floor at the first village, **Ferden** (1389m). Just 2km on, past the photogenic hamlet of **Kippel**, the main valley community is **Wiler**, home both of the tourist office (☎027 938 88 88, ⓦ www.loetschental.ch) and a cable car up to the **Lauchernalp**. This is the focus of skiing in winter, with access to pistes up to 3111m on the looming Hockenhorn (a one/six-day pass is Fr.45/225). The valley-floor road trickles on amidst increasingly wild and beautiful scenery past **Blatten** to end at the hamlet of **Fafleralp** (1788m), a scant 4km from the nose of the massive Langgletscher.

A handful of **hotels** and hikers' inns is dotted along the valley. The grand *Lötschberg* at Kippel (℡027 939 13 09, ⓦwww.hotel-loetschberg.ch; ❷) has been around since 1902; the *Sporting* at Wiler (℡027 939 13 77, ⓦwww.rhone.ch/sporting; ❷) and welcoming *Fafleralp* (℡027 939 14 51, ⓦwww.fafleralp.ch; ❷) are also good bets. The biggest of half-a-dozen **campsites** is *Lonzastrand* (℡027 939 14 16). The Lötschental is known around Switzerland for its tradition of mask-making, displayed to full effect in the week before Ash Wednesday for the extraordinary **Roitschäggättä**, when locals don grotesque, shaggy masks for a series of night-time parades through the villages in an ancient Lenten ceremony.

Brig and the Simplon

By virtue of its location, you may find yourself spending a night in the graceful old town of **BRIG** (Brigue in French; Briga in Italian). It's the fulcrum for a dizzying series of major road and rail routes: southeast through the Simplon train tunnel into Italy; southwest to Zermatt at the foot of the Matterhorn, and Saas-Fee; west to Lake Geneva; north through the Lötschberg Tunnel towards Bern; and northeast to the high Alpine passes.

The huge train station stands at the northern edge of the town, connected to Brig's broad cobbled central square – the focus of the Old Town and called in its various sectors **Stadtplatz**, **Marktplatz** and **Sebastiansplatz** – by the main shopping street of Bahnhofstrasse. Overlooking the square is the tiny **Sebastianskapelle**, built by local bigwig Stockalper (see below) in 1637, with a network of picturesque alleys winding behind and around it.

Lanes off the southeast corner of the square lead along Alte Simplonstrasse past many fine patrician town houses dating from the seventeenth and eighteenth centuries to the **Schloss Stockalper**. This grandiose Italianate palace – for much of its life the largest private residence in Switzerland – dominates the otherwise simple town. It was completed in 1678 to serve as the home of Kaspar Jodok von Stockalper, a merchant from Brig who first made a mint controlling the trade in silk over the Simplon Pass to Lyon, moved on to make another killing organizing mail transport between Milan and Geneva, and finally gained the monopoly in trading salt over the pass. You can stroll from the street into the triple-arcaded interior courtyard, especially beautiful when it catches the sun. Rearing up overhead are three giant corner towers topped by the onion domes that are visible from much of the town. **Entry** to the few rooms open to the public is by guided tour only (May–Oct Tues–Sun 9.30am, 10.30am, 1.30, 2.30 & 3.30pm; June–Sept also 4.30pm; Fr.5) – unless you're confident in reading the German notes, though, or you have an English-speaking guide, you'd best save your money.

Practicalities

Brig's **tourist office** is in the train station up a spiral staircase (July–Sept Mon–Fri 8.30am–6pm, Sat 9am–6pm, Sun 9am–1pm; rest of year Sat closes 1pm, closed Sun; ℡027 921 60 30, ⓦwww.brig-tourismus.ch). From the forecourt of Brig station, MGB **trains** depart for Zermatt, and also for Andermatt (see p.397), via Oberwald and the tunnel beneath the Furka Pass. "Glacier Express" panoramic trains (see p.42) use this line to reach Chur, Davos and St Moritz. For details of the Lötschberg Tunnel car-carrying train, see p.305.

Hotels in Brig are all moderately priced. The *Londres & Schweizerhof*, Bahnhofstrasse 17 (☎027 922 93 93, ⊛www.hotel-delondres.ch; ❸), is a comfortable old place, with pleasant rooms overlooking the main square. The graceful *Schlosshotel*, Kirchgasse 4 (☎027 922 95 95, ⊛www.schlosshotel.ch; ❷–❸), has bright and attractive rooms overlooking the Schloss Stockalper.

All the **cafés and restaurants** around the main square set tables outside during summer: pick of the bunch is *Zum Eidgenossen*, which offers fondues and meaty Walliser fare in a traditional atmosphere for around Fr.20. Nearby on Alte Simplonstrasse is the pleasant local bistro *Matza*, serving up pizzas and simple meals. Down by the station, as well as a self-service *Migros*, you'll find the *Hotel Victoria*, which offers good brasserie-style food, with some veggie options (Fr.15–20).

The Simplon Pass and Tunnel

The road over the **Simplon Pass** (2005m), southwest of Brig, was built by Napoleon as a military through-route between 1800 and 1808, immediately after he'd successfully crossed the Grand-St-Bernard with an army (see p.327). These days the old pass road is a modern, Swiss-engineered highway, and the pass itself isn't really worth a specific journey, with views nowhere near as impressive as those from the other great Alpine passes. What *is* worthwhile, though, is to explore the cobbled alleys and picturesque old houses of **Simplon-Dorf** on the other side – still in Switzerland – as well as, down towards the Italian border, the terrifyingly steep and narrow gorge leading to the frontier hamlet of **Gondo**; there are few places where the cliff walls feel so high and you feel so small. A stone next to the road commemorates the victims of a torrential mud slide which swept half the village away in 2000. An energetic two- or three-day **hike** covers the 35km Stockalper Road, from Brig to Gondo; this is the mule track completed by Stockalper for transport of goods between Italy and the Valais, and has inns aplenty dotted along its route, which is mostly away from the highway.

While you're standing on the pass heights, give a thought for those careering at speed on trains through the **Simplon Tunnel**, some 2400m beneath the Wasenhorn peak just to the east. Until the opening of the new Gotthard Base Tunnel (see p.399), this remains the longest rail tunnel in the world, entered just after leaving Brig station and emerging 19.8km later in Italy for the short run to Domodossola (from where Swiss trains connect on the Centovalli line to Locarno; see p.544), and on south to Milan. The completion of the tunnel in 1905 opened up an entirely new train route from London and Paris to Istanbul – the so-called **Venice–Simplon Orient Express** – which in turn led to a whole new era in pan-European travel.

The Simplon Pass road is kept open year-round, and offers an easy short-cut if you're driving to the Ticino. From the Italian border at Gondo, it's 22km to the town of **Domodossola**. Signage on the outskirts is poor, but if you aim for Masera, you'll pick up the road heading east towards **Santa Maria Maggiore** in the Val Vigezzo, which leads on to the Swiss border at Cámedo (roughly 26km from Domodossola). From Cámedo, the road continues to Locarno.

Zermatt

St Moritz may have the glamour, Verbier may have the cool, Wengen may have the pistes, but **ZERMATT** beats them all – Zermatt has the **Matterhorn**.

No other natural or human structure in the whole country is so immediately recognizable; indeed, in most people's minds the Matterhorn stands for Switzerland, like the Eiffel Tower stands for France.

Part of the reason the Matterhorn is so famous is that it stands alone, its impossibly pointy shape sticking up from an otherwise uncrowded horizon above Zermatt village, at 1620m. But you get the feeling that it would be famous even if it stood within a chain of peaks: there's just something about it that's bizarrely mesmerizing to see for real.

Emerging from Zermatt station is an experience in itself: this one little village – which has managed, much to its credit, to cling onto its old brown chalets and atmospheric twisting alleys – welcomes everybody, regardless of financial status, and the station square is where all worlds collide. Backpackers and hikers rub shoulders with high-

△ Horse-drawn carriage, Zermatt

society glitterati amidst a fluster of tour groups, electric taxis and horse-drawn carriages. Everyone has come to see the mountain. Zermatt has no off-season – it's busy year-round – yet the crowds never seem to matter. You may have to shoulder your way down the main street, but the terrain all around is expansive enough that with a little effort you could vanish into the wilderness, leaving everyone else behind.

The small area around Zermatt features 36 mountains over 4000m, a statistic as enticing to summer hikers as to winter skiers. As early as the 1820s, British climbers adopted the isolated hamlet as a base camp from which to scale the nearby peaks. The first hotel opened in 1838. All through the nineteenth century, word of the place spread, and the local community quickly saw the potential: grand hotels went up and public funds were diverted into construction of the Gornergrat rack railway at the turn of the century. The skiing boom of the 1960s saw the hamlet double in size, but today it's still acceptably small and low-key, rooted to the valley floor in a natural bowl open to the south. The Gornergrat railway lifts you up to a spectacular vantage point overlooking the **Monte Rosa** massif, with its summit the **Dufourspitze** (4634m) – the highest point in Switzerland. The skiing is superb, but in many ways the hiking is better, with some of the most scenic mountain walks in the whole country within easy reach of the village.

Arrival, orientation and information

The Matterhorn Gotthard Bahn (ⓦ www.mgbahn.ch) operates the **trains** from Brig and Visp to Zermatt; they're free to Swiss Pass holders. Although **Brig** is the starting point for MGB trains, mainline trains from the west (from Lake Geneva and Sion) are quite often timed to make the connection at **Visp** instead

ZERMATT

WINKEL MATTEN

OBER DORF

STEIN MATTE

HINTER DORF

Alpin Center

Alpine Museum

SCHLUHMATTSTRASSE

LUCHERNSTRASSE

STADELWEG

RIEDSTRASSE

STEINMATTSTRASSE

Matter Vispa

KIRCHSTRASSE

MATTERSTRASSE

BRUNNMATTGASSE

VISPASTRASSE

RIEDWEG

SEILERWESENSTRASSE

HOFMATTWEG

HOFMATTSTRASSE

MATTERSTRASSE

WIESTI-STR.

BAHNHOFSTRASSE

SPISS-STR.

Trockener-Steg

OBERDORFSTRASSE

J, K & Gornergrat

Sunnegga

0   100 m

Gornergrat Station

MGB Train Station

Campsite

EATING & DRINKING

Antares	1	North Wall	2
Café du Pont	3	Whymperstube	5
Elsie's Place	4	Z'Alt Hischi	6

ACCOMMODATION

Allalin	E	Matterhorn Hostel	C	Post	I
Alpina	H	Matterhornblick	F	Riffelalp	J
Bijou	A	Mischabel	L	Riffelberg	K
Bristol	D	Perren	M	Welschen	O
Jugendherberge	B	Pollux	N	Zermatterhof	G

(Viège in French); check the timetable carefully. At both Brig and Visp stations, MGB trains run on tracks laid in the street outside the front of the station, not from the usual platforms.

South of Visp, trains climb to **Stalden** (departure point for buses to Saas-Fee) and then enter the picturesque Mattertal, clinging precariously above the ravine as they rise higher and higher past a series of villages – as dramatic a prelude to the Matterhorn scenery as you could hope for. A minor **road** also runs along the valley: it's possible to drive as far as the village of **Täsch**, where vast car parks (see box) take care of all motorized transport, with everybody bundling onto trains, and extra Pendelzüge shuttles, for the final twelve-minute pull into Zermatt.

Zermatt's **train station** is a large, bustling place, with the usual left-luggage facilities, located at the northern end of the village's main street. The square outside is generally full of little **electric taxis**, which cost about Fr.15 for up to four people (more including luggage) to anywhere within the village. There are also two **electric buses**, free with a ski-pass (or around Fr.3), which serve all points. The **GGB Gorner-grat-Bahn** station is directly opposite the main station, while the underground funicular to **Sunnegga** leaves from the opposite bank (head east from the station beside the Gorner-grat tracks and over the river, then cut left for 100m).

Information

Zermatt's super-friendly, helpful **tourist office** is beside the station (mid-June to Sept Mon–Sat 8.30am–6pm, Sun 8.30am–noon &

Driving to Zermatt: long-term parking options

Zermatt is **car-free** – private vehicles are permitted no closer than **Täsch**, 6km away. From Täsch, trains, electric taxis and horse-drawn carriages shuttle passengers on into Zermatt.

However, it isn't necessarily the best policy to drive all the way to Täsch – especially if you have a Swiss Pass or similar (see p.41), which gives free or discounted train travel. Certain sections of the large parking garages at and near **Visp** station (27km from Zermatt) offer **free indefinite parking** if you get a permit at the train station ticket office when you buy your train ticket to Zermatt. Free parking only applies if you've parked in the right place: look for the marked "Matterhorn Gotthard Bahn park and ride" car parks to the east (covered) and west (open) of the station, and only use those areas marked with the **Matterhorn Gotthard Bahn logo** (*not* the SBB one). Check with the train station staff that you're in the right place before you head off or you'll be charged when you return. For your reference, the **full adult fare** by train from Visp to Zermatt is Fr.64 return (children under 16 pay half-price); however, the journey is **free** if you hold a Swiss Pass, Floxi Pass, Youth Pass or Swiss Card, or if you're using a Swiss Transfer Ticket to reach Zermatt.

If you do choose to drive up the valley, be aware (as the local residents are) of the **environmental impact** of driving in this fragile but highly touristed Alpine landscape: parking your car at Visp and taking the train is less environmentally damaging than driving to Täsch. From Visp, as from anywhere in Switzerland (and even from any airport in the world; see p.28), the train company will transport all your baggage independently for a small fee, letting you travel to Zermatt unencumbered. In addition, most Zermatt hotels will collect your bags from the station and deliver them to your room on request. It could hardly be easier.

If you're determined to drive, note that all the villages along the way are well aware of tourists' desire to get something for nothing, and all of them either charge for parking, or happily ticket offenders for parking illegally. In **Täsch**, the end of the road, there are a dozen large parking areas with space for 3000 cars, including the giant Matterhorn Terminal (🔢 www.matterhornterminal.ch); prices are reasonable (around Fr.7–11/day), but still more than the nothing you can get away with at Visp. The **shuttle train** from Täsch to Zermatt (which runs every 20min 6am–11.30pm) costs Fr.15.60 return. Plenty of **taxi** companies also operate from Täsch, most offering discounts on parking if you use them to reach Zermatt.

1.30–6pm; rest of year Mon–Sat 8.30am–noon & 1.30–6pm, Sun 9.30am–noon & 4–6pm; 📞 027 966 81 00, 🔢 www.zermatt .ch). A channel of cable TV within the village shows live pictures from local summits (including the Rothorn, Gornergrat and Trockener Steg) – handy for viewing weather conditions.

Accommodation

Accommodation in Zermatt is almost universally excellent. The village is so used to tourists – in fact, there *is* no village without the tourists – that service has been fine-tuned and facilities across all price brackets are good. There are dozens of hotels, so you shouldn't have any problem finding somewhere to suit; high season is an exception, when you should book as far ahead as possible. It must be said, too, that **Matterhorn views** from your balcony or window are truly worth paying for: the mountain is so magnificent that you won't get bored of opening your eyes to it each morning.

Apartments or **chalets** should also be booked well in advance (some places are reserved a year ahead). The standard rental period is a Saturday-to-Saturday week; only a handful of owners are willing to rent for less, and then only in the low season for a minimum three days.

Inexpensive hotels

Alpina ☎ 027 967 10 50, 🌐 www.alpina-zermatt .ch. Down in the Hinterdorf, with amiable staff and a calm atmosphere. ❸

Matterhornblick ☎ 027 967 20 17, 🌐 www .matterhornblick.ch. A modern place beside the church, drenched in light pine but living up to its name, with mountain views out back. ❸–❹

🏃 **Mischabel** ☎ 027 967 11 31, 🌐 www .zermatt.ch/mischabel. Another quality choice in quiet Hinterdorf, an old creaky-floored building with fresh, sunny rooms (none ensuite) and Matterhorn views. ❷

Post ☎ 027 967 19 31, 🌐 www.hotelpost.ch. Funky main-drag institution, with a popular bar, disco and youthful restaurant topped by a handful of comfortable, individually styled rooms. ❸–❹

🏃 **Welschen** ☎ 027 967 54 22, 🌐 www .reconline.ch/welschen. A real find, up on a hill beside the Sunnegga station, small, pleasant, atmospheric and family-run. ❸

Mid-range and expensive

🏃 **Allalin** ☎ 027 966 82 66, 🌐 www.hotel -allalin.ch. Acclaimed "garni" hotel beside the church, with modern decor and plenty of comforts. Service is outstanding, and there are balconies in all rooms (including ones facing south to the Matterhorn). ❹–❺

Bijou ☎ 027 966 51 51, 🌐 www.hotel-bijou.ch. Far away from the centre on a slope just next to the Matterhorn cable car, a small family-run place with some nice, cosy touches in the rooms. ❹–❺

Bristol ☎ 027 966 33 66, 🌐 www.hotel-bristol.ch. Excellent mid-range choice, with efficient, friendly service and cosy rooms – those facing south with picture-postcard views (go for the upper floors). ❹–❼

🏃 **Gornergrat Kulm** ☎ 027 966 64 00, 🌐 www.zermatt.ch/gornergrat.kulm. Solidly built mountain hotel alongside the terminus of the GGB Gornergrat line from Zermatt – reputedly the highest hotel in the Alps, at 3100m above sea level. It's a popular spot for day-trippers to gawp at the Matterhorn from the hotel terrace, or eat in the restaurant, but in the evening, after most of the crowds have departed, this can be a uniquely

atmospheric place to spend the night. It's also been totally revamped inside, with stylish, modern interiors. 45min by Gornergrat train from Zermatt. ❻

Perren ☎ 027 966 52 00, 🌐 www.hotel-perren.ch. Graceful, modern hotel on the riverbank, with an appealing stylishness to its well-appointed rooms. A bargain. ❺–❻

Pollux ☎ 027 966 40 00, 🌐 www.reconline.ch /pollux. Modern glitzy place bang on the main drag, with plenty of style and comfortable rooms, some facing off the street. ❺–❽

Riffelalp ☎ 027 966 05 55, 🌐 www.riffelalp .com. Superbly renovated mountain hotel, way up at 2222m on the slopes above the village – for decades a rather down-at-heel mountain inn, now a full-blown luxury resort, with spacious, stylish rooms and suites, and some outstanding Matterhorn views. 20min by Gornergrat train from Zermatt. ❽–❾

Riffelberg ☎ 027 966 65 00, 🌐 www.zermatt .ch/riffelberg. Another ten minutes up the Gornergrat train line past *Riffelalp* – a fairly standard three-star mountain hotel at 2585m, with cosy, comfortable rooms, priced high for the superb location. ❺–❻

Zermatterhof ☎ 027 966 66 00, 🌐 www.zermatt .ch/zermatterhof. The grandest hotel in the canton, and one of the finest in the country, built well over a century ago but glitteringly up to date inside. Manages to be effortlessly luxurious without a hint of tasteless resort swagger. ❽–❾

Hostels

Jugendherberge (HI hostel) ☎ 027 967 23 20, 🌐 www.youthhostel.ch. Large hostel, way out in Winkelmatten (beyond Steinmatte), with dorm beds, many with enticing Matterhorn views, from Fr.47 half-board (breakfast plus a packed lunch or dinner). Closed May & Nov. ❶

Matterhorn Hostel (SB hostel) ☎ 027 968 19 19, 🌐 www.matterhornhostel.com. In the same quarter as the HI hostel, but on the riverbank, with dorms from Fr.33 (breakfast extra). ❶

Campsite

Matterhorn ☎ 027 967 39 21. Good site located just north of the train station. June–Sept.

In and around the village

Zermatt's narrow main street, although picturesque, is packed all the way down with shops, hotels, restaurants and – for much of the year – people. To the east,

Skiing and snowboarding

There are three ski and board sectors, each accessed by its own transport route: pistes from **Sunnegga/Rothorn** link to the adjacent **Gornergrat/Stockhorn**, while the **Schwarzsee/Klein Matterhorn** sector, rising to 3900m, connects to the Italian resort of Cervinia. All of them offer satisfying runs at most levels of ability, with a healthy dose of blues and manageable reds around **Blauherd** above Sunnegga, and some good, scenic blues and reds at **Gifthittli** above Riffelberg; from here, long, leg-stretching reds take you down to **Gant** in the valley, which has lifts on both sides up to more choice runs. The spectacular **"Triftji Bumps"**, from Hohtälli above Gornergrat, is one of the most famous black runs in the Alps, but it also has a separate, less challenging red twin that meets it at the bottom.

Top destination has got to be the network of pistes and lifts above **Furi**, with some airy red and black runs around Schwarzsee and **Trockener Steg**, and a long blue dubbed **Gandegg**. The high-level red runs around **Testa Grigia** and the Klein Matterhorn station, well above 3800m, are superb, and there are plenty of options to ski down from here to **Cervinia** (passport needed). Up here on the Theodul glacier is also where you'll find the **Gravity Park**, Europe's biggest snow park, with a 200m super-pipe, half-pipe, kickers, rails and plenty more to keep boarders happy. These pistes also offer memorable **summer skiing** and **boarding**, in a sweeping area from the Klein Matterhorn at 3900m down to Trockener Steg at 2900m. A **ski-pass** for universal access at Zermatt and Cervinia is Fr.76/379 for one/six days. A pass for Zermatt's lifts only is Fr.68/336.

Schools include **Stoked** (Ⓦwww.stoked.ch), perhaps the best of Switzerland's new wave of ski and board academies; also check out Ⓦwww.skischulezermatt.ch and Ⓦwww.matterhornskiwochen.ch. Zermatt comes into its own with the array of heli-skiing (around Fr.300) and off piste possibilities all around the area; schools and the Alpin Center (see below) can advise.

Extreme sports, climbing and trekking

Zermatt's **Alpin Center** (☏027 966 24 60, Ⓦwww.alpincenter-zermatt.ch), on the main street, is the first place to come for advice and guides for extreme sports all year round. In addition to canyoning, ice-climbing, snowshoeing, heli-skiing and more, they run regular guided **climbs** up some of the nearby peaks. The Matterhorn itself is out, unless you have plenty of experience, all the professional apparatus, a week for training, and about Fr.1150 in fees. However, they do run daily guided excursions for Fr.100–200 that are suitable for beginners, including a four-hour trek from Klein Matterhorn across glaciers to Trockener Steg, an easy ascent to a 4000m peak such as the Breithorn, or a basic climbing course on the Riffelhorn. An individual who markets himself as "Jacques, your guide" runs short and long **mule treks** into the wilds (roughly Fr.40/hr per person; Ⓦwww .muletrekking.com).

One of the best **long-distance walks** – aside from the Haute Route to Zermatt from Chamonix (see p.329) – is the **Matterhorn Tour**. This comprises a 34-stage circular walk around the mountain, mostly on Alpine paths, crossing from the Mattertal into the Val d'Anniviers and Val d'Hérens, as well as into Italy; you'll need to hire a guide for two short stages, across the glacier-bound Theodul Pass and, further round, across a glacier above Arolla. It takes ten days to do in full, or you can select certain half- or full-day stages. The tourist office has a map and full details.

Perhaps the toughest **event** is the **Zermatt Marathon** (Ⓦwww.zermatt-marathon .ch), held in July on a regulation 42km course from St Niklaus (1085m) up to the Gornergrat peak (3010m).

7

VALAIS | Zermatt

alleys run down into **Hinterdorf**, an attractive old quarter by the river, full of old weathered-wood chalets and traditional *mazots* (barns raised on stone discs to protect against mice). Some 400m south of the station is the **church**, another main landmark, its riverside cemetery filled with memorials to attempts on the Matterhorn and other peaks gone wrong. From here a street doglegs east over the river to the district of **Steinmatte** on the opposite bank. The cable-car station up to **Trockener Steg** and Klein Matterhorn is 500m south of the church.

Beside the post office is the **Alpine Museum** (June–Oct daily 10am–noon & 4–6pm; Nov–May Mon–Fri & Sun 4.30–6.30pm; Fr.8) – worth a visit, with an interesting collection of mountaineering bits and bobs, as well as a room devoted to Edward Whymper, an English climber who led the first ascent of the Matterhorn on July 14, 1865, only for the rope to snap on the descent – four of his party of seven went over a precipice.

The Gornergrat railway

In summer, the slopes above Zermatt hold some of the country's most scenic hiking trails. The ever-popular GGB **Gornergrat Bahn** (Ⓦwww .ggb.ch) leads up from the village across the meadows of the Riffelalp to the **Gornergrat** itself (3130m) – get a seat on the right-hand side for magical Matterhorn vistas. The Gornergrat is the first point on a ridge that runs out to the Hohtälligrat (3286m) and, amidst a sea of ice, the **Stockhorn** (3407m), all linked by cable car from Gornergrat. The view from any of these peaks is terrific, with the entire Monte Rosa massif laid out in front of you, the vast Gornergletscher carving along at your feet, and the Matterhorn itself in isolation away to one side; at your back is the Rothorn (3103m), behind it the Dom (4545m), and behind the Dom the whole sweep of the Pennine Alps.

Hikes between the various stations on the Gornergrat railway are all very rewarding with, for example, three good trails leading out from the grand hotel alongside the station at **Riffelalp** (see "Accommodation"), easiest of which is the pleasant one-hour walk up to the **Riffelberg** hotel, on a spectacular exposed platform overlooking the valley. In summer (mid-June to mid-Sept), there are once-weekly dawn trains up to the Gornergrat so you can catch an awe-inspiring sunrise break on the Matterhorn.

Other mountain routes above Zermatt

From Zermatt village, an underground funicular tunnels up to **Sunnegga** (2300m), also on a plateau and linked to the **Rothorn** summit by gondola. Walks from Sunnegga are beautiful, weaving for a comfortable hour or two between the tiny lakelets of the Leisee, Moosjesee, Grindjisee and Stellisee out to **Fluhalp** (2616m).

From the south end of Zermatt village, cable cars run to **Furi** and on up to **Trockener Steg** (2939m), overlooking the gigantic Theodulgletscher, which slides over the Italian border at the foot of the Matterhorn. From Trockener Steg, another cable car runs up to the crest of the **Klein Matterhorn** – at 3820m, this is the highest cable car station in Europe. There's an ice pavilion and other bits and bobs on top; plans are afoot to construct a luxury hotel up here. From Furi, the cable car up to the little **Schwarzsee** gives what is commended as the most picture-perfect views of the Matterhorn, at close quarters *and* reflected in a pine-fringed lake. Again hikes abound, including a long but easy walk (7hr) back down into Zermatt village.

Eating and drinking

Considering the prices in some of Zermatt's hundred-plus **restaurants**, opting for picnic fare from the Co-op supermarket opposite the train station is a prudent move if you're on a tight budget. There are plenty of places where you can get diner-style fast food for under Fr.15: the *Hotel Post* is the best, incorporating the *Brown Cow* snack bar, a *Spaghetti Factory* and the famous *Broken* bar and pizzeria. The popular *North Wall* bar (Ⓦ www.northwallbar.com), on the other side of the river south of the *Bristol*, has pizzas from Fr.12 and draft beer at Fr.5/half-litre. There are a few equally inexpensive cafés beyond the church – best is the peaceful and pleasant ✝ *Café du Pont* on a nice corner. *Z'Alt Hischi*, down in Hinterdorf, is another, although it's more of a quiet place to savour a beer than anything else. *Elsie's Place*, opposite the church, is an unexpectedly cosy little nook, although a little over-glitzy in season; at least it offers light snacks to help your cocktail go down.

Moving up the scale, the *Antares*, on the other side of the river, serves quality fish dishes in its plush carved-wood dining room for around Fr.25. The *Rothornstube* in *Hotel Perren* is another comfortable place where you can select from a range of different *menus*, from Fr.25 to Fr.60 or more. The atmosphere in the *Buffet Royal* at the *Zermatterhof Hotel*, or the glorious Edwardian-style *Whymperstube* in the central *Hotel Monte Rosa*, is formal and restrained, but if you can afford the three-figure sums required, a meal at either of these places is likely to be at least as memorable as your ride to the Gornergrat. The three separate restaurants in the superb *Riffelalp* resort, partway up the Gornergrat line, are similarly outstanding, with the added benefit of the sensational views.

Saas-Fee

Lying in the next-door valley to Zermatt, **SAAS-FEE** (1800m) is sometimes overlooked, perhaps because it doesn't have any train access. However, were it not for the Matterhorn next door, the array of peaks around Saas-Fee would take centre-stage on any Alpine itinerary: the village is perched on a shelf of pasture at the base of a horseshoe of thirteen 4000m-plus peaks. Oozing out from between them is the giant Feegletscher – or Fairy Glacier – trickling its meltwater down through the village, and active enough in its various sectors to limit what would otherwise be spectacular skiing. (The danger of falling down a glacial crevasse if you stray beyond piste-markings is more pronounced in Saas-Fee than in most other resorts.) The village is heavily touristed, but can lay claim to unrivalled Alpine views and landscapes.

Throughout the village you may come across the name Zurbriggen on a number of shop signs; if the name sounds familiar, it's because Pirmin Zurbriggen, a local boy made good, was a downhill skiing world champion in the 1980s. Today, he owns a hotel in tiny Saas-Almagell up the valley, as well as another in Zermatt. Various branches of the family have kept their foothold in Saas-Fee.

Saas-Fee is one of four linked villages at the end of the Saastal. **Buses** from Brig pass through Visp and then **Stalden** (both on the train line) before branching off into the Saastal itself, passing first through **Saas-Balen**, then **Saas-Grund**, the main village on the valley floor; from here, a road branches up to Saas-Fee – which is car-free – while a few kilometres on down the valley is **Saas-Almagell**.

Sports and activities at Saas-Fee

With a preponderance of blue and red pistes, Saas-Fee is ideal territory for beginners or intermediates, and its snowboarding facilities have made it one of Switzerland's top boarding destinations. The focus of attention is the "Alpin Express" lifts serving the **Felskinn** (3000m); from here, there are plenty of good blue and red runs coming down the side of the huge glacial bowl that towers all around, plus a snowboarding half-pipe. From Felskinn, the "Metro Alpin" takes over, the highest underground funicular system in the world, that tunnels up to the **Mittelallalin** station (3500m), below the mighty Allalinhorn summit (4027m). Up here are the world's highest revolving restaurant (ⓦwww.drehrestaurant-allalin.ch) and ice pavilion (ⓦwww.eispavillon .ch), as well as a half-pipe, a hatful of scenic red runs on the Feegletscher and a long, exhilarating blue all the way down to **Längfluh** (2870m), which is served by its own lifts from the village via Spielboden. An alternative is the lift to **Plattjen** (2570m), from where red and another long blue wind back down to Saas-Fee. There's also **summer skiing** from the Mittelallalin. The **Hannig** (2350m) is barred to skiers, but has good sledge runs and winter walking trails.

Lift passes for one/six days cost Fr.61/303 for Saas-Fee alone, or Fr.65/327 for additional access to the limited runs above Saas-Grund and Saas-Almagell (ski bus included). Good discount deals for families are available. In addition to the official ski and snowboard school (ⓦwww.saas-fee.ch), check out ⓦwww.eskimos.ch. The **Mountain Guides** office (ⓦwww.mountain-life.ch) runs a host of adventure excursions, including husky tours, snowshoe trekking, snow-tubing, ice-climbing and more.

Hiking routes abound, both in summer, with long treks finding a way between the peaks into the Mattertal, and in winter, when some 30km of trails above the village remain open. The summer seven-day **hiking pass** (Fr.117, family Fr.234) covers all mountain transport in the Saastal and the Stalden–Saas-Fee postbus.

Practicalities

From the entrance to Saas-Fee, several quaint lanes lead down (southwest) into the heart of the village, full of shops and some boutiques, but still with much character and charm.

Saas-Fee is car-free, and there is a huge **parking** area at the entrance to the village (Fr.11.50/day, discounted with a visitor card issued by your hotel); parking at the base of the gondola in Saas-Grund, or at Saas-Almagell, is cheaper, but you'd do just as well to take advantage of the cheaper deals in Visp (see box p.347) and catch the bus in. Electro-taxis shuttle around all points in the village for Fr.12–18 or so. The **bus station** is beside the car park, as is the **tourist office** (Mon–Fri 8.30am–noon & 2–6.30pm, Sat 8am–7pm; ☏027 958 18 58, ⓦwww.saas-fee.ch). There's also a tourist office in Saas-Grund (Mon–Sat 8.30am–noon & 2–6pm, Sun 8.30–11am & 3.30–6pm; ☏027 958 66 66, ⓦwww.saastal.ch), and smaller offices along the valley.

Accommodation

The tourist office has an **accommodation**-booking line (☏027 958 18 68, Ⓔto@saas-fee.ch) that can reserve a room at any of the resort's hotels. Saas-Grund has several **campsites**, but only the simple *Bergheimat* site (☏027 957 20 66) stays open year-round.

Hotels

Burgener ☏027 958 92 80, ⓦwww.hotel -burgener.ch. Charming little hotel near the lifts,

with the quiet *Skihütte* restaurant adjoining. ❹–❺
Dolomit ☏027 957 24 89, ⓦwww.dolomit.ch. Well-run sport hotel, with modern, no-fuss rooms

and low prices. Runs guided hikes, mountain-bike rides, climbs and ski-tours. ➋–➌

Ferienart ☎ 027 958 19 00, ⓦ www.ferienart.ch. Top-rated five-star hotel bang in the heart of the village, with spa, sauna and solarium in addition to spacious, elegant rooms (many with a Jacuzzi) and superbly luxurious suites. ➑–➒

Jägerhof ☎ 027 957 13 10, ⓦ www.saas-fee .ch/jaegerhof. Fine mid-range option in a tranquil location right on the edge of the village – in winter, you can ski to the door. ➍–➏

🏃 **Romantik-Hotel Beau Site** ☎ 027 958 15 60, ⓦ www.beausite.org. Superb, central "wellness" hotel, with onsite spa and health centre. A fixture in the village for more than 100 years, with uniquely characterful rooms and attentive service. ➍–➐

Saaserhof ☎ 027 957 35 51, ⓦ www.saaserhof .ch. Modern, reliably accomplished and comfortable four-star hotel, very convenient for the lifts and right beside the slopes. ➏–➑

Tenne ☎ 027 957 12 12, ⓦ www.hotel-tenne.ch. Family hotel in a good, central location, with an upmarket restaurant and fresh, light-pine rooms. ➌–➎

Zur Mühle ☎ 027 957 26 76, ⓦ www.moulin -saas-fee.ch. Small, excellent-value place in an old burnt-wood chalet, with all rooms facing south and balconied. 500m southwest of the tourist office, close to all the lifts and on the riverbank. ➋–➌

Zurbriggen ☎ 027 958 91 58, ⓦ www.hotel -zurbriggen.ch. Another good mid-range choice, set in its own gardens close to the tourist office. ➍

Eating and drinking

Eating and drinking is a case of keep wandering until your stomach, or your eyes, tell you to stop. In the centre is *Boccalino*, doing decent pizzas and the like for Fr.12–15. The restaurant attached to *Hotel Zur Mühle* is a reliable proposition for inexpensive Walliser cuisine – mainly fondues and raclettes. Grab a table on the terrace of the *Skihütte* restaurant, attached to *Hotel Burgener*, for good local cooking and superb views. *Restaurant La Ferme*, near the tourist office, is a step up in quality, with good *menus* from Fr.25 and brave attempts at rustic decor. The sky's the limit for gourmet cuisine, exemplified by two temples to the art: the *Fletschhorn Waldhotel* (☎ 027 957 21 31, ⓦ www.fletschhorn.ch), out in the woods north of the village, and the *Cäsar Ritz* restaurant within the *Ferienart* hotel (☎ 027 958 19 00, ⓦ www.ferienart.ch), in the centre.

The Goms

The upper part of the Rhône valley, stretching from Brig to the high Alpine passes, is known as **the Goms** (ⓦ www.goms.ch). Winter sees thick snow covering the whole region, perfect for cross-country skiing at all levels. Traffic, at least in the warmer months, is often heavy on the valley road (which accesses the Furka, Grimsel and Nufenen passes), but drivers generally prefer to keep their foot down, zipping straight past the pine forests, wide-open meadows and the picturesque villages of traditional darkwood chalets without stopping. If you've got a car, it's worth taking a break at a couple of places on the long drive up the valley. Buses and local trains from Brig stop at all villages.

About 8km out of Brig you'll pass **Mörel**, with signs for cable cars rising west to **Riederalp** and, a little further on, **Betten**, with cable cars to **Bettmeralp**. Both these car-free resorts are perched on ridge-top plateaus, with lifts serving the unspoilt **Aletschwald**, one of the highest pine forests in Europe, which in turn overlooks the **Aletsch Glacier**, a mammoth ice sheet – longest in the Alps, and a UNESCO World Natural Heritage Site – which winds its way down 23km from the base of the Jungfrau. There are hiking possibilities galore around here, and tourist offices in Riederalp (ⓦ www.riederalp.ch) and Bettmeralp (ⓦ www.bettmeralp.ch) can provide details of specific trails, as well as of the network of inns and mountain huts. **Fiesch**, the next main town along the valley, has lifts up to the vantage point of the **Eggishorn**, above the hamlet of Kuhboden, offering the finest views of the glacier.

Above Fiesch, the Rhône is little more than a fast-flowing mountain brook, and the villages become smaller and more rural. Some 6km past Fiesch is the hamlet of **Niederwald**, which proudly announces its claim to fame with a US-style billboard: it was here, in 1850, that César Ritz, who went on to found the Ritz hotel chain, was born.

Some 3km further on is the little community of **MÜNSTER**. Away from the main road, the tranquil village is characterized by the traditional Valaisian-style chalets, all clustered together higgledy-piggledy, burnt a rich dark brown and decorated with pretty geranium window boxes. At their centre is a striking white church with a wood-panelled barrel-vault ceiling and florid Baroque interior – this is thought to be all that remains of a medieval monastery which once stood somewhere nearby. The handful of **hotels** in the village is worth passing over in favour of the ⚜ *Croix d'Or et Poste* beside the main road (☎027 974 15 15, ⓦwww.hotel-postmuenster.ch; ❷–❸), a marvellous old building dating from 1620. Up to 1900 or so it was the residence of the noble family of prince-bishops Von Riedmatten; these days, it's every bit as atmospheric as that sounds, its public rooms festooned with Victorian bric-à-brac, the few guest rooms more subdued but still characterful. Value for money extends to the cooking as well, with superb *menus* for Fr.20–25.

The high Alpine passes

Above Münster, you enter the **Obergoms** region (Upper Goms), and begin to approach the high Alpine passes. The guaranteed snow up here, and breathtaking scenery, makes for some outstanding cross-country skiing. Ulrichen, 4km on, has a turning southeast along the Agenetal to the **Nufenen Pass**, or Passo della Novena (2478m), which crosses into Ticino and the Val Bedretto (see p.537). The main road continues through **Oberwald** (1368m), where the Obergoms tourist office is located (☎027 973 32 32, ⓦwww.obergoms.ch), and then immediately begins to climb in a series of great looping switchbacks.

Way above Oberwald is the junction point of **GLETSCH** (1759m) – not really even a hamlet, but with a hotel, *Glacier du Rhône* (☎027 973 15 15, ⓦwww.glacier-du-rhone.ch; ❷; June–Sept), from which to enjoy the spectacular views. In summer, DFB (ⓦwww.furka-bergstrecke.ch) runs an antique **steam train** on a cogwheel track through spectacular scenery up to the Furka Pass via a short tunnel at Muttbach, heading on to Realp (see p.399). The round trip costs Fr.93. The long-awaited rail link from Oberwald to Gletsch is expected to enter service shortly.

To the Furka Pass

Northeast from Gletsch, heading up to the Furka Pass, the road sidewinds its way up the cliffside, coiling around the landmark **Hotel Belvédère** on the way (2300m; ⓦwww.gletscher.ch). In season, this once-grand edifice is swamped by the tide of traffic swarming up the road; it's not worth staying here, but it is worth stopping for the breathtaking views down into the valley, and also to explore the **Rhône Glacier**, which fills the head of the valley to the north. This is the source of the Rhône itself, which you can see spouting out as meltwater from beneath the glacier's eaves. Owners of a souvenir stall in the *Belvédère*'s car park have cashed in on the glacier's appeal – and its proximity to the road – by carving, fresh each year, a tunnel deep into the blueish ice for their many customers to walk along (June–Oct daily 8am–6pm; Fr.5). By the end of the

Car-carrying trains: the Furka and Oberalp passes

If you're heading east into Central Switzerland (or beyond) and would prefer to avoid the climb over the Furka Pass, note that **car-carrying trains** run daily year-round from Oberwald through the **Furka–Basis Tunnel** (15.4km) to Realp, at least every hour (6am–9pm); a one-way fare is Fr.25 (Oct–May Fr.30). Journey time is 15min. You can also avoid the climb over the **Oberalp Pass** by loading your car onto a train at Andermatt for the hour-long pull to Sedrun (Fr.65). Full information on both is at ⓦwww.mgbahn.ch.

summer, about a third of the tunnel's length has melted, as the glacier shifts by some 30m each year.

A short climb further is the **Furka Pass** itself (2431m; full account on p.399), beyond which lie Realp and Andermatt.

To the Grimsel Pass

The other road from Gletsch climbs west in ever tighter curves up to the **Grimsel Pass** (2165m), which marks the border between Valais and Canton Bern. There are three hotels on the top, and this is an extraordinarily dramatic place to spend the night, with the bare, snow-patched rocks rising all around, the summit Totensee ("Dead Lake") icy all summer, and stunning sunset views down over the Grimselsee just below. The ⚐ *Grimselblick* (☎027 973 11 77, ⓦwww.grimselpass.ch; ❶) is the best on offer, a cosy place once the daytime tour buses have departed, with one particularly enticing ensuite double room, complete with four-poster bed, that's worth asking for. On the other side of the lake is the simpler *Alpenrösli* (☎033 973 12 91; ❶). Three buses a day (July–Sept) run from Oberwald to Meiringen (see p.302) via the Grimsel Pass.

Travel details

Full timetables for all trains, buses, trams, boats and cable cars in Switzerland – as well as international connections – are searchable at ⓦwww.rail .ch. For details of trains to Zermatt and from Brig over the Furka and Oberalp passes, see ⓦwww .mgbahn.ch. For the route from Bern through the Lötschberg Tunnel to Brig and on into Italy, see ⓦwww.bls.ch.

Trains

Aigle to: Bex (hourly; 5min); Les Diablerets (hourly; 45min); Leysin (hourly; 25min); Martigny (every 30min; 20min); Geneva (twice hourly; 1hr 15min); St-Maurice (hourly; 10min).
Bex to: Aigle (hourly; 5min); Villars (hourly; 40min).
Brig to: Andermatt (twice hourly; 1hr 35min); Bern (hourly; 1hr 35min); Domodossola, Italy (twice hourly; 35min); Geneva (twice hourly; 2hr 20min); Martigny (twice hourly; 50min); Sion (3 hourly; 30min); Zermatt (twice hourly; 1hr 25min); Zürich (hourly; 2hr 40min).

Martigny to: Aigle (every 30min; 20min); Brig (twice hourly; 50min); Orsières (hourly; 25min); St-Maurice (twice hourly; 10min); Sierre (twice hourly; 25min); Sion (3 hourly; 15min); Verbier (hourly; 50min; change at Le Châble).
Sierre to: Brig (every 30min; 25min); Martigny (twice hourly; 25min); Montana (every 30min; 15min); Sion (twice hourly; 10min).
Sion to: Aigle (every 30min; 30min); Brig (3 hourly; 30min); Geneva (twice hourly; 1hr 45min); Martigny (3 hourly; 15min); Sierre (every 30min; 10min); Zermatt (hourly; 2hr; change at Visp).
Visp to: Zermatt (hourly; 1hr 5min).
Zermatt to: Brig (twice hourly; 1hr 25min); Visp (hourly; 1hr 5min).

Buses

Aigle to: Villars (every 2hr; 35min).
Brig to: Saas-Fee (hourly; 1hr 10min).
Le Châble to: Mauvoisin (July–Sept twice daily; 45min); Verbier (hourly; 25min).

7

VALAIS | Travel details

Crans to: Montana (continuously; 5min); Sion (hourly; 45min); Sierre (every 30min; 40–50min).

Les Diablerets to: Gstaad (5 daily; 50min); Villars (July–Sept 3 daily; 35min).

Leysin to: Château d'Oex (3 daily; 1hr 30min; change at Le Sépey).

Martigny to: Chamonix, France (hourly; 1hr 30min); Grand-St-Bernard Pass (1 daily; 2hr; change at Orsières).

Montana to: Crans (continuously; 5min); Sierre (every 30min; 40–50min).

Orsières to: Champex (every 2hr; 20min).

Saas-Fee to: Brig (hourly; 1hr 10min); Stalden (hourly; 40min).

Sierre to: Crans (every 30min; 40–50min); Montana (every 30min; 40–50min); Sion (hourly; 30min).

Sion to: Arolla (every 2hr; 1hr 20min; change at Les Haudères); Crans (hourly; 45min); Sierre (hourly; 30min).

Stalden to: Saas-Fee (hourly; 40min).

Villars to: Aigle (every 2hr; 35min); Les Diablerets (July–Sept 3 daily; 35min).

Visp to: Saas-Fee (hourly; 55min).

Luzern and Zentralschweiz

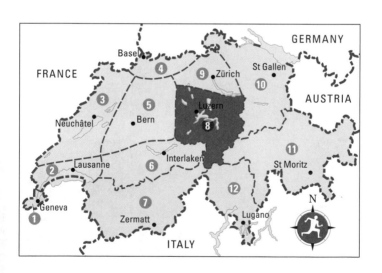

CHAPTER 8

Highlights

* **Vierwaldstättersee** Experience beautiful Lake Luzern from the deck of an old-time steamer. **See p.366**

* **Luzerner Fasnacht** The biggest carnival in Switzerland. **See p.369**

* **Sammlung Rosengart** Gallery of modern art in central Luzern, focusing on Picasso and Klee. **See p.372**

* **Pilatus** Craggy giant that rises just behind Luzern, easily accessible by rack railway and cable car. **See p.372**

* **Glasi Hergiswil** Small-town glassworks that offers a superb free tour. **See p.380**

* **Weg der Schweiz** Scenic lakeside walking route in William Tell country. **See p.383**

* **Titlis** Year-round skiing and snowboarding above the village of Engelberg. **See p.384**

* **Rigi** With three routes up, this is a popular way to take in the views from 2000m. **See p.386**

* **Einsiedeln** Benedictine monastery housing the venerated Black Madonna. **See p.393**

* **Gotthard Pass** Switzerland's most famous Alpine pass, dividing northern Europe from the south. **See p.398**

△ Luzern

Luzern and Zentralschweiz

T he oddly shaped **Vierwaldstättersee** ("Lake of the Four Forest Cantons") lies at the geographical and spiritual heart of Switzerland. It's the country's most beautiful and dramatic body of water by far, thickly wooded slopes rising sheer from misty wavelets, bays and peninsulas giving constantly changing views from vantage points on the decks of the steamers which ply to and fro. At the lake's western tip, **Luzern** (often anglicized to **Lucerne**) is an attractive town steeped in history that is a natural gateway to the diverse **Zentralschweiz** region all around.

Zentralschweiz – or, as it is often dubbed, **Innerschweiz** – is a land of tradition. Here, in the tidy villages of Switzerland's core, is where the founding myths of the country are nurtured. In the Middle Ages, the communities of the four so-called "forest cantons" dotted around the lake – **Uri**, **Schwyz**, **Nidwalden** and **Obwalden** (the last two often conflated into one as "**Unterwalden**") – guarded the approaches to the **Gotthard Pass**, key to the newly opened road between northern and southern Europe. When Habsburg overlords tried to encroach on their privileges, the communities formed an alliance at the lakeside Rütli Meadow in 1291 which was to prove the beginning of the Swiss Confederation. Luzern, as the principal market town for the region, was drawn into the bond shortly after, and tales soon began to circulate of a legendary figure from the Uri countryside named **William Tell**, who had pitted his wits against the local Habsburg tyrant and won. Today, the clifftop paths and shoreline trails of this region are trod less by foreigners than by a tide of Swiss tourists who make

---

The Vierwaldstättersee stutter

The large lake lying at the centre of Switzerland has five different names, depending on the language you happen to be speaking. In German, it is the Vierwaldstättersee; in French, Le Lac des Quatre-Cantons; in Italian, Il Lago dei Quattro Cantoni; and in Romansh, Il Lai dals Quatter Chantuns – all of which translate as "The Lake of the Four (Forest) Cantons". However, these tongue-twisters are all way too much for most English-speaking tourists, and so for as long as foreigners have been coming to the lake, it's been dubbed the **Lake of Lucerne** or **Lake Luzern** – names you'll never hear Swiss people using to one another.

LUZERN AND ZENTRALSCHWEIZ

Zürich ▲   Zürich ▲

Wädenswil   Zürichsee   Rapperswil
                              Pfäffikon

Olten ◄

Baar
Cham
                    Zug
        Zuger-
        see   Biberbrugg

        Unterägeri
                    Ägerisee   Sihl-
                    Wildspitz   see
        ZUG   1580m   Morgarten   Einsiedeln
Küssnacht SCHWYZ   1244m
                                        Gschwändstock
        Rigi   1616m
Luzern 1798m ▲ Arth
        Kaltbad   Goldau   Kl. Mythen
Kriens   ▲1811m
Emmental ◄ Weggis   Urmiberg   Gr. Mythen
        Vitznau   1899m
        Vierwald-   Schwyz
Kehrsiten   Gersau
Pilatus Bürgenstock   Brunnen
2120m Hergiswil   Ennetbürgen   Morschach
Stansstad   Buochs stättersee   Fronalpstock
        Beckenried   Seelisberg   1922m
Alpnachstad   Emmetten Rütli Sisikon
                    Klewenalp Urner-
Stans   Buochserhorn 1593m   see Tellsplatte
Brienz ◄ 1807m NIDWALDEN
        Dallenwil   URI   Bauen
Stanserhorn   Isleten
Sarnen 1898m   Brisen   Flüelen
        Gräfmattstand 2404m
        2050m   Altdorf
                    Uri-Rotstock   Bürglen
        NIDWALDEN ▲2928m
        OBWALDEN   Klausenpass
Heitlistock   Bälmeten
▲2146m   ▲2414m
Melchsee- Graustock Sunnigenstock
Frutt   2662m▲ Engelberg 2395m   Erstfeld
Hohmad   Schlossberg
2441m Jochpass Titlis 3133m
        Wendenstock 3239m Gross Spannort
        3042m   3199m
Meiringen ◄   Bristen
        Giglistock   ▲3072m
        ▲2900m Sustenpass
                Fleckistock
        BERN   3416m Wassen
        URI
        Hoch Horefellistock   Rienzenstock Disentis/
        ▲3175m Göschenen   2957m   Mustér
Diechterhorn   Oberalppass
3389m
        Galenstock   Spitzberg
Meiringen ◄ 3583m   2935m
        Winterstock Hospental Andermatt
        3203m
        Realp   Gemsstock   GRAU-
Rhonegletscher   2961m   BÜNDEN
Furkapass   TICINO
Grimselpass   URI Gotthardpass
BERN Oberwald Tällistock TICINO Lukmanierpass
VALAIS 2861m
        Saashorner La Fibbia
        Blashorn 3036m 2739m Airolo
        2777m
Brig ◄ Nufenenpass

N

0   10 km

Bellinzona ▼

the journey from their suburban homes to walk in the footsteps of William Tell and the semi-mystical founders of the nation.

Transport links around the region are excellent, with the fleet of lake steamers from Luzern running throughout the year, serving shoreside villages and small resorts tucked against the sugarloaf cliffs that have limited or no road access. In addition, a handful of rack railways serve mountain tops around the lake (most famously the **Pilatus** and the **Rigi**), and plenty of easy short- and long-distance hiking trails can get you well off the beaten path – although many also hop conveniently from one landing-stage to the next. Central Switzerland's long-standing tradition of tourism means that every hamlet has its choice of hotels and restaurants. The array of sights, excursions, museums and activities makes this one of the densest, and most rewarding, areas of the country to explore.

Luzern

There's nothing really wrong with Lucerne, except the people who go there.

John Russell, *Switzerland* (1950)

An hour south of Basel and Zürich, and boasting invigorating mountain views, lake cruises and a picturesque old quarter, **LUZERN** (**Lucerne** in French and English, Lucerna in Italian) has long been one of Europe's most heavily touristed towns. When Queen Victoria came for a long holiday in August 1868 (checking in under the pseudonym of the "Countess of Kent"), the town was already well known, and a century of steady growth has resulted these days in five million admirers passing through annually. Tourism is the leading source of income, which in recent years has led, in some quarters, to a rather blasé attitude towards visitors: although the city has retained a good deal of charm, the

△ The Hofkirche, Luzern

same can't be said of all its restaurant waiters and hotel staff. You may find your experience of the city, in the summer high season in particular, being coloured by association with the hordes of short-stay trippers that rush through on their way to the mountains.

The **River Reuss** splits the town, flowing rapidly out of the northwestern end of the lake. Both banks are clustered with medieval squares, frescoed houses, ancient guildhalls, churches and chapels, and filled with a commercially minded liveliness that belies the city's age. Aside from using Luzern as a base from which to explore the region, it would be easy to spend at least a couple of days taking in some of its quality museums – the outstanding **Rosengart gallery**, a unique **Picasso museum**, the impressive **Verkehrshaus** – in between walking on the medieval **battlements**, and exploring cobbled alleys and hidden garden courtyards.

But Luzern is no museum piece; the city's large population of young people love their café culture, and at midnight on a weekend night, the main Pilatusstrasse boulevard has the buzz of any European capital, with people bar-hopping, waiting for the last bus, or hanging out deciding where to go. Whether you're charmed by Luzern's sense of history and tradition, or by the misty lake at its doorstep and the snow-capped Pilatus rising above, or even by the nightlife, charmed is what you'll be.

Some history

Luzern's founding is lost in history. The town's name probably derives from the Celtic word *lozzeria*, meaning "a settlement on marshy ground", and that's more or less all Luzern was in the mid-eighth century when the small Benedictine **monastery** which existed here is thought to have come under the control of the Alsatian Abbey of Murbach. Nothing concrete is known about Luzern until 1178, when an abbot established a lay order at the Kapellkirche (now St Peter's Chapel), indicating that quite a substantial settlement must have existed in the area. Around 1220, the opening of the **Gotthard Pass** further south created new impetus for growth, with merchants and travellers setting sail from Luzern for the long trans-Alpine journey (the first lakeside road was built only in 1865).

Eyeing the prosperity flowing into the communities on the northern side of the new pass, Rudolf of Habsburg bought Luzern outright from Murbach in 1291, intending to subdue it and channel its profits into the imperial coffers. At the same time, though, the peasant farmers of Uri, Schwyz and Unterwalden on the eastern shores of the lake had formed a pact of mutual defence at **Rütli** (see box p.382) against the Austrian threat, and after some instability, Luzern joined them in 1332, the first major city to do so. This pact was the beginning of the Swiss Confederation, which survives today. Pro-Habsburg attempts to undermine the pact continued to flourish; one legend from the time tells of a boy who overheard conspirators meeting in the riverside marketplace at Unter der Egg. The plotters caught the boy and forced him to swear under oath that he would tell no living soul what he had heard them discuss, so the boy ran straight to a nearby guildhall and interrupted a Confederate meeting to tell his whole story to the tiled stove in the corner of the room. The confederates "overheard" the boy's tale, and so were able to thwart the plot. (The stove which stands today in the corner of the restaurant *Metzgern* on Weinmarkt is allegedly the self-same one.) The defeat of Austrian forces in the **Battle of Sempach** in 1386 severed the Habsburg claim to Luzern, and the city's elders reinforced their independence by building the Musegg fortifications, which are still standing.

Luzern remained Catholic throughout the Reformation and, like much of the country, was ruled by patrician families up until the late eighteenth-century revolutions. The early nineteenth-century quarrels in politics and religion led to civil war, with Luzern at the heart of the Catholic rebel **Sonderbund** (see p.569) – an association which, after Confederate forces had reasserted their control in 1847, led to Luzern being passed over for the choice of federal capital.

By this time, though, **tourism** to Switzerland had already begun, and with the cessation of hostilities Luzern became a focus for the increasing tide of foreign visitors, both for its own lakeside location, and as the gateway to the high Alps. In 1834, the mid-thirteenth-century Hofbrücke, which had linked the Hofkirche to the Old Town across a now-vanished marshy inlet, was torn down in favour of redeveloping the city centre and creating new lakeside promenades. Many old buildings and part of the medieval fortifications – with over forty towers and gates – were destroyed. The railway arrived in 1859, and over the following fifty years, Luzern's population quadrupled to forty thousand, with tourism, then as now, the mainstay of the city's economy.

All through the twentieth century, Luzern has clung tight onto its conservative, traditional roots: these days, the city is renowned as the heartland of Switzerland's SVP, an extreme right-wing political party with a strident and increasingly successful set of anti-immigration, anti-EU policies.

Arrival, information and lake transport

Luzern's giant **train station** – opened in 1991 to replace the grand nineteenth-century original which burned to the ground in 1971 (one arch survives, marooned in front of the new building) – is on the south bank of the Reuss, exactly at the point where the lake narrows into the river. Broad **Pilatusstrasse** runs southwest from Bahnhofplatz into the main shopping and commercial districts of the modern city. From the busy bus stops outside the station, the main Seebrücke takes traffic over the Reuss alongside the ancient **Kapellbrücke**, the latter marked by the distinctive stone Wasserturm (water tower). The pedestrian-only alleys of the Old Town occupy the northern bank, with the city walls ranged on the slopes above, as well as a small part of the southern bank.

Luzern's festivals

Luzern's two biggest festivals come from opposite ends of the cultural spectrum. February's **carnival** (see box p.369) features the biggest celebrations in the country, with six days and nights of continuous drinking and raucous partying. The city also plays host to one of Europe's most prestigious classical music events, the **Lucerne Festival** (@www.lucernefestival.ch), inaugurated in 1938 with a concert conducted by Arturo Toscanini in the grounds of Wagner's lakeside house at Tribschen. The festival comprises three separate elements. The "Sommer" event, in August and September, is the main one, a concert cycle held in venues ranging from the stunning KKL concert hall to town churches and even the Löwendenkmal that draws the world's finest soloists and orchestras. Smaller offshoots – "Ostern" at Easter, with a mix of classic and contemporary, sacred and secular music; and "Piano" in November, focusing on keyboard soloists in jazz and the classics – fill out the annual programme. Luzern also has an array of other music festivals, including two major blues events, in July and November. The fourth Saturday in June is the day of the **Altstadtfest** – the Old Town filled with oompah bands and food and beer stalls – while July sees prestigious international **rowing** regattas held on the Rotsee, a long, narrow lake 2km north of town.

LUZERN

ACCOMMODATION

Backpackers	P
City	K
Des Alpes	H
Des Balances	L
Falken	E
Hofgarten	C
Jailhotel	
Löwengraben	G
Jugendherberge	A
Krone	J
Montana	B
Palace	D
Pickwick	I
Schlüssel	N
The Hotel	O
Tourist	F
Wilden Mann	M

EATING & DRINKING

Bahnhof Buffet	17
Boa	25
Bodu	9
Galliker	13
Heini's Tearoom	5
Hug	11
Jazz Kantine	6
Korea-Town	19
Mahlzeit	20
Maihöfli	2
Opus	14
Parterre	22
Penthouse	18
Rathaus Brauerei	10
Reussbad	4
St Magdalena	7
Salü	21
Schiff	12
Seebar	16
Spaghetteria Valentino	8
Sunset Bar	3
Schüür	23
Sedel	1
Wärchhof	24
World Café	15

If you're **driving**, try to arrange parking with your hotel or leave your vehicle in the suburbs: Luzern is just about the most car-hostile city in Switzerland, with a fiendish one-way system woven tightly around the pedestrianized Old Town. There's little chance of finding a parking space on the street and the few, expensive parking garages are often full.

Information

The **tourist office** has entrances on platform 3 of the train station and at
Zentralstrasse 5 (mid-June to mid-Sept Mon–Fri 8.30am–7.30pm, Sat &
Sun 9am–7.30pm; May to mid-June & mid-Sept to Oct daily closes 7pm;
Nov–April Mon–Fri 8.30am–5.30pm, Sat & Sun 9am–1pm; ☎041 227 17
17, ⓦwww.luzern.org). With the vast quantity of tourists tramping through

the city, staff are well used to answering questions, and have stacks of information to impart – but you should be prepared to queue at peak times. Luzern's **guest card**, which you must get stamped by your hotel, is good value, giving discounts on entry to most museums and car rental; it also allows you to purchase a special Fr.14 three-day city bus pass (although Swiss Pass holders travel free anyway). The excellent two-hour city **walking tour** (May–Oct daily 9.45am; Nov–April Wed & Sat 9.45am; Fr.20) departs from the tourist office.

Lake transport

The Vierwaldstättersee, or **Lake Luzern**, is crossed year-round by the fine old boats of the SGV (☎041 367 67 67, ⊕www.lakelucerne.ch), free to Swiss Pass holders. All SGV boats – including their half-dozen paddle steamers (which incur no extra fare) – depart from the quay directly outside the station, stopping at places on both shores: **Alpnachstad** gives access to the Pilatus summit; **Weggis** and **Vitznau** to Mount Rigi; **Kehrsiten** to Bürgenstock, and from there to the Hammetschwand summit; and **Beckenried** to Klewenalp. All of these have limited road and rail connections, but at the far, eastern end of the lake, **Brunnen** (close to Schwyz) and **Flüelen** (close to Altdorf) are less than an hour's train journey from Luzern on the Zürich–Lugano main line, making it easy to construct half- and full-day round trips by boat and train.

In summer (June–Sept), at least seven boats daily make the full run from Luzern to Flüelen, with several more serving Brunnen, Vitznau and other intermediate points. In autumn (Oct) and spring (April & May), service is slightly curtailed in the evenings. Winter (Nov–March) sees two boats a day as far as Brunnen, with Flüelen served only by Sunday services. SGV also runs **cruises** and eat-aboard trips, including a three-hour summer sunset excursion.

Accommodation

Accommodation covers the gamut from dorms to palaces. Summer is especially busy, with double-room prices in many hotels rising almost fifty percent: an establishment we've listed at ❺ to reflect high-season prices might charge ❸ prices between October and April. Booking ahead is a priority across all price brackets.

Inexpensive hotels

Des Alpes Furrengasse 3 ☎041 410 58 25, ⊕www.desalpes-luzern.ch. Comfortable rooms, some with balconies, in an old building with a picturesque waterfront setting and a good restaurant. ❹

City Baselstrasse 15 ☎041 240 23 23, ⊕www .hotelguide.com. Basic place a little west of the centre on a busy street (so ask for a back room), with poky, generic rooms that are nonetheless kept clean. ❷

Falken Falkengasse 6 ☎041 410 37 37, ⊕www .hotel-falken.ch. Plain, decent, generic "garni" place in the Old Town, with compact, characterless rooms that just about do the job. Rates fall by thirty percent out of season (Nov–May). ❸

🏃 **Jailhotel Löwengraben** Löwengraben 18 ☎041 410 78 30, ⊕www.jailhotel.ch. Luzern's Old Town prison from 1862 to 1998, now

converted into a surprisingly classy budget hotel, with a hip, lively atmosphere. The staff frogmarch you down the long corridors to the refurbished cells – inevitably poky, but complete with ensuite shower cubicle and barred windows. Of the larger rooms, go for the panelled Director's Suite, the former prison governor's office, with a queen-size bed where the desk used to be, or the top-priced Falling Waters Suite, once the visiting room, also with a queen-size bed and sofa. ❷–❸

Pickwick Rathausquai 6 ☎041 410 59 27, ⊕www.hotelpickwick.ch. In spartan contrast to *Des Alpes* next door, an English-style pub with rooms above, sharing the excellent views but not the welcoming management style of its neighbour. No breakfast served. ❷

Schlüssel Franziskanerplatz 12 ☎041 210 10 61. The most characterful low-end accommodation in

town, and the oldest hotel in Luzern to boot. Only ten rooms, some of which overlook the quiet square of the Franciscan church and the formal gardens of the eighteenth-century Segesser mansion. ❷
Tourist St Karliquai 12 ☎041 410 24 74, 🌐www .touristhotel.ch. Clean, bright and very central, this has the atmosphere of a student dorm although the quality of the rooms (and the helpful management) speak more of a houseproud, good-value hotel. Some have suntrap balconies facing the river – peaceful, since the bankside road is quiet. ❷–❸

Mid-range and expensive
Des Balances Weinmarkt ☎041 418 28 28, 🌐www.balances.ch. A reverentially white lobby preludes a super-chic Old Town hotel, more reminiscent of midtown Manhattan than little Luzern. Understated elegance is the watchword. Back rooms overlook the water. ❻–❼

🏃 **Hofgarten** Stadthofstrasse 14 ☎041 410 88 88, 🌐www.hofgarten.ch. The best-value hotel in Luzern, and one of the most attractive small city hotels in the country. A centuries-old protected building set in a quiet courtyard near the Hofkirche, with an excellent vegetarian terrace restaurant and eighteen modern, individually decorated rooms, all fresh, bright and carefully furnished. ❺–❻

🏃 **The Hotel** Sempacherstrasse 14 ☎041 226 86 86, 🌐www.the-hotel.ch. Outstanding boutique hotel overlooking a quiet city-centre park, designed by architect Jean Nouvel and featuring chic, modern suites and studios decorated in dark, matt tones and brushed steel. Each guest room has a huge still image from a classic movie covering the ceiling, adding to the hip allure. ❼–❽
Krone Weinmarkt 12 ☎041 419 44 00, 🌐www .krone-luzern.ch. Friendly, bright boutique hotel in the heart of the Old Town, with spacious, contemporary styled rooms – crisp linen, wood floors and muted tones. ❺–❻

🏃 **Montana** Adligenswilerstrasse 22 ☎041 419 00 00, 🌐www.hotel-montana.ch. Exceptionally classy Art-Deco hotel on a hillside above the lake,

reached by its own funicular and boasting spectacular views. The 1920s-style decor is faultless, and rooms are generous and attractive. Often rated as the best four-star hotel in the country. ❻–❽
Palace Haldenstrasse 10 ☎041 416 16 16, 🌐www.palace-luzern.com. A giant Belle Epoque landmark catering to the ritziest of traditional five-star tastes, revelling both in wide-open views across the lake to Mount Pilatus, and the grandest of appointments to the broad, lofty guest rooms. With the huge *Kursaal* next door and the *Grand Hotel National* just beyond, these three edifices between them occupy half a kilometre of the city waterfront. ❽–❾

🏃 **Wilden Mann** Bahnhofstrasse 30 ☎041 210 16 66, 🌐www.wilden-mann.ch. Outstanding choice in this price-bracket, a historic hotel dating back to 1517 that occupies seven adjoining town houses amidst the atmospheric south-bank Old Town lanes: opposite is an antique pharmacy, behind is the medieval mint. Rooms are generous, tastefully decorated with plenty of rich wood, and quiet, while the service has an elusive blend of alertness and subtlety often lacking in grander places. Member of the Romantik group. ❻–❼

Hostels
Backpackers (SB hostel) Alpenquai 42 ☎041 360 04 20, 🌐www.backpackerslucerne.ch. Friendly former student house on the lakeshore 800m southeast of the station; take bus #6, #7 or #8 to Weinbergli, then head left for 150m. Pleasant dorms cost Fr.29; also basic doubles. ❶
Jugendherberge (HI hostel) Sedelstrasse 12 ☎041 420 88 00, 🌐www.youthhostel.ch. Quality hostel 1km northwest of town near the Rotsee lake; bus #18 to Jugendherberge. Dorms Fr.33.50. ❶

Campsite
Lido Lidostrasse 8 ☎041 370 21 46, 🌐www .camping-international.ch. Right by the Verkehrshaus, also with some dorm beds (Fr.20). Open all year.

The City

Evidence of Luzern's medieval prosperity is manifest in the frescoed facades of its **Old Town** and the two surviving covered wooden bridges which span the River Reuss, both formerly part of the city's fortifications (and so with higher defensive side walls facing away from the town) and both boasting unique triangular paintings fixed to their roof-beams. The **Sammlung Rosengart**, one of Switzerland's finest art museums, lurks on the busy Pilatusstrasse, while the excellent **Verkehrshaus** – an entertaining complex devoted to transport, also with an IMAX cinema – is just around the lakeshore.

The Kapellbrücke

Any tour of Luzern must begin with the fourteenth-century covered **Kapell-brücke** (Chapel Bridge), the oldest road bridge in Europe, angled around the octagonal mid-river **Wasserturm**. In deference to the fact that the city's development arose largely from defence of this bridge, its distinctive Wasserturm (formerly a lighthouse, a prison, a treasury and today serving as a meeting house) has come to stand as the symbol of Luzern. Disaster struck in the early hours of August 18, 1993, when a small boat moored alongside the bridge caught fire and the flames rapidly spread to engulf the whole structure. By dawn, virtually the entire bridge had been destroyed, with only the bridgeheads on both banks surviving. The authorities set about reconstruction, and an identical replacement was completed nine months later; today, it's easy to see where the old wood meets the new.

Before the fire, the principal historical interest of the bridge lay in its collection of double-sided triangular **roof panels**, painted in the seventeenth century with scenes from the city's past and present. Of the 111 panels, 65 were entirely ruined and had to be replaced with facsimiles, 30 were restored, and the remainder are still charred and impossible to make out. Each is numbered, and captioned with rhyming couplets, the idiosyncratic local dialect written out in obscure medieval gothic script. The most distinctive image is panel no. 31, which shows **William Tell** shooting the apple from his son's head, but it's fun to work your way slowly along. Panel no. 1 shows a giant, the first Luzerner; no. 3 Luzern in the earliest times, with the Hofkirche separated from the town by a bridged inlet; no. 4 the foundation of Luzern's monastery; no. 6 the town around 1600; no. 15 St Beatus (see p.299); no. 16 Einsiedeln (see p.393); no. 17 Luzern's Franciscan church; no. 26 local hero Winkelried slaying a dragon; no. 32 the Rütli oath; no. 38 the great fire of Luzern in 1340; and no. 58 the 1476 Battle of Grandson (see p.180).

Just downstream, the **Spreuerbrücke** is also worth a look for its macabre "Dance of Death" roof panels. These begin at the northern bankside with a little verse:

> All living things that fly or leap
> Or crawl or swim or run or creep
> Fear Death, yet can they find no spot
> In all the world where Death is not.

The succession of images shows a grinning skeleton leading kings, gallant princes, lawmen, nuns, merchants, prostitutes, peasants and maidens alike to their inevitable fate. The final panel, predictably enough, shows a majestic Christ vanquishing bony Death.

The Old Town

The north bank of the Reuss is home to the **Old Town**'s most atmospheric cluster of medieval houses, with Mühlenplatz, Weinmarkt, Hirschenplatz and Kornmarkt forming a compact ensemble of cobbled, fountained squares ringed by colourful facades. Modern commerce is definitely the motive force of the place these days, and it takes some imagination to conjure up the Middle Ages amidst the welter of shoppers and familiar brand-names.

Kapellplatz, at the bridgehead of the Kapellbrücke, encircles the tiny eighteenth-century **St-Peterskapelle**, built over a predecessor dating from as early as 1178. Some 150m west is **Kornmarkt**, site of the medieval public marketplace. On one side, overlooking the riverside market area of Unter der Egg, is the huge **Rathaus**, completed in 1606 in Italian Renaissance style but crowned with an incongruous Emmentaler-style roof. The market atmosphere survives today, with vegetable, fish and flower stalls doing a roaring trade every Tuesday and Saturday morning. Kornmarktgasse runs west to the atmospheric frescoed **Weinmarkt**, where Passion Plays were staged in the late Middle Ages.

Carnival!

Luzern's infamously raucous six-day all-in **carnival** (⊕ www.luzerner-fasnacht.ch), ending on Mardi Gras night, is the biggest and best in Switzerland, a genuinely participatory event which knocks Basel's stand-and-watch parades into a cocked hat. It's worth going a long way out of your way to visit, even though the streets of the Old Town get more and more crammed with revellers year-on-year.

Celebrations are focused around three "official" carnival days. The Thursday before Mardi Gras is dubbed **Schmotzig Donnschtig**, or Dirty Thursday; the following Monday is **Güdis Määntig**, or Fat Monday; while Mardi Gras itself (Fat Tuesday) is **Güdis Ziischtig**. *Güdis* comes from the dialect word *Güdel*, meaning belly, while *Schmotzig*, or dirty, has its roots in the word for grease or fat: carnival was traditionally a time for excess, to lay in some high-calorie *Fasnachtsküechli*, fried sweet layered pastry, before Lenten fasting.

Luzern's carnival is centred on the figure of **Fritschi**, mentioned as early as 1443 and later subsumed into the legends surrounding a victory at the Battle of Ragaz on March 6, 1446. (March 6 was the day of Fridolin, patron saint of Glarus, and Fritschi is a diminutive of Fridolin.) Originally Fritschi was a lifesize straw doll carried through Luzern accompanied by **Fritschene**, his "wife"; these days a costumed couple take their place. Around the middle of the eighteenth century, the two were joined on parade by a nanny, a jester named Bajazzo and some musicians.

To this day, Fritschi begins Luzern's carnival, at 5am on the morning of Dirty Thursday, when he and his entourage lean out of an upper window of the **Rathaus** on Kornmarkt as a cannon signals the start of festivities. From breakfast time onwards, bands of masked and costumed musicians, dancers and acrobats roam the Old Town streets, some performing **Guggenmusig** – comical oompah played on a handful of dented trombones and percussion – while others set up stages to give impromptu gigs to the promenading costumed crowds. The highlight of the day is the evening **Fritschi parade**, where Fritschi, Fritschene and the rest are paraded through the Old Town and around Löwenplatz, all the while flinging oranges out to carousing onlookers.

Friday, Saturday and Sunday aren't official carnival days, but nonetheless see plenty of activity: there are parties around the town on Friday and Saturday nights, with bars open late and lots of live music in the streets and clubs. **Fat Monday** is when carnival really takes off, with strolling musicians and *commedia dell'arte* pantomime players roaming the cafés and restaurants, and all the Old Town squares taken over by exuberant mass dancing. Monday night's raucously chaotic parade is broadcast live on Swiss TV, and Old Town bars are given special all-night licences in preparation for **Fat Tuesday**, Mardi Gras itself. The climax of carnival is a **Monsterkonzert**, the grand finale of all the bands performing together throughout the Old Town on the Tuesday night, accompanied by plenty of eating, drinking and merrymaking, a mighty blowout which lasts until 4am. Two hours later, street cleaners arrive to restore order, and respectably groomed and suited businesspeople return to Luzern's early-morning cafés to begin real life again amidst the exhausted revellers of the night before, many of whom will be nursing breakfast beers while still in their fancy dress and face paint.

Just off Kornmarkt, at Furrengasse 21, is Am Rhyn-Haus, a restored seventeenth-century building housing the fascinating **Picasso Museum** (daily: April–Oct 10am–6pm; Nov–March 11am–5pm; Fr.8; joint ticket with Sammlung Rosengart Fr.18; SMP; ⓦ www.kulturluzern.ch/picasso-museum): mainly late drawings, ceramics and a sheet-iron sculpture *Femme au Chapeau* (1963/64). The most striking works are a series of five tender portraits of Angela Rosengart – international art dealer and friend of Picasso – done over twelve years from 1954 to 1966. The highlight of the museum is an array of nearly two hundred intimate and often brilliant photographs of the artist's private life taken by American photographer David Douglas Duncan from 1956 until Picasso's death in 1973.

The battlements walk

A short stroll west from Weinmarkt along riverside St Karliquai past the sophisticated-looking hydroelectric turbines on the Reuss (which have had teething problems since they were installed, and still regularly clog up with silt) brings you to the **Nölliturm**, a fortified gate marking the southwestern extent of a lengthy stretch of the surviving fourteenth-century town walls. Pass through the gate and head right up the hill to gain access to the Musegg **battlements** (Easter–Sept daily 8am–7pm) and their impressive views. This is an oddly rustic corner of Luzern, cut off from the city behind the walls, and you may come across a cow or two quietly grazing back here, resident of a part-time urban farm. Stairs rise to the top of both the **Männliturm** and, further along, the **Luegisland-Turm**, but the battlements walk proper starts at the **Wachtturm**. From here, you can follow the parapets along to the **Zytturm**, with the oldest clock in Luzern (granted the honour of chiming one minute before all the others in the town). The bizarrely ugly statue down below is *Unweib* by local artist Rudolf Blätter, such an unpopular addition that the municipality had to unveil it in secret one evening a few years back. The rooftop walk continues to the adjacent **Schirmerturm**, gutted by an arsonist in 1994 and still bearing smoke-blackened stones. This is where the battlements walk runs out, but you can descend to follow the road through the Schirmerturm gate and down tranquil Museggstrasse through another breach in the old wall to the traffic-choked Löwenplatz.

Löwenplatz and around

Just northeast of Löwenplatz is one of the highlights of Luzern, the terribly sad **Löwendenkmal** (**Lion Monument**). This wounded beast – dubbed "the Dying Lion of Lucerne" – draped over his shield, with a broken spear sticking out of his flank, was hewn out of a cliff face in 1821 to commemorate the 700 Swiss mercenaries killed in Paris in 1792. On August 10 that year, French revolutionaries stormed the royal palace, the Tuileries; in the face of the mob, the Swiss palace guards were ordered to lay down their arms by Louis XVI and so were massacred. This would be a movingly tranquil spot, with its foliage and gently rippling pool in front, were it not for the fact that it's the single most touristed place in the entire city.

Adjacent are a handful of nineteenth-century tourist attractions, quaint and rather old-fashioned today. The "Lion Pass" **joint ticket** for all three of them costs Fr.17. The **Gletschergarten**, Denkmalstrasse 4 (Glacier Garden; daily: April–Oct 9am–6pm; Nov–March 10am–5pm; Fr.12; SMP; ⓦ www .gletschergarten.ch), holds within its grounds a fusty museum of old relief maps, a wonderful Mirror Maze (built in 1896 and restored in mock-Moorish style) and a set of geological potholes telling of the subtropical ocean beach that was

Luzern twenty million years ago. The **Alpineum** opposite (April–Oct daily 9am–12.30pm & 1.30–6pm; Fr.5; SMP; ⓦwww.alpineum.ch) is a relic from a bygone age: static models of Alpine scenes behind glass no doubt sparked the imagination of our great-grandparents, but today they barely merit a glance. More impressive is the **Bourbaki Panorama** (daily 9am–6pm; Fr.8; SMP; ⓦwww.bourbakipanorama.ch), a giant 110m-by-10m circular mural housed in a glass building on Löwenplatz; it depicts the retreat into Switzerland of the French Eastern Army under General Bourbaki during the Franco-Prussian War of 1870–71. Sound effects and good background information go some way to bridge the gap between nineteenth- and twenty-first-century attention spans.

The Hofkirche

Busy Löwenstrasse runs south from Löwenplatz to the riverside; just before you reach the Schweizerhofquai, the arrow-straight St-Leodegarstrasse cuts east to broad steps leading up to the **Hofkirche** (Sat–Thurs 10am–noon & 2–5pm). This grand structure sits on the site of the first monastery of Luzern, which dated from the mid-eighth century and was dedicated to St Leodegar (St Leger). The Romanesque church which replaced the monastery in the late twelfth century was burned to the ground on Easter Sunday 1633, the blaze reputedly sparked by the verger's careless shooting at birds. Only its twin **towers** escaped, and they survive today either side of a bizarrely incongruous Renaissance gable. The impressive main doors are carved with the two patron saints of Luzern: on the left is **St Leger**, a French bishop who was blinded with a drill (which he is holding), and on the right is **St Maurice**, a martyred Roman soldier-saint.

The interior design and furniture are almost wholly original Renaissance from the 1630s and 1640s, a unity rarely found in Swiss or European churches, most of which underwent Baroque renovation and embellishment. On the right, elaborate **pews** divided into individual seats were reserved for city councillors; plainer pews on the left were for the rank and file. Beyond the exceptionally fine **choir screen** – one of the earliest examples of strong three-dimensional perspective used to draw the congregation's attention forward – is the **high altar** in black marble, flanked by statues of the two patron saints. Above the Italianate depiction of the Agony at Gethsemane is a half-length figure of God. The carved choir stalls, as well as the beautiful pulpit, are the work of Niklaus Geissler. Against the north wall (left) is the lavish **Death of the Virgin altar**, showing Mary on a bed surrounded by disciples: dating from around 1500, this was the only relic to survive the 1633 fire. The mighty **organ**, bedecked in ornament, features 2826 pipes, along with a machine to mimic the sound of rain and a special register for thunder and hail.

The church is set amidst a lovely Italianate **cloister**, lined with the graves of Luzerner patrician families (who continue to be buried here to this day). Old houses all around the church still serve as the homes for canons of the parish. Just west of the church is the ancient **Rothenburgerhaus**, a teetering pile that's held to be one of the oldest wooden town houses in the country, dating from about 1500. On the slopes north of the church is the old cemetery, now a public park, while about 500m further north on the hilltop is the Capuchin monastery of **Wesemlin**, founded in 1584 and still functioning as the principal seat of the order in Switzerland.

The south bank

The Old Town extends to the **south bank** of the Reuss, comprising a triangular area known as the Kleinstadt, originally walled. Facing Unter der Egg is the huge **Jesuitenkirche**, dominating the riverside with its twin onion-domed towers. Completed in 1673, its astonishing interior is a frothy Rococo concoction of gilt stucco and marble. Among the profusion of frescoes is one on the ceiling that, intriguingly, depicts the church exterior as it was 300 years ago. A few steps west is the **Rittersche palace**, built in 1557 in Florentine Renaissance style as a private mansion but now the seat of Luzern's cantonal government. Behind it to the south is the **Franziskanerkirche**, the oldest building in Luzern, dating from 1270 (though much restored). It's unusually richly decorated for a Franciscan church, with Renaissance choir stalls and battle standards lining the walls – copies of those looted from battlefields through the centuries. A Baroque side-chapel is decorated with Italianate stucco and a host of kitschy, curly-haired angels. Continuing west, peaceful Pfistergasse curves to meet the south side of the Spreuerbrücke, where you'll spot the stout, sixteenth-century town arsenal, now home to the **Historisches Museum** (Tues–Sun 10am–5pm; Fr.10; SMP; ⓦwww.hmluzern.ch), filled with arms and armour, restored interiors, costumes and crafts telling the history of Luzern.

Sammlung Rosengart

Busy, traffic-heavy Pilatusstrasse, lined with shops, cafés and banks, storms southwest from the station, defining the limits of the Old Town. About 100m along, and the same distance south of the Kapellbrücke, is a solid Neoclassical building from 1923 – formerly the Luzern headquarters of the Swiss National Bank, and now renovated to house the outstanding **Sammlung Rosengart** (Rosengart Collection; daily: April–Oct 10am–6pm, Nov–March 11am–5pm; Fr.15; joint ticket with Picasso Museum Fr.18; ⓦwww.rosengart.ch). Art dealers Siegfried Rosengart and his daughter Angela – the latter born in Luzern in 1932 and still a resident – built up over forty years a collection of more than

Above Luzern – Mount Pilatus

The giant mountain looming above Luzern to the southwest is **Mount Pilatus** (2132m; ⓦwww.pilatus.com), an odd name supposedly deriving from the myth that the corpse of Pontius Pilate was flung into a lake on the mountain, his spirit forever after haunting the summit and certain to bring tempest and damnation onto Luzern if disturbed. (More prosaically, it's probably derived from the Latin *pileatus*, meaning "capped" – ie with clouds.) There are two means of transport to the top, making it easy to do a half- or full-day round trip from Luzern – simpler than in 1868, when Queen Victoria made the excursion on muleback.

Boats and local trains run from Luzern to **Alpnachstad**, from where the **steepest rack-railway in the world** runs at a gradient touching 48 percent directly to the top of the mountain – the journey up is half-an-hour, while the journey down takes a careful forty minutes. The second route up the mountain starts at **Kriens** (connected to Luzern's city centre by bus #1); from here a gondola rises to Krienseregg and Fräkmüntegg, and then a cable car to the summit (total 30min). The Kriens–Pilatus route runs year-round, while the Alpnachstad–Pilatus railway is summer only (mid-June to mid-Nov). Most tour groups follow a circuit going up from Kriens – so you might want to go up from Alpnachstad instead, to avoid the crush.

On the top are two hotels, the *Bellevue* and *Kulm*, but if you're looking for an overnight mountain-top stay, you'd do better on the nearby Rigi (see p.386). The walk to the highest point of the mountain, the Tomlishorn, takes less than thirty minutes from the top station, with expansive views the whole way along the clifftop path. It's also easy to walk back to Luzern from Fräkmüntegg (2hr 30min), or to make your way down from the summit to Alpnachstad or Hergiswil (3hr) or Kriens (3hr 30min).

200 key twentieth-century works. A small number of Picassos, donated by the Rosengarts, form the basis of Luzern's separate Picasso Museum (see p.370).

The **ground floor** is devoted to a magnificent overview of **Picasso**'s art, from early paintings – including a statuesque *Portrait Alice Derain* dated 1905, when Picasso was 24 – through to works full of light and space painted in Cannes in the mid-1950s, and five exuberant canvases dated 1967–69, a few years before the artist's death.

The **basement** holds one of the broadest collections of works by **Paul Klee** in private hands, a seamless chronological record showing the development of Klee's fluent and compelling fantasy world. In the first room – ahead at the bottom of the stairs – Klee's visit to Tunisia is reflected in a number of colourful North African landscapes and the many works with Arab and Jewish elements. His expressive imagination takes hold in the second room, which includes the unsettling *Ironic Fairytale* (#69), featuring two jesters on the edge of a nebulous wood beneath a furious moon. One of the most characteristic (and memorable) sketches is *Little X* (#117), in the third room – a dozen simple brushstrokes that create a universe of childhood experience, lost in a bigger, more serious adult world.

The **upper floor** features a creatively assembled array of Impressionist and Modernist works, amongst them a room of Chagalls – including *Night at the Window* (1950), a distinctive scene of blissful lovers looking out over a sleeping town – two fine Monets, and works by Renoir, Modigliani, Kandinsky, Matisse and others.

The KKL

On a plum waterfront site beside the station and alongside the quays stands Luzern's pride and joy, the multifunctional *Kultur- und Kongresszentrum Luzern*, known as the **KKL** (pronounced "kaka-el"; ⓦ www.kkl-luzern.ch). Within such a traditional-looking and -thinking city, Jean Nouvel's landmark architecture in glass and steel is a revelation. Reflecting pools all around draw the lake into the building, as an immense cantilevered roof floats high above. The atmosphere of the place changes according to the weather conditions: standing on the lakeside apron during a storm – exposed yet protected by the roof – is quite an experience. Parts of the building may be taken up with conferences when you visit, and the concert halls are off-limits, but there's nothing to stop you exploring the public areas, which are well signed.

On the station side rises a huge, glazed block, fenced in by an all-enveloping steel cage and penetrating deep beneath the dark roof; this is the **Kongresszentrum** wing, with a bistro at ground level and the Kunstmuseum on the top floor. Beside it, at the centre of the complex, is the **Luzernersaal**, a small hall used for concerts or meetings, with a drinks terrace atop its foyer. The easterly third of the complex is the **Konzertsaal**, one of the world's most acoustically advanced concert halls, and the principal venue for the Lucerne Festival. Adjoining it at ground level is the trendy *Seebar*.

On the top floor of the KKL's Kongresszentrum wing – from the train station, take the exit by platform 15 and cross the street – is the **Kunstmuseum** (Tues–Sun 10am–5pm, Wed until 8pm; longer hours in Aug & Sept during Lucerne Festival; Fr.10; ⓦ www.kunstmuseumluzern.ch). Lifts take you up to the ticket desk (press button "K"). The permanent collection – less-than-stunning canvases by Swiss artists of the nineteenth and early twentieth century, displayed in the first half-dozen rooms – is overshadowed both by the ground-breaking exhibitions of avant-garde contemporary art held in the dozen or so rooms beyond, and by the breathtaking architecture: more than once you cross between galleries on slender catwalks high up in the building's interior, bathed in natural and artificial light with the reflecting pools far below.

Out of the centre

Although many of Luzern's sights are packed close together in the city centre, there are a few incentives to venture further afield. Facing each other across the lake roughly 2km out of the centre are the **Verkehrshaus** (Transport Museum) on the northern shore, and the **Richard Wagner museum**, the composer's former home, on the southern shore. Buses run close to both, but the way to get there in style is by **boat**.

The Verkehrshaus

One of the main draws of Luzern is the **Verkehrshaus**, 2km east of the centre at Lidostrasse 5 (Transport Museum; daily 10am–6pm; Nov–March closes 5pm; Fr.24; joint ticket including one IMAX film Fr.32; discounts available for families and rail-pass holders; SMP; ⓦ www.verkehrshaus.org). If you're not arriving by boat, hop on bus #6 or #8, or take the pleasant twenty-minute stroll around the lakeshore.

This vast complex is devoted to Swiss engineering skill and could keep you amused all day: you'll need the free plan to navigate your way around. It's divided into several large areas, taking in Road Transport, Rail Transport, Aviation and Space Travel, Cableways and Tourism, and so on. Everything is in English, and "hands-on" is a rule, not an exception. Particular highlights include the **train** section, with dozens of giant locomotives on display (complete with evocative oily smell) and a well-presented walk-through account of the digging of the Gotthard tunnel, dramatized with slides and soundtrack. The airplane section has flight simulators, a mock-up of an airport control-tower and the **Cosmorama**, an interactive tour of the asteroid belt. The tourism bit has the **Swissarena**, a composite aerial photograph of the entire country covering the floor of a 200-square-metre hall. There's also a huge section devoted to communications, an excellent **Planetarium** and a separate, giant building housing an **IMAX cinema** (regular showings throughout the day for an extra Fr.16; ⓦ www.imax.ch).

The Hans Erni Museum

In an entirely different vein, a far-flung building on the edge of the Verkehrshaus site – regrettably overlooked by most visitors – houses a fine museum dedicated to the Luzerner artist **Hans Erni** (same hours as Verkehrshaus; admission included with Verkehrshaus ticket, or Fr.12 for Hans Erni Museum only; ⓦ www.hanserni.ch). Erni, born in 1909, has spent his long career producing art that is wonderfully warm and human, full of fluidity of figures and geometries that the museum blurb will try to convince you is linked in some spiritual way to the scientific prowess on display throughout the rest of the complex; however, his concern for human dignity in the face of modern technology stands more as a healthy counterpoint to all those displays of engineering skill. Erni is not well known outside Switzerland, but this museum – displaying 300 works – merits a special visit. Particularly outstanding are Erni's lithographs, made as illustrations for limited-edition books.

The Richard Wagner museum

Southeast of the city centre, in an idyllic location on a headland named Tribschen, is a villa that was **Richard Wagner**'s home from 1866 to 1872, and is now a **museum** to him (March–Nov Tues–Sun 10am–noon & 2–5pm; Fr.6; SMP; boat to Tribschen; bus #6, #7 or #8 to Wartegg, then 5min walk; or 40min walk from station; ⓦwww.richard-wagner-museum.ch). After many visits to Switzerland, the composer and his partner Cosima – Franz Liszt's daughter, who was still legally married to the pianist and conductor Hans von Bülow – spotted the derelict Tribschen villa in early 1866, made arrangements to rent it for an extended period, and moved in on April 15. "Nobody will get me out of here again," Wagner said, and it's generally agreed that this was the happiest and most productive time of his life, not least because Cosima's long-dead marriage was finally dissolved in 1870 and the couple were able to marry. The tranquillity of the lakeside house is still tangible today, as you wander through the rooms laid out with Wagneriana of all kinds – letters, pictures, original furniture, instruments and even his death mask – with Wagner compositions playing in the background.

Eating, drinking and nightlife

Luzern has a fine range of **eating and drinking** venues covering all budgets: the crowded, generic places that are in plain view tend to be least interesting, but a small amount of backstreet searching will turn up plenty of more rewarding options.

   Local specialities to keep an eye out for are led by the celebrated *Luzerner Kügelipastete* – spelled by many Old Town restaurant menus in dialect, along the lines of *Lozärner Chögalipaschtetli*, also often prefixed by *ächti* ("authentic"). This stomach-lining dish is a glorified vol-au-vent, a large puff-pastry shell filled with a super-rich concoction of diced veal and mushrooms in a creamy sauce; veggie versions omitting the veal aren't hard to find. Otherwise, fish is the thing, in endless varieties: you'll see *Forellen* (trout), *Egli* (perch), *Felchen* (a kind of white fish) and *Hecht* (pike) on most menus, virtually all of it plucked fresh from the lake. Wash it all down either with a *Kaffee fertig*, a coffee laced with Schnapps, or a *Kafi Luz*, traditionally seen in Canton Luzern outside the city but nowadays easy to find in the Old Town cafés. The right way to make one is to put a five-franc coin in a vase-shaped glass, pour hot coffee in until you can't see the coin, then add Schnapps until the coin becomes visible again. Stir in two large spoons of sugar, and you have the perfect farmers' pick-me-up.

Cafés and café-bars

Cafés and **café-bars** crowd the waterfront and the Old Town squares, and do a roaring trade amongst the flood of tour groups passing through the town. Better places, frequented by locals, abound in less-trod corners, such as Helvetiaplatz. The *Luzerner Barführer* (ⓦwww.barfuehrer.ch) is a free pocket appraisal of dozens of establishments.

North of the river

Alcatraz Löwengraben 18. Chic café-bar in the old prison, now the *Jailhotel* (see "Accommodation"), that's the in-place of the moment. Also serving full meals, moderately priced.

Heini's Tearoom Falkenplatz ⓦwww.heini.ch. Perfect place for cakes and pastries on a broad, people-watching corner in the Old Town.

Hug Mühlenplatz. Superb breakfast café, open from 7am, with warm fresh bread and croissants, that also has quality inexpensive lunch *menus* (around Fr.17). Closed Sun.

Jazz Kantine Grabenstrasse 8. Buzzing Old Town hub, open during the day for coffee and beers, and on into the late night as a hopping bar and meeting point, with DJs and live music downstairs.

Sunset Bar Seeburgstrasse 61 ⓦ www.sunsetbar .ch. Perfect lakeside café-bar opposite *Hotel Seeburg*, with just the right tone for summer lazing: deckchairs, music, spacious lawns, home-made ice-tea, dreamy views and its own landing-stage. Beware, though: the sharp-dressed regulars crowd in after 6pm. April–Oct only.

South of the river

Mahlzeit Corner Winkelriedstrasse and Waldstätterstrasse. Tiny Moroccan café with a friendly atmosphere and cheap couscous and falafel. Closed Sun.

Opus Bahnhofstrasse 16 ⓦ www .restaurant-opus.ch. Pricey but excellent waterside café, restaurant and wine-bar, with a bright, warm interior and a huge salad buffet (Fr.15 buys a ton of the stuff). Open daily until midnight (Fri & Sat 1.30am).

Parterre Mythenstrasse 7 ⓦ www.parterre.ch. Relaxed and inexpensive locals' hangout, open daily from breakfast until after midnight, with quality lunchtime *menus* (Fr.15). Try their English breakfast – it's satisfyingly filling, even if lacking a bit in authenticity.

Penthouse In the *Astoria* hotel, Pilatusstrasse 29. Rooftop bar with big views and bigger sofas.

Salü Helvetiaplatz. French-style daytime-only café, complete with *citron pressé* and *pain au chocolat* plus soups and salads for lunch. One of several options on this little square. Closed Sun.

Seebar Within the KKL complex. Pleasant daytime hangout, with waterfront views, snacks and sandwiches. Stays open into the night as a DJ-bar.

World Café Within the KKL complex. Bustling, airy place that does a rapid round of salads, light meals and drinks from breakfast until late.

Restaurants

There are hundreds of **restaurants** in Luzern, plenty of which need to do nothing more than occupy a panelled dining room and churn out a handful of traditional dishes to gone-tomorrow tourists in order to make money. A little searching can turn up more worthwhile eateries. If you're watching every franc, check out the shabby *Bahnhof Buffet* (see below) or grab a top-quality Thai **takeaway** from little *Sawasdee*, Zürichstrasse 38–40 (closed Sun).

Note that the much-advertised *Stadtkeller*, Sternenplatz 3, is the eye of Luzern's tourist hurricane, a folklore restaurant which lays on alphorn, yodelling and traditional dancing for dining tour groups – perfect if you're after a knee-slapping good time, but not the place for a romantic *tête-à-tête*.

North of the river

Bodu Kornmarkt 5 ☎ 041 410 01 77, ⓦ www .bordeauxwine.ch. Acclaimed French brasserie, with superb, authentic dishes sourced from Provence, Normandy and everywhere in between. Decor is pleasant, service attentive and the wine superb – but the location, with a fine river view, is the clincher. No closing day.

Hofgarten Stadthofstrasse 14 (see "Accommodation"). The city's best veggie food by miles, if a tad pricey, everything fresh and delicious whether from the buffet or ordered à la carte. A wonderful enclosed garden terrace and cheerful interior attract locals by the score. Reckon on at least Fr.25.

Maihöfli Maihofstrasse 70 ☎ 041 420 60 60. Marvellously relaxed and friendly little all-wood place 1km north of the centre – comfortable, cosy and atmospheric. The cuisine is fresh and modern, with a light, inventive touch, expertly presented, and servers are willing to help you decipher the menu with a recommendation or two,

or take the time to talk you through the range of post-prandial grappas on offer. Lean back on your chair and feel good about your dinner. Meals may set you back Fr.30–35. Closed Sun.

Reussbad Brüggligasse 19 ☎ 041 240 54 23, ⓦ www.reussbad.ch. Easygoing riverside joint to enjoy traditional cooking, relying on a renowned range of fresh fish dishes at around Fr.30. Otherwise, *menus* are around Fr.18. Closed Sun & Mon.

Schiff Unter der Egg 8 ☎ 041 418 52 52, ⓦ www .hotel-schiff-luzern.ch. Wonderful old wood-panelled hotel restaurant on the riverside, celebrated for three things: top-quality *Würst*, huge portions of *Chögelipastetli*, and twin Spanish waiters who've been serving in the place for twenty years. Summer sees tables set under the arcades directly on the waterfront. *Menus* are around Fr.25.

Schlüssel Franziskanerplatz (see "Accommodation"). Tiny old hotel offering a bargain three-course lunch *menu* for just Fr.13.

Spaghetteria Valentino Weinmarkt. Central pasta joint, with a range of risotto and other Italian dishes for under Fr.20. Closed Sun.

South of the river

Bahnhof Buffet Top floor of the train station ⓦwww.brl.ch. A low-budget gem. This greasy-table diner – replete with down-and-outs, smoking schoolchildren and drunken businessmen – charges budget prices for food which has been prepared next door in the kitchen of the adjacent *Au Premier* gourmet restaurant. A meal which might cost you Fr.50 in *Au Premier* may set you back a third of that in the *Bahnhof Buffet* – if you can stand the ambience, that is.

Galliker Schützenstrasse 1, at Kasernenplatz ☎041 240 10 02, ⓦwww.swisswindow.ch /galliker. Hearty, meat-heavy Swiss specialities in a tavern-like setting crammed with people, noise and smoke. The food is consistently excellent, with quality *Chögelipastetli* standing at the top of the pile, joined by *Cordon Bleu* (veal steak slathered with cheese and ham), and less palatable offerings such as *Kutteln* (tripe). Mains are Fr.30–40, not much more than lunchtime *menus*. Closed Sun & Mon, and Aug.

Korea-Town Hirschmattstrasse 23. Pleasant ambience and a good choice mark this Korean place out as something a little more worthwhile than average, with midday buffets from Fr.17 and a range of *menus* (veggie and not) from Fr.21.

Nightlife and entertainment

Luzern's **nightlife** scene is active, with plenty of arts centres and music venues around the Old Town and the rest of the city. The Panorama building on Löwenplatz houses the arthouse **Stattkino** (ⓦwww.stattkino.ch), where you can pick up listings magazines (also stocked at the tourist office).

Bars, clubs and music venues

Boa Geissensteinring 41 ⓦwww.boaluzern.ch. Arts and culture centre with a range of interesting events and music nights. Closed July to mid-Aug.

Jazz Kantine Grabenstrasse 8 ⓦwww.jsl.ch /kantine. Happening Old Town café-bar beside Luzern's jazz school, with DJs and live music (not only jazz) in the basement on weekends.

Rathaus Brauerei Unter der Egg ⓦwww .rathausbrauerei.ch. Wonderful echoing cross-vaulted beerhall below the Rathaus, where young enthusiastic drinkers come to sample a range of powerful, self-brewed beers.

Schüür Tribschenstrasse 1 ⓦwww.schuur.ch. Daytime bar with cheap weekday lunches which after dark becomes a frenetic venue for excellent live music (Fri & Sat until 4am).

Sedel Near the HI hostel ⓦwww.sedel.ch. A former women's prison outside the city, which now hosts noisy punkish/industrial bands and DJ nights at the weekend, with a kind of community-squat atmosphere during the week as bands practise in the graffitied cells.

Seebar Within the KKL complex. Daytime bar with DJs taking over for partying into the small hours.

St Magdalena Eisengasse 5 ⓦwww.magdalena .ch. Universally known as the Magdi-Bar, with a crowded ground-floor bar and a more sociable upstairs, although everything gets more and more raucous as the night veers wildly on.

Wärchhof Werkhofstrasse 11 ⓦwww.waerchhof .ch. Tiny co-op-run dive in an industrial area south of the station, with loud bands, DJs and alternative-style happenings for a college-age crowd.

Listings

Bike and skate rental In the station (June–Sept daily 7am–7.45pm; Oct–May Mon–Sat 7am–7.45pm, Sun 9.30am–7pm).

Boat rental SNG, Alpenquai 11 (☎041 368 08 08, ⓦwww.sng.ch), has pedalos and rowing-boats (about Fr.25/hr) and motorboats (about Fr.45/hr) for rent, all requiring a deposit (Fr.20–100). Prices rise after 7pm. Two competitors are Bucher at

Luzernerhof (☎041 410 20 55), and Herzog at Nationalquai (☎041 410 43 33).

Lost property The city office is at Hirschengraben 17b ☎041 208 78 08.

Markets Every Tuesday and Saturday morning, large and colourful food markets spill over both banks of the Reuss and under the arcades, with a supplementary fish market every Friday. There's a flea market every Saturday (May–Oct) on the south bank, and a monthly crafts market (April–Dec, first Sat of month) on Weinmarkt. In the modern part of town, Moosstrasse/Helvetiaplatz hosts a relaxed Saturday morning farmers' market of cheeses, organic vegetables, home-made jams and more.

Medical facilities 24-hour emergency room at the Kantonsspital, Spitalstrasse ☎ 041 205 11 11.

Post Main office is across from the station (Mon–Fri 7.30am–6.30pm, Sat 8am–noon).

Zentralschweiz

Zentralschweiz (Central Switzerland) is one of the most rewarding areas of the country in which to travel, with a host of different attractions to draw you off the beaten path. Routes around both shores of Luzern's lake give constantly changing perspectives, and even the shortest day-trip in the area will turn up places of great natural beauty. For details of the **boats** which crisscross the lake year-round – often the most convenient method of transport – see p.366.

The southern shore is quiet, characterized by country towns such as **Stans**, and offers clifftop hikes above the water. The excursion south to the once-grand resort of **Engelberg**, base station for the trip up to the summit of the **Titlis**, matches the Bernese Oberland's more famous rides up the Jungfrau and the Schilthorn for drama and natural beauty. The northern shore of the lake is studded by the lofty presence of the **Rigi**, with the old town of **Zug** behind; its easternmost finger, oriented north–south and dubbed the **Urnersee** (Lake Uri), channels the Föhn wind down from the high Alps, and so is a prime windsurfing spot. This is one of the country's most historically resonant areas, its wild and rocky shores the setting both for the legend of **William Tell** and for an ancient pact of mutual defence signed on a lakeside meadow – the **Rütli** – which laid the foundations for the Swiss Confederation as it survives today.

The southern lakeshore

The south shore of the lake – **Vierwaldstättersee–Süd** in German – is a land of broad green meadows and lush valleys interspersed with chunks of high forested plateau towering over the water. Once you gain some height, the views are magnificent, out across the whole shimmering expanse of blue. The shore forms part of the ancient canton of Unterwalden, divided for as long as anyone can remember into two small half-cantons, **Nidwalden** (the Lower Forest) and **Obwalden** (the Upper Forest). It's a perfect area for hiking and cycling, and it's easy to base yourself either in Luzern or in the main town of the region, tiny **Stans**.

Stans

The highest peak in the area is the beautiful Stanserhorn, rising to 1900m above the old village of **STANS**, capital of Nidwalden and on a direct train link with Luzern. The centre of the village lies behind the station. The hub, Dorfplatz, is overlooked by the large **Pfarrkirche St Peter und Paul**. From the Middle Ages onwards this was the sole house of worship in the canton, and so was expanded time and time again to accommodate the increasing population until it

Exploring Zentralschweiz

The **Tellpass** (April–Oct only; ⊕ www.tell-pass.ch) is the regional pass for Zentral-schweiz – but you'll need to cover plenty of ground to make it pay. The core region covers all boats on the lake, all routes to the Rigi and Pilatus, the train from Luzern to Engelberg, and cable-cars from Engelberg up to Trübsee and the Jochpass. With a **seven-day** Tellpass (Fr.140), you get two days' free travel in the core region, with half-price travel on all other lines, including trains to Zug, Einsiedeln, Brienz, Meiringen and Andermatt; a **fifteen-day** Tellpass (Fr.188) buys five days' free travel in the core region, with the remaining ten days at half-price. You can buy the pass from tourist offices throughout the region, and there's more information at ⊕ www .centralswitzerland.ch.

The **Snowpass** (Fr.999) is valid for the whole winter season throughout the entire Zentralschweiz region, covering lifts at Engelberg, Andermatt, the Rigi, Schwyz, Klewenalp and more – even Meiringen.

Adventure sports

Zentralschweiz is one of Switzerland's top **adventure sports** destinations. **Outventure** (☏ 041 611 14 41, ⊕ www.outventure.ch) is the leading local operator, offering bungee-jumps 130m out of the Titlis cable car (Fr.160), flying fox (Fr.90), canyoning (Fr.170), tandem paragliding (Fr.150), white-water rafting (Fr.100), mountaineering (Fr.160), mountain biking (Fr.110), glacier walks (Fr.170) and more. Every morning (8.30am) their shuttle bus runs from Luzern tourist office to each location, many of which are in and around Engelberg. One winter highlight, aside from snowshoe trek-king and tobogganing, is a two-day **igloo package**: build your own igloo, then sleep in it (dinner, mulled wine and breakfast included; Fr.240; minimum four people).

Another operator is the highly acclaimed **Trekking Team** (☏ 041 390 40 40, ⊕ www .trekking.ch) – with a branch in Ticino (see p.543) – which offers trekking, river raft-ing, a mountain-bike round-trip on the Klewenalp (including boat and cable car) for Fr.150, plus winter snowshoe trekking with and without huskies plus igloo-building. Their main draw is access to the vast **Hölloch caves** near Schwyz, 190km long and one of the largest such systems in the world; they run various excursions – including short individual visits (June–Sept Wed–Sun 3–4 daily; takes 1hr 30min; Fr.20; also year-round trips on request) – but the main attraction is long stays underground, exploring the cave network with a guide (all Nov–March only): from 7hr up to 16hr (Fr.159–249), or even overnighting below ground (2 days Fr.395; 3 days Fr.595).

Windsurfing Urnersee (☏ 041 870 92 22, ⊕ www.windsurfing-urnersee.ch) offers beginners' courses (5hr; Fr.280) and board rental, as well as packages including accommodation. Brunnen's Touch And Go (☏ 041 820 54 31, ⊕ www.paragliding .ch) is a respected operator running tandem **paragliding** flights from the Urmiberg (Fr.170; see p.390).

was completely renovated in 1647; the early Baroque building remains crowned by a Romanesque bell tower. Halfway up the hill behind the church is an 1865 fountain dedicated to **Arnold von Winkelried**, a native of the town, who is celebrated for diverting the attention of the Austrian army during the Battle of Sempach in 1386, thereby committing suicide but simultaneously opening a gap for his Swiss comrades to surge through to victory. The alleys surrounding Dorf-platz are worth a wander; east is quiet Schmiedgasse, while to the west is Altes Postplatz and the **Höfli**, or **Rosenburg House**, a medieval turreted building with a rear courtyard overlooked by beautiful Italianate loggias.

A couple of minutes beyond the Höfli is the station for the old-time cog railway up to the summit of the green and pleasant **Stanserhorn** (mid-April to Nov; ⊕ www.stanserhorn.ch), with views from the *Rondorama* revolving restaurant on top and the many trails on the summit taking in ten lakes as well as the close-at-hand high mountains around the Titlis. The zigzag walk back down to Stans takes about three and a half hours, or alternatively, you can head down the side of the mountain to Wirzweli (in 2hr 30min), from where a cable car deposits you at the village of **Dallenwil** for the bus ride back to Stans.

The **tourist office** for the region (Mon–Fri 9am–noon & 2–5pm; ☎041 610 88 33, ⓦwww.lakeluzern.ch) is above Stans train station, where there are bikes for rent. There are two pleasant **hotels** on Dorfplatz: the *Engel* (☎041 619 10 10, ⓦwww.engelstans.ch; ❷–❸), now totally renovated inside in a fresh, contemporary style, and the more traditional *Linde* (☎041 619 09 30, ⓦwww.hotel-linde.ch; ❸). Both have good **restaurants**, or you could plump for the *Wilhelm Tell* restaurant just off the square (*menus* Fr.15). Stans's top eating choice is the fine restaurant within the Höfli (*menus* around Fr.50; closed Mon & Tues; ⓦwww.rosenburg-stans.ch).

Hergiswil and beyond

On the train line midway between Luzern and Stans is the small lakeside community of **HERGISWIL**, for centuries a fishing village until it rose to fame for the **Glasi Hergiswil** glassworks, founded in 1817. For over a hundred years, the glassworks was one of the busiest in the country, yet by 1975 it was hopelessly obsolete, with no chance of matching the automated methods of more modern competitors. The "Glasi" would have closed altogether but for Roberto Niederer, a Ticinese glass designer who, backed by local people, bought it up and changed its products and its target market. Niederer's rejuvenation, continued today by his son, enabled the plant – and the village economy – to survive: it's a remarkable success story. The visitor-friendly Glasi now employs a hundred people, producing hand-blown pieces for sale as well as serving as a workshop for artists from around the world to design and work with glass using traditional craft techniques. The on-site **museum** (Mon–Fri 9am–6pm, Sat 9am–4pm; free; ⓦwww.glasi.ch) is excellent, focused around an engaging audiovisual walk-through history of glassmaking and the Glasi. The story ends as a door opens onto a gallery above the blazing-hot **factory floor**, where you can watch a team of glass-blowers do their stuff (although beware that they stop for lunch, and take a tea-break around 4pm).

Bürgenstock

East of Hergiswil rises a grand plateau, atop which is the private luxury resort of **BÜRGENSTOCK**, an odd little enclave owned by the handful of business-oriented hotels that occupy it, themselves mostly owned by a single family. Buses from Stans stop short at Obbürgen (from where a private toll road serves the resort), and the only way to access the area directly is by **boat** from Luzern to Kehrsiten, way down on the lake; from there, a **funicular** rises to Bürgenstock itself – Sophia Loren's summer getaway for many years, and a renowned setting for diplomatic negotiations and all kinds of international politicking. If you want to stay here, or eat here, or play golf here, you'll need a packet of money (double rooms start around Fr.300; ⓦwww.buergenstock-hotels.ch), but it doesn't cost anything to enjoy the views. Ignore the big cars and the well-cut suits clustering around the hotels, and instead strike out east on the Felsenweg path for a scenic twenty-minute clifftop walk to Europe's fastest outdoor elevator, which swishes you in seconds to the **Hammetschwand** summit (1128m), complete with a more affordable restaurant and stunning lake vistas. You can return to Bürgenstock via a steeper path zigzagging down the back of the Hammetschwand (35min), from where another path cuts down to the Kehrsiten boat station; or follow a four-hour trail east across the wooded hilltops down to Ennetbürgen and Beckenried, which gives expansive views over the lake and south to the high mountains.

Beckenried and Klewenalp

Just round the lakeshore from Kehrsiten, and accessible by bus from Stans (or boat), is **BECKENRIED**, from where a gondola rises to **Klewenalp** (1593m; ⓦwww.klewenalp.ch) and plenty more walking routes. This is touted strongly as **mountain-bike** territory, and you can rent at the gondola station, and from many outlets in Beckenried, Dallenwil and Seelisberg – around Fr.32 for a full day, or Fr.25 for a half-day. Two easy bike routes link Dallenwil and Beckenried (10km), and Emmetten and Seelisberg (7km), with harder ones climbing to Klewenalp and beyond to various mountain inns. One option is to rent from Beckenried, cycle to Seelisberg (about 12km) and then catch a boat from Treib, Seelisberg's boat station, back to Beckenried. The same route on foot would take about four and a half hours. You can **camp** west of Beckenried near Buochs (☎041 620 34 74; April–Sept).

Seelisberg and Treib

Beyond Beckenried, the main road enters a long tunnel beneath the cliffs and forests of the Seelisberg peninsula, emerging close to Flüelen (see p.396). Buses from Stans follow a minor road up onto the plateau itself, through the village of **Emmetten**, and on, with ever more spectacular lake panoramas, until you round a corner to be met with a sign reading "Welcome to the International Capital of the Age of Enlightenment". This is little **SEELISBERG**, a crow's nest of a place that is home to the Maharishi Ayur-Veda Health Centre (source of the sign). A funicular (ⓦwww.seelisberg.com) from the northern end of the main street shadows the steep path coiling down the cliff to the quaint old lakeside inn and boat station of **Treib** below, directly opposite Brunnen. Below the top funicular station, on the short path which ends up at the Rütli meadow (see p.382), you'll find an HI **hostel** (☎041 820 52 32, ⓦwww.youthhostel .ch; ❶; April–Oct), with simple dorms from Fr.19. Seelisberg has a handful of inexpensive **hotels**, including the comfortable, family-run *Montana* (☎041 820 12 68; ❷), and *Bellevue* (☎041 825 66 66, ⓦwww.bellevue-seelisberg.ch; ❸), a rather plusher option with lake views.

Engelberg

Situated at the southern end of the valley road and rail line from Stans in an enclave of Canton Obwalden, the top-quality ski resort of **ENGELBERG** (1050m) boasts an excursion to the highest point in central Switzerland – a station at 3028m, just below the distinctive crest-of-a-wave summit of the **Titlis** mountain (3239m). This, along with the village's huge Benedictine Kloster (monastery) and the faded grandeur of its hotel architecture, make Engelberg well worth a visit.

Arrival, information and accommodation

After a picturesque valley-floor ride, the Luzern–Stans–Engelberg (LSE) **train** pulls into the station in the middle of the village. Turn left on Bahnhofstrasse, and right onto the main central Dorfstrasse for the **tourist office**, in a sports

The Rütli meadow

On the western shore of Lake Luzern's "Urnersee" branch, below Seelisberg – and visible from Brunnen, across the water – is a flapping Swiss flag planted in the **Rütli meadow**, a sloping patch of grass above the shoreline that holds unique, almost mystical, significance for the Swiss. Legend and national pride says that it was here on August 1, 1291, that representatives from the three forest cantons around the lake (Uri, Schwyz and Unterwalden) met amidst continuing Habsburg repression to sign a pact of eternal mutual defence, thereby laying the foundation of the Swiss Confederation as it stands today. Nowadays, 1291 is taken as the birthdate of the nation, and August 1 is the official Swiss national holiday.

And yet, despite the proud flag which stands on the meadow today, and the crowds of parents who bring their children here to tell them the story of William Tell (see box p.394) and the birth of Switzerland, many historians doubt that anything very much happened at Rütli at all. Some pour scorn on the idea that such an obviously important document in formal Latin – now on display in Schwyz – would have been written and signed in a meadow (although England's grand Magna Carta was signed at Runnymede meadow in 1215), and cite evidence that the three representatives met at Rütli on November 7, 1307, simply in order to renew their formal written pledge of 16 years before. Other historians, yet more controversially, suggest that the Swiss Confederation developed organically, and that there was either no movement of resistance against the Habsburgs in 1291 at all, or that the Rütli oath was merely one in an array of other equally "eternal" or "perpetual" alliances between valley communities that came and went over the centuries. Nothing is certain, but most ordinary people have little truck with such trifling details anyway: the story has come to represent much more than its bare facts might suggest. The **Charter of Confederation**, as the Rütli document came to be known, has become as potently symbolic for the Swiss as the Declaration of Independence is for Americans, and the meadow itself has become a place of patriotic pilgrimage, focus of the country's national celebrations every August.

complex at Klosterstrasse 3 (July & Aug Mon–Sat 8am–6.30pm, Sun 9am–noon; May, June & Nov Mon–Fri 8am–6.30pm Sat 8am–5pm; Sept–Oct Mon–Sat 8am–6.30pm; Dec–April Mon–Sat 8am–6.30pm, Sun 8am–6pm; ☎041 639 77 77, ⊛www.engelberg.ch). Some 200m east of the tourist office rises the onion dome of the monastery, while the base station for the Titlis is 500m southwest of the station, well signposted on the south bank of the Engelberger-Aa stream. Dozens of **hotels** are dotted throughout the town and surrounding slopes.

Bollywood in the Alps

Engelberg stands at the centre of the biggest story in Swiss tourism in years: **Bollywood**. With ongoing conflict in Kashmir making location-shoots with a mountain backdrop impossible, directors from India's film industry (based in Mumbai, formerly Bombay – hence the name) have been discovering that it's easier and cheaper to fly cast and crew out to the Alps than it is to battle with bureaucrats for permits to film in the Indian or Nepalese Himalaya. Engelberg – less than two hours from Zürich airport, and with guaranteed snow cover on the Titlis all year round – is the top-choice destination, the *Hotel Terrace* in particular regularly hosting the biggest stars of Bollywood. Wealthy film buffs back home have been reading the credits closely, and these days India is one of Swiss tourism's biggest growth markets, dozens of tour groups paying to escape the torrid pre-monsoon months of April, May and June with a visit to Engelberg and other Alpine film locations to tread in the footsteps of the famous.

Weg der Schweiz (Swiss Path)

Appropriately enough, the **Rütli meadow** is the starting-point for the long-distance **Weg der Schweiz** (Swiss Path) walking route, inaugurated in 1991 as part of the 700th anniversary celebrations of the founding of the Swiss Confederation.

The scenic trail, which circumnavigates the Urnersee to **Brunnen** (see p.390), is almost 35km long, walkable in two days of roughly six hours each (with a midway overnight stop in **Flüelen** or **Altdorf**; see p.396), or is easily dividable into smaller chunks. Sections are: **Rütli to Bauen** (11km up and down; 3hr 30min); **Bauen to Flüelen** (a flat 10km; 2hr 45min); **Flüelen to Sisikon** (reasonably flat 8km; 2hr); and **Sisikon to Brunnen** (climbing and dropping 8km; 3hr). Distinctive yellow route markers – a Swiss cross incorporating an arrow – point the way (ignore whichever way the stylized arrow faces and follow the signpost's directional finger instead). **Boats** shuttle between Rütli, Bauen, Isleten, Flüelen, Sisikon and Brunnen, and **trains** run between Flüelen, Sisikon and Brunnen, enabling you to pick and choose which sections you fancy. Tourist offices around the region stock English guides to the route.

The idea behind the path is to provide a lasting reminder of the state of the nation in 1991. Marked stones along the route identify the 26 cantons in the order in which they joined the Confederation, with each canton allotted a length of the path proportionate to its population: meticulous attention to detail has calculated that every 5mm of the trail represents a single Swiss citizen. So the initial climb from the Rütli takes care of Uri, Schwyz, Nidwalden and Obwalden (who were co-founders in 1291, and are all lightly populated); then there's a section of 1.6km representing Luzern (which joined in 1332); then 6.1km, the longest section for the most populous canton, Zürich (1351), and so on. Just after Flüelen is the shortest section, 71m representing tiny Appenzell Inner-Rhodes (1513), while 3km further north is the **Tellskapelle** (see p.396), a handy resting-place. The final walk into Brunnen covers the most recent canton to join the Confederation, Jura (1979).

Hotels

Bänklialp Bänklialpweg 25 ☎041 639 73 73, ⊛www.baenklialp.ch. Good, straightforward, high-quality holiday hotel, in a useful location, with plenty of services and comfortable, functional rooms. ❸

Bellevue Bahnhofplatz ☎041 637 12 13, ⊛www.bellevue-engelberg.ch. A grand lobby preludes characterful old-style rooms that are excellent value – most are ensuite, and all have high ceilings and an air of faded grandeur. Many rooms are let to students during term time. ❸–❹

Cathrin Birrenweg 22 ☎041 637 44 66, ⊛www.cathrin-engelberg.ch. Pleasant, quiet place near the Titlis cable car, away from the bustle. ❸–❹

Edelweiss Terracestrasse 10 ☎041 637 07 37, ⊛www.edelweissengelberg.ch. Charming Art Nouveau hotel above the village, dating from 1901 and now in the hands of friendly and welcoming English-speaking owner/managers. Stylish, spotless rooms and broad valley views bring it head and shoulders above its competitors. ❸–❺

Engelberg Dorfstrasse 14 ☎041 639 79 79, ⊛www.hotel-engelberg.ch. Comfortable place on the pedestrianized main street, with warm and cosy rooms. ❸–❹

Europe Dorfstrasse 40 ☎041 639 75 75, ⊛www.hoteleurope.ch. Grandiose village-centre pile dating from 1905, with some of the bright, attractive rooms boasting wrought-iron balconies, chandeliers and fittings from an age of tourism long past. ❸–❹

St Jakob Engelbergerstrasse ☎041 637 13 88, ⊛www.st-jakobpension.ch. Small, simple family pension on the road west of the centre, also with dorms from Fr.38. ❶–❷

Terrace Terracestrasse ☎041 639 66 66, ⊛www.terrace.ch. Huge presence looming above the village, built in 1906 and newly renovated throughout, with a glorious sun terrace and comfortable rooms, accessible either by car or by its own tiny funicular. ❹–❻

Hostel

Jugendherberge (HI hostel) Dorfstrasse 80 ☎041 637 12 92, ⊛www.youthhostel.ch. Located 500m west of the station, with dorms from Fr.33 and excellent meals. Closed May & Nov.

Campsite
Eienwäldli ☎ 041 637 19 49, ⓦ www.eienwaeldli
.ch. Five-star site on the southeastern edge of the

village, about half-an-hour's walk from the centre.
Closed Nov.

In and around the village

Dominating the village is a huge Benedictine **monastery**. The first monks
arrived in the valley around 1120, and during the Middle Ages, the monastery
was key to the expansion of ascetic mysticism in Germany and Switzerland. The
buildings as they stand today date from a rebuilding after a fire in 1729. Until
1798, when French troops arrived in force, the monks ruled the whole valley,
which was independent of the Swiss Confederation and answered only to the
pope; the Revolution changed all that, and the monastery first joined Canton
Nidwalden in 1803, then changed its mind and switched to Obwalden twelve
years later. These days, the sixty or so monks teach high school and further
education courses, and have founded two affiliated monasteries in Missouri and
Oregon. The Rococo **church**, dating from 1730, is stunning – a vast, elegant
space with nine altars. A riot of ornamental stucco leads you through what
would otherwise be an austere interior to the dramatic high altar, framing a
luminescent painting of the Assumption. Guided **tours** of the whole complex,
including the church and several impressive halls within the monastery, run
year-round (in English: Wed–Sat 10am & 4pm; fewer in off-season; Fr.6;
ⓦ www.kloster-engelberg.ch).

To the Titlis

The monastery aside, Engelberg's attractions are all in the hills. The main
excursion, well worthwhile if the weather's clear, is the four-stage journey to

Sports and activities at Engelberg

Engelberg's skiing and boarding is focused on the **Titlis** (Ⓦ www.titlis.ch), specifically the area above **Gerschnialp**: on lower slopes is a network of fine blue runs, while further up, from the **Klein Titlis** station all the way down past **Stand** to the **Trübsee,** are plenty of red runs. There's excellent cross-country skiing around Trübsee as well, plus sledding at Gerschnialp. Way up at Klein Titlis – which benefits from summer skiing and snowboarding – is a hip boarder park, with another on the **Jochpass**. On the other side of the valley, the smaller **Brunni** sector (Ⓦ www.brunni.ch) features a cable car up to **Ristis**, from where a chairlift reaches the **Brunnihütte** (1860m), which has a cat's cradle of idyllic summer walks along the hillside meadows and down through forests to the village. In winter, a handful of blue ski runs swish you down easily to the valley floor.

The guest card gives discounts on **lift passes**, which are otherwise Fr.52/250 (one/ six days) for both sectors, or Fr.36/162 for Brunni only. The local school is at Ⓦ www .skischule-engelberg.ch.

Engelberg has an excellent reputation for **adventure sports**, with top operators Outventure (see box p.379) and Adventure Engelberg (Ⓦ www.adventure-engelberg .ch) organizing bungee-jumping, crevasse abseiling, canyoning, snowshoeing, igloo-building, ice-climbing, rafting, kayaking and more. Don't miss the Devil Bike, a huge, fat-tyred contraption with no pedals, which makes short work of the scenic downhill bike run from Jochpass to Trübsee.

the **Titlis** (Ⓦ www.titlis.ch). The first ascent crests a plateau to **Gerschnialp**, from where walking routes depart on both sides around back to the village and another lift brings you to the ridge above the small picturesque **Trübsee**. From the Trübsee station, you can detour on an easy stroll around the lake to the base station of a different cable car serving the **Jochpass** and **Engstlen**, a little-frequented corner. Back at Trübsee, a gondola rises on a breathtakingly exposed journey over the lake to **Stand**, perched way above the valley at 2428m, with its own sun terrace and restaurant. From here, you switch onto the "Rotair", the world's first revolving gondola; the broad cabin begins to rotate shortly after starting the ascent, and on the five-minute journey to the top station turns completely round once, giving you a 360° panorama of the ride over the vast and impressive Titlis Glacier. On top, you'll find the standard circus of souvenir shops, ice grottoes and the highest karaoke bar in Europe, but the views more than compensate. The hike up to the ice-bound Titlis peak takes a painstaking 45 minutes.

The full return **fare** Engelberg–Titlis is Fr.79, but as usual, walking some sections – notably from the Trübsee back down to the village (2hr) – can save plenty. Swiss Pass holders pay half-price, while the regional Tellpass brings a 50 percent discount to Trübsee only.

Eating and drinking

The *Coop* supermarket opposite the tourist office on Klosterstrasse has a budget self-service **restaurant** attached. Otherwise, there are plenty of places to fuel up along Dorfstrasse and through the centre. The *Alpenclub* (Ⓦ www.alpenclub.ch) shelters several different eating places, including an inexpensive pizzeria, a *Käse-tube* for fondue and the like, and a more formal restaurant with Swiss dishes for Fr.25 and up. Further east along Dorfstrasse, the *Café zur Alten Post* has basic stomach-filling *menus* for around Fr.15. The restaurant at *Hotel Bänklialp* does good Swiss staples for moderate prices. Twin hubs of the late-night après-ski scene are the *Yucatan* **bar** (❿www.yucatan.ch), which also offers good, filling evening meals for around Fr.18, and the *Spindle* (❿www.spindle.ch), within the *Alpenclub* on Dorfstrasse.

Routes to the Rigi

The titanic chunk of the **Rigi** (❿www.rigi.ch), which rises to 1798m between the lakes of Luzern and Zug, has long been famous as a majestic viewpoint. By itself, it's actually rather scrubby, a steep-scarped grassy ridge with several summits, but it stands alone dividing the two lakes, and offers wonderful views south to the Alps.

There are several transport options up the mountain, testifying to the scramble in the late nineteenth century to capitalize on burgeoning tourism to Luzern. Rival companies started laying track from **Vitznau** on Lake Luzern, and **Arth-Goldau** just south of the Zugersee, competing for who would be first to reach the summit. The Vitznau line – with the bonus of its accessibility from Luzern by boat – won out, but Arth-Goldau benefits from being a major junction-point on the Zürich–Gotthard mainline train route. Red trains from Vitznau and blue ones from Goldau converge at Staffel near the summit for the final pull to **Rigi-Kulm** at the very top. A third route up the mountain, a cable car from picturesque **Weggis**, also on Lake Luzern, rises to connect with the Vitznau trains at an intermediate stop named Rigi-Kaltbad. The popular method is to go up by one route and down by another. It's easy to make the Rigi a **day-trip from Luzern**; or you could just as easily spend a night on the summit to enjoy the sunrise over the Alps. If you're set on hiking to the summit, reckon on four hours for the trek up from Weggis.

Weggis

On a sheltered, south-facing bay, protected from cold northerly weather by the Rigi itself, **WEGGIS** basks in its own subtropical microclimate – the palm trees, figs and magnolias grow naturally. It looks out over the lake and across to the Bürgenstock cliffs, and has been a popular summer resort for a couple of centuries, with a dedicated older clientele returning year after year to soak up the sun.

The **tourist office** for Weggis, the Rigi region and the whole north shore of the lake is right beside the boat station, at Seestrasse 5 (May–Sept Mon–Fri 8am–6pm, Sat & Sun 9am–2.30pm; Oct–April Mon–Fri 8am–5pm; ☎041 390 11 55, ❿www.weggis.ch). There's no shortage of **accommodation**. Least pricey is the well-kept *Budget Hotel*, in a residential district a stiff walk uphill and west from the boat station (☎041 390 11 31, ❿www.budgethotel.ch; ❷). A couple of minutes east of the landing stage is the *Seehof Hotel du Lac* (☎041 390 11 51, ❿www.hotel-du-lac.ch; ❸–❹; closed Nov & Dec), a charming, quiet family-run place of some quality – it's worth splashing out for the lakeview rooms with balcony. Just beside it is the classy *Beau-Rivage* (☎041 392 79 00, ❿www.beaurivage-weggis.ch; ❺–❽; April–Oct), with plenty of creature comforts in the rooms and an enclosed lakeside lawn for sunny lounging. The cable-car station for Rigi-Kaltbad is northeast of the landing stage, well signposted.

Vitznau and Gersau

A couple of hours' stroll east from Weggis is the small village of **VITZNAU**, base station for Europe's oldest rack railway (inaugurated in 1871) running up to the Rigi-Kulm. Whereas Weggis can seem a trifle twee or over pretty, tranquil Vitznau – set in a sheltered west-facing bay close to the narrowest strait of the lake – has plenty of character, despite the hordes of day-trippers in the village centre. The train station for the Rigi is right opposite the boat station, with the **tourist office** beside it (Easter–Oct Mon–Fri 8.30am–12.45pm & 1.30–5.30pm, Sat 9am–noon; July & Aug also Sun 9am–noon; Nov–Easter Mon-Fri 9am–noon & 1.30–4.45pm; ☎041 398 00 35, ⓦwww.vitznau.ch). The cheapest **accommodation** is the *Schiff*, 300m west of the centre in a quiet location (☎041 397 13 57, ⓦwww.schiff-vitznau.ch; ❶; closed Nov), with six old-style rooms above the most pleasant of lakeside restaurants. A few hundred metres beyond is Vitznau's extraordinary *Park Hotel* (☎041 399 60 60, ⓦwww .parkhotel-vitznau.ch; ❾), a palatial Belle Epoque vision, with vast rooms, two gourmet restaurants, sauna, tennis courts and more. In the village itself, the *Rigi* (☎041 397 21 21, ⓦwww.rigi-vitznau.ch; ❸) is an attractive shuttered old house with renovated rooms.

Less than two hours' walk east from Vitznau is tiny **GERSAU**, a patch of sloping meadow that was, from 1390 until the French invasion of 1798, the smallest independent free republic in Europe, with all of two thousand inhabitants. Midway between Gersau and Vitznau there's a handy HI **hostel,** *Jugendherberge Rotschuo* (☎041 828 12 77, ⓦwww.youthhostel.ch; ❶; dorms Fr.28; March–Nov). Hourly buses connect Weggis, Vitznau and Gersau, while different buses run from Gersau on to Brunnen and Schwyz.

The Rigi

There are hiking routes all over the Rigi, most starting from **Rigi-Kaltbad** (1453m) or **Rigi-Klösterli** (1315m), the first accessible from both Weggis and Vitznau, the second a midway stop on the Arth-Goldau train line. Kaltbad is a peaceful traffic-free resort on a terrace of pastureland high above Weggis; there's a handful of hotels here, as well as relatively easy two- or three-hour hiking routes through the pine trees out to the Känzeli viewpoint, up onto the ridge at First, or to the Rotstock peak above Kaltbad (1659m). Red trains from Vitznau and blue ones from Arth-Goldau meet at Staffel for the final stretch to **Rigi-Kulm**, home of the *Hotel Rigi-Kulm* (☎041 855 03 03, ⓦwww.rigikulm .ch; ❸–❹; closed Oct & Nov), a bald 1950s creation replacing earlier incarnations dating back more than a hundred years. It's a rather dull place in itself, but has the incomparable selling point of offering a superb sunrise over the Alps. The summit is a 200m stroll from the hotel, and gives bird's-eye views over Luzern and the Vierwaldstättersee on one side, and Zug and the Zugersee on the other.

Zug

The town of **ZUG** (pronounced *tsoogk*), 22km from Luzern on the north side of the Rigi, is the richest place in Switzerland, which makes it very rich indeed. Tiny Canton Zug has some of the lowest tax rates in the country – about half the national average – which attracts flocks of multinational corporations; this, in turn, pushes average *per capita* net income up to an incredible Fr.70,000 (£31,000) a year. Zug's modern, business-driven existence proceeds without pomp amidst the glittering offices and malls of the new town, a world away from the picturesque medieval churches and cobbled waterfront lanes of the compact Old Town adjacent. The town's location on the crystal-blue Zugersee is very attractive, framed by the high wooded plateau of the Zugerberg rising 600m to the east and the peak of the Rigi (see above) on its southwest shores.

Arrival, information and accommodation

The ultra-modern **station** – with light installations by artist James Turrell – is about 400m north of the lakeshore, and the same amount again north of the Old Town, which ranges down the eastern shore of the lake. Zug is a rail junction, situated at the point where a line from Luzern in the west meets the main north–south route running from Zürich via Flüelen and the Gotthard Tunnel to Ticino. You emerge from the station at the head of Alpenstrasse, leading down (south) to the lake. Within the station is the **tourist office** (Mon–Fri 9am–7pm, Sat 9am–4pm, Sun 9am–3pm; ☏041 723 68 00, ⓦwww.zug-tourismus.ch).

SGZ **boats** (ⓦwww.zugersee-info.ch) tour the Zugersee from the Bahnhofsteg, at the foot of Alpenstrasse; check their posted timetable, which also has details of their numerous eat-aboard trips – everything from winter brunches to music-accompanied starlit dinners.

Zug's hoteliers – like most business people in the city – fairly glow with financial health: the combination of Zug's high business profile, its proximity to both Luzern and Zürich, and its chronic shortage of **accommodation** means that they can overcharge and still be rewarded with enviably high occupancy rates. Booking ahead is vital.

Hotels

Guggital Zugerbergstrasse 46 ☏041 711 28 21, ⓦwww.hotel-guggital.ch. Up on the slopes overlooking the town from the south: for the views and the service, the best mid-range choice. All rooms are modern and renovated, and virtually all face the lake for gorgeous sunsets (pay more for a balcony). Bus #11 stops outside. ❸–❹

Ibis Bahnhofstrasse 15, Baar ☏041 766 76 00, ⓦwww.hotelibis.com. Of the many motels and travel lodges off the Gotthard motorway near Zug, this is the most reliable – located at Baar train station, with parking. ❶–❷

Löwen am See Landsgemeindeplatz ☏041 725 22 22, ⓦwww.loewen-zug.ch. Attractive, renovated hotel in a car-free location on the main old-town square, just a stone's throw from the water. ❹–❺

Ochsen Kolinplatz 11 ☏041 729 32 32, ⓦwww.ochsen-zug.ch. A sixteenth-century gabled exterior and plush reception belie the rooms, which are less characterful than you might expect for a house venerable enough to have once hosted Goethe – the best are high up at the back overlooking rooftops and an internal courtyard. Go for one of the Japanese rooms, with roll-away futons. Weekdays you can barely move for suits; prices drop at weekends. ❹–❺

Hostel

Jugendherberge (HI hostel) Allmendstrasse 8 ☏041 711 53 54, ⓦwww.youthhostel.ch. Walk west along the lakefront Chamerstrasse, follow Allmendstrasse north under a railway bridge, and the hostel is to the right behind a petrol station. Dorm beds from Fr.31. ❶

Campsite

Innere Lorenzallmend "Brüggli" Chamer Fussweg 36 ☏041 741 84 22. Located 2km west of Zug on the lakeshore – take bus #4 from Bundesplatz to Brüggli (direction Hünenberg).

The Town

Alpenstrasse leads from the station past Bundesplatz straight down to the lakeshore jetty, from where there are splendid views of the Rigi and Pilatus. Vorstadt follows the eastern lakeshore to **Postplatz**, on the the edge of Zug's tiny Old Town.

From Postplatz, shop-lined Neugasse leads south to **Kolinplatz** and the striped-roof **Zytturm**, at 52m the Old Town's tallest building but these days tucked into a corner beside a busy traffic road and largely forgotten. Built in the mid-thirteenth century as a watchtower, it was renovated in 1557 and endowed with a clock in 1574. The shields below the clock face are those of the eight Swiss cantons at the time of the tower's construction (from left to right, Zürich, Bern, Luzern, Uri, Schwyz, Unterwalden, Glarus and Zug). There's a host of tiny details on the tower, including, under the archway, a beautiful late-Gothic wavy-haired angel. Just above the upper ledge, you'll spot a painting of a rat, made by medieval watchmen as a device to scare away the rats that stole their food during long nights on duty.

Opposite the Zytturm, Kolinplatz features a fountain dedicated to Wolfgang Kolin, standard-bearer of the Swiss army at their 1422 defeat by the Duke of Milan. Heading beneath the Zytturm brings you into the most atmospheric part of the Old Town, cobbled lanes lined with medieval gabled and balconied (and often frescoed) houses. Just behind the Zytturm is Zug's **Rathaus**, dating from 1509 and retaining much of its original woodwork, and a few steps north is the waterside **Landsgemeindeplatz**. From the Rathaus, the streets Unter-altstadt and Oberaltstadt both lead south to the tiny **Liebfrauenkapelle**, dating from 1266 but boasting a Baroque interior.

If you follow the alleys uphill from the chapel, and cross the main Graben-strasse, you'll spot St Oswaldsgasse leading left to the **Kirche St Oswald**, built between 1478 and 1545 and dedicated to St Oswald of Northumbria (605–642). Inside you'll find another lavish Baroque interior and a nineteenth-century mural; as you leave, look above the double portal to see a beautiful carved statue of Mary flanked by St Oswald and St Michael. It's a short walk from here up Kirchenstrasse to the **Burg**, a circular, top-heavy construction that was once the headquarters of the Kyburg and Habsburg governors, and now houses the town's **museum** (Tues–Fri 2–5pm, Sat 10am–noon & 2–5pm, Sun 10am–5pm; Fr.5, free on Sun; SMP; ⓦ www.museenzug.ch), worth a look for its model of medieval Zug. A few metres further up the hill is the **Kunsthaus**, with usually very good temporary art exhibitions. If you head along Dorfstrasse, and across the main Ägeristrasse, you'll spot a set of quiet, concealed steps leading up to the **chapel** of a Capuchin convent (1597), with an adjacent, well-tended walled cemetery. Tranquil covered steps bring you down to opposite the old **mint**, with Postplatz to the right.

Eating and drinking

The best concentration of places to **eat and drink** is in and around Landsge-meindeplatz: on sunny days, cafés and restaurants lay tables out on the water-front square, but there's also plenty of choice in the alleys all around. The lakefront road Vorstadt is shoulder to shoulder with restaurants, most offering fish of one kind or another.

Zug is famous around Switzerland for its cherries, which give rise both to many varieties of local **Kirsch** (cherry brandy) and to **Zuger Kirschtorte**, a delectably buttery almond tart saturated with Kirsch that breathes cherry fumes but, oddly, has not a single fruit adorning it. *Kirschtorte* is on offer all over town – the best is made fresh daily at Konditorei Meier, Alpenstrasse 16 (ⓦ www .diezugerkirschtorte.ch). Aside from coffee and a slice, they can box up a whole *Torte* for you to take away.

Restaurants

Liguria Fischmarkt 2 ⓣ 041 710 24 24 ⓦ www .liguria-zg.ch. Outstanding Italian fish restaurant occupying an elegant, historic lakefront building. Expect little change from Fr.100 a head.

Rathauskeller Oberaltstadt 1 ⓣ 041 711 00 58 ⓦ www.rathauskeller.ch. One of Canton Zug's top restaurants, housed in the historic Rathaus. Upstairs is the highest of *haute cuisine*, with a six-course evening *menu* around Fr.150, but the

ground-floor bistro serves simpler, more affordable dishes from the same kitchen. Closed Sun & Mon.
Speck Alpenstrasse 12 ⓦ www.speck.ch. Simple *menus* in the pasta-and-salad vein are around Fr.14, plus good *Kirschtorte*. Closed Sun.

🏃 **Widder** Landsgemeindeplatz 12 ☎ 041 711 03 16 ⓦ www.gasthaus-widder.ch. Excellent Old Town choice, with hot meals all day and terrace seating in summer. Relaxed South African owner-ship not only means the staff speak English, but also adds ostrich and springbok steaks (as well as spicy Sri Lankan curries) to the already full menu of Swiss specialities, quality pizzas and super-fresh lake fish.

Bars

Chaotikum Chamerstrasse 41. A shack beside the main road 1km west of town painted "CHAOS" where you can enjoy a good, solid meal for less than Fr.15 – if you don't mind the rough-edged crowd, wafting cannabis smoke and loud jangly music. Cheap beer too. Closed Mon.

Fischmärt Fischmarkt 15. Comfy Old Town bar with booths and a range of malt whiskies. Closed Sun.

Schiffbar Graben 2. Two different bars with the same name: much preferable is the upstairs one (self-dubbed the *Panorama*), with an elevated terrace aiding peaceful contemplation of the lake below.

Schwyzerland

Occupying the picturesque northeastern corner of Lake Luzern and extending north to the wild hills bordering the Zürichsee, unsung **Schwyzerland** takes in a series of broad, lush valleys enclosed between Alpine foothills and overlooked by the twin peaks of the Mythen. The gentle resort of **Brunnen** lies on the lake, while a short distance inland is the cantonal capital **Schwyz**, an old and grace-ful town with plenty of history. To the north, the ancient monastery church at **Einsiedeln** draws pilgrims from around the world to pay homage to the icon of the Black Madonna.

Brunnen

Of all the resort towns on the lake, **BRUNNEN** is perhaps most dramatically located, snug in a right-angled corner of the shore between the crests of the Rigi and the scarps of the Fronalpstock. Vistas from its jetty are stupendous, look-ing the length of the Urnersee south to the snowy peaks around the Gotthard; directly across to the misty cliffs of Seelisberg, with the Uri-Rotstock and Titlis behind; and east the length of the Vierwaldstättersee to far-distant Luzern. Brunnen basks at the head of a wind tunnel which draws the warm Föhn wind north from the Mediterranean, frequently turning the Urnersee choppy and stormy: rapidly fluctuating weather conditions mean that it's not unknown to look south to glorious sunshine on the high Alps and east to pelting rain over Luzern. Mad King Ludwig of Bavaria took a real shine to Brunnen in 1865; one of his favourite pastimes was ordering a team of alphorn-blowers to play to him while he sat in a small boat on the lake at midnight.

The easiest excursion from Brunnen is to the **Urmiberg** peak nearby (1140m; ⓦ www.urmiberg.ch), with stunning views both on the way up in the tiny cable car and from the summit itself. Hiking trails from the top include a steep path back down to Brunnen (1hr 30min; a gentler descent adds 1hr), and other trails down to Gersau or Goldau (both 3hr). There's a summit restaurant, and also the opportunity to take off on a **tandem paragliding** flight, cour-tesy of the local adventure operator Touch And Go (☎ 041 820 54 31, ⓦ www .paragliding.ch; Fr.170).

Practicalities

Brunnen's **train station** is set back from the lakeshore jetty, about ten minutes' walk inland on the main Bahnhofstrasse: you should allow plenty of time if you're switching from a boat to a train, or vice versa (switching at Flüelen is easier). Before you get to the station, you'll pass the **tourist office**, a short way from the jetty at Bahnhofstrasse 15 (June–Sept Mon–Fri 8.30am–6pm, Sat 9am–1pm; July & Aug also Sun 9.30am–3pm; Oct–May Mon–Fri 8.30am–noon & 1.30–5.30pm; ☎041 825 00 40, ⓦwww.brunnentourismus.ch): they can help you out with information for the whole area, including Schwyz (which only has a tiny information counter).

Top choice of lakefront **hotels** is *Waldstätterhof* (☎041 825 06 06, ⓦwww .waldstaetterhof.ch; ❺–❻), an elegant, five-star palace overhauled from top to bottom. Lakefront *Bellevue* (☎041 820 13 18, ⓦwww.bellevue-brunnen.ch; ❸) has stylishly modern rooms behind their ornate wrought-iron balconies. On the main street in the village, the seventeenth-century *Weisses Rössli*, Ludwig's old haunt, is due to reopen after having been gutted by fire; previously, its rooms – including a splendid Royal Chamber in Bavarian white, blue and gold – and its **restaurant** were excellent. Meanwhile, the Rôtisserie in the *Waldstätterhof* is the place to go for moderately priced seasonal cuisine. Aim for the *Park* restaurant, Gersauerstrasse 8 (☎041 825 47 47), for excellent veggie dishes. There's a handful of lively **café–bars**, including the popular *Mezcalito* on the lakefront Axenstrasse, with cocktails and pricey food.

Schwyz

A small but characterful town 5km northeast of Brunnen, **SCHWYZ** (pronounced *shveets*) is capital of its canton. First mentioned in a document dated August 14, 972, Schwyz was associated culturally and militarily with its neighbours Uri and Nidwalden from as early as 1144. After the combined confederate forces won a famous victory against the Habsburgs at nearby Morgarten in 1315, they all became collectively dubbed "Schwyzers" and the whole country – formerly Helvetia – became known instead as Schwyz (or Schweiz in modern High German), a name that stuck as the country grew. Throughout the Middle Ages and after, the men of Schwyz were sought after as particularly accomplished mercenaries, and many were able to return to their home town with fat wallets to build for themselves the fine town houses which characterize the old centre today.

Cutting a dash

In 1884, an impoverished young Swiss, Carl Elsener, believed he had spotted a gap in the market for dependable pocket knives, and founded the Swiss Cutlers' Association in order to supply knives and blades to the army. But times were hard: by 1893 his venture had collapsed, and a German competitor had started making knives more cheaply. Elsener persevered, making lighter and more elegant versions of his knives, which he patented in 1897. By word of mouth, the knives grew in popularity, and even without an official seal of approval, Swiss army officers began to ask for them specifically. Elsener had originally named his factory – located in Ibach, just south of Schwyz – after his mother Victoria, but when stainless steel was invented in 1921 and given the international designation INOX, Elsener combined the two into one. **Victorinox** knives (ⓦwww.victorinox.ch) gained official backing from the Swiss Army and, after World War II, from the US Army too. Today, in myriad varieties, they are the best-known brand of Swiss army knife. Tens of thousands are still churned out every day by the same factory in Ibach, about ten minutes' walk south of Schwyz town centre at Schmiedgasse 57. Its on-site **shop** sells the complete range of knives at discount prices (Mon–Fri 7.30am–noon & 1.15–6pm, Sat 8am–3pm).

Schwyz is best known for being the repository of the ancient documents embodying the history of the Confederation, on display in the **Bundes-briefmuseum**, Bahnhofstrasse 20 in the town centre (Museum of Federal Charters; May–Oct Tues–Fri 9–11.30am & 1.30–5pm, Sat & Sun 9am–5pm; Nov–April Tues–Fri same hours, Sat & Sun 1.30–5pm; Fr.4; SMP; ⓦwww .bundesbriefmuseum.ch). A joint ticket, valid for all three of Schwyz's museums, costs Fr.10. This small, beautifully simple 1936 building, with a garden and a cloister of attractive arches, houses banners, flags, coins and documents record-ing events in Swiss history – ask for the excellent English notes at the desk. The main treasure is upstairs, in a great hall lined with flags taken from various battlefields over the centuries. At the far end, lying alone in its own display case, is a small rectangular piece of parchment covered in close lines of text. This is the original **Charter of Confederation**, reputedly signed and sealed on the Rütli meadow on August 1, 1291; the wax seals of Uri and Nidwalden still dangle from it, but the seal of Schwyz was lost long ago.

The historical theme is continued in the inventive **Forum der Schweizer Geschichte** (Forum of Swiss History), a branch of the Swiss National Museum, in the town centre beside the bus station (Tues–Sun 10am–5pm; Fr.8; SMP; ⓦwww.musee-suisse.com). The ground floor is devoted to investigations of how people in both the countryside and the city used environmental resources throughout history; the middle floor concentrates on social history, with assess-ments of power structures and relations between the church and the state; and the top floor concentrates on why and how Switzerland survived in the way that it did. Plenty of videos and interactive displays keep you interested.

The central Hauptplatz square is a few steps east of the museum, dominated by two great buildings, both rebuilt after a town fire in 1642: on a terrace above is the large parish church of **St Martin**, with an ornate interior; while the foursquare **Rathaus** sits on the square itself, its facade decorated with frescoes painted in 1891 to celebrate the 600th anniversary of the Rütli oath. Alleys to the northwest bring you to the **Ital-Reding Haus** (May–Oct Tues–Fri 2–5pm, Sat & Sun 10am–noon & 2–5pm; Fr.4; SMP; ⓦwww.irh.ch), a splendid early seventeenth-century manor house set in its own gardens and with a magnifi-cent interior, its upper rooms bedecked with skilfully carved panelling on wall and ceiling. Across the garden – and within the same complex – is the ancient **Haus Bethlehem**, the oldest wooden house in the country, dating from 1287. Squeezing through its minuscule rooms makes you feel a bit like Alice.

Practicalities

Schwyz is rather awkward both to get to and to stay in, and you'd probably do better spending the night in Brunnen down the road. It's a **bus**-oriented town, with the main central bus station ("Schwyz-Post") handling arrivals from Brunnen. The **train station** is in the suburb of Seewen, some 2km west of Schwyz centre; buses run from outside to Schwyz-Post. The **tourist office** is by the bus station at Bahnhofstrasse 4 (Mon–Fri 6.30am–6.30pm, Sat 7.30am–noon; ☎041 810 19 91, ⓦwww.wbs.ch & ⓦwww.schwyz-tourismus.ch).

Hotels include the *Hirschen*, Hinterdorfstrasse 14 (☎041 811 12 76, ⓦwww .hirschen-schwyz.ch; ❶), a cosy old place also with dorms (Fr.26); and the classier *Wysses Rössli*, Hauptplatz 3 (☎041 811 19 22, ⓦwww.roessli-schwyz .ch; ❹), with large pleasant rooms and an excellent **restaurant**, especially strong on fish specialities (*menus* Fr.24). *Ratskeller*, Strehlgasse 3 (closed Sun & Mon; ☎041 811 10 87, ⓦwww.ratskeller.ch), is another quality restaurant, with a less expensive bistro area to one side (*menus* Fr.19).

Mountain
excursions

**Although it barely needs saying, the Swiss
mountains are sensationally beautiful.
Few visitors leave without journeying to at
least one summit during their stay – and,
fortunately, peaks all across the country
are easily accessible to non-mountaineers,
thanks to a network of mountain railways
and cable cars.**

The Cardada cable car, Locarno

Wherever you start from, it's rarely more than a couple of hours' journey to the mountains. There are few areas that have no means of getting to the top of at least one local peak, and even relatively unsung Swiss summits can offer breathtaking panoramic views.

Furthermore, the experience of being effortlessly lifted out of everyday life into the high mountains – a world of fresh air and bright colour, clear sunlight pouring from saturated blue skies, pure, cool lakes and the uncluttered landscapes above the treeline – is so powerful and extraordinary that it is worth putting up with any amount of discomfort to achieve. Fortunately, with the smoothness and efficiency of Swiss public transport, discomfort is kept to a barely discernible minimum.

Most mountains that can be accessed by public transport also feature at least one summit **restaurant** or **terrace café**; often, there are several to choose from. These tend to be popular getaways: if you're seeking solitude and tranquillity, you generally have to hike away from the summit station, or choose a mountain where the only means of reaching the top is Shanks's pony.

Timetable practicalities

Descending funicular, Muottas Muragl

The online timetable ⓦwww.rail.ch gives timings for every train, bus, boat, funicular, cable car, gondola and chairlift in the country, displaying detailed information on connections between each.

Fares – except on the flagship tourist routes such as to the Jungfraujoch or the Titlis – aren't excessive, and are usually discounted if you hold a Swiss travel pass: 25–50 percent is common.

Where printed timetables or station noticeboards don't show exact timings (often because cable cars or chairlifts run continuously), they at least note the first **ascent** (Bergfahrt, montée, salita) in the morning, the frequency of service throughout the day, and the final **descent** (Talfahrt, descente, discesa) in the evening.

On the highest peaks you may have to leave the top station in mid-afternoon, say 3–4pm, if you want to reach the valley without having to hike or ski part or all of the way down.

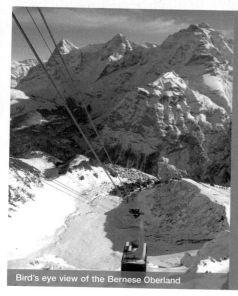

Mountain transport terms

- **Cable car** Seilbahn or Luftseilbahn, téléphérique, funivia.
- **Chairlift** Sesselbahn, télésiège, seggiovia.
- **Draglift** Schlepplift, téléski, sciovia.
- **Funicular** Standseilbahn, funiculaire, funicolare.
- **Gondola** Gondelbahn, télécabine, cabinovia.
- **Mountain transport network** Bergbahnen, remontées mécaniques, impianti di risalita.
- **Rack railway** Zahnradbahn, chemin de fer à crémaillère, ferrovia della cremagliera.

Bird's eye view of the Bernese Oberland

Switzerland's best mountain excursions

The following is a selection of some of the **best mountain journeys** Switzerland has to offer. It is a subjective list that, by necessity, omits much. Most of these journeys do not operate outside high season – for details, see p.27. Some advice about planning walks in the mountains is given on p.69, while p.581 has information on Alpine flora and fauna.

Ski-lift station, Gornergrat

Western Switzerland

Grand-St-Bernard Pass p.327. A historic inn and hospice marks the high-altitude border between Switzerland and Italy.

Les Diablerets p.319. A scenic branch line train winding up from the valley floor to this quiet Alpine village is topped by the sensational cable car ride up to 3000m for glacier panoramas.

Rochers de Naye p.160. Prominent rocky summit perched high above Montreux and Lake Geneva.

The central Alps

Four Passes p.399. A full-day outing by postbus, driving Europe's highest roads and taking in famous passes such as the Furka, Grimsel and Gotthard.

Gornergrat p.350. A rack-railway from Zermatt that crawls its way up impossible slopes to view the Alpine giants close-up.

Jungfraujoch p.294. Flagship tourist route from Interlaken to Europe's highest train station, at 3454m.

Klausen Pass p.472. Unsung pass road (open summer only) between Uri and Glarus, above Lake Luzern, which offers a magnificent drive through classic Swiss scenery.

Piz Gloria revolving restaurant, Schilthorn

Allmendhubel funicular, Mürren

Klein Matterhorn p.349. Perhaps Switzerland's single best cable car; a heart-stopping ride in several stages above Zermatt, ending at a fairytale razor-edge peak at 3900m – Europe's highest cable car station, perfectly positioned opposite the mesmeric Matterhorn. Unforgettable.

Pilatus p.372. The steepest rack-railway in the world is a popular route climbing high above Luzern.

Rigi p.386. Alpine giant looming above Lake Luzern, notable for its ease of access from, among other points, Arth-Goldau, a rail junction on the Zürich–Luzern–Lugano main line.

Schilthorn p.288. Superbly scenic cable car trip above Interlaken – quicker, cheaper and more spectacular than the Jungfraujoch.

Schynige Platte p.281. Another outstanding route from Interlaken, by rack-railway up to all-round panoramic views over lakes, towns and mountains.

Titlis p.384. Snowbound giant above Engelberg, south of Luzern, with a rotating cable car up to the summit.

Trümmelbach falls p.284. Take a detour from Interlaken to this stunning set of mountain waterfalls that have carved their way through the rock face.

Graubünden and the east

The Albula railway p.493. This incredibly well-engineered section of track – also followed by the Glacier Express panoramic train – links St Moritz with the gorges and ravines of central Graubünden via a high pass route.

Arosa p.489. A stunning journey up to this acclaimed Alpine resort by road or rail from Chur.

The Bernina railway p.484. Another superb train ride from St Moritz, over the ice-bound Bernina Pass and down into Italy.

Muottas Muragl p.518. Of the many high-altitude rides above St Moritz, this is perhaps the best – a viewpoint that is lower than most, but with inch-perfect positioning on a crag facing directly along the funnel of the beautiful Engadine valley, threaded with lakes and forests and flanked by the tallest peaks in the eastern Alps.

Säntis p.471. The highest peak in eastern Switzerland, an easy journey up from Appenzell, near Lake Constance but well off most tourist routes.

Ticino

Cardada p.541. Mountain station above Locarno: within minutes, you can leave the lakeside bustle behind for the cool pine forests on the slopes above.

Monte Generoso p.559. Ticino's only rack-railway climbs high above Lake Lugano for spectacular views out over northern Italy, as far as Milan and Turin.

Einsiedeln

The small village of **EINSIEDELN** (900m), in the hills of northern Schwyz 25km northeast of Brunnen, has been Switzerland's most important site of pilgrimage for a thousand years, and still draws a quarter of a million devout believers every year. The village itself is unremarkable, but the mighty Benedictine **Kloster** (monastery) which dominates it is exceptional, and worth a detour whether you're drawn by faith or curiosity.

Einsiedeln means hermitage, and is named for **St Meginrat**, who withdrew to what was then wild forest in about 828 AD. After his death in 861, hermits maintained Meginrat's self-built altar, forming a **Benedictine** community in 934 at the behest of a provost of Strasbourg cathedral, who invited the Bishop of Konstanz to perform the consecration of a new church on the site – the bishop was about to do so, when a voice was heard ringing through the church, insisting three times over that Christ himself had already consecrated the church. The pope declared this to be a **miracle**, and issued a papal bull blessing the pilgrimage to Einsiedeln.

From then on, the monastery enjoyed special privilege, with large royal grants and positions of honour for the abbots. By 1286 a Chapel of Our Lady, built over the remains of Meginrat's cell, was already a focal point; it was adorned after a destructive fire in 1468 with a statuette of Mary with the infant Christ, carved in wood some time before 1440. It is this figure, blackened by smoke from the candles of centuries, which became the focus for pilgrimage, and which has retained its numinous power to this day as the Black Madonna.

The church

The monastery complex was rebuilt from 1704 to 1726 in the most lavish of late-Baroque styles. As you emerge from the cluster of the village centre, the vast **Klosterplatz** opens out in front. The rather plain sandstone front of the church, with its twin towers rising from an immense 140m-long facade, is framed by unusual semi-circular sunken arcades. The ornate **Well of Our Lady** in the square taps the water of Meginrat's spring – pilgrims traditionally drink from each of the 14 spouts in turn on their approach to the church.

The interior, designed by Kaspar Moosbrugger, one of the monks, is breathtaking, although with the regular cycle of services continuing daily you may not get a chance to wander round admiring it. The nave is decorated with detailed **frescoes** by Cosmas Damian Asam, and every part of the lofty white interior is detailed in lavish gold. An intricate wrought-iron choir screen gives into the stunning pink Rococo **choir**, its ceiling bedecked with animated sculptures of angels. However, the focus of all the pilgrims' attention is the black marble **Chapel of Our Lady**, positioned in a huge octagonal bay just inside the main portal. The invading French destroyed the chapel in 1798 (although the monks had already removed the Black Madonna to the Tyrol for safekeeping), and the present chapel building dates from a Neoclassical reconstruction in 1817. The **Black Madonna** itself, a little over a metre tall and usually dressed in a jewelled and tasselled golden dress donated by Canton Uri in 1734, stands illuminated within at the centre of attention.

Einsiedeln remains a fully functioning monastic community (🌐www.kloster -einsiedeln.ch), with around a hundred priests and brothers. **Mass** is celebrated several times a day. Of the many annual **pilgrimage festivals**, the most colourful is the Feast of the Miraculous Dedication on September 14, which culminates in a candlelit procession around the square.

Practicalities

Trains run every hour from Luzern to Biberbrugg, where you have to change for the climb to Einsiedeln; trains from Brunnen require an extra change at Arth-Goldau. Einsiedeln's **train station** is a ten-minute walk from the church: from Dorfplatz out front, head east along Hauptstrasse. The **tourist office** is just off Klosterplatz at Hauptstrasse 85 (Mon–Fri 8.30am–5pm, Sat 9am–4pm, Sun 10am–noon; ☎055 418 44 88, ⓦwww.einsiedeln.ch). Almost every building in sight of the church is a **hotel**: on the square, *Linde* (☎055 418 48 48, ⓦwww.linde-einsiedeln .ch; ❸–❹) is a good mid-range choice, while just off the square is *Storchen*, Hauptstrasse 79 (☎055 412 37 60, ⓦwww.hotel-storchen.ch; ❹), a comfortable place with a good restaurant. There are plenty of places to **eat** – ranging from the simple *Pizzeria Zia Teresa*, Hauptstrasse 21 (closed Mon & Tues), up to the quality restaurants on and near Klosterplatz (such as *St Georg*) with Fr.23-ish *menus*.

The legend of William Tell

The legend of **William Tell** is the central defining myth in Swiss national consciousness. Most schoolchildren, whether in Switzerland or elsewhere in the West, know at least the bare bones of the story, but whereas in most cultures it is little more than one folktale among many, in Switzerland it has come to embody the very essence of Swissness.

The story

At a time soon after the opening of the Gotthard Pass in the thirteenth century, when the Habsburg emperors of Vienna sought to control Uri and thus control trans-Alpine trade, a new bailiff, **Hermann Gessler**, was despatched to Altdorf. The proud mountain folk of Uri had already joined with their Schwyzer and Nidwaldner neighbours at Rütli in pledging to resist the Austrians' cruel oppression, and when Gessler raised a pole in the central square of Altdorf and perched his hat on the top, commanding all who passed before it to bow in respect, it was the last straw. **William Tell**, a countryman from nearby Bürglen, either hadn't heard about Gessler's command or chose to ignore it; whichever, he walked past the hat without bowing. Gessler seized Tell, who was well known as a marksman, and set him a challenge. He ordered him to shoot an apple off his son's head with his crossbow; if Tell was successful, he would be released, but if he failed or refused, both he and his son would die.

The boy's hands were tied. Tell put one arrow in his quiver and another in his crossbow, took aim, and shot the apple clean off his son's head. Gessler was impressed and infuriated – and then asked what the second arrow was for. Tell looked the tyrant in the eye and replied that if the first arrow had struck the child, the second would have been for Gessler. For such impertinence, Tell was arrested and sentenced to lifelong imprisonment in the dungeons of Gessler's castle at Küssnacht, northeast of Luzern. During the long boat journey a violent storm arose, and the oarsmen – unfamiliar with the lake – begged with Gessler to release Tell so that he could steer them to safety. Gessler acceded, and Tell cannily manoeuvred the boat close to the shore, then leapt to freedom, landing on a flat rock (the **Tellsplatte**) and simultaneously pushing the boat back into the stormy waters.

Determined to see his task through and use the second arrow, Tell hurried to Küssnacht. As Gessler and his party walked along on a dark lane called Hohlegasse on their way to the castle, Tell leapt out, shot a bolt into the tyrant's heart and melted back into the woods to return to Uri. His comrades were inspired by Tell's act of bravery to throw off the yoke of Habsburg oppression in their homeland, and to remain forever free.

Every few years, the monastery stages a mass **open-air** production of the *Great World Theatre* – a religious drama by Pedro Calderón de la Barca that was premiered at the Spanish court in 1685. Some 600 villagers take part, coached by the monks themselves. Check Ⓦwww.welttheater.ch for details of the next production.

Uri and the Alpine passes

The mountainous **Canton Uri** occupies the land between Lake Luzern and the barrier of the high Alps. Although Uri shares borders with Bern, Valais, Ticino, Graubünden and Glarus, it is cut off from them all by 2000m–plus

The legend

Walter Dettwiler, in his book *William Tell: Portrait of a Legend* (1991), outlines the impact of the Tell legend over the centuries. The basis of the story – a marksman forced by an overlord to shoot an object from the head of a loved one – first appears in **Scandinavian sagas** written centuries before the Swiss version was first committed to paper in the fifteenth century. It was an epic song, however, composed in 1477 about the founding of the Swiss Confederation and including a section on the story of Tell, which accounted for the widespread circulation of the legend. During the **French Revolution**, the popularity of Tell rose to a peak: he was viewed as a freedom fighter in the noblest of traditions and the tale was held up as a justification for the killing of Louis XVI – all the more so because Tell and the French revolutionary armies shared a common enemy, the Austrian Habsburgs. In the 1770s and 1780s, the German poet Goethe had travelled extensively throughout Switzerland, later telling his friend, the playwright **Friedrich Schiller**, of his journeyings. Schiller's famous play *Wilhelm Tell* (1804) drew from Goethe's first-hand accounts as well as from ancient Swiss chronicles to set the Tell legend in stone, and over subsequent decades, to broadcast the story to a wide European public. **Rossini**'s opera *Guillaume Tell*, which premiered in Paris in 1829, did for the Romance-language countries of Europe what Schiller's play had done for the Teutonic.

With the final unification of Switzerland in 1848 after half-a-century of war, a mood of national liberation and communal purpose became crystallized around the enduring significance of William Tell, who began to be portrayed with increasing idealism, notably in the **Tell monument** in Altdorf, which was unveiled in 1895. **Ferdinand Hodler**, most famous of Swiss artists, drew directly on this monument for his seminal portrait of Tell as a godlike figure, emerging from a gap in the clouds with arm outstretched (see p.257). Throughout **World War II**, the image and notion of a deeply moral, fervently nationalistic Tell hardened the resolve of ordinary Swiss to resist domination by Nazi Germany, and contributed to Switzerland's self-imposed exclusion from the co-operative international organizations – specifically the United Nations and the European Union – which arose after 1945.

However, the **700th anniversary** of the Confederation, celebrated in 1991, brought dissenting voices to the fore for the first time, with revisionist historians searching for more pragmatic reasons for the survival of Swiss culture than the doings of a single male hero. The annual retelling of Schiller's drama on an open stage in touristic Interlaken (see p.279) to an audience increasingly made up of foreigners is, too, beginning to ring hollow, and in a new century, popular perception has become increasingly cynical over the continuing appropriateness of William Tell as an icon for a 21st-century Switzerland.

mountain passes, and the only cantons with which it has easy exchange of influence are its old partners from the 1291 Rütli oath, Schwyz and Nidwalden. It's no coincidence that Uri is the setting for the medieval legend of **William Tell** (see box pp.394–395), absorbed into Swiss consciousness as near fact and serving to define the essence of Swissness to the rest of the world. The small cantonal capital **Altdorf** was where Tell did his apple-shooting.

Uri also holds the keys to the great trans-Alpine **Gotthard** route, one of the main Alpine passes. For centuries, people and traffic have followed the ancient road up and over the mountains, although these days massively long tunnels draw trains and most of the cars swiftly to and from Ticino and Italy. **Andermatt**, on the south side of the Gotthard, is uniquely located at an Alpine crossroads, with six high-level routes passing through or near the town.

Flüelen, Altdorf and Bürglen

FLÜELEN is the farthest point of the Vierwaldstättersee from Luzern, a picturesque little town with the train station right beside the landing stage. Fast trains from Flüelen serve both Luzern and Zürich (with alternate services requiring a change at Arth-Goldau), as well as heading south through the Gotthard to Ticino. It's also the southern terminus of the **Axenstrasse**, the narrow road which clings below the cliffs of the eastern shore of the Urnersee south from Brunnen. The road was only completed in 1865, and enabled travellers to approach the Gotthard for the first time by land, instead of forcing them to take ship from Luzern or Brunnen. Some 3km north of Flüelen – and accessible only by car, boat or on foot (no buses use the Axenstrasse) – is the **Tellsplatte**, a flat rock onto which William Tell is purported to have leapt to escape the clutches of Gessler (see box pp.394–395). Beside it is a restaurant and, beautifully framed amidst the trees, the **Tellskapelle** (see p.383), a tiny monument

built in 1880 with arched loggia featuring vivid frescoes depicting the story of Tell. Boats serving this point from Brunnen also pass the **Schillerstein**, a 25m high natural obelisk near the Rütli which was inscribed in 1859: "To Friedrich Schiller, the Chronicler of Tell".

Buses from Flüelen station run into central **ALTDORF**, some 3km south (Altdorf's own train station is inconveniently located 1km west of the centre). At the traffic-bound heart of Altdorf is the Rathausplatz, dominated by the impressive **Telldenkmal** (Tell Monument) – a much-photographed icon erected in 1895 that depicts a sturdy, bearded Tell raising his eyes fearlessly to the horizon, while his son, embodiment of the Swiss people, accepts his father's protecting arm and gazes trustingly upwards at him. This square is reputedly the scene of the

△ The Tell Monument, Altdorf

apple-shooting event commemorated in the legend. Nearby alleys have retained plenty of character, but if the Tell bug has bitten you, grab a bus (from the square, or from Altdorf-Post, 100m south on Bahnhofstrasse) to **BÜRGLEN**, a village 2km northeast on the Klausen road, which is celebrated as Tell's birthplace. The **chapel** which sits beside Bürglen's village church on the site of Tell's house was dedicated as early as 1582, with interior frescoes depicting the legend dating from the 1750s. Around the corner from the 1786 Tell fountain out front is the **Tell Museum** (daily: July & Aug 9.30am–5.30pm; May, June, Sept & Oct 10–11.30am & 1.30–5pm; Fr.5; SMP; Ⓦ www.tellmuseum.ch), a worthwhile little place crammed with Tell curiosities; ask them to set up the informative twenty-minute slide-show (in English) on the history of the legend.

What's remarkable about the Altdorf area is the understatedness of its Tellmania: you get the feeling that Tell, although something of a caricature to non-Swiss, is far too important to the locals to start a whole tourist circus. Tellsplatte, Altdorf and Bürglen are all out-of-the-way places, little visited by foreigners, and you may well find that the only tourists are Swiss families, spending a weekend in the area to give the kids a glimpse of their heritage.

The road through Bürglen continues up on a spectacular drive – followed by buses in summer – to the **Klausen Pass** (see also p.472) and over to Linthal in Canton Glarus. This is one of the most scenic pass routes in the country, with dizzy views constantly distracting you from the business of keeping on the narrow road.

Practicalities

Altdorf's **tourist office**, with information on the whole canton, is just off the main square at Schützengasse 11 (Mon–Fri 9–11.30am & 1.30–5.30pm, Sat 9–11.30am; ℡041 872 04 50, Ⓦ www.altdorftourismus.ch & Ⓦ www.i-uri.ch).

For accommodation in **Flüelen**, aim for the serviceable *Weisses Kreuz*, opposite the landing stage at Axenstrasse 2 (℡041 870 17 17, Ⓦ www.weisseskreuz -fluelen.ch; ❷). The campsite (℡041 870 92 22, Ⓦ www.windsurfing-urnersee.ch), fifteen minutes' walk from the station, doubles as a windsurfing centre.

The best-value hotel in **Altdorf** is the *Schwarzen Löwen*, Tellsgasse 8 (℡041 874 80 80, Ⓦ www.hotel-loewen-altdorf.ch; ❸), which has renovated rooms, all clean and pleasant (choose one off the street) – one room has retained the original furniture from when Goethe stopped by in the 1770s.

The most characterful accommodation choice of the lot is the ⚇ *Gasthaus Adler* in the centre of **Bürglen** (℡041 870 11 33; ❶), a fine old sixteenth-century roadhouse inn, with wooden eaves bedecked in ivy and a handful of alluringly creaky guest rooms above a *gutbürgerliche* restaurant.

Andermatt and around

If you're travelling south by fast train, you're likely to miss the small town of **ANDERMATT** (1444m), surrounded by the high Alps on all sides, since it lies beyond the entrance to the Gotthard Tunnel at **Göschenen** (see p.398). This once-great staging post for four major Alpine crossings is now even bypassed by the motorway, which plunges into its own tunnel, also at Göschenen. However, as the hub of many long-distance hiking routes, Andermatt still sees plenty of visitors in the short Alpine summer (June–Sept), and equal numbers in the winter skiing season, with red and black runs galore off the nearby **Gemsstock** summit (2963m), and an abundance of cross-country routes. The Gemsstock is also the best summer viewpoint in the area, since the town is too close to the valley sides to offer any panoramas of its own. Andermatt also serves as the Swiss Army's principal Alpine training centre: you may find an over-preponderance of military types around and about, and it's prudent to check with the tourist office that your chosen route is open before you set off on any long-distance hikes.

Andermatt's train station is 400m north of the town centre; turn left outside for the **tourist office**, in the same building as the postbus booking centre (July–Sept & Dec–March Mon–Sat 9am–noon & 2–5.30pm; rest of year Mon–Fri same times; ☎041 887 14 54, ⓦ www.andermatt.ch). **Accommodation** is clustered around the picturesque main Gotthardstrasse, which can get crowded in summer: *Sonne*, at no. 76 (☎041 887 12 26, ⓦ www.hotelsonneandermatt.ch; ❸), is a cosy old wooden place, while the *Drei Könige & Post*, at no. 69 (☎041 887 00 01, ⓦ www.3koenige.ch; ❸–❹), has modern, comfortable rooms.

The high passes all round offer possibilities for spectacular round-trip **driving tours** – you can follow the route from Andermatt over the Gotthard, Nufenen and Furka passes by postbus in summer; or it's equally possible to strike out with your own transport over the Susten, Grimsel and Furka passes, with an intermediate stop for lunch in Meiringen (see p.302). To the east, the Oberalp Pass leads to Disentis/Mustér (see p.497).

The Gotthard Pass and tunnels

The most famous of all the Alpine passes, the **St Gotthard** or **San Gottardo** (2108m) is also the most memorable to visit. The turbulent Schöllenen Gorge, a few kilometres north of Andermatt, was first bridged in the thirteenth century, allowing traffic to penetrate up the full length of the Reuss valley from Flüelen to the pass itself, from where a continuation road followed the valley of the River Ticino all the way south to Bellinzona and Milan. Today, three daily buses (July–Sept only) follow the new road from Andermatt up to the pass and on down to Airolo. The old cobbled road, which branches off partway up, is much quieter and more picturesque. Both meet on top, where you'll find a wild windswept spot with a handful of buildings clustered around a small lake that's become an unfortunately popular picnicking spot for day-tripping families. The pass is one of Europe's watersheds: rain or snowmelt on the north side ultimately ends up in the Rhine and the North Sea, while moisture on the south side flows into the Po and the Mediterranean.

The old **hospice** beside the road now houses the engaging **Museo Nazionale del San Gottardo** (May–Oct daily 9am–6pm; Fr.9; SMP), which outlines the history of the pass with models, reliefs, paintings and audiovisual slide-shows. Across the road, there are simple modern rooms available at the often-busy ⚷ *Albergo San Gottardo* (☎091 869 12 35, ⓦ www.gotthard-hospiz.ch; ❷; May–Oct). From the pass, most traffic follows the new road down to Airolo, but the old cobbled road that snakes down behind the *albergo* off the back of the pass into Ticino is truly spectacular, with terrific vistas all the way down into the Val Tremolo ("Valley of Trembling"). If you're **hiking**, it's a three-hour walk to Airolo this way, or six hours by an off-road route through Val Canaria; on the north side, Andermatt is three hours away via the small village of Hospental, or six by a more scenic route through the deserted valleys around Maighels.

The Gotthard tunnels

Foot traffic has used the Gotthard Pass since about 1200, and the first carriage crossed in 1775. Less than a century later, in 1872, after decades of debate over routes and costs, work began on a **rail tunnel** beneath the pass. Over seven years and 277 lives later, the bores which had begun simultaneously from

Göschenen and Airolo met midway on February 29, 1880. The first trains ran through the 15km-long tunnel in 1882.

This line is still a vital north–south artery, carrying at peak times an average of one train every six minutes – with five million passengers and 25 million tonnes of freight carried to and fro each year. The Gotthard journey is one of Switzerland's great train rides, not so much for the long stretch of blackness as you swoosh beneath the Alps, but for the spectacular approach. South of Flüelen, you climb slowly and dramatically up the wild valley, passing through dozens of straight tunnels and, around **Wassen**, a series of tightly spiralled tunnels, which gain maximum altitude at minimum gradients. Wassen's little onion-domed church, prominent on its rock, is a famous landmark: you'll pass it three times, first high above you, then on a level, and finally far below you before you're plunged into darkness shortly afterwards at **Göschenen**. Trains emerge at Airolo (see p.537) for the long journey down to Bellinzona.

The 16.3km Gotthard **road tunnel**, completed in 1980, which runs in parallel from Göschenen to Airolo, was the longest road tunnel in the world until a Norwegian project overtook it in 2000. Although prone to hideous kilometres-long jams on both approaches, it remains open year-round, while the pass road above is impassable in winter.

Work is now well under way on the new **Gotthard Base Tunnel**, part of an ambitious project to upgrade high-speed train routes beneath the Alps in order to take freight off the roads and shorten long-distance rail journeys. When the tunnel opens in 2012, trains will enter at Erstfeld, a few kilometres south of Altdorf, speeding through the deep tunnel at up to 250kph to the exit at Bodio, 58km south. Cutting out the long climb up to Göschenen and the long descent from Airolo will shave a full hour off Zürich–Milan journey times. Legislation is also in place to force pan-European road freight onto the new line, thus clearing the N2 highway in the upper Reuss and upper Ticino of its appalling traffic-jams and easing environmental degradation. Full information and progress reports are at Ⓦ www.alptransit.ch.

The Furka Pass

Summer postbuses from Andermatt cross the **Furka Pass** (2431m; see also p.354) westwards into Canton Valais, while mainline passenger and car-carrying trains use the year-round Furka-Basis Tunnel beneath the pass. Buses aside, the main draw on the Uri side is a volunteer-run antique mountain **steam train**, the DFB (Ⓦ www.furka-bergstrecke.ch), which in summer puffs its way from **Realp** – a hamlet an easy hour-and-three-quarter walk from Andermatt – up to a station near the pass and on through the short Muttbach tunnel to Gletsch. The round trip costs Fr.93.

Between Realp and the pass is *Hotel Tiefenbach* (☎041 887 13 22, Ⓦ www .tiefenbach-hotel.ch; ❷), with quality dorms from Fr.40, also open in winter

---

Car-carrying trains: the Furka and Oberalp passes

If you're heading west into Valais and would prefer to avoid the climb over the Furka Pass, note that **car-carrying trains** run daily year-round from Realp (near Andermatt) through the **Furka-Basis Tunnel** (15.4km) to Oberwald, at least every hour (6am–9pm); a one-way fare is Fr.25 (Oct–May Fr.30). Journey time is 15min. You can also avoid the climb eastwards over the **Oberalp Pass** into Graubünden by loading your car onto a train at Andermatt for the hour-long pull to Sedrun (Fr.65). Full information on both routes is at Ⓦ www.mgbahn.ch.

as base camp for some fine cross-country skiing. On the pass sits the historic *Furkablick* (☎041 887 07 17; ❷; June–Sept), a fine old inn bought in the 1990s by gallery-owner Marc Hostettler, who has preserved much of the charm (and original features) of the century-old interior – not least the library, now crammed with books on contemporary art. Dutch architect Rem Koolhaas worked on part of the renovations, and the interior is decorated with "Furkart", left by artists invited to stay up here by Hostettler.

The Oberalp Pass

Directly east of Andermatt is the **Oberalp Pass** (2044m) into Canton Graubünden, kept passable to trains year-round. This is the route of the famous Glacier Express (see p.42) between Zermatt and St Moritz, which runs via the Furka-Basis Tunnel, Andermatt and the Oberalp on its way to Chur. Local trains from Andermatt to Disentis/Mustér (see p.497) can drop you on the pass itself, trailhead for a host of high-country summer hikes. Two scenic routes run through the bleak and invigorating high country down to Andermatt, one via the Lolenpass (5hr 30min), the other via the Maighelspass (6hr 30min), while an easier one heads out to Fellilücke, and from there to Nätschen and Andermatt (5hr).

Travel details

Full timetables for all trains, buses, trams, boats and cable cars in Switzerland – as well as international connections – are searchable at ⓦ www.rail.ch. For details of trains from Andermatt over the Furka and Oberalp passes, see ⓦ www.mgbahn.ch.

Trains

Andermatt to: Brig (hourly; 2hr); Disentis/Mustér (hourly; 1hr 10min); Flüelen (hourly; 50min; change at Göschenen); Oberalppass (at least hourly; 25min).

Arth-Goldau to: Lugano (hourly; 2hr 10min); Luzern (3 hourly; 25min); Rigi Kulm (hourly; 40min); Zürich (hourly; 40min).

Brunnen to: Altdorf (hourly; 10min); Flüelen (every 30min; 10min); Luzern (twice hourly; 45min; some change at Arth-Goldau); Zug (every 30min; 35min).

Einsiedeln to: Luzern (hourly; 1hr; change at Biberbrugg); Zürich (every 30min; 45min; change at Wädenswil).

Engelberg to: Luzern (hourly; 1hr 5min).

Flüelen to: Andermatt (hourly; 50min; change at Göschenen); Brunnen (every 30min; 10min); Lugano (hourly; 2hr 15min); Luzern (every 30min; 55min; some change at Arth-Goldau); Schwyz (every 30min; 15min); Zürich (every 30min; 1hr 10min; some change at Arth-Goldau).

Luzern to: Basel (hourly; 1hr 10min); Bellinzona (hourly; 2hr 15min); Bern (twice hourly; 1hr 5min); Brienz (hourly; 1hr 35min); Brunnen (twice hourly;

45min; some change at Arth-Goldau); Einsiedeln (hourly; 1hr; change at Biberbrugg); Engelberg (hourly; 1hr 5min); Flüelen (every 30min; 55min; some change at Arth-Goldau); Hergiswil (4 hourly; 10min); Interlaken Ost (hourly; 1hr 55min); Lugano (hourly; 2hr 45min; some change at Arth-Goldau); Stans (every 30min; 20min); Zug (3 hourly; 20min); Zürich (twice hourly; 45min).

Stans to: Engelberg (hourly; 35min); Hergiswil (every 30min; 10min); Luzern (every 30min; 20min).

Vitznau to: Rigi Kulm (twice hourly; 30min).

Zug to: Brunnen (every 30min; 35min); Lugano (hourly; 2hr 30min); Luzern (3 hourly; 20min); Zürich (twice hourly; 25min).

Buses

Altdorf to: Bürglen (hourly; 5min); Flüelen (hourly; 10min).

Andermatt to: Airolo via Gotthardpass (July–Sept 3 daily; 50min); Oberwald via Furkapass (July–Sept 2 daily; 1hr 30min).

Brunnen to: Schwyz (every 10–20min; 10min).

Flüelen to: Altdorf (hourly; 10min); Linthal via Klausenpass (July–Sept 4 daily; 2hr 20min).

Gersau to: Schwyz (hourly; 25min); Weggis (hourly; 25min).

Göschenen to: Meiringen via Sustenpass (July–Sept 2 daily; 1hr 45min).

Schwyz to: Brunnen (every 10–20min; 10min).

Stans to: Beckenried (twice hourly; 20min); Seelisberg (hourly; 45min).
Weggis to: Gersau (hourly; 25min); Vitznau (hourly; 10min).

Boats

Following is a summary of April–Oct services; fewer boats run in other months, quite often only on Sun, if at all. Full details are at ⓦ www.lakelucerne.ch (for Zug, see ⓦ www.zugersee-info.ch).
Brunnen to: Luzern (approx hourly; 1hr 50min–2hr 40min); Vitznau (approx hourly; 1hr–1hr 15min).

Flüelen to: Luzern (approx 7 daily; 2hr 50min–3hr 40min).
Luzern to: Alpnachstad (6 daily; 1hr 30–45min); Beckenried (approx hourly; 1hr 20min–2hr); Brunnen (approx hourly; 1hr 50min–2hr 40min); Flüelen (approx 7 daily; 2hr 50min–3hr 40min); Kehrsiten-Bürgenstock (6 daily; 35min); Vitznau (approx hourly; 40min–1hr 10min); Weggis (approx hourly; 35-50min).
Vitznau to: Brunnen (approx hourly; 1hr–1hr 15min); Luzern (approx hourly; 40min–1hr 10min).
Zug to: Arth-am-See (3–6 daily; 45min–2hr).

9

Zürich

CHAPTER 9

Highlights

✳ **Grossmünster** Zürich's "Great Minster", from where Zwingli preached the Reformation. **See p.421**

✳ **Kunsthaus** World-class gallery of art, unmissable if only for the vast array of works by Alberto Giacometti. **See p.422**

✳ **Chagall windows** Marc Chagall's breathtaking stained glass in the lofty choir of the Fraumünster will have you spellbound. **See p.427**

✳ **Uetliberg** Steep-sided ridge rising above the city, with stunning views and wooded walking trails. **See p.429**

✳ **Zürich West** Hotbed of the city's counterculture, centred on the buzzing Langstrasse. **See p.429**

✳ **Café Schober** Lacy, old-fashioned confectioner and tearoom that could bring out the little old lady in anyone. **See p.432**

✳ **Blinde Kuh** Quirky, highly successful restaurant where you eat in complete darkness. **See p.433**

✳ **The Zürichsee** An easy escape from the city is by boat for the short trip to the "City of Roses", Rapperswil. **See p.439**

△ Zurich West

9

Zürich

Zürich's relationship to the world is not of the spirit, but of commerce.

C.G. Jung

Not so long ago, **ZÜRICH** was famed chiefly for being the cleanest, most icily efficient city in Europe: apocryphal stories abound from the 1970s of the calm and order of the midweek lunch hour in the financial district, of tourists embarking on efforts to find a cigarette butt or an empty crisp packet discarded on the streets – and drawing a blank every time. Things have changed. If you live in a big city yourself and are tiring of Switzerland's picture-perfect country towns, visiting Zürich will be like coming home: finally you can walk on crowded, multi-ethnic streets, buy a kebab, get a drink after midnight, feel a lived-in urban buzz.

Zürich is still best known for a phrase coined as a response to the city's collective sense of superiority. After World War II, Zürich's foreign exchange speculators had become so powerful and secretive that irritated British ministers, amidst the 1964 sterling crisis, spoke of them as gnomes, scurrying about in the corridors and vaults of the private banks manipulating the outside world and forever counting their gold. Their reference to "**the gnomes of Zürich**" stuck, and journalists reporting on Switzerland's often-murky banking and finance industries still reach for the phrase today. Aptly, Zürich now hosts the world's most important market for trading **gold** and precious metals, and boasts the fourth-largest stock market, after New York, London and Tokyo. Exceptional affluence tends to define the area these days and yet, despite its wealth and status as Switzerland's biggest city (population 360,000), Zürich is not a flashy place at all. The ghost of the bible-thumping Reformer Huldrych Zwingli still stands at the shoulder of the bankers, industrialists and business people who live and breathe the city's ingrained Protestant work ethic – yet it's the freedom of thought that Zwingli encouraged which continually bubbles to the surface. Wry Zürchers like to make much of how apt it is that you have to tut, purse your lips and clear your throat just to say the city's name (*tsoorikh* in dialect), but they're deliberately pandering to a long-outdated stereotype.

You're likely to find plenty to keep you occupied in this most beautiful of cities, poised astride the River Limmat, adorned with over a thousand medieval and modern fountains, and turned towards the **Zürichsee**, a lake so crystal-clear the Swiss authorities have certified its water safe to drink. Following a period of notoriety in the early 1990s as one of Europe's hard-drug capitals, Zürich has, in recent years, undergone a boom in arts and popular culture, expressed most tangibly in a host of chic new restaurants and dance clubs. The medieval **Old Town**, characterized by the steep, cobbled

Within the map:

Olten

Baden

Dielsdorf

▲ Schaffhausen   ▲ St Gallen

Winterthur

Kloten

Kyburg

✈

Oerlikon

Zürichberg
▲676m

Dübendorf

ZÜRICH

Pfäffikon

AARGAU
ZÜRICH

Uetliberg
▲870m

Greifensee

Uster

Adliswil

Kilchberg

Küsnacht

Reuss

Pfannenstiel
▲853m

Thalwil
▲791m
▲880m

Zürichsee

Albishorn
909m

Horgen

Stäfa   Rapperswil

N

Pfäffikon

ZÜRICH
ZUG

Wädenswil

Sihl

0   10 km

Cham

Baar

ZÜRICH AND AROUND

Zug
988m

Gottschalkenberg
1164m ▲

Biberbrugg

Luzern ▼   ▼ Schwyz

Schwyz ▼ ▼ Einsiedeln

---

alleys and attractive, small-scale architecture of the **Niederdorf** district, comprises a substantial part of the city centre and is perfect for exploratory wanderings. With a handful of medieval churches to take in, including the mighty **Grossmünster** and graceful **Fraumünster**, the superb **Kunsthaus** art gallery and the most engaging café culture in German-speaking Switzerland, you could easily spend days here.

Some history

The **Romans** were the first to fortify the area, creating a customs post on the Lindenhof in the first century BC and naming it *Turicum*. The legend of the city's foundation dates from the martyrdom of **Felix and Regula**, deserters from a Roman legion based in Valais.

During the eleventh and twelfth centuries, Zürich's traders built up fabulous wealth, mainly from textiles such as wool and silk – but in 1336 a visionary burgomaster, **Rudolf Brun**, shuffled the merchant nobility out of power, handing control instead to workers' guilds (which were to keep a hold on the city until the nineteenth century). Shortly after, still under Brun's direction, Zürich joined the nascent Swiss Confederation.

The thriving city experienced its zenith of power and prestige in the sixteenth century, when it became the first Swiss city to embrace the **Reformation**. The city's spiritual father, Huldrych **Zwingli** (see box p.422), preached in the Grossmünster from 1519 until his death in 1531. With the abolition of the

Too rich!

Political activism within Zürich's youth movement during the 1970s culminated in major riots in 1980–81 and the police closure of the city's autonomous youth centre. The counterculture regrouped around two large community **squats**, the activities of which have passed into the city's collective memory. The first, known as **Wohlgroth**, took over an empty commercial building next to the train tracks on Zollstrasse; the squatters immediately erected a placard on the roof to greet trains rolling into the city with a huge imitation SBB station sign reading not "Zürich" but "*Zu reich*" ("Too rich"). At a stroke, this guaranteed them fame – admiring chuckles mixing equally with establishment fury. The Wohlgroth developed into a thriving centre for arts, music and alternative culture, and such was its popularity that, after some years of hand-wringing at the loss of rent on such a prime site, the chief executive of the corporation which owned the building personally came visiting with the offer to donate another, less embarrassingly visible building to the collective. His offer, needless to say, was rejected, and shortly afterwards, in October 1993, the police evicted the place with tear gas and water cannon. Perhaps the greatest legacy of the Wohlgroth, aside from their classic *Zu reich* prank, is that the neighbourhood has now become the heart of the city's new subculture.

The second big squat of the early 1980s was of the **Rote Fabrik**, a former silk mill in a beautiful lakeside location south of the city, owned by the municipality. Whereas similar city-owned places squatted in Bern and Geneva have remained illegal and on the radical fringes of city life to this day, it's a mark of discreet Zürcher pragmatism that in 1987 the Rote Fabrik collective voted to apply for legal status and an arts subsidy from the city council. This was granted, millions of francs flowing into their coffers shortly after. These days, although its alternative heart still beats, the Rote Fabrik is able to develop and stage avant-garde dance and drama that gets taken seriously by the *Neue Zürcher Zeitung*, the city's most conservative newspaper. The flipside, of course, is that a mere mention of the place makes the committed radicals in Bern roll their eyes and start muttering about a sell-out.

Catholic Mass in 1525, Zürich became a centre for dissident intellectuals from all over Europe. After 1549, when Calvinist doctrine was adopted over Zwinglian, the city experienced a slow fading in its fortunes. The French Revolution of 1789 sparked **pro-libertarian** demonstrations at Stäfa, south of Zürich, but the city itself remained a backwater.

A late-nineteenth-century city councillor, **Alfred Escher**, is credited with reinventing Zürich as the economic capital of Switzerland, by his legislative innovations boosting tourism, banking and local manufacturing industry. Strict neutrality during World War I again made Zürich a refuge for dissidents, and for some months in 1916 and 1917, the city was home to **Lenin**, mulling over the future Russian Revolution, **James Joyce**, holed up near the university writing *Ulysses*, and a band of émigré artists calling themselves "Dada", who spent their evenings lampooning Western culture at the famous **Cabaret Voltaire**.

Zürich's exact role during and after **World War II** remains murky, but the city emerged post-war to flourish, becoming one of the world's leading financial centres. More recently, following a relaxation of licensing laws, Zürich is discovering a new will to party. Alongside all its sights and its lakeside beauty, Zürich is reinventing itself again, and a gritty and engaging subculture – centred in the up-and-coming district of **Zürich West** – is thriving beneath the city's slick, monied surface.

Arrival and information

Zürich's **airport** (ⓦ www.zurich-airport.com) is 11km northeast in Kloten. Its subterranean **train station** is clearly signed. Trains depart roughly every ten minutes for the city's main station, Zürich HB (takes 10min; last train 12.15am); some go nonstop, others have an intermediate halt at Zürich-Oerlikon. Beware that a few stop at suburban stations but avoid Zürich HB – check the departure boards carefully. You can buy a ticket from the machines (Fr.5.80; press the red button), but note that if you intend to stay a day or two in Zürich, it may be more economical to get a ZürichCARD (see p.412) from a staffed counter.

Frequent fast trains also go direct from the airport to points all over the country – major destinations like Basel, Bern, Luzern, Interlaken, Lausanne and Geneva, as well as other cities including Baden, Winterthur, St Gallen, Fribourg and Brig (for Zermatt), cutting out the need to change at Zürich HB. Check timetables at ⓦ **www.rail.ch**.

Many Zürich **hotels** will pick you up at Arrivals and drive you to the door – ask about this service (which is often free) when you book your room. A **taxi** into the city centre costs Fr.60 or more.

By train

Zürich's main station, or **Hauptbahnhof** (HB), has trains arriving continuously from all corners of Switzerland and around Europe. It's a massive beehive of a place located in the heart of the city, extending three storeys below ground and taking in a shopping mall, supermarket and some good restaurants. Most trains arrive at **street level** (platforms 3–18), where the echoing station concourse is home to a scattering of fast-food stalls and cafés, a post office and, at the far end beyond the

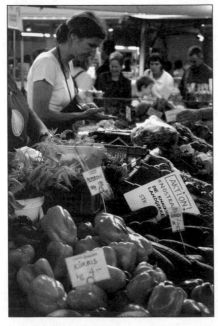

giant clock, the tourist office (see below). Out of sight behind the travel bureau are the bike rental office and left-luggage counter.

One level down you'll find luggage lockers, while going down again brings you to the **shopping level**, with a warren of echoing subterranean passageways stretching off in all directions. **S-Bahn** suburban trains leave from the lowest level (platforms 1–2 and, separately, 21–24) to local destinations such as Uetliberg and Adliswil; the huge information boards on the street-level concourse list S-Bahn departures separately from mainline departures (*Fernverkehr*). Some S-Bahn trains depart from platforms 51–54, located at street level halfway along platform 3. S-Bahn services to nearby towns such as Winterthur and Baden are slower than mainline trains, but

△ Weekly market, Hauptbahnhof   go more frequently.

By car and bus

Parking is difficult and expensive. All of the Old Town, plus chunks of the central commercial district, are off-limits to cars, and although there are nine parking garages in the centre, pinpointed at ⓦwww.parking.ch, they can be prohibitively expensive, often more than Fr.30 a day. It's a good idea to ask your hotel in advance about parking: some can reserve free or discounted spaces for guests. International **buses** arrive at the open bus park on Sihlquai opposite the *Walhalla* hotel, 50m behind the station. Domestic Swiss postbuses terminate in the suburbs.

Information

On the street-level concourse of the city's main train station, Zürich HB, sits the excellently equipped **tourist office** (April–Oct Mon–Sat 8am–8.30pm, Sun 8.30am–6.30pm; Nov–March Mon–Sat 8.30am–7pm, Sun 9am–6.30pm; ☎044 215 40 00, ⓦwww.zuerich.com). Staff can book you onto a two-hour **guided walk** through the old town in English (Easter–Oct Mon–Fri 3pm, Sat & Sun 11am & 3pm; Nov–Easter Wed & Sat 11am; Fr.20), or a two-hour **city tour** on a bus done up as a vintage trolley-bus, where you listen to a headphone commentary (daily 9.45am, noon & 2pm; Fr.32). There's a host of other tours available by bus and/or boat, generally costing Fr.30–40. The tourist office also stocks, for free, *Züritipp* (ⓦwww.zueritipp.ch), the best weekly **what's-on** paper, in German only.

City transport

One of the great advantages of Zürich is that you can enjoy all the buzz of big city life in a compact setting that's no larger than a single *arrondissement* of Paris: covering the city **on foot** is perfectly feasible. The main Bahnhofstrasse, which extends from the station to Bürkliplatz, is only a bit over 1km long. Nonetheless, Zürich's **city transport** system is legendary for its efficiency, punctuality and convenience, with the city centre and surrounding suburbs linked by a cat's cradle of routings.

After a referendum in the 1970s, in which Zürchers rejected a proposal to build an underground metro, the city has focused on its eco-friendly and ubiquitous **trams**, while easing most cars off the city-centre streets. Tram lines weave through the centre, and dozens of **bus** routes fan out from suburban termini to outlying districts. **S-Bahn** suburban trains, most originating from or passing through the main station, add a third dimension, linking to Zug and Einsiedeln in the south and Winterthur, Schaffhausen and Stein-am-Rhein in the north, as well as serving the nearby Uetliberg summit. **Boats** crisscross their way up and down the Zürichsee. There's even a **free bike-rental** scheme (see p.439).

Taxis, in a city where even millionaire bankers use the tram, are an extravagance, with a Fr.6 flagfall plus Fr.3.50 per kilometre. There are numerous public ranks, or you can order one from, for example, Taxi 444 (☎0 444 444 444) or Alpha Taxi (☎044 777 77 77).

Ticketing and fares

Ticketing is organized by zone, with the city centre covered by Zone 10 (the airport is in neighbouring Zone 21; Uetliberg in Zone 55). All tickets can be used for all transport – both land- and water-based – within each zone, with unlimited changes permitted. Trams, buses and S-Bahn trains operate daily from

▲ *Airport & Winterthur*

▲ *Airport & Winterthur*

FLUNTERN

KRAFTSTRASSE

BERGSTRASSE

BERGSTRASSE

KANTSTR

GLORIASTRASSE

STRASSE

MOUSSON

VOLTASTRASSE

PLATTENSTRASSE

FREIESTRASSE

HOTTINGERSTRASSE

University

RÄMISTRASSE

UNIVERSITÄTSTRASSE

KÜNSTLERGASSE

SEILERGRABEN

HIRSCHENGRABEN

LEONHARDSTRASSE

HIRSCHENGRABEN

SEILERGRABEN

CENTRAL

NIEDERDORF

Grossmünster

MÜNSTERGASSE

LIMMATQUAI

Limmat ◀

Hauptbahnhof

BAHNHOFQUAI

BAHNHOFPLATZ

BAHNHOFSTRASSE

RENNWEG

BAHNHOFSTRASSE

NEUMÜHLE QUAI

MUSEUMSTR

SIHLQUAI

GESSNERALLEE

see Zürich West map

URANIA

TALSTR

Selnau
Station

Sihl ◀

ZÜRICH

9

ACCOMMODATION	
Dolder Grand	B
Dolder Waldhaus	C
Jugendherberge	E
Lady's First	D
Zürichberg	A
EATING & DRINKING	
Blinde Kuh	1

Botanischer Garten

Stadelhofen Station

see Central Zürich map

Johann Jacobs Museum

Chinese Garden

Zürichhorn Park

Zürichsee

N

0   250 m

Arboretum

Voliere

Sukkulenten-Sammlung

Museum Rietberg

Enge Station

▶ Rapperswil

▶ Rote Fabrik

▶ *Zug*

411

The ZürichCARD

If you haven't already got a Swiss transport pass, the **ZürichCARD** represents excellent value (Fr.15 for 24hr; Fr.30 for 72hr). It is buyable at the tourist office, train stations (including the airport station) or at hotels, and is valid for **free public transport** by train, bus, tram, boat or funicular throughout the city centre (extending as far as the airport, Uetliberg and short trips on the lake), **free admission** to over forty museums, and a host of **discounts**, including on the tourist office's guided walking tour, purchases of Swiss army knives, car rental at Europcar, rental of inline skates, and more. In addition, it gets you a **free drink** at lunch or dinner at twenty restaurants around the city.

around 5.30am to after midnight. Full information on ticketing and fares is at ⓦ www.vbz.ch (English option).

If you hold a **Swiss Pass** (see p.41) or a **ZürichCARD** (see box above), all public transport in the city is **free**.

Otherwise, of the tickets buyable with coins from the machines at all tram and bus stops, the most useful Zone 10 ticket is the Fr.7.60 **Tageskarte** (press the green button), valid for 24 hours' travel. The blue "**Stadt Zürich**" button gives a Zone 10 ticket valid for an hour (Fr.3.80), while the yellow "**Kurzstrecke**" button gives a short-hop one-way ticket (Fr.2.40), good for half-an-hour within a radius of five stops: the black panel lists the stations for which it is valid. If you hold a Swiss Card, press "1/2" to get your discount. The **9-Uhr Tagespass** (9 O'Clock Day Pass, valid Mon–Fri after 9am, Sat & Sun all day; Fr.22) is good for an off-peak day-trip, valid throughout the whole region north to Winterthur (Zone 20) and the Rhine falls (Zone 16) and south to Rapperswil (Zone 80); to get one, key ★141 on any ticket machine. Several other passes and combi-tickets are available.

There are regular spot-checks on trams, trains and buses by plain-clothes ticket inspectors. If you're caught without a valid ticket, you must pay a **fine** of Fr.80.

Boats

Zürich has plenty of **boat** trips. The tourist office has full information, as does the Lake Zürich Shipping Company (ZSG; ☎ 044 487 13 33, ⓦ www.zsg.ch). Full timetables are posted at the company office at **Bürkliplatz**, from where almost all boats depart. Note that most of the trips mentioned below operate only in summer (April–Oct); in winter, service is reduced and is dependent on good weather.

There's a host of **pleasure cruises**, including circular sightseeing trips (*Rundfahrten*) on the lake from and to Zürich-Bürkliplatz without stopping (*Kleine* 1hr 30min Fr.7.60; *Mittlere* 2hr 30min Fr.18.80; *Grosse* 4hr Fr.22). **Eat-aboard cruises** – in daylight and after dark – are also popular. Meanwhile, regular boats ply the length of the lake from Zürich to **Rapperswil** (see p.440; 1hr 45min) and beyond, stopping at just about every shoreside town on the way.

One of the best short trips is on the **Limmat-Schiff**, which departs from the Landesmuseum for the scenic upriver journey through the heart of the city, including a short trip on the lake and the return journey down the Limmat again. Departures are every half-hour (July & Aug daily 10am–9pm; May, June & Sept Mon–Fri 1–9pm, Sat & Sun 10am–9pm; shorter hours in April & Oct; takes 1hr; Fr.3.80).

Zürich's festivals

Zürich's biggest party is August's massive **Street-Parade** (⊛ www.street-parade.ch), a tumultuous three-day techno weekend of floats, costumes, dancing in the streets and general hedonism.

The **Sechseläuten** (⊛ www.sechselaeuten.ch) is Zürich's spring festival, held on the third Monday in April, and is the only time in the year that the city's establishment preens its feathers in public: the highlight is a parade through the city centre by the traditional guilds, dressed in costume. The festival culminates at 6pm precisely with the burning of the Böögg – an effigy stuffed with fireworks – on Sechseläutenplatz next to Bellevue, to symbolize the end of winter. Throughout the evening the guilds take turns to visit each other in their respective guildhalls (most of which have now been turned into rather good restaurants). Not long after, Sechseläutenplatz is taken over by the regular month-long May residency of the Swiss National Circus, **Circus Knie** (⊛ www.knie.ch).

Zürich's February **Fasnacht** (Carnival) is a boisterous affair, fun if you happen to be in the city. The July **Züri Fäscht** (⊛ www.zuerifaescht.ch), held every three years (next in 2007 and 2010), is worth making a diversion for, with the whole city throwing itself into fairground revelry. The annual **Festspiele** (⊛ www.zuercher-festspiele .ch) is a festival of theatre, opera, music and art, held from late June into mid-July, with special productions, concerts and exhibitions all over the city. Late August's **Theaterspektakel** (⊛ www.theaterspektakel.ch) also packs out the city's stages and sees lakeside marquees set up on Mythenquai for avant-garde drama from around the world. A weekend in mid-September is taken as a local holiday for the rather odd **Knabenschiessen** (⊛ www.knabenschiessen.ch), a shooting competition for teenagers held on the Albisgütli amidst a huge and colourful fair. There's a citywide international **jazz festival** every November. One evening in the week before Christmas sees the **Lichterschwimmen**, a tradition of launching floating candles from the Rathausbrücke onto the river, to the accompaniment of gingerbread and *glühwein*.

Accommodation

Zürich has a full range of **accommodation** and – despite its being one of the most expensive cities in the world – if you book ahead you'll have a strong chance of finding somewhere good within your price range. Prices at the higher-end places, though, can be frightful, and some mid-range hoteliers take this as carte blanche to overcharge: you'd be well advised to take nothing for granted and investigate what you'll be getting for your money before you check in. Nearby **Baden** (see p.221) and **Winterthur** (see p.448), as well as some of the Zürichsee lakeside towns such as Küsnacht or Stäfa, offer equally characterful accommodation at more affordable prices. It's worth checking with the tourist office about any weekend or off-season promotions, which can slash walk-in rates.

All these establishments are **keyed on the maps** – either of the city (p.410), the central area (p.418) or Zürich West (p.430).

Hotels

The greatest concentration of **inexpensive hotels** is in the Old Town's Niederdorf district. None is more than ten minutes' walk from the station, or you could hop on tram #4 (direction Tiefenbrunnen): it runs south down Limmatquai, stopping at Central, each of the three river bridges and Bellevue.

To reach Zürich West, tram #3 from the station (direction Albisrieden) stops at Bezirksgebäude, at the southern end of Langstrasse, while tram #13 (direction Frankental) stops at Limmatplatz and Escher-Wyss-Platz. Be warned that many of the cheap hotels on and off Langstrasse double as brothels.

Mid-range hotels in Niederdorf are generally quiet and characterful, although universally pricey and often renovated, while those elsewhere in the city tend to offer better value but have noisier or more mundane surroundings. Unless you're devoted to urban living, withdrawing to one of the good-value hotels in the wooded hills to east and west is a sound ploy.

Zürich has any number of **expensive hotels**, chain- and private-owned palaces catering chiefly to executives and glitterati who demand luxury at any price.

Inexpensive hotels

Niederdorf

Goldenes Schwert Marktgasse 14 ⓣ 044 250 70 80, ⓦ www.gayhotel.ch. Excellent value, with a uniquely easygoing atmosphere. This is the only hotel in Zürich which makes a selling-point of its gay- and lesbian-friendliness. The comfortable rooms are large, bright, individually decorated and inexpensive, but you should insist on the fifth floor to avoid noise from the bars and nightclub. They also have quality apartments for Fr.200 or less. ❸–❹

Limmathof Limmatquai 142 ⓣ 044 267 60 40, ⓦ www.limmathof.com. Although this is one of the cheaper options overlooking the river, you'd do well to eschew the noisy river-view rooms for the newer, quieter ones at the back. Either way, you may have problems swinging a cat. With two restaurants onsite, one of which (the *Pot au Vert*) is vegetarian. ❸

Martahaus Zähringerstrasse 36 ⓣ 044 251 45 50, ⓦ www.martahaus.ch. Renovated budget hotel in a slightly dodgy neighbourhood, but a safe, clean and thoroughly respectable place to rest your head for minimal franc outlay. Some rooms are ensuite, but you should go for a back room to avoid street noise. Also has good, partitioned dorms. An annexe out west on Lutherstrasse is women-only (check-in at *Martahaus*). ❷–❸

🏃 **Otter** Oberdorfstrasse 7 ⓣ 044 251 22 07, ⓦ www.hotelotter.ch. Best in this bracket by miles, relaxed, friendly and great value, with an unconventional clientele of students and artists. Uniquely colourful rooms, all with plump, comfy beds, are decked in murals, drapes and plants, ones higher up with lovely rooftop views. Shower and toilet are shared between the three rooms on each floor. A good indication of the mood of the place is that breakfast only happens from 9am (10am weekend). The top-floor apartment, for Fr.190, feels like home. ❷–❸

Splendid Rosengasse 5 ⓣ 044 252 58 50, ⓦ www.hotelsplendid.ch. Gloomy unrenovated small hotel on a central alley, with no TVs, no ensuite facilities, no decoration and no lift. Quiet, ordinary and honestly cheap. ❶–❷

Villette Kruggasse 4 ⓣ 044 251 23 35. Friendly little place above an award-winning fondue restaurant just off Bellevue. Plain rooms (most ensuite) are clean enough and adequate for simple tastes – the breakfast is notably good – and the owner of the place (who also does the fondues) is full of jolly stories and banter. ❷

Zic-Zac Marktgasse 17 ⓣ 044 261 21 81, ⓦ www.ziczac.ch. Ordinary cheapie which has taken some marketing advice and reinvented itself as a "rock hotel", dubbing their poky and rather depressing rooms (some with shared bathrooms) the "Bryan Adams" or the "Pink Floyd". Lively atmosphere in the bar. ❷–❸

Zürich West

Etap Technoparkstrasse 2 ⓣ 044 276 20 00, ⓦ www.etaphotel.com. Budget international chain. Generic, functional rooms in the heart of the old industrial quarter, priced identically – and very low. Located alongside the *Ibis* and *Novotel* hotels, just behind the trendy Schiffbau arts centre. ❶

Haus zur Stauffacherin Kanzleistrasse 19 ⓣ 044 241 69 79. Clean, airy, fresh rooms in a wheelchair-accessible building off lively Helvetiaplatz, with kitchen and laundry facilities. Discounts for long stays. Women only. ❸

Regina Hohlstrasse 18 ⓣ 044 298 55 55. The least dodgy of Langstrasse's many dodgy hotels, although the prevalence of over-friendly single women in the hotel bar tells its own story. Nonetheless, the rooms are fine, clean but smallish, and Fr.20–30 cheaper than similar places elsewhere in the city. ❸

Rothaus Sihlhallenstrasse 1 ⓣ 044 241 24 51, ⓦ www.hotel-rothaus.ch. Bang on the honky-tonk

Langstrasse, replete with sex cinemas and pick-up joints, but if you can overlook that, you can save Fr.30–40 on perfectly adequate, secure ensuite rooms, equipped with all facilities and sound-proofed windows. **❷**

Walhalla Limmatstrasse 5 ☎044 446 54 00, ⓦwww.walhalla-hotel.ch. Reasonable value in a useful but unromantic location, just 50m behind the train station, with large, pleasantly decorated rooms. Cheaper rooms available in a nearby annexe. **❸–❹**

X-tra Limmatstrasse 118 ☎044 448 15 95, ⓦwww.x-tra.ch. In the same building as the popular *X-tra* bar and nightclub, just off the Limmatplatz in a young and lively part of town. Rooms are compact, but come with postmodern decor and all facilities. **❸**

Out of town

Central Poststrasse 10, Küsnacht ☎044 910 08 04. Small, family-run option in this pleasant

town south of Zürich (see p.440), with rooms both ensuite and not. **❷–❸**

Formule 1 Heidi Abel-Weg 7 ☎044 307 48 00, ⓦwww.hotelformule1.com. Chain motel that is clean and functional but completely character-less. All rooms are identical – generically plasticky – sleeping one, two or three people, with shared bathrooms, and all are priced rock-bottom. Located north of town midway from the airport, alongside the *Ibis* hotel, a block from the Messe conference centre and autobahn exit. Tram #11. **❶**

Gasthof zur Metzg Bergstrasse 82, Stäfa ☎044 928 18 88, ⓦwww.zur-metzg.ch. Simple inn a little up the hill from this quiet lakeside community south of town; they'll come and collect you from Stäfa station on request. Rooms are cosy and there's an affordable menu of rustic cooking on offer. **❷–❸**

Mid-range hotels

In town

Adler Rosengasse 10 ☎044 266 96 96, ⓦwww.hotel-adler.ch. Very clean, light and pleasant hand-decorated rooms set right in the heart of the Niederdorf buzz above a famous fondue restaurant. Service is good, the pastel interior is modern, and rates undercut similar places on the west bank. Weekend discounts. **❹**

City Löwenstrasse 34 ☎044 217 17 17, ⓦwww .hotelcity.ch. A quiet, unremarkable business-style hotel in the shopping district just off Bahnhof-strasse, reasonably priced and efficiently staffed. Rates drop at weekends. **❹**

Franziskaner Niederdorfstrasse 1 ☎044 250 53 00, ⓦwww.hotel-franziskaner.ch. Charming small city hotel in classic style, with dark-wood decor and a popular outdoor terrace on a square in the heart of the old town. A little pricey for what you get, but the top-floor rooms, sharing a spacious rooftop terrace, are delightful. **❺**

Kindli Pfalzgasse 1 ☎043 888 76 76, ⓦwww .kindli.ch. A building dating from the sixteenth century that has provided lodging since (at least) 1774, in a tranquil location on the steep cobbled lanes below the Lindenhof. These days it's one of Zürich's most charming hotels, renovated through-out. Rooms are not spacious, but are elegant and characterful. **❼**

Lady's First Mainaustrasse 24 ☎044 380 80 10, ⓦwww.ladysfirst.ch. Upmarket designer hotel near the lake south of the Opera House, with spacious, airy singles and doubles displaying style and a good attention to detail. Billed as "for

dynamic women and modern men". Spa, sauna and solarium; also cosmetic and massage treat-ments. **❺–❻**

Limmatblick Limmatquai 136 ☎044 254 60 00, ⓦwww.limmatblick.ch. Completely renovated hotel right on the riverfront close to Central, with airy, contemporary-styled rooms (some with balcony) that are good value despite some traffic noise. **❹**

Rössli Rössligasse 7 ☎044 256 70 50, ⓦwww .hotelroessli.ch. Super-chic choice on a quiet Niederdorf lane. The spartan wood-and-stone rooms with crisp white styling are spotlessly clean, and service is friendly and attentive. **❺**

Out of town

Sonne Seestrasse 120, Küsnacht ☎044 914 18 18, ⓦwww.sonne.ch. A fine hotel, part of the Romantik group, set in lakeside gardens south of Zürich, also with a couple of good restaurants. **❺–❻**

Uto Kulm Uetliberg ☎044 457 66 66, ⓦwww .utokulm.ch. Hotel and restaurant atop the forested Uetliberg ridge (see p.429), towering over the city and lake from the west. Its chic, contemporary rooms offer considerably better value for money than similar city-centre hotels, especially when you throw in the tranquillity, the Alpine vistas and plentiful walking routes close at hand. Eight romantic suites feature oversized circular bathtubs, balconies and – in the Tower Suite – a separate conservatory. No cars: take the train to Uetliberg, from where the hotel is a short walk (luggage collection on request). **❺–❽**

🏃 **Zürichberg** Orellistrasse 21 ☎044 268 35 35, ⓦ www.zuerichberg.ch. Comfortable, attractive hotel, opened in 1899 way up in the wooded hills east of the city. Renovated for its centenary, and now featuring bright, spacious rooms, most with balconies and all with full facilities. Alongside is a low, curved annexe sheathed in wood which has attracted much architectural acclaim; accessed only by a subterranean corridor from the main building, it's designed around an airy atrium and a cool, Guggenheim-style elliptical interior ramp. All its rooms have private balconies. Tram #6 to Zoo. ⑤–⑧

Expensive hotels

Baur au Lac Talstrasse 1 ☎044 220 50 20, ⓦ www.bauraulac.ch. One of Zürich's oldest hotels, in the same family since 1844, and recently completely renovated. Set in a private park on the lakeshore adjacent to Bahnhofstrasse, it fairly shimmers with opulent grandeur. From Fr.750. ⑨

Dolder Grand Kurhausstrasse 65 ☎044 269 30 00, ⓦ www.doldergrand.ch. An extraordinary nineteenth-century palace perched atop a hill overlooking the city and accessible only by private funicular. Towers, cupolas, spires and turrets sprout from all sides of the elegant building; inside, the high-ceilinged rooms are unsurpassable. Completing the picture are a private nine-hole golf course, a full-size pool with wave machine, one of Switzerland's top *haute cuisine* restaurants, and plenty of walking trails into the parks and forest all around. Closed at the time of writing for major renovation work, complete in late 2007. ⑨

Dolder Waldhaus Kurhausstrasse 20 ☎044 269 10 00, ⓦ www.dolderwaldhaus.ch. Quiet, more residential annexe in the woods just down from the *Dolder Grand*, with just as stunning views over the city and lake, plus plenty of activities (tennis courts, golf, swimming pools and an ice-rink). Rooms are vast and well appointed. ⑦–⑧

St Gotthard Bahnhofstrasse 87 ☎044 227 77 00, ⓦ www.hotelstgotthard.ch. *Grande-dame* of the city-centre hotels, in the same family since 1889, with bags of charm and a perfect location steps from the station. The understated elegance of the dark-wood-and-leather lobby, however, isn't matched in the rooms, which are spacious and comfortable but have been done up in a rather cloying chintzy style. A bargain, considering the competition. ⑧

🏃 **Widder** Rennweg 7 ☎044 224 25 26, ⓦ www.widderhotel.ch. Top choice in this bracket, for its cool elegance and superb modern design. On a quiet Old Town street, a row of eight medieval houses has been gutted – at a cost of Fr.100m – to make this stylish and innovative, effortlessly classy hotel; the stunning lobby, in granite, wood and steel, sets the tone. The attention to detail, both architecturally and in the interior decor, is meticulous, and the array of several hundred single malt whiskies in the bar – which also stages live jazz – adds to the appeal. From Fr.650. ⑨

Easy day-trips from Zürich by train

Braunwald p.472. Car-free Alpine hideaway for rapid battery-recharge. Change at Ziegelbrücke and Linthal. 1hr 45min.

Einsiedeln monastery p.393. Centuries-old site of pilgrimage up in the hills. Change at Wädenswil. 45min.

Luzern p.361. Exquisite Old Town plus breathtaking lake-and-mountains scenery. Direct. 45min. Either train back, or boat Luzern–Flüelen then train Flüelen–Zürich.

Rapperswil p.440. Gentle, easy-going Zürichsee waterfront town, perfect for a lazy afternoon. Direct. 35min (or 1hr 45min by boat).

Rhine falls p.456. Europe's biggest waterfall. Change at Winterthur for Schloss Laufen or Neuhausen. 50min.

Rigi p.386. A popular ride up the nearest high mountain to Zürich (1798m). Change at Arth-Goldau. 1hr 40min.

Schaffhausen p.452. Fascinating, little-visited Old Town; combine it with a river trip to Stein-am-Rhein. Direct. 55min.

Uetliberg p.429. Zürich's "home mountain", with a network of easy walking routes. Direct. 20min.

Winterthur p.448. Relaxed city with high-quality art museums. Direct. 25min.

Camping and hostels

The one **campsite** within easy reach is *Seebucht*, Seestrasse 559 (☎044 482 16 12, ⓦwww.camping-zurich.ch; May–Sept); take bus #161 or #165 from Bürkliplatz south along the western shore of the lake to Stadtgrenze.

City Backpacker/Hotel Biber (SB hostel)
Niederdorfstrasse 5 ☎044 251 90 15, ⓦwww
.city-backpacker.ch. A good atmosphere, plum
central location and super-friendly management.
A dorm bed is Fr.34 excluding breakfast. Some
singles and doubles are available, along with free
kitchen use, laundry service and other services. ❶

Jugendherberge (HI hostel) Mutschellenstrasse
114 ☎043 399 78 00, ⓦwww.youthhostel.ch.
Suffers from a rather depressing institutional feel
and is awkwardly situated in a humdrum southwestern suburb. Dorm beds are Fr.38, and a few
parking spaces are free. Take tram #7 (direction
Wollishofen) to Morgental, then walk five minutes
(follow the signs). ❶

The City

Because the River Limmat divides the **Old Town** into two distinct halves, it makes more sense to consider the two banks of the river separately rather than concentrate on a New Town/Old Town split.

The alleys of the east bank – known as **Niederdorf** or the "Dörfli" – are full of cafés and small shops, with the enormous twin towers of the **Grossmünster** as a centrepiece. The slender spire to the north belongs to the Predigerkirche with, above it on a hill to the east, the grandiose architecture of the university.

Opposite, the **west bank** is the oldest part of the city, centred around the raised platform of the **Lindenhof** and characterized by expensive fashion outlets and offices. Nearby rise the graceful spires both of **St Peter's**, featuring the largest clock face in Europe, and the **Fraumünster**, a medieval church decorated in the last century with beautiful stained glass by Marc Chagall. The long, curving **Bahnhofstrasse** follows the ancient course of the western city wall, and is now one of Europe's most prestigious shopping streets, packed with jewellers and designer boutiques.

The best of the city's clutch of **museums** are the Kunsthaus on the fringes of the Niederdorf, and the Schweizerisches Landesmuseum (Swiss National Museum) in a park on the west bank.

The east bank

It's a walk of only 100m from the station across the Bahnhofbrücke to the east bank of the Limmat and a large square bedecked with tram wires, known as **Central**. On one side of the square is the bottom station of the **Polybahn funicular**, which has connected the city with the university buildings on the hill 40m above since 1889. Normal city transport tickets are valid for the two-minute ride.

Niederdorf

From Central, the **Niederdorf** district stretches south along the riverside for about 1km. A more engaging walk than the busy riverside Limmatquai is to fork one block inland onto the narrow pedestrianized **Niederdorfstrasse**; the tackiness of its initial stretches – replete with fast-food stalls and lowlife beer-halls – soon mellows, and there are plenty of opportunities for absent-minded exploration of cobbled side-alleys, many of which open onto secluded court-yards adorned with medieval fountains.

CENTRAL ZÜRICH

EATING AND DRINKING

Altstadt	37
Amsterdam	19
Babalu	7
Ban Song Thai	36
Bodega Española	30
Bona Dea	2
Cranberry	17
Le Dézaley	33
Haus zum Rüden	32
Helvetia	12
Hiltl	13
James Joyce	23
Jelmoli	6
Jules Verne	8
Kantorei	16
Kaufleuten	27
Kronenhalle	42
Kropf	34
Lions	10
Manora	5
Mère Catherine	31
Mövenpick	39
Nelson	3
No	15
Noble Dubliner	24
Odeon	41
Oepfelchammer	22
Oliver Twist	21
Pigalle	25
Rathaus	26
Reithaus	9
Rheinfelder Bierhalle	4
Sala of Tokyo	1
Santa Lucia	18
Schlauch	29
Schober	28
Spaghetti Factory	14
Sprüngli	38
Weisser Wind	40
Zähringer	11
Zeughauskeller	35
Zunfthaus zur Schmiden	20

ZÜRICH

▶ *Rapperswil*

Zürichsee

200 m

Schauspielhaus

Kunsthaus

Stadelhofen Station

Opera House

Grossmünster

Helmhaus

Wasserkirche

Rathaus

St Peters-Kirche

Zunfthaus zur Meisen

Frauminster

Augustinerkirche

James Joyce Foundation

Beyer Museum

Tonhalle Concert Hall

Völkerkundemuseum

Park zur Katz

RAMISTRASSE
HOTTINGERSTR.
ZELTWEG
HEIM-PLATZ
HIRSCHEN-GRABEN
KREUZBÜHLSTRASSE
HOHENBÜHLSTR.
PROMENADENGASSE
SCHANZ.
HEIMSTRASSE
KANTONSSCHULSTRASSE
FLORHOFGASSE
OBMANNAMTSGASSE
HIRSCHEN-GRABEN
THEATERSTRASSE
STADELHOFER-PLATZ
STADELHOFERSTRASSE
RAMISTRASSE
OBERDORFSTRASSE
BELLEVUE-PLATZ
UTOQUAI
FALKENSTRASSE
SCHIFFLÄNDE-PLATZ
HECHT-PLATZ
LIMMATQUAI
STÜSSIHOFSTATT
THORGASSE
NEUSTADTGASSE
KIRCHGASSE
OBERE ZÄUNE
UNTERE ZÄUNE
BLATTENGASSE
SPIEGELGASSE
RINDERMARKT
MÜNSTERGASSE
NEUMARKT
PREDIGERG.
FROSCHAUG.
ZÄHRINGERPLATZ
NIEDERDORF
MARKTGASSE
MÜNSTER-HOF
MÜNSTERBRÜCKE
MÜNSTERGASSE
QUAIBRÜCKE
STADTHAUSQUAI
WEIN-PLATZ
WÜHRE
RATHAUSBRÜCKE
STORCHENGASSE
FRAUMÜNSTERSTRASSE
POSTSTRASSE
BÖRSENSTR.
KAPPELERGASSE
BÜRKLI-PLATZ
BAHNHOFSTRASSE
IN GASSEN
STRELGASSE
MÜNSTERGASSE
ST PETERHOFSTATT
PARADE-PLATZ
TALSTRASSE
BÄRENGASSE
STRASSE
ST PETERSTRASSE
TALACKER
AUGUSTINERGASSE
KUTTELGASSE
LINDENHOF
FORTUNAGASSE
STRELGASSE
BAHNHOFSTRASSE
PELIKANSTRASSE
PELIKAN-PLATZ
NÜSCHELER-STRASSE
PELIKANSTRASSE
SIHLSTRASSE
ST ANNAGASSE
FUSSLISTR.
URANIA-STRASSE
TALSTRASSE
SIHLPORTE
BRANDSCHENKESTR.
SELNAUSTRASSE
BEETHOVENSTRASSE
STOCKERSTRASSE
DREIKÖNIGSTR.
BLEICHERWEG
CLARIDENSTRASSE
GLARNISCHSTR.
GENERAL GUISAN QUAI
GOTTHARDSTR.
GLÄRNISCHSTRASSE

ACCOMMODATION

Adler	I
Baur au Lac	R
City	F
City Backpacker	H
Franziskaner	K
Goldenes Schwert	N
Kindli	L
Limmatblick	E
Limmathof	B
Martahaus	D
Otter	P
Rössli	O
St Gotthard	C
Splendid	G
Villette	Q
Walhalla	A
Widder	J
Zic-Zac	M

Dada in Zürich

At the same time as both a pre-Revolution Lenin and a *Ulysses*-obsessed Joyce were staying in Zürich, a group of maverick European intellectuals was also seeking refuge in the city from the bloodshed and misery of World War I. In 1915, **Hugo Ball**, a writer and theatre director, had arrived from Munich with his partner **Emmy Hennings**, a dancer and singer. It seemed to them, as to many horrified by the brutality of war, that Western civilization had finally lost all reason; with a group of like-minded friends, they made an arrangement with the owner of the *Meierei* tavern at Spiegelgasse 1 to use the pub's backroom for a "literary cabaret" to demonstrate to the people of Zürich and the world the moral bankruptcy of Western culture. On Saturday, February 3, 1916, Ball, Hennings, the Romanian poet **Tristan Tzara**, **Hans Arp** (an artist from Franco-German Alsace), and a handful of other émigrés inaugurated the "**Cabaret Voltaire**" with a night of wild music, poetry and dance, intended to satirize art and literature by placing unreason against reason, anti-art against art. On June 15, they published a magazine with contributions from Kandinsky, Modigliani and others, and presented themselves as "**Dada**", the most significantly meaningless name they could find, picked at random out of a dictionary (*dada* is French for "hobby-horse").

Dada's poignant absurdities aptly expressed the mood of dislocation and crisis seizing Western society, and the movement spread rapidly. In **New York**, Dada was centred at Alfred Stieglitz's gallery "291", meeting point for Man Ray, Marcel Duchamp and others. In **Berlin**, Dadaists such as George Grosz relentlessly lampooned high society, and were the initiators of the brand-new technique of photomontage. In **the Netherlands**, Dada became *De Stijl*, led by Mondrian. In 1920, some of the Zürich Dadaists moved to **Paris** and there formed the Surrealist movement, which later attracted artists such as Dalí and Miró.

The greatest legacy of Dada was its liberating influence in overturning previously unquestioned strictures of style and order, not only in art and writing but across society as a whole. What is both appropriate and extraordinary is that such a movement should have emerged from – of all places – neutral, bourgeois Zürich.

A short way down on the left is **Rindermarkt**, where Gottfried Keller – generally thought of as Switzerland's national poet – lived (at no. 9) and drank (at the *Oepfelchammer* opposite; see p.436). A little further along, tiny

Spiegelgasse enjoyed a burst of fame during World War I: Lenin and Krupskaja stayed for fourteen months at no. 14, in the home of Titus Kammerer, a cobbler, before returning to Russia in April 1917 to lead the revolution, while diagonally opposite, at no. 1, is the updated *Cabaret Voltaire* café-bar and arts centre (ⓦ www.cabaretvoltaire.ch), on whose site the Dada art movement was born (see box).

Niederdorfstrasse, which becomes **Münstergasse**, leads on to the **Grossmünster** and beyond, as Oberdorfstrasse, out to the open **Bellevue** plaza, dominated on its south side by the lavish opera house. A short distance up the hill to the left – by the main Rämistrasse or any of the back alleys (tiny **Trittligasse** is the most alluring) – lies the Kunsthaus (see p.422), while a pleasant walk south along the lake brings you after 1km to the Zürichhorn park.

△ Niederdorfstrasse

The Grossmünster

With its distinctive twin sugar-loafed towers, and a venerable history at the heart of the Swiss-German Reformation, the **Grossmünster**, or Great Minster (daily 9am–6pm; Nov–Feb 10am–5pm; ⓦ www.kirche-zh.ch), dominates Zürich's skyline. In a tight-packed city of generally modest, small-scale architecture, it is dauntingly gigantic; and yet, caught half a millennium ago in the eye of a tight-lipped theological hurricane, its interior has been denuded of virtually all its decorative grandeur. Today it's as bare as a cellar inside, but the beauty – as the Reformers would have wanted – is all in its lofty austerity, and its associations. In twelve years preaching from the Grossmünster's pulpit in the sixteenth century, **Huldrych Zwingli**, a contemporary of Luther's and the initiator of the Reformation in Switzerland (see box, p.422), transformed Zürich from a sparsely populated hinterland town into a religious centre attracting students and theologians from around Europe. Quite aside from the architecture, the sense of history in the church is compelling.

After its foundation by **Charlemagne** in the ninth century on a site of long-established religious significance (recent excavations below the church suggest the existence of a **Roman** cemetery), the church was constructed in its present form between 1100 and 1230. At that time, the north tower was higher than its twin, since it held, and still holds, the bells. In the fifteenth century, the south tower was brought up to the same height and adorned on its south side with a statue of a seated Charlemagne. After a **fire** in 1763, the spires and upper sections of the towers were demolished, and reconstruction shortly after produced the Gothic belfries, watchrooms and octagonal cupolae which survive today. The fire also gave impetus to much **Baroque** alteration to the church interior, and the nineteenth and twentieth centuries saw a continuous programme of restoration of its original Romanesque character.

The building is skewed from the river bank, its broad front facing northwest. The most impressive approach is across paved **Zwingliplatz**, with the main North Portal featuring capitals adorned with animals, birds and, on the extreme left, a fiddle player. To the right, at the base of the North Tower, is a modern statue of Heinrich Bullinger, Zwingli's successor.

Inside, the overriding impression is of the loftiness of the galleried space and its austerity; aside from some **capitals** decorated with battle scenes – and, on the third pillar on the north side, Charlemagne's discovery of the graves of Felix and Regula – almost no decoration survives. The altar paintings were removed in 1524 at Zwingli's behest, as were the church treasures. Most decorative elements which survive today are replacements, including the pulpit (1851) and the organ (1960). The **stained-glass** windows were made in 1933 by Augusto Giacometti and stand alone for their artistic accomplishment. It's worth ducking into the **crypt**, a long triple-aisled hall, the largest of its kind in Switzerland, dominated by the fifteenth-century statue of Charlemagne taken from the South Tower (the one up there now is a replica) and also featuring some well-preserved brush wall drawings dating from 1500. You can **climb** the 187 steps of the 62-metre South Tower for a spectacular view over the city (March–Oct daily 9.15am–5pm; Fr.2).

To the right as you leave the Grossmünster onto Zwingliplatz is a door set into the wall of what was once the chapterhouse, now the university's Theological Institute. This gives into the atmospheric **cloister**, originally built in 1170–80, partly demolished in 1848 and renovated in the 1960s. Aside from strolling through the vaulted bays around a central garden, it's worth visiting to see the twelfth-century capitals and spandrels of the arched windows, decorated with grotesque faces, monkeys, dragons and centaurs.

At the vanguard of the Reformation, **Huldrych** (or Ulrich) **Zwingli** (1484–1531) is one of the most radical anti-establishment figures in European history, a dedicated and eloquent humanist who developed a passion for the liberty of individuals to decide the course of their lives free from the strictures of the past. An archetypal "red under the bed" fifth columnist, he used his position of authority in the church to undermine and reinvent the power structures of the church itself. He died at 47 fighting for his cause.

As did his contemporary, **Martin Luther**, Zwingli came to his personal revolution through education, studying in Basel, Bern, Vienna and possibly Paris, and absorbing the humanist ideas of the Dutch philosopher Erasmus. After ten years as a pastor, his study of scripture led Zwingli to begin questioning the teachings of the Catholic Church; after 1518, when he was appointed to the Grossmünster, he began to develop his controversial ideas from the pulpit, proclaiming the sole authority of the word of God as revealed in the Bible and preaching against church practices. Zürich's congregation, democratically inclined and politically autonomous, was receptive. Barely a year had passed since Luther had nailed his 95 theses to the door of the Wittenberg church.

In 1523, with mounting tension fuelled by an increasingly vocal opposition to clerical celibacy, monasticism, the observance of Lent and the whole structure of papal control, Zwingli was summoned to a public disputation in Zürich with a papal representative. It says a great deal for Zwingli's powers of persuasion (and the city council's courage) that, at a time of profound religious and political turbulence, Zürich's councillors came down on the side of their preacher. The papal representative returned to Rome the loser, and Mass was celebrated at the Grossmünster for the last time in 1525.

Zwingli's ideas spread rapidly, and by 1529 Bern, Basel and St Gallen had all embraced the Reformation. Opposition came from two sides: the Anabaptists, who wanted even more radical reform, and the Swiss "Forest Cantons" around Lake Luzern that had taken up arms in loyalty to Rome. War broke out in 1531; Zwingli went into battle and was killed at Kappel.

Zwingli's lead in Zürich was followed by his son-in-law **Heinrich Bullinger**, but after 1536 the impetus for reform in Switzerland passed to **Jean Calvin**, a young preacher working in Geneva. Calvin initially followed Zwingli's doctrine, but then developed his own strict theology. Today, thanks in no small measure to the voyages of Calvinist Puritans to the New World, Calvin is much better-known than his predecessor, but it was the unsung Zwingli who paved the way, forging ideas of personal liberty, and using them to strike at the very heart of the institutionalized hierarchy that had been taken for granted throughout Europe for centuries.

The Wasserkirche and Helmhaus

Near the Grossmünster, down on the riverside, stands the beautiful late-Gothic **Wasserkirche**, site of the martyrdom of Zürich's patron saints, Felix and Regula, but still used mostly for services (visiting hours Wed 9–11am & 2–5pm). Alongside is the Baroque **Helmhaus** (guildhall), Limmatquai 31 (Tues–Sun 10am–6pm, Thurs until 8pm; free; ⊛www.helmhaus.org), now converted to an art gallery, staging temporary exhibits of mainly Swiss painting. This marks the Münsterbrücke, which leads across the river directly to the **Fraumünster** (see p.427).

The Kunsthaus

Five minutes' walk east up the hill from Bellevue is a square formally dubbed Heimplatz but known to every Zürcher as "Pfauen" (Peacocks), after the peacock statue over the famous Schauspielhaus theatre. The adjacent café was for decades known as the Pfauen Café, and was James Joyce's favourite watering hole; it still has a peacock as its inn sign.

Dominating the square is the **Kunsthaus**, Switzerland's finest gallery (Tues–Thurs 10am–9pm, Fri–Sun 10am–5pm; permanent collection Fr.10, free on Wed; temporary exhibits Fr.10–17; joint tickets available; audioguide Fr.6; ⓦwww.kunsthaus.ch). As well as a large permanent collection, the Kunsthaus hosts a continuous flow of top-flight temporary exhibitions, advertised widely around town. If you visit just one art museum in Switzerland, this should be it.

The collection begins even before you get inside: beside the main door is **Rodin**'s vivid *Gate of Hell*, while sculptures by **Moore**, Maillol and others dot the grounds. Inside, most of the ground-floor galleries house whatever temporary exhibit is on, aside from one whole wing of the ground floor which is given over to a permanent display of the widest array of Alberto **Giacometti**'s sculpture in the world.

Elsewhere, you'll find Dutch and Flemish painting represented by **Rubens**, **Rembrandt**, **Hals** and others, the Venetian room showing **Canaletto** and **El Greco**, and canvases from the Italian and Dutch Baroque. There's a complex of rooms devoted mainly to Swiss artists of the nineteenth century, including many works by Anker, Böcklin, Segantini and **Füssli**, who lived and worked for many years in London. Only a tiny fraction of the massive **Graphische Sammlung**, comprising 80,000 graphic works, is on display at any one time.

The collection of twentieth-century art is stunning. A broad selection of pop, concrete and abstract expressionist art is headed by a number of works by **Warhol**, a **Rothko**, a gigantic wall-sized installation by Baselitz, geometric constructivist sculpture and works by Bacon and Twombly. A collection of French sculpture since Rodin is dominated, unusually, by **Matisse**. Cubism, Fauvism and **Dada** are all represented, and works by Miró, Dalí and De Chirico head an impressive **Surrealist** overview. **Picasso**, **Chagall** and **Kandinsky** are all represented, there are two of **Monet**'s most beautiful water-lily canvases, while **Van Gogh**, Gauguin, Cézanne and the largest **Munch** collection outside Scandinavia top an extraordinary journey. Last but not least is the rare chance to revel in the powerful, mystical landscapes of Alps and lakes by the Swiss painter Ferdinand **Hodler**.

At the university

If you follow Rämistrasse uphill from the Kunsthaus, you'll soon come to the university quarter. At Rämistrasse 73 is the **Archäologische Sammlung** (Archeological Collection; Tues–Fri 1–6pm, Sat & Sun 11am–5pm; free; ⓦwww .archinst.unizh.ch), with a range of impressive pieces. Aside from the wealth of Etruscan ware, the most interesting artefacts come from the Middle East, with an entire case devoted to the stunning Egyptian Fayoum portraits from the first centuries BC–AD; wall-sized steles from ninth-century BC Nimrud (in modern Iraq); a complete mummy, and dozens of statuettes of ancient Egyptian deities (including some memorable cats); and many Roman and Hellenic pieces. Close by, the **Graphische Sammlung der ETH**, Rämistrasse 101 (entrance on Karl Schmid-Strasse; Mon–Fri 10am–5pm, Wed until 7pm; free; ⓦwww .gs.ethz.ch), houses thousands of woodcuts, etchings and engravings from all periods, particularly strong on Dürer, Rembrandt, Goya and Picasso.

Before you reach these, partway up Rämistrasse at the junction with Zürich-bergstrasse stands the **university's law library** (Rechtswissenschaftliches Institut; ⓦwww.rwi.unizh.ch/bibliothek; Mon–Fri 8am–8pm, Sat 8am–4pm), at no. 74. Unremarkable from the street, it boasts a stunning modern interior,

△ Calatrava's law library

designed by architect **Santiago Calatrava** – a vast, six-storey interior atrium encircled by smooth curves and flooded with natural light. It is a cathedral-like space, hugely impressive to explore.

South to the Zürichhorn

The lakeside promenades running south from Bellevue are crowded with people all summer long, blading, strolling and chatting in the sunshine. Following them south brings you past the **Johann Jacobs Museum**, Seefeldquai 17 (Fri 2–7pm, Sat 2–5pm, Sun 10am–5pm; free; Ⓦ www.johann-jacobs-museum .ch), a mildly diverting place in an elegant lakeside villa, devoted to the cultural history of coffee. Selections of Rococo and Neoclassical porcelain ware, silver

---

Parks and gardens

Zürich is not a big city, and there are plenty of green spaces close-at-hand to escape to, aside from the attractive **Zürichhorn** park and **Botanischer Garten** on the east bank (see opposite), the **Platzspitz** park north of the station (see p.428), and the **Park zur Katz** west of the centre (see p.428).

A few minutes' walk west of Bürkliplatz is a waterside **Arboretum**, beside which is the 150-species-strong aviary **Volière**, Mythenquai 1 (Tues–Sun 10am–noon & 2–4pm; free; Ⓦ www.voliere.ch). From here, it's about ten minutes' walk south along the lake to the **Sukkulenten-Sammlung**, Mythenquai 88 (daily 9–11.30am & 1.30–4.30pm; free; Ⓦ www.sukkulenten.ch), a jungle of desert plants and cacti that forms one of the world's most important collections of succulents (water-retaining plants).

A little over 3km west of the centre, past the giant Sihlfeld cemetery, you'll find luscious orchids and a steamy little tropical forest complete with birds and turtles in the fragrant **Schauhäuser der Stadtgärtnerei**, Sackzelgasse 25 (daily 9–11.30am & 1.30–4.30pm; tram #3 to Hubertus; free; Ⓦ www.stadtgaertnerei.ch).

Zürich's **Zoo**, Zürichbergstrasse 221 (daily 9am–6pm, Nov–Feb closes 5pm; Fr.22; tram #5 or #6; Ⓦ www.zoo.ch), stands high on a hill about 4km northeast of the centre; it's large, with a good variety of animals and the popular **Masoala rainforest** experience, but you may find that a stroll in the **Zürichberg** woods behind the zoo is a more peaceful way to spend the afternoon.

coffeepots, painting, prints and drawings are fleshed out by videos of TV coffee ads – and free coffee to drink.

Just beyond is the lovely **Zürichhorn** park, a popular place for soaking up some sunshine that also boasts the fine *Heureka* sculpture by Jean Tinguely and a visually striking, but underwhelming, walled **Chinese garden** (April–Oct daily 11am–7pm; Fr.4; Ⓦ www .chinagarten.ch), a gift from Zürich's twin city of Kunming, featuring scarlet gateways, a traditional zigzag bridge and pavilions, and the three symbolic species of pine, bamboo and cherry. The grand Zürichhorn Casino building has a popular terrace café for refreshments, and a jetty from where boats shuttle to and from Bürkliplatz. A couple of blocks inland from the Zürichhorn is the pleasant, open **Botanischer Garten**, Zollikerstrasse 107 (Mon–

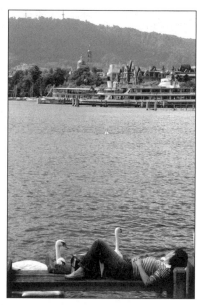

△ The lakeside

Fri 7am–7pm, Sat & Sun 8am–6pm; shorter hours in winter; tram #2 or #4 to Höschgasse; free; Ⓦ www.bguz.unizh.ch), a riot of colour in spring and summer, with three tropical planthouses and a café.

South of the Zürichhorn park is the **Sammlung E.G. Bührle**, a small, very high-quality private fine-art collection, at Zollikerstrasse 172 (Tues, Wed, Fri & Sun 2–5pm; tram #2 or #4 to Wildbachstrasse, then walk 10min; Fr.9; Ⓦ www .buehrle.ch). The paintings are mostly by French Impressionists and Post-Impressionists, displayed in a tastefully furnished mansion. Manet, Van Gogh (including an 1887 self-portrait) and Cézanne's landscapes form the centrepiece, but other artists represented include Monet, Renoir, Sisley, Degas, Toulouse-Lautrec, Seurat, Matisse, Braque and Picasso. Filling out this extraordinary collection are works by Rembrandt, including *Portrait of Saskia*, a rare painting of his wife.

The west bank

Emerging on the south side of the station into hectic Bahnhofplatz, you're met by a statue of Alfred Escher, a prominent nineteenth-century politician and industrialist who is credited with single-handedly leading Zürich into the modern business age. In an inspired piece of statue placement, he gazes down **Bahnhofstrasse** (Ⓦ www.bahnhofstrasse-zuerich.ch), one of the most prestigious shopping streets in Europe, an enduring symbol of Zürich's wealth and a fascinating counterpoint to the quaintness of the Niederdorf alleys. This is the gateway into the modern city, and is where all of Zürich comes to walk, snack and shop, whether to browse at the inexpensive department stores that crowd the first third of the street, or to sign away Fr.30,000 on a Rolex watch or a Vuitton handbag at the understated super-chic boutiques further south. At no. 31, below the Beyer watch and jewellery shop, is the **Uhrenmuseum Beyer** (Mon–Fri 2–6pm; Fr.5; Ⓦwww .beyer-ch.com), filled with examples of timekeeping, from sundials and an ancient Egyptian water-clock onwards.

Two-thirds of the way along the boulevard is **Paradeplatz**, a tram-packed little square offering some of the best people-watching in the city. It's around here that the frippery retreats and Zürich's serious money begins: the streets off Paradeplatz are home to more financial institutions, insurance companies and top-name designer outlets than you could shake a stick at, as well as the headquarters of many Swiss banks. Bahnhofstrasse ends at the unromantic, paved **Bürkliplatz**, departure point for all boat trips on the lake and boasting a fabulous view of the Zürichsee and its eastern "Gold Coast", named for the mansions and grandiose public buildings lining the shore that bask all summer long in the afternoon sunshine.

Around the Lindenhof

Between Bahnhofstrasse and the river lies the western portion of the Old Town; there are many picturesque alleys to explore here. Rennweg branches off Bahnhofstrasse, and a short walk left from it up the hill brings you to the **Lindenhof**, the oldest part of Zürich and site of a Roman customs post. The broad space is quiet now, occupied mostly by chess-playing old-timers, and gives a fine panorama over the rooftops. Down on the riverside is **Schipfe**, one of Zürich's oldest quarters, once the centre of the city's silk industry, packed with artisans' shops and little cafés. On the Lindenhof's other side, **Pfalzgasse** descends steeply into a dense network of cobbled lanes, where **Augustinergasse**, with its romantic oriel-windowed houses, leads to tiny Münzplatz overlooked by the beautiful **Augustinerkirche**, dating from 1274. Spare and simple inside, the church was secularized during the Reformation in 1524 and became the town's mint, but it was renovated and re-dedicated in the nineteenth century and is now used by the Christ Catholic Church (see p.239).

Nearby, the top floor of the Strauhof literary museum is home to the **James Joyce Foundation**, Augustinergasse 9 (Mon–Fri 10am–5pm; free; Ⓦwww .joycefoundation.ch; on Mondays, ring the bell), which has a creaking library and reading room crammed with research materials and one of Europe's most

comprehensive collections of Joyceana. Joyce wrote *Ulysses* during his wartime exile in Zürich (1915–19); he returned in 1940, and died on January 13, 1941, laid to rest in Fluntern cemetery next to the zoo, where there is now a statue to him. The Foundation can direct you to his various haunts around town, and they also hold regular open readings – free to all – from *Ulysses* (Tues 5.30–7pm) and *Finnegans Wake* (Thurs 4.30–6pm & 7–8.30pm).

Augustinergasse leads on to the **St Peters Kirche** (Mon–Fri 8am–6pm, Sat 9am–4pm; Ⓦwww.st-peter-zh.ch), dating from the thirteenth century but much altered in 1705. The fact that it boasts the largest clock face in Europe (8.7m in diameter; 1534) is less interesting than the unusual sight, above the pulpit amidst Baroque bas-relief, of the name of God in Hebrew lettering, legacy of the

△ Joyce's grave, Fluntern cemetery

Reformers' desire to reclaim the fundamental sources of Christianity. A stepped alley adjacent to the church, **Thermengasse**, has a catwalk taking you over an excavated Roman baths. A short distance south is the Münsterhof, with the grand Baroque **Zunfthaus zur Meisen** housing the National Museum's ceramics collection (Tues–Sun 10.30am–5pm; Fr.3), including some impressive eighteenth-century porcelain and faience.

The Fraumünster

The Münsterhof is dominated by the graceful, slender-spired **Fraumünster** (daily 10am–6pm; Nov–March closes 4pm), a beautiful church boasting a breathtaking series of stained-glass windows by Marc Chagall and Augusto Giacometti that should not be missed.

It's not known when the church was founded, but on July 21, 853, King Ludwig the German signed over to his daughter Hildegard a convent which already stood on the site. In 874, Hildegard's sister Bertha consecrated what was probably a simple, towerless basilica, and built a crypt beneath to house the relics of **Felix and Regula**, Roman Christians and the patron saints of Zürich. During the eleventh century, the convent abbesses gained considerable rights, and the present structure was built during the thirteenth century. The convent was suppressed under Zwingli's Reformation, and in 1524 all the icons, ornaments and the organ were destroyed. During the following centuries, the minster became a place of worship for Veltliner and Huguenot refugees, was temporarily a Russian Orthodox church, and – between 1833 and 1844 – hosted both Catholic and Protestant services. There was much renovation during the twentieth century, and in 1967, **Marc Chagall** – then 80 – accepted the commission to make new stained glass for the five 10m-high windows of the Romanesque choir. The stunning artistry of the work he produced makes them one of the highlights of Zürich.

The Chagall windows

Entrance is into the transept through the small east door beneath the spire, and attention is so concentrated on the Chagall windows that you may well find the rest of the church has been roped off.

The Romanesque **choir** dates from 1250–70; it is extremely high (18m) and has a wonderful simplicity of design that would make it a magical place even without its windows. Chagall's blood-red **"Prophets"** window, on the north wall (left), features Elisha at the bottom watching Elijah mount to heaven in a chariot of fire; above, drenched in a divine blue, sits Jeremiah. The **"Law"** window, on the opposite wall, has Moses looking down upon the disobedience and suffering of the people, who are following a horseman into war. Below is Isaiah in the arms of a seraph, preparing to proclaim his message of peace to the world.

Of the three main windows, the left, known as the **"Jacob"**, window, shows the patriarch's struggle with the angel and his dream of a ladder to heaven. The yellow **"Zion"** window on the right shows an angel trumpeting the beginning of eternity and the descent of New Jerusalem from the heavens; below are a radiant King David and Bathsheba. Finally, the central **"Christ"** window shows Joseph, standing at the bottom beside a huge tree – the tree of life, and the family tree of Christ. Floating in its upper branches is a vision of Mary holding the baby Jesus with the Lamb of God at her feet. Scenes from Jesus' life and parables culminate in an associative depiction of the crucifixion; a cross is barely visible, and Christ is already floating free of the world towards the source of luminescence above.

Giacometti's 1940s work in the 9m-high window in the north transept, visible as you head out, is equally stunning. Were it not for the Chagall windows, this vision of God and Christ, with eight prophets below, and Matthew, Mark, Luke and John framed by ten angels, would take pride of place; as it is, it's doomed to play second fiddle.

West of Bahnhofstrasse

The shopping streets to the west, between Bahnhofstrasse and the River Sihl, hold little interest. Very near Pelikanplatz, in the **Park zur Katz** (Mon–Fri 7am–7pm, Sat & Sun 7am–6pm; shorter hours in winter) – once the city's botanical garden, and still boasting an octagonal glasshouse – is the **Völkerkundemuseum**, Pelikanstrasse 40 (Tues–Fri 10am–1pm & 2–5pm, Sat 2–5pm, Sun 11am–5pm; free; Ⓦwww.musethno.unizh.ch), a highly acclaimed museum of non-European cultures. Not far away, at Selnaustrasse 25, the **Haus Konstruktiv** (Tues–Fri noon–6pm (Wed until 8pm), Sat & Sun 11am–6pm; Fr.14; Ⓦwww .hauskonstruktiv.ch) hosts changing exhibits of concrete and constructivist art.

Schweizerisches Landesmuseum

Behind the train station, and unmistakeable in its mock-Gothic, purpose-built castle, is the **Schweizerisches Landesmuseum** (Swiss National Museum; Tues–Sun 10am–5pm; Fr.5; SMP; Ⓦwww.musee-suisse.com). This massive building has a varied collection covering the range of Swiss history, and is well worth investigation. The collection is so vast, and the layout of the place so labyrinthine, that you'd do best to consult a (free) floor-plan at the door and then head straight for those areas which interest you rather than to try and absorb everything. An ongoing programme of major renovation work (due to last until 2013) means that various parts of the building – and its collections – may be off-limits when you visit.

The museum begins with a series of rooms devoted to **sacred art** from the ninth to the sixteenth centuries, displaying medieval wood carvings, painted altar pieces, a wheelable model of Christ on an ass (used in Palm Sunday processions), and 65 copies of the 153 panels that adorn the ceiling of the church at Zillis (see p.494). Fifteenth-century **stained glass** has been installed in a room which also displays a sequence of images of some less well-known saints (including St Vitus, patron saint of bedwetting). Rooms lead you past a reconstruction of an eighteenth-century **apothecary** and an intricately detailed sixteenth-century bestiary; up some stairs are several watches and clocks, and a display on **exploration** crowned by a spectacular two-metre-high globe dating from 1570. Pieces showing the life of the Swiss **nobility** include a decorated gentleman's sleigh from seventeenth-century Luzern. Stairs lead up again to a tower, with dozens of cases of **costumes**, some pieces of silver and eighteenth- and nineteenth-century **toys**. Returning back down the same stairs brings you to a sequence of **Baroque** and Rococo rooms, including a ceremonial hall from a Zürich house of 1660. There's also a section on **military history**, as well as an **archeological collection**, comprising a wealth of finds from Roman Zürich. Pick of the Iron Age collection is a stunning embossed golden bowl from 600 BC; Neolithic and Bronze Age artefacts bring you back round to the entrance again.

Stretching behind the museum, the small, shady **Platzspitz** park (daily 6am–9pm), where the Sihl meets the Limmat, was once known as Needle Park, crunching underfoot with used syringes from the flaked-out junkies all around. These days it's been entirely cleaned up, and is good for a pleasant wander framed by the two rivers.

One of the best short trips out of the city is to the hill of **Uetliberg**, a twenty-minute train ride away and a favoured getaway for the locals to do a spot of sledding (winter) or picnicking (summer). Uetliberg – popularly known in dialect as "Üezgi" – is also one end of a popular hiking route, running about two hours south along a forested ridge overlooking the lake to Felsenegg, from where a cable car can deliver you 300m down to Adliswil village to catch a train back to Zürich. Swiss Pass and ZürichCARD holders travel free; otherwise, press *131 on the ticket machine for an all-inclusive day-pass ("AlbisTageskarte") or 8138 for a ticket to Uetliberg only.

From Zürich HB, S-Bahn **trains** depart at least every half-hour to Uetliberg. At the tiny end station, an information hut stocks a free hiking map of the area identifying plenty of short and long trails. The trail which begins at Uetliberg station is dubbed the *Planetenweg* (Planet Path), and features models of the planets on a scale of 1:1 billion, with the distances between them also to scale. From the station, it's about a ten-minute walk uphill to the **summit**, passing the Sun, Mercury, Venus, Earth and Mars on the way; Pluto is about 5km away at Felsenegg.

From the top of the summit's 30m viewing tower, which boosts your altitude to 900m, there are terrific 360-degree views over Zürich, the whole curve of the lake and, on a clear day, east into Austria and as far southwest as the Jungfrau. Also on the summit is the *Uto Kulm* hotel (see p.415) and **restaurant**, a handy spot for refreshment. The panoramic walking route from *Uto Kulm* to Felsenegg and beyond passes another couple of restaurants. A **cable car** (daily: May–Sept 8am–10pm; Oct–April 9am–8pm) runs every fifteen minutes between Felsenegg and Adliswil, from where it's less than ten minutes' walk to Adliswil train station.

Museum Rietberg

The impressive **Museum Rietberg** (Tues–Sun 10am–5pm; April–Sept Wed until 8pm; Fr.6, plus about Fr.6 for any special exhibits; SMP; Ⓦ www.rietberg .ch) comprises two villas set in a lush park southwest of the centre, which together house a splendid collection of non-European art. Signs from the Rietberg stop on tram #7 direct you up into the park; a right-hand fork takes you to the Villa Wesendonck, a left-hand fork to the Park-Villa Rieter. Reconstruction and expansion work is creating a futuristic new glass wing for the museum.

For now, the main collection is housed in the grandiose **Villa Wesendonck**, where the composer Richard Wagner lived for a time in 1857. Once inside, head left for a chronological tour, through rooms of Indian and Chinese Buddhist art and sculpture from between the third and sixteenth centuries – look out for the blissfully serene lovers' faces, in glorious contrast to the mournfulness on display in the Landesmuseum's European art of roughly the same period. A four-armed dancing Shiva in bronze, surrounded by a ring of fire, is particularly stunning. Upstairs are some intricate Tibetan bronzes, Chinese ceramics, and a host of American, African and Australasian pieces. The smaller **Park-Villa Rieter** houses on two floors changing selections from the museum's enormous collection of exquisite Asian painting: Indian art on ground level, Chinese and Japanese art upstairs.

Zürich West

For a clean break from the sometimes overly packaged Zürich of cobbled alleys, medieval guildhalls and glitzy shopping, you need to head west. The new home of the city's underground is the residential and post-industrial area comprising the postal districts of 8004 (*Kreis 4*) and 8005 (*Kreis 5*), together known as **Zürich West**.

▲ Hardturm

ZÜRICH WEST

HARDTURMSTRASSE

FÖHRLIBUCKSTR

ESCHER-WYSS PLATZ

Limmat

INDUSTRIE-

Schiffbau ❶

Kunsthalle & Migros Museum

HARDSTRASSE

Daros Exhibitions

❷

QUARTIER

JOSEF

PFINGSTWEIDSTRASSE

NEUE HARD

GEROLDSTR

VULKANSTR

Hardbrücke Station

HARDBRÜCKE

ERNASTRASSE

SIHLFELDSTRASSE

STAUFFACHERSTR

Rail Freight Station

HOHLSTRASSE

AUSSERSIHL

HOHLSTRASSE

SEEBAHNSTRASSE

LIMMAT

LIMMATSTRASSE

LIMMAT-PLATZ

Museum für Gestaltung

LETTENVIADUKT

SIHLQUAI

KORNHAUSBRÜCKE

WASSERWERKSTRASSE

KLOSTER

AUSSTELLUNGSSTRASSE

KONRADSTRASSE

ZOLLSTRASSE

LAGERSTRASSE

Haupt-bahnhof

ACCOMMODATION

Etap	A
Haus zur Stauffacherin	F
Regina	D
Rothaus	D
Walhalla	C
X-tra	B

0   200 m

❸
❹
❺ ❻

Ⓑ

Ⓐ

Ⓒ

Ⓓ

Ⓔ

Ⓕ

❼

❽

❾

LANGSTRASSE

STAUFFACHERSTRASSE

ANWANDSTRASSE

KANZLEISTRASSE

HELVETIA PLATZ

BADENERSTRASSE

ZEUGHAUSSTRASSE

N

KASERNENSTR

GESSNER BR

LÖWEN-PLATZ

SIHL

Sihl

SIHLBR

ZWEIER-PLATZ

EATING & DRINKING

4. Akt	2
El Parador	3
Helvetia	10
Kanzlei	8
La Salle	1
Lily's Stomach Supply	6
Reithalle	9
Riff Raff	5
Sala of Tokyo	7
Santa Lucia	4

▼ Wiedikon

Paradeplatz ▼

The north–south artery of **Langstrasse** is where the daily dramas are played out, a seedy but absorbing mile-long strip of designer bars, videogame parlours, independent cinemas, clubwear outlets and cheap eateries. Trams #2 or #3 to Bezirksgebäude deliver you to the respectable southern end of Langstrasse around **Helvetiaplatz**, relaxed home of the *Xenix* bar and cinema. Strolling north, the street narrows and the mood changes: this was once Zürich's red-light district, and although some of the unpleasantness survives (there's still a fair spread of sex cinemas and prostitution), the worst of the vice trade has moved on. In its place has developed a downmarket ethnic and social mix that is a universe away from the homogeneous collection of expensive suits and fur coats parading the Bahnhofstrasse not a kilometre east: lowlife bars rub shoulders with avant-garde galleries, smells of greasy kebabs mix with wood-fired pizza and aromatic marijuana, and the whole street is a mingle of Swiss-German voices with French-African, Portuguese, Turkish, Balkan, Latin American, Haitian and more.

Two-thirds of the way along, Langstrasse dips beneath the train tracks; the style north of the underpass is different again, with residential side-streets increasingly attracting artists and creative types who have, in turn, spawned plenty of hip bars, high-quality restaurants and designer boutiques on and off the stretch leading to the major **Limmatplatz** junction (served by trams #4 and #13). A short walk east, set amongst streets packed with independent galleries and design studios, is the celebrated **Museum für Gestaltung**, at Ausstellungstrasse 60 (Design Museum; Tues–Thurs 10am–8pm, Fri–Sun 10am–5pm; Fr.12; SMP; Ⓦwww.museum-gestaltung .ch), with exhibits relating to design, the visual arts, advertising and the media.

The Industrie-quartier

More interest lies in wandering the streets west of Limmatplatz; from here all the way out to the football stadium at Hardturm is the old **industrial quarter**, still largely unreclaimed. Trains and heavy traffic pass on viaducts way above the roofs of working depots, old factories and business parks, while in between thrives a lively subculture focused on industrial spaces reclaimed as galleries and restaurants, and anonymous-looking bunkers that double as some of Zürich's best dance clubs.

West of the the rail viaduct off Ottostrasse stands the old Löwenbräu brewery, a vast brick building at Limmatstrasse 268–270 that now houses, aside from five small galleries and an art bookshop, the acclaimed contemporary-art shows of the **Kunsthalle** (Tues–Fri noon–6pm, Sat & Sun 11am–5pm; Fr.8; Ⓦwww .kunsthallezurich.ch), the **Migros Museum für Gegenwartskunst** (Contemporary Art; same hours; Fr.8; Ⓦwww.migrosmuseum.ch) and **Daros Exhibitions** (Thurs–Sun noon–6pm; Fr.5; Ⓦwww.daros.ch).

Close by is the busy **Escher–Wyss–Platz**, its swirl of cars, bikes, buses and trams smothered by a traffic overpass: high overhead, stressed-out city-centre workers speed home to the suburbs while down at street level, locals relax in the clutch of trendy bars and cafés on and off Hardstrasse. Signed just off the

△ The Schiffbau

street is perhaps the city's most impressive architectural space, the **Schiffbau**, a huge plant which once built parts for ships; now, with bare concrete largely left unadorned and heavy machinery still hanging in the ceiling, it houses, in its various sectors, two drama stages of the Schauspielhaus, *Moods* jazz club and *LaSalle*, one of the city's best restaurants. It's open for exploration throughout the day.

You can get back to Zürich HB either on tram #4 or #13 from Escher-Wyss-Platz, or by train from Hardbrücke station, located 300m south of the Schiffbau.

Eating and drinking

As you might expect from a city like Zürich, there's a wealth of variety in **eating and drinking** possibilities, with as much available citywide at the bottom end of the market as at the top.

All the places reviewed here are **keyed on the maps** – either of the city (p.410), the central area (p.418) or Zürich West (p.430).

Cafés and café-bars

Zürich has an enormous variety of both **cafés** and **café-bars**; as ever, the difference between them, and between a café and a restaurant, is blurred. Bars and pubs are listed on p.436.

There's any number of places all through the **Niederdorf** alleys where you can sit and watch the world go by over a coffee or glass of beer. Don't stick – as many visitors do – to the slightly seedy cafés along Niederdorfstrasse itself; Zürich's most alluring café culture takes place further south, at the pavement cafés along the riverside Limmatquai and the cobbled squares, such as Hechtplatz and Schiffländeplatz, that open onto it. This is also where you'll find international names, including *Starbucks*.

The west bank of the river, **around Bahnhofstrasse**, is less of a draw, not least because this is shopping territory: long expanses of shop windows don't make the streets especially amble-friendly, although a bit of poking around in the old-town alleys between Bahnhofstrasse and the river can turn up trumps.

Niederdorf

Altstadt Kirchgasse 4 ⓦ www.hotel-altstadt .ch. Cool jazzy café-bar, open from breakfast time onwards, that's gaining a reputation as an old-town meeting point away from the sleaze.

Odeon Limmatquai 2 ⓦ www.odeon.ch. Compact café-bar on Bellevue, where Lenin once sat and watched the world go by. There's little sign of revolutionary activity these days – although the bar prices would spark a popular uprising anywhere other than Zürich.

Rathaus In the Rathaus on Limmatquai. Pleasant place with an outside terrace alongside the old Town Hall, sandwiched neatly between the river and the Limmatquai trams.

Schlauch Münstergasse 20 (upstairs). Quiet, friendly and relaxed diner-bar, perfect to catch your

breath from the Niederdorf scrum. Sizeable plates of health-conscious food (veggie and not), and a snooker hall adjacent attract a young, vaguely alternative crowd. Closed Mon & Tues.

Schober Napfgasse 4. A memorable old confectioner's and café that's straight out of Mary Poppins – a riot of frothy white lace, flowers and choice treats. Head through to the capacious interior for quite simply the best mug of hot chocolate (with whipped cream) you will ever have tasted. It's even a shame to spoil it with a slice of home-made apple strudel – but then again…

Zähringer Spitalgasse at Zähringerplatz. Long-standing cooperative-run bastion of Zürcher counterculture, attracting an alternative clientele for snacks, herbal teas and beer. Mon 6pm–midnight, Tues–Sun 8am–midnight (Fri & Sat until 12.30am).

Around Bahnhofstrasse

Amsterdam Schwanengasse 4. Tiny, colourful old town café for fresh juices and healthy snacks. Closed Sun & Mon.

Mövenpick Paradeplatz 4. Perfect people-watching café, with a great selection of teas and coffees from around the world, plus snacks and full meals all day long.

No Kuttelgasse 7. Purportedly Japanese teahouse (although little more than a standard café done up with some paper screens and a tinkling miniature water-garden), nonetheless cool and relaxing, conveniently located in the alleys just off Bahnhofstrasse. Offers a good range of refreshments and light lunches.

Sprüngli Bahnhofstrasse 21 ⓦwww .confiserie-spruengli.ch. Main branch of the world-famous confectioner's, in this location since 1859, displaying cabinets full of the most exquisite chocolates and cakes imaginable, plus their own speciality, Luxemburgerli, cream-filled pastry bites that are truly drool-worthy. Enjoy it all in the upstairs café-patisserie overlooking Parade-platz, the city's most atmospheric tearoom, where Zürich's ladies come to gossip discreetly over coffee and cake. Free choc with every espresso.

Restaurants

Traditional Zürich cuisine is rich and heavy with meat, epitomized in the city's trademark dish *Züri Gschnetzlets* – diced veal in a creamy mushroom sauce, generally served alongside *rösti*. There's a host of good-quality inexpensive **restaurants** in every corner of the city that can do you a filling lunch for Fr.15–20, or a full evening meal for roughly twice that; Niederdorf is shoulder to shoulder with them. As a general rule, the area around Bahnhofstrasse is livelier than Niederdorf at lunch time, while in the evening the reverse is true. There's also no shortage of expensive places, where you'd be lucky to come away with change from Fr.75 per person, and are probably looking at almost twice that for a full meal.

Inexpensive and mid-range restaurants

Niederdorf and east bank

Adler's Swiss Chuchi Rosengasse 10 ☏044 266 96 96, ⓦwww.hotel-adler.ch. Landmark Swiss restaurant below the *Adler* hotel, freshly renovated in bright, modern style (although it's located on a particularly sleazy section of Niederdorf-strasse). Good-value fondue or raclette (Fr.25–30) are what to go for; the bargain lunch specials have a careful, home-cooked touch as well, but cheese is the thing – you'll sniff the place before you see it.

Ban Song Thai Kirchgasse 6 ☏044 252 33 31, ⓦwww.bansongthai.ch. One of the city's better Thais, small and pleasant with a varied menu. Lunch specials start from Fr.15, evening meals more than twice that. Closed Sun.

Blinde Kuh (literally "Blind Cow", German for Blind Man's Buff), Mühlebachstrasse 148

☎044 421 50 50, ⓦ www.blindekuh.ch.
Remarkable restaurant offering a unique experience.
The food is excellent, down-to-earth cuisine that
gains acres of new depth by being served in absolute
darkness: after the foyer (there are lights here and in
the toilets), you're led into the pitch-dark, smoke-free
dining room where you can't see a thing, not your
hand in front of your face. The restaurant – a small
place, seating 48 at eight tables – is run as a way for
sighted folk to sample the experience of losing their
sight for a couple of hours. The menus (one meat,
one fish and one vegetarian, all moderately priced)
change each week. The waiters are blind or partially
sighted; the head chef is sighted, but the sous chef
is blind. It's a very popular place: you'll need to book
several weeks ahead. Open every evening, and also
Tues–Fri for lunch.

Bodega Española Münstergasse 15 ☎044
251 23 10. Small, dark-wood place dripping
with atmosphere that's been here since 1892,
concealed from the street behind its attached wine
shop. Upstairs is the restaurant, with a long menu
ranging from *tortilla catalana* to an unmissable
paella (around Fr.40 for two). The buzzing tapas bar
downstairs is also outstanding, with a huge range
from Fr.5.

Le Dézaley Römergasse 7 ☎044 251 61 29,
ⓦ www.le-dezaley.ch. Excellent Swiss-French
restaurant nestling in a quiet alley at the foot of
the Grossmünster's north tower. House specialities
are pricey Vaudois dishes such as fondue bourguignonne (with a cellarful of Vaudois wines to boot),
but there are many inexpensive options available.
Interior decor is attractive, and there's also a lovely
little courtyard garden. Closed Sun.

Kantorei Neumarkt 2 ☎044 252 27 27, ⓦ www
.restaurant-kantorei.ch. Warm and pleasant,
award-winning young restaurant, occupying a
600-year-old building in a little-visited part of the
Old Town and serving unpretentious, but excellently
prepared, modern Swiss cuisine. Doubles as a
tranquil café between mealtimes.

Mère Catherine Nägelihof 3 ☎044 250 59 40,
ⓦ www.commercio.ch. Pleasant little place in a
hard-to-find courtyard below the Grossmünster,
brightly done up and touting itself as *"un peu
provençal"* – salads and seafood are the main
draw, with especially good bouillabaisse. Menus
change monthly.

Pinte Vaudoise In *Hotel Villette*, Kruggasse 4
☎044 251 23 35. Traditional dark-wood den
serving what has been voted several times as the
best fondue in Zürich. The jovial owner/manager/
chef is used to tourists and can explain the range
of fondues on offer (around Fr.22). Closed Sat in
summer, & Sun.

Santa Lucia Marktgasse 21 ☎044 262 36 26,
ⓦ www.santalucia.ch. Simple Niederdorf Italian
with a wide selection of good-value pasta and pizza,
plus the bonus of late-night service until 2am.

Spaghetti Factory Niederdorfstrasse 5 ⓦ www
.spaghettifactory.ch. Straightforward pasta restaurant in the heart of the Niederdorf buzz, good and
cheap. Daily until 2.30am. Also at Schifflände 6,
behind Hechtplatz, and Theaterstrasse 1, south of
Bellevue.

Weisser Wind Oberdorfstrasse 20 ☎044 251 18
45, ⓦ www.weisserwind.ch. Comfortable, traditional setting for Italian and Swiss specialities, with
plenty of vegetarian options, for around Fr.20–30. A
beerhall in all but name. Closed Sun.

Around Bahnhofstrasse

Bona Dea Bahnhofplatz 15 ☎044 217 15 15,
ⓦ www.bahnhofbuffet.ch. Excellent, no-smoking
vegetarian buffet restaurant attached to the train
station, with loads of choice. Note that, despite the
location, this is a dainty, upmarket kind of place
(and, at Fr.35 a head, priced accordingly).

Hiltl Sihlstrasse 28 ☎044 227 70 00,
ⓦ www.hiltl.ch. Top-quality vegetarian
restaurant, a city institution since 1898 but now
completely renovated with bright decor, calm,
friendly service and excellent fare. Sample the à
la carte options, or plump for the expansive and
great-value hot and cold buffet. During 2006, while
the Sihlstrasse location was being renovated,
a temporary *Hiltl* opened in the Alten Börse at
Bleicherweg 5, off Paradeplatz; this may become a
going concern in future, too.

Kropf In Gassen 16 ☎044 221 18 05. An atmospheric listed building, boasting a frescoed interior
which dates from its conversion into a restaurant
in 1888, and which stands a little askance with the
solid *bürgerliche* cooking on offer: Bacchic revels
may be erupting all around, but only in picture
form on the ceiling. Meat, potatoes and dumplings
in various forms, along with tripe, are staples, and
yet standards are high and the food is never dull.
Closed Sun.

Zeughauskeller Bahnhofstrasse 28a at
Paradeplatz ☎044 211 26 90, ⓦ www
.zeughauskeller.ch. A wood-ceilinged room dating
from the fifteenth century that's now the city's top
beerhall, a sometimes chaotic place serving hearty
meat dishes and plenty of the amber nectar. One of
the most extensive sausage menus around – over
a dozen different varieties, served with onion sauce
and fresh potato salad – is crowned by a one-
metre giant (around Fr.80) that should keep four
people occupied for some time. Although the menu
is in English (and ten other languages), this place

is still very popular with Zürchers of a certain bank balance – a long way from the rough-and-ready beerhalls of Niederdorf.

Zürich West

El Parador Luisenstrasse 43 ☎043 366 88 85, ⓦwww.elparador.ch. Acclaimed Spanish restaurant, on the quiet corner with Heinrichstrasse, with a small, select menu of authentic dishes. Food is expertly prepared – the *paella* and *crema catalana* are both sublime – but don't expect to pay less than about Fr.50 a head. Closed Sat lunch & Sun.

Lily's Stomach Supply Langstrasse 197 ☎044 440 18 85, wwww.lilys.ch. Clean, modern place in the heart of the Langstrasse district, always busy, churning out authentic Asian dishes fresh-cooked in the open kitchen – anything from Tamil chicken curry or Pakistani panji renga to Japanese yaki soba, Thai noodles or hong shao tofu, washed down with Filipino beer. Seating is at long, communal tables with benches. The German menu marks dishes that are extra-spicy !!! and those that are an acquired taste ***. Phone ahead for a takeaway. Food served Mon–Thurs 11am–midnight, Fri & Sat 11am–1am, Sun 3pm–midnight.

Reithalle Gessnerallee 8 ☎044 212 07 66, ⓦwww.restaurant-reithalle.ch. Formerly the military riding school, this complex of buildings along the Sihl has been turned into a theatre and centre for performing arts, with one long, stone-floored hall serving as a combination bar and restaurant. It attracts a lively and eclectic crowd of twenty-somethings with a varied menu of light, modern dishes (many vegetarian), and a relaxed, share-a-table attitude. Saturday nights they crank up the music for late-night dancing.

Santa Lucia Luisenstrasse 31, corner Josefstrasse ☎044 272 58 93, ⓦwww.santalucia.ch. Bright, airy Italian on a quiet residential street, with a wood-fired pizza oven and excellent fresh pasta. The friendly, accommodating service makes it popular with the locals. Daily until midnight.

Expensive restaurants

Haus zum Rüden Limmatquai 42 ☎044 261 95 66, ⓦwww.hauszumrueden.ch. Splendid thirteenth-century riverside *Zunfthaus* (guildhall), complete with vaulted ceiling and late-Gothic decor; book in advance for a window table. The food covers most of the standard Zürich bases – plenty of meat and rich sauces, including the famous *Züri Gschnetzlets* (Fr.52), prepared with care and skill. Bank on Fr.80 a head. Closed Sat & Sun.

Hummerbar In *Hotel St Gotthard*, Bahnhofstrasse 87 ☎044 227 77 00, ⓦwww.hotelstgotthard.ch. A wonderfully romantic place for *Hummer* (lobster) and a host of other seafood (including Iranian caviar), all flown in fresh daily and prepared in pristine style for consumption amidst a formal, *fin-de-siècle* setting. Prices – compared with others under this heading – are reasonable, but who's counting when you're contemplating fresh oysters? Lobster and seafood speciality mains are around Fr.70–80, or plump for the menu of oysters in butter followed by clam chowder, a half-lobster in Champagne sauce and dessert, for Fr.80.

Kronenhalle Rämistrasse 4 ☎044 262 99 00, ⓦwww.kronenhalle.com. Despite the impressive array of the twentieth century's great and good who've licked their chops appreciatively here, the ambience of this classically grand place, bedecked with original Picassos, Matisses and Braques, remains amiable rather than stiff. (With at least one hors d'oeuvre on the menu over Fr.100, they can afford to be amiable.) The cuisine is outstanding but undramatic – there's little on the menu that you won't have seen before – but where the place scores is in its down-to-earth attitude to those who decide to spurn the champagne and truffles in favour of enjoying the atmosphere over a sausage and a glass of beer instead. A classic Zürich restaurant: discreet and hearty.

LaSalle In Schiffbau building, off Hardstrasse ☎044 258 70 71, ⓦwww.lasalle-restaurant.ch. Amazing place set within a huge glass cube on the factory floor of the old Schiffbau (see p.432); you eat beneath a giant glowing Murano chandelier suspended on high. It's far from downmarket, though – all white tablecloths and silver service – and is a breath of fresh air after the stuffiness of traditional city-centre restaurants. The modern European cuisine is outstanding (Fr.50 or so per head), but the surroundings are just as alluring as the food. Unmissable, whether you come to gawp or dine. Closed Sat & Sun lunch.

Petermann's Kunststuben Seestrasse 160, Küsnacht ☎044 910 07 15, ⓦwww.petermanns.grandestables.ch. Universally acclaimed as one of Switzerland's top five restaurants, replete with two Michelin stars, several international awards (including the title "Best Restaurant in Europe", as assessed by 8250 diners for Zagat) and pages of gushing reportage from foodie journalists. To cut to the chase: if you're prepared to invest Fr.125 per head for lunch, or twice that in the evening – plus the cost of getting to and from Küsnacht, 8km south of town – then you'll get a meal to remember for years to come. The dining-room setting is classy, sophisticated with a light, arty touch, and chef Horst Petermann is constantly at work refining his menu. You'll need to book several weeks ahead. Closed Sun & Mon, also early Sept and late Feb.

Sala di Tokyo Limmatstrasse 29 ℡ 044 271 52 90, ⓦ www.sala-of-tokyo.ch. You'd never know it, but this dowdy, anonymous building at the station end of a busy traffic street hides one of Switzerland's best Japanese restaurants. Prices are very high (Fr.80 for lunch, Fr.130 in the evening), but the quality of the traditional cuisine, using the freshest

of ingredients, is outstanding. Closed Sat lunch, Sun & Mon; also late July to early Aug.

Zunfthaus zur Schmiden Marktgasse 20 ℡ 044 250 58 48, ⓦ www.zunfthausschmiden.ch. The guildhall of the smiths, dating from 1520, and now a splendid setting in the heart of Niederdorf in which to linger over the richest of Swiss-German cuisine, meat-heavy platters and top Zürcher specialities such as *geschnetzeltes Kalbfleisch* (veal in a white wine and cream sauce), everything in mighty portions. Closed Sat & Sun; also closed mid-July to mid-Aug.

Nightlife and entertainment

For a city that's a minnow in world terms, Zürich has a surprisingly wide range of **nightlife and entertainment**. Live rock and jazz – although easy to find most nights of the week – take second place to the city's dynamic club scene, which covers the gamut from techno to salsa. Zürich is also home to a top-flight orchestra, a world-famous opera company, and one of the German-speaking world's premier theatres. You can find complete what's-on **listings** for the week ahead in *ZüriTipp* (ⓦ www.zueritipp.ch), the Friday supplement to the *Tages Anzeiger* newspaper, available free at the tourist office.

Pubs and bars

Niederdorf

Babalu Schmidgasse 6. Tiny postmodern-style bar, its chic denizens quaffing bottled beers and cocktails amidst an onslaught of deep beats.

Cranberry Metzgergasse 3 ⓦ www.cranberry.ch. Popular and lively old-town bar – predominantly gay.

Oepfelchammer Rindermarkt 12 ⓦ www .oepfelchammer.ch. A 200-year-old building, all creaking timbers and lop-sided ceilings, famous for its association with the city's literary son, Gottfried Keller. The reason to visit is for beer in the tiny low-beamed upper front room, which is invariably

△ Zürich West bar

packed. Legend has it that if you can swing up and wriggle your way through the gap between beam and ceiling, your beers are on the house: Keller may have done it, but few have succeeded since. Closed Sun & Mon.

Oliver Twist Rindermarkt 6 @ www.pickwick.ch. Snug little pub on a Niederdorf back alley, a mecca for expats and Anglophiles in search of pints, English conversation and football on the telly.

Pigalle Marktgasse 14 @ www.pigalle.ch. Legendary little campy bar filled with the elegantly wasted, or at least those who are aspiring.

Rheinfelder Bierhalle Niederdorfstrasse 76. Best of the many beerhalls at the northern end of the street. With wooden benches, zero decoration and bright lights, this is a place to get shamelessly, sociably drunk, laugh loudly and clap strangers on the back. The food is cheap and hearty: daily specials for around Fr.13 are padded out by their infamous "Jumbo Jumbo Cordon Bleu" – a slab of deep-fried cheese-slathered meat so big it dangles off the plate on both sides. Closed Sun.

Wüste Oberdorfstrasse 7 @ www.wueste.ch. Mellow, comfortable bar below the *Otter* hotel, decorated in ethnic style and dotted with candles.

Around Bahnhofstrasse

Helvetia Stauffacherquai 1. Loud and jovial locals' haunt – nicknamed the Helvti-Bar – just across the Sihl; the only bar in town where you can get full table service after midnight (closes 1am weekdays, 2am weekends). A little pricey for everyday consumption, but very civilized for a nightcap or three.

James Joyce Pelikanstrasse 8 @ www .jamesjoyce.ch. For many years this stood as the ultimate memorial to one of Zürich's best-known residents. The pub then comprised the original nineteenth-century "Antique Bar" of Dublin's Jury Hotel, saved from the developers in the 1970s, transported here piece by piece and reassembled to stand as a relic of a bygone age. Its location – in the heart of the financial district – let it down, but it retained the ring of authenticity. Tragically, it is now under new management, who have installed black leather seats, shiny metal tables and generally tarted the place up to be just another wine-bar. Not a shred of atmosphere remains. Go, if only to weep into your Zinfandel. Closes Sat 6pm and all day Sun.

Jules Verne Access through *Brasserie Lipp*, Uraniastrasse 9 ☎ 043 888 66 66, @ www .jules-verne.ch. Intimate little city-centre bar in the stubby-domed observatory building, done up with canvas decor to mimic the basket of a

hot-air balloon and boasting superb panoramic views across the rooftops and steeples – worth the price of refreshment. Phone ahead to reserve a table facing south towards the mountains for twilight. Take the lift to the tenth floor, and then climb another 17 steps. Closes midnight Mon–Thurs, 1am Fri & Sat, 11pm Sun.

Kaufleuten Pelikanstrasse 18 @ www .kaufleuten.com. Modish venue for mixing with Zürich's burgeoning "in" scene. Designers, musicians, bankers and the idle rich flock here, and to the club next door. A pricey beer is worth it for the buzz.

Lions Oetenbachgasse 24. Pleasant English pub just off Bahnhofstrasse by the Orell Füssli English bookshop – larger, quieter and much more comfortable than other pubs in the area. Also with a daily food menu.

Nelson Beatengasse 11 @ www.thenelsonpub .com. Massive, noisy pub seconds from the station, crammed on weekend nights with Zürich's sizeable contingent of teenage au pairs and exchange students on the pull. Cheap beer, late opening, live music, DJs, and TV sport make for a heady, if predictable, brew. Sun–Wed until 2am, Thurs–Sat until 3 or 4am.

Noble Dubliner Talacker 43/Talstrasse 82. Good beer, good service and a talkative atmosphere make this cramped mock-Irish pub – with doors front and back – hugely popular with locals and expats alike.

Zürich West and south

4. Akt Heinrichstrasse 262 @ www.4akt.ch. Deeply cool bar at the Hardstrasse junction, with plenty of outside tables, a good, up-to-date music selection, and a small food menu (about Fr.20).

Riff Raff Neugasse 57 @ www.riffraff.ch. Small cinema attached to a trendy bar, a few steps off Langstrasse. The building has a longer history than it seems; it showed silent movies back in the early days, and has now been taken over by a cooperative dedicated to restoring its reputation and promoting independent film-making. The walls, like the clientele, are floor-to-ceiling matt black, and the bar stands between two small auditoria.

Ziegel oh Lac At the Rote Fabrik arts centre, Seestrasse 395 @ www.ziegelohlac.ch. One of the most appealing bar/restaurant-spaces in the city, with a light, open interior and waterside seating in summer but way south of the centre, far from the crush. Signs declare "Smoking Cannabis is Illegal", but to little effect. The food is quality, balanced fare (Fr.12–22). Closed Mon.

Zürich has a thriving **gay and lesbian** scene, probably the best established and most diverse in the country. No hotel will turn a gay or lesbian couple away; however, the *Goldenes Schwert* (see p.414) is the only hotel to make a selling point of its gay- and lesbian-friendliness; handily enough, it occupies the same building as *T&M* (ⓦwww.gaybar.ch), one of the best gay bar/cabaret/disco venues in the city, dark, campy and cruisey. The huge *Barfüsser*, Spitalgasse 14 (ⓦwww.barfuesser.ch) – recently reinvented as a "Café-Bar-Sushi" joint – is Europe's longest-running gay bar, established in 1956 and embracing all scenes, while *Cranberry* (see p.436) is a more relaxed, talkative meeting place for non-scene types. The "Bermuda Triangle" is a cruisey area around Mühlegasse. For more **information**, check ⓦwww.zuerigay .ch or contact HAZ, Sihlquai 67, 3rd floor (Wed 2–6pm; ☎044 271 22 50, ⓦwww.haz .ch). Zürich's Christopher Street Day Parade website (ⓦwww.csdzh.ch) has loads of useful links.

9

ZÜRICH | Nightlife and entertainment

Clubs and live music

Zürich's **club** and **music** scene has skyrocketed recently, helped by legislation permitting some all-night opening: you'll find the city's dance venues heaving with a new-found energy lacking in most European cities. At the heart of the new subculture are the cosmopolitan bars, chic bistros and crowded alternative hangouts of **Zürich West** – particularly on and off Langstrasse and Hardstrasse – although you'll find that the northern half of **Niederdorf**, bang in the city centre, has some of the same vibe. The **industrial quarter** northwest of Langstrasse is where the best underground clubs hide themselves; venues move, nights change and new places open virtually every month. Check flyers at the bars up and down Langstrasse.

Bands and DJs

Abart Manessestrasse 170 ⓦwww.abart.ch. Eclectic programme of local and foreign bands, plus celebrated dance parties.

Dynamo Wasserwerkstrasse 21 ⓦwww.dynamo .ch. Bills itself as a "youth culture centre" and, as well as a disco and jazz school, hosts live bands with an alternative, punkish bias. Also excellent club nights.

Kanzlei Kanzleistrasse 56 at Helvetiaplatz ⓦwww .kanzlei.ch. Groovy lounge bar and club just off Langstrasse, with a full programme of DJ events.

Kaufleuten Pelikanstrasse 18 ⓦwww.kaufleuten .com. Plush city-centre nightspot, its housey, groovey beats drawing an unusual blend of hardcore clubbers and work-to-play young professionals. Voted one of the world's best party venues by the *Wall Street Journal* (which says it all). Dress to impress.

Oxa Andreasstrasse 70 ⓦwww.oxa.ch. Premier venue for trance and house, with two dance floors, a garden and even a restaurant; famous for its after-hours parties (Sun 5–11am).

Rohstofflager Duttweilerstrasse, corner Pfingstweidstrasse, ⓦwww.rohstofflager.ch. Lively mix of DJs and live bands.

Rote Fabrik Seestrasse 395 ⓦwww.rotefabrik .ch. Alternative-style arts complex, in old graffitied industrial buildings on the lakeshore some 5km southwest of town, hosting a continuous flow of bands famous and unknown from all musical genres, as well as big-name DJs. Bus #161 or #165 from Bürkliplatz (last bus returns after midnight).

Toni Molkerei Förrlibuckstrasse 109 ⓦwww .tonimolkerei.com. Eclectic, highly acclaimed and popular house club and relaxed DJ-bar occupying a vast 3000-square-metre industrial space. As well as a great vibe, it has the unique attribute of high-quality bar food as well.

X-tra Limmatstrasse 118 ⓦwww.x-tra.ch. Hugely popular multipurpose venue just off Limmatplatz, with triphop and funky sounds entertaining a youngish crowd. Bar and restaurant adjacent, and hotel upstairs.

Live jazz

Casa Bar Münstergasse 20 ⓦwww.casabar.ch. Zürich's longest-running jazz venue, still featuring live music nightly in the Niederdorf.

Moods In Schiffbau building, off Hardstrasse ⓦwww.moods.ch. The city's premier jazz club, with a good restaurant attached, pulling in top-flight names.

Classical music, opera and ballet

The acoustically superb **Tonhalle** concert hall, Claridenstrasse 7 (ⓦwww .tonhalle.ch), inaugurated by Brahms in 1895, has a programme of world-class **classical music** of all kinds from both the resident Tonhalle and Zürich Chamber orchestras and guest performers. Many of Zürich's **churches** – principally the Grossmünster, Fraumünster, Predigerkirche and St Peter's – host regular concerts of organ, choral and chamber music, as does the **Conservatory** (Florhofgasse 6; ⓦwww.hmt.edu) and the Kunsthaus. The city's majestic **Opera House** (ⓦwww.opernhaus.ch) has an impressive programme of both **opera and ballet** – performances sell out quickly.

Listings

Bike rental The station has the usual paid bike-rental facilities (daily 6am–10.50pm), but you can also take advantage of the *Züri-Rollt* scheme (ⓦwww.zuerirollt.ch), a free bike-rental scheme to help unemployed people get back to work. There are pick-up points around the city (all daily 7.30am–9.30pm): the main one is "Velogate" at the train station, next to platform 18 (open year-round), and the most accessible others (all May–Oct only) are at the Globus department store at Theaterplatz, and by the Opera House off Bellevueplatz. You must leave your passport and Fr.20 as a deposit; various machines are available, from multigeared city bikes to mountain bikes, electric bikes, scooters and skateboards.

Books Zürich's best English bookshop – complete with Rough Guides – is Orell Füssli, Bahnhofstrasse 70. The Travel Bookshop, Rindermarkt 20, is another good source.

Consulates Ireland, Claridenstrasse 25 ☎044 289 25 15; UK, Hegibachstrasse 47 ☎044 383 65 60, ⓦwww.britain-in-switzerland.ch; USA, Dufourstrasse 101 ☎043 499 29 60, ⓦbern .usembassy.gov. Other English-speaking countries

are represented by their embassies in Bern (see p.251) and/or consulates in Geneva (see p.111).

Flights Zürich-Kloten airport flight enquiries ☎0900 300 313, ⓦwww.zurich-airport.com. For a train ticket to the airport from the city centre, press 8058 on the ticket machines.

Lost property The city office is at Werdmühleplatz 10 (Mon–Fri 7.30am–5.30pm; ☎044 216 51 11). The station office is near the head of platform 17 (daily 7am–6pm).

Medical facilities Most convenient is the Permanence Medical Centre at Bahnhofplatz 15 (daily 7am–11pm, but with a 24-hour emergency room; ☎044 215 44 44). Alongside it is the Bahnhof Apotheke pharmacy (daily 7am–midnight).

Police Headquarters is at Bahnhofquai 3 ☎044 216 71 11.

Post office Zürich's main post office is the Sihlpost, poised over the River Sihl next to the main station at Kasernenstrasse 95 (Mon–Fri 6.30am–10.30pm, Sat 6.30am–8pm, Sun 10am–10.30pm). There's also a post office within the station and dozens more around town.

Around the Zürichsee

A pleasant day-trip leads out of the city around the long, slender **ZÜRICH-SEE**, which nestles between the parallel ridges of the Uetliberg to the west and the Pfannenstiel opposite. Basing yourself in lakeside communities such as **Küsnacht** or **Rapperswil** has obvious benefits of tranquillity and value for money over staying in the centre of Zürich; the restaurants in these lakeside communities are also of a very high standard. Kids aren't forgotten either, with a waterpark at **Pfäffikon** and petting zoo in Rapperswil.

The best way to go is by **boat** – ZSG ferries (see p.412) stop at every lakeside town in summer – while picturesque S-Bahn **train** lines run the length of both shores. Küsnacht is a scant ten-minute train ride out of town, Rapperswil a half-hour more. The lake beyond Rapperswil is known as the **Obersee**, served by boats and trains as far as Schmerikon.

The eastern and western shores

Heading along the **eastern shore**, you leave the city and plunge directly into a comfortable, leafy world of trimmed hedges and car dealerships. The unremarkable suburb of **KÜSNACHT**, 7km south, is made significant by the outstanding *Sonne* hotel (see p.415) and *Petermann's Kunststuben* restaurant (see p.435). Some 15km south lies **STÄFA**, a mildly picturesque village clustered at the foot of the Pfannenstiel, in the largest vine-growing region in the canton. From Stäfa, Rapperswil is 12km south.

From Zürich's Bürkliplatz, it's 6km along the lake's **western shore** by bus #165, boat or S-Bahn train to the dormitory town of **KILCHBERG**, unremarkable but for the fragrant presence of the huge Lindt & Sprüngli **chocolate factory**, part of which is open for public visits (closed for renovation at the time of writing; formerly Wed–Fri 10am–noon & 1–4pm; free). The company refuses to let anyone near the production line; instead, you're diverted to a small museum, shown a video and then escorted out (after a free sample or two) to the adjacent shop. As you head south, suburbia fades away, replaced by evidence of a more down-to-earth, rural existence that feels a long way from the Zürich hubbub. Past the old warehouses of **Wädenswil**, from where trains branch off into the hills to Einsiedeln (see p.393), is **PFÄFFIKON**, 23km south of Kilchberg in an outpost of Canton Schwyz (and so named on timetables as "Pfäffikon SZ" to differentiate it from another Pfäffikon nearby). Here sits the popular **Alpamare waterpark** (Tues–Thurs 10am–10pm, Fri 10am–11pm, Sat 9am–11pm, Sun & Mon 9am–10pm; day-pass Fr.46, four-hour pass Fr.36; ⓦwww.alpamare.ch), replete with slides, flumes, heated wave pools and saunas. Rapperswil is a short distance across the lake by road or rail.

Rapperswil

Lying 37km south of Zürich, the small lakefront town of **RAPPERSWIL** repays a gentle afternoon's exploration. Avoid the modern part of town and lose yourself in the quiet Old Town alleys, which weave around and between a succession of plazas. Prettiest is **Fischmarktplatz**, not least because it's open to the lake, lined with terrace cafés and has a shaded promenade alongside a little marina. A lane or two back is a Capuchin monastery dating from 1597, with, beside the main gate, a delightful walled **rose-garden** – one of a handful around town that support Rapperswil's moniker "City of Roses". Alleys climb to the dour thirteenth-century **castle**, with its small museum (April–Oct daily 1–5pm; Fr.4; ⓦwww.muzeum-polskie.org) devoted to Switzerland's Polish community. Signposted south, a short walk from the station, is the **Knies Kinderzoo** (Children's Zoo; March–Oct daily 9am–6pm; Fr.10; ⓦwww.knieskinderzoo.ch), with animals to pet and feed and elephants and ponies to ride.

The **train station** stands on the edge of the Old Town; head left and cross the road to reach Fischmarktplatz, where, behind Parkhaus 1 See, is the **tourist office** (daily 10am–5pm; Nov–March 1–5pm; ☏0848 811 500, ⓦwww.zuerichsee.ch). The most characterful **hotel** is the attractive *Hirschen*,

Fischmarktplatz 7 (☎055 220 61 80, ⓦwww.hirschen-rapperswil.ch; ❸–❹), not far from the characterful, easygoing *Jakob*, Hauptplatz 11 (☎055 220 00 50, ⓦwww.jakob-hotel.ch; ❸). A little way inland near Jona is an HI **hostel**, *Jugendherberge Busskirch*, Hessenhofweg 10 (☎055 210 99 27, ⓦwww .youthhostel.ch), with dorm beds for Fr.32.

Best **restaurant** is *Schloss Rapperswil* (☎055 210 18 28, ⓦwww.schloss -restaurant.ch), with a fine location within the castle and outstanding fish and seafood that has won it a Michelin star; expect Fr.60 for the set lunch, Fr.140 in the evening. *Marsala/San Marco*, Marktgasse 21 (☎055 211 22 24, ⓦwww .san-marco-rappi.ch), is a good, mid-priced Italian with a modern ambience, or you could opt for the convivial restaurant within the *Jakob* hotel on the main square.

Travel details

Full timetables for all trains, buses, trams, boats and cable cars in Switzerland – as well as international connections – are searchable at ⓦ www.rail .ch. Details of the boat service on the Zürichsee are at ⓦ www.zsg.ch.

Trains

Zürich HB to: airport (4–7 hourly; 10min); Baden (every 30min; 15min); Basel (every 15min; 55min); Bern (3 hourly; 1hr); Biel/Bienne (twice hourly; 1hr 10min); Chur (twice hourly; 1hr 15min); Einsiedeln (every 30min; 45min – change at Wädenswil); Flughafen/Airport (4–7 hourly; 10min); Fribourg (every 30min; 1hr 25min); Geneva (every 30min; 2hr 45min); Interlaken Ost (twice hourly; 2hr 5min); Lausanne (twice hourly; 2hr 10min); Lugano (hourly; 2hr 55min); Luzern (twice hourly; 45min); Neuchâtel (3 hourly; 1hr 35min); St Gallen (every 30min; 1hr 5min); Sargans (twice hourly; 55min); Schaffhausen (twice hourly; 40min); Solothurn (twice hourly; 55min); Uetliberg (every 30min; 20min); Winterthur (4 hourly; 20min); Zug (twice hourly; 25min); Zürich airport (4–7 hourly; 10min).

Boats

Zürich (Bürkliplatz) to: Rapperswil (hourly; 1hr 45min).

10

Ostschweiz and Liechtenstein

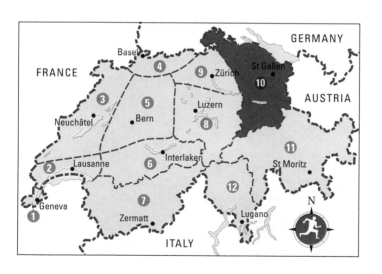

GERMANY

Basel

FRANCE

❹ ❾ Zürich St Gallen

❸ ❺ 10 AUSTRIA

Neuchâtel Bern Luzern

❽

❻ Interlaken ⓫

❷ Lausanne St Moritz

⓬

❼ Lugano

❶ Geneva

Zermatt N

ITALY

10

OSTSCHWEIZ AND LIECHTENSTEIN

CHAPTER 10

Highlights

* **Winterthur** Easygoing city with an array of world-class art museums. See p.448

* **Schaffhausen** Beautiful but little-visited market town, crammed with superb medieval architecture. See p.452

* **Rhine falls** The Wagnerian spectacle of Europe's largest waterfall. See p.456

* **Stein-am-Rhein** Switzerland's most picturesque village square, ringed by frescoed facades. See p.457

* **Abbey library, St Gallen** A splendid Rococo interior, lined with books from floor to ceiling. See p.466

* **Appenzell** Quiet, rustic village set amidst the craggy Alpstein range. See p.469

* **Braunwald** Remote car-free mountain hideaway. See p.472

* **Klausen Pass** Spectacular pass road, one of the country's most scenic drives. See p.472

△ Stein-am-Rhein

Ostschweiz and Liechtenstein

Switzerland's rural northeast – known as **Ostschweiz** – is one of the least celebrated areas of the country, and is often sidelined by tourists anxious to get to the famous Alpine regions further south. Which, of course, means that you can enjoy the mountains and lakes, medieval town centres and verdant countryside in relative peace, free from hard-sell tourism and the glitz and glamour of big-name resorts. Most visitors haven't even heard of the main city of the northeast, **St Gallen**, and yet its magnificent Baroque cathedral and well-preserved medieval town centre make it a major cultural landmark. Just to the west, **Winterthur** has a set of excellent museums to complement its urban neighbour, Zürich.

Immediately south of St Gallen lies the hilly backcountry of **Appenzell**, sheltering a close-knit, still largely isolated community of farmers and craftspeople occupying the foothills of the Alpstein range. The Säntis peak tops 2500m – mediocre in Swiss terms, but still tall enough to enjoy plenty of snow, vistas stretching to the horizon and quality hiking in the web of valleys beneath it. Further south, walled in by Alpine giants, is isolated **Glarnerland**.

Exploring Ostschweiz

Local Swiss, German and Austrian tourist boards market the region strongly, focusing on the main draw for tourists from their own countries: the Bodensee. There are several different passes that give discounts to attractions all round the lake. Best is the **Bodensee Erlebniskarte** (April–Oct only; ⓦ www.bodenseeferien.de), which comes in different varieties, most comprehensive of which is the *Seebärenkarte* (3/7/14 days €69/89/119, less for children). This gives free transport on all boats on the lake and the Rhine; free admission to Insel Mainau, the St Gallen abbey library, museums in Appenzell and Stein-am-Rhein, and dozens more attractions; free travel up the Säntis and other mountains; and so on. It's available from tourist offices. Alternatives worth investigating, with complex zone networks and tariffs, are the four-country **EuRegio Tageskarte** (ⓦ www.euregiokarte.com) and the Switzerland-only **Ostwind Tageskarte** (ⓦ www.ostwind.ch). For information on the whole region (which excludes Winterthur), contact **Ostschweiz Tourismus** (☎ 071 227 37 37, ⓦ www.ostschweiz.ch).

THE NORTHEAST & LIECHTENSTEIN

GERMANY

Innsbruck

Bregenz

Langenargen

Lindau

St Margrethen

Heiden

Altstätten

Rorschach

Friedrichshafen

Trogen

Gäbris
1247m

APP. A.R.

Horn

Arbon

APP. I. R.

Immenstaad

Bodensee

Romanshorn

Hagnau

Meersburg

Kesswil

St Gallen

Überlingen

Mainau

Konstanz

Münsterlingen

Gossau

Stein

Überlingersee

Kreuzlingen

Herisau

Radolfzell

Reichenau

Untersee

Steckborn

Weinfelden

Wil

Singen

Stein
am Rhein

Warth

Thur

THURGAU
ST GALLEN

Kartause
Ittingen

Frauenfeld

Rhein

Herblingen

Büsingen

Dachsen

Andelfingen

Winterthur

Schaffhausen

Neuhausen

Rhine
Falls

Stühlingen

Hallau

Rhine

Zürich

Wettingen

Dietikon

N

Stuttgart

Stuttgart

Basel

Baden

▲ Innsbruck   ▲ Davos

10 km

AUSTRIA

Feldkirch

Rhine

LIECHTENSTEIN

Schaan
Vaduz
Triesen

Landquart

Chur

Fehrenbühl 1506m
Hoher Kasten 1795m
Schellenberg

Rhine

Buchs

Fulfirst 2384m

Sargans

Bad Ragaz

Ebenalp 1640m
Seealpsee
Kreuzberge 2065m
Meglis
Santis 1663m
Silberplatten 2158m
Kronberg 1530m
Stockberg 1781m
Säntis 2501m
Lütispitz 1987m

Gamser Rugg 2076m
Gamsberg 2385m
Hinterrugg 2306m
Brisi 2279m
Gross Güslen 1833m

Alt St Johann

ALPS

Alvier 2343m

Walenstadt

Flums

Hochfinster 2421m

Hangsackgrat 2634m

Ringelspitz 3247m

Surenstock 3056m

ST GALLEN
GRAUBÜNDEN

Flims

Laax

Ilanz

APP A.R.
ST GALLEN
1521m
1590m

Umäsch

TOGGENBURG

Golmen 1789m
Speer 1950m

Walensee

Firstock 1923m

Näfels

Nüenchamm 1904m

Glarus

Elm

Kärpf 2794m
Hausstock 3158m

Regelstein 1315m
1374m
Tanzboden 1443m

Rautispitz 2283m
Bächistock 2914m

GLÄRNISCH

Braunwald

Linthal

GLARUS
GRAUBÜNDEN

Bifertenstock 3421m

Planggenstock 1675m

Rapperswil

Tödi 3614m

URNERBODEN

Einsiedeln

Schwyz

Klausenpass

SCHWYZ
URI

Altdorf

▼ Thusis

▼ Disentis/Mustér

▼ Gotthard

Zug

ZÜRICH
ZUG

Küssnacht
Weggis

Luzern

Stans

Engelberg

447

The River Rhine, which bulges out into the huge **Bodensee** (**Lake Constance**) in Switzerland's northeast corner, throws a protective loop around this part of Switzerland, forming international frontiers with Germany to the north, and Austria and the tiny independent statelet of **Liechtenstein** to the east. At the westernmost tip of the lake, the cosmopolitan German city of **Konstanz** is divided from its Swiss twin of **Kreuzlingen** only by an arbitrary frontier between buildings. The beautiful river journey west from Kreuzlingen runs past **Stein-am-Rhein**, an almost perfectly preserved medieval village boasting spectacular sixteenth- and seventeenth-century frescoes and one of the country's best small historical museums, and ends at the atmospheric medieval town of **Schaffhausen**, dubbed "Rheinfallstadt" for its proximity to the mighty **Rhine falls**, the largest waterfall in Europe.

Winterthur

A peaceful city of almost 100,000, set in rolling countryside on the River Töss 25km northeast of Zürich, **WINTERTHUR** boasts a volley of impressive art museums, displaying Old Masters, classic Modernists, Impressionists and contemporary photography. It lies in Canton Zürich, slightly west of what is usually termed Ostschweiz.

Evidence of a nearby settlement, Vitudurum, goes back to the first century, but the city dates its history from 1264, when it was granted status by the Habsburg king Rudolf. The Industrial Revolution powered meteoric growth during the nineteenth century, and after 1848 Winterthur also became the centre of Switzerland's democratic movement. Local architects and engineers visited England in mid-century to study designs for factories and workers' housing, bringing English ideas back to Winterthur's booming textile and railway industries. Most Swiss today still indelibly associate Winterthur – the country's sixth-largest city – with industry: it has pulled off the transition into hi-tech, and remains a dynamic place. It's also surprisingly green, and the combination of bicycles, green hills and world-class art galleries can make for a pleasant day or two.

Arrival, information and accommodation

Winterthur lies on the main road and rail lines between Zürich and St Gallen, at a junction of routes north to Schaffhausen and Stein-am-Rhein. The **station** is centrally located, and hosts the helpful **tourist office** (Mon–Fri 8.30am–6.30pm, Sat 8.30am–4pm; ☎052 267 67 00, ⓦwww.winterthurtourism .ch). Weekly food **markets** are held in Steinberggasse (Tues & Fri 6–11am).

Travel between Winterthur and Zürich

Winterthur is viable as an alternative base for exploring Zürich – cheaper, smaller and quieter than its neighbour. Travel between the two cities is straightforward: **trains** run roughly every ten minutes all day. The S-Bahn route **S12**, with half-hourly service, takes just 16min to reach **Zürich Stadelhofen** station (centrally located near Bellevueplatz) and another 3min into **Zürich HB**. Other S-Bahn trains, on **S8**, also half-hourly, go a slightly longer way round into Zürich HB (27min). In addition, several intercity trains each hour run from Winterthur direct to **Zürich Airport** (15min) and on to Zürich HB (25min). The **last train** back from Zürich (HB or Stadelhofen) to Winterthur departs around 12.20am.

Map labels:

▲ *Schaffhausen & Frauenfeld*

N

Sammlung
Oskar Reinhart
Am Römerholz

WINTERTHUR

ACCOMMODATION
Albani	**D**
Grüntal	**F**
Hessengüetli	**A**
Krone	**C**
Loge	**E**
Wartmann	**B**

EATING & DRINKING
Gleis 11	**2**
Gotthard	**4**
Kraftfeld	**8**
Obergass	**5**
Paddy O'Brien's	**3**
Titbits	**1**
Typisch Thai	**6**
Walliser Kanne	**9**
Widder	**7**

Kunstmuseum

Museum Oskar
Reinhart Am
Stadtgarten

Station

Kunsthalle

Stadtkirche

Fotomuseum

Villa
Flora

0   250 m

10

OSTSCHWEIZ AND LIECHTENSTEIN | Winterthur

▶ *St Gallen*

Accommodation is geared largely towards business people, though prices are still lower than Zürich. You should always book ahead.

Hotels

Albani Steinberggasse 16 ☎052 212 69 96, Ⓦwww.albani.ch. Budget hotel above the famous Old Town club and music venue just south of Kirchplatz. The OK rooms are big and well kept, but aren't ensuite and there's no breakfast. Free entry for gigs downstairs. Don't bother phoning before 3pm. ❷

Grüntal Im Grüntal 1 ☎052 232 25 52, Ⓦwww .restaurant-gruental.ch. Solid country inn at a quiet crossroads 4.5km southeast of town, with hospitality, good service, basic, pleasant rooms and free parking. Bus #6 to Grüntal. Phone ahead, as it's closed for walk-in arrivals Tues & Wed. ❷

Hessengüetli Oberfeldstrasse 10 ☎052 224 32 32, Ⓦwww.hessengueetli.ch. A small, family-run hotel attached to an high-end Asian restaurant 1.5km northwest of the centre, with a stream on one side and the wooded Brüelberg rising behind. Their ensuite rooms are excellent value, and parking is free. Bus #2 to Feldtal. ❷

Krone Marktgasse 49 ☎052 208 18 18, Ⓦwww .kronewinterthur.ch. Historic renovated building in the Old Town, with stylish and comfortable three-star rooms. Significant weekend discounts. ❸–❹

Loge Graben 6 ☎052 268 12 00, Ⓦwww .hotelloge.ch. Modern and very quiet three-star Old Town hotel – excellent value. Go for the light,

449

top-floor rooms with panoramic balcony. On-site parking. ④ **Wartmann** Rudolfstrasse 15 ☎052 260 07 07, ⓦ www.wartmann.ch. Quality business hotel in a renovated building dating from 1894, just behind the train station. Two standards of rooms; prices on both drop at weekends. ③–④

The Town

Winterthur's main draw is its excellent **museums**, principally the two separate Oskar Reinhart art collections – one housed in the town centre ("Am Stadtgarten"), the other on a hill near the town ("Am Römerholz") – and the Kunstmuseum. The Fotomuseum and Villa Flora are close runners-up. A Museumspass (see box) grants free admission. Note that all Winterthur's museums are **closed on Mondays**.

The pedestrianized Old Town has some charm once you get off the main shopping streets – the elegant medieval Stadtkirche, for example, with its kitschy modern murals, is worth a look. If Victorian industrial architecture lights your fire, head southwest under the tracks into the **Sulzer-Areal** district, where hulking brick-built factories are slowly being reclaimed as atmospheric theatre spaces, bars and skating arenas.

The Oskar Reinhart museums

Oskar Reinhart was born into a local trading family in 1885. Aged 41, he withdrew from business and moved into the hilltop villa "Am Römerholz" to devote himself to his passion for art. When he died in 1965, part of his collection – one of the leading private art collections assembled in Europe in the twentieth century – passed to the municipality (and is now housed in the Stadtgarten museum), and the remaining 200 paintings and his villa at Römerholz were bequeathed to the nation.

The **Sammlung Oskar Reinhart "Am Römerholz"**, Haldenstrasse 95 (Tues–Sun 10am–5pm, Wed until 8pm; Fr.10, joint ticket with "Am Stadtgarten" Fr.12; SMP; ⓦ www.roemerholz.ch), is an idiosyncratic mingling of styles and periods, brought together more for each piece's artistic qualities than as an attempt to form a representative overview of any one artist or genre. There are works from fifteenth- and sixteenth-century German masters, including Matthias Grünewald, Lukas Cranach the Elder and Hans Holbein the Younger; a small group of Italian and Spanish works, including by El Greco and Goya; and fifteenth- to seventeenth-century Dutch and Flemish painting dominated by Brueghel, Rubens, Hals and Rembrandt. Works by French Baroque, Neoclassical and Romantic artists – including some of Delacroix's best portraits – lead on to Reinhart's marvellous Impressionist collection, covering Renoir, Manet, Degas and many more. The museum has a lovely sunny café.

> ## Winterthur's festivals
>
> The most popular event is the **Albanifäscht** (ⓦ www.albanifest.ch), a weekend of live rock music in late June. The August **Kyburgiade** (ⓦ www.kyburgiade.ch) is an international chamber music festival in the romantic setting of Kyburg castle, outside town. The **Musikfestwochen** (ⓦ www.musikfestwochen.ch), in late August, see Winterthur's Old Town taken over for live music of all kinds. If you're around in May, ask at the tourist office about the **Eschenberg-Schwinget**, a folksy festival of traditional wrestling held in a nearby meadow, and/or **Jodlersonntag** (Yodelling Sunday). Whitsun is celebrated in Winterthur as **Afro-Pfingsten** (ⓦ www.afro-pfingsten.ch), a mini-carnival of African music, dance and food.

To get to and from the Römerholz collection, some distance from town on a hilltop, the city runs a **Museumsbus**. Minibuses depart from the station (Tues–Sun hourly 9.45am–4.45pm), picking up at the town-centre Stadtgarten and nearby Kunstmuseum a few minutes later, and dropping off at the gates of the Römerholz gallery. Departures from there back to town are on the hour 10am to 5pm. On Sundays the bus makes extra stops at the Villa Flora and the Fotomuseum. The Fr.5 **fare** is valid all day, but is waived if you hold a **Museumspass**, buyable from the tourist office or any museum, which gives free entry to all the city's museums for one/two/three days (Fr.16/25/28). Otherwise, reaching the Römerholz collection involves city bus #3 to Spital and a stiff ten-minute walk up the hill.

Back in town, the **Museum Oskar Reinhart "Am Stadtgarten"**, Stadthausstrasse 6 (Tues 10am–8pm, Wed–Sun 10am–5pm; Fr.8; SMP; Ⓦ www .museumoskarreinhart.ch), is of less general interest, concentrating on German, Swiss and Austrian artists from the eighteenth to the twentieth centuries. On the ground floor are a few rooms of portraits by local artists including Graff and Füssli. On the floor above are Romantic Swiss landscapes, and up another floor are fine studies of children by the Swiss artist Albert Anker, and works by Hodler, Segantini and Giovanni Giacometti. The top-floor extension features changing exhibitions.

Other museums

Just across the Stadtgarten lies the **Kunstmuseum**, Museumstrasse 52 (Tues 10am–8pm, Wed–Sun 10am–5pm; Fr.10; SMP; Ⓦ www.kmw.ch), with a splendid collection covering international art over the last century. The tour begins upstairs, with a room devoted to Van Gogh, Monet, Rousseau and sculpture by Picasso and Rodin. Hodler and a Cubist room lead on to a Surrealist selection topped by Miró and a rare self-portrait by De Chirico. Works by Brancusi lead into the high-ceilinged, white-walled extension, dominated by Mondrian, American artists and sculpture by Alberto Giacometti. The **Kunsthalle**, nearby at Marktgasse 25 (Wed–Fri noon–6pm, Sat & Sun noon–4pm; free; Ⓦ www .kunsthallewinterthur.ch), stages changing shows of contemporary art.

The critic Paul Graham has called Winterthur's **Fotomuseum**, Grüzenstrasse 44 (Tues–Sun 11am–6pm, Wed until 8pm; Fr.9; SMP; Ⓦ www.fotomuseum.ch), "the most beautiful museum of photography in Europe", and it's easy to see why. Housed in a brick-built renovated former warehouse, it's light, bright and open, and benefits further from its policy of staging five or six top-notch annual exhibitions each year. It lies a walkable 400m southeast from the Old Town, off Tösstalstrasse (or bus #2 to Schleife).

Nearby is the **Villa Flora**, Tösstalstrasse 44 (Tues–Sat 2–5pm, Sun 11am–3pm; Fr.10; Ⓦ www.villaflora.ch), which houses the private collection of Hedy Hahnloser, built up between 1907 and 1930. It comprises a small but high-quality selection – on continuous rotation – of French Post-Impressionism, Fauvist and Nabi works (Bonnard, Matisse, Vallotton and more) fleshed out with earlier works by Cézanne, Van Gogh and others.

Eating, drinking and nightlife

You'll have no trouble finding places in the Old Town to **eat and drink**. **Nightlife** can be surprisingly good, with the excellent *Albani* bar and venue, plus some lively music bars on Neumarkt.

Restaurants and cafés

Gleis 11 At *Hotel Wartmann*, Rudolfstrasse 15. Chic and elegant upmarket hotel restaurant, with warm, contemporary decor and a pleasant atmosphere. Great value mid-priced lunch buffets of salads and hot mains. Open daily.

Obergass Schulgasse 1, corner Obergasse. Quiet easy-going café to eat, read and drink in, with a wide range of food, veggie and not, for Fr.14–25. Closed Sun.

Tibits Oberer Graben 48. Local branch of the excellent Swiss chain of chic, stylish eateries – loads of buffet salads, sandwiches, soup and light bites, plus fresh-squeezed juices, gourmet coffees and more. Open daily from breakfast time to around midnight.

Typisch Thai Neumarkt 3. Full range of Thai dishes, with friendly service and plenty for veggies. Fr.12–15 for lunch, double in the evenings. Closed Mon.

Walliser Kanne Steinberggasse 25. Quality Swiss specialities, served in classic style, with subdued decor and a calm atmosphere. Around Fr.35. Closed Sat lunch, Sun & Mon eve.

Widder Metzggasse 9. Subculture Old Town café-bar, with long wooden tables and loud music. Good cheap food, well prepared and in massive portions for under Fr.15. Fri & Sat until 2am.

Bars and clubs

Albani Steinberggasse 16. Smallish Old Town bar and venue well able to draw Zürchers out into the sticks with a quality programme of DJs and live music – previous headliners have included Pearl Jam and Sheryl Crow. Weekend nights are packed. Fr.15 or so for bands.

Gotthard 1900 Untertor 34, opposite station Ⓦ www.gotthard1900.ch. Switzerland's first-ever 24-hour bar, a young, friendly joint that's a peaceful café during the day; at night it attracts a few lowlifes but avoids the sleaze of its Bahnhofplatz neighbours.

Kraftfeld Lagerplatz 18, off Tössfeldstrasse in Sulzer-Areal industrial quarter, 100m beyond Brockenhalle junk shop Ⓦ www.kraftfeld.ch. Alternative artists' community which lays on excellent DJ nights featuring experimental drum'n'bass, plus bands, films and happenings. Wandering around the nearby streets will turn up similar post-industrial venues: the *Plan B Bar* (Ⓦ www.planb-bar.ch), the excellent Aussie-styled *Outback Lodge* bar/BBQ-diner (Ⓦ www.outback-lodge.ch), and others.

Paddy O'Brien's Merkurstrasse 25 Ⓦ www .paddyobriens.ch. Quality Irish pub five minutes north of the station to warm your jaded cockles, with 12 beers on tap, TV football and enough of a reputation to pull in The Dubliners for a gig now and again. Daily 3pm–2am.

Schaffhausen and around

Capital of the northernmost Swiss canton of the same name, **SCHAFF-HAUSEN** can boast one of the most captivating medieval town centres in the whole of Switzerland as well as, just 4km downriver, the mighty **Rhine falls** – and yet it remains uncelebrated, as if too far north to be of concern to most visitors. (For the record, trains from Zürich take 38 minutes.) Adding to the allure is the splendid medieval village of **Stein-am-Rhein**, within easy reach upriver.

A bankside docking point had already developed into the thriving market town of Scafusun by 1045 (the name of the town probably derives from its many riverside boathouses). It grew rapidly, handling salt and grain from Bavaria and the Tyrol and joining the Swiss Confederation in 1501. The town maintained steady growth, its eighteenth-century merchants indulging in the fashion for adding ornate **oriel windows** to the Gothic or Renaissance buildings, both to demonstrate their wealth and good taste, and also to give people inside a clear view up and down the street. With 170-odd examples on show, Schaffhausen's nickname *Erkerstadt* ("City of Oriel Windows") is well-earned.

Hydroelectric works, built to exploit the flow of the Rhine, brought the area into the industrial age. During **World War II**, Schaffhausen was the only Swiss town to be bombed by Allied aircraft: about 100 civilians were killed by American bombers on April 1, 1944. The US claimed that pilots had mistakenly identified Schaffhausen – the only sizeable chunk of Swiss territory on the north bank of the Rhine – as a German target. They apologized profusely and paid out compensation… only to make the same mistake again on February 22, 1945, this time killing sixteen in Schaffhausen and nine in Stein-am-Rhein. Records that could throw light onto the allegation that the bombings were in fact a deliberate Allied response to Schaffhausen's munitions industries supplying arms to the Nazis in breach of Swiss neutrality are, as yet, still classified. In recent years, Schaffhausen has capitalized on its position to act as a commercial and cultural bridge between Germany and Switzerland, and has absorbed a high number of Sri Lankan immigrants and asylum seekers, leading to an unusually broad ethnic mix on the streets.

Arrival, information and accommodation

Schaffhausen's **train station** is at the northwestern edge of the compact Old Town, served by both Swiss SBB and German DB trains. One block east is bustling Fronwagplatz. Just south at Herrenacker 15 is the **tourist office** (June–Sept Mon–Fri 9.30am–6pm, Sat 9.30am–4pm; July & Aug also Sun 9.30am–3.30pm; Oct–May Mon–Fri 9.30am–5pm, Sat 9.30am–1.30pm; ☎052 632 40 20, ⓦwww.schaffhausen-tourismus.ch), with an excellent guided **walking tour** of the Old Town (April–Sept Tues, Thurs & Sat 2pm; Fr.12), which includes a tasting of five wines in a vintner's at the end.

The best way to arrive is **by boat** from further up the Rhine. At least three boats a day (May–Sept; see p.460) make the beautiful journey along the river from Kreuzlingen via Stein-am-Rhein, a peaceful ride between wooded banks

ACCOMMODATION
Fischerzunft   D
Jugendherberge Belair B
Jugendherberge Dachsen F
Kronenhof   C
Löwen   A
Park Villa   E

SCHAFFHAUSEN

EATING & DRINKING
Bambus   2
Falken   4
Fass-Beiz   1
Kammgarn   9
Manora   5
Theaterrest   7
Zum Frieden   8
Zum Schäfli   6
Zum Weissen Rössli 3

on just about the only stretch of the Rhine that is free of heavy industry. They dock at Freier Platz, at the southeastern corner of the Old Town.

Hotels

Fischerzunft Rheinquai 8 ☎ 052 632 05 05, Ⓦ www.fischerzunft.ch. Schaffhausen's most characterful choice, an excellent modern Relais & Châteaux hotel on the riverfront. Its ten rooms have been done up in a rather flouncy style, with Asian touches; it's definitely worth splashing out on one of the more restrained, tasteful suites. ❺–❻

Kronenhof Kirchhofplatz 7 ☎ 052 635 75 75, Ⓦ www.kronenhof.ch. Slick, modern business-class rooms in a central location, also with some good, spacious suites. ❸–❹

Löwen Im Hösli 2, Herblingen ☎ 052 643 22 08. Comfortable old guesthouse in a suburb 3km north (bus #5), with modern, renovated rooms. ❷

🏃 **Park Villa** Parkstrasse 18 ☎ 052 635 60 60, Ⓦ www.parkvilla.ch. Atmospheric old mansion on the edge of Schaffhausen's Old Town, with 25 individually decorated rooms, complete with chandeliers and Persian carpets. Splash out on the Royal Suite for the rooftop balcony and fine, wood-panelled bedchamber with four-poster bed, or dine in the wonderful Louis XVI salon. ❸–❹

Hostels

Jugendherberge Belair (HI hostel) Randen-strasse 65 ☎ 052 625 88 00, Ⓦ www.youthhostel .ch. Award-winning hostel, housed in a sixteenth-century manor house 1km northwest of the station that featured in Hermann Hesse's 1914 novel *Rosshalde*. Dorm beds from Fr.25.50. March–Oct. ❶

Jugendherberge Dachsen (HI hostel) Schloss Laufen ☎ 052 659 61 52, Ⓦ www.youthhostel .ch. Older hostel in an annexe of Schloss Laufen, a castle overlooking the Rhine falls 4km west of town (with its own train station). Dorm beds Fr.26. Mid-March to mid-Oct. ❶

The Town

Schaffhausen's beautiful riverside Old Town is crammed full of well-preserved architecture, lending the cobbled streets considerable charm. A good place to begin is the central **Fronwagplatz**, the town's marketplace during the Middle Ages. Dominating the long square is the **Fronwagturm**, within which hung the market's massive scales; the clock and astronomical device on the top dates from 1564. Beside it is the distinguished, late-Baroque **Herrenstube**

△ Zum Steinbock

town house, although the facade of the **Zum Steinbock** house, 100m west at Oberstadt 16, is even more impressive, covered in stucco Rococo curlicues.

Strolling north on Fronwagplatz, past the square's two medieval fountains – the **Metzgerbrunnen** (1524), topped by a statue of a Swiss mercenary, and the **Mohrenbrunnen** (1535), with a Moorish king – you'll come to the **Zum Ochsen** house at Vorstadt 17, one of the most grandiose in the city. The late-Gothic facade of this former inn was remodelled in 1608 and decorated with striking Renaissance frescoes of classical heroes. The oriel window is especially graceful: it shows, in five panels, a woman embodying each of the senses: holding a mirror (sight), a glove (touch), a flower (smell), a stringed instrument (hearing) and a cake (taste).

North of the Zum Ochsen, a short detour past the frescoes of the **Zum Grossen Käfig** house at Vorstadt 43, which shows the triumphal parade of the medieval Mongol king Tamerlane, brings you to the northern gate of the city, the **Schwabentor**. The tower dates from 1370, but on the outer face is a small panel added during renovations in 1933, which shows a boy with a pig under his arm dodging the traffic. The dialect inscription *Lappi tue d'Augen uf* translates as "Knuckleheads should keep their eyes open" – a reference to the danger of newfangled motorized traffic.

Vordergasse and the Munot

Karstgässchen leads from opposite the Zum Ochsen house into **Platz**, its fountain sporting another grim-faced mercenary. From here, alleys bring you south onto the main **Vordergasse**, a shopping street sloping downhill to the east. On the corner of Münstergasse is Schaffhausen's most celebrated house, the **Zum Ritter**, its facade covered in an intricate design dating from 1570 that is acclaimed as the most significant Renaissance fresco to survive north of the Alps (the original is now preserved in the town museum; this is a 1930s copy). The fresco depicts, over three storeys, various elements of knightly virtues (*Ritter* means "knight"): the central panel shows Odysseus in the Land of the Lotus-Eaters, tempted by a voluptuous woman, while above is a Roman knight who sacrificed himself for the glory of his country. Below is a trusting girl, symbolizing virtue, protected by a king (the government) and a woman holding a mitre (the church). From the Zum Ritter, alleys head southwest to another of Schaffhausen's broad, open squares, **Herrenacker**, surrounded by tall, dignified facades and, on the west side, the massive **Kornhaus** (1679).

From the Zum Ritter house, Vordergasse continues east to the Gothic, five-naved **Kirche St Johann** (Mon–Sat 9am–6pm; Oct–March 10am–5pm), expanded six times since it was begun in the eleventh century. In a niche on the south side of the tower is a small statue of the Madonna and Child without feet: they were removed during the Reformation when a wall was built to hide the image. A few steps east, in front of a fountain statue of William Tell, is the magnificent double-fronted Rococo mansion **Zur Wasserquelle und Zieglerburg**.

Some 50m north is a footbridge over the main Bachstrasse road, which brings you onto steps climbing the hill to the **Munot**. This is Schaffhausen's trademark circular fortress, built by forced labour in 1564 after the religious wars of the Reformation. The interior (daily 8am–8pm; Oct–April 9am–5pm; ⓦwww .munot.ch) is gloomy, with massive stone vaulting strong enough to support the 40,000-tonne superstructure. An internal spiral ramp leads up to the circular roof of the bastion, with good views over the town. A different door exits onto stairs running through the vines planted on the Munot hill, down to the small riverside quarter known as **Unterstadt**; Schaffhausen's annual Old Town shindig, held on a weekend in late June, still passes on alternate years between the salt-of-the-earth folk of the Unterstadt and their toffee-nosed neighbours of the town centre further west.

Münster zu Allerheiligen

Schaffhausen's lofty **Münster zu Allerheiligen** (All Saints' Minster; Tues–Sun 10am–noon & 2–5pm; Ⓦ www.muenster-schaffhausen.ch) is the focus of the Old Town. The first church on the site dated from 1049, replaced in 1103 by the building which still stands today. The beautifully restored Romanesque tower gives a hint of the interior, in which twelve huge columns of Rorschach sandstone line the austere nave. Beside the cathedral, the Romanesque-Gothic **cloister** is the largest in Switzerland, a lovely broad walkway circling the Junkernfriedhof (noblemen's cemetery). In the cathedral courtyard sits the huge **Schiller Bell**, cast in 1486; the German poet Friedrich Schiller never set foot in Schaffhausen, but was inspired to compose his *Song of the Clock* by Goethe's record of this bell's Latin inscription: *vivos voco, mortuos plango, fulgura frango* ("I call on the living, lament the dead, shatter the lightning"). Just beyond is an atmospheric little herb garden.

In the same complex is Schaffhausen's main historical museum, the **Museum zu Allerheiligen** (Tues–Sun 11am–5pm; Fr.9; Ⓦ www.allerheiligen.ch). The ground floor is mostly given over to a vast archeological collection but, as with the rambling historical collections spread over this and the upper floors, there's little coherence. The place is like a labyrinth, and you could either wander, enjoying the surprise of coming across a roomful of early medieval religious art or a restored Gothic chapel, or instead cut your losses and head for the topmost floor, which holds an engaging collection of art by Swiss painters and sculptors of the last five centuries.

Hallen für Neue Kunst

Baumgartenstrasse marks the southern boundary of the cathedral quarter. In a giant old textile factory at no. 23 is the outstanding **Hallen für Neue Kunst** (Contemporary Art Spaces; Tues–Sat 3–5pm, Sun 11am–5pm; Fr.14; SMP; Ⓦ www.modern-art.ch). This impressive gallery focuses on American and European art from the 1960s to the 1990s, spread over several vast floors. Particularly striking in such airy surroundings are the geometrical games in two and three dimensions of Robert Mangold, and Sol LeWitt's dazzling cube installations. Check the website for details of the regular guided tours in English.

The Rhine falls

Schaffhausen's best excursion is the short trip westwards to the **Rhine falls** (Ⓦ www.rhinefalls.com), Europe's largest waterfalls. They are truly magnificent, not so much for their height (a mere 23m) as for their impressive breadth (150m) and the sheer drama of the place, with the spray rising in a cloud of rainbows above the forested banks. The turreted castle **Schloss Laufen** on a cliff directly above the falls to the south completes the spectacle. August 1 – the Swiss National Day – sees a mighty fireworks display staged on the riverside.

The 4km riverside **walk** from Schaffhausen to the suburban town of **NEUHAUSEN**, where the falls are located, takes about 45 minutes; or you could take city **bus** #1 or #6 to Neuhausen Zentrum, from where the well-signposted falls are five minutes' walk away. Schloss Laufen has a **train** station (April–Oct only), served by hourly trains between Schaffhausen and Winterthur, but Neuhausen's own station is awkwardly far away.

Once you're within sight of the falls, you're inevitably brought down to earth by the hordes of tourists crowding both banks in search of the best camera angle, and by the circus of souvenir stalls and dismal restaurants all around. The worst of it is on the north (right) bank; crossing by the arched footbridge over to the south (left) bank – which can still get crowded – at least means you can experience the power of the falls at close quarters. Damp **steps** (Fr.1) lead down from the souvenir shop at Schloss Laufen (ⓦwww.schlosslaufen.ch) past the **Bellvedere** and **Fischetz** lookout points to the **Känzeli** platform at the very edge, from where the roaring waters tumble inches from your nose.

Another great view can be had from one of the daredevil **boats** which scurry around in the spray; their top excursion, termed a *Felsenfahrt*, docks at the craggy rock in the centre of the cataract. Both Rhyfall Mändli (ⓣ052 672 48 11, ⓦwww.maendli.ch) and Schiff Mändli (ⓣ052 659 69 00, ⓦwww .schiffmaendli.ch) run trips continuously all day (May–Sept) for as little as Fr.5. Boats depart from easy-to-spot jetties on both banks.

Eating and drinking

Schaffhausen has a good range of places to **eat**, from the self-service *Manora* diner just off Fronwagplatz upwards. Cafés and **bars** line all the Old Town squares. *Fass-Beiz* (see below) is a quiet little nook to savour a beer or three, while there's a lively café-bar (closed Mon & Tues) attached to the *Kammgarn* arts centre, Baumgartenstrasse 19 (ⓦwww.kammgarn.ch).

Bambus Vorstadt 9 ⓣ052 624 09 05, ⓦwww .bambus.sh. Informal Thai restaurant above a WWF shop, offering good food (including veggie menus) for around Fr.15. Closed Mon eve & Tues.

Falken Vorstadt 5. Quality Swiss food in this congenial Old-Town restaurant for around Fr.20. Open daily from breakfast until around midnight.

Fass-Beiz Webergasse 13 ⓦwww.fassbeiz.ch. Cosy cooperative-run café-bar which offers the best budget dining in town: plenty of wholesome, home-cooked veggie dishes for under Fr.15. Closed Sun eve.

Fischerzunft Rheinquai 8 ⓣ052 632 05 05, ⓦwww.fischerzunft.ch. Outstanding restaurant, best in town by miles and rated in the top half-dozen in the country. The setting is superb, a Rhineside dining room decorated creatively with luxurious fabrics and fresh flowers – or you can opt to eat on the open terrace. The cuisine is sensational, a unique blend of French and East Asian elements. Menus range from Fr.100 up to the memorable five-course Menu Yin/Yang, at Fr.265 (including a different wine with each dish). Closed Tues (Jan–March also Mon).

Theaterrestaurant Herrenacker 23 ⓣ052 625 05 58, ⓦwww.theaterrestaurant. ch. Highly acclaimed establishment offering an informal bistro at ground level (open from 9am) and an excellent, GaultMillau-recognized restaurant above. The bistro serves salads and light meals for moderate prices in cool, pleasant surroundings, while the restaurant has classic dishes such as fillet of perch, veal or steak (expect around Fr.60–80 a head) in an attractive, modern, pastel-toned dining room. The wines – many from in and around Schaffhausen – are outstanding. June–Sept closed Sun & Mon.

Zum Frieden Herrenacker 11 ⓣ052 625 47 15, ⓦwww.wirtschaft-frieden.ch. An atmospheric tavern-style place with a good-value *Stübli* at ground-floor level and a pricier formal restaurant upstairs serving Frenchified mains for around Fr.40. Closed Sun lunch & Tues.

Zum Schäfli Unterstadt 21. Typical of the cheerful, inexpensive places on Unterstadt that are generally full of hearty locals; *menus* of standard Swiss fare cost from Fr.15.

Stein-am-Rhein

Positioned on the Rhine 20km east of Schaffhausen, little **STEIN-AM-RHEIN** is an almost perfectly preserved medieval village, famed for the intricacy of the sixteenth-century **frescoes** which adorn houses in the village. It's well worth a visit, but sees so many tour buses during the frantic summer season – about a million people pass through annually – that to enjoy the place you should stay overnight: it's only after 5pm and before 10am that there's much peace.

From the Schifflände quay, if you head east and then cut north on tiny Schwarzhorngasse, you'll come in a minute's stroll to the **Rathausplatz**, often acclaimed as the most picturesque square in Switzerland, ringed by medieval half-timbered buildings vying with each other for the lavishness of their **frescoes** and the gracefulness of their oriels. Standing alone at the head of the square is the Rathaus, built in 1539–42: the half-timbered top storeys are original, the middle floor dates from a 1745 renovation, and the ground floor facade and entranceway were added in 1865. The line of facades along the south side of the square is dazzling, each one sporting a fresco illustrating the house name: these are, from left to right, the *Hirschen* (stag), *Krone* (crown), *Vordere Krone* (foremost crown, which sports an especially lofty gable), *Roter Ochsen* (red ox, the town's oldest tavern, with a Gothic facade), *Steinerner Trauben* (stony grapes), *Sonne* (sun, the oldest hotel in the village but with twentieth-century frescoes), and the *Schwarzer Horn* (black horn). Opposite are the *Adler* (eagle) and, most impressive of all, the *Weisser Adler* (white eagle), bedecked in the town's oldest frescoes, a Holbein-esque series painted in 1520–25.

The rest of the village pales in comparison, but there are plenty of picturesque narrow lanes and alleys to explore, ignored by most visitors. A manor house at Understadt 18, dating from 1279 and renovated in 1819, has been converted into the **Museum Lindwurm** (March–Oct Mon & Wed–Sun 10am–5pm; Fr.5; SMP; ⊕www.museum-lindwurm.ch), with surprisingly interesting displays on Stein-am-Rhein's bourgeois and agricultural life in the nineteenth century. The desk keeps extensive English notes. A great deal of work has been done to re-create the living conditions of the wealthy upper-class family who owned the house: walking through the cobbled stables, the Empire-style drawing room and the spartan servants' quarters under the eaves, feels like stepping back in time.

Practicalities

At least six **boats** a day in summer arrive at Stein-am-Rhein, three from Kreuzlingen upriver and three from Schaffhausen downriver. The **train station** is on the southern bank of the Rhine, a couple of minutes' walk from the bridge. The tiny **tourist office** is at Oberstadt 9 (Mon–Fri 9.30am–noon & 1.30–5pm; July & Aug also Sat 9.30am–noon; Jan–March closed Fri; ☎052 742 20 90, ⊕www.steinamrhein.ch).

Hotels

Adler Rathausplatz ☎052 742 61 61, ⊕www .adlersteinamrhein.ch. Directly on Rathausplatz, with a brilliantly decorated facade sheltering pine-decor rooms which are surprisingly plain and ordinary, though comfortable enough. ❸

Chlosterhof Oehningerstrasse 2 ☎052 742 42 42, ⊕www.chlosterhof.ch. An unattractively modern building just to the east of the village centre that is quite a surprise for this corner of Switzerland – inside, rooms are spacious, tastefully decorated in contemporary style and many have balconies over the Rhine, some with four-poster beds. ❺–❻

Rheinfels Rhigass 8 ☎052 741 21 44, ⊕www .rheinfels.ch. Fine old Rhineside inn, dating from the sixteenth century, with atmospheric public areas and sixteen comfortable, modernized rooms, all with a river view. Closed Jan & Feb. ❸–❹

Rheingerbe Schifflände 5 ☎052 741 29 91, ⊕www.rheingerbe.ch. Old wood-beamed inn with some rooms overlooking the Rhine. ❷–❸

Hostel

Jugendherberge (HI hostel) Hemishoferstrasse 87 ☎052 741 12 55, ⊕www.youthhostel.ch. Good hostel about fifteen minutes' walk due east from Rathausplatz, via Understadt. Dorms from Fr.26. March–Oct. ❶

Eating and drinking

The village is crammed with **eating** places. There's an inexpensive crêperie at Understadt 10, while the historic *Rheinfels* inn (see opposite) has an atmospheric all-wood dining room (closed Wed) specializing in excellent fish; *menus* are around Fr.35. The gorgeous interior of the *Rother Ochsen* on Rathausplatz (☎052 741 23 28, ⓦwww.rotherochsen.ch; closed Mon) suits its outstanding Swiss food, made from only local ingredients. Top choice is the *Sonne*, also on Rathausplatz (☎052 741 21 28, ⓦwww.sonne-steinamrhein.ch; closed Tues & Wed), with the ground-floor *Weinstube* serving excellent daily *menus* (around Fr.25) prepared in the same kitchen as the gourmet cuisine costing Fr.60 or more in the restaurant upstairs.

Kartause Ittingen

A fine detour with picnic possibilities is to the **KARTAUSE ITTINGEN** (ⓦwww.kartause.ch), a former Charterhouse (Carthusian monastery) set amidst hop fields and open farmland 6km south of Stein-am-Rhein over a hilly ridge.

From 1461 until 1868, the old buildings, arrayed around a large, peaceful courtyard, were home to a community of between twelve and fifteen monks; today, the **Ittinger Museum** (Mon–Fri 2–6pm, Sat & Sun 11am–6pm; Oct–March closes 5pm; Fr.7) sheds light on the life of the order. The monks lived a life of extreme austerity, taking all meals except Sunday lunch alone in their cell and remaining committed by oath to silence. The Rococo **church** has a long nave, divided into four and flanked by intricate choir stalls carved around 1700, and a dramatic high altarpiece depicting St Bruno, founder of the order. There's no organ, since the Carthusian Mass is sung without accompaniment. Beside the church is the **Little Cloister**, prelude to a series of decorated and partly furnished rooms once used by the monks, including the Refectory (room 4), with seventeenth-century portraits ringing the walls. The fifteen monks' cells lie off the **Great Cloister**. Upstairs rooms include a tiny **prison** with barred window, and an unusual upper-level gallery in the church. Some rooms are given over to the **Kunstmuseum des Kantons Thurgau** (ⓦwww.kunstmuseum .ch), showing twentieth-century Swiss art.

The on-site **restaurant**, *Zur Mühle*, has quality, affordable modern cuisine (*menus* Fr.20–25), but the farmland all around is prime picnic territory; pick up some home-made goodies from the little **shop**, which sells vegetables, fresh-baked bread, fragrant *eaux-de-vie* and bottles of 🍺 lip-smacking Klosterbräu beer, brewed from hand-picked hops. Part of the Kartause has been renovated as a modern conference-style **hotel** (☎052 748 44 11; ❹) – all exposed brick and bright, functional comforts. The *Herberge* section adjacent has simpler shared-bath rooms (❷). The Kartause hosts an internationally renowned **festival of chamber music** every Whitsun.

From Stein-am-Rhein take a bus to **Warth**, fifteen minutes' walk (or a two-minute bus ride) from the Kartause. From Winterthur or Zürich take a train to **Frauenfeld**, from where several buses a day run direct to the Kartause; alternatively you could rent bikes from Frauenfeld station for the ride 4km north to the monastery – the station tourist office (Mon–Fri 9am–noon & 2–6pm, Sat 9am–noon; ☎052 721 31 28, ⓦwww.frauenfeld.ch) has maps and information.

The Bodensee (Lake Constance)

Forming a natural border between Switzerland and Germany, the long **Bodensee** – often anglicized to **Lake Constance** – is a huge bulge in the course of the Rhine, some 67km from end to end. Unlike most of the Swiss lakes, it doesn't have the benefit of shoreline mountains, and so is exposed to winds year-round and has particularly rough weather in the winter. If there is heavy rain further south in the Alps combined with unusually rapid snowmelt, the Bodensee's lakeside towns are the first to feel the effects: spring and summer floods have been an increasingly common event in recent years.

Three countries border the Bodensee. The head of the lake, at its southeastern corner, is **Austrian**, focused around the genteel town of **Bregenz**. The largest settlement on the northern, **German** shore is the cosmopolitan city of **Konstanz**, separated from its contiguous Swiss suburb of **Kreuzlingen** only by an arbitrary international frontier. Haze and lingering fog can often mask the views across the water, but this hasn't stopped the lakeshore becoming one of Germany's main summer–holiday destinations; this rubs off on the southern, **Swiss** shore, too, where the scattering of soporific little resorts such as **Rorschach** and **Arbon** have a strong Teutonic air about them.

Kreuzlingen and around

At the northwestern corner of the Bodensee, the small Swiss town of **KREUZLINGEN** is an anomaly, nothing more than a southern suburb of the cosmopolitan German city of **Konstanz**; the international frontier separating them runs arbitrarily between buildings. Kreuzlingen is like border towns everywhere, full of traffic streaming through without stopping and imbued with a feeling that the exciting stuff is happening elsewhere, just out of sight. It has little history of its own, but is worth stopping in, both as a base from which to spend a day or two exploring Konstanz, and for its own **Kirche St Ulrich**, 150m south of the centre on Hauptstrasse. This Baroque church houses the remarkable Ölbergkapelle, containing a 1780 wood carving of the Passion

---

Boats on the Bodensee

All three countries' **boat operators** have formed a joint body, the VSU (ⓦwww .vsu-online.info). The Swiss partners are the **SBS** (☎071 466 77 88, ⓦwww.sbsag .ch), operating between Rorschach and Kreuzlingen; **Untersee & Rhein** (☎052 634 08 88, ⓦwww.urh.ch), operating between Kreuzlingen, Stein-am-Rhein and Schaffhausen; and the **Schifffahrtsbetrieb Rorschach** (☎071 846 60 60, ⓦwww .schifffahrt-rorschach.ch), operating short trips from Rorschach to Rheineck. The German shore is served by Bodensee-Schiffsbetriebe (ⓦwww.bsb-online.com), while Austrian Railways also runs a fleet (ⓦwww.bodenseeschifffahrt.at).

There are dozens of **excursion cruises** all round the lake during the summer season (April–Oct), most of them round-trips and many with refreshments on board. In the peak season (June to mid-Sept), it's possible to spend **a day on the lake**, leaving Rorschach at 10.50am for the two-hour cruise to Kreuzlingen, where you have time for lunch before departing at 3pm on the leisurely journey down the Rhine to Schaffhausen, arriving at 6.45pm. The other way, going upstream, takes from 9.10am to 6.35pm. In addition to the numerous passenger services, year-round **car ferries** run between Romanshorn and Friedrichshafen, and between Konstanz and Meersburg. You'll need to show your **passport** on international ferries. **Swiss Pass** holders travel free. See p.445 for details of regional passes.

comprising around 300 individual figures; the sculpture is teeming with intricate detail, and is surmounted by a fifteenth-century cross (*Kreuz* in German) which has survived three major fires. The church itself is no less dazzling, with a stunningly ornate choir screen in green and gilt.

Kreuzlingen's main station, the **Hauptbahnhof**, is 150m south of the international border; head east (left) out of the station to reach the traffic lights on Hauptstrasse. The **tourist office** is 50m away, just behind Hauptstrasse at Sonnenstrasse 4 (Mon–Fri 9–11.30am & 2–4pm; ☎071 672 38 40, ⓦwww .kreuzlingen-tourismus.ch). From these traffic lights, Hafenstrasse continues east to the lakeshore, where you'll find the harbour and the **Hafenbahnhof** train station. Nearby is the old Villa Hörnliberg, housing an HI **hostel**, Promenadenstrasse 7 (☎071 688 26 63, ⓦwww.youthhostel.ch; ❶; March–Nov); dorms are Fr.29. South along the lakeshore is the *Fischerhaus* **campsite** (☎071 688 49 03; April–Oct). Opposite the Hauptbahnhof, friendly *Bahnhof-Post* **hotel**, Nationalstrasse 2 (☎071 672 79 72, ⓦwww.hotel-bahnhof-post.ch; ❷–❸), has pleasant ensuite rooms. *Zapfenzieher*, Hauptstrasse 44 (ⓦwww.zapfen.ch), is an amiable **café-bar** with terrace (closed Sun eve), while *Seegarten*, Promenadenstrasse 40 (☎071 688 28 77, ⓦwww.seegarten.ch; closed Mon, Sept–April also closed Tues) is a high-class **restaurant** at the marina, with sophisticated cuisine for Fr.50 and up.

Konstanz and Insel Mainau

The main point of coming to Kreuzlingen is to visit **KONSTANZ** just over the German frontier. This ancient city straddling the Rhine has been an important ecclesiastical hub for centuries: the Council of Konstanz (1414–18), which tried and failed to heal divisions within the Church, met in the huge **Münster**, originally a Romanesque basilica, set amidst a web of characterful alleys now lively with students from the city's university. The **tourist office** beside the station (April–Oct Mon–Fri 9am–6.30pm, Sat 9am–4pm, Sun 10am–1pm; rest of year Mon–Fri 9.30am–12.30pm & 2–6pm; ☎0049 1805 133030, ⓦwww .konstanz.de) has an English booklet detailing a self-guided walking tour. **Trains** take three minutes from Kreuzlingen's main station, but it's really no hardship to walk the fifteen minutes or so; either way, you'll need to show your **passport**.

Just 8km north in Germany – accessible by direct ferry from Swiss and German ports – is **INSEL MAINAU** (daily 7am–8pm; Oct–April 9am–6pm; €11.90; ⓦwww.mainau.de), a forested island occupied by a Baroque castle and beautiful gardens.

Münsterlingen

About 2km east of Kreuzlingen lies the village of **MÜNSTERLINGEN**, worth stopping in to visit its sixteenth-century Baroque church, originally part of a Benedictine convent. The interior is beautifully decorated, with a lavish altarpiece flanked by twisted gilt and turquoise columns, and a cupola overhead painted with a *trompe l'oeil* fresco: the abbess of the convent in the 1680s was related to master sculptor Christof Daniel Schenck from Konstanz, and brought him in to do some of the decoration and to sculpt the wood figures still on display in the church. An altar curtain dating from 1565, used during Lent to hide the glory of the altar, hangs to one side.

The church's most interesting tale begins in the sixteenth century when, it is said, the lake froze solid six or seven times. One winter, in the early years of the Reformation, a church official from **Hagnau**, on the German bank opposite, walked across the frozen lake to Münsterlingen, where the church was being

Friedrichshafen airport (☏0049 7541 28401, ⓦwww.fly-away.de) is a few kilometres inland from the town. Taxis (€11) and hourly trains shuttle from the airport through the city (Stadt) to the harbourside (Hafen) train station (€1.60; takes 12min; last train to harbour 7.45pm, to city 11.20pm; ⓦwww.bob-fn.de). From Friedrichshafen harbour, ferries run hourly to **Romanshorn** (40min; last ferry 8.40pm, July & Aug Fri & Sat 10.40pm; ⓦwww.sbsag.ch), where trains depart regularly from the main station near the dock to destinations all over Switzerland, including St Gallen (last 11.30pm), Zürich (last 10.30pm), Bern, Luzern, Interlaken and Brig. From Friedrichshafen-Stadt, German railways has fast trains direct to Basel (last 7pm).

stripped of its decoration. He saved a statuette of John the Baptist and took it back to Hagnau for safekeeping. When the lake froze again some years later, he remembered his journey and brought the statuette back. Ever since then, a freezing of the lake has precipitated a solemn procession across the ice to carry the statuette to the opposite shore. In 1830, Münsterlingen's clergy and villagers delivered the figurine to Hagnau, where it remained until the harsh winter of 1963, when the ice was solid enough to return it to Münsterlingen church. There it still sits, in the crypt (a copy is on display), awaiting the next icy spell.

Romanshorn and around

Along the shore is **ROMANSHORN**, a run-of-the-mill lakeside resort, arrival point for boats from **Friedrichshafen** on the German bank opposite. About 7km east is the ancient village of **ARBON**, reputedly the point at which Columba and Gallus (see p.464) stepped ashore. Walk left from the station for about ten minutes to reach the tranquil centre, marked by the spire of the **Kirche St Martin**, with, in its grounds, the tiny eleventh-century Galluskapelle. Adjacent is the sixteenth-century **Schloss Arbon**, housing a pleasant little restaurant (ⓦwww.zumschloss.ch; closed Sun). The old streets nearby hold a number of half-timbered buildings, most seventeenth- or eighteenth-century; on Kapellgasse is a chapel built in 1390, but deconsecrated in 1777 and now daubed with graffiti.

Rorschach

A couple of hours' walk southeast of Arbon, the pleasant lakeside resort of **RORSCHACH** occupies a bay below the grassy Rorschacherberg, 9km from St Gallen. It has three train stations. The main Rorschach-HB (Hauptbahnhof) is awkwardly located 1km east of the harbour and town centre. Coming from St Gallen, trains stop first at **Rorschach-Stadt**, a short walk above the harbour. Trains from Romanshorn, though, stop first at **Rorschach-Hafen** (harbour), directly on the lakefront alongside the old **Kornhaus**, emblem of a once-thriving grain trade between St Gallen and Germany. From the Hafenbahnhof, **Hauptstrasse** heads east, flanked by fine sixteenth- to eighteenth-century houses with attractive oriel windows. The **Kolumbanskirche** just off the street is a broad, white, late-Baroque church dedicated to the Irish monk Columba, with much gilded glitter inside. A rack railway (ⓦwww.ar-bergbahnen.ch) winds up from the Hafenbahnhof to the hill resort of **Heiden**, which offers views and hiking trails. As well as regular Bodensee ferries, the local boat operator

(ⓦ www.schifffahrt-rorschach.ch) runs short pleasure trips to Rheineck, on the Austrian border just east of town.

Rorschach's **tourist office** is opposite the Hafenbahnhof, Hauptstrasse 63 (April–Oct Mon 2–5.30pm, Tues–Fri 9.30–11.45am & 2–5.30pm; June–Sept also Sat 9.30am–noon; Nov–March Mon–Fri 2–5pm; ☎071 841 70 34, ⓦ www .tourist-rorschach.ch). There's a pleasant HI **hostel** on the lake, Churerstrasse 4 (☎071 844 97 12, ⓦ www.youthhostel.ch; ❶; April–Oct; dorm beds Fr.35). The lakefront **hotel** 🍴 *Mozart*, 150m west of the Hafenbahnhof (☎071 844 47 47, ⓦ www.mozart-rorschach.ch; ❸), has comfortable, renovated rooms and an excellent **restaurant** for midpriced daily menus and convivial Sunday brunches.

As a footnote to the town, the famous **Rorschach Ink-Blot Test**, in which a subject under therapy is asked to describe the images they see in the random shape of a blot, was named after its deviser, Swiss psychologist Hermann Rorschach. He was born in Arbon in 1884 but, as far as records show, never set foot in Rorschach itself.

St Gallen

The main urban centre of eastern Switzerland, **ST GALLEN** is a relaxed and conservative provincial city set amidst rolling countryside between the Appenzell hills and the Bodensee. It's a gentle place, with a busy modern centre and a beautiful Old Town. The centrepiece is an extraordinarily lavish Baroque abbey, declared a UNESCO World Heritage Site: its cathedral is impressive

ST GALLEN

Station

ACCOMMODATION
Dom   C
Einstein   E
Elite   B
Jugendherberge   F
Vadian   D
Weisses Kreuz   A
RESTAURANTS
Am Gallusplatz   6
Da Franco   5
Hörnli   4
New White Swan   1
Seeger   2
Zum Goldenen Schäfli   3

Textilmuseum

Waaghaus

St-Laurenzenkirche

Cathedral   Klosterhof

Abbey Library

0   100 m

enough alone, but the **abbey library** is celebrated as Switzerland's finest secular Rococo interior and contains a world-class collection of ancient books and manuscripts.

Some history

St Gallen owes its existence to the religious community which remains at its core. In around 612, the Irish monk **Gallus** – a follower of Columba – was travelling south from the Bodensee into the forest. Legend has it that he either fell over, or stumbled into a briar patch, or told a bear to fetch some firewood whereupon it obeyed; whichever, Gallus felt he had received a sign from God, and so chose that spot to build his hermitage. In the eighth century, a follower named **Otmar** established a monastic community around Gallus's cell, and founded a school of scribes and translators. In the 830s, Abbot Gozbert established the great **library**, and St Gallen's reputation as a centre of culture and learning grew. By the thirteenth century, St Gallen had become an important market town and its reputation as a centre of learning was being superseded by its reputation as a producer and exporter of high-quality **linen**. By the end of the Middle Ages, it was the only Swiss town to have trade representatives resident in foreign cities, and was linked by stagecoach to centres of textile processing in Nuremberg and Lyon.

In 1529, Joachim von Watt – known as **Vadian** – introduced the Reformation, sparking iconoclastic riots which forced the monks temporarily to flee; the abbey survived, however, as an independent Catholic walled enclave within the Protestant city.

In the eighteenth century, St Gallen's weavers switched to the new fashion for **hand-embroidery**: by 1790, some 40,000 women were working from home to embroider cotton and muslin for export – notably to the young United States. The invention of embroidery machines brought a golden age, although production remained centred in the home. By 1913, embroidery was Switzerland's largest export industry, with St Gallen accounting for around half of the entire world production of textiles. These days, that figure is down to just 0.5 percent, but Swiss embroidery remains a highly valued, luxury commodity, with small, highly specialized companies supplying designs and finished products to *haute couture* fashion houses: Lacoste's famous crocodile logo, for instance, is Swiss-embroidered. Nonetheless, St Gallen's embroidery industry – now almost entirely computerized – still relies on two thousand local women working from home, hand-sewing detailing that is impossible to achieve by machine.

Arrival, information and accommodation

St Gallen's **train station** is 200m southwest of the Old Town, with the **tourist office** across the square at Bahnhofplatz 1a (Mon–Fri 9am–6pm, Sat 10am–1pm; May–Oct Sat until 3pm; ☎071 227 37 37, ⊛www.st.gallen-bodensee .ch). Staff can supply information on the whole Ostschweiz region, and run an excellent two-hour guided **walking tour** (May–Oct Mon–Sat 2pm; July & Aug also Sun 2pm; Fr.15, includes admission fees and a drink). The **OpenAir** pop festival (⊛www.openairsg.ch), on the last weekend in June, pulls in a varied range of international performers from Van Morrison to Metallica. **Accommodation** includes a clutch of business hotels at the station, and a few more characterful choices.

Hotels

Dom Webergasse 22 ℡071 227 71 71, ⑭www
.hoteldom.ch. Pleasant little hotel on an Old Town
lane, with decent enough rooms, both ensuite and
shared-bath, that are uniquely decorated with
original works of *art brut*, or naïve art. Parking on
site. ❷–❸

Einstein Berneggstrasse 2 ℡071 227 55 55,
⑭www.einstein.ch. The city's top choice, a grand
old hotel housed in a former textile factory, with
generously appointed rooms and quality service. ❻

Elite Metzgergasse 9 ℡071 222 12 36, ⑭www
.hotel-elite.ch. Plain and serviceable rooms near
Marktplatz, both ensuite and not. ❷–❸

Vadian Gallusstrasse 36 ℡071 228 18 78,
⑭www.vch.ch. House-proud little "garni" hotel on
a quiet street near the cathedral, with pleasantly
renovated rooms, some ensuite. ❷–❸

Weisses Kreuz Engelgasse 9 ℡071/223 28 43.
Entirely renovated family-run hotel, unprepossessing from the outside, cool and modern within. ❷

Hostel

Jugendherberge (HI hostel) Jüchstrasse 25
℡071 245 47 77, ⑭www.youthhostel.ch. Take the
Trogenerbahn narrow-gauge train from outside the
main station to the Schülerhaus stop, and walk up
the hill. Dorms are Fr.28.50. March to mid-Dec. ❶

The City

St Gallen's Old Town is roughly circular, crossed by the main pedestrian streets
of **Vadianstrasse/Multergasse** leading east from the station, and **Marktgasse**
running south from Marktplatz, a hub for buses and shoppers. The attractive
streets and alleys are adorned with 111 elaborate **oriels**, or small projecting bay
windows, most of which are younger than the houses to which they're attached:
a fashion for them in the eighteenth century meant that many were carved from
wood, painted, and then stuck onto the stone facade to satisfy the whim of the
nouveau-riche merchant who lived within. Some of the finest can be found at
Schmiedgasse 15 (House of the Pelican) and 21 (House of Strength); Kugelgasse
8 (House of the Ball) and 10 (House of the Swan); Hinterlauben 10 (House of
the Deep Cellar); and Spisergasse 22 (the Camel Oriel). Along **Gallusstrasse**
you'll also find half-timbered cottages from the Middle Ages rubbing shoulders
with Baroque town houses and grand nineteenth-century dwellings put up
during St Gallen's golden age of textile production.

The **Textilmuseum**, Vadianstrasse 2 (Mon–Sat 10am–noon & 2–5pm, Sun
10am–5pm; Fr.5; SMP; ⑭www.textilmuseum.ch), has an interesting and well-
presented collection, focusing on handmade embroidery and lace, along with
explanations of the growth and decline in the industry locally. The tall, steepled
St-Laurenzenkirche on Marktgasse (Mon 9.30–11.30am & 2–4pm, Tues–Sat

Schoggi Land chocolate factory

A short way west of St Gallen is the **Maestrani chocolate factory** – dubbed in Swiss
German (in which gg is pronounced as ck) "**Schoggi Land**", Toggenburgerstrasse
41, Flawil (Mon–Fri 9am–noon & 2–6pm, Sat 9am–noon; ℡071 228 38 64, ⑭www
.schoggi-land.ch). You can wander through displays on the history of Maestrani
(which is one of the oldest Swiss chocolate firms, founded in 1852), and are allowed
onto a gallery above the factory floor to watch the production lines running (they do
not operate on Friday afternoons or Saturdays); video screens give additional information. There's also a shop. During the summer months, you can opt to join a **guided
tour** (April–Oct Wed 3pm; Fr.3), where you watch a movie on chocolate-making and
then are guided around the site. Book ahead for their chocolate-tasting courses and
other events. To **get there**, take a train to **FLAWIL** from St Gallen (14min) or Zürich
(59min), then switch to a bus (direction Lütisburg, Ganterschwil or Bütschwil) for the
five-minute ride to the factory's own "Flawil Maestrani" bus stop. By car, take the
Uzwil exit off the A1 (Zürich–St Gallen); the factory lies between Flawil and Wattwil.

9.30am–4pm) dates from the ninth century, and originally stood within the monastic enclosure of the cathedral and abbey. Renovated in Neo-Gothic style in the mid-nineteenth century, and restored in the 1970s according to the 1845 plans, it has a narrow, lofty nave flanked by Gothic pointed side arches.

The cathedral

St Gallen's giant Baroque **cathedral** (Mon–Sat 9am–6pm, Sun 12.15–5.30pm) is unmissable, its twin towers visible from most points. Designed by one Peter Thumb from Bregenz, it was completed in 1767 after just twelve years' work. Easiest access is through the west door on Gallusstrasse, although it's worth making your way through the church and out into the enclosed Klosterhof, at the heart of the complex, where you can gaze up at the soaring **east facade**. To the left is the palace wing, still the residence of the Bishop of St Gallen.

The **interior** is vast, a broad, brightly lit white basilica with three naves and a central cupola. Although not especially high, it has a sense of huge depth and breadth thanks to its accomplished architecture: from the sandstone of the floor and wood of the pews, fanciful light-green stuccowork – characteristic of churches in the Konstanz region – draws your eye up the massive double-width pillars to the array of frescoes on the ceiling, which are almost entirely the work of one artist, Josef Wannenmacher. Above the western end of the nave is a panel showing Mary surrounded by angels. The central cupola shows paradise, with the Holy Trinity, apostles and saints. Details throughout the rest of the cathedral are splendid: the lavish, mock-tasselled pulpit; the ornate choir screen; the richly carved walnut-wood confessionals; the intricate choir stalls; and, far away at the back of the choir, the high altar flanked by black marble columns with gold trim. The south altar features a bell brought by Gallus on his seventh-century journey from Ireland, one of the three oldest surviving bells in Europe.

The abbey library (Stiftsbibliothek)

Within the same complex of buildings as the cathedral, and just adjacent to it, is the **abbey library** (Stiftsbibliothek; Mon–Sat 10am–5pm, Sun 10am–4pm; Dec–March closed noon–1.30pm; closed for 2 weeks in late Nov; Fr.7; SMP; Ⓦwww.stibi.ch), one of the oldest libraries in Europe, and famous both for

its superb Baroque interior and for its huge collection of rare and unique medieval books and manuscripts. You enter beneath a sign reading ΨΥΧΗΣ ΙΑΤΡΕΙΟΝ (*psyches iatreion*, Greek for "Pharmacy of the Soul"). Ranged beside are dozens of oversized felt slippers; slip your shoed feet into a pair, to save the inlaid wooden floor of the library from scuffing.

The 28-by-10-metre room is acclaimed as Switzerland's finest example of a Baroque secular interior, and the first glimpse of it as you enter is dizzying. Designed by the same Peter Thumb who worked on the cathedral, the library dates from slightly later: its orthodox Baroque architecture is overlaid with the opulent decoration of the Rococo period which then held sway. The four **ceiling frescoes** by Josef Wannenmacher depict with bold *trompe l'oeil* perspectives the early Christian theological councils of Nicaea,

△ The abbey library, St Gallen

Constantinople, Ephesus and Chalcedon. Amongst the wealth of smaller frescoes set amongst the ceiling stucco, in the far southeast corner you'll spot **The Venerable Bede**, a seventh-century English monk from Northumbria who wrote one of the first histories of England: he is shown as a scholar, with, beside him, a magic number square. This four-by-four sequence, where the numbers add up to 34 horizontally, vertically, diagonally and from the four corners, is thought to have been invented by Pythagoras in ancient Greece, but took on a new mystical power for early Christians who understood Christ to have died at 34 years of age.

The **books** are ranged on floor-to-ceiling shelves all around, originally organized by subject (indicated by the cherubs at the head of capitals around the library), but now arranged alphabetically. Inside the recessed panels between each bookcase are registers of books in the nearby shelves, with space to leave your name: the library still operates as an ordinary lending library and study centre, with some 140,000 volumes focused on the Middle Ages. Its list of cultural treasures is extraordinary. There are more **Irish manuscripts** in St Gallen than there are in Dublin, fifteen handwritten examples including a Latin manuscript of the Gospels dating from 750. Other works include an astronomical textbook written in 300 BC; copies made in the fifth century of works by Virgil, Horace and other classical authors; texts written by Bede in his original Northumbrian language; and the oldest book to have survived in German, dating from the eighth century. Various of these and other treasures of the library's upstairs manuscript room (no public access) are displayed in glass cases dotted around the main library area. An ancient Egyptian **mummy** in the library dates from 700 BC and was a gift to the mayor of St Gallen in the early nineteenth century; unsure of what to do with the thing, he plonked it in this corner, where it has sat incongruously ever since.

Eating, drinking and nightlife

St Gallen has a good range of **eating and drinking** places. Look out for stalls selling St Gallen's famous pale Olma sausage, eaten ketchup- and mustard-free in a *Bürli*, or bread roll. A feature of St Gallen dining is the handful of traditional tavern-restaurants on the upper floor of old town houses.

Am Gallusplatz Gallusstrasse 24 ☎071 223 33 30, ⓦwww.gallusplatz.ch. The city's best restaurant, serving high-quality French cuisine amidst suitably stout decor. Your best option is to come for lunch, when *menus* are lighter in tone and cost less (around Fr.25). In the evening, expect Fr.50-plus. Closed Sat lunch & Mon.

Da Franco Webergasse 23. A decent Italian, with loads of pastas and pizzas, plus a choice of 25 different risottos. Eat well for Fr.18.

Hörnli Marktplatz 5 ☎071 222 66 86, ⓦwww .hoernli.ch. Easygoing restaurant specializing in market-fresh salads and delicious *rösti*, with some *menus* around Fr.15. Its fondues – served all winter long – are delicious local varieties, with Williams (pear schnapps) or Kirsch (cherry schnapps). Also several beers on tap.

New White Swan Metzgergasse 24. Fast-paced little diner serving up huge portions of steaming

Asian-style stomach fillers to students and others on tight budgets.

Seeger Oberer Graben 2 ⓦwww.seeger -restaurants.ch. Elegant big-windowed café with inexpensive food, playing classical music during the day to a twenty-something crowd relaxing on the leather sofas inside, or at tables on the pavement terrace.

Zum Goldenen Schäfli Metzgergasse 5 ☎071 223 37 37. Best known of St Gallen's upper-floor restaurants, with low ceilings, wood panelling all around and creaking floors. The food is all hearty local fare, with plenty of offal on the menu – the house speciality is calf's liver – and other local dishes such as sautéed lake fish. *Menus* start from a very reasonable Fr.15 or so. Closed Sun in summer.

Students attending the University of St Gallen, on a hillside campus north of town, feed the **nightlife**, although locals have no compunction about jumping on a train to Zürich for a wider choice. There's live **jazz** nightly at *Gambrinus* (⊛www.gambrinus.ch), at the Kastanienhof, Kreuzbleicheweg 2; *Seeger*, a café-cum-**DJ bar** at Oberer Graben 2, hosts pumping weekend dance parties; *Birreria*, Favrestrasse 7 (⊛www.birreria.ch), has dozens of beers on tap and a hard-rock sound system; and *Stadtkeller* on Spisermarkt is a popular **club**.

Appenzellerland

The residents of **Appenzellerland** are the butt of many a Swiss joke, regarded by cosmopolitan urbanites as country bumpkins and mercilessly mocked for their folksy ways. Yet although a sophisticated Lausannois or Basler might chortle to hear it, this rustic region is something of a sensuous delight: as you cross the verdant hills south from St Gallen, the pungent smells of cows and cheese assault your nose; on a wander through the villages, busy embroidery and the fussily net-curtained windows of wooden houses delight the eye; and local cooking, particularly rich with butter and cream, has a delicious silkiness on the tongue.

Encircled by rolling hills, with the snowy peaks of the Alpstein ridges to the south, Appenzell has for centuries been a land apart. Monks from St Gallen colonized the area in the tenth century, calling it *Abtszell* ("Abbey Cell"), but the fiercely independent local peasantry threw off ecclesiastical control in a series of wars in the fourteenth century. Although surrounded by St Gallen's territory, Appenzell joined the Swiss Confederation in 1513, long before its more powerful neighbour. Shortly afterwards it split into two tiny autonomous half-cantons – Protestant **Appenzell Ausserrhoden** (abbreviated to "AR"), and Catholic **Appenzell Innerrhoden** ("AI"). For touristic purposes, the two half-cantons are together dubbed "Appenzellerland", but the divisions between them remain to this day, with Ausserrhoden's dynamic economy based on manufacturing industry and Innerrhoden's slower one based on tourism and the preservation of traditional culture.

Appenzell village, capital of Innerrhoden, the least populous Swiss canton, is the main draw for its quaint, traditional air – preserved even amidst the high-season day-trippers. Other than **Stein**'s excellent museum and show-dairy, surrounding villages hold few attractions, but there's plenty of good **hill-walking**,

---

Exploring Appenzell

If you book to stay in the region for three nights or more, you receive, free of charge from your hotel, the **Appenzeller Ferienkarte** or Appenzell Card (⊛www.appenzell.ch), which covers transport on local buses and trains (including to and from St Gallen), as well as the cable cars to Ebenalp, Kronberg and Hoher Kasten, admission to museums, a cheese-tasting session at the Stein show-dairy and other benefits.

If you just want to visit for a day, the local train company Appenzeller Bahnen (⊛www.appenzellerbahnen.ch) has the **AB Tageskarte** (Fr.21), which covers free travel on their network and also cuts the cost of bike rental at Appenzell station to Fr.5/day; buy it from any AB station (including St Gallen).

with routes crossing the velvety slopes towards the rocky peaks of the Alpstein and its highest point, the snowy **Säntis** (2502m).

Appenzell

The main street of **APPENZELL**, 20km south of St Gallen, is car-free Hauptgasse, running from a bridge over the River Sitter at the entrance to the village west for 300m or so to the broad, open **Landsgemeindeplatz**; it's worth wandering along to admire the intricately painted old wooden houses – notably *Löwen Drogerie*, a pharmacy at no. 20 – with their rows of small, closely packed windows. During the nineteenth century, the embroidery industry of nearby St Gallen relied upon thousands of women working by hand from home, with the intricate work of Appenzell particularly highly prized: the upstairs rooms in these buildings, flooded by daylight through the lines of windows, were used as workshops. Hand-embroidery flourished into the first half of the twentieth century, and is still carried on by a few specialists here and there, with workshops often located on characterful back alleys.

In the same building as the tourist office is the **Appenzell Museum**, Hauptgasse 4 (April–Oct daily 10am–noon & 2–5pm; Nov–March Tues–Sun 2–5pm; Fr.7; SMP; ⓦ www.museum.ai.ch). This interesting exhibition of local crafts is spread out over six floors, spilling over onto the upper floors of the arcaded Rathaus next door: highlights include many examples of Appenzell hand-embroidery, as well as militaria from Claux Castle, the ruins of which are visible on a nearby hilltop. Don't miss the short videos shown on demand in a viewing room on the ground floor: the one on local musical traditions is especially good. A few steps away is the church of **St Mauritius**, much more ornate than you would expect for a country village; its Baroque interior, the high altar flanked by gold figures, is oddly asymmetrical.

Museum Liner stands on the edge of the village, Unterrainstrasse 5 (April–Oct Tues–Fri 10am–noon & 2–5pm, Sat & Sun 11am–5pm; Nov–March Tues–Sat 2–5pm, Sun 11am–5pm; Fr.9; SMP; ⓦ www.museumliner.ch). This gallery, devoted to the work of father-and-son local artists Carl August Liner and Carl Walter Liner, is interesting mainly for its boldly conceived design in steel by the Zürich partnership of Annette Gigon and Mike Guyer. Exhibitions of the Liners' uninspiring modernistic art are made more appealing by additional exhibits of Swiss contemporary works.

Practicalities

Appenzeller Bahnen runs two narrow-gauge **train** lines to Appenzell (free to Swiss Pass holders; ⓦ www.appenzellerbahnen.ch), one direct from outside St Gallen station, the other from Herisau. Appenzell's **station** is 200m south of the centre. The friendly **tourist office** is at Hauptgasse 4 (Mon–Fri 9am–noon & 1.30–6pm, Sat & Sun 10am–noon & 2–5pm; Nov–March Mon-Fri 9am–noon & 2–5pm, Sat & Sun 2–5pm; ☎071 788 96 41, ⓦ www.appenzell .ch). On many summer Fridays, *Hotel Säntis* stages an evening of traditional folkloric **music**.

Accommodation

Appenzell's **accommodation** is neat, quiet and characterful, to suit the village. Not many people seem to stay, but it's definitely worth doing so, not least because the village is set on a sloping patch of meadow tipped westwards towards low hills, and on clear summer evenings the tranquil streets are filled with lingering twilight until 10pm.

Adler Adlerplatz/Hauptgasse 1 ☎071 787 13 89, ⓦwww.adlerhotel.ch. Attractive, well-run family hotel overlooking the river, with a range of quality rooms both modern and traditionally styled. ❸

Appenzell Landsgemeindeplatz ☎071 788 15 15, ⓦwww.hotel-appenzell.ch. Characterful, heavily gabled old building on the south side of the square, with chunky wooden beds in spacious and comfortable rooms. ❸–❹

Freudenberg Riedstrasse 57 ☎071 787 12 40, ⓦwww.hotel-freudenberg.ch. It's worth making your way up the hill behind the station to find this place, not so much for the rooms, which are pleasant but unremarkable, but for the views from the balconies over the village and surrounding countryside. Closed Nov. ❷–❸

Säntis Landsgemeindeplatz ☎071 788 11 11, ⓦwww.saentis-appenzell.ch. Top choice in town, on the north side of the main square, and a member of the prestigious Romantik group. Some rooms feature canopied or four-poster beds and there's polished wood everywhere; smaller attic rooms are priced attractively. ❹–❺

Eating and drinking

Of all the local specialities – including *Chäshörnli* (cheese-and-potato mini-dumplings), *Birnebrot* (pear bread), a sweet liqueur named *Alpenbitter*, and a fragrant herb-based Schnapps dubbed *Kräuter* – the most ubiquitous is ripe **Appenzeller cheese**, advertised widely with rustic images of gap-toothed kids and milkmaids. It's powerful stuff: if you buy some, take the shopkeeper's advice and have it vacuum-sealed, otherwise you'll find the pong seeping its way into everything else in your bag.

Many hotels offer quality **eating and drinking**. The best value is *Hotel Appenzell* (closed Tues lunchtime): go through the *confiserie* shop into the non-smoking restaurant behind. *Menus* are from Fr.17, excellently prepared with a light touch; the house speciality is a range of fresh vegetarian and health-conscious food. Elsewhere, traditional fare abounds, relying heavily on pork,

Appenzell traditions

More than most areas of the country, Appenzell has clung on to its many rural **traditions** as modern, living elements of local culture: although you may be tempted to dismiss demonstrations of local crafts or evenings of folkloric music as phoney touristic kitsch, in fact such events are put on as much for the benefit of locals as for visitors. Weddings, dances and celebrations of all kinds count as excuses for locals to don **traditional dress**, with the women in stiff-winged caps and lace-edged dresses, and the men in elaborate embroidered scarlet waistcoats, with tight black trousers and a silver earring dangling from their right ear.

It seems as if everything Appenzell does is just plain different: up until 1988, the Appenzell **school year** began in the spring, instead of in the autumn as everywhere else. The village of **Urnäsch**, 10km west of Appenzell, celebrates New Year's Eve (Silvesterklausen) twice, once on December 31 and again, in order to keep faith with the long-abandoned Julian calendar, on January 13. Even the ornate silver **pipes** smoked by Appenzeller old-timers are idiosyncratic, curving down at the end instead of up, with the tobacco kept in place by a little sliding lid.

In politics, too, Appenzell stands alone. It was only in 1990 that the men of Ausserrhoden finally, and reluctantly, allowed **women** to have the vote in cantonal affairs. Innerrhoden held out for another year, and remains one of the last Swiss cantons to use the **Landsgemeinde**, the ancient embodiment of Swiss direct democracy (Glarus – see p.472 – is the only other), in which citizens gather in traditional dress once a year in the town square of the cantonal capital to vote by brandishing a short sword (the badge of citizenship) in response to a series of shouted yay-or-nay questions. It takes place on the last Sunday in April and is a nationally televised event.

potatoes and creamy sauces. The bustling old-fashioned restaurant in *Gasthaus Hof*, Engelgasse 4 (ⓦ www.gasthaus-hof.ch), concentrates on a host of excellent cheese dishes, including *Käseschnitte* (cheese-on-toast). *Hotel Säntis* has the swankiest dining in town, although the ground-floor *Stübli* and terrace is considerably cheaper and much less formal than the upstairs restaurant with its Gallic-accented menu.

Around Appenzell

Walking in the pretty countryside **around Appenzell** can be rewarding, with inns and guesthouses dotting the landscape – so many that you could walk for days from inn to inn without encountering a town and without having to carry food. The Appenzell tourist office has plenty of maps, trail guides and mountain-bike routes, including details of *Barfuss durchs Appenzellerland*, a trail which you can follow **barefoot** through grassy meadows from Appenzell village up to **Gonten**, a couple of hours west, scene of June's cantonal Schwingen (traditional wrestling) championships.

Most hiking trails are crammed into and around the narrow valleys sandwiched between the three great rock walls of the **Alpstein** range. The small village of **Wasserauen**, a short train ride or a couple of hours' walk south of Appenzell, is the base station for a cable car running up to **EBENALP** (ⓦ www.ebenalp.ch; 1640m), from where a high-level route takes you five hours along the ridge to the Säntis. Another route from Wasserauen runs up for an hour into the narrow valley of the beautiful **SEEALPSEE** (1141m). This isolated tarn is the site of a celebrated annual folkloric festival which culminates in a yodelling of Mass on Assumption Day morning (Aug 15; ⓦ www.hobbysaenger.ch). The attractive *Berggasthaus Forelle* on the lakeshore (ⓣ071 799 11 88, ⓦ www.gasthausforelle .ch; ❶; April–Oct) has comfortable, traditional-style rooms as well as dorms, while around the lake is the simpler *Berggasthaus Seealpsee* (ⓣ071 799 11 40, ⓦ www.seealpsee.ch; ❶; April–Oct). Both have terrace tables at which to enjoy succulently prepared lake fish. Beyond Seealpsee, a two-hour trail hairpins its way steeply up to tranquil **MEGLISALP** (1517m), with its own rustic *Berggasthaus Meglisalp* (ⓣ071 799 11 28, ⓦ www.meglisalp.ch; ❶; May–Oct), focus of a weekend of folkloric dancing in late July.

Appenzell's most famous peak is the **Säntis** (2502m), well below the proportions of the Alps but nonetheless the highest point for miles around. Trains run from Appenzell to the small town of **Urnäsch**, departure point for hourly buses which follow a winding road up to **Schwägalp**, from where a cable car (Fr.36 return; ⓦ www.saentisbahn.ch) rises to the Säntis summit. This is a popular daytrip, especially in summer: if you're staying for lunch, you'd do best to aim for the older, more atmospheric *Berggasthaus* on top (ⓦ www.berggasthaus-saentis .ch), rather than the newer canteen-style diner – both, though, have terraces offering spectacular panoramas. From the summit, it's an easy three-and-a-half-hour hike along to Ebenalp, from where there's transport back to Appenzell.

Stein

Herisau, capital of the half-canton Appenzell Ausserrhoden (AR), and connected to Appenzell village by train, is a workaday town, handy for its bus link to St Gallen via the backcountry village of **STEIN** (often dubbed "Stein AR"; not to be confused with Stein-am-Rhein). Stein hosts the engaging **Appenzeller Volkskunde Museum** (Folklore Museum; Mon 1.30–5pm, Tues–Sat 10am–noon & 1.30–5pm, Sun 10am–5pm; Fr.7; SMP; ⓦ www .appenzeller-museum-stein.ch). The highlight is on the top floor, which is devoted to Appenzell's **folk art**, made by nineteenth-century farmers who decorated furniture, milk pails and other implements with ornate designs, painting scenes from daily life on canvas and wood. Johannes Müller is the most prolific of these uncelebrated artists; he lived all his 91 years in Stein as a clockmaker, and his simple paintings are characterized by vibrantly green hills crisscrossed by long lines of cattle led by herders in traditional dress.

Next door is the **Appenzeller Schaukäserei** (Show Dairy; daily 9am–7pm; Nov–April closes 6pm; free; Ⓦwww.showcheese.ch), where you can watch the various processes of cheesemaking from a gallery above the huge vats and churns – try to time your visit to coincide with the main cheesemaking procedures (which stop at 2pm). Cheese-lovers won't want to miss the Sunday morning all-you-can-eat breakfast buffet (9–11am; Fr.23).

Glarnerland

Switzerland's least-known and hardest-to-reach region is **Glarnerland**, centred on Canton Glarus, a tract of mountain territory featuring just a handful of widely spaced settlements and very low-key tourism. Its isolation is its main attraction: this is a place to turn your back on the crowds and head for the wilderness.

The slender, cliff-girt **Walensee** is pretty much bypassed by both the N3 autobahn and Zürich–Chur trains. **Ziegelbrücke**, at the lake's western tip, marks the start of routes squeezing southwards. The main **tourist office** is on the autobahn, near Ziegelbrücke at the Niederurnen rest-stop (July & Aug daily 8am–6pm; rest of year Mon–Fri 8.15am–noon & 1.30–5.30pm, Sat 8am–5.30pm, Sun 8am–1pm; ☎055 610 21 25, Ⓦwww.glarusnet.ch); their wide range of outdoorsy deals includes two days' all-in hill-trekking on horseback (Fr.130). **GLARUS**, the picturesque little capital, lies 12km south, dwarfed by the looming Glärnisch massif; there's little reason to stay, unless you're here on the first Sunday in May for the **Landsgemeinde**, a traditional form of direct democracy when cantonal affairs are decided by public voting in the main square.

The main road continues south to scenic **Linthal**, base station for a short funicular ride up to the unsung gem of the region – the car-free mountain resort of **BRAUNWALD**; there are few quieter, more refreshing places to rest up, take in the Alpine views and get out into nature. As you emerge from the top station, you'll see map-boards of the village and its surrounds; the **tourist office** (July–Oct & Christmas–Easter Mon–Fri 8am–noon & 1–5pm, Sat 8am–2pm; rest of year Mon–Fri 8am–noon; ☎055 653 65 65, Ⓦwww.braunwald.ch) can advise on routes: there are lifts to higher slopes as well as a host of walks around Braunwald's plateau. **Hotels** all have balconies and sun-terraces; the *Alpenblick* (☎055 643 15 44, Ⓦwww.alpenblick-braunwald.ch; ❸–❹) is conveniently beside the funicular station, and there's a good **hostel**, *Adrenalin* (☎079 347 29 05, Ⓦwww.adrenalin.gl; ❶; Fr.35).

The Klausen Pass

Beyond Linthal, the road climbs west over the **Klausen Pass** (1948m) towards Lake Luzern. This is a simply stunning drive through breathtaking scenery, but is little used: the road is only open in summer (June–Oct) and is mostly very narrow – just about two car-widths between the cliff and the ravine. Tortuous hairpin bends mean that you should reckon on at least an hour and a half to cover the 47km to **Altdorf** (see p.396).

After some steep climbing out of Linthal, you emerge into the lovely, high, enclosed valley of **URNERBODEN**, dotted with a few farms and dozens of wandering cows; to the left is the Clariden (3268m), to the right the cliffs of the Ortstock (2717m). The road meanders its way past a couple of inns, including the sturdy *Urnerboden* (☎055 643 14 16; ⓦwww.urnerboden.ch; ❷), which is open year-round – in winter, there's some fine cross-country skiing up here. Faced by a sheer cliff at the head of the valley, the road somehow jinks its way up and around to the pass itself, where there's a refreshment kiosk; a kilometre down the other side – just before the truly awesome scenery kicks in – is the century-old *Hotel Klausenpasshöhe* (☎041 879 11 64, ⓦwww.klausenpasshoehe .ch; ❶), with century-old rooms to match. The route from here all the way down to Altdorf is a battle: you'll constantly be having to drag your eyes away from the spectacular views to concentrate on the road.

Postbuses run both ways on the "Historic Route Express" between Linthal and Altdorf in summer (June–Sept; reserve on ☎041 870 21 36, ⓦwww .postbus.ch), and from Linthal up to Urnerboden all year round.

Liechtenstein

The Principality of **LIECHTENSTEIN** (*Fürstentum Liechtenstein*, abbreviated to "**FL**") is the world's fourth-smallest country, a chip of green only slightly larger than Manhattan island squeezed between the Rhine and the Austrian Alps. It's a quiet, unassuming place, home to 35,000 mostly Catholic Liechtensteiners, who take an impressive 22 days public holiday a year, sing their own German words to the tune of "God Save the Queen" as the national anthem, and regard themselves as entirely separate from the Swiss, with whom neighbourly relations only began in 1923. This said, you won't notice many differences and, inevitably, the main reason to visit is the novelty value. There are some rustic spots outside the toytown capital **Vaduz** to enjoy, as well as lonely walks and family-friendly skiing in the craggy mountains.

Regular **postbuses** run to Vaduz from **Sargans** and **Buchs**, both of them on the main SBB train line between St Gallen and Chur. Austrian Railways (ÖBB, or OeBB) operates a few **trains** a day between Buchs and Feldkirch (Austria) which stop at Schaan, 3km north of Vaduz, from where buses shuttle into the capital. The principality's biggest event is **Staatsfeiertag** (National Holiday; ⓦwww.staatsfeiertag.li), on August 15, which culminates in a huge fireworks display.

Some history

Liechtenstein is the only country in the world to have been named after the person who bought it. After the Romans came through in 15 BC, the area

---

Exploring Liechtenstein

Postbuses (ⓦwww.lba.li) serve all points. A one-week bus pass costs Fr.18, but Swiss transport passes are valid for journeys into and around Liechtenstein (apart from the Austrian trains from Buchs to Schaan). Otherwise, the best deal is the **Erlebnispass Liechtenstein**, covering unlimited bus transport, a city-train tour in Vaduz, the Malbun chairlift, admission to all museums, a wine-tasting at the Hofkellerei des Fürstens, and other attractions. A two-day pass (valid 10 days) is Fr.25; a six-day pass (valid 30 days) is Fr.45.

St Gallen

Ruggell
Schellenberg
Feldkirch
Mauren
Eschen
Schaanwald
Nendeln
Planken
Drei Schwestern
2052m
Kuhgrat
2123m
AUSTRIA
Galinakopf
2198m
Buchs
Schaan
Margelchopf
2163m
Vaduz
Schönberg
2104m
SWITZERLAND
Alvier
2343m
Triesenberg
Steg
Ochsenkopf
2286m
Fundlkopf
2401m
Triesen
Malbun
2091m
Sareiserjoch
2000m
Gonzen
1830m
Balzers
2222m
Panüelerkopf
2859m
Mittlerspitz
1897m
Naafkopf
2570m
Falknis
2562m
Sargans
0   5 km

Chur   Maienfeld

Rhine
Toggenburg
Zürich
Innsbruck
N

was passed from pillar to post until 1699, when Johann Adam Andreas of the **Von Liechtenstein** family of Vienna purchased the Lordship of Schellenberg, and then in 1712 the County of Vaduz, in order to get a seat for himself in the imperial German Diet of Princes. Shortly after, the little patch was renamed after him. Liechtenstein won independence in 1866, the Prince taking an active political role within a so-called **democratic monarchy** linked to Austria-Hungary. After that empire's war defeat, the principality negotiated a customs treaty with Switzerland in 1923, since when borders between the two neighbours have been open and unmarked. The next milestone was 1984, when women got the vote.

The current head of state is His Serene Highness **Prince Hans Adam II von und zu Liechtenstein**, who – unlike most European monarchs – makes a point of regularly speaking his mind on political matters. He guided Liechtenstein's entry into the UN (1990) and the sub-EU European Economic Area (1995), both of which controversially created a gulf in relations with more reticent Switzerland, and in 2003 won a referendum which handed him significant new powers to appoint judges, veto parliamentary decisions and dismiss the government. The bitterly divisive campaign which led up to the vote exposed

Although Liechtenstein uses Swiss francs, it has its own telephone country code ☎423, completely separate from the Swiss phone system. For more, see p.62.

serious fault-lines in Liechtensteiner society: shortly afterwards, in 2005, in an unprecedented snub to the entrenched power of the Catholic Church, the people voted in another referendum to legalize abortion. Although Prince Hans Adam retains power, since 2004 he has placed his son, **Crown Prince Alois**, in charge of day-to-day affairs.

Meanwhile, the principality gets on with what it does best: making **money**. Tens of thousands of international companies are nominally headquartered in Liechtenstein, purely to take advantage of the favourable tax regime. The **banks** – which hold assets of Fr.80 billion or more – were reformed in 2000 after international investigations concluded that their system of anonymous numbered accounts was facilitating money-laundering by organized crime. High finance aside, Liechtenstein has also made a mint from producing highly collectable **postage stamps**. Its industries sound wonderfully quirky – they include the making of sausage skins and false teeth – and the countryside has noticeably escaped scarring by heavy industry; nonetheless, they bring in a cool Fr.4 billion or so annually. Liechtensteiner villages have a neat, bourgeois atmosphere about them, rather disappointing if you've come expecting to see signs of an ancient monarchy stuck somewhere in the Middle Ages.

Vaduz

You have to feel sorry for **VADUZ**. It could have been a quiet and pleasant Rhineside provincial town like Sargans on the Swiss bank opposite; instead, it labours under the unreasonable weight of being capital of an historical oddity. The little town bulges with glass-plated banks and squadrons of whistle-stop foreigners aimless with anti-climax.

Occupying a sleek, dark building at Städtle 32 is the impressive **Kunstmuseum** (Tues–Sun 10am–5pm, Thurs until 8pm; Fr.8, joint ticket with Landesmuseum Fr.12; Ⓦwww.kunstmuseum.li). Temporary shows from its collection embrace modern and contemporary art, particularly strong on sculpture: you may find a Courbet landscape alongside a Giacometti bronze opposite a spindly Arte Povera installation. Running simultaneously are exhibits taken from the private collection inherited and added to by the Prince, which includes works by Rubens, Van Dyck, Rembrandt and others.

VADUZ

ACCOMMODATION
Gasthof Löwen — C
Jugendherberge — B
Real — D
Säga — E
Sonnenhof — A

RESTAURANTS
Cesare — 2
Café Amann — 3
Torkel — 1

Rathaus
Schloss Vaduz
Kunstmuseum
Briefmarken Museum
Landesmuseum
Bus station

0 — 200 m

Triesen & Ⓔ

△ Schloss Vaduz

The juxtaposition is particularly engaging, played out in such a well-designed space.

A stroll away, at Städtle 43, is the **Liechtensteinisches Landesmuseum** (National Museum; Tues–Sun 10am–5pm, Wed until 8pm; Fr.8; ⓦwww .landesmuseum.li), with themed displays covering archeology, history, contemporary life and more. Otherwise, aside from a wander in the older streets north of the centre, interest is thin. Philatelists will love the **Briefmarkenmuseum** (Postage Stamps; daily 10am–noon & 1–5pm; free; ⓦwww.pwz.li). Perched picturesquely on the forested hillside above Vaduz is the Prince's photogenic restored sixteenth-century **Schloss Vaduz**, off-limits to the public. Knots of people gather at the castle gates to admire the doughty towers and turrets. Groups of ten or more can book a guided tour of the **Hofkellerei des Fürsten von Liechtenstein**, the Prince's own vineyard and cellars, situated just north of Vaduz (reservations essential ☎232 10 18, ⓦwww.hofkellerei.li; price varies), or individuals can taste wines for free during the onsite shop's opening hours (Mon–Fri 8am–noon & 1.30–6pm, Sat 9am–1pm).

Practicalities

The helpful **tourist office** is at Städtle 37 (daily 9am–noon & 1.30–5pm; Oct–April closed Sat & Sun; ☎239 63 00, ⓦwww.tourismus.li). Most of their time is taken up banging souvenir Liechtenstein stamps into visitors' passports (Fr.2) – an entirely unnecessary novelty.

The best-value **hotel** is the spotless, family-run ⚲ *Säga* (☎392 43 77, ⓦwww .saega.li; ❸), 6km south in the countryside near Triesen. In Vaduz, period furniture adds to the atmosphere of the 600-year-old *Gasthof Löwen*, Herrengasse 35 (☎238 11 44, ⓦwww.hotel-loewen.li; ❺–❻), while the top choice is the *Park-Hotel Sonnenhof*, set in its own grounds at Mareestrasse 29 (☎239 02 02, ⓦwww.sonnenhof.li; ❼–❾). Beside *Säga* is the quiet *Mittagsspitze* **campsite** (☎392 36 77). Dorm beds are Fr.31 at the HI **hostel** *Jugendherberge*, 2km north of Vaduz near Schaan, Untere Rüttigasse 6 (☎232 50 22, ⓦwww.youthhostel .ch; ❶; March–Oct; bus to Mühleholz).

Within the Kunstmuseum an attractive little **café** serves salads, light bites and sushi. The **restaurant** *Cesare*, Städtle 15 (closed Sat & Sun; ⓦ www.adler.li), has good Italian *menus* for Fr.20. Incognito *Café Amann*, Äulestrasse 56 (closed Sun), is worth a look for its value meals and a breath of local atmosphere, while *Torkel*, amidst the vineyards off Hintergasse (closed Sat eve & Sun; ⓦ www.torkel .li), is owned by the Prince, a perfect place to sample old-style Swiss/Austrian specialities (*menus* from Fr.30). One of the best restaurants in the country is in *Hotel Real*, Städtle 21 (☎232 22 22, ⓦ www.hotel-real.li), with an arty, creative take on traditional Liechtensteiner cuisine; presentation is superb and quality is exceptional.

Around Vaduz

Attractions around the principality are low-key, and aside from the mountain resort of Malbun, almost entirely untouristed. North of Schaan is the Unterland region, with some pleasant walks through the rolling countryside and dark woods. From **Nendeln**, a path climbs for an hour through the forest to **Planken**, Liechtenstein's smallest village (pop. 374), from where a steep two-hour route takes you up to spectacular views at the **Gafadurahütte** at 1428m (☎262 89 27, ⓦ www.alpenverein.li). Further north is tiny **SCHELLENBERG**, overlooked by the ruins of the medieval Obere Burg castle set amidst lush forest. Its sole hotel is the simple, cosy *Krone* (☎373 11 68, ⓦ www.hotelkrone .li; ❷), where children get a discount.

South of Vaduz is the Liechtensteiner Oberland, with workaday Triesen overshadowed by pretty **TRIESENBERG**, perched on a sunny hillside above the Rhine and best known as the adopted home of a community of Walser people, who left their homes in Wallis (German-speaking Valais) in the thirteenth century to spread out across central Europe. Many of the houses are old wooden chalets built in the Walser style. The modern, well-presented **Walser Heimatmuseum** (Tues–Fri 1.30–5.30pm, Sat 1.30–5pm; June–Aug also Sun 2–5pm; Fr.2; ⓦ www.triesenberg.li) documents Walser history and culture. A fine, scenic walk leads through Gnalp and Masescha and back (3hr).

Malbun

From Triesenberg, a back-country road climbs through a long tunnel beneath an Alpine ridge to **STEG** and on to **MALBUN**. This quiet hamlet at 1600m is Liechtenstein's only ski resort, with half-a-dozen little lifts (ⓦ www .bergbahnen.li) and a handful of gentle runs where Prince Charles and Princess Anne learned their snowploughing technique, back in the days before Klosters became the British royals' choice resort. Steg is the trailhead for a web of **cross-country ski** routes through the Valüna valley to the south. In summer, the area has a wealth of lonesome high-country **hikes**: a classic full-day mountain trek from Steg rises south through the Valüna valley up to the Naafkopf (2570m), before returning via the Augstenberg and Malbun. From Malbun, a rewarding three- or four-hour hike begins with a journey up the Sareis chairlift and then heads south along the Austrian border to the scenically positioned **Pfalzerhütte** at 2108m (☎263 36 79).

Malbun has a little **tourist office** (June–Oct & mid-Dec to mid-April Mon–Sat 9am–noon & 1.30–5pm; ☎263 65 77). The most congenial **place to stay** is *Berggasthaus Sücka* near Steg (☎263 25 79, ⓦ www.suecka-erlebnis .li; ❶; dorms Fr.32), also with good food. In Malbun the *Alpenhotel* (☎263 11 81, ⓦ www.alpenhotel.li; ❷–❸) is an attractive budget choice, while the chalet-style *Kulm* (☎237 79 79, ⓦ www.hotelkulm.com; ❸–❹) has some very comfortable balconied rooms. **Eating and drinking** is in the handful of hotel restaurants, or at the *Bergrestaurant Sareiserjoch* (Ⓦ www.sareis.li) – the top station of the Sareis chairlift (2000m), or an hour's hike up from Malbun – which has a scenic terrace and hearty Swiss dishes that rely heavily on the local Malbuner smoked ham.

Travel details

Full timetables for all trains, buses, trams, boats and cable cars in Switzerland – as well as international connections – are searchable at Ⓦ www.rail.ch. For details of the boat service on the Bodensee (Lake Constance), see p.460.

Trains

Appenzell to: St Gallen (every 30min; 45min).
Kreuzlingen to: Romanshorn (every 30min; 25min); Rorschach (every 30min; 50min); Schaffhausen (hourly; 55min).
Romanshorn to: Arbon (every 30min; 10min); Kreuzlingen (every 30min; 25min); Rorschach (every 30min; 15min); St Gallen (every 30min; 25min); Schaffhausen (hourly; 1hr 25min); Stein-am-Rhein (hourly; 55min).
Rorschach to: Chur (hourly; 1hr 15min); Kreuzlingen (every 30min; 50min); Romanshorn (every 30min; 15min); St Gallen (3 hourly; 15min).
St Gallen to: Appenzell (every 30min; 45min); Bern (twice hourly; 2hr 10min); Chur (hourly; 1hr 35min); Rorschach (3 hourly; 15min); Sargans (hourly; 1hr 10min); Schaffhausen (3 hourly; 1hr 30min; some change in Winterthur); Stein-am-Rhein (hourly; 1hr 25min); Winterthur (3 hourly; 35min); Zürich (3 hourly; 1hr).
Schaffhausen to: Kreuzlingen (hourly; 55min); Schloss Laufen (twice hourly; 5min); Stein-am-Rhein (every 30min; 25min); Winterthur (3 hourly; 25min); Zürich (twice hourly; 40min).

Stein-am-Rhein to St Gallen (hourly; 1hr 25min): Schaffhausen (every 30min; 25min).
Winterthur to: Bern (every 30min; 1hr 30min); St Gallen (3 hourly; 35min); Schaffhausen (3 hourly; 25min); Zürich (6 hourly; 20min).

Buses

Frauenfeld to: Kartause Ittingen (every 2hr; 10min); Stein-am-Rhein (hourly; 30min).
Stein AR to: St Gallen (hourly; 15min).
Stein-am-Rhein to: Frauenfeld (hourly; 30min); Warth (hourly; 20min).
Vaduz to: Buchs (every 20min; 15min); Malbun (hourly; 30min); Sargans (every 20min; 30min).

Boats

(Following is a summary of May–Sept services.)
Kreuzlingen to: Romanshorn (at least 2 daily; 1hr 15min); Schaffhausen (at least 3 daily; 3hr 45min); Stein-am-Rhein (at least 3 daily; 2hr 25min).
Romanshorn to: Arbon (at least 3 daily; 30min); Friedrichshafen, Germany (at least hourly; 40min); Kreuzlingen (at least 2 daily; 1hr 5min); Rorschach (at least 3 daily; 55min).
Rorschach (Hafen) to: Romanshorn (at least 3 daily; 55min).
Schaffhausen to: Kreuzlingen (at least 3 daily; 4hr 45min); Stein-am-Rhein (at least 3 daily; 2hr).

Graubünden

CHAPTER 11

Highlights

⁂ **Rhätische Bahn** The local train company has a superbly scenic network. **See p.484**

⁂ **Arosa** Outstanding small resort, high in the mountains above Chur. **See p.489**

⁂ **Flims-Laax** Top destination for snowboarders. **See p.495**

⁂ **Davos and Klosters** Two of the biggest names in the Alps. **See p.498**

⁂ **Lower Engadine** Fairy-tale high-sided valley, lined with deep, dark forests. **See p.504**

⁂ **Parc Naziunal Svizzer** The country's only national park, with a network of fine walking trails. **See p.507**

⁂ **Müstair** Remote village huddled round a frescoed abbey. **See p.510**

⁂ **Upper Engadine** Perhaps the most beautiful valley in the Alps, with over 320 days of sunshine a year. **See p.510**

⁂ **St Moritz** One of Europe's best-known ski resorts, not just for the rich and famous. **See p.511**

⁂ **Muottas Muragl** Gaze on the mighty Bernina range and a string of valley-floor lakes from this lofty viewpoint. **See p.518**

△ Halfpipe, Davos

Graubünden

GRAUBÜNDEN (Ⓦwww.graubuenden.ch), Switzerland's largest canton, occupies the entire southeast of the country, encompassing a sparsely populated area that borders Austria to the north and Italy to the east and south. Its folded landscape of deep, isolated valleys, sheer rocky summits and thick pine forests makes it the wildest and loneliest part of Switzerland, more difficult than most to get around in, but also more reward- ing, with some of the finest scenery in the Alps. Glaciers oozing from between the high mountains launch two of Europe's great rivers – the Rhine and the Inn – on their long journeys to the North Sea and the Black Sea respectively, while two smaller rivers water pomegranates, figs and chestnuts in secluded southern valleys en route to the Po and the Adriatic.

The canton – once the Roman province of Rhaetia Prima – is officially **trilingual**, known as Graubünden in German, Grigioni in Italian and Grischun in **Romansh**, the last of these a direct descendant of Latin which has survived locked away in the mountain fastnesses far from the capital **Chur** since the legions departed 1500 years ago. You'll also come across the canton's French name of **Grisons**, although there are no French-speaking communities.

Until the nineteenth century, **Rhaetia** was entirely separate from its western neighbour of Helvetia. As Helvetia began to experience stirrings towards inde- pendence in the thirteenth and fourteenth centuries, the population of Rhaetia also began to organize themselves. The impenetrable landscape was on their side: as one historian, Benjamin Barber, accurately noted, "an army occupying Chur no more controls Graubünden than does one in Milan or Vienna." The 1367 League of the House of God was the first of these popular associations, soon followed by the **Grey League** in 1395 (formed by a band of highland shepherds dubbed "the grey farmers" for their woollen cloth) and, in 1436, the League of the Ten Jurisdictions. These three came together in 1471 to pledge mutual assistance, and were soon able – with the spur of the Reformation – to seize political power from the nobility. Since then the people have been free, and they relish the fact more than most other Swiss. It was only in 1803 that the united "**Graubünden**", or Grey Leagues, finally assented to join the Swiss Confederation, and to this day Bündners consistently vote in large numbers against joining the EU.

The canton's resorts – headed by **St Moritz**, **Klosters** and **Davos** – are some of the most famous names in the Alps and offer world-class skiing and top-qual- ity hiking, but they're far from the whole story. The beautiful **Engadine valley** runs for almost 100km along a southern terrace of the Alps, bathed in glittering sunlight that pours from blue skies for well over 300 days a year. This is the heartland of Romansh culture, with its own language, style and architecture.

South of the Alps, three of the canton's most enticing valleys – **Bregaglia** and **Poschiavo** in particular – are Italian-speaking, filled with a Mediterranean lushness in their flora and cuisine that might tempt you to leave the mountains behind and just keep heading south.

Chur and around

Sitting in a deep valley carved by the Rhine, **CHUR** (pronounced *koor*), the lively cantonal capital, is much overlooked: it has a characterful Old

Vaduz
LIECH.
Fläsch
HEIDILAND
Maienfeld
Jenins
Landquart
PRÄTTIGAU
Chrüz
2196m
Madrisahorn
2826m
Wannenspitz
1970m
Küblis
Glattwang
2376m
Parsenn
2200m
Klosters
Chur
Mattjischhorn
2461m
Weissfluh
2844m
Weisshorn
2653m
Tiejerflue
2781m
Davos
Churwalden
Valbella
Hörnli
2512m
Arosa
Sandhubel
2764m
Jakobshorn
2590m
Flüelapass
Lenzer-
heide
Parpaner
Rothorn
2861m
Rinerhorn
2528m
Schwarzhorn
3146m
Lhisur
Hoch Ducan
3063m
Bühlenhorn
2808m
Tiefencastel
Bergün
Savognin
Corn da Tinizong
P. Vadret
3229m
Schanf
Preda
Albulapass/
Pass d'Alvra
Zuoz
Marbegnas
2670m
P. Bleis
Marsha
3128m
Piz d'Err
3378m
Samedan
Il Corn
2959m
P. Nair
3057m
Celerina
Muottas
Muragl
2453m
P. Platta
3392m
Julierpass/
P. dal Güglia
St Moritz
Piz Vadret
3199m
Pontresina
Mazzaspitz
3164m
Bivio
Silvaplana
P. Rosatsch
3123m
Bormio
Juf
Stallerberg
2774m
Sils
Munt Arlas
3127m
Diavolezza
2973m
P. Paradisio
3302m
P. Duan
3131m
Maloja
VAL BREGAGLIA
Pso. del
Maloja
P. Bernina
4049m
Pso. del
Bernina
ITALY
Stampa
Promontogno
Piz Palü
3905m
VAL POSCHIAVO
Poschiavo
Brusio
Tirano
Sondrio & Lake Como

AUSTRIA
Ischgl
Galtür
Piz Rotz
3097m
Samnaun
Muttler
3294m
Fluchthorn
3399m
Martina
Landeck
P. Campatsch
2920m
Tschlin
Inn
Piz Buin
3312m
VEREINA
Pischahorn
2979m
Piz Cotschen
3030m
Ftan
Scuol
Ramosch
TUNNEL
Piz Cotschen
3030m
Guarda
Ardez
Tarasp
LOWER ENGADINE
P. Lischana
3105m
Susch
P. Arpiglias
3027m
P. Nair
2951m
Zernez
P. Sesvenna
3205m
Piz Terza
2682m
PARC
NAZIUNAL
SVIZZER
Ofenpass/
Pass dal Fuorn
Piz Daint
2968m
VAL MÜSTAIR
Müstair
Sta.
Maria
ENGADINE
Munt
Cotschen
3104m
Livigno
UPPER

11
GRAUBÜNDEN | Chur and around

0   10 km
N

Town, full of medieval cobbled alleys, secret courtyards and solid, four-square town houses, that is dominated by a huge **cathedral** symbolizing the rule of the bishop-princes of years gone by. Aside from offering "the best shopping between Zürich and Milan" (debatable), Chur serves as the linchpin of transport routes, with buses and trains sneaking their way through the high, narrow valleys of Central Graubünden to Davos and St Moritz, and west through Surselva to the high Alps around Andermatt. In a remote mountain fastness southeast of the town sits the picturesque resort of **Arosa**, while the gentler foothills to the northeast are cloyingly dubbed "**Heidiland**".

Graubünden's **Rhätische Bahn** (RhB; ⓦ www.rhb.ch) has one of the most scenic train networks in the world. Superbly engineered, with tracks spanning deep valleys on soaring viaducts and crossing several mountain passes, it can get you to sights and views far off any roads. Many of the most dramatic routes are marketed as attractions in their own right (see p.42), although bear in mind that, despite the hype, they're all served by regular, scheduled trains at **standard fares**; the only extra costs are seat reservations (always advisable, for a few francs), surcharges to sit in panoramic coaches, upgrades to first class and/or reservations for the dining car that often accompanies longer journeys. Otherwise, all RhB trains are **free** to Swiss Pass holders.

The RhB **regional pass** is good value. The **summer** versions (May–Oct) cost Fr.120/150 for 7/14 days, with 2/4 days of free travel on RhB trains and postbuses, and the remaining days at half-price (mountain transport is half-price throughout). The **winter** version (Nov–April) costs Fr.90 for seven days: train travel is free for two days and half-price for the remainder, buses are half-price throughout, and you get one mountain trip for free (up and down). Both are buyable from local stations.

Despite the excellent train service, if you want to cover a lot of ground independently, Graubünden merits **renting a car**. Buses penetrate to the most remote valleys and hamlets, but often only every two hours, and journeys can be long and tortuous. Driving means you can pull over at will, or detour to outlying corners that might otherwise take up a full day on public transport.

Special train journeys

Although these are the headline routes, it's easy to cherry-pick the most attractive or convenient bits of any of them to construct your own itinerary. The **Glacier Express** runs from St Moritz and Davos to Chur and then west over the Alps to Zermatt. The **Bernina Express** runs from Chur to St Moritz, then over the high Bernina Pass to Tirano, switching to a postbus for the journey around Lake Como to Lugano. The **Heidi Express** heads from Landquart through Klosters and Davos, linking in with the Bernina route to Tirano and Lugano. The **Aqualino** runs from Landquart through Klosters to Scuol, tying in with day-packages at the Bogn Engiadina spa. The **Arosa Express** does the run from Chur to Arosa. Finally, the **Engadin Star** (June–Oct only) runs from Landquart through Klosters to St Moritz.

The RhB also runs its own **Pullman** coaches on various scenic full-day routes, on selected days in summer only (June–Sept), as well as similar outings pulled by **steam-engines**. Perhaps the most fun journey of the lot is on the **Railrider**, a roofless train completely open to the elements, which shuttles the forty minutes between Filisur and Preda on the steep, dramatic Albula route every Sunday in July and August (Fr.15; no reservation needed).

Other package deals

Freizeit Graubünden (ⓦ www.freizeit-graubuenden.ch), an association of tourist offices, has put together a number of **package** deals: two nights' B&B in a three-star hotel in Chur, including entry to museums, city tour and other perks, costs Fr.181 per person in a double room. One of their best **hiking** packages follows the restored Via Spluga trail in five stages from Thusis to Chiavenna: five nights' B&B, including maps, four packed lunches, admission to the Viamala gorge and baggage transport from hotel to hotel, costs from Fr.349 per person in a double room.

Chur is the oldest continuously inhabited city north of the Alps, with archeological finds dating back to 11,000 BC. Situated on prime north–south routes of commerce and communication, Curia Rhaetorium was founded by the **Romans** after their conquest of 15 BC. **St Luzius**, a missionary, is reputed to have brought Christianity to the region in the fourth century, and the first **bishop** of Chur to be positively documented was Asinio, in the year 451. A few centuries on, the bishop had become a powerful political ruler, enjoying the patronage of Holy Roman Emperors, and by 1170, the post was officially recognized as a Prince-Bishopric. With the populist movements of the fourteenth century, the Prince-Bishops' power began to erode, and when the **Reformation** took hold in 1526, Chur's wealthy merchants and crafts-workers took over all significant political decision-making for themselves. Today, from his palace beside the cathedral, the bishop of Chur still controls a diocese covering Graubünden, all the central Swiss cantons and Zürich, and students flock to the adjacent St Luzi theological seminary to train for the priesthood.

Arrival, information and accommodation

Chur's **train** and **postbus station** – resplendent beneath a vast, fully glazed arching roof, reminiscent of nineteenth-century railway architecture – is at the head of Bahnhofstrasse, five minutes northwest of the Old Town. The **tourist office** at Grabenstrasse 5, 100m east of Postplatz (Mon 1.30–6pm, Tues–Fri 8.30am–noon & 1.30–6pm, Sat 9am–noon; ☎081 252 18 18, ⓦwww .churtourismus.ch), has pamphlets explaining the red and green footprints painted on the pavements, which show the routes of self-guided walking tours: the longer red route is the better of the two. The tourist office also offers its own excellent **guided walk**, starting from the Rathaus (April–Oct Wed 2.30pm; Fr.8).

Hotels

Drei Könige Reichsgasse 18 ☎ 081 354 90 90,
ⓦ www.dreikoenige.ch. A 200-year-old inn steps
from the tourist office in the Old Town, characterful
and pleasant, also with some budget backpacker
rooms. ❷–❸
Franziskaner Kupfergasse 18 ☎ 081 252 12 61,
ⓦ www.franziskaner.biz. Freshly renovated rooms
in the heart of the Old Town, both ensuite and
shared-bath. ❷–❸
Freieck Reichsgasse 44 ☎ 081 255 15 15,
ⓦ www.freieck.ch. Comfortable mid-range place
spread across a couple of old renovated
buildings, with some good rooms updated in pine
and pastel. ❸
Rebleuten Pfisterplatz 1 ☎ 081 257 13 57,
ⓦ www.rebleuten.ch. Lovely guildhouse dating
from 1483, with elaborate scrollwork on its facade,
an excellent, sophisticated restaurant and cosy,
attractive rooms. ❷–❸
🏃 **Stern** Reichsgasse 11 ☎ 081 258 57 57,
     ⓦ www.stern-chur.ch. Nicest hotel in town.
An historic inn and member of the Romantik group,
with top-quality service, modern, wood-beamed
rooms and parking. The excellent restaurant is a
particular asset. ❹–❺

The Town

Chur's picturesque Old Town nestles in the shadow of the cathedral, which
looms on high ground to the southeast. The alleys and fountained squares are
characterized by their terraces of old houses, traditionally built without shut-
ters and fronted in rather dour, greyish Scalära stone. The main north–south
thoroughfare **Poststrasse** bisects the Old Town; at its northern end is busy
Postplatz, overlooked by a large villa housing the **Bündner Kunstmuseum**
(Tues–Sun 10am–noon & 2–5pm, Thurs until 8pm; Fr.8; SMP; ⓦ www
.buendner-kunstmuseum.ch), featuring paintings by Graubünden artists Angelika Kauffmann and Giovanni and Alberto Giacometti. Something of a feminist
icon during her lifetime and afterwards, Kauffmann was born in Chur in 1741,
and moved to London at the age of 25. She quickly established a solid reputation there, becoming one of the most popular artists of the time, and was one
of the founding members of the Royal Academy in 1768. Although she was
best known in her day for the kind of dramatic narrative painting exemplified
in *Hector and Paris* (1770), viewable here, art historians now tend to reject such
works as overly sentimental and favour instead her portraits, of which there are
also plenty on show, not least a graceful self-portrait (1780). The museum also
stages high-quality temporary exhibitions.

Following Poststrasse 100m south brings you to the arcaded courtyard of the
fifteenth-century **Rathaus**. One street to the east is Reichsgasse, an atmospheric old alley with, at no. 57, a plaque commemorating Angelika Kauffmann's
birthplace. Reichsgasse ends in the attractive open square of Arcas, dominated
by the Gothic **Kirche St Martin**, dating from 1491 and now sporting three
beautiful stained-glass windows by Alberto Giacometti. Arcas hosts the lively
Gänggelimarkt flea market (1st Sat of month). Opposite the church, bustling
Oberegasse – site of a weekly food market (May–Oct Sat morning) – runs west

---

Above Chur – Brambrüesch and the Dreibündenstein

Chur is proud of the fact that it's the only Swiss city with its own hiking and winter-
sports area accessible directly from the city centre. The **Brambrüesch** (ⓦ www
.brambruesch.ch) rises immediately southwest of the Old Town: its cable-car station
is on Kasernenstrasse, five minutes' walk west of the Obertor. Brambrüesch (1600m)
is one of the three peaks of the **Dreibündenstein** (2174m), and has plenty of summer
hiking routes, as well as paragliding and a summer toboggan run. In winter, a **ski
pass** (Fr.24/36 half/full day) also covers chairlifts above Brambrüesch, giving access
to easy pistes and tobogganing.

to the **Obertor** gate, a remnant of Chur's medieval fortifications. Behind the church rises the hill upon which the cathedral sits; just to the left, in a quiet courtyard at Hofstrasse 1, is the impressive **Rätisches Museum** (Tues–Sun 10am–noon & 2–5pm; Fr.6; ⓦwww.rm.gr.ch), housing the canton's historical collections on six floors.

The cathedral

Chur is dominated physically and spiritually by its huge **cathedral** (daily 8am–7pm; ⓦwww.bistum-chur.ch), constructed between 1151 and 1272 in late-Romanesque and Gothic styles. Still hived off from the town by a thick gated wall, which reflects the bitterness of the disputes that flared around the Reformation, the cathedral is the focus of the **Hof**, a complex of eighteenth-century buildings in the heart of the city protecting Chur's religious elite from contact with the mob. Extensive preservation works are in train, and access may be limited for the next few years.

The **interior** is vast and gloomy, with Romanesque capitals above the massive columns showing grotesque creatures and gargoyle-like demons. To the left of the main nave is a blank space where once stood the **altar of St Laurentius**: thieves broke in through the crypt a few years back and destroyed the altar; its paintings were recovered and are now under restoration. Looking back from the **choir steps**, it becomes apparent that the nave is out of alignment with the choir. Many stories are put about as to why this should be, the most fanciful being that the nave was deliberately angled to match the droop of Christ's head on the cross. High up opposite the Baroque **pulpit** is a tiny gallery: this is one end of a "secret" passage from the bishop's palace next door, allowing the bishop to enter the House of God at a suitably lofty altitude and without soiling his shoes on the courtyard outside. The elaborate winged **high altar**, carved in 1486–92, is under restoration until at least 2008.

Eating and drinking

Chur's Old Town has a good range of places to **eat**, many of them offering the classic regional dish of *Bündnerfleisch*, prime beef air-dried in an open attic or under the eaves of a barn, served sliced paper-thin to adorn a *Bündnerteller* – a carefully presented plate of cold meats. *Bündnerfleisch* also takes centre-stage in *Bündner Gerstensuppe*, a creamy barley soup with vegetables. Hunting is still popular in the countryside, and you'll see game on autumn menus, including stews of deer or chamois. Another local speciality is Passugger **mineral water**, bottled in Passugg 2km south; however, it's not worth paying for, since the same stuff flows out of every tap and street fountain in town. As the location of the canton's only matriculation college, Chur has loads of pre-university students packing the **bars** around the Obertor.

Restaurants

Alten Zollhaus Malixerstrasse 1 ☏081 252 33 98. Right beside the Obertor, with plain, hearty meals served downstairs in its cosy *Stübli* from Fr.12, and more formal dining in the upstairs restaurant, from Fr.22 or so.

Controversa Steinbruchstrasse 2. A classy, modern restaurant with an excellent salad buffet and plenty of light pasta meals with veggie options (Fr.15–20). Closed Sun lunch.

Drei Könige Reichsgasse 18. Attractive

wood-panelled dining room that draws a fair range of locals to sample its hearty, well-priced cuisine. Makes a point of its "Backpacker Menu", a full-blown set meal for Fr.15 or less.

Duc de Rohan Masansterstrasse 44 ☏081 252 10 22, ⓦwww.ducderohan.ch. Comfortable old manor house 400m north of the centre – a pleasant, sophisticated atmosphere to enjoy creative takes on international and regional specialities, with some Asian influences. Various lunch menus from Fr.25; at least double that in the evenings. Closed Sun.

The story of the Swiss gypsy people, known as the **Jenisch** (or Yenish), and how they have been treated over the last century by the Swiss authorities, is shocking, and exposes a calculated policy of Nazi-style eugenics carried out in Switzerland behind closed doors well into the 1970s. For almost fifty years, the Swiss government advocated and funded the wholesale kidnapping of Jenisch children, separating more than six hundred babies and toddlers from their families in what was nothing less than a determined attempt to completely wipe out Jenisch culture. Ghosts have not been put to rest and the scandal remains a source of national shame and anger.

The Jenisch (⊛www.jenisch.info) are one of the three main groups of central European gypsies, along with the Sinti and the Roma. During and after the great waves of gypsy migration in the seventeenth and eighteenth century, many arrived in Switzerland and specifically in Graubünden, where they lived a generally quiet, if socially ostracized, life. Following the tide of nationalism that swept through Europe after World War I, the science of **eugenics** gained widespread credibility, with its notion of state-sponsored "cleansing" of the racial gene pool by the forced removal from society of those with mental illnesses, physical disabilities and other characteristics seen as socially aberrant. Along with Jews and homosexuals, people with a lifestyle centred on travelling were singled out for special treatment. In 1926, the Swiss government approved a project set up by the children's charity Pro Juventute intended to eliminate vagrancy. Entitled **Kinder der Landstrasse** ("Children of the Road"), it effectively sanctioned child abduction: police seized Jenisch newborns and infants from their mothers and carted them off to orphanages run by Pro Juventute. Some children were handed on to foster parents, effectively to vanish into society; others ended up shunted from pillar to post until their adulthood. As a result of personality assessments by appointed psychologists, large numbers of children were consigned to mental institutions, one of the most notorious of which was the Waldhaus clinic in Chur. Parents were not only kept in the dark about their children's whereabouts, they were actively barred from making inquiries.

Kinder der Landstrasse was founded and directed by **Alfred Siegfried**. One of the aims of the project, according to Siegfried's own admission, was effectively to eliminate the Jenisch people altogether: "We must say that we have already achieved much if these people do not start a family, do not reproduce without restraint and bring new generations of degenerate and abnormal children into the world." As late as 1964 Siegfried was writing, "Nomadism, like certain dangerous diseases, is primarily transmitted by women... Anyone wishing to combat nomadism must aim to destroy the travellers' communal existence. Hard as it may seem, we must put an

Han Kung Rabengasse 6. Chinese with three-course lunch *menus* for well under Fr.20. Closed Mon.
Migros Gäuggelistrasse 28. Big self-service diner behind the station. Closed Sun.

🎿 **Rebleuten** Pfisterplatz 1 ☎081 257 13 57, ⊛www.rebleuten.ch. Excellent place for quality regional cooking under an innovative young manager who – rather than faking antiques – has brought in modern furniture and a fresh style to the medieval surroundings of a formal, wood-panelled guildhall dining room. An adjacent "bistro" room has lower prices and a more relaxed atmosphere. Restaurant closed Sat lunch, Sun & Mon; bistro open daily.

Stern Reichsgasse 11 ☎081 252 35 55, ⊛www.stern-chur.ch. Top-choice hotel restaurant for characteristically meaty Bündner specialities, with a cosy, intimate atmosphere. *Menus* around Fr.20.

Bars

American Sports Bar Rabengasse 7. Convivial joint for familiar beers and TV sport.
Controvini Steinbruchstrasse 2. Chur's first wine-bar, still a chic, popular spot offering over thirty wines by the glass.
Giger Bar Comercialstrasse 23 ⊛www.gigerbar.ch. A blank cube tucked anonymously between office buildings 1.5km west of the Old Town in a business-park area of furniture showrooms and

end to their family community. There is no other way." Under Siegfried's guidance, boys were forced into apprenticeships or onto farms as cheap labour, and girls were often either sent to convents or simply kept under lock and key: **Uschi Waser**, chair of **Naschet Jenische** (ⓦ www.naschet-jenische.ch), a foundation set up to campaign for Jenisch rights, was placed in 23 different institutions in 18 years. Jenisch were not just forbidden from marrying other Jenisch, they were imprisoned for attempting it. **Mariella Mehr**, a Jenisch writer (ⓦ www.mariellamehr.com), described her treatment at the hands of the scientists: "When I was three years old, they realised I didn't want to talk. They decided to force me. They used a kind of bath-tub... The patients were made to lie in the tub and covered with a plank so they couldn't get out. Only their heads were above water. They were kept there in freezing-cold water for up to twenty hours."

In 1972, the Swiss weekly *Der Schweizerischer Beobachter* exposed the Kinder der Landstrasse project, to universal public outrage. Pro Juventute closed the operation down a year later, and yet, according to official reports, there were about a hundred victims of Kinder der Landstrasse still incarcerated in clinics and institutions in 1988, after the Swiss state had formally acknowledged its moral, political and financial responsibility for the abductions and apologized to the Jenisch. Although Pro Juventute's own summations of individual cases remain under a 100-year embargo, the findings of an **official report** into the whole affair were published in 1998. Ruth Dreyfuss, then Swiss president, commented that "the conclusions of the historians leave no room for doubt. Kinder der Landstrasse is a tragic example of discrimination and persecution of a minority." The effects of the revelations on Swiss society have been devastating: along with accusations of collaboration with the Nazis before and during World War II and evidence from historians undermining the treasured notion of Swiss neutrality, the Kinder der Landstrasse report delivered a body blow to the image of a wholesome, morally upright Switzerland.

Meanwhile, about 5000 of Switzerland's 35,000 Jenisch still head out on the road each summer, working as antique dealers or craftspeople, handing on their skills and the Jenisch language to new generations. They have been assigned caravan grounds all over the country, and their children can even study while on the road with correspondence courses offered by many Swiss schools for the purpose. The majority of Jenisch however – often light-skinned and fluent in Swiss-German – live a settled life in mostly low-income housing on the edge of many Swiss cities, completely cut off from their culture. Pro Juventute, though it dissociates itself from the Kinder der Landstrasse project these days, remains in operation.

petrol stations, but nonetheless much-vaunted for its owner and designer, the Swiss-born, Oscar-winning special-effects supremo H.R. Giger (see p.139). The interior is kitted out in the style of Giger's greatest creation, *Alien*, with sleek, sci-fi power-chairs, jet-black decor and a limbless, writhing female torso hoisted above the bar. Oddly enough, if you go expecting to plug into an exciting cutting-edge subculture, you'll be disappointed: despite the movie-set decor, it's an utterly ordinary after-work bar for local business folk, with its radio tuned to a light-melodies channel. Brad Pitt did stop by once, though. Mon–Thurs 8am–8pm, Fri & Sat 8am–midnight; bus #1 to Agip.

Toms Beer Box Unteregasse 11/Goldgasse ⓦ www.toms.ch. Hole-in-the-wall joint which stocks 140 bottled beers from around the world.

Arosa

AROSA was discovered by the outside world in 1883 when Dr Otto Herwig-Hold, on a skiing tour of the mountains south of Chur, came across the remote hamlet – a perfect spot to build his new tuberculosis sanatorium. The chest patients of old have long since given way to sports enthusiasts, and the isolated village has developed into one of Graubünden's most acclaimed resorts, yet it's still small enough to have retained its atmosphere and lacks even a trace of the hotshot swagger of Davos or St Moritz.

Arosa lies at the end of a single, spectacular mountain road which cuts its way up into a sheer and narrow valley southeast of Chur, passing on the way through a succession of idyllic terraced villages and offering vistas breathtaking enough to make you want to stop and gape every three minutes – which you could do, but for the fact that in the 32-kilometre journey, there's a total of 244 switchbacks. It's frankly less nerve-racking to take the **Arosa Express** train, which departs from the forecourt of Chur station and shadows the road all the way up.

Beware that almost everything – shops, hotels, attractions, walking routes – is **closed during off-season** (mid-April to mid-June & mid-Oct to mid-Dec). We've specified months of opening only when they differ from this pattern.

Arrival, information and accommodation

The town consists of two areas: the main resort is **Ausserarosa**, clustered around the train station and the Obersee lakelet; while the older village at the upper end of the valley is dubbed **Innerarosa**. The **train station** borders the Obersee, with the **tourist office** five minutes' walk away, uphill on Arosa's only proper road, Poststrasse (May–Nov Mon–Fri 8am–noon & 1.30–6pm, Sat 9am–1pm; Dec–April Mon–Fri 8am–6pm, Sat 9am–5pm, Sun 4–5.30pm; ☎081 378 70 20, ⓦ www.arosa.ch). All buses within the village are free, and private cars are banned between midnight and 6am (except to arrive or depart). Some **hotels** charge extra if you stay less than three nights, especially in the winter season – but prices in summer can be up to fifty percent cheaper than at the winter peak, and also include free use of the cable cars.

Sports and activities in Arosa

Arosa occupies the broad sunny bowl of the Schanfigg, surrounded on all sides by snowy peaks. The **Weisshorn** (2653m) is the main focus, due west of the resort, along with the **Hörnli** (2512m) to the south and the **Brüggerhorn** (2401m) to the north.

The **skiing** is small-scale but high-quality, with over 70km of mostly blue and red pistes sidewinding down the gentle sunny slopes; beginners will feel especially at home. There's also 25km of cross-country pistes and a **snowboard** halfpipe up above 2000m. Lifts and a gondola rise from the Obersee to the Weisshorn (with a chairlift from halfway up branching over to the Brüggerhorn), and at the very top of the village in Innerarosa there's another gondola connecting to the Hörnli. A pass for one/six days costs Fr.55/256. For lessons, try ⓦ www.sssa.ch or ⓦ www.bananas.net.

In **summer**, there are several good high-country hikes: from the Weisshorn summit, a scenic and easygoing four-hour trail heads over the Carmenna Pass and through the lonely Urden valley to Tschiertschen, connected to Chur by postbus; or you could head across the meadows from the Weisshorn middle station to Alpenblick and the tranquil Schwellisee before returning to Arosa (3hr). Another fine route leads off the back of the Hörnli summit and across the peaks to the Parpaner Rothorn (2861m), from where cable cars run down to Lenzerheide, near Valbella 12km south of Chur, and connected to Chur by bus. You can rent **mountain bikes** from the station to tackle any of the five marked MTB trails, which include circular routes as well as downhill runs.

Hotels

Allegra Isla Neubachstrasse 30 ☎ 081 377 12 13, Ⓦ www.allegra-isla.ch. Pleasant, efficient three-star place on a quiet street between the Obersee and its lower twin, the Untersee, on the edge of the forest. Go for the superb corner room. ❹–❺

Arosa Kulm Innerarosa ☎ 081 378 88 88, Ⓦ www.arosakulm.ch. Super-luxurious palace at the very top of town, on the edge of the slopes. Facilities are excellent, with a range of formal restaurants and rooms boasting picture windows and balconies. ❽–❾

Arve Central Hubelstrasse 252 ☎ 081 378 52 52, Ⓦ www.arve-central.ch. Unusually open all year round, offering cut-price bargains in spring, summer and autumn. Friendly staff, a couple of good restaurants and attractive rooms (go for the south-facing ones). Also with a "backpackers' chalet" dorm annexe. ❸–❹

🏃 **Eden** Ausserarosa ☎ 081 378 71 00, Ⓦ www.edenarosa.ch. The most characterful hotel in town, on a quiet street close to the station, with an array of chic Design Rooms, individually decorated Art Rooms (which, despite names like The Muse's Kiss, Tiger Lily and Time Machine, manage to live up to their hype) and trendy Classic–Nouveau Rooms on the top floor that revel in 1970s design features and decor. A handful of "normal" rooms are cheaper, but this place is worth a splash. ❹–❼

Prätschli ☎ 081 377 18 61, Ⓦ www.praetschli .ch. If you're here to relish the winter snows, this is the place to be – a romantic old winter hotel in a unique location plum on the slopes high above the Obersee, with road access but truly out in the wilds. Mid-Dec to mid-April only. ❻

Sonnenhalde Innerarosa ☎ 081 378 44 44, Ⓦ www.sonnenhalde-arosa.ch. Good-quality inexpensive hotel near the skating rink, excellently located for the winter-only Carmenna and Tschuggen lifts, with super-friendly service and surprisingly well-appointed rooms. ❷–❸

Suveran ☎ 081 377 19 69, Ⓦ www.suveran .ch. Quiet, simple pension on a street above the Catholic church, with shared-bath rooms and low prices. ❶–❷

Hostel

Backpackers Arosa ☎ 081 378 84 23, Ⓦ www .backpackers-arosa.ch. Three linked hostels, dotted around the resort. The main, well-equipped "Downtown" hostel is on Seewaldweg – from the tourist office, turn off partway down the main road – with the "Chalet" and the "Mountain Lodge" up on the slopes (both only for groups in summer). Dorm prices vary. ❶

Campsite

Arosa ☎ 081 377 17 45. Tranquil site below the main resort, on a path winding down from the tourist office.

Eating and drinking

In general, **eating and drinking** options are down-to-earth to suit the majority of Arosa's clientele, with a handful of simple diners around the Obersee and the lower reaches of Poststrasse, including the landmark *Orelli's* (closed Wed), where you can fill up on fish dishes, *Röschti* or salad for Fr.15 (also with veggie meals). *Pizzeria Grottino*, just down the road from it, has quality pizza/pasta staples for Fr.15–20. Otherwise you're looking at hotel dining: *Hold*, up near the Hörnli cable car, is a popular, traditional place offering raclette *a gogo* (all-you-can-eat) every week, while *Quellenhof* (closed Sun & Mon), near the tourist office, has good, *Röschti*-rich *menus* for under Fr.20. Otherwise, aim for the *Arve Central*, which has two restaurants offering excellent, inventive cuisine with local ingredients, or the luxury *Arosa Kulm*, with a handful of top-rated dining options, including an excellent Thai restaurant (open winter only).

Heidiland

The Rhine valley north of Chur winds through lush meadowland to the small industrial town of **Landquart** – an important rail junction for the line to Davos – and on to **Bad Ragaz**, a rather graceful spa resort full of cheery elderly folk strolling happily along the neat boulevards feeling much better than they used to, thanks to the town's hot springs, which are famed for soothing away rheumatic and circulatory problems. The hills above Bad Ragaz are where the ruthlessly marketed **Heidiland** region got its name (Ⓦ www.heidiland.com):

Swiss author Johanna Spyri set her wholesome classic of children's literature *Heidi* in and around the village of **MAIENFELD**, and the place milks its claim to fame mercilessly.

A gentle half-day trail leads from Maienfeld station past the pretty central square and the **tourist office** (Mon–Fri 10am–noon & 1.30–5pm, Sat closes 4pm; ☎081 302 58 58, ⓦwww.maienfeld.ch), which stocks plenty of Heidi kitsch, and then on up the hill to the hamlet of Oberrofels, now cruelly renamed **Heididorf** (ⓦwww.heididorf.ch). Regardless of the lack of firm evidence linking Spyri's story with any particular house, one old chalet near the execrable *Heidihof Hotel* has been reborn as "the original **Heidi's House**". A scenic and, thankfully, rarely-tramped trail leads from Heididorf further up into the high pastures, past another lone chalet designated Peter the Goatherd's Hut, up to **Heidi Alp** and down through lush meadows to the village of Jenins, and back to Heididorf.

The Bündner Herrschaft

The east bank of the Rhine around Maienfeld, taking in the adjacent villages of Fläsch, Jenins and Malans, is one of Switzerland's more unusual winemaking areas, dubbed the **Bündner Herrschaft** (ⓦwww.buendnerherrschaft.ch). In what would otherwise be far too inhospitable a climate, luscious red Pinot Noir (Blauburgunder) grapes – introduced in the seventeenth century by the Duc de Rohan – are nurtured by the warm southerly Föhn wind, which can sometimes raise summer temperatures well above 25°C. The villages are linked by footpaths, generally quiet once you're out of the range of Heidi-seekers, and have good rustic inns at which to enjoy a carafe of local wine alongside a square meal. Schloss Brandis, a medieval castle on the edge of Maienfeld (☎081 302 24 23, ⓦwww.schlossbrandis.ch), has a renowned **restaurant** and an impressive cellar, and the *Landhaus* in Fläsch (closed Mon & Tues), *Alter Torkel* in Jenins (closed Tues & Wed; ⓦwww.torkel.ch), and *Zum Ochsen* in Malans (closed Mon & Tues; ⓦwww.donatsch-malans.ch) all concentrate on their wines as much as on their mid-priced *menus*.

Central Graubünden

The **Central Graubünden** region south of Chur is the canton's wildest area, characterized by deep, narrow valleys, ancient forests, mountain torrents and a succession of quiet old villages that feel as if they've seen few visitors since the Romans – who are known to have used the two main Alpine passes of the area, the **Julier** and the **Splügen**. Aside from simple inns in most villages and a couple of low-key, family-oriented Alpine resorts – Valbella/Lenzerheide is one, Savognin another – there are few facilities for tourists, and not even many side routes by which you can escape into the wilderness. The most convenient way to experience the area is through the window of a train or a postbus, both of which offer scenic rides through different valleys – notably the sensational ride up to the **Albula** pass by train. Note that, in winter, the Albula road is closed above Preda, but the Julier pass road is kept clear.

Thusis and Tiefencastel

The train from Chur to St Moritz heads west to the road and rail junction of **Reichenau** before cutting south into the Hinterrhein valley to the village of **RHÄZÜNS**. On a forested rise down by the river, ten minutes' walk north of Rhäzüns, is the isolated Carolingian chapel of **Sogn Gieri** (St George; Ⓦ www.kirchgemeinde-rhaezuens.ch), its interior covered with amazingly fresh fifteenth-century frescoes (chapel kept locked; key and map at Rhäzüns station). Further south, the valley sides close in, opening out again beyond Rothenbrunnen below the sharp ridges of the **Domleschg** to the east that crest 2500m, and the gentler slopes of the **Heinzenberg** to the west.

Some 12km south of Rhäzüns is the town of **Thusis**, loomed over by precipitous mountains and thick forest. From here, the main road continues south via the **San Bernardino Pass** and tunnel (see p.494). Another road swings east, shadowed by the train line which coils into the deep ravine of the **Albula** valley for a memorably dramatic journey to St Moritz, passing below sheer cliffs, through 16 tunnels and over 27 bridges, including the famous Landwasser viaduct near Filisur, its lofty arches adorning most RhB publicity material. An alternative route, followed by postbuses, is via the **Julier Pass**.

Roads and the rail line meet at the small valley-bottom crossroads town of **TIEFENCASTEL**, its prominent white church saving it from being lost altogether in the thick pine forests on all sides. Aside from Thusis, 12km west, every route from Tiefencastel is up: north 35km to Chur, south to the Julier Pass, southeast to the Albula Pass, and northeast 37km to Davos. About ten minutes east of Tiefencastel by train, you pass over what must be the most photographed bridge in Switzerland, the elegant, six-arched **Landwasser Viaduct**, which carries the curving track a soaring 65m above the valley floor into the Landwasser Tunnel, drilled out partway up the sheer cliff face. From the train window you see the vertiginous drop, but from a bend on the main Davos road, between Alvaneu and Schmitten villages, you can stand below the viaduct for the full, photogenic effect.

The Albula route

Trains towards St Moritz branch off to climb south into the beautiful **Albula** valley (Ⓦ www.albula.ch), marked by the little station at **FILISUR** (1084m). The line from here up to Preda (1792m) is renowned for its extraordinary engineering: the line gains over 700m in a distance, as the crow flies, of around 13km. The road, which runs alongside, is extremely steep, while the rail track coils around on itself in a series of tight hairpins, especially pronounced after **BERGÜN**, a pretty little village clustered around a photogenic central square. Above Bergün the track switchbacks eight times in a series of corkscrew tunnels back and forth, crossing five viaducts; the engineering achievement is mind-boggling. At **PREDA**, little more than a hamlet, the train enters a short tunnel – the highest rail tunnel in the Alps, at 1820m – emerging in the Val Bever for the short ride down to **Samedan**, in the Engadine Valley. The road, though, continues above Preda, breaking the treeline to the 2312m **Albula Pass** (June–Oct) – which has a restaurant on top – before coiling sharply down to the valley floor at La Punt.

Bergün tourist office (☎081 407 11 52, ⓦwww.berguen.ch), on the main street, has details of local walking routes and information about one of Switzerland's most famous winter **toboggan runs**: you rent wooden sleds from Preda station for the rapid 5km slide to Bergün, from where trains cart you back up to Preda for another go (Fr.33 for a day ticket). Trains run late into the evening, so you can sled the illuminated route by night (not Mon).

The Julier route

On a different, train-free route, south of Tiefencastel, a dramatic road climbs in a series of broad plateaux – each more beautiful than the last – towards the Julier Pass, an often-busy route favoured by trucks. The major resort, just beyond Cunter, is Romansh-speaking **SAVOGNIN**, a family-friendly spot in the broad, sunny Surses valley. Its chairlift up to Somtgant (2112m) gives access to a "Veia Panorama" trail (2hr 30min) to Radons and down to the chairlift mid-station of Tigignas. Mountain-bike routes abound, as well as, in winter, some very scenic blue and red ski runs down from Piz Martegnas (2670m), plus tobogganing, boarding and snowshoeing. The **tourist office**, on the main road Stradung (☎081 659 16 16, ⓦwww.savognin.ch), has full details.

Further up at 1769m, past the startlingly beautiful Lai da Marmorera set amongst the pines and rocky crags, lies **BIVIO**, the only settlement north of the Alps with an Italian-speaking majority – although in true Swiss style this little village also has Romansh and German speakers and Catholic and Protestant churches. Bivio sits near the treeline amidst dramatic upland country, and has plenty of outdoorsy activities: the little **tourist office** (Mon–Fri 8.30–11am & 3–5.30pm; ☎081 684 53 23, ⓦwww.bivio.ch), within the Banca Cantonale, can advise. The cosy **hotel** *Solaria* (☎081 684 51 07, ⓦwww.hotelsolariabivio.ch; ❸) is known for its summer **horse-riding** packages, which include a guided ride over the isolated Septimer Pass (2310m), including full board and baggage transport (Fr.480/600 for two/three days).

About 10km south is the **Julier Pass** (Pass dal Güglia; 2284m), the heights of which are still marked by the column stumps of a long-demolished Roman temple. Silvaplana (see p.520) lies on the other side.

The San Bernardino route

Some 5km south of Thusis, the main road plunges into a ravine, with sheer rock walls barely 10m apart rising some 500m from the bed of the foaming Hinterrhein. This **Via Mala** (Evil Road) was first constructed in 1473, various improvements since then resulting in a web of bridges spanning the gorge. At one point, you can descend 321 steps to the valley floor to see both the ancient original road and the bridges lined up way overhead (daily: May–Oct 8am–7pm, March, April & Nov 9am–6pm; Fr.5; ⓦwww.thusis-viamala.ch). See also ⓦwww.viaspluga.com for details of hikes in the area.

The gorge opens up 3km further at the farming village of **ZILLIS** (Ziràn in Romansh), whose small **Kirche St Martin** (Baselgia Sontg Martegn; ⓦwww .zillis-st-martin.ch) – sporting a huge external mural of St Christopher, patron saint of travellers – has a remarkable twelfth-century wooden ceiling, divided into 153 painted panels (there's a stack of mirrors by the door to save you cricking your neck). Around the edge runs a depiction of the sea, with angels in the corners representing the four winds. The interior panels feature stories from the life of Christ, which start at the east (choir) end and run row by row to the west (door). Christ crowned with thorns is the last of the biblical scenes, since the final row, instead of depicting the Crucifixion and Resurrection, is devoted to scenes from the life of St Martin, implying that the original artist was, for some reason, unable to complete his intended story-cycle.

The main road bends west 6km south of Zillis. From **Andeer**, a lonely road penetrates some 25km up the remote Val Ferrera, flanked by 3000m-plus peaks. After a handful of waterfalls and widely spaced hamlets comes **Juf**, a cluster of farmhouses which, at 2126m, claims the title of the highest permanently occupied village in Europe. Tough full-day hiking routes lead over the mountains to Bivio.

Splügen and the San Bernardino Pass

The road from Zillis heads through the deep Rheinwald forest to the dourly picturesque village of **SPLÜGEN**, with a jumble of traditional slate-roofed houses, a **tourist office** (☎081 650 90 30, ⓦwww.splugen.ch), a year-round **campsite** (☎081 664 14 76) and four **hotels**, including the *Pratigiana*, an old smugglers' haunt (☎081 664 11 10; ❸). See p.484 for details of a long-distance hike that passes this way. The **Splügen Pass** (2113m), 10km south of the village and reached via a twisting minor road, marks the Italian border; postbuses head on to **Chiavenna**, 30km south, from where different buses run back into Switzerland up the Val Bregaglia (see p.521) to St Moritz.

From Splügen, the main road climbs west in the shadow of the giant Zapport-gletscher, one of the sources of the Rhine, to the **San Bernardino Pass** (2065m). The pass route (closed in winter) is undercut by a road tunnel (open year-round), which feeds south into the long, Italian-speaking Valle Mesolcina on the route to Bellinzona (see p.521): once you're out of the mountains, vines, fig trees and chestnut forests spring up all around, giving a hint of the lushness of Ticino spreading out below.

Surselva

A straight road west from Chur shadows the train line into the big, broad wooded valley of the River Vorderrhein, a patch of countryside known in Romansh as **Surselva**, the High Forests. The linked ski and sports resorts of **Flims–Laax–Falera** are within easy reach of Chur. Further west, a handful of quiet towns is capped at the end of the valley by a Benedictine abbey at **Disentis/Mustér**, staging post for journeys south into Ticino over the Lukmanier Pass (Lucomagno), and west towards Andermatt via the Oberalp Pass.

Flims-Laax-Falera

On a hillside above the Rhine 18km west of Chur, the attractive resort of **FLIMS** is well known to the Swiss, who consistently pack the place out every season, but is much less known abroad, although it offers some of the best snowboarding facilities in the canton. There are two parts: **Flims-Dorf** is the older, original village with most amenities and the base station for the ski lifts, while on a slightly higher elevation 1km south is **Flims-Waldhaus**, a newer, quieter area set amidst beech and larch woods, with most of the hotels. Some 5km south of Waldhaus is the village of **LAAX**, with tiny **FALERA** up a 3km branch road completing the picture. All three share the extensive **Alpenarena** ("Alpine Arena") ski region.

Along with most of the Romansh-speaking areas of Graubünden, Surselva has kept hold of many ancient **customs** rooted in pagan, Roman or early Christian seasonal rites. These generally hold more significance for those taking part than for outside observers, but there are some rituals – most notably winter ones – which are worth looking out for. At Epiphany (Jan 6), the village of **Breil/Brigels** 12km west of Ilanz resounds to traditional songs as groups representing the Three Wise Men deliver the Christmas message. After nightfall on Easter Sunday, young men gather on the hillside above two hamlets beside Breil/Brigels, **Dardin** and **Danis-Tavanasa**, and ceremonially fling discs of burning wood known as *trer schibettas* down into the valley while pledging their love to a particular woman; tradition has it that it's possible to predict the success or failure of the match depending on the flight of the disc. Carnival in **Domat/Ems**, 6km west of Chur, is celebrated as Tschaiver with masked festivities on both Mardi Gras (*margis bel*, or Beautiful Tuesday) and the following Thursday (*gievgia grassa*, or Fat Thursday).

No trains pass this way, but Flims is served by regular postbuses from Chur. The main **tourist offices** are in Flims Dorf and Waldhaus (Mon–Fri 8am–6pm, Sat 8am–4pm; Dec–April also Sun 8am–noon; ☎081 920 92 00, ⊛www.alpenarena.ch), with branch offices in Laax and Falera. All local transport is free with the Guest Card.

Best reason to **stay** is to experience the stunning, hi-tech 🏂 **Riders Palace** (☎081 927 97 00, ⊛www.riderspalace.ch; ❸–❺), near the Murschetg base station in Laax, perhaps the coolest hotel in the Swiss Alps. The architecture is striking, an innovative juxtaposition of untreated larch wood and glittering walls of glass, giving floor-to-ceiling panoramic views over the forest and slopes. Everything is geared to a young, sporty clientele: all room rates include a lift pass (which is also valid for the day you arrive and the day you check out), whether you opt for a bed in a shared room, a double or a Starck-designed suite. The slick, minimalist guest rooms and the 24-hour hotel bar feature plasma-screen TVs, sound systems, games consoles and more, while the basement club hosts international DJs every weekend throughout the winter (past residences have included Ministry of Sound and Cream).

Less trendy options include the tiny, modern *Uaul Pign* in Waldhaus (☎081 911 13 39, ⊛www.kpage.ch/garni.htm; ❷), in a tranquil location well away from the road, its ten balconied rooms looking into the forest; and, in Laax, the quiet *Bellaval* (☎081 921 47 00, ⊛www.hotelbellaval.ch; ❸), with pleasant, well-appointed rooms. There are also plenty of dorm places, including the SB **hostel** *Backpacker Deluxe/Capricorn* in Laax (☎081 921 21 20, ⊛www.caprilounge.ch; ❷; dorms Fr.34) and the *Mountain Hostel* in an unbeatable location on the Crap Sogn Gion (☎081 927 73 73, ⊛www.mountainhostel-laax.ch; ❷).

Ilanz to Disentis/Mustér and beyond

Some 5km west of Laax is **ILANZ**, known in Romansh as **Glion**. These days it's a lively commercial and cultural hub, but in times gone by this was one of the most important towns in Graubünden. From the train station, a short wander through the centre will turn up a surprising number of stately sixteenth- and seventeenth-century town houses. The town's few **hotels** include the unassuming *Rätia*, Via Centrala 5 by the bridge (☎081 925 23 93, ⊛www.hotel-raetia.ch; ❷), with a nice little restaurant serving regional cuisine.

Sports and activities in Flims–Laax–Falera

The **Alpenarena** is a huge winter-sports area, the largest in Graubünden, with access from all three villages. From Laax-Murschetg, on the edge of Laax village, there's the choice of a cable car to the **Crap Sogn Gion** summit (2228m), or a gondola to the halfway point of Curnius (also accessed from Falera), from where a chairlift continues to the top. From there, a cable car continues to **Crap Masegn** (2477m) and on up to the **Vorab** (2570m), a glacier region with year-round skiing and snowboarding courtesy of T-bars rising to 3018m. From Flims-Dorf a combination of chairlifts and a cable car serve various points on the adjacent **Cassons Grat** (2634m). Aside from the host of blue and reasonably testing red ski runs all over the mountain – and a huge 14km run from Vorab all the way down to Flims – there's plenty for freeriders, with 40km of marked but unprepared runs, and superb facilities for **snowboarders**, with seven halfpipes and boarderparks, including ones way up at 3000m and, allegedly, the world's largest halfpipe (up to 6.7m height). Passes cost Fr.62/306 for one/six days.

In **summer**, the hiking network is extensive, plenty of trails winding their way through the forest. Alternatively, take the chairlift up to the broad, level plateau atop the Cassons Grat, where there's a pleasant three-hour circular walk offering Alpine panoramas. The three-hour trek from Falera up to Crap Sogn Gion, and 3.5km along the crest to Crap Masegn, is especially beautiful too. Swissraft (ⓦwww.swissraft.ch) runs **white-water rafting** trips between Ilanz and Reichenau.

West of Ilanz, there's little to stop for until, after 28km, the huge white abbey of **DISENTIS** (also known by its Romansh name of **MUSTÉR**) hoves into view. A Benedictine community was founded here, at the foot of Alpine pass roads, in the eighth century, only to be sacked by a marauding Saracen army in 940. Later churches were replaced in the late seventeenth century by the current Baroque building, which today houses about forty priests and novices. The white interior of the great **abbey church** (ⓦwww.kloster-disentis.ch) is immediately impressive, not least because of the startling contrast of such lavish ornament with the wild countryside all about. Built in 1712 by Kaspar Moosbrugger, architect of the church at Einsiedeln, it is covered in gilt and ornate stucco, with light flooding in from high windows and a deep choir. An internal passageway in the west wall signposts the way through corridors and up stairs to the still and silent Marienkirche, its triple apse surviving as the only remnant of the tenth-century church sacked by the Saracens.

From Disentis, the road and rail line climb west to **Sedrun** and on over the **Oberalp Pass** (2033m; see p.400) to Andermatt, while a branch road cuts south from Disentis to cross the **Lukmanier Pass** (1914m; see p.536) to Olivone.

Vals

From Ilanz, a couple of minor roads penetrate two beautiful side valleys, known for their meadowland and cherry trees. One climbs through the Romansh-speaking **Val Lumnezia** to the hamlet of Vrin, while the other splits off into the deep, high **Valsertal**, named for its thirteenth-century Walser colonizers and still German-speaking today. The valley rises to the village of **VALS** (1252m), best known as the source of Valser bottled water, where the architect Peter Zumthor has built one of Switzerland's finest modern buildings, the spectacular ⚘ **Therme Vals** baths and hotel (☎081 926 80 80, ⓦwww.therme-vals.ch; ❹–❼; closed May & Nov). The building – composed of 60,000 bonded slabs of local quartzite – is effortlessly sleek and sensuous, all water, natural light, wood and polished stone. The **spa** (Mon 11am–9pm, Tues–Sun 11am–8pm; Fr.30) has

⑪

GRAUBÜNDEN | Surselva

every facility, including therapy treatments. Guests at the stylish attached **hotel** benefit from extended hours and discounts – as well as a visit to remember. This place is very much worth the detour.

Davos and Klosters

From the junction point of **Landquart**, north of Chur, roads and rail lines meander up the Prättigau ("Meadow Valley") to two of the most famous names in the Alps, enjoying some of the best skiing in the world: first **Klosters**, then, beyond the Wolfgang Pass, **Davos**. Walser migrants arrived in the valley in the thirteenth century, and the area – surrounded on three sides by Romansh – remains German-speaking today. The focus is fair and square on outdoorsiness: skiing and snowboarding in the winter, hiking and mountain-biking in the summer.

Sports and activities in Davos and Klosters

The options for outdoors activity are almost limitless: the best advice is to check ⓦ www.davosklosters.ch for up-to-date details. Look out for good-value winter and summer package deals at hotels, which often include a free lift pass.

Winter
The **skiing** is outstanding. Although the two resorts are quite far apart, they share the same ski area and lift pass; the prime attraction is being able to swoosh down broad, well-tended pistes which go on and on, for more than 10km in many cases from mountaintop to valley bottom. There are 99 downhill pistes, totalling an impressive 321km – half of them intermediate (red), a third beginner (blue) and the rest expert (black).

The big focus of attention is the **Parsenn** ski area on the north side of Davos and the west side of Klosters, centred on the Weissfluh summit. It has only three methods of access. The **Parsennbahn** funicular starts from Davos-Dorf and rises to the Weissfluhjoch saddle just below the summit; the little **Schatzalpbahn** funicular (ⓦ www.schatzalp.ch) from Davos-Platz takes you to a broad snow shelf, from where you must switch to chairlifts and gondolas for the journey further up; while the **Gotschnagrat** cable car rises from Klosters station to a ridge just east of the Weissfluh. On the mountain are plenty of draglifts serving dozens of blue and red runs, including giant, weaving pistes from the summit down through the trees to hamlets such as Küblis, Saas and Serneus. For more testing runs, you could attempt the notorious Gotschnawang or a handful of black runs on the lower, steep slopes above Davos-Dorf and Wolfgang.

Moving onto one of the four other ski sectors can take you away from the crowds. From Davos-Platz, cable cars rise to the **Jakobshorn**, with a hatful of scenic blues and reds. Bus #1 from Davos-Dorf serves Dörfji, the base station of the cable car up to **Pischa**, while a gondola from Davos-Glaris (bus #7) rises to the **Rinerhorn**, which has lifts going higher to access blues, reds and a testing black run. A gondola from Klosters-Dorf climbs east to **Madrisa**, also with plenty of long, exciting reds on pistes which hug the Austrian border. **Snowboarders** should aim principally for the Parsenn, although the Jakobshorn is the focus of a hip boarding fraternity and there's scope for experimentation on the Madrisa as well.

Passes, considering the range on offer, are excellent value. A RegionPass for all areas (excluding use of Schatzalpbahn) for 3/6 days is Fr.169/282. A day pass for

If you stay overnight in either resort, you'll receive a very useful **Guest Card**, which gives free transport locally plus a range of other discounts. Beware that almost everything in both resorts – shops, hotels, attractions, walking routes – is **closed during off-season** (mid-April to mid-June & mid-Oct to mid-Dec). We've specified months of opening only when they differ from this pattern.

Davos

Twinned in a touristic masterstroke with Aspen, Colorado, **DAVOS** (1560m) is the antithesis of a peaceful Alpine ski village. It's a bustling, sometimes impatient town, famous for its toothpaste-fresh air and its consistently excellent snow cover. It has been attracting **skiers** for generations and has gained new life (and hipness) with the seal of approval of Switzerland's **snowboarding** cognoscenti. In summer, the snows recede to reveal a surrounding of lush countryside and the town takes on a new lease of life – not least because hotel prices plummet. The location, in a high, narrow valley between two lines of peaks, is stunning.

the Parsenn and Gotschna is Fr.60, for the Jakobshorn Fr.55, for Madrisa, Pischa or Rinerhorn Fr.47. Part-day and selected-day tickets are available. **Schools**, which vary in facilities and prices, include, in Davos ⓦwww.ssd.ch and ⓦwww.newtrenddavos .ch; in Klosters ⓦwww.bananas.net and ⓦwww.adventure-skiing.ch.

Both resorts have tons of other diversions, including indoor swimming, ice-skating, tobogganing and snowshoe-trekking. Tandem **paragliding** flights cost around Fr.160 at ⓦwww.luftchraft.ch or ⓦwww.fs-grischa.ch. Major **winter events** include the international ice-hockey Spengler Cup (late Dec; ⓦwww.spenglercup.ch).

Summer

In summer, the opportunities for **hiking** and **mountain-biking** are excellent. The "**Davos Inclusive**" scheme grants free travel on all mountain transport plus local trains (including Klosters) with a Guest Card, obtainable if you stay overnight in the resort.

Both tourist offices run full-day guided **walks**, free with a Guest Card, that cover some difficult territory – over the Vereina pass, for instance – but it's easy to strike out alone. From the Weissfluhjoch, accessed by the Parsennbahn (or a 3–4hr walk up), the views of Piz Buin and beyond are spectacular, even better from the Weissfluhgipfel summit, served by a cable car from the funicular top-station. Invigorating walks head down to Davos (2hr) or Klosters (4hr), or there's a testing route over to Arosa (6hr). From the Gotschnagrat, a fairly tough hike leads to Casanna Alp, then Serneuser Schwendi and on down to Klosters (3hr). Easier walks abound, not least in the meadows and woods around the little Davosersee. A stroll from the top of the Schatzalpbahn brings you to the **Alpinum**, a hillside botanical garden (mid-May to mid-Oct daily 9am–5pm; Fr.5). There are some leg-stretching trails from the Pischa and Jakobshorn summits back to Davos (2–3hr). Top choice from Klosters is the **Madrisa Rundtour**, a two/three-day walk into Austria and back; the price (from Fr.94) includes B&B and cable cars.

There are plenty of **mountain-bike** routes around Davos, including several routes along the valley floor west as far as Wiesen (31km round trip), and a classic 20km run from the Weissfluhjoch down to Küblis. ⓦwww.bike-erlebnis.ch has more. Other activities include tandem paragliding, curling, inline skating, sailing, volleyball, windsurfing, golf, clay-pigeon shooting, horse riding, mule- or llama-trekking and tons more. Major **summer events** include the gruelling Swiss Alpine Marathon (late July; ⓦwww.alpine-davos.ch).

△ Snowboarder, Davos

Davos achieved fame as a **health resort**, its high altitude and long hours of sunshine easing the suffering of tuberculosis patients: by 1900, ten years after the railway arrived – and long before winter sports were even thought of – there were 700,000 overnight visitors a year. The consumptive Robert Louis Stevenson completed *Treasure Island* while resident at a Davos sanatorium in 1882; Sir Arthur Conan Doyle stayed in 1894–95 and was the first person in Davos to ski; and in 1912, Thomas Mann was inspired while visiting Davos to write *The Magic Mountain*. Although many clinics have now closed, a few remain: modern science has confirmed the beneficial effects of high altitude on respiratory and dermatological complaints. The town also has one of the world's best-equipped **high-altitude sports training** facilities, used by athletes and international football teams to improve fitness and stamina.

Another hat worn by Davos is that of a major international **conference** venue: in the last week of January each year, presidents, prime ministers and assorted mega-suits of the World Economic Forum meet at Davos under the gaze of the world's media to discuss global cashflow and set the financial agenda for the year ahead, regularly sparking anti-capitalist demonstrations in the process.

Arrival, information and accommodation

The two contiguous halves of the town, **Davos-Platz** and **Davos-Dorf**, are strung along a four-kilometre ribbon of low-key development in the Landwasser valley. Approaching from Klosters, you'll pass the picturesque little Davosersee before arriving at Dorf, generally the quieter district. The main street, **Promenade**, lined with shops and hotels, feeds traffic one-way from Dorf past the huge Congress Centre to bustling Platz, home to most of the nightlife; parallel one block downhill (south) is quieter **Talstrasse**, which is one-way from Platz to Dorf. The Weissfluh (2844m) rises immediately to the north, flanked by the Strelagrat (2545m) and Schwarzhorn (2670m). The Jakobshorn (2590m) looms on the other, south, side of the town. There are outlying suburbs on both sides, linked to Davos by bus and train, but they're quiet communities with few facilities: east of Dorf is Davos-Wolfgang and Laret, west of Platz is Davos-Glaris and Frauenkirch.

Davos lies at the far end of a circular **train** line from Chur: the eastern half runs from Landquart through Klosters, the western half from Filisur. Service is half-hourly but almost always requires a change: the only through trains are the Glacier Express and Bernina Express. **Davos-Platz** is the main terminus, although all trains to and from Klosters/Landquart also stop at Davos-Dorf. **Postbuses** run direct from Chur.

There are two branches of the **tourist office** – the main one at Promenade 67 in the middle of Platz (Mon–Fri 8.30am–6.30pm, Sat 9am–5.30pm; April

to mid-June & mid-Oct to Nov Sat closes noon; Dec–March also Sun 10am–
noon & 3–5.30pm; ☎081 415 21 21, ⓦwww.davos.ch), plus a branch office
opposite Dorf station (slightly curtailed hours). VBD **city buses** (free with a
Guest Card) stop at all points of interest, and also run out to Wolfgang, Glaris
and the Pischa base station.

Hotels

Alte Post Berglistutz 4, Platz ☎081 413 54 03,
ⓦwww.davosklosters.ch. Serviceable little two-
star place beside Platz station that offers cut-price
winter weekend deals. ❸

Bahnhof-Terminus Talstrasse 3, Platz ☎081 414
97 97, ⓦwww.bahnhof-terminus.ch. Large, airy
rooms and private parking directly opposite Platz
station. ❸–❹

Berghotel Schatzalp On Schatzalp above Platz
☎081 415 51 51, ⓦwww.schatzalp.ch. This old
Jugendstil sanatorium (now a three-star hotel)
is the most characterful accommodation around,
perched on a tranquil terrace 300m above the town
and only accessible by funicular. Views over the
Jakobshorn and beyond from the ranks of balconied rooms – which boast up to four more hours of
sunshine per day than the town – are well worth
paying for. ❹–❻

🏃 **Bünda** Museumstrasse 4, Dorf ☎081
417 18 19, ⓦwww.buendadavos.ch.
Outstanding three-star hotel a short walk from
the Parsennbahn at the foot of the slopes in a
perfectly peaceful location. Service is friendly and
helpful, and the rooms – whether the smaller ones
in the main building, or bigger, better ones in the
connected Residenz alongside – are characterful
and well-equipped. ❸–❺

Davoserhof Berglistutz 2, Platz ☎081 414
90 20, ⓦwww.davosklosters.ch. Comfortable,
well appointed three-star hotel alongside Platz
station that has an discreet air about it. A well-
managed blend of luxury with a rustic, country
atmosphere. ❸

Edelweiss Rossweidstrasse 9, Platz ☎081 416
10 33, ⓦwww.edelweiss-davos.ch. One of the
best in this price range, with private parking and a
welcoming, comfortable atmosphere. ❸–❹

Pischa Strelastrasse 2, Platz ☎081 415 50 50,
ⓦwww.hotel-pischa.ch. Pleasant, quiet hotel, way
up above Platz (with a free shuttle bus up and
down the hill) and freshly renovated throughout:
rooms are airy and spacious. Relatively small price-
hike makes it good value in winter. ❹–❺

Soliva Symondsstrasse 7, Platz ☎081 416 57 27.
Small, quiet family-run B&B opposite the Congress
Centre. ❷

Hostel

Jugendherberge "Youth Palace" (HI hostel)
Horlaubenstrasse 27, Dorf ☎081 420 11 20,
ⓦwww.youthhostel.ch. Huge, 260-bed former
sanatorium that only does half-board deals,
summer and winter: dorm bed plus two meals from
Fr.45. ❷

The Kirchner Museum

Prime attraction for non-sports fans is the **Kirchner Museum**, 600m east of
the Platz tourist office at Promenade 82 (Tues–Sun: July–Sept & Christmas–
Easter 10am–6pm; rest of year 2–6pm; Fr.10; SMP; ⓦwww.kirchnermuseum
.ch). This impressively airy structure – designed as a series of cubes, with opaque
glass admitting diffuse daylight – houses a vibrant collection of artworks by the
German Expressionist painter Ernst Ludwig Kirchner. Born in 1880, Kirchner moved to Berlin in 1911, but after an intensive period of work his health
deteriorated rapidly. He emigrated to Davos in 1917 and lived in shacks out in
the countryside, where he painted prodigiously. In 1936, his work was tagged
"degenerate" by the Nazis and two years later in Davos, in a deep depression,
he committed suicide. The museum displays work from all periods of Kirchner's
life, including starkly stylish woodcuts and sketches from his time in Berlin and
dozens of expressive, highly colourful works painted in Davos.

Eating and drinking

Budget **eating** options include the *After Hours* convenience store, open 24
hours at Promenade 64. The ultra-swish *Choccolino*, Promenade 45, is a *confiserie* and café, with classical music at Sunday brunch time and a proper cup of

▲ Schatzalp

DAVOS

SCHATZALPSTRASSE

PRAVIGANWEG

EDENSTR.

OBERWIESSTRASSE

OBERE STRASSE

HOLSBERGWEG

OBERE STRASSE

Ⓐ

ⓘ 1

2

OBERE STRASSE

PROMENADE

SPORTWEG

**Kirchner
Museum**

BUOLSTR.

BUOLSTR.

PROMENADE

PROMENADE

GUGGERBACHSTRASSE

SCHULSTR.

TOBELMÜELISTRASSE

EISBAHNSTRASSE

KURGARTENSTRASSE

PROMENADE

3

**DAVOS
PLATZ**

**Sports
Centre**

PROMENADE

BAHNHOFSTR. PL.

BÜELSTUTZ

4

TOBELMÜELISTRASSE

**Congress
Centre**

Ⓓ **Platz
Station**

Ⓔ

6

TALSTRASSE

RIEDSTR.

MITTELSTR.

FLUESTR.

LINARDSTR.

HEIMSTR.

TALSTRASSE

HERTISTRASSE

BRÄMABÜELSTRASSE

DAMMSTRASSE

DAMMWEG

SKISTRASSE

SKISTRASSE

Glaris & Filisur ◀

Filisur ◀

◀

← Landwasser

MATTASTRASSE

LÄRCHENRING

FÖHRENWEG

MATTASTRASSE

▼ Jakobshorn

tea. There's a handful of simple pizza/pasta restaurants where you can eat for around Fr.20: *Albana*, Talstrasse 18, is one of the cosier options; *Dischma*, Promenade 128, is another, also with good *rösti* and fondues. The large *Hotel Europe*, Promenade 63, shelters the bright and modern *Scala* restaurant, with inexpensive pizzas and daily *menus*. The *Goldener Drachen* restaurant in *Hotel Bahnhof-Terminus* is the best Chinese in town, serving authentic cuisine for around Fr.25. The *Hotel Bünda* restaurant has excellent Bündner specialities, including game.

Although Davos has several **gourmet restaurants**, for the best local dining experience you need to head out towards Wolfgang: *Hubli's Landhaus* (☎081 417 10 10, Ⓦwww.hublis.ch; closed Mon) is a cosy, attractive country inn with a Michelin-starred restaurant, offering light, creative international cuisine for less than you might expect (around Fr.60 per head).

Focus of Platz's buzzing **nightlife** is the *Ex-Bar*, Promenade 63 by the tourist office, which only really gets going after 2am. The *Chämi*, 200m east, is another very popular choice. There are pool tables in the *Hotel Montana's* lively bar, and cocktail pianists in the *Hotel Europa*, which also hosts the *Cabanna* club and a swanky casino.

Klosters

Instantly recognizable to Britons as being the favoured winter getaway of Prince Charles and his family, little **KLOSTERS** (1190m) – about 9km northeast of Davos, below the Wolfgang Pass – steals quite a march on its neighbour in terms of ambience. Where Davos has traffic, bright lights, street bustle and concrete multistorey hotels, Klosters has peace and quiet, an appealing huddle of dark-wood chalets and a village atmosphere. It's linked to Davos's Parsenn ski slopes, and the two share a lift pass covering each other's pistes and mountain transport: in choosing a base, you could do worse than shun Davos altogether. Details of sports and activities are on p.498.

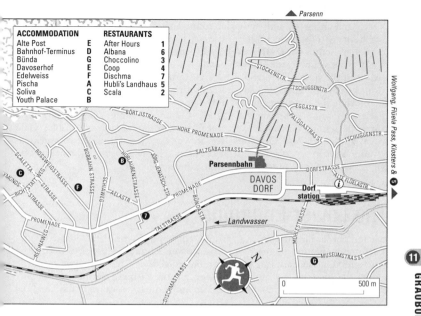

ACCOMMODATION		RESTAURANTS	
Alte Post	E	After Hours	1
Bahnhof-Terminus	D	Albana	6
Bünda	G	Choccolino	3
Davoserhof	E	Coop	4
Edelweiss	F	Dischma	7
Pischa	A	Hubli's Landhaus	5
Soliva	C	Scala	2
Youth Palace	B		

STOCKENSTR.
TSCHUGGENSTR.
EGGASTR.
PALÜDASTRASSE
TSCHUGGENSTR.
BÖRTJISTRASSE
HOHE PROMENADE
SALZGÄBASTRASSE
DORFSTRASSE
SCALETTA
ROSSWEIDSTRASSE
BOBBAHN STRASSE
OBERLAUBENSTRASSE
JÖRG-JENATSCH-STR.
PROMENADE
Parsennbahn
DAVOS DORF
ALTE FLÜELASTR.
Dorf station
i
YMONOS...STRASSE
RICHT..STRASSE
SCHIAWEG
AELASTR.
PROMENADE
BONDASTR.
TALSTRASSE
← *Landwasser*
MÜHLESTRASSE
PROMENADE
REGINAWEG
DISCHMASTRASSE
N
MUSEUMSTRASSE

0   500 m

Klosters Platz is the centre of things, and has the main train station; the smaller, quieter **Klosters Dorf** sits 2km north, with its own station. Both are on the Landquart–Davos line, and are also linked by town buses, which are free with the resort's Guest Card. The main **tourist office** is in Platz, by the station (Mon–Fri 8.30am–6pm, Sat & Sun 8.30am–4pm; shorter hours in off-season; ☎081 410 20 20, ⓦ www.klosters.ch). There's a branch office at Albeina Sport in Dorf, keeping similar hours.

Klosters has many fewer hotels than Davos, with a greater proportion of upmarket properties. The cosy HI **hostel** *Soldanella Jugendherberge* is at Talstrasse 73, a fifteen-minute climb above Platz (☎081 422 13 16, ⓦ www.youthhostel .ch; ❶; dorms Fr.29). The weathered-wood *Sonne*, Hauptstrasse 155 (☎081 422 13 49, ⓦ www.sonne-klosters.ch; ❷), is one of the best low-end **hotels**, with simple shared-bath rooms, some with balcony. The family-run *Silvapina*, on the edge of Dorf near the Madrisabahn, Silvapinaweg 6 (☎081 422 14 68, ⓦ www .silvapina.ch; ❷–❹), is a fine choice, with attractive guest rooms and good service. *Chesa Grischuna*, Bahnhofstrasse 12 in Platz (☎081 422 22 22, ⓦ www .chesagrischuna.ch; ❺–❻), may look like a tumbledown old chalet from the outside, but is one of the liveliest and chicest places in town, with a good deal

Car-carrying trains: the Vereina Tunnel

The **Vereina tunnel** (see ⓦ www.rhb.ch) runs under the Alps between **Selfranga** (just outside Klosters) and **Sagliains** (a little west of Scuol). It is over 19km long, the longest narrow-gauge rail tunnel in the world. Drive-on drive-off **car-carrying trains** run through the tunnel all year round (daily every 30min 5.30am–9pm; takes 20min; a car plus 9 people costs Fr.27 summer, Fr.35 winter, Fr.40 midwinter weekends; no reservations). The parallel Flüela Pass road is closed in winter.

of style and character, with cut-price rooms in a chalet annexe. Prince Charles's establishment of choice is the *Walserhof*, Landstrasse 141 (☎081 410 29 29, ⓦ www.walserhof.ch; ❺–❼), a relatively small, cosy Relais & Châteaux hotel that displays a superb attention to detail.

Most of the hotels listed above have **restaurants** attached: the *Sonne* (closed Mon & Tues) is a good budget choice, with good regional *menus* starting from Fr.16, while the *Vereina* restaurant in the heart of Platz serves quality pizzas. The modest *Wynegg*, Landstrasse 205 (☎081 422 13 40; winter only), enjoys royal patronage, serving beer and hearty meals that are surprisingly affordable; while to eat at chichi *Chesa Grischuna* (see above), you should book two weeks in advance and expect to lose a fistful of francs. The *Walserhof* restaurant has two Michelin stars for its outstanding cuisine and service.

The Lower Engadine

Beyond the mountains, in the farthest corner of Switzerland – and requiring some dedication to reach – is the **Lower Engadine** (Engiadina Bassa in Romansh, Unterengadin in German). Remote from Chur, let alone from the rest of the country, this attractive valley nurtures a quite distinct, thoroughly Romansh culture that has flourished in isolation for centuries: although the

---

Romansh

Romansh is the fourth language of Switzerland and the principal everyday tongue of some 70,000 people in Graubünden. If you stick to the main tourist centres of Chur, Davos and St Moritz, you'll probably see and hear only Swiss German, but if you venture to smaller countryside towns, you'll find signs to the *staziun* pointing along Via Principala, and hear people greeting each other with "Allegra!" or "Bun di!" in what sounds like Italian with a Swiss-German accent. For a glossary of Romansh words and phrases, see p.608.

History
Romansh can trace its roots directly back to Latin, fountainhead for all the Romance languages of Europe. After the Roman conquests, so-called **Vulgar Latin**, spoken by soldiers, merchants and officials, slowly merged with the pre-existing languages of conquered areas, giving rise to four main linguistic groups: Ibero-Romance, including Spanish, Catalan and Portuguese; Gallo-Romance, mainly French; Italian; and **Rhaeto-Romance**, comprising Friulian and Ladin, two languages spoken by around 750,000 people in the extreme north of Italy, and Romansh, spoken only in Graubünden. The first significant inroads made by outsiders into the isolated Romansh-speaking mountain communities was in the thirteenth century, when German-speaking Walsers from Canton Valais settled in some of the high valleys; their legacy survives to this day, with Davos (once called Tavau, the Romansh word for "alp") still majority Swiss-German, and German-speaking communities clustered together in otherwise Romansh Surselva. In 1464, a huge fire destroyed Chur; the arrival of craftspeople from the north to rebuild virtually erased the town's Romansh culture and language.

In the mid-nineteenth century Romansh was still counted as the native tongue of over half the population of Graubünden, but the development of roads and railways penetrating remote valleys led to greater and greater erosion, as the Romansh people themselves realized that their language was an impediment to getting well-paid

Austrian Tyrol is just a few kilometres away on the north side of the Piz Buin range, it might just as well be on the other side of the continent. The succession of hamlets which cling to the banks of the foaming **River Inn** (**En** in Romansh), tumbling its way towards Innsbruck, the Danube and eventually the Black Sea, show their Latin origins as much as does the language of their inhabitants: thick-walled houses stuccoed in cream abound, complete with small, deep-set windows and scarlet geraniums sprouting from every window-box, reminiscent of Mediterranean village architecture found much further south. Everywhere you'll see the characteristic *sgraffiti* decoration: ornate, curli-cued designs, pictures and even mottoes or dedications etched into the white stuccoed facade of a house to reveal a darker, coloured layer beneath. The beautifully decorated cottages and quaint cobbled squares, set against a tremendous backdrop of dark pine forests and looming mountains, combine to give the valley a uniquely fairy-tale air.

Scuol is the main town of the valley, prefaced by a succession of charming cliffside villages such as Guarda and Ftan. **Zernez** serves as the gateway for exploration of the **Parc Naziunal Svizzer**, the sole national park, a vast chunk of highland wilderness. Beyond the park in tiny **Müstair** village is one of Switzerland's greatest cultural treasures, a Carolingian church sporting perfectly preserved medieval frescoes.

Transport isn't easy. Trains from Landquart and Klosters run through the Vereina tunnel to the terminus at Scuol, while others from Pontresina or

work outside their traditional communities. With schools, churches and communes slowly switching over to German, a conscious effort began to preserve Romansh, with cultural groups promoting the language nationwide. In 1938, an amendment to the Swiss Constitution confirmed the status of Romansh as a **national language**. In 1996 a second constitutional amendment elevated Romansh to the status of a **semi-official language**, thereby preserving its status amongst Romansh communities, guaranteeing its appearance on official documents such as passports and in legislation affecting Romansh areas, and eliminating the requirement for Romansh-speakers to use any other language.

Dialects

Romansh is not a unified whole: there's a welter of dialects, which can vary dramatically. The word for "cup", for example, in German is *Tasse*, in Italian *tazza*, but in the **Sursilvan** dialect of Romansh, spoken west of Chur, it is *scadiola*; in the **Sutsilvan** of the Hinterrhein valley, *scariola*; in the **Surmiran** of the Julier and Albula valleys, *cuppegn*; in **Putèr**, spoken in the Upper Engadine, *coppa*; and in **Vallader**, spoken in the Lower Engadine, *cuppina*. In 1980, the **Lia Rumantscha**, a leading Romansh cultural organization (@www.liarumantscha.ch), put forward a proposal to regularize this mishmash. The result was the creation of **Rumantsch Grischun** ('Graubünden Romansh'), a composite written language formed by averaging out words across all five dialects. (Under this new system, "cup" became *cuppin*.) Nonetheless, despite the lack of a Romansh capital city able to provide a cultural and linguistic focus for the language, and the consequent reliance of Romansh-speakers on German-language companies for work and media for information, there was still some resistance to forming a hybrid in this way; today, local communities still stick to their own dialect in everyday life, and presenters on Radio Grischa and Radio Piz, Graubünden's two Romansh stations, speak their own dialects. @**www.mypledari.ch** is an online English-Romansh dictionary covering all five dialects plus Rumantsch Grischun.

Customs in the Lower Engadine

The communities of the Lower Engadine keep alive many ancient local **customs** as an expression of their Romansh heritage. In Ramosch and Tschlin, two hamlets 10km east of Scuol, the **Mattinadas**, held on January 2, can overshadow even Christmas and New Year. During the day, the local children parade through the village dragging a decorated sledge behind them and collecting home-made sweets and candy (*mattinadas*); after a communal feast, everyone then embarks on an evening of dancing, whereupon the kids sit down to another banquet, this time of traditional butter biscuits smothered in whipped cream. The whole procedure is then repeated either the next day, or on the Saturday following, by the young men of the village. Epiphany celebrations (Jan 6) take the form of **Bavania** or **Buania**. In the afternoon, the village girls gather together and draw lots to choose a lover; they then visit their allotted man and, to mark their conquest and Fate's irrevocable decision, they tie a red ribbon round his neck. Later that night, at the village dance, the girls are chaperoned by their ribboned partner... presumably happily ever after. In Scuol, the first Saturday in February sees the ceremonial torching of the **Hom d'strom** ("Man of Straw"), probably as a symbolic banishment of the winter. On March 1 many villages stage the children's festival of **Chalandamarz** or **Calonda mars**. This originates in the Roman New Year celebration *Calendae Martii*, which these days takes the form of a colourful spring parade with cowbell-ringing and traditional songs.

St Moritz (changing at Samedan) serve Zernez. To reach the Austrian border or Müstair, you're reliant on postbuses – but timetables can leave you waiting a couple of hours between buses: unless you're on an extended walking tour of the valley, driving is the transport of choice, allowing you to enjoy the sunset in Müstair and still make it to St Moritz by bedtime.

Scuol and around

The dramatic road from Davos over the icy Flüela Pass drops down into the Engadine at **Susch**, a perfect introduction to the valley, its cobbled alleys filled with the rushing noise of the River Inn. Set picturesquely amidst its *sgraffitied* houses is the Baselgia San Jon, with one tower Romanesque, the other late-Gothic. To the east, beyond the ruined hilltop castle of Chaschinas, rears the giant Piz Arpiglias (3027m). The road to Scuol continues through tremendous scenery between the high, wooded valley walls, past a string of alluring little villages. Some 7km northeast of Susch on a lofty perch above the river, **Guarda** is especially attractive, its architecture and traditional *sgraffiti* meriting a federal order of protection. Just beyond, **Ardez** and **Ftan** are both equally worthy of a stop.

Some 22km east of Susch, the lively town of **SCUOL** (pronounced *shkwol*), known as Schuls in German, is beautifully located in a sunny, open part of the valley at the end of the train line. Its reputation is built on its history as a spa town, and the main draw today is the pristine, modern **Bogn Engiadina** complex (Engadine Spa; daily 9am–10pm; ⓦ www.scuol.ch; Fr.25). It has a range of warm and hot pools, and offers treatments including saunas, massages and Finnish baths. Alternatively, you can opt for the works: warm and hot rooms, vapour baths, massages, mineral plunge pools and a heavenly two-hour session in the Roman-Irish baths (reserve one day ahead; Fr.66). You'll see "**Badekombi**" day-packages to the spa advertised widely, taking in train transport (often on the **Aqualino** train), bus transfers and admission, for Fr.55–65 from Davos, Klosters or St Moritz, Fr.76 from Chur. Behind the spa, quiet streets head down into Scuol's pretty **Old Town**, filled with traditional houses, tinkling fountains and a photogenic village square. The view of **Chaste Tarasp** (Tarasp Castle) on the opposite bank is now overshadowed by a modern hotel; the view from Ftan is better. The Motta Naluns **ski** area (2146m, with lifts up to 2800m) offers plenty of easy and intermediate runs, including long reds from Piz Champatsch 12km back down to Scuol, and plenty for snowboarders.

Practicalities

The valley has plenty of **places to stay**. In Ftan are the charming *Engiadina* (☎081 864 04 34, ⑩www.engiadina-ftan.ch; ❸–❹) and the superb, modern-styled *Haus Paradies* (☎081 861 08 08, ⑩www.paradieshotel.ch; ❺–❼). Both have outstanding restaurants, the latter with two Michelin stars. More modest, and remarkably good value, is the *Piz Buin*, at the edge of Guarda village (☎081 861 30 00, ⑩www.pizbuin.ch; ❸), a member of the "Silence" group. Cross the river from Ardez on a covered wooden bridge to Sent, location of the ultimate in tranquil campsites, *Sur En* (☎081 866 35 44), open year-round.

Scuol's **train station** is over 1km west of the centre, which is a bus ride or a ten-minute downhill walk away. The **tourist office** is on Stradun (Mon–Fri 8am–noon & 2–6.30pm, Sat 10am–noon & 2–6pm, Sun 10am–noon; shorter hours in off season; ☎081 861 22 22, ⑩www.scuol.ch). Scuol's main drag has plenty of ordinary **hotels**, but there are a couple of traditional *sgraffitied* gems on Plaz, the old village square: the lovely *Gabriel*, Rablüzza 159a (☎081 864 11 52, ⑩www.hotel-gabriel.ch; ❷–❸; closed May & Nov), is a rambling old house with terraces and roof gardens; *Engiadina*, Rablüzza 152 (☎081 864 14 21, ⑩www.engiadina-scuol.ch; ❸–❹; closed May & Nov), retains its oriel-windowed exterior.

Samnaun

East of Scuol, postbuses penetrate to the Austrian border and on to Landeck. Just before the frontier, a minor road curls back to climb into an isolated side-valley, at the end of which sits German-speaking **SAMNAUN** (1840m), a duty-free area and so crammed with banks, shops and cut-price petrol stations, all open long hours. In winter, Samnaun's snow facilities – which include the world's only double-decker cable car – link in with the network of pistes above the Austrian resort of **Ischgl** on the other side of a wall of 3000m peaks, taking in Europe's single largest snowboarding area; a six-day VIP pass valid on both resorts' lifts is Fr.270. Samnaun-Dorf **tourist office** (☎081 868 58 58, ⑩www .samnaun.ch) has full details. The best of the summer hikes from Samnaun is a tough, multi-day trail to Ischgl over the Zeblasjoch Pass.

Parc Naziunal Svizzer

Some 6km south of Susch sits the graceful little town of **ZERNEZ**, the slender white steeple of its church marking a junction of valleys: north is the Lower Engadine, south is the Upper Engadine, while to the east, a road leads through the **PARC NAZIUNAL SVIZZER** to the Ofenpass/Pass dal Fuorn and on into the Val Müstair. Although attractive enough in its own right, Zernez comes into its own as a staging post for hikes into the park, a pint-sized Alpine wilderness stretching for 169 square kilometres either side of the Ofen/Fuorn road.

Established in 1914, the park's credo is to leave nature well alone: absolutely everything, from the tiniest lichen to the breeding pairs of golden eagles, is protected. Forest fires are monitored but allowed to burn; injured animals are left to their own devices; and roaming wardens will impose fines should you so much as pick a flower. You're allowed to **walk** in the park (provided you don't step off the marked trails), but prominent noticeboards publish stringent **regulations** prohibiting everything from littering to making loud noises – with the result that the park remains pristine. Red and roe deer, ibex and chamois roam freely, as do hares, foxes and huge numbers of marmots. Wolves, lynxes and brown bears are all predicted to re-establish a permanent presence in the area in forthcoming years. Aside from the golden eagles, there are also bearded vultures, kestrels, ravens, various woodpeckers, grouse, partridge and skylarks. The venomous northern viper or adder is also around (but you'd have to tiptoe to come upon one unawares). Pine and larch forests grow up to 2300m, beyond which Alpine meadows are carpeted in springtime with edelweiss, gentians and a host of other high-altitude flowers. Further up still are bare rocky areas and permafrost.

Access, information and accommodation

Entry to the park is free. If you're **driving**, head along the main road to any one of nine free parking areas within the park boundaries, from all of which long and short trails twist out to north and south. **Postbuses** running hourly between Zernez and Müstair also stop at each parking area. Cycling is prohibited in the park.

The best place for information is the **National Park House**, located about 1km east of Zernez and open the same hours as the park itself (June–Oct daily 8.30am–6pm, Tues until 10pm; ☎081 856 13 78, ⓦwww.nationalpark .ch). This office is overflowing with maps, trail guides (including coverage of multi-day hikes) and useful information on animal sightings, all in English. A **tourist office** on Zernez main street can also help with maps and general guidance (Mon–Fri 8.30am–noon & 2–5.30pm; July–Oct until 6.30pm, plus Sat 8.30am–noon & 2–4pm; ☎081 856 13 00, ⓦwww.zernez.ch).

There are only two **places to stay** within the National Park, both of which need reserving in advance. *Hotel Il Fuorn*, beside Parking 6 (☎081 856 12 26, ⓦwww.ilfuorn.ch; ❷–❸; June–Oct), is a comfortable old lodge with shared-bath rooms, and has a newer wing with ensuite rooms. In the middle of the park, at the junction of several trails, is *Chamanna/Blockhaus Cluozza* (☎081 856 12 35; June–Oct), a simple hut with dorm beds (Fr.31).

In Zernez, the **campsite** *Cul* is 500m behind the station (☎081 856 14 62, ⓦwww.camping-cul.ch; May to mid-Oct), and there are plenty of **hotels**: *Spöl* (☎081 856 12 79, ⓦwww.hotel-spoel.ch; ❷; closed Nov) is a characterful low-end choice within ten minutes' walk of the park entrance. About 7km beyond Zernez just outside the park boundary before Parking 1 is *Naturfreundehaus Ova Spin* (☎081 852 31 42, ⓦwww.nfhouse.org; dorms Fr.18; June–Oct).

Walks in the National Park

There are 21 marked **walking** trails in and around the park, ranging from full-day mountain ascents to brief roadside strolls. The following are some of the more straightforward scenic routes that have easy access at either end; always check on trail conditions at the National Park House before you start. Note that, on high-summer weekends in particular, paths can get crowded. One of the best could involve overnighting in the wilds: **trail 7** (3hr) leads from Zernez into the Cluozza gorge, directly to the *Chamanna Cluozza* (see above), from where **trail 8** (3hr 30min) brings you out on a different route via a steep ascent to Praspöl, emerging at Parking 3 ("Vallun Chafuol"). Both these can be done in reverse. The circular **trail 9** (2hr) leads from Parking 3 through heather and pine forest to Margun Grimmels and back. The tougher **trail 15** (5hr) leads from Buffalora (1968m), just outside the boundary at Parking 10, on a simple ascent of Munt la Schera (2091m) and down to *Hotel Il Fuorn* at Parking 6.

Hiking in the Engadine valley

The 94km **Engadine valley**, with its numerous tributaries and adjacent valleys, offers a wealth of opportunities for walks of all degrees of seriousness, as well as the modest ascent of several peaks with commanding summit viewpoints. Maps which cover the area are the LS 249, 259, 268, and 269, all of them 1:50,000. Valuable reading are two books by Kev Reynolds: *Walking in the Alps* and *Walks in the Engadine* (see p.587).

In the Lower Engadine, behind **Scuol** to the south is Val S-charl, leading to **S-charl**, a tiny summer-only hamlet at a confluence of glens. From here, walkers could cross Fuorcla Funtana da S-charl to the Ofen Pass/Pass dal Fuorn (3hr 30min); the Pass da Costainas to Santa Maria in Val Müstair (5hr); or take an easy 1hr stroll to Alp Sesvenna among streams and pastures that are full of Alpine flowers in early summer.

Further up-valley, the charming village of **Guarda** gives access to Val Tuoi, near the head of which stands the *Tuoi Hut/Chamanna Tuoi* (☎081 862 23 22) below Piz Buin. This is gained in about 2hr 30min from Guarda, while strong walkers could continue across the right-hand ridge at the 2735m Furcletta and descend through Val Tasna to **Ardez** – a total of 7hr 30min. The **Parc Naziunal Svizzer** has any number of walks from which red and roe deer, marmots, chamois and ibex may be seen. The best base for an exploration is the *Blockhaus Cluozza*, reached in 3hr from **Zernez**, since an overnight there enables you to cross into neighbouring valleys by a choice of passes.

In the Upper Engadine, **Maloja** offers several rewarding walks, especially up to the lovely alp hamlets of Grevasalvas and Blaunca (1hr). Above them lies Lägh da Lunghin, birthplace of the River Inn, and a path which climbs to Piz Lunghin (2780m) in 3hr 30min from Maloja. From that elevated point both Engadine and Bregaglia are spread out below. Across the valley, Val Fex gives gentle walking in idyllic surroundings, while a belvedere path above its entrance makes a high traverse round to **St Moritz-Bad** (up to 5hr from Sils Maria). From St Moritz a classic walk crosses the 2755m Fuorcla Surlej for a stimulating view of Piz Bernina and Piz Roseg (*Berghaus Fuorcla Surlej* ☎081 842 63 03), then descends into Val Roseg and continues to **Pontresina** (up to 6hr). Walkers staying in Pontresina should visit the *Coaz Hut* (☎081 842 62 78) and neighbouring *Tschierva Hut* (☎081 842 63 91), the first in 4hr 30min, the second in an hour less: both give close views of glaciers and their icefalls. The *Boval Hut* (☎081 842 64 03) is another unmissable 3hr 30min walk, giving stupendous high mountain and glacier scenery for much of the way, while the easy but steep ascent of the 3262m Piz Languard directly above Pontresina (up to 4hr) is the best place to enjoy an Alpine sunrise or sunset.

In **Val Bregaglia**, one of the most notable villages is **Soglio**, which sits on the right-hand hillside gazing south to Val Bondasca, Piz Badile and the blade-like Sciora aiguilles. Paths leading out of Soglio climb the hillside to Alp Tombal, to Pass da Cam and Pass Düana for the most breathtaking views. These are steep trails, while a slightly less severe path (of 4hr) entices the walker from **Promontogno** below Soglio into Val Bondasca and up to its inner recesses where the *Sciora Hut* (☎081 822 11 38) stands immediately below the pinnacles after which it is named, with Piz Badile towering above to the southwest. Experienced mountain walkers could continue for four hours over the exposed Colle Vial below Badile to the *Sasc Furä Hut* (☎081 822 12 52), or cross the high Cacciabella Pass in the east to reach the *Albigna Hut* (☎081 822 14 05) in 4hr 30min.

Three of the simpler routes (marked as suitable for children) include **trail 1** (2hr 30min), a circular walk from Parking 1 ("Champlönch"), taking in the view from Alp Grimmels; **trail 13** (2hr), leading from Parking 1 on an easy countryside path to *Hotel Il Fuorn* at Parking 6; and **trail 10** (3hr 30min), a riverside forest walk that loops from Parking 3 through the tranquil Spöltal to Parking 4 ("Punt la Drossa").

Val Müstair

As you crest the Ofenpass/Pass dal Fuorn 20km south of Zernez, spread out in front is the idyllic **Val Müstair** (Münstertal in German), a lush, peaceful valley pointing the way south into Italy. This finger of Switzerland, cut off by the mountains from the rest of Graubünden and entirely surrounded by Italy, is determinedly Romansh in language and culture. Half-a-dozen hamlets dot the green slopes on the 8km descent to **Santa Maria**, the main village of the valley, with a Gothic church just off its narrow main street. However, the chief attraction is **MÜSTAIR** (pronounced *moosh-tire*), 4km further, where virtually the last buildings before the Italian frontier are a Carolingian monastery and church, the **Claustra Son Jon**, or Klosterkirche St Johann (daily 8am–7pm; ⓦwww.muestair.ch). This function-ing Benedictine convent was reputedly founded by Charlemagne himself around 800 AD, and has been named a UNESCO World Heritage Site for the array of brilliantly coloured Romanesque frescoes adorning the interior of its monastery church. The style and detail of the frescoes, which depict stories such as the ston-ing of St Stephen and the Dance of Salome, are breathtaking, and the atmosphere of the church, its adjacent cemetery and cobbled courtyard make the journey well worthwhile. A small **museum** off the courtyard has chunks of Carolin-gian carving and Baroque statues and icons (May–Oct Mon–Sat 9am–noon & 1.30–5pm, Sun 1.30–5pm; Nov–April Mon–Sat 10am–noon & 1.30–4.30pm, Sun 1.30–4.30pm; Fr.12, including guided tour).

Müstair **tourist office** (May–Oct Mon–Sat 9am–6pm, Sun 1.30–6pm; ☏081 858 50 00, ⓦwww.val-muestair.ch) has information on the valley. In Santa Maria is a characterful HI **hostel**, *Chasa Plaz* (☏081 858 56 61, ⓦwww.youthhostel.ch; ❶; dorms Fr.28.50; closed April, May & Nov), while in Müstair there's the good-value *Landgasthof Münsterhof* (☏081 858 55 41, ⓦwww.muensterhof.ch; ❷–❸), its old rooms filled with antiques.

The Upper Engadine

"I have never seen light as it is up here: it's fantastic!"

Ferdinand Hodler, Swiss painter

The **Upper Engadine** (Engiadin'Ota in Romansh, Oberengadin in German) is one of the most scenic valleys in Switzerland, a heart-stoppingly beautiful array of forests, snowy mountains and silvery lakes, raised high at 1800m and looking southwest directly into the crispest and clearest sunshine in the Alps. The long, straight 55km run southwest from Zernez takes in a handful of attrac-tive little resorts, all of them overshadowed by **St Moritz**, which holds court in mid-valley. In point of fact, many of the smaller fry – such as **Pontresina**, **Celerina** and **Silvaplana** – have as much, if not more, to offer than their world-famous neighbour, but for a century past and probably for a century to come, the Moritz name is the one that sells.

Crossing the two major mountain passes that lead on from St Moritz delivers you into small valleys sticking out into Italy that are entirely unlike the rest of Graubünden. To the southwest, the **Maloja Pass** heralds the deep and lush **Val Bregaglia**, while to the southeast, a road and rail line crosses the icy **Bernina Pass** into the idyllic **Val Poschiavo**. Both are thoroughly Italian, in language, culture and flora, and both offer a taste of Mediterranean-style living that's like a revelation after the rustic ambience of the high mountains.

If you're keen to avoid difficult mountain driving, winter or summer, see the note on p.493 regarding **car-carrying trains** on the Albula pass route. Beware that almost everything – shops, hotels, attractions, walking routes – is **closed during off-season** (mid-April to mid-June & mid-Oct to mid-Dec). We've specified months of opening only when they differ from this pattern.

St Moritz

ST MORITZ is all you expect and more – a brassy, in-your-face reminder of the hotshot world beyond the high valley walls. For a century or more, it's been the prime winter retreat of social high-flyers, minor European royalty and the international jetset, who've sparked the creation of a mini-Mayfair of Vuitton and Armani in this stunningly romantic setting of forest, lake and mountains. When the tourist office trumpets the "champagne climate", they don't necessarily mean the sparkling sunshine – although there's plenty of that as well, an unbeatable 322 days of it a year on average.

Not unlike its twin, Vail, Colorado, this can be the kind of town to give money a bad name. It's neither cosmopolitan, characterful nor especially attractive; indeed, after the rural, traditional villages to west and east, even this little place can come across as exhaustingly built-up. And yet its name glisters better than gold, enough for the tourist board to make "St Moritz" a patented registered trademark. Presidents and princes, Hollywood starlets, nobility and *nouveaux riches* clamour to be associated with it, and the town gladly responds, turning on the razzle all winter long with an endless round of banquets, celebrations and spectacles centred on the frozen lake. Summer is downtime, when the hoi polloi arrive to hike and relax in the sunshine.

△ Shopping, St Moritz

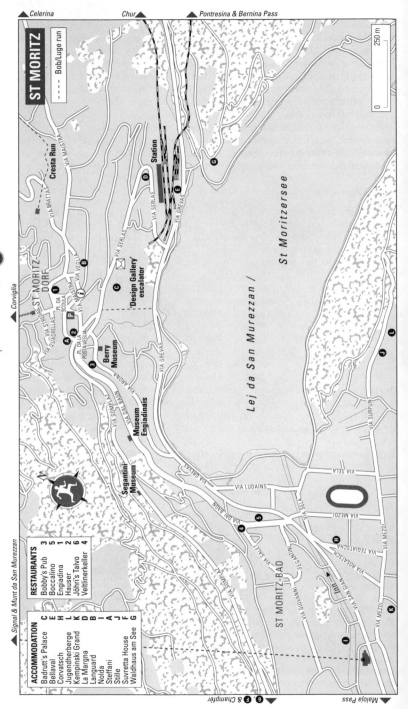

There's been a spa here since the Bronze Age, although the tale really begins in 1864, when local hotelier Johannes Badrutt laid down a challenge to a party of English summer-only regulars: spend a winter here, he said, and I'll foot the bill. They came, brought their friends the year after, and since then Badrutt has been quids in (the family's hotel is still the most expensive in town).

St Moritz is set amidst some of the world's most beautiful mountain scenery. Once you've arrived, head out as quickly as possible.

Arrival, information and accommodation

The town spans two villages: when people refer to St Moritz, they're talking about **St Moritz-Dorf**, a cluster of hotels, restaurants and boutiques on the hillside above the lake. **St Moritz-Bad**, far removed from the glitz 2km southwest down on the lakeshore, is a less attractive mini-sprawl of concrete apartment blocks and sports halls. Via dal Bagn connects the two. The **train station** is located below Dorf, on the opposite side of the lake from Bad. Via Serlas winds up from the station past the **postbus** station to the linked central squares of Dorf. The **tourist office** is signposted 100m east at Via Maistra 12 (mid-June to mid-Sept & mid-Dec to mid-April Mon–Fri 9am–6.30pm, Sat 9am–6pm, Sun 4–6pm; rest of year Mon–Fri 9am–noon & 2–6pm, Sat 9am–noon; ☏081 837 33 33, ⓦ www.stmoritz.ch).

Few bargains come wrapped with the St Moritz name, and **accommodation** is no exception: prices are high across the board, and during the winter season they go stratospheric. There are more affordable alternatives at neighbouring Celerina, Pontresina and Silvaplana, as well as up at the Muottas Muragl *Berghotel* (see p.518).

Inexpensive and mid-range hotels

Bellaval Via Grevas 55, Dorf ☏081 833 32 45, ⓦ www.bellaval-stmoritz.ch. Some of the least expensive rooms in Dorf. Conveniently situated beside the station and lake, modest but pleasant. Ensuite and shared-bath available. Open year-round. ❷–❸

Corvatsch Via Tegiatscha 1, Bad ☏081 837 57 57, ⓦ www.hotel-corvatsch.ch. Excellent family-run hotel, located out of the hustle in peaceful Bad (with parking); an unromantic exterior preludes very pleasant, well-kept rooms with handcarved wooden furniture. Back rooms have views of the lake and mountains. Service is outstanding, and the onsite restaurant is a bonus. ❸–❹

Languard Via Veglia 14, Dorf ☏081 833 31 37, ⓦ www.languard-stmoritz.ch. Comfortable, friendly little family hotel in the middle of Dorf that keeps a tighter lid on its winter surcharges than its near neighbours. ❸–❹

Nolda Via Crasta 3, Bad ☏081 833 05 75, ⓦ www.nolda.ch. Pleasant enough pack-'em-in hotel next to the Signal cable car, with pine-clad rooms that do the job. Also has a nearby, more upmarket *Noldapark* annexe. ❸–❺

Stille Beside the hostel in Bad ☏081 833 69 48, ⓦ www.hotelstille.ch. Quiet, modern, well-run sports hotel, popular with skiers and snowboarders, who crowd out its no-frills rooms. ❷

Waldhaus am See Via Dim Lej 6 ☏081 836 60 00, ⓦ www.waldhaus-am-see.ch. Large, quiet lodge in an idyllic location, just five minutes' walk from the station and slightly above the lakeshore, but far enough away from the road to be utterly peaceful. It's a modern, bustling, three-star establishment, so the atmosphere inside is more holiday-hotel than country-retreat – but if you choose one of the six spacious double-view corner rooms, with superb panoramas over the whole lake and forest, you won't care. Add in the fact that the bar has the widest choice of whiskies in the world – more than 2500 varieties – and you may decide to hole up here for the winter (or summer). ❸–❺

Expensive hotels

Badrutt's Palace Via Serlas 27, Dorf ☏081 837 10 00, ⓦ www.badruttspalace.com. Legendary five-star behemoth, one of Switzerland's – and Europe's – swankiest hotels. You may not even get past the flunkey on the door: men must wear a jacket just to stand in the lobby after 7.30pm. If you do get in, make the most of it – this is the haunt of filmstars, princesses (real and wannabe) and more fur coats than live in the forest. Staying here involves tossing zeros around like confetti. ❾

Don't be misled into thinking that the Upper Engadine is all St Moritz-style glamour: there's a vast range of sports and activities that take advantage of the valley's natural beauty. Check ⓦ **www.bergbahnenengadin.ch**.

Winter

There are three main ski and snowboard sectors. On the north side of the valley is the sunny, south-facing **Corviglia–Piz Nair**; with three access routes. From St Moritz-Bad, a cable car rises to Signal, with chairlifts up to the Munt da San Murezzan (2659m), where there's a halfpipe. From St Moritz-Dorf a funicular runs via Chantarella to Corviglia itself (2486m), from where a cable car continues to the soaring Piz Nair summit (3057m). A gondola from nearby Celerina rises to **Marguns** (2278m), which gives access to testing runs off Las Trais Fluors and Piz Glüna, as well as linking directly by chairlift to Corviglia. Across the valley is **Corvatsch–Furtschellas**: a cable car from Surlej, 3km south of St Moritz-Bad, and a chairlift from nearby Alp Surlej both arrive at Murtèl (2702m), from where a cable car rises to Piz Corvatsch (3451m). Again, long sweeping reds are plentiful, while dropping through the trees is the testing 8km Hahnensee black run. A cable car from Sils Maria 4km south of Surlej serves Furtschellas (2800m), neatly linked by chairlifts to Murtèl. Finally, 12km south of St Moritz – with easy access from Pontresina – is **Diavolezza–Bernina**, with some steep, difficult runs from Diavolezza (2978m) on the south side and off Piz Lagalb (2959m) opposite, including the Minor black run.

A peak-season **pass**, valid for 3/6 days in all areas, is Fr.188/339. A half/full day pass for Corvatsch or Corviglia is Fr.66/54, for Diavolezza Fr.56/47. Discounts apply out of peak season, and selected-day and afternoon-only passes are available. **Schools** include ⓦ www.skischool.ch.

There are some legendary bob and toboggan runs, including an exhilarating 4.2km toboggan from **Muottas Muragl** into the valley, a vertical drop of 700m (you can rent a sled at the top). Fr.210 buys you an adrenalin-fuelled "taxi ride" down the 1.6km **Olympia bob run** (ⓦ www.olympia-bobrun.ch), the world's only natural-ice bobsleigh run, between St Moritz and Celerina, while for Fr.450 you can do five skeleton runs in a season (Christmas–Feb) on the most famous luge course in the world, the death-defying 1.2km **Cresta Run** (ⓦ www.cresta-run.com) – which, for no good reason, is barred to women. See p.494 for details of the excellent, inexpensive **Preda–Bergün** toboggan run. ⓦ www.boarders-valley.com is the best local **snowboarding** site.

Other attractions include skiing by moonlight, heli-skiing, snow-tubing, skating, curling, paragliding, hanggliding and winter walking. ⓦ www.bergsteiger-pontresina .ch offers a range of tough, long-distance guided skiing excursions, and ⓦ www .bananas.net has exhilarating back-country boarding for experts. **Horse-drawn sleighs** wait for business beside the Catholic church in St Moritz-Bad; their route crosses the frozen lake into the forest (Fr.95/hr). Winter events held on the lake include show-jumping, polo, "White Turf" horse races, cricket and greyhound racing,

Kempinski Grand Hôtel des Bains Via Mezdi 27, Bad ☎081 838 38 38, ⓦ www.kempinski -stmoritz.ch. Sensational five-star hotel in traditional style down at the spa complex in St Moritz-Bad, entirely fitted out from scratch in 2002 within the shell of the original 1864 grand hotel. Rooms are spacious and modern, many with balconies or terraces. ⑨

La Margna Via Serlas 5, Dorf ☎081 836 6600, ⓦ www.lamargna.ch. Fine old

stalwart hotel, built in 1907, just above the station, with good views over the lake and mountains. Rooms are spacious and solidly comfortable, service is warm and efficient and the lounge offers stout, wing-backed armchairs arranged around the stone fireplace, with picture windows facing south. Fine, traditional quality. ⑤–⑦

Steffani Plazza da la Posta Veglia 1, Dorf ☎081 836 96 96, ⓦ www.steffani.ch. Very comfortable, along with ski-jumping, various bob and luge championships and the **Engadin Ski Marathon** in early March (ⓦwww.engadin-skimarathon.ch), 42km down the valley from Maloja to S-chanf.

Summer

One of the best round-trip summer **walks** starts from **Muottas Muragl** (2453m). A Höhenweg (high-level route) leads across Val Muragl and then splits: a steep path heads up to the Segantini Hütte (2731m), where the painter died, and then comes down to meet the easier path – which has stayed fairly flat – at Unterer Schafberg (2231m) before continuing to the restaurant at Alp Languard (2325m; total 2hr 30min), where a chairlift takes you down to Pontresina. Ask for the discounted Höhenweg ticket at the Punt Muragl funicular. Above St Moritz, **Marguns**, **Signal** and **Corviglia** are hubs for a network of trails, including a panoramic route from Corviglia to the isolated Chamanna Saluver hut and on down to Samedan (3hr 30min). A fairly easy trail runs from Marguns to Corviglia and down via Alp Giop to Signal, or via Alp Nova to Chantarella (1hr 30min); from either, it's a further hour down to St Moritz. A quieter route to the valley floor runs from Marguns to Alp Laret and then into the cool **God da Blais forest** to Celerina (1hr 30min) – or you can detour from Alp Laret to St Moritz. Top long-distance route is the **Via Engiadina**, a reasonably flat high-level trail across the whole region; simplest access is at Marguns or Corviglia, from where you walk for six full hours above the spectacular lake scenery to Maloja (19km). A testing alternative is the full-day trail from Piz Nair down to the **Suvrettasee** – with a stunning view of Piz Julier and the Bernina range – and on via the Suvretta Pass into Val Bever, ending at Spinas train station; an alternative leads up from the Suvrettasee around the south face of Piz Nair back to Corviglia (2hr). A lovely half-day walk leads from the **Furtschellas** top station to Marmorè, from where two routes lead back to Sils Maria; the direct option is 1hr 30min, but if you divert down to Curtins, you can trace a path through the meadows of the **Val Fex** to Sils Maria via the frescoed chapel at Fex-Crasta (2hr 30min). There are plenty of easy walks from Murtèl, including a circuit to and from the restaurant at **Fuorcla Surlej** (1hr); a tougher trail leads from there into the Val Roseg to Pontresina (3hr 30min), while another heads down to St Moritz-Bad via the Hahnensee (3hr). At **Diavolezza**, the best route involves a two-hour round trip from the top station up to the spectacular **Munt Pers** (3207m), overlooking the Morteratsch glacier.

There are tons of other activities. ⓦwww.stmoritz-experience.ch runs canyoning, glacier walking and multisports, including abseiling, flying fox, sailing, tubing and more, as well as rock climbing and multi-day **trekking** itineraries. There's also rafting, horse riding, go-karting in Celerina and a spectacular **mountain-bike** route from Lagalb (2893m) way down 22km to Poschiavo (1000m). The Innline Engadina is a marked **inline skating** and **cycling** off-road path that follows the river 8.6km from La Punt to S-chanf. Silvaplana is known for its **windsurfing** (ⓦwww.windsurfing -silvaplana.ch) and **kitesurfing** (ⓦwww.kitesailing.ch).

bustling hotel on the central square, with a few airs and graces but efficient and welcoming nonetheless. Open year-round. ⑥–⑧
Suvretta House Via Chasellas 1, Suvretta ☎081 836 36 36, ⓦwww.suvrettahouse.ch. Vast luxury hotel located amidst the forests west of St Moritz itself, with uniquely elegant, understated guest rooms and an exquisite attention to detail. Service is formal, but not stiff. ⑨

Hostel

Jugendherberge Stille (HI hostel) Via Surpunt 60, Bad ☎081 833 39 69, ⓦwww.youthhostel .ch. Excellent quality, but dorm beds – including obligatory half board – cost a moritzy Fr.46. Open year-round. ①

Campsite

Olympiaschanze ☎081 833 40 90. Good site, about 1km southwest of Bad. Mid-May to Sept.

The Town

St Moritz's town museums are worth making time for – although beware their different closing days. About 1km west of Dorf on Via Somplaz, the terrace road, is the domed, church-like **Giovanni Segantini Museum** (June–Oct & Dec–April Tues–Sun 10am–noon & 2–6pm; closed Mon; Fr.10; SMP; ⓦwww .segantini-museum.ch), displaying the beautiful work of this largely self-taught Symbolist. Segantini (1858–99) is acclaimed as the definitive painter of Alpine life, and spent the twelve years before his sudden death at the age of 41 working to portray the clear mountain light of the Upper Engadine. Although many of the works on display are excellent – including an intense self-portrait, drawn three years before his death – the highlight is the Alpine Triptych, shown upstairs in the circular domed room designed for the purpose. This sequence of vast, luminous canvases, each between three and four metres long, covers *Birth*, *Life* and *Death*. Segantini had studiously sketched all three in entirety as preparation (the sketches are also displayed), and was working on the final touches of the complete painted triptych when he died.

On the terrace below is the **Museum Engiadinais**, Via dal Bagn 39 (Mon–Fri 9.30am–noon & 2–5pm, Sun 10am–noon; closed Sat; Fr.6), housed in a solid stone *sgraffitied* building that's one of the few surviving pieces of vernacular architecture in the town. Inside are reconstructed interiors of farmhouses and patrician mansions, along with interesting displays on the history of the spa and Engadine culture.

Just off the central square, the **Berry Museum**, Via Arona 32 (Mon & Wed–Sun 10am–1pm & 4–7pm; closed Tues; Fr.15; ⓦwww.berrymuseum.com), is devoted to the painter and doctor Peter Robert Berry (1864–1942), housed in the family's former home. The excellent audioguide gives background to Berry's paintings, which were very much influenced by Segantini. Berry spent many winters in the mountains painting out-of-doors, and the best of his work captures the light and ethereal nature of the Alpine landscapes. Look out, particularly, for *The Great Silent Glow* (1910), a panoramic view over the Bernina Pass.

The **St Moritz Design Gallery** is the grandiose name for an exhibition of posters on changing themes which lines a long covered escalator running between Level 4 of the lakefront parking garage and Via Serlas up in the town centre. It is freely accessible 24 hours a day.

Eating and drinking

You'll find few bargains **eating and drinking** in St Moritz. The big hotels all have super-swanky dining rooms – exclusive, expensive and cloying to a fault. More down-to-earth establishments might take a bit of sniffing out. Die-hard romantics shouldn't miss the chance to book ahead for a window table at the Muottas Muragl restaurant (see p.518).

Similarly, there's a plethora of upmarket **bars**, discos, nightclubs and drinking dens, most of which are either for members only, shielded by sky-high entry fees, or simply dull and expensive. The *Roo Bar*, at Hotel Hauser, on Dorf's main square, is an exception, as is *Bobby's Pub*, Via dal Bagn 52. Alternatively, you could settle in at the eye-popping *Devil's Place*, the bar of *Hotel Waldhaus am See*, Via Dim Lej 6 (daily 4pm–12.30am), which holds the world's largest selection of **whiskies**.

Restaurants

Boccalino Via dal Bagn 6 ☎081 832 11 11. Lively, bustling place with a range of quality wood-fired pizzas for under Fr.20, as well as pasta dishes. Home-made tiramisu fills out the menu.

Corvatsch Via Tegiatscha 1, Bad ☎081 837 57 57. Down-to-earth, cosy restaurant attached to an attractive, mid-priced hotel, well out of the chic part of town, but with a carefully compiled menu and well-presented local cuisine, with wines to match.

Engiadina Plazza da Scoula 10 ☎081 833 32 65. Popular place in the middle of Dorf that concentrates on fondue – pay about Fr.30 for the ordinary version, or considerably more for the house special with extra champagne. Closed Sun.

🏃 **Hauser** Via Traunter Plazzas 7 ☎081 837 50 50, www.hotelhauser.ch. Occupying a perfect location in the middle of Dorf, on the central square, with a lovely terrace that soaks up the sun's rays: if the sun is shining, you can eat lunch outside in shirtsleeves, even if the thermometer reads well below freezing. The food is good, too, with a choice of Rösti – including with smoked salmon and sour cream (around Fr.20) – and a range of Piöda: steaks (or the veggie tofu

equivalent) grilled on hot stones at your table (around Fr.40).

Jöhri's Talvo Via Gunels 15, Champfèr ☎081 833 44 55, ⓦwww.talvo.ch. Perhaps the finest restaurant in the valley, 3km west of St Moritz in neighbouring Champfèr, specializing in superb fish and lobster dishes and also offering classic, elegant takes on heavier local cuisine. Be prepared to pay hundreds of francs for the privilege.

Mathis Food Affairs Corviglia funicular top station ☎081 833 63 55, ⓦwww.mathisfood.ch. Book well ahead for a meal to remember at the *Marmite* restaurant, high above town on the Corviglia slopes – think caviar and truffles at 2500m.

Veltlinerkeller Via dal Bagn 11 ☎081 833 40 09. A perennial favourite; ignore the hunting trophies on the walls, and concentrate on the quality, lightly prepared food in front of you – excellent pastas, fish dishes and grilled meats with *menus* starting at around Fr.22.

⑪

Celerina and around

Just 2km – a half-hour walk – east of St Moritz is **CELERINA** (Schlarigna in Romansh). This pleasant small town on the banks of the Inn, base station for a gondola rising to the ski slopes of Corviglia, has an atmospheric old cobbled quarter of traditional Engadine architecture. It's also the end-point of both the infamous Cresta Run luge course and the Olympia Bob-Run (for both, see p.514). On a grassy knoll 1km east of the centre is the isolated **Baselgia San Gian**, with a Romanesque choir and a painted wooden ceiling dating from 1478 (mid-June to mid-Oct Mon 2–4pm, Wed 4–5.30pm, Fri 10.30am–noon; Dec–March Wed 2–4pm; free).

Beware that there are **two train stations**: the one on the St Moritz–Samedan line is on the north side of the centre; the other (dubbed "Celerina Staz") on the St Moritz–Pontresina line is 700m south, just over the river. The straight Via da la Staziun links the two; halfway along it, at the central crossroads with Via Maistra, is the **tourist office** (Mon–Fri 8.30am–6.30pm, Sat 9am–noon & 3–6pm, Sun 4–6pm; May, June & Nov Mon–Fri 8.30am–noon & 2–6.30pm; ☎081 830 00 11, ⓦwww .celerina.ch). Inexpensive **accommodation** includes the excellent *Inn Lodge* hostel (☎081 834 47 95, ⓦwww .innlodge.ch; dorms from Fr.35). The most characterful upmarket hotel is *Chesa Rosatsch*, a 350-year-old riverside inn (☎081 837 01 01, ⓦwww.rosatsch .ch; ④–⑥).

△ Engadine architecture

Muottas Muragl

Across from Celerina rises the ridge of **MUOTTAS MURAGL** (2456m), accessed by a steep **funicular** from **Punt Muragl**, which is on the Celerina–Pontresina road, served by buses and trains. The panoramic view from the top, some 700m above the valley, is unmissable summer or winter, offering an uninterrupted gaze southwest up the length of the Engadine, its string of lakes glittering in the sunlight between high peaks. The summit *Berghotel* has reinvented itself as a fine 🍴 **restaurant** (☎081 842 82 32, ⓦ www.muottasmuragl .ch), with an excellent menu of regional and international cuisine complemented by an outstanding wine list and spectacular views: book in advance for a window table. Lunch is a reasonable Fr.35 or so, rising to Fr.75 or more per head in the evening. Throughout the season, the funicular runs every half-hour until 11pm. The *Berghotel*'s spotlessly clean, fresh but simple shared-bath **rooms** are a rare bargain (❷–❸); guests benefit from discounts on the funicular. The mountain also offers great walks and a winter toboggan run.

Pontresina and beyond

Less than 2km up the Bernina Pass road from Punt Muragl is the swish resort of **PONTRESINA**, lying in a privileged, wind-sheltered position on a southwest-facing terrace amidst meadows and fragrant pine and larch woods. Access to the Diavolezza slopes is easy from here, and the scenery of high rocky peaks to east and west interspersed with glaciers – most notably the huge **Morteratsch glacier**, sidling down from Piz Bernina (4049m) – is impressive; the town stares directly across to the **Val Roseg**, complete with its own glacier. Pontresina is curiously split between its St-Moritzy aspirations, with half-a-dozen luxury palace hotels and a glitteringly modern main street, and its tough reputation as the best place in the area for adventure sports and hiking; the local mountaineering school is the largest in Switzerland.

From the station, it's a short walk across the river and up to the **tourist office**, housed in the landmark Rondo conference centre (Mon–Fri 8.30am–6pm, Sat 8.30am–noon & 3–6pm, Sun 3–6pm; shorter hours in off season; ☎081 838 83 00, ⓦ www.pontresina.com). Via Maistra slopes upwards into the centre of town, location of most **hotels**, including simple *Pensione Valtellina* (☎081 842 64 06; ❷), but you'll find more character in the narrow lanes of the Old Town,

△ View, Muottas Muragl

the other direction on Via Maistra. Here are the *Grand Hotel Kronenhof* (☎081 830 30 30, Ⓦ www.kronenhof.com; ❽–❾), a vast Baroque-style palace set around its own courtyard with lawns and tastefully luxurious guest rooms; and the delightful *Saratz* (☎081 839 40 00, Ⓦ www.saratz.ch; ❼), a similarly grand hotel that has been superbly renovated and updated: rooms are styled in tasteful contemporary decor that feels like a breath of fresh air. Down by the station is the reliable non-ensuite *Bahnhof* (☎081 838 80 00, Ⓦ www.hotel-bahnhof .ch; ❷), alongside the HI **hostel** *Jugendherberge Tolais* (☎081 842 72 23, Ⓦ www .youthhostel.ch; ❶; dorms Fr.46 including half board), where you can get advice on hikes and adventure sports. The **campsite** *Plauns/Morteratsch* (☎081 842 62 85, Ⓦ www.campingplauns.ch; closed May & Nov) is in a lovely countryside location.

Walks and skiing aside, the most enjoyable excursion from Pontresina (June–Oct only) is by **horse-drawn carriage** from the station for an hour to the tastefully renovated **Hotel Roseggletscher** (☎081 842 64 45, Ⓦ www .roseggletscher.ch; ❸; dorms Fr.35), 7km up the car-free Val Roseg at the foot of the glacier. There is a scheduled timetable – up to five carriages a day (Fr.26 return) – but booking is essential (Luigi Costa Carriages ☎081 842 60 57). Otherwise, it's an easy, scenic **walk** (2hr). The views from the hotel are stunning, and plenty of high-level trails lead on deeper into the mountains.

Val Poschiavo

From Pontresina, the high **Bernina Pass** (2328m) is about 15km southeast. This route is served by ordinary trains as well as the Bernina Express (see p.42), an excursion in panoramic carriages from Chur, Davos and St Moritz into the idyllic **Val Poschiavo** (Puschlav in German) and down to the Italian border town of Tirano, from where you switch onto a postbus around the shores of Lake Como, ending up back in Switzerland at Lugano. However you travel in the valley, it's still gorgeous. A classic vantage-point is **Alp Grüm**, on the train line but not the road (reachable after a two-hour walk from the car park at the *Ospizio Bernina* inn on the pass; Ⓦ www.bernina-hospiz.ch): from here, at 2091m, you can see clear down the valley to the Lago di Poschiavo and beyond. The *Belvedere* hotel and restaurant (☎081 844 03 14, Ⓦ www.belvedere -engadin.ch; ❷–❸; dorms Fr.40; May–Oct), ten minutes' walk from Alp Grüm station, provides refreshment.

The railway joins the road again at the village of **San Carlo**, watched over by its ancient church tower, and heads on 2km to **POSCHIAVO** (pronounced *poss-KYA-vo*). The difference between this laid-back, photogenic Italianate town and the huddled Alpine resort of Pontresina the same distance north of the pass couldn't be more striking. Poschiavo's tranquil old quarter, across the river from the train station, is filled with tall, foursquare eighteenth-century shuttered mansions in various shades of pastel, overlooking stone-paved plazas ringed with terrace cafés. The place is perfect for soaking up some sunshine – of which there's plenty – filling up on risotto instead of fondue, and savouring a carafe of Valtellina wine from the Italian regions bordering. On the north side of the central Piazza Comunale is the seventeenth-century Protestant church of **Sant'Ignazio**, which holds an inscription stating that the town was *riformata da gli errori e superstizioni* in 1520. Despite this claim, the Catholic **San Vittore**, dating from the late fifteenth century, remains a powerful presence 200m away on the south side of the square. The same square holds the **tourist office** (Mon–Fri 8am–noon & 2–6pm; July & Aug also Sat 9am–noon & 2–5pm; ☎081 844 05 71, Ⓦ www.valposchiavo.ch). Of the **hotels**, *Croce Bianca*, a five-minute walk south (☎081 844 01 44, Ⓦ www.croce-bianca.ch; ❷–❸), and

Suisse, on Via da Mez (☎081 844 07 88, ⓦwww.suisse-poschiavo.ch; ❷–❸), are both long-standing fixtures in the town, with decent rooms.

Beyond the Lago di Poschiavo and the village of **Brusio** – with its famous, much-photographed circular viaduct bringing trains gently down to the valley floor – is the Italian border at **Campocologno**, 16km south of Poschiavo. Some 4km further is **TIRANO**, terminus of Swiss trains. The Swiss station and its Italian counterpart (with trains to Milan roughly every 2hr) sit beside each other, separated by passport control. Swiss **postbuses** to Lugano – the second leg of the Bernina Express – depart from round the corner (signposted). Tirano's residential Old Town, dead ahead on the west bank of the river, has cobbled, arcaded courtyards and tiny sloping lanes leading up to the medieval Porta Bormina. The pilgrimage church of **Madonna di Tirano**, commemorating an appearance of the Virgin in 1504, lies 1km northwest of the centre, its shrine focused around a statue of Mary dressed in a silk and gold robe donated by local people in 1746.

Silvaplana and beyond

The Engadine continues to rise gently for 16km beyond St Moritz, past little **Champfèr** to the village of **SILVAPLANA**, on a bulge of land between the diminutive Lej da Champfèr and the grand Lej da Silvaplauna (Silvaplanersee in German). Due to a particular feature of the local summer climate – in which morning thermals rise more quickly than in neighbouring St Moritz or Sils, thus creating the consistently strong, warm "Malojawind" that sweeps across the surface of the lake during the day – Silvaplana is home to some outstanding watersports: it has hosted the windsurfing and kiteboarding world championships. Opposite the village is tiny **Surlej**, base station for the cable car up to Piz Corvatsch.

In the centre of Silvaplana – on the main road up to the Julier Pass (see p.494) – is the **tourist office** (Mon–Fri 8.30am–noon & 1.30–6pm, Sat 9am–noon & 4–6pm; Dec–March also Sun 4–6pm; ☎081 838 60 00, ⓦwww.silvaplana .ch). Of the **hotels**, youthful *Julier Palace* (☎081 828 96 44, ⓦwww.julierpalace .com; ❶–❸) has a lively atmosphere, good prices and an excellent bar. Champfèr's four-star *Chesa Guardalej* (☎081 836 63 00, ⓦwww.chesa-guardalej .ch; ❹–❻) has perks like a free ski bus and free parking but stands out for its superb-value summer rates. The acclaimed *Landgasthof Bellavista* (☎081 838 60 50, ⓦwww.bellavista.ch; ❺–❼) is in a peaceful location near the Surlej cable car, with a stunning view and a fine restaurant.

Sils and Maloja

Beyond the Lej da Silvaplauna lies the quiet village of **SILS** (Segl in Romansh), with an alluring, rural atmosphere lacking in either Silvaplana or St Moritz: **Sils Baselgia** offers ethereally beautiful views over the Lej da Segl, acclaimed by a century of artistic and literary visitors – not least Hermann Hesse, Marc Chagall and Richard Strauss – while 200m south, **Sils Maria** was the summer home of the philosopher Friedrich Nietzsche for eight creative years. His modest house has been turned into the **Nietzsche–Haus** museum (Tues–Sun 3–6pm, closed May & Nov; Fr.6; ⓦwww.nietzschehaus.ch), where you can see manuscripts, photos, death masks and the room where Nietzsche wrote his most celebrated work, *Also Sprach Zarathustra*. In the Chesa Cumünela on the nearby village square is the well-equipped **tourist office** (Mon–Fri 8.30am–6pm, Sat 9am–noon & 4–6pm, Sun 4–6pm; shorter hours in off season; ☎081 838 50 50, ⓦwww.sils.ch). Traffic is barred from circulating between Maria and Baselgia: there's a large underground car park in Maria and, in winter, free local buses which also serve the base-station of the Furtschellas cable car. A handful of grand old hotels include the stunning Art Nouveau *Edelweiss* (T081 838 42 42, W www.hotel-edelweiss.ch; ❺–❼), Sils's oldest hotel, with a renowned restaurant. Less lavish options include simple *Schulze* (T081 826 52 13; ❷).

From Sils Maria, horse-drawn "buses" run on a schedule into the romantic, car-free **Val Fex** (June–Oct at least 2 daily; Fr.30 return; reserve on T081 826 52 86) to the peaceful *Hotel Fex* at the end of the valley (T081 826 53 55, W www.hotelfex.ch; ❸–❹).

In summer, a small **motorboat** – dubbed "Europe's highest ferry" – chugs around the Lej da Segl, 1800m above sea level, stopping a few times on its way to the village of **MALOJA** (July–Sept; 3–4 daily; takes 40min; Fr.20 return; reserve on T081 826 53 43), whose church cemetery holds the grave of painter Giovanni Segantini. Tough hiking trails to the north climb into the mountains to the Lunghin Pass, a rare triple watershed: from this point, the Inn flows into the Danube and the Black Sea; the Julier flows via the Rhine to the North Sea; and the Maira flows into the Po and the Mediterranean. In Maloja is a useful HI **hostel** *Jugendherberge* (T081 838 28 44, W www.youthhostel.ch; ❶; dorms Fr.32).

Val Bregaglia

From the **Maloja Pass** (1815m), the road suddenly tumbles off the cliff edge and down in a series of concertina switchbacks into the beautiful **Val Bregaglia** (Bergell in German), one of Graubünden's three Italian-speaking valleys (along with Mesolcina and Poschiavo). Suddenly, everything is different: the crisp air of the Alps is replaced by the warm breezes of the south, pine forests and rocky, snowy crags by lush, green vegetation, and *sgraffitied* bungalows by flinty cottages. Roughly 14km from the pass is the main village, **Vicosoprano**, an attractive, quiet place bypassed by the main road which heads on south through tiny **STAMPA**, birthplace of the painter Augusto Giacometti and his better-known son, the sculptor Alberto, and home to the valley's **tourist office** (T081 822 15 55, W www.bregaglia.ch). The road shadows the river, coiling on down the valley past ruined hilltop castles and isolated, crumbling roadside churches.

From **Promontogno**, 3km west of Stampa and about the same distance east of the border village Castasegna, postbuses follow a narrow branch road which climbs the north wall of the valley to **SOGLIO**. This eyrie of a hamlet, its narrow, cobbled alleys lined with close-set stone buildings, offers tremendous panoramic views: its lofty terrace sits opposite the Pizzo Badile (3300m), and is backed by the equally lofty Piz dal Märc and Piz Duan. The village is the focus of a wealth of mountain walks, easy ones following a valley-side route down to Stampa (2hr), as well as longer high-level hikes back to Vicosoprano, or up through the treeline behind the village. But there are lazier reasons to spend a day or three in Soglio: the 🌲 *Palazzo Salis* in the village (T081 822 12 08, W www.palazzosalis.ch; ❸–❺; March–Nov) is one of Switzerland's more extraordinary **hotels**. Soglio was the seat of the Von Salis family long before 1630, when the *palazzo* was constructed, and the hotel is still owned by the same family today. The whole place is an eye-opening experience, from the echoing vaulted hall, crammed with antique furniture, *chaises longues*, open fireplaces and suits of armour, to its grand guest rooms (some ensuite), stone-floored down below, wood-floored above, complete with four-poster beds and antique stoves.

Travel details

Full timetables for all trains, buses, trams, boats and cable cars in Switzerland – as well as international connections – are searchable at ⓦwww.rail.ch. For details of the Rhätische Bahn's flagship panoramic routes, see ⓦwww.rhb.ch.

Trains

Arosa to: Chur (hourly; 1hr).
Chur to: Arosa (hourly; 1hr); Davos Dorf & Platz (twice hourly; 1hr 30min; change in Landquart or Filisur); Disentis/Mustér (hourly; 1hr 15min); Klosters (hourly; 1hr 10min); Maienfeld (twice hourly; 15min); St Gallen (hourly; 1hr 35min); St Moritz (hourly; 2hr); Sargans (3 hourly; 20min); Thusis (twice hourly; 30min); Tiefencastel (hourly; 50min); Zürich (twice hourly; 1hr 15min).
Davos (Platz & Dorf) to: Chur (hourly; 1hr 30min); Klosters (twice hourly; 25min).
Klosters to: Chur (hourly; 1hr 10min); Davos Dorf & Platz (twice hourly; 25min); Scuol (hourly; 45min).
Pontresina to: St Moritz (hourly; 10min).
Poschiavo to: St Moritz (hourly; 1hr 40min); Tirano (hourly; 45min).

St Moritz to: Pontresina (hourly; 10min); Poschiavo (hourly; 1hr 40min); Tirano via Bernina Pass (hourly; 2hr 30min); Zernez (hourly; 45min; change at Samedan).

Buses

Andeer to: Juf (5 daily; 55min).
Chur to: Bellinzona via San Bernardino Tunnel (every 2hr; 2hr 15min); Flims (twice hourly; 45min); St Moritz via Julier Pass (1–2 daily; 2hr 40min); Splügen (every 2hr; 1hr); Zillis (every 2hr; 40min).
Davos (Platz & Dorf) to: Zernez via Flüela Pass (July–Oct every 2hr; 1hr).
Disentis/Mustér to: Biasca via Lukmanier/Lucomagno Pass (June–Sept 2 daily; 1hr 55min).
Flims to: Chur (twice hourly; 45min); Laax (twice hourly; 10min).
St Moritz to: Lugano via Chiavenna, Italy (1–2 daily; 4hr); Soglio (every 2hr; 1hr 25min; change at Promontogno).
Tiefencastel to: Bivio (hourly; 55min).
Zernez to: Davos via Flüela Pass (July–Oct every 2hr; 1hr); Müstair via Pass dal Fuorn (every 2hr; 1hr 10min).

12

Ticino

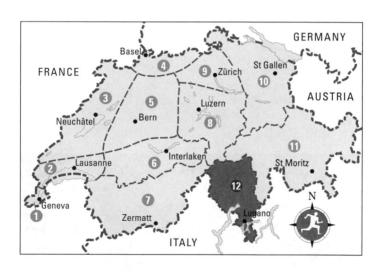

CHAPTER 12

Highlights

* **Bellinzona** Atmospheric, often-bypassed town, dominated by its three castles. See p.529

* **Alto Ticino** There's some excellent walking on offer in these remote, high valleys. See p.534

* **Locarno** Ticino's most stylish lakeside resort – a hint of the Mediterranean. See p.538

* **Cardada** Lofty viewpoint above Locarno, set amidst cool, fragrant, pine forests. See p.541

* **Valle Maggia** Tortuous valley system north of Locarno that culminates in isolated trailheads and a serene Alpine chapel at Mogno. See p.543

* **Centovalli** Highly memorable train ride, winding above a ravine west of Locarno. See p.544

* **Isole di Brissago** Two tiny dots of green in the glittering Lago Maggiore. See p.547

* **Lugano** Chic lakeside city, overlooked by, sugarloaf hills rising from a palm-fringed lake. See p.549

* **Monte Generoso** Ticino's only rack railway climbs above the Lago di Lugano. See p.559

△ Observation platform, Cardada

Ticino

It is strange how different the sun-dried, ancient, southern slopes of the world are, from the northern slopes. It is as if the god Pan really had his home among these sunbleached stones and tough, sun-dark trees. So I was content, coming down into Airolo...

D.H. Lawrence

The Italian-speaking canton of **TICINO** (*Tessin* in German and French) occupies the balmy, lake-laced southern foothills of the Alps. It's radically different from the rest of Switzerland in almost every way: culture, food, architecture, attitude and driving style owe more to Milan than Zürich, and the famously sunny skies even draw in fog-bound Milanese for a breath of air.

The place is simply irresistible: a short train ride under the Alps and you emerge – often in glittering sunshine – to a tiny corner of the Italian Mediterranean that is forever Switzerland, peopled by expressive, stylish, hot-blooded folk as different from the stolid farmers of the north as they could possibly be. And it's no wonder they're hot-blooded. As an ethnic and linguistic minority of eight percent in their own country and nothing more than a quaint irrelevance to the urban hotshots of Milan next door, the Ticinesi consistently have to struggle to get their voices heard in the corridors of power.

Exploring Ticino

Train services in Ticino, run by **FFS** (the Italian abbreviation for SBB, Swiss Federal Railways) or smaller local operators, are fine for accessing the three major towns, Bellinzona, Locarno and Lugano, with **local buses** from each of them serving points close at hand. However, if you want to explore the hinterland, relying on public transport can be frustrating: **postbuses** penetrate to the remotest hamlet, but on schedules that may leave a two-hour gap between services. **Renting a car** might be a better option, but you should bear in mind that all three major towns, and the roads between them, are choked with **cars**, and it can be literally impossible to find a parking space in the town centres.

The **Lugano Regional Pass** (April–Oct only; Ⓦwww.utp-lugano.ch), buyable from train stations, hotels and tourist offices, gives free travel on trains, buses and boats on and around Lago di Lugano, with half-price discounts on trains, buses and boats around Locarno, plus other benefits, for three/seven days (Fr.72/96). **Ticino Turismo** (Ⓦwww.ticino-tourism.ch) has more details.

TICINO

Splügen Pass/
Passo d. Spluga

Splügen

Passo del San
Bernardino

Mesocco

VALLE MESOLCINA

P. di Strega
2912m

VAL CALANCA

S. Vittore

P. Terri
3149m

P. Cassimoi
3129m

GRAUBÜNDEN
TICINO

Torrone Alto
2950m

Osogna

RIVIERA

Marumo
2790m

2787m

2670m

VAL MALVAGLIA

Malvaglia

Biasca

Ticino

Campo

Olivone

Aquila

Torre

VAL BLENIO

P. Medel
3211m

Disentis/Mustér

2195m

Brenno

Acquarossa

2505m

2445m

Il Madone
2395m

Passo del
Lucomagno/
Lukmanierpass

Acquacalda

P. di Campello
2660m

P. Molare
2585m

Giornico

2577m

2520m

P. di Vogorno
2442m

P. dell'Uomo
2663m

Schenadü
2747m

Faido

2518m

VAL VERZASCA

P. Blas
3019m

Sole
2773m

LEVENTINA

P. Forno
2907m

Sonogno

2304m

Madone
2130m

Lavertezzo

VAL PIORA

VALLE

Quinto

P. Campolungo
2713m

P. Campo
Tencia
3072m

la Marcia
2454m

Brione

Madone
di Giove
2265m

GRAUBÜNDEN
URI

Oberalppass

Disentis/Mustér

P. Taneda
2666m

VAL CANARIA

P. Centrale
3001m

Airolo

Corona di Redorta
2804m

P. Rasia
2684m

Maggia

Andermatt

Göschenen

GOTTHARD TUNNEL

Fusio

Mogno

Peccia

V. DI

Broglio

M. Zucchero
2736m

VALLE MAGGIA

Pso. del S. Gottardo/
St. Gotthardpass

Il Madone
2756m

Ponciona di Braga
2864m

P. Malora
2640m

Bignasco

Ticino

Bedretto

VALLE BEDRETTO

S. Carlo

VAL BAVONA

P. Alzasca
2262m

Furkapass

P. Rotondo
3192m

Basodino
3274m

P. di Sofógna
2698m

P. d'Orsalietta
2476m

Bosco/Gurin

Rosso di Ribia
2541m

Nufenen Pass/
Pso. della Novena

AGENETAL

Meiringen

Grimselpass

Oberwald

BERN
VALAIS

ITALY

FURKA TUNNEL

12

527

The glamour of their canton, and its stunning natural beauty – lushly wooded hills rising from azure water, palm trees swaying against deep blue skies, red roofs framed by purple bougainvillea – often seem to blind outsiders with romance. The German-speaking Swiss in particular fall head over heels for the Latin paradise on their doorstep. It takes just three hours from the grey streets of suburban Zürich to the fragrant subtropical gardens of Lugano, and from March till November German Swiss come in their thousands to sit beneath vine-shaded outdoor terraces of simple *grotti* or *osterie* (rustic local taverns) and choose polenta, risotto or herb-scented salads from bilingual Italian-German menus, sample a carafe of Merlot del Ticino, and still pay with familiar francs at the end.

Ticino is divided topographically in two by the **Monte Ceneri** range (1961m), two-thirds of the way down: the area to the north is the **Sopraceneri** ("Above Ceneri"), that to the south is **Sottoceneri** ("Below Ceneri"). The main attractions are the lakeside resorts of **Locarno** and **Lugano**, where mountain scenery merges with the subtropical flora encouraged by the warm climate, although the cantonal capital **Bellinzona** and the quiet valleys of **Alto Ticino** also hold a great deal of charm. Ticino is known for its plethora of ancient churches, many of them Romanesque and containing medieval frescoes, and most also featuring huge external murals of St Christopher, patron saint of travellers. **Architecture and design** have been taken seriously for centuries past, with a string of world-class architects emanating from the Ticino; for more, see p.578. Much time and money is devoted to architecture, with towns and villages throughout the canton full of sympathetic, subtle restoration of ancient buildings; kitschy Alpine chalets are confined to *Oltre Gottardo*, the locals' some-what disparaging term for the rest of Switzerland "beyond the Gotthard".

Some history

Although linguistically, culturally and temperamentally Italian, the Ticino has been controlled by the Swiss since the early 1500s, when Uri, Schwyz and Unterwalden moved to secure the southern approaches of the **Gotthard Pass** against the dukes of Milan. For three centuries the Ticinesi remained under the thumb of the tyrannical northerners, until **Napoleon** arrived in 1798 to reorganize the area under his new Cisalpine Republic. But faced with a mere exchange of overlords, the Ticinesi held out for independence, and under the banner *Liberi e Svizzeri!* ("Free and Swiss!"), the **Republic of Ticino** joined the Confederation as a new canton in 1803.

Since then, the Ticinesi – appearances notwithstanding – remain resolutely Swiss, and have little truck with foreigners calling them Italian, although it's also almost impossible for an outsider to tell the locals apart from the 36,000 Italian *frontalieri* who cross into Ticino daily to work for salaries well below the Swiss average. A cruel irony of life here is that Ticino suffers some of Switzerland's highest **unemployment** rates even while its service industries thrive, staffed by Italians and paid for by thousands of Swiss-German tourists and second-homeowners. Similarly, young people, who would naturally gravitate towards universities or jobs in nearby Milan, have been forced by their lack of an EU passport to go north into culturally and linguistically "foreign" Switzerland instead. The reality behind Ticino's glamorous front is a tale of fifty years or more of social dislocation and a draining, deep-rooted frustration with chiefly Swiss-German-inspired isolationism.

Sopraceneri

The **SOPRACENERI** region takes in the whole of the northern two-thirds of the canton. Road and rail lines stream down from the Alpine tunnels, bypassing the Ticinese hinterland and funnelling into the cantonal capital **Bellinzona**, a quietly elegant place often passed over in favour of the lakeside resorts – the latter exemplified by shades-and-*gelati* **Locarno**, revelling in its location at the tip of the idyllic **Lago Maggiore**. The heart of this rugged region, however, lies in the very hinterland that most people see hurtling past at 110kph. Unspoilt **Alto Ticino**, comprising a network of wild, Prealpine valleys and mountain-top lakelets glittering in clear, crystalline sunshine, holds some of the best walking in the country.

Bellinzona

Few people bother with **BELLINZONA** – their loss, since this graceful and beautiful old town is the perfect place to draw breath before hitting the lakeside glitz further south, and is a mellow introduction to the easy pace of the Ticino.

A fortress since **Roman** times, Bellinzona occupies a prime valley-floor position, controlling the great Alpine passes of the Novena (Nufenen), Gottardo (Gotthard), Lucomagno (Lukmanier) and San Bernadino. In 1242 it was bought by the Visconti family, dukes of Milan, who built a new **castle** atop the hill plum in the middle of the valley, while their allies, the Rusconi family of Como, built another castle slightly up the hillside. In the late fourteenth century, the newly independent Swiss confederates north of the Gotthard Pass, who had successfully thrown off Habsburg rule, started to look to secure their position by conquering the territory on the south side of the pass. They began a violent campaign against the Milanese in the 1420s, which spurred the Sforza dynasty – then in the ascendant in Milan – to reinforce the two existing castles

---

Bellinzona's Saturday market

It's worth making a special trip to Bellinzona for the colourful, atmospheric **Saturday market** of breads, local cheeses, wines, fruit and veg and handicrafts, held in the alleys of the Old Town (8am–1pm). Many local restaurants take the opportunity to offer polenta or risotto for a civilized Saturday lunch al fresco. Also don't miss the annual cheese market in early October, where all the Ticinese Alpine producers parade their wares.

Bellinzona's festivals

Bellinzona's February carnival, known as **Rabadan** (ⓦ www.rabadan.ch), takes in a huge masked parade and festivities in and around the Old Town, starting on the Thursday before Mardi Gras and continuing all weekend. Early June sees the **Spada nella Rocca** (ⓦ www.laspadanellarocca.ch), a medieval festival at Montebello. The town also hosts several music festivals, including **Piazza Blues** (ⓦ www.piazzablues .ch), an open-air event in late June; past performers include such big names as Albert Collins, B.B. King and Screamin' Jay Hawkins.

at Bellinzona and build a third, even higher up the hillside. A massive chain of fortifications cut right across the Ticino valley at Bellinzona… but to no avail, since the Swiss won the town under the Treaty of Arona in 1503. Three centuries of oppression followed, with Swiss overlords posted to Bellinzona to keep control of the peasantry until Ticino won its **independence** in 1803.

Bellinzona has gained a reputation as the poor relation of Locarno and Lugano. This is undeserved, since it might lack a lake, but it also lacks the hectic pace, the crowds and the touristic sheen of its bigger neighbours. This gentle town is blessed with medieval architecture and picturesque churches, and also serves as the main access point for excursions into the wild Alto Ticino region. Its grand trio of castles – **Castelgrande**, **Montebello** and **Sasso Corbaro** – together comprise a UNESCO World Heritage Site.

Arrival, information and accommodation

Bellinzona's **train station** is 500m northeast of the Old Town. Note that the cobbled streets of the Old Town, from the post office south to Piazza Indipendenza, are banned to private vehicles from 7.30pm to 6am.

The **tourist office** is in the Palazzo Civico on Piazza Nosetto (Mon–Fri 9am–6.30pm, Sat 9am–noon; ☎091 825 21 31, Ⓦwww.bellinzonaturismo.ch). They have good information on architecture as well as walking routes and driving itineraries in the higher valleys, and also stock the scholarly *Castles of Bellinzona* booklet by Werner Meyer (in English). You can take a self-guided **walking tour** with the **Bellinzona ArtKey audioguide** (Fr.5), available from the tourist office and all three castles and usable by two people at the same time.

Bellinzona's **accommodation** wins few prizes for style or imagination. Of the **hotels**, *San Giovanni*, Via San Giovanni 7 (☎091 825 19 19; ❷), has a few well-kept rooms above a Ticinese restaurant. *Internazionale*, Piazza Stazione 35 (☎091 825 43 33, Ⓦwww.hotel-internazionale.ch; ❷–❸), is the most pleasant of the station hotels, with comfortable, serviceable rooms; *Garni Moderno*, Viale Stazione 17b (☎091 825 13 76; ❷), is a clean, modern alternative. *Unione*, Via Generale Guisan 1 (☎091 825 55 77, Ⓦwww.albergo-unione.ch; ❹; closed Jan), is Bellinzona's best, with efficient service and renovated rooms. The HI **hostel** *Ostello/Jugendherberge* is in the grand Villa Montebello, at Via Nocca 4 (☎091 825 15 22, Ⓦwww.youthhostel.ch; ❶; dorms Fr.35).

The Town

The elegant Renaissance buildings of **Piazza Collegiata** mark the centre of the Old Town, dominated by the lavish Collegiata church, built by the same architect who worked on Como's cathedral and decorated with Baroque frescoes and stucco. Narrow, shaded lanes branch out all around: arcaded **Piazza Nosetto** is just south, with the Cà Rossa house on the way featuring a striking red terracotta facade – a style fashionable in early nineteenth-century Milan. From Piazza Nosetto, a gateway leads into the courtyard of the **Palazzo Civico** or **Palazzo del Comune**, rebuilt in the 1920s in Renaissance style, with loggias winding attractively around both upper floors.

Castelgrande

High on Bellinzona's central rock rise the massive towers and walls of **Castelgrande** (Mon 10am–6pm, Tues–Sun 9am–10pm; free), most impressive of the town's three medieval castles. Known to have been occupied as far back as the Neolithic age, the hill was fortified first by the Romans, and then again in the thirteenth century by Milanese forces to protect the valley routes to and from the Alpine passes. For three centuries between the Swiss conquest and Ticinese independence, Castelgrande was known as the Castello di Uri after its trans-Alpine occupiers (Montebello was the Castello di Svitto (Schwyz), while Sasso Corbaro was the Castello di Untervaldo). Just to confuse things further, the rock on which the castle sits is known as **Monte San Michele**.

The hilltop complex has been imaginatively and sympathetically restored by architect Aurelio Galfetti. He added a free-to-use public **lift** that is dramatically

Bellinzona has two **museum passes** with overlapping validities. A combi-ticket for admission to all three castles is Fr.8. Alternatively, the **CulturaPass Bellinzona** grants admission to the three castles plus the Villa dei Cedri art gallery, for Fr.13. Both are buyable at any of the museums or the tourist office.

recessed deep into the bedrock of the hill behind the central **Piazza del Sole** and emerges at a purpose-built modern fortification on an upper terrace of the castle.

The castle grounds are serene, overlooked by the slender thirteenth-century **White Tower**, with two upper windows on all four faces, and the fourteenth-century **Black Tower**, with three windows on its longer side. Despite their names, both, like the castle itself, are grey granite, and between them run lines of distinctive Lombard-style **winged battlements**, which you'll see on castles all over Ticino. You can also walk part of the way round the walls (daily 10am–7pm, Nov–March until 5pm).

Off Castelgrande's central lawns is an entrance to the **Museo Storico** (daily 10am–6pm, Nov–March until 5pm; Fr.4; see box p.531 for pass details; SMP). The archeology section offers a tour through Bellinzona's ancient past, including an excellent audiovisual show (in English) presenting the history of the town. The pride and joy, in the artistic section, is a set of murals made in 1470 to decorate the wooden ceiling of a villa in the town, depicting a complex set of allegorical themes dealing with love, faith and virtue.

Atmospheric steps wind down the hillside from Castelgrande to Piazza Collegiata.

South to the Villa dei Cedri

Peaceful **Piazza Indipendenza** is 100m south of Piazza Nosetto and sports a 1903 obelisk commemorating the first century of Ticinese independence. On the east side of the square is the small, atmospheric church of **San Rocco**, built in 1330 and renovated in 1478.

Following Via Lugano south from Piazza Indipendenza for 600m brings you to Piazza San Biagio, and the gates of the **Villa dei Cedri** art gallery (Tues–Fri 2–6pm, Sat & Sun 11am–6pm; Fr.8; see box p.531 for pass details; SMP; ⓦwww.villacedri.ch), set in beautiful grounds. The modest collection focuses on nineteenth- and twentieth-century Swiss and Lombard art. Beside the villa, the frescoed church of **San Biagio** dates from the twelfth century and has a mural of St Christopher beside the door.

Beside a disused convent 100m west across the tracks is **Santa Maria delle Grazie**, which was severely damaged by fire after a nativity scene caught alight on New Year's Eve 1997; restoration is well under way on its enormous late-fifteenth-century interior fresco of the Crucifixion.

Montebello and Sasso Corbaro

Behind the Collegiata church, on the eastern side of Piazza Collegiata, a path rises to the picturesque **Castello di Montebello** (daily 8am–8pm; free), some 90m higher in elevation than Castelgrande, with suitably impressive views of the town. From a vantage point on the lofty ramparts, it's easy to trace the line of defensive fortifications which link the two castles across the width of the Ticino valley. The castle itself is impressive, with a fifteenth-century courtyard and residential palace surrounding an older central portion dating from the thirteenth century, the latter now housing the modern **Museo Archeologico e Civico** (April–Oct daily 10am–6pm; Fr.4; see box p.531 for pass details).

A stiff 45-minute climb further up will bring you to **Castello di Sasso Corbaro** (Easter–Oct Mon 10am–6pm, Tues–Sun 10am–10pm; free), some 230m above Bellinzona, designed and built in six months in 1479 by a military engineer brought in from Florence after the Swiss defeat of Milanese troops at the Battle of Giornico. It shelters a particularly welcome vine-shaded courtyard *osteria* and has a spectacular rampart panorama; its **museum** (April–Oct daily

Walks around Bellinzona

There are plenty of picturesque **walks** near Bellinzona which could fill a pleasant afternoon. One of the best begins in nearby **Roveredo** (in Graubünden's Val Mesolcina and served by postbuses from Bellinzona), from where an old cart track on the "quiet" side of the river heads through tiny San Giulio and into the woods opposite San Vittore, before crossing the river at a little bridge in Lumino and heading on through the forest to Arbedo on the outskirts of Bellinzona. You'll come across plenty of peaceful shady *grotti* on the way. Side roads off the main Via San Gottardo lead through Arbedo and under the tracks to the picturesque Chiesa Rossa, an ancient red-washed church sitting lost and forgotten beside industrial warehouses on Via del Carmagnola backing onto the tracks (total 2hr walking). Buses can run you the final 1.5km south into Bellinzona centre.

The walk to **Prada** begins in the car park of the hospital in Ravecchia, a southern suburb (city bus #5) – cobbled alleys lead you alongside vineyards to a mule track which climbs gently beneath the looming Castello di Sasso Corbaro to the tiny, isolated church of San Girolamo di Prada, set amidst the ruins of Prada village (45min). Tougher paths lead on from Prada through forests into the secluded Val Morobbia, an old smugglers' route; two or three postbuses a day from Bellinzona to the last village in the valley, **Carena**, bring you to the trailhead of a tough, but deserted, five-hour circular hike up to the Passo di San Jorio (2014m), marking the Italian frontier, and back.

10am–6pm; Fr.4; see box p.531 for pass details) includes a gallery showing changing exhibits by contemporary Ticinese artists.

To avoid the climb, catch bus #4 from the centre to Artore, near Castello di Sasso Corbaro, and then wend your own path back down the hillside.

Eating and drinking

Within Castelgrande are two **restaurants** (both closed Mon): you can eat well for Fr.20 at the ⚜ *Grotto San Michele*, which spreads itself over the panoramic terrace and also has an interior room; while the formal *Castelgrande* restaurant (☎091 826 23 53, ⊛www.castelgrande.ch), all black leather and tubular steel furniture, is a much snootier affair – you'll get little change from Fr.60 for its modern, Ticino-inspired cuisine. The atmospheric *Osteria Sasso Corbaro*, in Bellinzona's topmost castle (☎091 825 55 32; closed Mon & Nov–March) – recommended by the "SlowFood" guide for its authentic ingredients and preparation – serves up Ticinese fare accompanied by plenty of wine at stone tables in the shady castle courtyard, or in a great hall within; *menus* are Fr.25 or so.

Down in the town, *Locando Orico*, Via Orico 13 (☎091 825 15 18, ⊛www .locandaorico.ch; closed Sun & Mon), is a fine gourmet restaurant in an atmospheric old wood-beamed house, with a lunch menu for Fr.40 and a six-course *menu degustazione* for Fr.105 (excluding wine). *Portici*, a pleasant *osteria*/pizzeria in the Old Town at Vicolo Muggiasca 4 (closed Sun lunch & Mon), serves palatable food in its shady courtyard to a young, easy crowd of regulars for Fr.20 or less. Cheap self-service nosh is at *Manora* on Viale Stazione. *Birreria Corona*, Via Camminata 5 (closed Sun), is an atmospheric café-bar fronting quite a good restaurant in the back, with *menus* also around Fr.20.

Pavement **café-bars** abound, especially around Via Codeborgo, where you'll see (or hear) the jumping *Amadeus Pub* on Vicolo Torre (closed Sun) and the equally lively *Peverelli* at Codeborgo 12 (closed Mon).

Alto Ticino

The most pristine part of this sometimes tiresomely touristic canton is **ALTO TICINO** (Upper Ticino), north of Bellinzona – a region of wild, lonesome valleys cutting deep into the landscape on the approach to the high Alps, dotted with rustic stone-built hamlets teetering on steep slopes. As throughout the rest of the canton – though less obtrusively here – many of the original Ticinese communities, which laboured so long to scrape a living from the land, are now financially enriched (even if culturally challenged) by the presence of many German and Swiss-German second-homeowners seeking refuge from the pressures of city life. The villages and the scenery nonetheless survive unscathed, and if getting off the beaten path is your aim, Alto Ticino is a perfect choice.
Biasca is the gateway to the region, a small town at the junction of the scenic **Val Blenio** – which heads north from Biasca up to **Olivone**, then cuts over to the Lucomagno Pass – and the main **Valle Leventina**, which bends northwest up to the foot of the Gottardo Pass and the quiet town of Airolo, where the rural Val Bedretto splits off west to the Novena Pass.

You'd do well to check your planned itinerary with the tourist office in Bellinzona before you set off: although information and maps are much the same wherever you go, staff in the regional tourist offices in Biasca, Olivone and Airolo are less likely to be fluent in English.

Biasca

The small town of **BIASCA** sits in a grand location at the junction of three valleys: the Valle Leventina, the Val Blenio, and to the south towards Bellinzona a part of the Ticino valley called the **Riviera**, which crams in side by side a motorway, a main road, a minor road, a train line and several footpaths, all snaking between wooded mountainsides rising 1500m above your head. High above the town to the southeast, commanding an eagle's-eye view of all routes in and out, is the imposing thirteenth-century church of **San Pietro e Paolo**, with a sixteenth-century portico tacked on to its simple, Romanesque facade. Collect the key from the newer parish church halfway up the hillside. Inside, the irregular Romanesque floor plan – architects seem to have struggled with the sloping bedrock – is unchanged, and the interior walls are covered in medieval frescoes.

Biasca's **train station** is 750m south of the centre. The **tourist office** is just off Piazza Centrale on Piazzetta Cavalier Pellanda (Mon–Fri 8.30am–noon & 2–6pm; May–Oct also Sat 8.30–11.30am; ☎091 862 33 27, ⊕www.biascaturismo .ch). Stairs up to the church rise directly behind the tourist office. The modern **hotel** *Al Giardinetto*, Via Pini 21 (☎091 862 17 71, ⊕www.algiardinetto.ch; ❸), is located in the centre. Look out for the regular Saturday **market**, showcasing fresh produce from the upper valleys.

Val Blenio

Quiet **Val Blenio** heads north from Biasca, away from the main Leventina routes, a broad open valley that basks in generous sunshine. The valley floor is dotted with villages, themselves marked by *rustici*, stone-built peasant dwellings, sometimes little more than shacks, that are topped with rough slate roofs. A lot of these are now holiday cottages, renovated and rented out for tidy sums to nature-starved northerners, but the valley has nonetheless made sure to protect its most valuable assets – peace, quiet and unspoilt natural beauty. Oddly enough, the Bleniesi have been known throughout Europe for centuries as culinary entrepreneurs, a skill probably picked up in Milan sometime in the Middle Ages and passed on through the

A two-week walking **Tour of Ticino** explores the finest valleys and most remote landscapes in the upper part of the canton. The granite massifs of the Lepontine Alps, as these mountains are known, are among the least visited of any in Switzerland: you can wander for hours, even in the height of summer, and see no one. The scenery is charming: clear streams tumble through the valleys, numerous tarns add a sparkle to the crags, and deep green pools in hidden corners invite walkers to pause for a well-deserved midsummer bathe. Accommodation is sometimes sparse in the villages but there are plenty of mountain huts (*capanne*). As ever, it's easy to pick out **shorter walks**: from the Valle Santa Maria through Val Piora to Airolo, for instance, or from Bignasco to Fusio. **Maps** to pack are the LS 265, 266, 275 and 276 (all 1:50,000); *Walking in the Alps* and *Walking in Ticino*, both by Kev Reynolds (see "Books", p.587), are essential reading.

The tour begins either in **Torre** or **Dangio**, two adjacent villages in the upper Valle di Blenio 4km south of Olivone. The route heads through Val Soi on a path which climbs to **Capanna Adula** (☏091 872 15 32) at the southern end of Val Carassina. Day two leads through Val Carassina to a small dammed lake, then descends to **Olivone** before following a mule track through a defile into Val Camadra. On the western hillside the path leads to **Capanna Boverina** (☏091 872 15 29). Next day you continue up to Passo di Gana Negra, cross Valle Santa Maria and make a steady ascent to Passo Colombe. An enjoyable descent from there takes the route into the gentle tarn-glistening Val Piora where sits the **Capanna Cadagno** (☏091 868 13 23). Day five crosses Bochetta di Cadlimo to Pian Bornengo at the head of Val Canaria, then descends this glen to **Airolo**. On the south side of Valle Leventina the way resumes on a belvedere trail known as the Strada degli Alpi Bedretto, but on reaching the alp hutments of Piano di Pesciüm it cuts into Val Torta and climbs to **Capanna Cristallina** (☏091 869 23 30). The following stage makes a crossing of the Cristallina massif to **Capanna Basòdino** (☏091 753 27 97) by one of two wild, rocky routes, both of which feature several tarns.

On day eight, an easy downhill walk descends through the woods and pastures of Val Bavona to **Bignasco** at the head of the Valle Maggia. It's a glorious walk leading past tiny hamlets and feathery waterfalls to a confluence of valleys. From Bignasco on day ten, the suggested route goes through Val Cocco and over Passo del Cocco at its head, before dropping to the remote, unstaffed **Capanna Alpe d'Osola**. The way now negotiates Bochetta di Mugaia in the south ridge of Monte Zucchero, before descending 1600m to **Sonogno**. Day eleven crosses Passo di Redorta (2181m) to Val di Pertüs, whose stark walls plunge into the depths of a gorge. Val di Pertüs feeds into Val di Prato, and this in turn spills into Val Lavizzara where you spend the night in **Prato-Sornico**. The tour heads north to **Fusio**, a short journey on linking trails that avoids most of the road between the two villages. On such a short stage it would be worth diverting up to Lago di Mognola high on the eastern hillside, at the northern end of which an airy path makes a traverse before plunging steeply to the valley near Fusio. The final (thirteenth) day's walk leads back to Valle Leventina via Passo Campolungo. The pass is more than 1000m above Fusio, while the descent to **Rodi-Fiesso**, 10km south of Airolo, is a steep 1300m, but the path is mostly good and there are consistently fine views on both sides.

generations. In 1600 one Signor Bianchini from the valley was no less than head chef to the King of Spain; in 1849, a Signor Baggi won an award for selling the best ice cream in France; while the Gatti family – also from the Blenio – owned and managed 230 restaurants and cafés throughout late-Victorian England.

The Sentiero Basso is the main valley-floor path: the walk from Biasca to **Acquarossa** on the west bank of the river is a gently rising 13km, taking a little under four hours. On the east bank just north of Biasca is **Malvaglia**, whose village church boasts a huge fresco of St Christopher; from here a tortuous branch road climbs in a series of hairpins into the lonesome **Val Malvaglia** amidst tremendous scenery of steep wooded slopes dropping away into a seemingly bottomless ravine. From a point on the road, it's possible to park and walk across a bridge spanning the valley, on the other side of which a dramatic mule track penetrates for a couple of hours' walk to **Dagro**, a hamlet on the northern side of the valley with broad views.

As you rise into the Blenio, the lush green slopes begin to close in. The main town at the head of the valley, below the sharp-peaked Sosto on one side and the Töira on the other, is **OLIVONE**, a little place 24km north of Biasca that reflects the valley's once-noble pretensions in its array of grandiose, if worn, eighteenth- and nineteenth-century mansions – rather out of place amidst the orchards and increasingly wild high-valley scenery. The **tourist office** (☎091 872 14 87, ⓦ www.blenio.com) has information on the valley. Up in the village is the *Osteria Centrale* (☎091 872 11 07; ❶), which serves tasty home-cooked fare and has a few simple rooms. Down a short hill beside the main road is the post office and bus stop with, alongside, the *Albergo San Martino* (☎091 872 15 21; ❷), also with excellent traditional food and pizzas plus a choice of rooms.

A five-hour walk from Olivone climbs to the **Lucomagno Pass** (1914m). The road over the pass from Olivone to **Disentis/Mustér** in Graubünden (see p.497) is perhaps the most scenic route in and out of Ticino.

Valle Leventina

From Biasca, the motorway, the main road and rail line all blaze a trail northwest into the **Valle Leventina**, heading for the **Passo del Gottardo** (Gotthard Pass) and tunnels (see p.398) at the end. There's no doubt that this is a spectacular route, whether heading north or south, but its heavy usage is its downfall: hemmed in by the high valley walls, the hiss and rumble of traffic noise from the motorway can seem obtrusively loud to valley-floor walkers and cyclists. This situation will change in 2012, when the **Gotthard Base Tunnel** (see p.399) opens: most of the road and rail traffic will enter the new tunnel at **Bodio**, just north of Biasca, thereby restoring peace and quiet to the upper Leventina.

Giornico

Make time for **GIORNICO**, a small town 9km northwest of Biasca. It was here in 1478 that a Swiss force numbering 600 defeated a 10,000-strong Milanese army, thereby linking Ticino's subsequent history to Switzerland rather than Italy. Giornico is lovely, a typical Ticinese village built on the gentle slopes either side of the tumbling River Ticino, with cobbled alleys running picturesquely between old stone-roofed houses, and a photogenic hump-backed bridge crossing to a wooded island mid-river, and from there to the west bank, where rises the campanile of **San Nicolao**, one of the most impressive and atmospheric of Ticino's many Romanesque churches. Its external walls are decorated with Lombardic designs, while inside is a fresco-decorated choir placed above a beautiful triple-apsed half-sunken crypt. After exploring the village, visit the *Osteria Giornico* on the main street (☎091 864 22 15; closed Wed) to pick up the keys for **La Congiunta**. This blank structure, stuck in the fields 300m north of Giornico's little train station, is an art gallery, dedicated to the sculpture of Zürich artist Hans Josephsohn – though you'd never know from the outside: it looks like a concrete bunker. The raw, oddly tranquil interior holds three rooms of lumpy metal reliefs and a few sculptures in bronze dating from 1950 to 1991.

The architect Peter Märkli's deserted, deconstructed setting suits Josephsohn's brutalist art perfectly.

Giornico has a couple of terrific *grotti*, both of them full of atmosphere and serving up the kind of simple, lovingly prepared food you wouldn't expect to be able to buy. The *Grotto dei Due Ponti* is the one everyone goes to, perfectly located on the mid-river island, its shaded terrace overlooking the rushing water. ☂ *Grotto Pergola* (ⓦ www.grottopergola.ch), tucked away on the west bank of the river and south of San Nicolao, though with a less alluring garden, serves even better food.

Airolo

Some 28km north of Giornico is **AIROLO**, first town in the Ticino for the millions who pour out of the Gottardo train and road tunnels each year heading south. Thankfully bypassed by the main routes, it's a quiet town with a handful of hotels serving as staging post for summer journeys up to the **Gotthard Pass** (see p.398), or into the **Val Bedretto** and up to the **Novena** (Nufenen Pass; see p.354). The town is also the trailhead for plenty of high-altitude walks, especially into the stunning **Val Piora**, outlined in the box on p.535. Winter

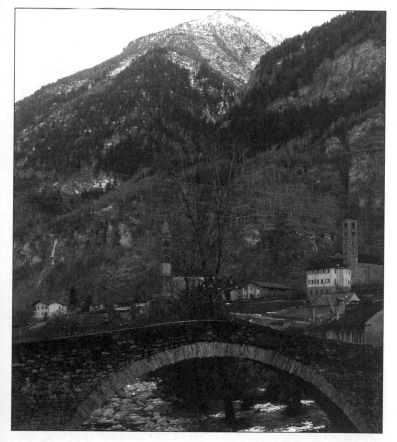

△ Giornico

sees Airolo transformed into a modest ski resort. The Leventina's **tourist office** is also here (☎091 869 15 33, ⓦ www.leventinaturismo.ch).

Locarno

Trains and often packed minor roads head west from Bellinzona for some 15km to **Lago Maggiore** and its principal Swiss resort, **LOCARNO**. This characterful old town enjoys the most glorious of locations, on a broad sweeping curve of a bay in the lake, and also clocks up the most sunshine hours of anywhere in Switzerland. The arcades and piazzas of the town centre are overlooked by subtropical gardens of palms, camellias, bougainvillea, cypress, oleanders and magnolias, which flourish on the lakeside promenades and cover the wooded slopes which crowd in above the town centre.

Locarno slumbered under Swiss occupation after 1503, but with independence in the nineteenth century it found its feet as the most elegant of the country's lakeside resorts. In 1925 its backdrop of Belle-Epoque hotels and piazza cafés served as the setting for the **Treaty of Locarno**, signed by the European powers in a failed effort to secure peace following World War I. The town went from strength to strength during the 1950s and after, growing in chic-ness year on year. These days, Locarno focuses its considerable resources on tourism, and draws in two very different sets of customers: one, from the German-speaking north, arrive to test out their hiking boots, while the other, from fog- and smog-bound Milan, come to test out their sunglasses. The cobbled alleys of Locarno's Old Town, lined with Renaissance facades, can get entirely overrun with the rich and wannabe-famous on summer weekends, yet still – in the midst of the hubbub – the place manages to retain its sun-drenched cool.

Turn to p.545 for an account of Locarno's neighbour, **Ascona**.

Arrival, information and accommodation

Locarno's **train station** is 100m north of the lakeshore landing-stage and 150m northeast of Piazza Grande; mainline FFS trains depart from ground level, while

---

Festivals in Locarno and Ascona

Locarno and Ascona host events and festivities all summer long. After the **Festa delle Camelie** in early April, the season kicks off with the **Artisti di Strada** festival (ⓦ www.artistidistrada.ch) in Ascona, celebrating mime, busking and all kinds of entertainment. The popular **New Orleans Jazz Festival** (ⓦ www.jazzascona.com) takes place in Ascona in late June, followed in mid-July by Locarno's **Moon and Stars** rock festival (ⓦ www.moonandstarslocarno.ch) – international stars such as Eric Clapton, Bryan Adams and The Who have played here in past years.

The world-class **Locarno International Film Festival** (ⓦ www.pardo.ch), held over ten days in early August, is stealing a march on Cannes for both movie quality and star appeal, and is now rated among the top five film festivals in the world. Catch major offerings on the huge open-air screen in Piazza Grande, playing to 7500 people nightly (around Fr.22), or at one of the 12 daily screenings in the city's cinemas (around Fr.15). A universal festival pass is Fr.210 or so.

Throughout September, Ascona and Locarno host the **Settimane Musicali** ("Music Weeks"; ⓦ www.settimane-musicali.ch), a cycle of prestigious classical concerts held in churches and other venues, and drawing in major world orchestras and soloists.

Cardada ▲

ORSELINA

LOCARNO

Santuario della Madonna del Sasso

Sant'Antonio

Chiesa Nuova

Casa Rusca

San Francesco

Castello Visconteo

MURALTO

Station

San Vittore

Lago Maggiore

EATING & DRINKING

Bar del Pozzo	7
Cantina Canetti	6
Centenario	3
Cittadella	4
Funicolare	1
Lungolago	8
Manora	2
Svizzero	5

ACCOMMODATION

Camelia	A
Città Vecchia	D
Navegna	B
Nessi	C
Ostello	F
Schlosshotel	G
Vecchia Locarno	E

0 ———— 250 m

Bosco Isolino

Ascona, Isole di Brissago & Italy ▼

the local transport company Ferrovie Autolinee Regionali Ticinesi – unfortunately abbreviated to **FART** – operate trains on the Centovalli line (see p.544) from a separate station below ground. The municipality of Locarno itself is quite small, and the city also includes the contiguous districts of **Muralto**, in which the station is located, **Minusio** further east, and **Orselina** on the slopes above.

The efficient but often crowded **tourist office** is in the Casino complex on Via Largo Zorzi, 100m southwest of the station (April–Oct Mon–Fri 9am–6pm, Sat 10am–6pm, Sun 10am–1.30pm & 2.30–5pm; Nov–March Mon–Fri 9am–12.30pm & 2–6pm; ☎091 791 00 91, ⓦ www.maggiore.ch). The **guest card** has wide validity, covering discounts on local transport and museums as well as bonuses for walkers exploring the high valleys, such as cheap stays at Alpine huts and reduced fares on cable cars.

Hotels

Camelia Via Nessi 9, Muralto ☎091 743 00 21, ⓦ www.camelia.ch. Elegant, eager-to-please family hotel set in fragrant floral gardens and offering spacious rooms, some with balcony and lake view. March–Oct. ❸–❹

Città Vecchia Via Torretta 13 ☎091 751 45 54, ⓦ www.cittavecchia.ch. Centrally placed B&B ("garni") hotel, with dorms (see overleaf) and simple, shared-bath rooms. March–Oct. ❶–❷

Navegna Via alla Riva 2, Minusio ☎091 743 22 22, ⓦ www.navegna.ch. About 1.5km east of the centre, directly on the waterfront, with modern, stylishly renovated rooms, private parking and an excellent restaurant. March–Nov. ❹–❺

Nessi Via Varenna 79 ☎091 751 77 41, ⓦ www.garninessi.ch. Welcoming little family-run place a short bus ride west of the centre, with its own pool and underground parking. Rooms are fresh and decent, with better, bigger ones on higher floors. ❸

Schlosshotel Via San Francesco 7a ☏ 091 751 23 61, ⓦ www.schlosshotellocarno.ch. Large, comfortably old-fashioned rooms in a well-kept Old Town pile. March–Nov. ❸–❹

Vecchia Locarno Via Motta 10 ☏ 091 751 65 02, ⓦ www.hotel-vecchia-locarno.ch. Scruffily characterful Old Town gem, with both shared-bath and ensuite rooms above a courtyard restaurant and wine bar. ❷

Hostels

Città Vecchia (see p.539). Good Old Town option, with dorms from Fr.29.

Ostello/Jugendherberge Palagiovani (HI hostel) Via Varenna 18 ☏ 091 756 15 00, ⓦ www.youthhostel.ch. Modern hostel with dorms from Fr.33.50, but it's in an awkward western location – take bus #31 or #36 (direction Centovalli) to Cinque Vie. ❶

Campsite

Delta ☏ 091 751 60 81, ⓦ www.campingdelta.com. Excellent site, a fifteen-minute walk south along the lakeshore. March–Oct.

Boats on Lago Maggiore

Boats run by NLM (April–Oct only; ⓦ www.navigazionelaghi.it) crisscross the Swiss shores of the exceptionally beautiful **Lago Maggiore**, as well as continuing down the lake into Italy. Note that Maggiore is the only major lake in Switzerland to be **excluded** from the Swiss Pass.

For fare purposes, the Swiss part of the lake is divided into two: a **day pass** for the area *either* north *or* south of Ascona is Fr.13.40, or for the whole Swiss basin is Fr.23. Examples of **point-to-point** tickets include Locarno to Ascona Fr.6.70, Locarno to the Isole di Brissago Fr.11.90. A **Lago Maggiore Holiday Card** gives free transport on the whole of Lake Maggiore and half-price travel on Lake Lugano; one/three/seven days cost Fr.35/57/86. Various **day-trip excursion** tickets into Italy are also available, which include boat transport and admission fees for major attractions such as the splendid gardens of Isola Bella or Villa Táranto, or the cable car from Stresa to the Mottarone peak. Don't forget your **passport**.

The combination ticket **Il Lago e la Montagna** (Fr.55; valid 10 days) includes a day-pass for boats on the Swiss sector, admission to the Isole di Brissago, the funicular to Madonna del Sasso and the cable scar to Cardada and Cimetta.

Lago Maggiore Express

For its simplicity, diversity and superb scenery, the **Lago Maggiore Express** ticket (ⓦ www.lagomaggioreexpress.com) is worth looking at. It comprises three sectors, all of them great journeys in their own right: the stunning **Centovalli rail line** between Locarno and Domodossola (see p.544), a **fast train** from Domodossola to Stresa, and a long **boat trip** on the lake. It runs only in spring (mid-March to May Fri–Sun) and summer (June–Sept daily, generally excluding Wed). The schedules are flexible: you make your own choice of connections, and you can do the trip in either direction. The whole thing could take as little as six hours – or you could dawdle over it for a couple of days.

Note that this is not a tour: you travel on your own, using **public transport**. You should carry your **passport** and also check the timetables carefully for the validity of each part of the trip. You must reserve ahead for any **hydrofoil** journeys (and pay a small supplement). On certain boats – marked on the timetables – **lunch** is available.

Fares are great value. The complete round-trip in one day, in either direction and from any starting-point, costs Fr.44. The two-day pass, which allows you to break your journey overnight anywhere on the route and also covers unlimited boat travel on the whole of Lake Maggiore, is Fr.54. Brochures and the website list various itineraries. Starting from Locarno or Ascona, choose either **Itinerary 14**, which involves the Centovalli line first, then a fast train to Stresa, then a boat back; or **Itinerary 4**: a boat to Stresa, a train to Domodossola, and then the Centovalli.

The Town

The focus of town is **Piazza Grande**, an attractive arcaded square just off the lakefront that is lined with pavement cafés and serves as the town's meeting point, social club and public catwalk. Warm summer nights serve up some great people-watching, as exquisitely groomed locals parade to and fro, all the cafés a-buzz and fragrant breezes bringing in the scent of flowers from the lakeside gardens.

From the west end of Piazza Grande, lanes run up to Via Cittadella in the **Old Town** and the Baroque **Chiesa Nuova**, decorated with a huge statue of St Christopher outside. The tiny arcaded courtyard, reached through a side door, is a charming spot away from the bustle of the alleys. Following the atmospheric Via di Sant'Antonio brings you to the rather sombre church of **Sant'Antonio**, dating from the seventeenth century but rebuilt following a fatal roof collapse in 1863. Beside the church, the eighteenth-century **Casa Rusca** (Tues–Sun 10am–5pm; Fr.5) houses a worthwhile art museum focusing on the paintings and sculptures of the twentieth-century Swiss artist Jean Arp.

Alleys lead south to the tall **San Francesco**, consecrated as part of a monastery in the fourteenth century. Sixteenth-century renovation added frescoes, most of which are now fading badly. Further down sits the stout thirteenth-century **Castello Visconteo**, now home to the **Museo Archeologico** (April–Oct Tues–Sun 10am–noon & 2–5pm; Fr.5), worth visiting if only for its collection of beautiful Roman glassware and ceramics.

On the other side of town in Muralto, 100m east of the station, is the austere twelfth-century Romanesque basilica of **San Vittore**, built over a church first mentioned in the tenth century and now surrounded by generic suburban housing redevelopments of the late-twentieth. Medieval fresco-fragments inside and the Renaissance relief of St Victor on the bell tower are a diverting contrast to the uninspiring views over the train station.

Madonna del Sasso

Most striking of all Locarno's sights is the Franciscan **Santuario della Madonna del Sasso** church (daily 6.30am–7pm), an impressive ochre vision floating above the town on a wooded crag – *sasso* means rock – and consecrated in 1487 on the spot where, seven years earlier, the Virgin had appeared to Brother Bartholomeo da Ivrea from the San Francesco monastery in the town. The twenty-minute walk up through the wooded ravine of the Torrente Ramogno and past a handful of decaying shrines is atmospheric enough in itself; or you could take the half-hourly **funicular** from just west of the main train station to Ticino's greatest photo-op, looking down through the palms to the sunlit arcaded main front of the church and glittering blue lake behind.

Within the complex is a small **museum** of icons (Easter–Oct Sun–Fri 2–5pm; Fr.2.50), but the church **sanctuary** is the focus of all the pilgrims' attention. On the way through the complex you'll pass several striking terracotta sculpture groups of biblical scenes. The low, Baroque interior of the church features a number of paintings, two of which stand out: Bramantino's emotionally charged *Fuga in Egitto* (Flight to Egypt, 1522) and local artist Antonio Ciseri's *Trasporto di Cristo al Sepolcro* (1870). The statue of the Virgin on the high altar was sculpted for the church's consecration by an unknown artist.

Cardada and Cimetta

When sweltering, overcrowded Locarno (210m) gets too much, it's easy to make an escape into the cool, wooded hills above. By the top station of the Madonna del Sasso funicular in Orselina (395m) is the lantern-like base station

– designed by architect Mario Botta – of a futuristic cable car that rises on an ear-poppingly steep course to the plateau of **Cardada** (1350m; ⓦ www.cardada .ch). A short stroll left from the top station, set amidst fragrant pine woods and fresh breezes, is the "Observation Platform", a gracefully designed catwalk suspended off a huge A-frame that extends out over the edge of the hill above the treetops; from the end, an eagle-eye view takes in Ascona, much of Lago Maggiore and the mountains. There's a couple of simple restaurants up here and some easy strolls in the pine forest – many of them wheelchair accessible.

Turn right from the top station, and it's ten minutes or so through the woods to a spectacular chairlift that whisks you even higher, right through the trees up to the flower-strewn meadows of **Cimetta** (1672m), where there's a restaurant/ guesthouse with a terrace view that you won't forget in a hurry. Some longer, tougher walks include one up to the nearby summit of Madone (2039m).

A return **ticket** from Orselina to Cardada is Fr.27, to Cimetta Fr.33. If you're coming up from Locarno, ask for a discounted ticket at the base station of the Madonna del Sasso funicular that includes the whole round trip (to Cardada Fr.30, to Cimetta Fr.35).

Eating and drinking

Piazza Grande is full of cafés and pizzerias buzzing from morning until after midnight, but **eating** and **drinking** is more atmospheric in the Old Town alleys. Fresh fish plucked from the lake is Locarno's speciality – look out for trout (*trota*), perch (*persico*), pike (*luccio*) and whitefish (*coregone*).

Bar del Pozzo Piazza Sant'Antonio. Friendly local café-bar on a quiet Old Town square, a little out of the tourist crush.

Cantina Canetti Off Piazza Grande. Plain local cooking (Fr.15) in a noisy diner, with the added bonus of live accordion on Friday and Saturday nights.

Centenario Lungolago 13, Muralto ☎ 091 743 82 22. One of Locarno's best restaurants, serving internationally acclaimed *nouvelle cuisine* in an appealing blend of French and Italian styles. A lakeside terrace and three-figure bills come as standard. Closed Sun & Mon.

Cittadella Via Cittadella 18 ☎ 091 751 58 85. The popular trattoria section at ground level is excellent, serving pizzas, pasta and simple fish dishes for Fr.20 or less, while upstairs the formal restaurant concentrates on fish alone – and does it well (*menus* Fr.30–35). Closed Mon.

Funicolare Beside funicular top station in Orselina. Quiet, simple place that benefits from a spectacular secluded terrace garden overlooking Madonna del Sasso at which to savour their fish specialities. Closed Thurs in winter & Nov–Jan.

Lungolago Via Bramantino 1. Classy pizzeria, *paninoteca* and pub where locals go to flee the invasion of white-kneed northerners.

Manora Via della Stazione. Good self-service salads and plain cooking in this busy spot across from the train station, open late and Sundays.

Navegna (see "Hotels"). A little east of town in Minusio, but right on the lakefront and highly acclaimed for its delicately prepared and presented Ticinese cuisine (*menus* Fr.45). Closed Nov–March.

Svizzero Piazza Grande. Best of the many pizzerias and diners on the square, with affordable fresh-made pasta, wood-fired pizza and plenty of Italian staples. Bustling from breakfast till the small hours.

Locarno's valleys

The valleys around Locarno are packed with hiking possibilities, and offer some of the most beautiful scenery in the whole canton – which means that trails can get a little overcrowded in the summer season. **Val Verzasca** and **Valle Maggia** both lead north from Locarno, while the gorgeous **Centovalli** runs west on one of Switzerland's most scenic and dramatic train rides. Locarno's neighbour **Ascona** is covered on p.545.

There are some excellent opportunities for **adventure sports** around Ticino, all of which need to be booked in advance. **Trekking Team** (Ⓦwww.trekking.ch) is a top local operator that runs what is perhaps the star attraction: the highest bungee-jump in the world, off the 220m-high Verzasca Dam (see p.544), as performed by James Bond in the opening scene of *Goldeneye*. It takes some nerve just to venture out onto the dam to watch, let alone do the leap yourself. Your first jump costs Fr.255, including training and free drinks; a second on the same day is a cut-price Fr.125, and in high summer, you can jump by moonlight. They also do bungee-jumps off the 70m Intragna railway bridge (see p.545; one Fr.125, two Fr.195), as well as canyoning in the Centovalli, Val Onsernone, Val Verzasca, Valle Maggia and elsewhere. **Swiss Challenge** (Ⓦwww.swisschallenge.ch), based at Roveredo near Bellinzona, organizes canoeing around Cresciano and on Lago Maggiore, and canyoning in Val Malvaglia or around Cugnasco. **Swissraft** (Ⓦwww.swissraft.ch) has an office near Bellinzona, organizing river rafting from Cama through Roveredo, canyoning, mountain biking and more. Locarno's **The Wave** (Ⓦwww.watersports.ch) runs wakeboarding and waterskiing. **Adventure's Best** (Ⓦwww.asbest.ch) is Lugano's biggest operator, with a full range of adventure sports including canyoning, rap jumps, freeclimbing, paragliding, mountain biking and more.

Walks around Locarno
The tourist office brochure *Sentieri della Collina* pinpoints the route of two pleasant walking paths on the hillside just above the town. The **Sentiera Collina Bassa** is 5.4km long, and takes you from the Madonna del Sasso funicular east through Orselina and onto the Via Panoramica through the suburb of **Brione** above Minusio, before gently coming down to the lakeshore in **Tenero** (1hr 40min), from where buses and trains return you to Locarno. The **Sentiera Collina Alta** runs for 6.3km from **Monte Brè**, the next hill west of Orselina (bus #32), on a scenic, winding path through the foothills to **Contra**, and down to Tenero (2hr).

Valle Maggia

The **VALLE MAGGIA** comprises a complex valley system stretching north of Locarno into the high Alps. This is wild countryside, not easy to explore: about 30km into the main valley, roads split to follow three separate upper valleys, the Val Rovana, Val Bavona and Val Lavizzara, which are cut off from each other and which all eventually come to a stop against impassable rock. It is, however, superb territory for **walking**: the long-distance route outlined in the box on p.535 passes through, and there are some fine short walks in remote corners.

North from Pontebrolla, a village above Locarno at the junction of the Centovalli, the valley is deep, rugged and very narrow. It opens out further along around Gordevio and the village of **Maggia**, home of the local tourist office (☎091 753 18 85, Ⓦwww.vallemaggia.ch); across the river from Maggia at Aurigeno is the SB hostel *Baracca* (☎079 207 15 54, Ⓦwww.backpacker.ch; ❶). At **Cevio** (416m), the largest town in the valley, a road branches west into the **Val Rovana**, climbing to the village of **BOSCO/GURIN** (1503m). This is the highest settlement in Ticino, and also its only German-speaking community, founded in the Middle Ages by ex-mercenaries from the upper Valais; the locals still speak an odd combination of Oberwalliser and Locarnese dialects. With lift access up to 2400m, the remote village has become a centre for winter sports, and there are some good walks in summer in and around Grossalp (Ⓦwww.grossalp.ch).

Just 2km north of Cevio (30km north of Locarno) is the idyllic village of **BIGNASCO** (438m), where the valley divides. Of a handful of lovely restaurants here, the *Turisti* has excellent food and a shaded terrace, as well as some rooms (T091 754 11 65; ❶). Northwest from Bignasco, a road climbs into the wild **Val Bavona**, a strip of valley floor 10km long that is hemmed in by sheer scarps on both sides. There are twelve rustic hamlets in the valley, including **Foroglio**, with a restaurant huddled next to a splendid waterfall. A short climb above **San Carlo** (960m), the final hamlet, characterized by tall, narrow sixteenth-century stone houses, is a cable car up to the eyrie of **ROBIEI** (1905m), overlooked by the Basodino glacier. The top station has a terrace restaurant and accommodation (T091 756 50 20, W www.robiei.ch; ❶; dorms Fr.25); one of the most scenic walks heads west into the Val Fiorina (45min).

From Bignasco, another road climbs northeast into the **Val Lavizzara**. After Peccia (849m) – renowned for its marble quarries and sculpture school – the switchbacks get tighter up to the hamlet of **MOGNO** (1180m), where, across the way on your right, you'll spot the tilted circular roof of the church of **San Giovanni Battista** through the trees. The church, reached by a short path climbing from a parking area, was designed by Mario Botta after an avalanche destroyed a pre-existing chapel on the same spot in 1986: Botta has said that when the locals came to him saying they didn't want to give the future generation a place poorer than the one they knew, he responded by offering to build a church that would last a thousand years. His achievement, in this remotest of places, is dazzling. It is a small building, set on a marble plaza. The interior is supremely elegant, bare and silent, encircled in striped marble, the transparent roof bathing the altar in sunlight. Lingering here is mesmeric; walking back out into the pine forest, amidst chirping birds and log cabins, is a revelation.

Val Verzasca

About 1.5km east of Locarno on Lago Maggiore is the suburb of **Tenero**, standing at the head of the **VAL VERZASCA**, the shortest of the major valleys around Locarno. The southern end of the valley, high above Tenero, is blocked by the gigantic **Verzasca Dam**, scene of the world's highest bungee-jump (see box p.543). Even if you're not jumping, it's worth stopping here to wander out into the middle of the dam; on one side is a dizzying 220m drop down to bare rock, on the other a tranquil, blue lake is framed by classic Alpine scenery.

The road continues beyond the dam, passing below **Corippo** (530m) at the end of the lake, a beautiful cluster of old stone cottages crowned by a tall campanile; 3km north is **Lavertezzo**, site of perhaps the most photographed bridge in Switzerland, a graceful seventeenth-century double arch that leaps from bank to island to bank. Many quieter trails head off into side valleys from Lavertezzo, while the valley cuts deeper for another 14km up to **Sonogno** (909m), passing on the way through **Brione**, located on a plateau at a junction of valleys; the views are pretty and the church boasts fourteenth-century Giotto-style frescoes.

The Centovalli

Locarno is the eastern terminus of the wonderful **Centovalli** railway (W www.centovalli.ch), one of Switzerland's most scenic rides (see p.42). Little trains run by Locarno's FART company depart from beneath Locarno station into the spectacular valley – so named for its "hundred" side valleys – most of the time winding slowly on precarious bridges and viaducts above ravine-like depths (sit on the left for the best views). The area is renowned for its natural beauty,

and with **walking maps** from Locarno tourist office (also available at ⓦwww
.procentovalli.ch) you could get out at any of the villages en route, pick up a
trail and head off into the hills. There's no lack of *grotti*, cafés and simple budget
accommodation. One neat way to see the route is with the **Lago Maggiore
Express** pass (see p.540).

Past Pontebrolla, tiny **Verscio**, 4km northwest of Locarno, is a lovely stone-
built village which also houses the **Teatro Dimitri** (ⓦwww.teatrodimitri.ch),
a highly acclaimed international mime school founded by Ascona-born clown
"Dimitri", a protégé of Marcel Marceau. The small theatre, in a cobbled lane
off the village square, stages performances by students and professionals almost
nightly (March–Dec), and is also the training ground for the excellent Circus
Monti, which tours Swiss towns and cities every year. Also on site is the small
Museo Comico (open on performance days 5pm–midnight; Fr.5, free with
theatre ticket), with costumes and memorabilia.

Some 3km down the line, the train clanks over a graceful iron viaduct spanning the 75m gorge of the Isorno torrent. This was the scene of Switzerland's
first-ever bungee-jump, in 1993, and remains a choice spot for leaping (see box
p.543), on the outskirts of **INTRAGNA**, its church marked by the highest
steeple in Ticino (65m), built in 1775. An excellent walk starts from Intragna
station, crossing a medieval bridge and joining a mule-track which climbs
gently across the meadows to **Rasa**, an isolated stone-built hamlet with no
road access, from where a tiny cable car swoops back over the valley down
to **VERDASIO** station. From Verdasio, another cable car scales the opposite,
northern valley wall to **Monte Comino**, 600m above (ⓦwww.comino.ch);
from here, you could follow a two-hour circuit of the summit, or a more taxing
6km path back to Intragna.

After Verdasio, the train rolls on through dense chestnut forests to the quiet
border village of **Cámedo** (passport needed) and on through the rustic villages
of the Italian **Valle Vigezzo** for the climb to Santa Maria Maggiore, the
highest point of the line (830m). The terminus lies 20km on, at the bustling
valley-floor Italian town of **DOMODOSSOLA**. Fast Swiss trains from here
run west through the Simplon/Sempione Tunnel to Brig and on to Bern, Basel
and Geneva, while Italian trains head south to Milan. If you have time to kill
between trains, head 200m west from the station into the old part of town, set
around a series of attractively crumbling arcaded piazzas.

Ascona

On the south-facing side of the Maggia delta, 3km southwest of Locarno,
ASCONA has been a magnet for idealistic, sun-starved northerners for a
century. The place was nothing more than a fishing hamlet until the 1890s,
but since then it has grown into a cultured, artistically inclined small town, an
enticing blend of character, natural beauty and good shopping.

But Ascona faces a serious problem, stemming from its popularity as a holiday
centre. The influx of German-speakers, as summer tourists and second-homeowners, has been so great in recent years that Ascona has noticeably lost its way.
Since most of the visitors have, at best, rudimentary Italian, staff in hotels and
restaurants are now accustomed to speak to guests in German first. Even the
poshest menus are bilingual. Shops frequently advertise special offers in German
before Italian, and some cultural activities – readings or gallery openings
– take place in German. With general Ticinese disquiet at German-speaking

△ Lakefront, Ascona

dominance of Swiss affairs, Asconesi are becoming uneasy: voices are being raised for the cantonal government to step in and force Ascona's businesses to prioritize Italian.

The town

Ascona's *tour de force* is **Piazza Motta**, the cobbled lakefront promenade, south-facing and fully 500m long: the airy views down the lake, flanked by wooded peaks, to the Brissago islands are sensational. There are few better places to watch the day drift by: the morning mists on the water, the clarity of light at midday, the sunsets and peaceful twilight are simply mesmerizing.

Word of Ascona began to spread a century or more ago, when a slow but steady influx began of philosophers, theosophists and spiritualists, most of whom believed that a return to nature was the best remedy for the moral disintegration of Western society. At the turn of the century the artists Henri Oedenkoven and Ida Hofmann established an esoteric, vegetarian artists' colony

Into the Gambarogno

The 13km of shoreline opposite Locarno and Ascona is known as the **Gambarogno**, and comprises a line of quiet shoreside villages backed by rugged mountains. **VIRA** holds the local **tourist office** (July & Aug Mon–Fri 8am–6.30pm, Sat 9am–noon & 3–5pm, Sun 9am–noon; rest of year Mon–Fri 8am–noon & 2–6pm, plus Sat 9am–noon in June, Sept & Oct; ☎091 795 18 66, ⓦwww.gambarognoturismo.ch). From Vira, a tightly coiled road leads for 17km over the bleak **Alpe di Neggia** pass (1395m) – with an inn boasting spectacular views – way up to the isolated hamlet of **INDÉMINI** (930m), on the mountain border with Italy. This stone-built village clinging to the valley sides has recently attracted artists and sculptors; workshops are often open, and the simple *Ristorante Indeminese* (☎091 795 12 22) is a great lunch stop. The road continues for 18km through some spectacular mountain terrain, with sensational viewpoints high above the lake, down to the Italian town of **Maccagno**, 9km south of the lakeside border at Pino/Zenna. Buses also serve Indémini from the ferry stop at Magadino, beside Vira.

on the hill of **Monte Verità** beside Ascona. An array of European fringe intellectuals followed, including practitioners of the new arts of psychology and psychoanalysis. In 1913, Rudolf von Laban set up his nudist School of Natural and Expressive Dance within the Monte Verità community, attracting Isadora Duncan among others, and during and after World War I artists and pacifists flocked to Ascona. The buildings atop the peaceful wooded hill are now used mostly for conferences, but a few have been preserved as a **museum** of the movement (Tues–Sun: July & Aug 3–7pm; April–June, Sept & Oct 2.30–6pm; Fr.6; ⓦ www.monteverita.org). It's a short walk up the hill from the bus stop (bus #33) to the **Casa Anatta**, with two floors of the original wooden house given over to papers and photos commemorating the artists' exploits. A walk past the main Bauhaus conference centre and into the woods brings you to the tiny **Casa Selma**, used as the community's retreat, and on further to the **Elisarion**, housing a circular painting by Elisar von Kupffer depicting the spiritual liberations of communal life.

Central Ascona's attractive cobbled lanes leading back from the lakefront are full of artisans' galleries, jewellers and craft shops. The **Museo Comunale d'Arte Moderna**, in a sixteenth-century *palazzo* at Via Borgo 34 (March–Dec Tues–Sat 10am–noon & 3–6pm, Sun 4–6pm; Fr.7; ⓦ www.museoascona.ch), has a high-quality collection focused on Marianne von Werefkin, one of the many artists attracted to Ascona in its heyday and joint founder of Munich's expressionist *Blaue Reiter* movement; look out for her terrifying, Munch-like *Il Cenciaiolo* (The Rag-Man, 1920).

The **Italian border** lies 8km south of Ascona, past the rather soulless little resort of **Brissago**. About 5km further is the characterful and attractive old town of **Cannóbio** – well worth a visit.

Isole di Brissago

Twin islands 4km south of Ascona, the **ISOLE DI BRISSAGO** (April–Oct daily 9am–6pm; Fr.8 in addition to boat ticket; ⓦ www.isolebrissago.ch) are accessible by hourly boats from Locarno and Ascona, and by more regular shuttles from **Porto Ronco**, the nearest point on the mainland. These tiny dots of green in the shimmering lake overflow with luxuriant subtropical flora basking in the hot sun (this is also the lowest point in Switzerland, 193m above sea level). The main island, St Pancras – about ten minutes' stroll end to end – is given over to a fine botanical garden. At one end is an attractive 1929 villa, now a conference centre and quality **restaurant** (☎091 791 43 62): a long lunch here, followed by a siesta under the palms, makes for a most un-Swiss-like afternoon. Note that the signs identifying each plant species are in Italian, French and German – but not English. Only groups can stay overnight; everyone else must leave on the last boat (around 6pm). The small island, St Apollinaris, has no public access.

Practicalities

Ascona's **tourist office** is at the top of the old quarter, on Via Papio (April–Oct Mon–Fri 9am–6pm, Sat 9am–5pm; Nov–March Mon–Fri 9am–noon & 1.30–5.30pm; ☎091 791 00 91, ⓦ www.ascona.ch). There are literally dozens of **hotels**, with eight on the waterfront Piazza Motta alone, ranging from two to four stars: a good choice here is the characterful, family-run 🍴 *Tamaro* (☎091 785 48 48, ⓦ www.hotel-tamaro.ch; ❸–❹). If money's no object, aim for the *Eden Roc*, Via Albarelle 16 (☎091 785 71 71, ⓦ www.edenroc .ch; ❾), one of Switzerland's top luxury hotels, where a south-facing room is a cool Fr.750 a night, or the sensuously opulent five-star spa retreat *Albergo Giardino*, Via Segnale 10 (℡091 785 88 88, Ⓦwww.giardino.ch; ❾), set in lavish gardens.

Eating, too, is a case of following your nose along the waterfront: every café and restaurant lays tables outside. The *Tamaro* offers dining in the pleasant internal atrium, the *Elvezia* is a good spot for inexpensive pizza and fish dishes, or you could fill a gap with the excellent ice cream at the *Mövenpick*. At all of these, Fr.25–30 will cover a meal. Back in the old town, the *Della Carrà* (℡091 791 44 52) has an atmospheric courtyard off the cobbled Via Carrà dei Nasi, serving excellent fish dishes and novelties such as chicken in whisky sauce; reckon on Fr.50 or more. *Al Torchio* on Contrada Maggiore (℡091 791 71 26; closed Nov) has good local specialities, similarly priced, and the allure of live jazz nightly.

Sottoceneri

The **SOTTOCENERI** region south of Bellinzona and Locarno is much more developed than the Sopraceneri, with dozens of neat, prosperous towns crammed in between the narrowing international borders to east and west. The principal draw is the sophisticated and stylish city of **Lugano**, sited on a bay of the glorious **Lago di Lugano**, which twists out into Italy on both sides. Jutting out into the lake just a stone's throw from the city is the sun-drenched **Ceresio peninsula**, dotted with idyllic Italianate country villages and crisscrossed by some of the loveliest easy walks in the canton.

Monte Tamaro

North of Lugano, alongside the autostrada and rail exit from the Monte Ceneri tunnel, gondolas rise from the town of **RIVERA** (469m) up to **Alpe Foppa** (1530m), located on a shoulder of **Monte Tamaro** (1961m; Ⓦwww.montetamaro.ch). Just by the gondola top station, to one side of a restaurant and information centre, is one of Ticino's most celebrated new buildings, the church of **Santa Maria degli Angeli**, designed by Mario Botta. The project was commissioned by the owner of the Monte Tamaro resort in remembrance of his wife, and it's an effortlessly graceful building, with symmetrical stairs, arches and a long walkway, everything in beautiful porphyry stone. From the belvedere, a crucifix faces out over an infinite view above the Ticino valley. The intimate interior of the cylindrical chapel, with black plastered walls, is filled with indirect light from low windows and the tiered ceiling, and culminates in an ethereal blue fresco by Enzo Cucchi of two cupped hands.

There's some skiing up here in winter, and in summer you'll find plenty of walks – not least from Alpe Foppa up to the Tamaro summit (1hr 40min) or down to Rivera (2hr 15min). The most spectacular heads on an isolated route along the ridge west to **Monte Lema** (1624m; Ⓦwww.montelema.ch) on the Italian border (4hr 30min), from where a cable car runs down to Miglieglia and a combination of buses can return you to Lugano.

Lugano

With its compact cluster of Italianate piazzas and extensive tree-lined promenades, **LUGANO** is the most alluring of Ticino's lake resorts, much less
touristy than Locarno but with, if anything, double the chic. Even Milanese
style-junkies, who give very little quarter to their own provincial towns, bring
friends over to Lugano for some shopping, a lakeside *apéro* and a good meal. The
ever-aspiring Luganesi return the compliment by dropping in to Milan – just
50km south – for a taste of big city highlife and fashion-conscious clubbing.
Their home town is nonetheless an exciting, sassy place, full of energy and style.
Set on a south-facing bay of the cerulean blue **Lago di Lugano**, its lake vistas
are astonishing: the city is framed on all sides by wooded, sugarloaf hills rising
from the water that have led to its being dubbed the "Rio of the Old World".
Both **Monte Brè** to the northeast and **San Salvatore** to the south are served
by funiculars, and both give spectacular views over to the snow-capped Alps.

In terms of status as a centre for banking in Switzerland, Lugano vies with
Geneva for second place behind Zürich, and the city centre reflects this, with
none of Locarno's Belle-Epoque stuffiness: these old alleys and winding lanes are
full of commerce, whether in the form of enticing delicatessens and boutiques
or graceful, villa-style hotels and apartment buildings. Ancient churches and
art galleries are draws in themselves, quite aside from the simpler pleasures of a
stroll under the lakeside palms. If there is a drawback to Lugano, it's the **traffic**
– unpleasantly heavy most of the time, especially along the lakefront corniche,
and marked by alarming Italian-style driving. But at night, looking down from
the summit of Brè amidst a warm southerly breeze, with the toot and rumble
of cars rising from a bed of twinkling lights, you could feel yourself a long, long
way from Switzerland.

Arrival, information and accommodation

Lugano's **train station** overlooks the town from the west. From within the
station, a funicular (Fr.1.10) trundles down to pedestrianized **Piazza Cioccaro**
in the centre; on foot, you could head out of the station and follow steps down
to Via Cattedrale, which connects to Piazza Cioccaro. Narrow lanes link this with
the main **Piazza della Riforma**, one block back from the waterfront. The train
station is also the arrival and reservations point for the Palm Express **postbuses**
from St Moritz through Italy; all other postbuses depart from Piazza Rezzonico,
adjacent to Riforma in the centre. **Parking** is truly a nightmare. Don't bother
battling to find a space in the city-centre car parks (or on the streets); you'd do best
paying Fr.25/day at either of the long-term car parks flanking the train station.

Lugano's little **airport** is 4km west of the city in Agno. Shuttle buses wait for
flight arrivals; the driver will drop you at your hotel or any point in the centre
(Fr.10 one-way including luggage). On departure, you must book a pick-up at
least one hour in advance (☎079 221 42 43, ⓦwww.shuttle-bus.com). A taxi is
around Fr.35. **Milan Malpensa** airport, 40km southwest of Lugano in Italy, is
served by shuttles operated by Star Bus (☎091 994 88 78, ⓦwww.starbus.info;
daily hourly; Fr.60 return).

Lugano's **tourist office** is in the Palazzo Civico on Riva Albertolli, directly
opposite the main landing-stage (April–Oct Mon–Fri 9am–7pm, Sat 9am–6pm,
Sun 10am–6pm; Nov–March Mon–Fri 9am–noon & 2–5.30pm, Sat 10am–
12.30pm & 1.30–5pm; ☎091 913 32 32, ⓦwww.lugano-tourism.ch). Their
excellent **guided walk** (in English) around the city, starting from Santa Maria
degli Angioli on Piazza Luini, is free (April–Oct Mon 9.30am; 2hr). TPL **city**

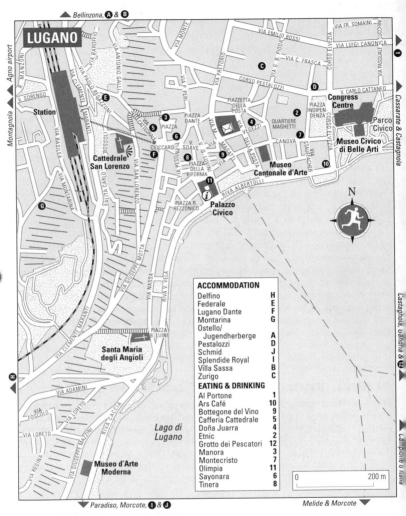

LUGANO

Bellinzona, **A** & **B**

Agno airport

Montagnola

Station

Cattedrale
San Lorenzo

PIAZZA
DANTE

PIAZZETTA
DELLA
POSTA

QUARTIERE
MAGHETTI

PIAZZA
INDIPEN-
DENZA

Congress
Centre

Parco
Civico

Museo Civico
di Belle Arti

CANOVA

PIAZZA
DELLA
RIFORMA

Museo
Cantonale d'Arte

RIVA ALBERTOLLI

PIAZZA R.
REZZONICO

Palazzo
Civico

N

Santa Maria
degli Angioli

PIAZZA
B. LUINI

*Lago di
Lugano*

Museo d'Arte
Moderna

Paradiso, Morcote, **I** & **J**

Melide & Morcote

Cassarate & Castagnola

Castagnola, Gandria & **12**

Campione o Italia

ACCOMMODATION	
Delfino	H
Federale	E
Lugano Dante	F
Montarina	G
Ostello/	
Jugendherberge	A
Pestalozzi	D
Schmid	J
Splendide Royal	I
Villa Sassa	B
Zurigo	C
EATING & DRINKING	
Al Portone	1
Ars Café	10
Bottegone del Vino	9
Cafferia Cattedrale	5
Doña Juarra	4
Etnic	2
Grotto dei Pescatori	12
Manora	3
Montecristo	7
Olimpia	11
Sayonara	6
Tinera	8

0   200 m

buses cost Fr.1.20–1.90 per trip, or Fr.5 for a day pass. See the note on p.525 regarding the excellent-value **Lugano Regional Pass**.

The city includes a number of adjacent districts: the modestly named **Paradiso** is just around the lakeshore south of the centre; **Cassarate** is just east of the centre at the foot of Brè, the slopes of which are covered by the mansions and private palaces of the seriously wealthy **Castagnola** district. To complicate things further, locals – and some maps – refer to the Lago di Lugano by its Latin name, **Ceresio**.

Inexpensive hotels

Montarina Via Montarina 1 ☎091 966 72 72, ⓦwww.montarina.ch. Efficient little place in a nice garden just behind the station, with clean,

all-new rooms and helpful management. Closed Jan. **2**

Pestalozzi Piazza Indipendenza 9 ☎091 921 46 46, ⓦwww.attuale.com/pestalozzi.html. Quality

Lugano's festivals

Lugano has a number of prestigious festivals, many of them centred around music. The season opens in mid-April with the **Primavera Concertistica**, a classical programme of international soloists and orchestras performing in the main Congress Centre. In early July, **Estival Jazz** (Summer Jazz; ⓦ www.estivaljazz.ch) covers a series of free concerts in Mendrisio, Tesserete and Lugano. It's been running for decades: in the 1950s, Dexter Gordon, Max Roach and Ornette Coleman all played at Lugano, and in the 1960s the festival featured some of Keith Jarrett's earliest performances. The **Blues to Bop Festival** in early September (ⓦ www.bluestobop .ch) is another free event, with international blues, jazz, rock and gospel artists performing on the lakefront and at venues around town.

choice bang in the centre, 150m from the lakeshore, with serviceable rooms in an Art Nouveaustyle building. ❷–❸

Schmid Via delle Scuole 9 ☎ 091 994 91 21. Clean, pleasant family-run place beside the Salvatore funicular in Paradiso, the rooms aren't modern, but are atmospheric, and some bigger ones with double balconies are a bargain. ❸

Zurigo Corso Pestalozzi 13 ☎ 091 923 43 43. Central, very clean and well-kept place, with modern, renovated rooms, private parking and a trace of style as well. ❷–❸

Mid-range and expensive hotels

Delfino Via Casserinetta 6 ☎ 091 985 99 99, ⓦ www.delfinolugano.ch. Pleasant, welcoming, small family-run hotel, with secure private parking and a pool. Something of an institution, and with a good reputation to uphold; rooms are functional rather than characterful, and the food is of a high standard. ❸–❹

Federale Via Regazzoni 8 ☎ 091 910 08 08, ⓦ www.hotel-federale.ch. Impressive town house set in the quiet leafy district immediately below the station, well away from traffic and with lake views from upper floors; quality modern rooms are characterful and good value. ❸–❹

Lugano Dante Piazza Cioccaro 5 ☎ 091 910 57 00, ⓦ www.hotel-luganodante.com. High-quality option bang in the heart of the pedestrianized city centre, with good service, comfortable rooms and no trouble from street noise. Private parking. ❺–❻

Splendide Royal Riva Caccia 7 ☎ 091 985 77 11, ⓦ www.splendide.ch. Lugano's best and most expensive establishment, with public and guest

room interiors that live up to the hotel's name. Accept nothing less than one of the vast rooms on the top floor, offering some of the best views in the city. ❾

Villa Sassa Via Tesserete 10 ☎ 091 911 41 11, ⓦ www.villasassa.ch. An excellent-quality modern four-star hotel in the hills just north of the city centre. Hotel rooms – which are large, airy, quiet and with contemporary styling – look out onto the gorgeous pool area, with a superb view over the city and lake. Service is cheerily efficient. Private parking. ❼–❽

Hostels

Montarina (see above). Good low-budget central hotel that also has dorms (Fr.25).

Ostello/Jugendherberge Figino (HI hostel) Via Casoro 2, Figino ☎ 091 995 11 51, ⓦ www .youthhostel.ch. A good alternative to the suburban Savosa hostel is this option in an idyllic former fishing village on the Ceresio peninsula, offering dorms from Fr.27. Hourly postbuses from outside the Lugano tourist office go to Casoro, a stop beside the hostel (20min). Mid-March to mid-Oct. ❶

Ostello/Jugendherberge Savosa (HI hostel) Via Cantonale 13, Savosa ☎ 091 966 27 28, ⓦ www.youthhostel.ch. One of Switzerland's best-value hostels (complete with swimming pool), with dorms from Fr.31. Take bus #5 to Crocifisso from the stop 200m left out of the train station. March–Nov. ❶

Campsite

La Piodella Muzzano ☎ 091 994 77 88. Lakeshore site 3km west of town near Agno airport – best of five that are in close proximity. Closed Nov.

The Town

The centre of Lugano is the broad, spacious **Piazza della Riforma**, a huge café-lined square perfect for eyeballing passers-by over a cappuccino. The lake is a few metres away behind the Neoclassical **Palazzo Civico**, as are the characterful steep lanes of the Old Town on the opposite side of the square. Wandering through the dense maze of shopping alleys northwest of Riforma, you're bound to stumble on the photogenic Gabbani delicatessen, whose fame spreads far beyond Lugano – the interior is an Aladdin's Cave of fine *salsiccia* made especially for the shop, cabinets full of Alpine cheeses from the farmers of Alto Ticino, pastries and foodie delights galore. From bustling Piazza Cioccaro just past the deli, the atmospheric stepped Via Cattedrale doglegs steeply up to **Cattedrale San Lorenzo**, characterized by an impressive Renaissance portal, fragments of fourteenth- to sixteenth-century interior frescoes, and spectacular views from its terrace.

The narrow **Via Nassa** – one of Switzerland's top addresses for chic, international designer-label fashion – heads southwest from Riforma through a string of picturesque little squares to the medieval church of **Santa Maria degli Angioli** on Piazza Luini. This plain little building beside a disused funicular track was founded in 1490 as part of a Franciscan monastery (suppressed in 1848 during Switzerland's civil war). Inside, the wall separating the nave from the chancel is entirely covered with a monumental Leonardo-esque fresco painted in 1529 by **Bernadino Luini** that depicts, in intricate and gory fashion, the Passion and Crucifixion, as well as St Sebastian, graphically pierced by

Boats on Lago di Lugano

More even than other Swiss lakes, the idyllic **Lago di Lugano** merits taking to the water simply for the pleasure of it. SNL (☎091 971 52 23, ⓦwww.lakelugano.ch) provides the service; their ticket booth is at the main Lugano jetty opposite the tourist office. This landing-stage is known as **Lugano-Centrale**; some services depart from **Lugano-Giardino** 100m to the east. Within Lugano, boats also call in at Cassarate and Castagnola to the east, and Paradiso to the south.

Between April and October boats run roughly every 45min over to **Gandria** on the eastern arm of the lake, while others depart every two hours south to **Campione d'Italia**, **Morcote**, **Porto Ceresio** (Italy) and on around the peninsula to **Ponte Tresa**, stopping at most places on the way. One boat a day heads east to **Porlezza** (Italy), while one morning boat connects at **Capolago** for the rack railway up to Monte Generoso.

A panoramic two-and-a-half-hour **cruise** around the whole lake, with commentary in English, runs daily (April–Oct) in mid-afternoon, and there are also plenty of cruises throughout the day offering on-board meals, drinks and/or music. In **winter**, a skeleton service operates three boats daily to Morcote, and a few each week over to Campione and Gandria. **Passes** for one/three/seven days cost Fr.36/54/65. All SNL boats are free to Swiss Pass and Lugano Regional Pass holders.

Como e Lugano

The pass **Como e Lugano: Due Laghi per Sognare** ("Two Lakes for Dreaming"; April–Oct only) – buyable from the tourist office or the SNL boat ticket kiosks – covers a circular tour by land and water through the neighbouring regions, with time to stop and sightsee (as well as eat) on the way. Starting from Lugano, a one-day trip on **route A** involves a 2.15pm boat to Porlezza, a bus to Menaggio on the shores of Lake Como and a boat to Como, from where a train returns you to Lugano by 9pm. Doing the same thing in reverse counts as **route B**, starting with a 9.45am train to Como, a boat to Menaggio, a bus to Porlezza, and a boat return to Lugano by 5.30pm. On both routes, the pass is valid for **two days**, allowing you to break the journey wherever you like. The fare is Fr.46 – a great-value way to see and experience both lakes and the landscapes between them. Don't forget your **passport**.

arrows. Frescoes of unnamed towns cover the three arches through to the chancel: beneath one is a depiction of Jerusalem. On the left-hand wall is another fresco by Luini, this time of the Last Supper.

In the lakefront park opposite is a bust of one "**Giorgio**" **Washington**, placed here by a nineteenth-century Swiss entrepreneur who'd made his fortune in the United States. Some 100m south on the lakefront is the **Museo d'Arte Moderna**, Riva Caccia 5 (admission varies; ⓌHwww.mdam.ch), which puts on one or two annual fine-art exhibitions of world-class quality; watch for the posters around town.

East of Piazza della Riforma

Five minutes walk east from Riforma brings you to the **Museo Cantonale d'Arte**, a fine old villa at Via Canova 10 (Tues 2–5pm, Wed–Sun 10am–5pm; Fr.7, more for temporary shows; Ⓦwww.museo-cantonale-arte.ch). Inside are paintings by Klee and Renoir among local depictions of peasant life by Swiss and Italian artists of the nineteenth and twentieth centuries. Another 100m east is the attractive waterfront Parco Civico; within the park, the nineteenth-century **Villa Ciani** – with some sumptuously decorated ceilings – houses the **Museo Civico di Belle Arti** (Tues–Sun 10am–noon & 2–6pm; Fr.5), showing works by Cranach, Giovanni Serodine and Henri Rousseau among plenty of Impressionist and Modernist canvases.

Eating and drinking

Lugano is blessed with plenty of pleasant, atmospheric places to **eat**, and you'll have no difficulty finding somewhere to suit. The many bars and cafés around Riforma all offer good, inexpensive food at lunch and dinner – yet although they get packed with evening **drinkers**, hip, bar-hopping Luganesi prefer to tuck themselves away elsewhere, filling out a handful of vibrant bars off the main streets of the centre.

Cafés and snacks

Ars Café Riva Albertolli 5. Chic bistro-style café on the edge of the lake, with great views – perfect for lingering over a drink or a light meal of Mediterranean-style salad or pasta. The interior is airy, with contemporary styling and service is warm and courteous. Closed Sun.

Bottegone del Vino Via Magatti 1. Old-style wine bar centrally located beside the main post office, with waiters in proper white aprons and a huge range of wines on offer by the glass or bottle. Closed Sun.

Cafferia Cattedrale Via Cattedrale 6. Small, friendly café dispensing espresso as it should be.

Montecristo Via Canova, junction Stauffacher. Hip café-bar, reasonably laid-back during the day but crammed to the rafters most nights, when even the sound system fails to drown the conversation.

Olimpia Piazza della Riforma. Venerable old institution housed in one wing of the Palazzo Civico, and best of the many cafés around the square for its surprisingly good, inexpensive food. *Menus* of Italian staples, steaks and a few more interesting dishes rarely go for more than Fr.20.

Restaurants

Al Portone Viale Cassarate 3 ☎091 923 55 11. Gourmet restaurant that manages to keep a pleasantly relaxed ambience alongside its spectacular, inventive new Italian cuisine. Top quality commands top prices. Closed Sun & Mon.

Doña Juarra Via Vegezzi 4 ☎091 922 03 65. Popular, well-respected evening and late-night place serving good-quality mid-priced Mexican food (*menus* Fr.25 or so). Closed Mon.

Etnic Quartiere Maghetti, east of the post office. A great, inexpensive bamboo-and-candlelight eatery tucked away in an unlikely looking purpose-built warren of shops and pharmacies. The menu is all Mediterranean, with Greek and Lebanese specialities around Fr.15, or you could plump for a beer or a banana daiquiri from the bar instead. Either way, the atmosphere is happy, studentish and relaxed. Closed lunchtimes.

Grotto dei Pescatori Caprino ☎091 923 98 67. Alluring little *grotto* located near the hamlet of Caprino, across the lake from Lugano – and inaccessible by road. The only way to get here is

A funicular run by FMB rises from Cassarate, ten minutes' walk east of the centre, to the summit of **Monte Brè** (ⓦ www.montebre.ch), a sheer 660m directly above the city (also accessible by car), offering spectacular views from the summit café over the lake, the curve of Lugano's bay overlooked by the sugarloaf San Salvatore, and due west to the snowy Monte Rosa massif, behind which lurks the Matterhorn. Bracing walks lead off all over the mountain, including a four-hour circuit out to Monte Boglia and back. A short walk from the summit is Brè village, through which is dotted a series of outdoor art installations; ⓦ www.montebre.com has details, and the Lugano tourist office has an English pamphlet to guide you through the village.

by boat: a handful head over from Lugano, and smaller craft shuttle across from Gandria. The means of arrival and the isolation are the main attractions, but the atmosphere of the place – and the food – match up: tables are laid out under the shade of the trees, directly on the waterfront. Plump for the succulent perch in butter and sage, or a heartier dish such as beef with polenta. Prices are moderate – around Fr.25. Closed Oct–April.

Manora Simple but excellent self-service fare on an upper level of the Manor department store beside the lower terminus of the station funicular – fresh salads, good pizzas and pasta, hot staples such as chicken, fish and rice, plenty of cakes and desserts with coffee. Always packed at lunchtime. Closes 6pm (Thurs until 9pm).

Sayonara Via Soave 10. Fast-paced central diner offering inexpensive pizza and pasta options, along with filling staples like polenta for around Fr.15.

Tinera Via dei Gorini 2. Very popular rustic *grotto*-style restaurant, specializing in Ticinese and Lombard dishes such as *pollo alla cacciatora* (spicy chicken stew) and home-made pasta, along with an array of excellent local merlots. *Menus* around Fr.20. Closed Sun & Aug.

Villa Sassa Via Tesserete 10 ☎091 911 41 11, ⓦ www.villasassa.ch. Outstanding *haute cuisine* restaurant attached to this luxury hotel in the hills just north of the city centre. The restaurant terrace offers a spectacular view over the city and the lake. The romance is kept up by the service – white-tuxedoed waiters gliding by – and the food, formal European/international cuisine with a north Italian twist: superb lake fish, delicately flavoured filled pastas and the like. Prices are high – rarely less than Fr.50 per head.

Around Lugano

The possibilities for getting out into the countryside around Lugano and the lake are plentiful: the tourist office has sheets on 21 cycling routes and 28 walking trails out of the city, both long and short, taxing and easy. The best area to head for is the hilly countryside of the **Ceresio peninsula**, extending directly behind the San Salvatore mountain opposite Lugano, with lake views to east, south and west that are continually captivating. Postbuses and/or boats from Lugano serve all villages on the peninsula.

East of Lugano across the Italian border is the little lakeside stretch of the **Valsolda** – a cluster of attractive villages on the way to **Porlezza** and on to Menaggio on Lake Como. The **Malcantone**, west of Lugano, is for the most part residential and light-industrial: before the border at Ponte Tresa and another stretch of lakeside villages in Italian territory, there's the memorable attraction of a visitable Swiss chocolate factory at little **Caslano**.

Gandria and east to Lake Como

From Castagnola, just east of Lugano city centre, a pleasant stroll heads east around the base of Monte Brè, joining the Sentiero di Gandria footpath through the **Parco degli Ulivi**, a Mediterranean-style lakefront park shaded by olive trees, cypress, laurels, oleander and deliciously fragrant rosemary. This whole south-facing horn of Monte Brè is protected as an area of special scientific interest, revelling in a semi-tropical microclimate of near-continuous sunshine and just a handful of rainy days a year.

After less than an hour's walk from Lugano (or five minutes in the car), you come to the picturesque village of **GANDRIA**, rising straight from the water 5km east of the city. At the top of the village, off the main road, are parking areas: there is no access to the village by car – the slopes are far too steep. Wandering down through the quiet, narrow alleys, past palm trees growing out of the rocky walls, you come to the landing-stage (served by regular boats from Lugano), around which is crowded a handful of terrace **restaurants**: there are few quieter, more alluring corners at which to hole up. Views down this little-explored eastern arm of the lake frame the pinnacle of Monte dei Pizzoni – and, beside it, Monte Bronzone – sweeping down into the water, with precipitous wooded slopes opposite that are almost completely devoid of habitation. The silence is wonderful. Should you decide to **stay**, *Hotel Moosmann* can oblige with a lake-view room (℡091 971 72 61, ⓦwww.hotel-moosmann-gandria .ch; ❸–❹; April–Oct).

Opposite Gandria, with its own landing-stage served by boats from Gandria itself as well as Lugano centre (there are no roads here), is the **Museo delle Dogane Svizzere** (Customs Museum; April–Oct daily 1.30–5.30pm; free), with an interesting collection of customs-related bits and bobs that lack decent English notes, although the displays relating to smuggling methods speak for themselves.

Valsolda and Porlezza

From Gandria, the main road heads east for 1.3km to the international border; after 500m of no-man's-land between Swiss and Italian customs, you emerge into the **Valsolda**, a stretch of lakeside villages headed by **Oria** and, almost immediately east, **Albogasio**, both of them cheerful little places – thoroughly Italian, and quite unlike Gandria just the other side of the frontier. **San Mamete** is especially picturesque, with its twelfth-century bell tower.

A quarter-hour east of Gandria, and 8km from the border, is **PORLEZZA**, the main town on this Italian branch of Lago di Lugano – but, in truth, it's not much of a place. The views, facing directly west over the water, are sensational, but Porlezza's lakefront is ramshackle and disorganized, and the town itself is unremarkable. Menaggio, on the shores of Lake Como, lies just 11km east.

Campione d'Italia

Just across the lake from Lugano is the enclave of **CAMPIONE D'ITALIA**, which opted out of the campaign for independence in 1798 and so formed a part of Italy when all around it became Swiss. The village – for that's all it is, even though it's very swish – is part of the Provincia di Como; it has Italian police driving around in Swiss-registered cars and uses Swiss francs rather than euros. There is no passport control. Ambitious plans to build a cable car to the mountain-top above the town – and thereby make it possible, for the first time in centuries, to reach Campione directly from Italian territory – were recently shelved on grounds of cost.

By road, you enter at a modern **arch**: there is a strict one-way system, so you must go right round the town centre before turning back along the lakeshore.

Campione's landmark building is its giant **casino** (daily 3.30pm–3.30am or later; Ⓦ www.casinocampione.it), with a huge, almost windowless extension by Swiss architect Mario Botta. Unlimited stakes apply here, and – despite recent liberalization of Swiss gaming law – this is still where Lugano's many high rollers come to dally after dark.

Previously the town was famous for its stonemasons, the Maestri Campionesi, whose skills were sought for buildings all over northern Italy; the only example that has survived unscathed in Campione is the little, glassed-in church of **San Pietro**, just off the central **Piazza Roma**. From here, Via Marco da Campione runs south along the lake, back to the arch. About 700m along, and 100m before the arch, is the church of **Santa Maria dei Ghirli** (April–Oct daily 9am–6pm; Nov–March Sat & Sun 9am–4.30pm). *Ghirli* means "swallows" and refers to Campione's well-travelled masons, who returned home only rarely. The church – which shows its best side to the lake – is filled with thirteenth-century **frescoes**; especially striking are the scenes on the south wall, showing Salome and Herodias in courtly medieval dress.

Boats dock at Piazza Roma, just near the casino and opposite a row of busy, cheerful and unmistakably Italian (as opposed to Swiss) cafés churning out coffees and full meals: *La Taverna* is a good choice (closed Wed). Campione's poshest **restaurant** is *Da Candida*, Via Marco da Campione 4 (☎091 649 75 41, Ⓦ www.dacandida.com; closed Mon & lunch on Tues; closed July): the chef prepares his own foie gras, and imports his own oysters and other seafood from Brittany. Expect a bill well into three figures.

The Ceresio peninsula

From Paradiso, ten minutes south of Lugano city centre, a funicular run by FMS rises to **San Salvatore** (Ⓦ www.montesansalvatore.ch), a rugged rock pinnacle offering especially good 360-degree panoramas from the roof of the little church on the summit, a short climb from the funicular station. A terrace café by the top station attends to refreshment needs. This is also the starting point for a number of walks south into the **Ceresio peninsula**: it's about an hour and twenty minutes through Carona village to Morcote (see opposite) on the tip of the peninsula.

Although San Salvatore is the most obvious landmark hereabouts, it shares the peninsula with the lower **Collina d'Oro**, or Hill of Gold – about 4km southwest of central Lugano – named as such not for its minerals but for its sun-drenched tranquillity.

Montagnola

On the top of the Collina d'Oro sits the village of **MONTAGNOLA**, home for 43 years to the writer Hermann Hesse. Hesse was born in Germany in 1877, and came to Montagnola in 1919 following traumatic separation from his family after World War I. He rented the **Casa Camuzzi**, an ornate villa, where he lived for twelve years, and where, in an extraordinary outpouring of creativity, he wrote his classic works *Klingsor's Last Summer*, *Siddhartha* and *Steppenwolf*, among many others. In 1924, he was granted Swiss citizenship, and then, in 1931, he moved across the village to the Casa Bodmer, where he wrote *The Glass Bead Game*, which won him the Nobel Prize for Literature in 1946. Hesse died in Montagnola in 1962.

The Casa Camuzzi now houses the **Museo Hermann Hesse** (March–Oct Tues–Sun 10am–12.30pm & 2–6.30pm; Nov–Feb Sat & Sun same hours; Fr.6; Ⓦ www.hessemontagnola.ch). There are no signs to the museum from the

Montagnola bus stop; with the village post office behind you, walk down the slope and aim through a narrow passage leading ahead off the square. The house is five minutes further on the right. Walking around the old villa is interesting, although the modest displays – Hesse's umbrella, Hesse's table – are labelled in Italian and German only. What makes the entry fee worthwhile is an excellent 45-minute video in English on the writer's life in Montagnola that the staff can set up for you.

Melide: Swissminiatur

On the eastern side of the peninsula, at the point where the train tracks, main road and autostrada all cross the lake on a low bridge, sits the village of **MELIDE**, home to the kitschy but rather fun **Swissminiatur** (mid-March to Oct daily 9am–6pm; Fr.15; ⓦ www.swissminiatur.ch). This small park features 1:25 scale models of just about every attraction in Switzerland, from Geneva's cathedral to Zürich airport circa 1958. The reproductions are excellent, and moving model boats, trains and cable cars liven the static models up no end. A wander past all 113 exhibits might take an hour or two – buy the English leaflet (Fr.2) for a brief rundown.

Morcote and Vico Morcote

At the peninsula's southern tip, 4km south of Melide, lies the captivating village of **MORCOTE**, once a fishing community and now eking out a living as a lakeside attraction. Its photogenic arcaded houses – and slightly tacky antiques shops – are strung along the shoreline road, with a web of tranquil, stepped lanes leading up the hill behind to **Santa Maria del Sasso**, a fifteen-minute climb (April–Oct Mon–Fri 8am–6pm, Sat & Sun 9am–6pm; Nov–March Mon–Fri 1.30–6pm, Sat & Sun 9am–6pm). The atmospheric hillside church has well-preserved sixteenth-century frescoes, and boasts great views. Several walks explore the lush woodlands nearby, including a long trail back up to San Salvatore (2hr 30min).

Morcote has a handful of hotels, but also suffers from a great deal of tourist attention. One way to escape is to aim for the tinier village of **VICO MORCOTE**, on the hard-to-reach hillside above and 1km north of Morcote. Here, although the church is just as picturesque and the tiny village piazzas are lined with old stone-built houses that are just as beautiful, unlike in Morcote you can actually hear the fountains tinkle, smell the camellias and stand alone in the middle of the street to absorb the atmosphere. On a junction within the village beside the rustic *Osteria al Böcc* (gnocchi or spaghetti Fr.15), you'll find the tranquil ⚐ *Bellavista* (☎091 996 11 43; ❹–❺). Its impressive **restaurant** is run by a highly accomplished team, who serve exquisite, lightly prepared local cuisine on a beautiful terrace high above the lake; *menus* are around Fr.70. The **hotel** rooms to one side are outstanding, the bargain of the region – fresh, modern, with contemporary furnishings, and flooded with sunlight. Their top-floor luxury suite, huge and spotless, with white tiled floor, billowing curtains and a private terrace, is utterly romantic. Another split-level suite is in the adjacent building, with similarly impressive decor and views.

Porto Ceresio and around

From Capolago, on the east shore of the lake, a minor road cuts west through the medieval village of **RIVA SAN VITALE** and around the perimeter of **Monte San Giorgio**, a wooded mountain that has been made a UNESCO World Natural Heritage Site for its unspoilt environment and its fossils. From

BRUSINO ARSIZIO, an attractive village 5km from Riva, with a handful of lazy terrace cafés that soak up the afternoon sun, a **cable car** rises to Serpiano on a shoulder of the mountain for lonesome forest rambling. Before you reach Brusino, the road rounds the headland of **POJANA**, occupied by the broad, shady terrace of the restaurant *Terminus*. It's an unromantic establishment that can only stretch to plastic garden chairs under the trees, but the location is marvellous, looking beyond Lugano to the high peaks behind.

The Italian border lies 2km beyond Brusino; 1500m further brings you to the genial lakefront town of **PORTO CERESIO**, gazing back at Morcote, just a short hop across the water. The town has built a boardwalk on stilts over the water to facilitate the lovely late-afternoon *passeggiata*, which extends either side of the main lakefront **Piazza Bossi**, and takes in several enticing little pockets of west-facing sandy beach. There's not much else to do; boats stop in here two or three times a day from Lugano.

The Malcantone

Little red trains run by FLP start from open platforms opposite Lugano's main rail station on a scenic but circuitous route west through the **Malcantone** district. After circling the airport at **AGNO**, they hug an arm of the lake, bound for Ponte Tresa. Above Agno are a succession of hill-villages and some fine, lonely walks. A trail from Monte Tamaro (see p.548) ends up here at Monte Lema, connected by cable car with the village of **Miglieglia**.

Trains head on to the undistinguished town of **CASLANO**, unlikely home of the **Alprose chocolate factory** (Mon–Fri 9am–6pm, Sat & Sun 9am–5pm; Fr.3; ⓦwww.alprose.ch), on an industrial estate at Via Rompada 36; to find it from Caslano station, follow the tracks in the direction of Ponte Tresa for about 200m and cut left. As you enter you're greeted, Willy Wonka-like, by a fountain bubbling with fragrant molten chocolate; a guide will swoop a breadstick through and hand it to you. The museum is refreshingly free of corporate hard sell: you'll wander past some old coin-op machines and knick-knacks, including a Meissen porcelain chocolatier, plus there's a short video. The best bit is that you're allowed onto a catwalk above the production line, to watch the mixing machines and conveyor belts shuttling bars and ingredients around the factory floor. You can buy the full Alprose range at discounted prices in the onsite shop.

Caslano is loomed over by the bulbous **Monte Caslano**, which almost chokes this corner of the lake: there is just a narrow, reedy strait between the mountain and the opposite, Italian, shore which allows **boats** to access **PONTE TRESA**, the rail terminus 3km south of Caslano. This is a schizophrenic little place, divided by the River Tresa, along which runs the **international border**. The Swiss half of town is placid and neat, with an air of repose, but crossing the bridge for which the town was named throws you into its Italian twin – a mini-maelstrom of cars negotiating a complex one-way system around a shop-filled town centre. South around the lakeshore lies Porto Ceresio.

The Mendrisiotto

South of Lugano, main roads and trains shoot through the hot, dry region known as the **Mendrisiotto**, after **MENDRISIO**, largest town in the area and a major wine-growing centre. There's not a great deal to stop for in the town, although its centre is picturesque; the main draw is the giant **Foxtown outlet mall** (ⓦwww.foxtown.ch), prominently signposted alongside the autostrada, where you can pick up designer label fashions – Prada, Gucci, Versace, Dolce & Gabbana, and loads more – at between thirty and seventy percent off.

Some 6km on, and 23km south of Lugano, the Italian frontier is marked by **CHIASSO**, an unprepossessing border town, with a large train station on the edge of a desultory town centre and swarms of motorized and foot traffic passing through during the morning and evening rush hours. **Como**'s suburbs begin immediately on the other side, trickling on for 5km to the city centre and lakefront.

Monte Generoso and the Valle di Muggio

Just north of Mendrisio, from alongside **Capolago** train station (274m) at the head of the lake (also accessible by boat from Lugano), Ticino's only rack railway climbs on a slow, scenic route up to the summit of **MONTE GENEROSO** (1704m; Ⓦ www.montegeneroso.ch). For the views alone, this trip is worth taking: from the steep summit – a short climb above the Vetta (top) station – you can see out across virtually the whole of northern Italy, in an amazing panorama. Milan and Turin are both visible; Lake Como and Lake Maggiore are both in plain sight, as is the distinctive pyramidal Matterhorn; and you can even see as far as the mountain pass in the Apennines above Genoa. The restaurant by the top station is the starting-point for an array of **walks**, including down to Mendrisio one way (2hr 40min) or Muggio another (2hr 15min); you can pick up maps and information at the ticket office in Capolago.

Near Mendrisio, the village of Morbio Inferiore marks a branch road that climbs into the last valley in Switzerland, the tranquil **Valle di Muggio** (Ⓦ www.valledimuggio.ch). Thickly wooded, with seemingly inaccessible hamlets clinging to the steep side opposite the road, this is a lovely, rarely visited backwater; **MUGGIO** (666m), 7km in, has a few taverns where you can grab a bite, and a steep trail leading up to the Generoso summit. The best **accommodation** option is 🍴 *Osteria La Montanara* (☎091 684 14 79; ❷), a welcoming little inn in **MONTE**, across the valley from Muggio.

Travel details

Full timetables for all trains, buses, trams, boats and cable cars in Switzerland – as well as international connections – are searchable at Ⓦ www.rail.ch.

Trains

Bellinzona to: Airolo (hourly; 50min); Biasca (twice hourly; 15min); Locarno (3 hourly; 20min); Lugano (3 hourly; 25min); Luzern (twice hourly; 2hr 10min); Zürich (twice hourly; 2hr 30min).
Locarno to: Bellinzona (3 hourly; 20min); Domodossola, Italy (approx. hourly; 1hr 45min); Intragna (twice hourly; 20min); Verscio (hourly; 15min); Zürich (approx. hourly; 3hr).
Lugano to: Basel (hourly; 3hr 55min); Bellinzona (3 hourly; 25min); Caslano (every 20min; 25min); Como, Italy (twice hourly; 45min); Luzern (hourly; 2hr 40min); Zürich (hourly; 2hr 55min).

Buses

Airolo to: Andermatt via Gottardo (July–Sept 3 daily; 50min); Oberwald via Novena/Nufenen Pass (July–Sept 2 daily; 2hr 45min).
Ascona to: Brissago (every 30min; 10min); Locarno (every 15min; 15min).
Bellinzona to: Biasca (hourly; 25min); Chur via San Bernardino (every 2hr; 2hr 15min); Giornico (hourly; 40min); Locarno (hourly; 50min).
Biasca to: Bellinzona (hourly; 25min); Disentis/Mustér (June–Sept 2–3 daily; 1hr 20min; change at Lucomagno Pass); Giornico (hourly; 10min); Olivone (every 2hr; 40min).
Locarno to: Ascona (every 15min; 15min); Bellinzona (hourly; 50min).
Lugano to: Melide (approx. hourly; 15min); Montagnola (hourly; 20min); Morcote

(approx. hourly; 30min); St Moritz via Italy (Palm Express; 1–3 daily; 4hr); Vico Morcote (every 2hr; 35min; change at Olivella).

Boats

Following is a summary of April–Oct services. See ⓦ www.navigazionelaghi.it (Lago Maggiore) or ⓦ www.lakelugano.ch (Lago di Lugano).

Ascona to: Isole di Brissago (hourly; 15min); Locarno (approx twice hourly; 20–30min).
Locarno to: Ascona (approx twice hourly; 20–30min); Isole di Brissago (hourly; 45min–1hr).
Lugano to: Gandria (approx. every 45min; 35min); Morcote (every 2hr; 1hr).
Porto Ronco to: Isole di Brissago (every 40min; 5–10min).

Contexts

Contexts

History

Switzerland is often dismissed as an irrelevance in the broader picture of European history: because the country is peaceful today, the underlying suspicion is that it either wasn't subject to the same tide of events as elsewhere, or that the place is just somehow inherently tranquil. Both ideas are false.

The Swiss difference came in solving the same problems that everyone else had in entirely different, co-operative ways. Decentralization, consultation and cooperation are still key Swiss attributes, as they were in 1291 at the start of the country's history. Until 150 years ago, Switzerland was the most unstable country in Europe, with a history spanning centuries of internecine conflict. The Alpine calm of today came at the price of almost a millennium of war.

Early civilizations

In Appenzell and near the Rhine in Schaffhausen are scattered remains of the **Paleolithic** civilizations that occupied the area of Switzerland between the long periods of prehistoric glaciation. Around 10,000 years ago, at the end of the last major Ice Age, hunter-fisherfolk moved in to occupy the Mittelland, soon afterwards building villages on the shores of the lakes of Zürich, Neuchâtel, Geneva and others. During the **Bronze Age** and early **Iron Age** the settled villagers began to make contact with neighbouring populated regions. In the first millennium BC, the **Celts** advanced into Switzerland from the west, bringing with them a new culture and new sophistication, as exemplified in the fortified Celtic township discovered at **La Tène**, near Neuchâtel.

The Romans: 58 BC–400 AD

In 58 BC at Bibracte in modern France, a **Roman** army under Julius Caesar defeated the **Helvetii** – a group of Celtic tribes resident in the fertile area between the Alps and the Jura – and forced them to move en masse to western Switzerland. After also conquering **Rhaetia** (modern Graubünden), the Romans gradually opened up the country, building the first roads over the major Alpine passes – most significantly the **Grand-St-Bernard**, as well as the Julier and Splügen further east – and founding provincial towns at Nyon, Augst near Basel, and Avenches, the last of which became the Roman capital, with over fifty thousand inhabitants in its heyday. For two centuries or more, Switzerland enjoyed peace and prosperity: agriculture flourished, and the population was a cosmopolitan mix of native Celts and settled Roman officials. The peace was shattered in 260, when the **Alemanii** – a group of Celtic tribes from the area of modern Germany – broke through the Romans' fortified northern border. Amidst increasing turmoil, Helvetia and Rhaetia were reduced to impoverished frontier regions.

The roots of freedom: 400–1516

Around 400, Rome withdrew its legions from the area of Switzerland, and Germanic tribes moved in to take control. In the western regions, the originally Germanic **Burgundians** settled and adopted both the Christianity and the Latin language of the local Gallo-Roman tribes. On the south side of the mountains, and in the closed Alpine valleys of Rhaetia, Lombardic and

Romansh peoples retained close cultural and linguistic links with their former Roman overlords. Elsewhere, **Aleman** tribes from the north settled the forests of central and northeastern Helvetia, halting their advances at points where the land was already populated by Latin-speaking Burgundians. The Germanic Alemans had had little contact with Rome and Christianity, and so continued to use their own native language and follow their own customs. In this way, a **border** of language and culture slowly developed along a line running roughly north–south, marking the easternmost limit of Latinate Burgundian territory and the westernmost limit of Alemanic territory. This language border survives today as the frontier between French- and German-speaking Switzerland.

Around 600, both the Alemans and the Burgundians were conquered by the **Franks**, who absorbed them into their empire under first **Merovingian** and then **Carolingian** kings. The Frankish Empire greatly expanded Latin Christianity throughout Switzerland – and especially into the pagan Alemanic areas – with a network of **monasteries**, including those which still flourish at Romainmôtier, Einsiedeln, Engelberg and St Gallen. **Feudalism** also spread: local warrior nobles took control over an agrarian society of lords, vassals and a vast, impoverished peasantry. In 870, **Charlemagne**'s empire was split, with the dividing line running right through the middle of modern Switzerland. Conflict erupted, and it wasn't until around 1050 that peace and order returned, nominally under the Holy Roman Emperor.

The birth of the Confederation

During the twelfth century, about a third of the central Swiss forests were cleared; noble dynasties – among them the houses of **Habsburg**, **Zähringen**, **Savoy** and Kyburg – established towns such as Bern, Fribourg, Murten and Winterthur from which to assert their control over the increasingly prosperous countryside.

Around 1220, the road over the **St Gotthard Pass** was opened for traffic, and those communities lying on the northern approaches to the pass – specifically Uri and Schwyz – suddenly took on massive importance to the imperial rulers. A resurgence in **trade** with the Mediterranean world after almost a millennium of isolation led to luxury goods making their way across the Alpine passes into northern Europe. Local lords, merchants, princes and the valley communes squabbled with each other for control of the lucrative pass routes. The situation needed resolution, and the Holy Roman Emperor himself stepped in, granting to Uri in 1231 and to Schwyz in 1240 the privilege of freedom from feudal overlordship. The Austrian house of **Habsburg** had extended its influence over much of Switzerland, but the proud, independent people farming the remote valleys of Uri and Schwyz, and their neighbours in forested Unterwalden, remained self-reliant.

The death in 1291 of the ruler **Rudolf of Habsburg** sparked popular revolts, directed against entrenched power bases (such as the monasteries). In response, a number of Swiss communities forged new partnerships, or renewed old ones, to give themselves a degree of protection against an uncertain future. The legendary **founding of the Swiss Confederation** on the Rütli meadow on August 1, 1291, by representatives of Uri, Schwyz and Unterwalden, was just one of these alliances, and is thought to have been a renewal of an earlier agreement of unknown date declaring that an attack on any one of the partners was an attack on them all. The legend of **William Tell** probably arose both as a justification of the sporadic rebellions that followed the death of Rudolf, and as a way to embody the concept of Swiss liberty in a single heroic figure; there is no mention either of Tell or of any organized resistance to the Habsburgs in contemporary thirteenth-century chronicles. The name the Swiss gave themselves after 1291 – **Eidgenossen** – is untranslatable in English (approximating to "comrades bound by oath into a cooperative"), but retains a special significance. Switzerland still calls itself the *Eidgenossenschaft*, and the word *Eidgenosse* is listed in dictionaries as a synonym for "Swiss".

Consolidation and growth

Revolts continued against symbols of Habsburg power. In 1315, at **Morgarten** near Schwyz, an army of peasants from the newly formed Confederation defeated a force of Austrian knights. Ludwig of Habsburg was forced to concede yet more privileges to the three cantons. The Habsburgs then tried to force the burgeoning market town of **Luzern**, transport hub for the journey to and from the Gotthard Pass, to take up arms against its lakeside neighbours. Luzern instead threw in its lot with the "Schwyzers", and joined the Confederation in 1332. Unable to bring the Swiss to heel, Habsburg bailiffs withdrew altogether in about 1350 and left the hard-nosed peasants to their own devices. The local economy continued to flourish.

The feudal system began to collapse under pressure from an increasingly prosperous and ambitious free peasantry, who formed an array of democratic rural communes. This went hand in hand with a rise in the power of urban workers: **Zürich**, where the guilds had already overthrown the city's ruling nobility, joined the Confederation in 1351. Tiny **Glarus** and **Zug** were roped into the Confederation to secure overland transport routes; and then **Bern**, which was looking to expand its territory westwards, joined in 1353 to defuse the possibility of attack from the east by the increasingly powerful Confederation.

Suddenly, in a little over sixty years, the insignificant Schwyzers – born out of a pact of farming folk – were able to call on an army of over 100,000, and had control of a large swathe of former Habsburg territory across the northern foothills of the Alps. Similar leagues of alliance among ordinary farmers in impenetrable Rhaetia to the east were coalescing into an organized opposition to noble Habsburg rule. While blue-blooded Habsburg armies swept victorious through the great cities of Swabia, in southern Germany, the very same armies experienced crushing defeats in Switzerland by the Confederate soldiery, most notably at **Sempach** in 1386 and **Näfels** in 1388 – both battles which retain resonance today for the Swiss. The eight cantons formed an independent state within the Habsburg empire that was ruled – uniquely – by urban burghers and merchants and founded on principles of social cooperation, at a time when elsewhere across Europe kings, princes and noble dynasties held unchallenged sway.

Military conquest

The fifteenth century saw continued expansion. Forces from Uri and Obwalden crossed the Gotthard to seize the **Valle Leventina** south to Bellinzona, crushing the armies of the dukes of Milan as they did so, while the Confederation took advantage of popular uprisings against the abbot of **St Gallen** to extend their influence eastwards, and of a dispute between Austria and Luxembourg to seize control of the fertile northern lands of **Aargau**.

After 1460, Swiss **mercenaries** became known and feared throughout Europe for their bravery and military skill, tested on battlefields fighting Charles the Bold of **Burgundy**. Victories at Grandson, Murten and Nancy in 1476–77 effectively wiped Burgundy from the map as a regional power, but led to the first of many disputes within the Confederation over the balance of power between towns and countryside. Rural cantons were loath to see Bern – principal victor against Charles – become any more powerful, and only accepted the entry of **Fribourg** and **Solothurn** to the Confederation in 1481 on condition that they took a role of arbitration to moderate urban expansionism. Following Zürich's victory in the **Swabian War** of 1499 – which won complete freedom for the cantons from the German Empire – both **Basel** and **Schaffhausen** joined the Confederation (1501), followed by tiny **Appenzell** in 1513. By then, the thirteen cantons possessed extensive subject territories, including Aargau, Thurgau and a swathe of Ticino. The first Swiss parliament, the **Diet**, met regularly in Baden as a forum to bring Confederate opinion together, both by discussion and – even at this early date – by majority voting.

Reformation and religious conflict: 1516–1798

The **Reformation**, which began in Germany in the early sixteenth century, was sparked in Switzerland by **Huldrych Zwingli**, a lay priest in Zürich. City after city overthrew its ecclesiastical overlords in favour of the new **Protestantism**: St Gallen, Basel, Biel, Schaffhausen and, in 1528, Bern. In each place, the urban guilds were the motive force behind the overthrow, and once Catholicism had been ejected, each city government gained new power and authority over the countryside surrounding it, thus fuelling rural resentment. With the Church's land around Zürich parcelled out to the city authorities, the rural peasantry saw no benefit from the change, and many switched support to the extreme, but largely ineffectual, **Anabaptist** movement, which sought the abolition of serfdom altogether. When Zwingli promulgated the controversial notion of reorganizing the Confederacy under the twin **city** leadership of Zürich and Bern, many rural Catholics resisted strongly, feeling both their religious faith and their political voice to be under threat. Conflict broke out in 1531, in which Zwingli was killed and the Catholic forces won a right of veto in the Diet.

The Reformation continued to spread: with the help of Bernese forces, Geneva won its independence from Savoy in 1530 and accepted the Reformation shortly afterwards, along with Neuchâtel, Lausanne and rural Vaud. In 1536, the French priest **Jean Calvin** settled in Geneva, establishing a rigid Protestant theocracy that spread the city's reputation for religious zeal and tolerance Europe-wide.

The situation became further entrenched in the 1550s and 1560s, with the coalescing of the Reformation around Calvinist doctrine, and the consequent launch of the **Counter-Reformation** in a bid to preserve Catholic territory and reassert Catholic rights. With the support of Spain – a major world power – the Catholic cantons retained their religious identity (in 1597 Appenzell split into two half-cantons, one Protestant and one Catholic), but they increasingly nurtured an inferiority complex towards the Protestant cities, which held a grip on political authority and the economy. The latter had started to take on new vitality, boosted by the presence of skilled Huguenot and Veltliner craftspeople – **Protestant refugees** from Catholic regimes in France and Italy.

The seventeenth century

Throughout the tense seventeenth century, it was only shared economic interests that kept the Swiss Confederation together: a lucrative system of **textile processing** developed, in which merchants in the cities (generally Protestant) supplied raw materials to peasants in the countryside (generally Catholic), who worked up the finished product and delivered it back to the city merchants for trading on or export. Politics, however, remained in deadlock. No new regions could be admitted to the Confederation, since to do so would upset the delicate balance between Catholic and Protestant cantons. Mistrust on the part of Catholics of a perceived Protestant agenda for domination of the Confederation prevented reorganization or redistribution of jointly administered subject territories, which included Graubünden and Valais.

This wariness filtered over into foreign policy, with the continuing traffic in mercenaries entangling the Confederation in a complex web of **armed neutrality**. All the cantons had pledged to supply France with manpower; in addition, the Catholic ones had links with Spain and Savoy, the Protestant ones with various German principalities and the Netherlands. (The Battle of Malplaquet in 1709 between France and Holland is the most famous example of Swiss mercenaries taking to the battlefield against each other.) The Confederation stayed out of the **Thirty Years' War** (1618–48) – the first significant test of its neutrality – but still imposed new taxes to strengthen its frontier defences. In 1645, a peasants' rebellion against the new austerities was suppressed with violence. In 1653, after the currency was devalued without warning, wiping out the meagre savings of the rural peasantry overnight, a full-scale **Peasants' Revolt** set out to reclaim ancient rights enshrined in agreements from the early days of the Confederation. The urban patricians of Bern and Luzern called in the army to crush the revolt, and then launched a campaign to reform the Confederate charter in favour of themselves. This was blocked by the rural cantons, who then went to war to safeguard their interests. In a mark of the turbulence of the period, Protestant urban aristocrats and Catholic rural aristocrats first combined to crush the peasantry, then within a few years turned to face each other in bloody conflict. After two battles at **Villmergen**, in 1656 and 1712, Catholics conceded Protestant rights both in confederal matters and in administering the joint dependencies.

The build-up to revolution

The Protestant victory in 1712 – which ended Catholic hegemony in confederal affairs – also ended two centuries of religious conflict, and resulted in a **social and economic shift** in favour of the largely Protestant cities. Catholic regions, which had remained free from the dour influence of Calvin, enjoyed relative freedom in personal conduct but were industrially backward, while Protestant areas benefited from a better-educated populace and the presence of Protestant artisans from around Europe. French Huguenots in particular, their name a corruption of *Eidgenosse*, were the motive force behind a growth in urban manufacturing industries such as **watchmaking** in the northwest and **textiles** in the east. During the Swiss industrial revolution of the eighteenth century, **commercial farming** also began to take hold in the rural cantons.

The second half of the century saw the liberal **Enlightenment** replacing the rigours of Calvinism, with writers and thinkers such as Jean-Jacques Rousseau and Heinrich Pestalozzi feeding a new spirit of Helvetic nationalism which brought Catholics and Protestants together in their patriotic concern for the nation.

However, political life became increasingly **conservative**. Fearful of a repetition of the peasants' uprising, urban patrician dynasties asserted their traditional prerogatives and concentrated power in their own hands. Increasing prosperity and the influence of liberal philosophies in towns and countryside alike led to growing intolerance of patrician rule: in Lausanne in 1723, in Geneva in 1737, in Bern in 1749, in Ticino in 1755, and in Geneva again throughout the 1760s, popular insurrections against entrenched systemic injustice demonstrated a grassroots desire for change.

Revolution and civil war: 1798–1848

The impact in Switzerland of the **French Revolution** of 1789 was enormous. The Confederation itself remained neutral in the battles that followed, but popular revolutionary demonstrations throughout Vaud – at that time a Bernese colony – and at Stäfa near Zürich acted as a spur to a full-scale **French invasion** in 1798 by armies under Napoleon. Revolution swept through the country. In Ticino, Aargau and the lower Valais, the old patrician establishment was swept away; urban residents of Basel, Zürich and Schaffhausen at a stroke won equality before the law; Vaud declared itself independent from Bern; and the brief burst of resistance to the French mounted in central areas was violently suppressed. On March 5, French forces entered Bern, marking the fall of the *ancien régime* in Switzerland.

Within weeks, Napoleon promulgated a new constitution intended to replace the archaic patchwork of communities and privileges, decentralized authority and internecine mistrust that had prevailed since the Middle Ages. His brave new **Helvetic Republic**, "unitary and indivisible", did away with cantons altogether and instead vested centralized power, French-style, nominally in the people but actually in a five-man executive. This showed just how drastically Napoleon underestimated the Swiss, who broke the habit of centuries by coming together – liberal and conservative, Catholic and Protestant alike – in unanimous rejection of his imposed new order. A series of *coups d'état* prompted Napoleon to withdraw his troops from the country in short order in 1802. Civil war broke out, and Napoleon stepped in as arbitrator, this time prudently urging the Swiss themselves to come up with a constitution. This shortlived **Mediation**, as it was called, restored the notion of autonomous cantons, and in addition conferred full cantonal status on six areas previously under joint administration: St Gallen, Graubünden, Aargau, Thurgau, Ticino and Vaud. It also gave the country the new title of the **Swiss Confederation**, a name it bears today.

After Napoleon

The calm was shortlived: once Napoleon was defeated at Waterloo, the democratic balance in Switzerland collapsed. The 1815 **Congress of Vienna** reasserted old patrician privileges throughout Europe, not least in Switzerland, where aristocratic families regained control over local and federal politics. Geneva, Neuchâtel and Valais entered the Swiss Confederation as new cantons, and Bern was granted the Jura as compensation for its losses in Aargau and Vaud. For fifteen years, the political situation simmered, until street-fighting in Paris in 1830 sparked in Switzerland the **Regeneration**, a similar movement of liberalization. This led to seizures of power by united bands of peasants, urban merchants, and craftspeople, who drew up cantonal constitutions enshrining equality and political rights for all – rural and urban alike – and instituted democratic elections to the cantonal governments. In 1831, the patricians of **Basel** condoned a localized civil war, and the division of the canton into two antagonistic half-cantons, rather than surrender any of their powers to radical activists.

Switzerland nonetheless enjoyed an **economic** boom. Unlike in Britain – the only country in Europe more industrially advanced – Switzerland experienced no rush to the cities by an impoverished proletariat. Swiss factories, where they existed, were in rural areas, and drew their labour from the local peasantry, who often came to work after tending to their herds in the fields. Cottage industries, where textiles were processed or watches assembled by individuals working in their own homes under contract from urban suppliers, remained a mainstay of Swiss economic development. The piecemeal, individual-driven Swiss textile industry was efficient enough to stave off competition from Britain's "dark satanic mills" throughout the first half of the century. In addition, new and diverse fields of expertise in chemical production, chocolate-making and tourism boosted national confidence and the image of the country in the eyes of the world.

The Sonderbund War

After the upheavals of the early 1830s, conflict between **radical** liberals and **conservative**, generally Catholic, activists led to increasingly bitter squabbles. After Aargau overturned religious equality in 1841 and ordered all religious buildings in the canton to be shut down, outraged Catholics in neighbouring Luzern nullified their own canton's newly drafted liberal constitution and – in a move intended to provoke – invited the **Jesuit** order to run the schools. This, in turn, outraged radical opinion, which valued liberal education highly and viewed Jesuit control of the schools as nothing less than a step backwards into superstition.

Violent, radical-led scuffles soon broke out, aimed at Luzern's Catholics. In response, the Catholic cantons – Luzern, Zug, Schwyz, Uri, Obwalden, Nidwalden, Fribourg and Valais – formed an illegal resistance force, dubbed the **Sonderbund** (Separatist League), which threatened to destabilize the country. During 1846, a series of localized revolutions put radicals in control of more and more cantons nationwide until, by 1847, with a majority in the Diet, they demanded the expulsion of the Jesuits from the country, the drafting of a new democratic constitution and the forced dissolution of the Sonderbund. **Civil war** was inevitable, and – as much to head off intervention by the great European powers as anything else – the federal commander-in-chief General Henri Dufour took the opportunity to strike. In a month-long campaign during November 1847 he took Fribourg and Zug, and then Luzern, crushing the heartland of the Sonderbund with minimal casualties. The remaining Catholic cantons soon capitulated.

Reconciliation: 1848–1918

The postwar **Federal Constitution of 1848** – still in effect today – marked the birth of the modern Swiss state. It enshrined a host of liberal measures designed to limit patrician power and to permit continued expansion of industry and the economy. For the first time, Switzerland had a **central government**, with a directly elected bicameral parliament. To a background of revolutions breaking out all over Europe during 1848, the radical liberals – conscious of the centuries of Swiss conflict behind them – devised a constitution that was able to defuse the age-old Catholic fears of Protestant domination. They did so principally by **dividing power** between the centre and the cantons, thereby allowing the majority Protestants and the minority Catholics to engage in democratic debate together, in the knowledge that each needed the other to survive. Devolution of power to self-governing cantons – **federalism** – allowed the retention of strong Catholic communities at the cantonal level and the creation of strong Protestant-led institutions at the national level. And, following 25 years of peace and consolidation, the formal adoption in 1874 of the **referendum** as the prime tool for consultation of the people – on matters of local, cantonal and national interest alike – ensured that politicians remained directly accountable.

Amidst steady economic growth in railways, tourism, chemicals, engineering and heavy industry, **national reconciliation** was allowed to develop organically over the second half of the century, and with it came further democratization, with the adoption of proportional representation in cantonal elections and the growth of consultation and compromise at executive level in the federal government. With a mood of reconciliation after 1848, ever-increasing numbers of **tourists** exploring the newly fashionable Alps, huge national celebrations of six hundred years of Swiss history in 1891, and the unveiling of the idealistic monument to William Tell in Altdorf in 1895, a new, specifically **Swiss national identity** began to develop.

Although the appeal of Swiss national unity was strong, **nationalism** threatened – paradoxically – to split the country apart again. The alluringly woolly ideas that developed at this time of race, social darwinism and the mystical destiny shared by all people who shared a particular language (exemplified in the concept of uniting Europe's German-speaking *Volk*), held a romantic, supranational appeal. German Swiss looked towards the achievements of Germany, with its booming economy, military prowess and advanced social-welfare policies, and felt themselves to be part of it, distanced from their French-speaking compatriots. Similarly, French Swiss looked towards the cultural achievements of *fin-de-siècle* France, and saw their Swiss–German neighbours as foreign. Italian-speaking Swiss in particular felt the arbitrary international border between them and the "rest" of Italy to be increasingly absurd. At the dawn of the twentieth century, the Swiss had stopped talking to each other.

World War I and after

Officially, Switzerland stayed out of **World War I**. In practice, the army had been "thoroughly Prussianized", as Jonathan Steinberg puts it, and its commanders saw no reason not to support Germany. As soon as war broke out in the summer of 1914, Switzerland began passing military intelligence to Berlin. The mood within the country soured, as German and French Swiss retreated from each other, both backing opposite sides in the war. In an echo of the trenches of northern France, a *Graben*, or trench, opened up along the language border between the two. French Swiss were increasingly outraged by their army's pro-German bias.

Economic conditions were hard, compounded by the need to maintain a frontier force and to support a growing number of refugees and asylum-seekers. In 1915 and 1916, Lenin, Trotsky and Zinoviev were all resident in Switzerland, and the influence of their revolutionary socialist agitation, as well as subsequent news of the successful Russian Revolution, spurred Swiss workers on to a **General Strike** in November 1918. For three days the Federal Council dithered, then called in the army. The strikers capitulated soon afterwards and went back to work, but had made their point: in a referendum in 1919, the Swiss people approved the adoption of proportional representation in national elections – a major plank of the workers' concerns, since majority voting had effectively excluded the Socialist Party from real power. The Federal Council acknowledged the benefits of compromise, and met the strike committee face-to-face. Soon after, policies on welfare expansion and a 48-hour working week became law.

Neutrality and World War II: 1918–1945

The rise in power of a socialist-minded proletariat after the war prompted a corresponding rise in the old forces of Catholic conservatism: rural farmers

quickly won a place on the Federal Council alongside the urban Radicals. As elsewhere, the economic bubble of the 1920s burst in the early 1930s, with a crippling **depression** halving output, decimating incomes and causing huge unemployment. At the same time, cosy domestic coalitions were breaking down under the influence of proportional representation, which brought a myriad of economic and political interest groups into parliament. After **Hitler**'s rise to power in Germany in 1933, sympathetic Nazi "fronts" emerged, gathering support nationwide from right-wing conservatives and hard-hit petty bourgeois merchants who together proposed revision of the Federal Constitution. But both a devaluation of the franc in 1936 (which boosted Swiss industry in the run-up to war) and a new partnership of liberals and social democrats – who, in the face of spreading fascism, had together abandoned the ideal of class war – were effectively able to sideline these authoritarian movements in favour of continued democratic debate. As war became more and more likely, Switzerland bolstered its own national institutions, affirming the status of **Romansh** as a national language, authorizing widespread official usage of **Swiss-German** as a distancing measure from the High German of the Third Reich, and showcasing home-grown achievements at a **National Exhibition** in 1939. In addition, it readied its economy and industry for war, passing a series of laws to protect individual earnings should mobilization become necessary, and introducing anonymous **numbered bank accounts** to protect the savings of German Jews from seizure by the Nazis.

Switzerland and the Jews

As across Europe, **anti-Semitism** worked its way into official Swiss policy over decades. Freedom of residence and civic and legal equality had been granted to Jews in Switzerland only in 1866, and even in the glow of pan-Helvetic pride in diversity around the 1891 national anniversary, a referendum was passed in 1893 banning Jewish ritual slaughter of animals on ostensibly compassionate grounds (ritual slaughter remains illegal in Switzerland today). Russian pogroms in the 1880s resulted in floods of destitute Jews heading west across Europe, and subsequent concerns about **Überfremdung**, or foreign infiltration, of Switzerland showed themselves in discriminatory immigration policies that required assimilation before civic protection could be conferred: in virtually all cases, Jews who applied for refugee status were deemed to be alien to Swiss society and thus unassimilable.

As the European situation worsened during the 1930s, Switzerland searched for a way to keep the Jews out – as did many European governments – without being seen to compromise their reputation for neutrality and tradition of providing asylum. In 1938, in response to a specific request to the Gestapo made by Switzerland's police chief, Germany ordered that the passports of all "non-Aryan" Germans – that is, Jews – be stamped with a "J" to identify them to border guards, who were then instructed to turn them back. After August 1942, racial persecution alone was deemed to be not sufficient grounds for emergency admission to the country, and the borders were effectively closed. Only twelve Jews in each year of the war were granted Swiss naturalization papers, and of some 300,000 refugees who were accepted into Switzerland, just ten percent were Jewish. Surviving records testify to 25,000 Jews being turned back at the borders, but the real figure must have been vastly higher.

By autumn 1942, the Red Cross in Geneva knew unequivocally of the systematic murder of Jews in Nazi death camps. Under pressure from the Swiss government, it did and said nothing. The borders remained closed. A few individuals within Switzerland were working against the policies of the

government, but the official line was that – in the notorious words of Federal Councillor Eduard von Steiger – "the lifeboat is full".

World War II

In the summer of 1939, Switzerland mobilized between ten and twenty percent of its entire population in preparation for **war**. Germany had already invaded Austria in 1938 under the pretext of "union" (*Anschluss*), and by June 1940, Denmark, Norway, Holland, Belgium, Luxembourg and France had all succumbed. Mussolini's Fascist Italy lay to the south. Switzerland was surrounded. An invasion by the Axis powers seemed imminent, and on July 25, 1940, following a controversial speech hinting at advantages to be gained by collusion with Berlin, the Swiss commander-in-chief **General Guisan**, along with the entire Swiss officer corps, took ship in Luzern for the **Rütli** meadow, semi-mythical scene of the founding of the Confederation in 1291. There, at this most resonant spot, Guisan reaffirmed the Swiss commitment to resistance and neutrality, and conducted a ceremony at which all officers did the same. Rumblings of discontent among junior officers at the hints of collaboration in the upper echelons of command were thus quelled.

And yet it is now clear that collaboration continued apace. Unlike in the previous war, this time the flouting of Swiss neutrality was usefully concealed beneath a glow of national pride and unity, fuelled by the Rütli declaration. The role of Switzerland in World War II is still highly controversial, but historians now accept that the country escaped Nazi invasion not simply through the doggedness and tenacity of its troops (as Swiss history books have long maintained). Both the Allied and the Axis powers were very well served by having an ostensibly neutral, stable Switzerland at the heart of war-torn Europe. The country's role as a **banking and financial centre** was pivotal: both sides needed to buy war *materiel* and resources, and during the war the only truly convertible currency accepted for payment worldwide was the Swiss franc. Basel's Bank of International Settlements – a bank of national banks, with board members drawn from the US, Britain, France, Germany and elsewhere – kept the wheels of international capitalism turning, and was the only place where **high-level meetings** continued in extreme secrecy between Allied and Axis officials, meetings that were treasonous by the standards of both. Right up until the fall of Berlin in 1945, the Swiss National Bank accepted **gold** from Germany in exchange for Swiss francs, in the full and certain knowledge that Berlin would then use the money to keep the Axis war machine supplied, and that the ingots arriving at Bern had been looted from the banks of invaded countries and/or melted down from the possessions and even the teeth of dead Jews. In addition, Hitler needed a peaceful Switzerland to keep the **Alpine passes** that linked Germany and Italy open, and also benefited from Swiss **industry**, which continued to supply the Third Reich with guns, ammunition and heavy artillery, in exchange for essential raw materials and food.

After the Rütli gathering General Guisan ordered Swiss frontier defence positions to withdraw from the national borders in order to fortify positions within the high Alpine chain. The *réduit national* ("**Fortress Switzerland**") took shape: at almost any point after 1940, Hitler could have crossed the frontier and taken the entire populated lowlands – Basel, Zürich, Bern, Geneva and the countryside – without a fight, and reduced independent Switzerland to a scattering of snowbound bunkers in the high Alps. But such an invasion would have impoverished the Reich. In reality, Switzerland was safe: the military kudos to be gained by Hitler's having a subdued, occupied Switzerland subject to Allied bombing was vastly outweighed by the material benefit of his nurturing a

nominally neutral, independent Switzerland that remained enthusiastically open for business. The moral consequences of this for the Swiss themselves are only now being felt, decades later.

Sonderfall Schweiz: 1945–2001

Patrick Kury, a historian at the University of Basel, has written: "After World War II, the lack of experience of war made Swiss people believe that they were a kind of chosen people living outside history. This strange belief goes together with the misconception that between 1933 and 1945 Switzerland had followed a humanitarian tradition, and had never practised an anti-Jewish [policy]. In the postwar period, neutrality – the number one state maxim – also helped to neutralize analysis and discussion."

The glow of national pride in having reached war's end unscathed – despite the fact that Switzerland's citizen army had merely kept its head down, and that neither Allied nor Axis powers had had the slightest intention of invading – was intoxicating, and the Swiss felt themselves to be special: the term **Sonderfall Schweiz**, or "Switzerland as a Special Case", is often used to describe the period. The extent of official collaboration with both warring parties was widely known by foreign governments – who shunned Switzerland immediately postwar – but was generally not even suspected by ordinary Swiss.

In Switzerland things continued after the war much as they had done before. While the new world order expressed itself in the establishment of the **United Nations** in 1945, Switzerland stuck tight to its neutrality and stayed out. By 1946 international diplomatic relations had been repaired, and Switzerland – with its intact industry, low taxes, and socio-political stability – took on the role of catalyst to European reconstruction. At a time of austerity, Swiss banks were able to draw on large capital reserves (thanks in large part, it is now clear, to their wartime policy of accepting looted gold from Berlin).

With the **Cold War**, fear of the spread of Communism took over from fear of the spread of Fascism. Swiss political parties that were already rooted in concordance moved together into a rock-solid national consensus. Dubbed after 1959 the "**magic formula**", this ensured two seats on the Federal Council went to the moderate-left Liberals, two to the moderate-right Christian Democrats, two to the left-wing Social Democrats and one to the right-wing People's Party; four were reserved for German-speakers and three for French- and Italian-speakers, reflecting the language division in the country.

Along with most of the rest of Western Europe, Switzerland experienced a cycle of economic fortunes: consolidation in the 1950s, boom in the 1960s, recession in the 1970s, entrenchment and readjustment in the 1980s, streamlined growth in the 1990s. However, despite massive advances in personal and national wealth, and success in adapting traditional industries to the new era – exemplified by the launch of **Swatch**, a slick, new company that dragged the Swiss watch industry out of its fustiness – it took until the 1990s for Switzerland to bring itself fully into line with European conceptions of social modernity. **Women** got the vote in national elections only in 1971, decades behind most other European countries; as late as 1991, one canton (Appenzell Inner-Rhodes) had to be forced to accept women onto the cantonal electoral roll by the Federal Supreme Court.

As the Western European powers drew together in an ever-closer **common market**, the insular Swiss looked on, the national mood still one of "Fortress Switzerland": throughout the postwar period, Switzerland consistently voted against joining international bodies of political cooperation. (In 1986, a proposal for **United Nations** membership received a resounding "no" from 76 percent of Swiss voters.) Since 1960, Switzerland had been a member of the European Free Trade Area (EFTA), a purely commercial body without political ambitions. When its EFTA partners Sweden, Finland and Austria applied to join the **European Union** in 1992, Switzerland was forced to follow suit. Put to the vote, the national margin of defeat was narrow, but analysis of the figures showed that 70 percent had voted yes in francophone Romandie, but just 44 percent had voted yes in German-speaking areas; roughly similar figures taken as a national whole split pro-EU urban voters away from anti-EU rural voters. The figures reignited national soul-searching over the age-old social and linguistic divide, and Switzerland shelved its application.

After 1992, this soul-searching was exploited by a new bloc of strident, right-wing opinion shaped and led by the notorious **Christoph Blocher**, leader of the Zürich section of the SVP (Swiss People's Party), who campaigned throughout the 1990s on a platform of anti-EU, anti-immigration rhetoric, wrapped up in a cloak of pro-Swiss, pro-neutrality platitudes. Amidst a floundering economy following the rejection of EU membership – Switzerland had the weakest growth rate in western Europe in the period 1992–2001 – parliamentary time was taken up with endless amendments to bring Swiss law into line with EU law: popular opinion notwithstanding, the country simply couldn't afford to ignore the direction its neighbours were heading in. The Swiss government, forced to seek unorthodox methods of cooperation, embarked on talks with the EU to draw up a series of bilateral accords. Meanwhile, the cosy "magic formula" began to crumble: in the 1999 elections, Christian Democrat support dropped away, while Blocher's SVP won the largest share of the vote.

Blocher's rise was boosted by a series of **scandals** throughout the 1990s that sent the country reeling. Suddenly, as if from nowhere, the squeaky-clean image that postwar generations had of themselves and their country was shown to have been an illusion. In 1989, **Elizabeth Kopp**, the first woman to serve as a Federal Councillor – and something of an icon of the new Switzerland – had to resign when it was revealed that she had tipped off her husband about ongoing investigations into his financial dealings. The same year it emerged that the Swiss **secret police** had been keeping files on 200,000 individuals, under the guise of monitoring anti-patriotic activity. An accountant in the defence department under investigation in a multimillion-franc **fraud** case – the largest in Swiss history – turned out to be an intelligence agent, and claimed he had withdrawn the money on the orders of his boss to fund the secret training of a shady battalion of highly armed agents for purposes unknown.

But the story that hit the international headlines, and brought Switzerland into the uncomfortable glare of global attention, concerned its **wartime** record.

Wartime reappraisal

With the end of the Cold War in 1989, former Communist countries in Eastern Europe opened their borders and their state archives. **Jews** who had survived the Holocaust began petitioning the governments in Warsaw, Budapest, Prague and elsewhere – often with the help of international Jewish organizations such as the New York-based **World Jewish Congress** (WJC) – for return of property that had been seized by the Nazis. In 1995, the fiftieth anniversary of the end of World War II prompted apologies from many Western governments for their activities during wartime. Swiss President Kaspar Villiger officially **apologized** for the introduction of the "J" stamp in the passports of German Jews and for Switzerland's closing its borders to Jewish refugees at the height of the Final Solution. Meanwhile, WJC researchers had been recording case after case of Holocaust survivors being refused access to their dead relatives' accounts in Swiss banks, often on spurious grounds such as not providing a death certificate. They began to smell a rat, and turned to the US National Archives, which held official wartime government records tracking the flow of money through Switzerland. They uncovered records showing that the Swiss banks were not just sitting on the assets of dead Jews, but that they had also accepted vast quantities of obviously looted **gold** as part of a hitherto only guessed-at secret, semi-official network of economic collusion with the Third Reich.

The story rapidly hit the headlines, and pressure built for official investigations to begin. In 1996, the **Swiss Bankers' Association** disingenuously announced it had uncovered a mere Fr.39 million in heirless accounts. Pressure built throughout the year, with the WJC and other organizations – Jewish and not – demanding full access to banks' archives to get to the bottom of the story. In 1997, a security guard working at UBS, **Christoph Meili**, made public the fact that the bank was secretly shredding large quantities of prewar documents. Meili was fired for violating the bank's secrecy and prosecuted shortly afterwards, but became something of a folk hero, not least to liberal-minded Swiss who were getting increasingly uncomfortable with the banks' attitude. It was becoming clear to the Swiss establishment that the game was up: the president, Arnold Koller, attempted to head off the oncoming onslaught by proposing the financing of a Fr.7 billion fund from the gold reserves of the Swiss National Bank to support Swiss and foreign victims of oppression and natural disaster – the so-called **Swiss Solidarity Foundation**. Then a local newspaper revealed that Credit Suisse – another major Swiss bank – had opened an account for the Nazi SS during the war and that the Bank for International Settlements in Basel had acted as a safe conduit for much of the Reich's looted gold. The WJC publicized documents from the US National Archive stating that **Japan**, wartime ally of the Nazis, had also used Swiss banks. Meanwhile, the banks themselves were scrabbling to prove their good faith: Fr.17 million that had lain in dormant accounts since the war was returned to the descendants of account holders.

The affair was souring international relations. Switzerland made official complaints to the BBC over a documentary entitled "Nazi Gold". Canada was forced to admit that it had laundered at least six tons of Nazi gold via Switzerland and Portugal. US president Bill Clinton and the US Congress granted the bank security guard Christoph Meili asylum, and UBS dropped the case against him in the Swiss courts and apologized. Amidst the tide of accusation and counter-accusation, the **Red Cross** issued an unprecedented statement admitting a "moral failure" in not having spoken out during the war against the ongoing genocide of the Jews.

In 1997, a committee of historians chaired by **Jean-François Bergier** reported that, in addition to the $389 million of gold purchased from Nazi Germany by the Swiss National Bank (approximately $4 billion in modern-day terms), some $61 million of Nazi gold had been bought by the Swiss commercial banks (among which were UBS and Credit Suisse), three times more than previously thought. The Bergier commission confirmed that the Swiss National Bank had known that much of the gold they were buying had been looted from occupied countries, and also that officials had been aware that the Nazis were robbing Jews and other persecuted groups before exterminating them.

With an array of lawsuits brought by tens of thousands of Holocaust survivors making their way slowly through the US courts, and escalating threats of a Swiss–US trade war, the international pressure on the Swiss banks to acknowledge culpability for their wartime activities and their subsequent attempts to block investigation was inexorable. In 1998, desperate to see an end to the story, the three largest banks, Credit Suisse, UBS and SBC, offered $1.25 billion, the so-called **global settlement sum**, to settle all claims connected with Holocaust-era assets. According to a poll, less than half the Swiss population declared itself content with the outcome, most of them believing the figure to be too high. Meanwhile, the damaging revelations continued to emerge, most notably when the Red Cross was forced to acknowledge deep regret over the fact that it issued **Josef Mengele**, the infamous doctor at the Auschwitz death camp, with a permit to travel through Switzerland in 1949.

In 1999, two official commissions set up to look into the whole affair issued reports. The **Volcker Commission**, which examined Swiss bank accounts from the Nazi era, found almost 54,000 accounts that had been opened between 1933 and 1945, and, in addition to the thousands of names already declared, advised the banks to publish a further 25,000 names of account holders suspected to have been victims of the Nazis. It estimated that, at current prices, these accounts totalled between $200 million and $440 million. The report of the **Bergier Commission**, set up to investigate Switzerland's wartime treatment of refugees, merely confirmed what many already knew, that Switzerland had deliberately blocked the entry of refugees, condemning Jews and others to certain death at the hands of the Nazis. It identified a strain of "cultural, social and political" anti-Semitism that ran through the country at the time. The report prompted Swiss president **Ruth Dreifuss** – the only Jewish woman to have served in the post – to reiterate the government's official apology of 1995. The commission's final report in 2002 stated explicitly that "the [Swiss] refugee policy contributed to... the Holocaust."

The end of "Sonderfall Schweiz"

The whole sorry saga of the 1990s struck deep at the heart of Swiss self-confidence. Statements like those issued by the Bergier Commission that "Switzerland declined to help people in mortal danger" ran counter to all the notions of ethical behaviour that postwar Swiss generations learned from their parents, from each other and from their history books. For some, it has been almost too much to bear: the anger and frustration that has been stirred up in the proudly nationalistic working people of the inner cantons of the country in particular has coincided with the rise of the right-wing demagogue Christoph Blocher, who has channelled it into a coherent, extremist political strategy directed against foreigners of all kinds, embodied – in his philosophy – in the EU, the UN and the many asylum seekers and guest workers resident in Switzerland.

The Nazi gold brouhaha died down after 1998, but a series of crises followed, hammering away at Swiss self-confidence. The most serious erupted in 2001, when the national airline **Swissair** – having squandered millions on an ill-advised policy of acquisitions of failing European carriers, after the rejection of EU membership in 1992 had denied it equal competition rights under EU law – defaulted on its loans and was declared bankrupt. The sight of Swiss travellers marooned at foreign airports and the flag humiliated in public, not to mention the economic failure of a core institution, felt to many Swiss like a national disaster. For six months, bankers and industrialists worked on a rescue package, and in 2002, the new national carrier **Swiss** appeared. Nonetheless, another Swiss icon, and key marker of Swiss reliability, had been shown to be fallible. In 1999, 21 people were killed while canyoning near Interlaken, and eleven people died in a 2001 fire in the St Gotthard road tunnel, further undermining faith in Swiss safety standards that were previously thought to be unimpeachable.

This devastating combination of scandal and national humiliation effectively punctured, in five short years, the self-assurance – and, some said, smugness

– that had shaped Swiss national consciousness over the previous five decades. Commenting on the country's wartime role, the Geneva newspaper *Le Temps* finally spoke a painful truth: "The Swiss were no better or worse than anyone else." It was clear that the idea of *Sonderfall Schweiz*, Switzerland as a "Special Case", was dead.

Switzerland today

Although the *Sonderfall* notion persists, in the ugly shape of Christoph Blocher and the SVP, modern Switzerland has gained a new, rejuvenating humility. This has been most tangibly expressed in the vote in 2002 to finally apply for membership of the **United Nations**; the country was accepted as the UN's 190th member state the same year. The yes vote was hailed as a sign of an end to Swiss isolation; the government still struggles with continuing rejection of European Union membership in referenda, but brought into force in 2002 seven **bilateral accords** between Switzerland and the EU, on such matters as trade and free movement. Progressive liberalization in some areas will be complete by 2014, whether the Swiss people ever vote for EU membership or not.

Asylum and immigration remains a hot topic, fuel to the reactionary fire. Connected with this, and tied up in lingering notions of the core values of Swissness being eroded by foreign influence, is an inexorable rise in the use of **English** throughout the country, in education, business and popular culture. English is now the first foreign language studied in primary schools in Zürich and other cantons, supplanting French; much to the chagrin of those trying to build cultural bridges between the four language communities, it is increasingly seen as Switzerland's *lingua franca*.

With the demise of the *Sonderfall* image, Switzerland continues to search for a contemporary identity. On the one hand, Swiss **architecture** and design lead the world, and a keen awareness of environmental protection shows itself most dramatically in two new trans-Alpine **rail tunnels** – the 35km Lötschberg Base Tunnel and 56km Gotthard Base Tunnel. Both are part of a concerted multibillion-euro effort to conserve the Alpine environment and shift pan-European freight off the roads. On the other hand, Switzerland remains a conservative, traditionalist and – perhaps most surprisingly – deeply militaristic society: it is now the only European country to have **universal male conscription**. The new century has seen the breakdown of the old consensus politics, and the abandonment of the cosy "magic formula" in favour of an unusually divisive oppositional dynamic. Switzerland has gained new self-knowledge after the crises of the 1990s, but it has also lurched to the right. The old guard are digging in.

Contemporary architecture

With its intrinsic faith in modernity and traditional support for innovation, Switzerland has developed a cultural climate that has fostered some of the most important contemporary architects of the last twenty years. Private and state sponsorship, coupled with an understanding of the value of quality design, has led the country to become a model for contemporary architecture, where home-grown talent constructs alongside international stars. Private commissions and public competitions alike generate a dynamic environment for both new and established architects.

Having largely escaped the upheavals associated with the world wars of the twentieth century, Swiss culture has had the freedom to grow organically, avoiding many of the ruptures and traumas suffered by its neighbours. The **Modern** movement of the 1930s, with its philosophy of cost-effective architecture coupled with a certain pride in the use of rational techniques, was the basic model for construction across the country for more than three decades.

The Ticino School

International recognition for Swiss architecture came with the **Ticino School**. In the 1960s, renewed economic prosperity swept across the country; this boom was manifested in the Ticino region by a mushrooming of small factories and private houses with no building or urban planning restrictions. The Ticino School emerged out of this uncontrolled situation with a sense of optimism in the capability of architecture to provide a solution to the chaos and ruin of the landscape.

The central influences on the movement were the theoretical arguments that were developing across the border in Italy, focused around the Milanese architect and critic Aldo Rossi. Rossi held that modern architecture should essentially be a social discipline where individuality is replaced by the use of a few identifiable and unchangeable components, elementary geometrical volumes with the capacity to become monuments and so give sense and order to the surrounding territory.

The ideals of the Ticino School found probably their clearest expression in the work of **Luigi Snozzi**. Snozzi has been responsible for construction in the village of Monte Carasso, just outside Bellinzona, since 1977, attempting to break down any differences between urban planning and architecture. His aim has been to give the village a distinctive identity, since it was in danger of becoming merely a dormitory town. By refurbishing existing structures, designing public spaces and constructing new buildings with a monumental capacity he has created focal points for the spatial organization of the village.

Another high-profile example of Ticino School architecture that deals with the central themes of identity, memory and monumentality in a groundbreaking way is the work of **Aurelio Galfetti** at Castelgrande in Bellinzona (1981–91). His restoration of this historic fortification was begun by pulling down the "non-original" interventions, including the surrounding vegetation, and inserting modern elements into the ancient fabric. The project created a new reference for the treatment of historical monuments and sensitive heritage sites across the country.

The most famous architect from the Ticino School at an international level is **Mario Botta**. His renown is now linked with large projects all over the world, most notably the San Francisco Museum of Modern Art (1989–95). But, although his buildings are ubiquitous in Switzerland, it's in his smaller works that he best reveals a sensitive and evocative relationship with the environment. This is best illustrated in the church of San Giovanni Battista at Mogno (1986–96) and the chapel of Santa Maria degli Angeli at Alpe Foppa on Monte Tamaro (1990– 97). The creation of the Centre Dürrenmatt, near Neuchâtel (1992–2000), with a subterranean intervention that doesn't compromise the integrity of the writer's old house, illustrates his ability to work in particularly delicate situations.

Swiss German architecture

Since the early 1990s, the attention of international critics has shifted from the Ticino School to the architecture of **German Switzerland**. A fresh genera- tion of architects have created a new language and an approach to architecture that is resulting in elegant, emblematic buildings across the world. Rather than concentrating on the concept of architecture as a symbolic act – so central to the theory of the Ticino School – they focus on architecture as a purely constructive act.

The most important practitioners are three studios that have become interna- tionally renowned in recent years. **Herzog & de Meuron** is perhaps the best known office, having worked across Europe and in the US as well as on numer- ous high-quality projects at home. The studio's architecture is characterized by a sophisticated intellectualization of architectural problems that are often solved through collaboration with contemporary artists. **Peter Zumthor** has entered the public consciousness in a very different way. A cabinet-maker by trade, his exquisite interventions in often rural and culturally sensitive communities have won him a reputation for an unparalleled level of craftsmanship and attention to detail. The younger duo of **Annette Gigon and Mike Guyer** have produced a clutch of buildings that embody the self-confident simplicity associated with contemporary Swiss architecture.

One of the main focuses of this Swiss-German school is the use of everyday materials, which were previously thought of as banal, or at least, not suitable for refined or noteworthy architecture. Herzog & de Meuron's Ricola Storage Building (1986–87) in Laufen, south of Basel, perfectly illustrates this attitude: panels of fibre-cement sheeting were chosen for the facade and stacked verti- cally to create a sophisticated, free interpretation of the piles of freshly sawn wooden boards lying outside the sawmills in the surrounding valley. To clad the facade of the extension to the Oskar Reinhart gallery "Am Römerholz" in Winterthur (1993–98), Gigon & Guyer used large panels of prefabricated concrete mixed with Jura limestone and copper powder to obtain a material that will gradually develop a green patina and slowly age in keeping with the rest of the buildings.

The central question is not just what material to use but how to use it in a way that is free of conventions and preconceptions. In **Therme Vals** (1990–96), Peter Zumthor employs traditional stone in an elegantly detailed manner to finish both the interior and exterior, creating a sublime building of closed spaces and sensual lighting, protected from the harsh surrounding landscape. The pivotal point in this case is the very Swiss attitude of an obsessive attention to detail and craftsmanship: architecture as the art of constructing well. Zumthor is also the author of the chapel of San Benedetg in Somvitg, near Disentis/ Mustér (1987–88), a replacement for a hillside church that had been destroyed by an avalanche. The texture of traditional wooden cladding contrasts with the abstract, sculptural shape of the deceptively simple geometrical building. The chapel is wrapped in strips of larch which weather and gradually change colour over time, altering the perception of the volume.

This concentration on shape in contemporary Swiss-German architecture has been defined as the creation of "**Forceful Forms**". The buildings are conceived as intense, geometric volumes with a simplicity that exalts their shape, material, texture and colour – an attitude towards design that is clearly heavily indebted to the artistic movements of Concrete Art, Abstractism and Minimalism. Gigon & Guyer's Museum Liner in Appenzell (1996–98) is a saw-tooth roofed volume clad uniformly with sandblasted sheets of stainless steel. The sophisticated result is both an everyday industrial-looking building and an enigmatic structure dominating this small village. One of the numerous projects commissioned by Swiss Federal Railways is Herzog & de Meuron's signal box on the edge of the train tracks at Basel SBB station (1989–94). A concrete box wrapped with copper bands to form a Faraday cage, this abstract object stands laconically detached among the unruly overhead cables, railway tracks and train sheds. It is not simply a building but a presence in the urban landscape.

Critics have described these designs as "**Swissbox architecture**", maligning the emphasis put on the envelope of the building and the lack of interest in the creation of internal space. There are undeniably numerous projects where the design focus is very firmly on the treatment of the facade, but, more often than not, this is a strength more than a detraction. In Herzog & de Meuron's Ricola production and storage building in Mulhouse (1992–93), just north of Basel in France, the design on the exterior transforms a conventional warehouse into a representative focus. In their university library in Eberswalde, Germany (1994–99), the unassuming bulk of an anonymous building is defined by the histori-cal and artistic photographs printed on the panels of the facade. In both these cases, by choosing to screen-print on such everyday materials as polycarbonate or prefabricated concrete panels, the architects have shifted attention from the conventional interior spaces and transformed relatively modest construction opportunities into truly emblematic buildings.

Crossing borders

The natural consequence of the international acclaim of the 1990s has been some exciting commissions abroad for Swiss architects. Herzog & de Meuron have been building across the globe: their numerous high-profile projects include the remodelling of Bankside power station in **London** into the Tate Modern gallery (1995–99), and the masterly Dominus Winery in the Napa Valley, **California** (1995–98). Peter Zumthor has taken his expressive poeticism across the Swiss frontier to the Kunsthalle in **Bregenz**, Austria (1989–97), and to a Diocesan Museum on a sensitive, historical site in **Cologne** (1997–2004).

Hand-in-hand with the rise in profile for Swiss architecture have been invita-tions to foreign architects to contribute to the built fabric of Swiss cities. In 1990 **Jean Nouvel** won the first architectural competition in Switzerland that was not restricted to Swiss residents. With its over-sized canopy, his striking KKL complex (1992–98), in a splendid location on the shore of Lake Luzern, creates a powerful new urban space. **Renzo Piano** followed up his serene Fondation Beyeler in Riehen, near Basel (1991–97), with an impressive project for the Paul Klee Centre in Bern (1999–2005) – the building's undulating roof has been conceived as a sculptural modification of the landscape. And to confirm the opinion that architecture has become an international showbiz affair, **Daniel Libeskind**'s popular fragmented gestures have been employed in the huge Westside leisure complex on the outskirts of Bern (2001–06).

by Lucy Ratcliffe

Alpine flora and fauna

F rom valley floor to mountain summit Switzerland enjoys a wide range of wildlife and botanical habitats. Thanks to the huge difference in altitude, climate and vegetation zones, there's nearly always something of interest to see, whether you're a dedicated naturalist, expert botanist or just a visitor with an interest in the overall mountain environment.

Fauna

In the distant past the Swiss Alps were inhabited by such creatures as the cave bear, cave lion and panther; not more than a few hundred years ago the most prolific animals found in the Alpine valleys included the lynx and wildcat, and the wolf. Periods of glaciation drove the first group from the mountains, while hunters reduced the numbers of the latter: the last wolf in Switzerland was thought to have been shot in 1947, but a handful of recent suspected sightings of wolves in the Valais are under investigation by naturalists. Hunting is still popular today, but is generally under strict controls. The **Parc Naziunal Svizzer** in the Lower Engadine (Swiss National Park) is a haven for numerous resident and migratory animals, and is perhaps the country's most rewarding location for the casual wildlife observer, since something like half of the seventy species of mammals found in Switzerland can be seen there.

Alpine fauna is noted for its extreme shyness, which is why observation can be difficult, but many animals that inhabit the more remote regions of the high Alps also descend to lower altitudes. The following survey, though by no means comprehensive, picks out the highlights.

Mammals

The **red deer** (*Cervus elaphus*) had disappeared from much of the country before the National Park was established in 1914, but natural migration from neighbouring regions of Austria saw a steady repopulation in the forested valleys of Graubünden. The adult male dominates a harem of several hinds, and vigorously defends them against all challengers. Fawns are born in May or June and are suckled for three or four months, remaining within easy reach of forest shelter. In summer the adult coat is reddish brown, turning grey-brown in winter. The much smaller **roe deer** (*Capreolus capreolus*) has similar colouring, is timid but also very inquisitive, and can be found roaming around the upper timber line. The best time to observe roe deer is in the early morning, or towards dusk when they stray from tree cover to open meadows and favoured drinking pools. The adult male sprouts slender horns, which are shed during the autumn, at the end of the rut.

The **red squirrel** (*Sciurus vulgaris*), like its American grey cousin in England, favours a woodland habitat and is fairly common throughout Switzerland. Despite the name its coat is dark brown, or almost black, and the female produces up to seven young, born naked and blind in a spherical drey. The **European lynx** (*Lynx lynx*) was reintroduced into the Swiss Alps in 1970. Weighing 20–30kg, it lives in the forests where it preys on birds and mammals up to the size of a roe deer, which it kills with a bite through the neck. Casual sightings are extremely rare. The **wildcat** (*Felis silvestris*) is another elusive forest animal. Larger than the domestic cat, it nevertheless has a purr not unlike that of an ordinary moggie, but a miaow that is deeper and more powerful. A few specimens were released into the wild near Interlaken, and others in the Jura, but it is still by no means common. The **Alpine hare** (*Lepus timidus*) has a wide distribution in northern Europe and is found in open country both below and above the tree line, to about 3000m. In winter its coat is white; in summer, brown with white patches. Thanks to the production of two, and sometimes three, litters a year, the hare manages to maintain its numbers against the ravages of a variety of carnivores.

Throughout the Alps the shrill, high-pitched alarm whistle of the **marmot** (*Marmota marmota* – or *Murmeltier* in German) will be heard from late spring until early autumn. One of the most widespread of all Alpine rodents, it is ever wary of such predators as the fox and eagle, for which it forms the chief food source. Living in burrows, mostly above the tree line, the marmot hibernates in a "nest" of dried grasses for as many as seven months a year in the upper regions around 3000m, or five to six months at lower altitudes. At the end of hibernation pairing occurs almost at once, and after a 33-day gestation period the young are born, naked and with eyes closed. The young do not emerge from their burrows much before the end of July, by which time they've grown a covering of fur, and are able to attack the coarse meadow grasses with their razor-like teeth. An adult grows to a length of 48–56cm, with a 16–20cm tail, and by September weighs around 4–6kg, although some males can weigh up to 9kg. They live to approximately ten years, although some have been known to reach twenty.

The **chamois** (*Rupicapra rupicapra* – or *Gemse* in German) is found not only in the Alpine regions, but also in the lower Jura mountains of the west and northwest of Switzerland. Although sought by hunters in the autumn, in select areas it has enjoyed protected status since the sixteenth century. The Engadine is thought to have one of Europe's largest populations of this handsome antelope-like ruminant with short hooked horns and a russet coat sometimes lightening to fawn-grey in summer. Noted for its agility, it is also prone to disease, especially the notorious chamois-blindness that occasionally devastates complete herds. The rut finishes in November and the young are born between mid-May and mid-June after a gestation of 160–180 days. A fully grown chamois reaches 1.10–1.30m in length and weighs up to 50kg (male) or 30–35kg (female). Longevity is about twenty years. They can be seen, either singly or in herds, throughout the Swiss Alps – but rarely at close quarters.

While the chamois has short but graceful horns, the stockier male **ibex** (*Capra ibex* – or *Steinbock* in German) has large, knobbly, scimitar-shaped horns which are used as weapons during the battles for dominance that accompany the autumn rut. Defeated males must then wait their turn for sexual maturity until they are able to defend a harem of their own. Although the chamois ranges high in the mountains, the ibex zone is even higher: some have been sighted at over 4000m. For the greater part of the year it lives above the tree line, often roaming to the high snows in summer, but occasionally descending to the forests in winter. Weighing up to 100kg, the ibex negotiates narrow rock ledges with confidence and precision despite its stocky body and comparatively short legs, and apparently displays great care when crossing slopes threatened by avalanche. A sizeable herd roams the upper slopes of Piz Albris near Pontresina in Val Bernina, another can be seen high above Val de Bagnes in the Valais, often grazing close to the Sentier de Chamois hiking trail.

Birds

woodlands of the Alpine foothills, and in the Jura, the bizarre call of the ~caillie (*Tetrao urogallus*) rattles in the early hours of a spring dawn: first ᵗhen another, followed by a quickening succession that precedes what can only be described as a cork being drawn from a bottle. The capercaillie is scarce enough in the Alps to create a thrill of excitement when heard or seen – its dark shape has easy camouflage in a beech, larch or pine wood where it can feed on assorted berries, buds and needles, but where it can also fall prey to such predators as the fox and marten, while the young are sometimes taken by a goshawk or golden eagle.

Game birds of the forest regions are notoriously difficult to observe except when accidentally flushed out of cover. The hazel hen (*Tetrastes bonasia*), black grouse (*Lyrurus tetrix*), ptarmigan (*Lagopus mutus*) and rock partridge (*Alectoris graeca*) are all found in the National Park, as is the long-billed woodcock (*Scolopax rusticola*), in marshy ground near the tree line. Other woodland birds found in Switzerland include a number of **owls**: the eagle owl, tawny, long-eared, pygmy, and small, golden-eyed tengmalm's owl (*Aegolius funereus*), which takes over the abandoned nests of woodpeckers. There are several species of **woodpecker** too, notably the green, great-spotted, black, and rare three-toed woodpecker (*Picoides tridactylus*), all of which are found at some time or other in the forests of the National Park.

There's no shortage of songbirds, most of which are widely distributed throughout Europe, but it is the mountain specialists that are notable in the high Alpine regions and whose presence adds an extra dimension to the climber's day: the **alpine accentor** (*Prunella collaris*), for example, whose nest has been discovered above 3000m and whose song resembles that of the lark, as does its mating flight. Another is the brightly coloured **rock thrush** (*Monticola saxitilis*) that returns to the Alps in mid-May after wintering in tropical Africa. Then there's the **alpine chough** (*Pyrrhocorax graculus*), whose aerial acrobatics, yellow beak and strident call are familiar to all who visit the hikers' huts in the high mountains, where this gregarious bird comes as a scavenger after leftover scraps of food.

The **golden eagle** (*Aquila chrysaetus*) builds its eyrie on inaccessible rock ledges high in the mountains, and with no shortage of sites to choose from, and no shortage of prey either, there's a fair chance of spotting one of these graceful predators sailing over the high pastures in search of food. The golden eagle has a broad appetite: although its basic diet in the summer consists of marmot, it will also strike grouse and mountain hare, and may even try to take the young of chamois and red deer. Since it makes short work of sick and weak animals, its contribution to the maintenance of strong, healthy species is significant.

Flora

The range of **plants** found in Switzerland is enormous, as one might expect in a country whose soil, habitat, climate and altitude varies from region to region and, in some cases, from one valley to the next. Igneous rocks may dominate in one district, with more plant-friendly limestone in another. Habitats vary from damp grassland to semi-arctic rockface, from desert-like scree to shady woodland, from glacial moraine to the marshy fringe of a mountain lake, from a sunny cliff or stretch of limestone pavement to an acid valley bog. Each has its own specific flora. Mountains create their own microclimate: one side may be damp, the other protected in a rain shadow. A south-facing hillside will be different from the opposite, north-facing slope, and on a mountainside the seasons change, not by the calendar, but by altitude. All these factors have an effect on the plant life, as do grazing and cultivation of the soil.

In the lower valleys **soldanellas**, **primulas**, **crocus**, **anemones** and others come into flower early in the year as the snow melts, and having bloomed they wither and all but disappear, with only their leaves remaining hidden beneath the new grass of the meadowlands. But as the season advances and the snow recedes, so the same flowers appear higher up the hillside. By mid-June or July, alongside many other plants, they colour the "alps" – the upper pastures – before cattle are brought up for summer grazing. Before the end of July most of the pasture flowers will have gone, but it is then that the screes, moraine walls and rockfaces display their own special Alpine flora.

Of the early pasture and meadowland flowers the **pasque flower** comes in several forms. *Pulsatilla vernalis*, or the spring pasque flower, has its white petals often flushed a pale violet on the outside, while the alpine pasque flower (*Pulsatilla alpina*) is protected from the cold by a coating of tiny hairs. The tiny **alpine snowbell** (*Soldanella alpina*) on the other hand has no apparent protection, even though it often pushes its way through the melting snowfields. Its tassled petals vary from violet to pink-blue depending on habitat, for it may be found on sites as diverse as shallow pockets of limestone, and damp pastures up to 3000m. The **lily** family is another pasture and meadowland favourite that comes in many forms, including asphodel, crocus, fritillary and scilla. The claret-headed martagon lily (*Lilium martagon*) appears in shady woodland glades of the Jura, while the extravagant, showy orange lily (*Lilium bulbiferum*) adorns grassy terraces above Urnerboden.

If the lily family has spawned a variety of species, the **gentian** is even more numerous, and in Switzerland is represented by such extremes as the tall, multi-flowered great yellow gentian (*Gentiana lutea*), whose starry flowers burst from an upright stem, to the tiny, delicate blue favourite, the spring gentian (*Gentiana verna*), and deep royal blue – almost navy – of the trumpet gentian (*Gentiana kochiana*), that sometimes appears to have practically no stem at all, but produces flowers almost as it emerges from the turf.

The low-growing, evergreen **alpenrose** shrub (*Rhododendron ferrugineum*) has a remarkably wide range throughout the Alps, flowering pink to deep red on hillsides up to 3200m between June and August, and where it forms a carpet the summer display can be extremely attractive. The **creeping azalea** (*Loiseleuria procumbens*) is a member of the same family and has similar colouring. But this plant prefers exposed peaty sites, and is often found on acid soils, growing at altitudes of 1500–3000m. Forming cushions over rocks and screes, the **moss campion** (*Silene acaulis*) is a mass of pink in a bed of deep green, an eye-catching beauty, while the rosettes of the **common houseleek** (*Sempervivum tectorum*) can decorate otherwise drab moraines when they produce their stalk of bright pink flower heads in summer.

And of course there's the **edelweiss** (*Leontopodium alpinum*), whose woolly grey flowers have for some reason become prized above all other mountain plants. Found usually, but not exclusively, on limestone, it may be seen clustered in short grass overlooking a glacier, or thrusting from a cliff face. Its distribution in Switzerland ranges from the Engadine to the Bernese and Pennine Alps, flourishing between 1700 and 3400m.

by Kev Reynolds

C

CONTEXTS | Alpine flora and fauna

Books

t's surprisingly hard to find books about Switzerland. Go to any large book-store, and you'll see plenty of shelves devoted to the history and politics of Germany, France, Italy and the rest of Europe, but you'll be lucky to find a single work on Switzerland. Literature is the same, with Swiss authors rarely reaching audiences in their native languages outside the borders of their own country, let alone getting translated into English for a wider market.

Pro Helvetia, the federally funded Arts Council of Switzerland, publishes a range of slim paperbacks giving erudite background to the country and its culture in English; subjects covered include music, theatre, literature, compos-ers, dance and ballet, media, cinema, architecture, philosophy, politics, social structure, refugees, multilingualism, and more. You can get any or all of them for free by contacting your nearest Swiss embassy, or order online at ⓦwww.pro-helvetia.ch.

Publishers are listed below in the form of UK publisher/US publisher, where both exist. "UP" stands for University Press, "o/p" signifies out of print. "Bergli" refers to **Bergli Books** (ⓦwww.bergli.ch), an English-language Swiss publisher which produces and distributes a range of books on Switzerland. Books tagged with the 🛪 symbol are particularly recommended.

Travel

Early travellers

When the first *Murray's Handbook* to Switzerland appeared in 1838, there had already been a couple of centuries or more of **travelogues** telling of adventures had while on long crossings of the Alps; throughout the nineteenth century, the trickle of memoirs became a flood. Most of these venerable tomes are now long out of print, and the list below is a small selection of more widely available works.

Peter Arengo-Jones *Queen Victoria in Switzerland* (Robert Hale). Absorb-ing transcript of Victoria's diaries from her incognito stay in Luzern in August 1868, along with a commen-tary weaving events into the context of historical and political events of the day.

Trevor Braham *When the Alps Cast Their Spell* (Neil Wilson). Subtitled "Mountaineers of the Alpine Golden Age", this is an award-winning account of the early days of Alpine conquest, with detailed chapters on the life and career of each of the major nineteenth-century players – Stephen, Whymper, Mummery and the rest. Fascinating and comprehensive.

Mavis Coulson *Southwards to Geneva* (Alan Sutton). Well-researched survey of two centuries of English travellers' musings on Geneva and the Swiss, including excerpts from the writings of Boswell, Maria Edgeworth, Byron, Shelley and more, along with plenty of pictures, engravings and sketches.

Elma Dangerfield *Byron & the Romantics in Switzerland 1816* (Thomas Lyster). Slim account of the travels, passions and writings of Byron, Shelley et al on their famous visit to Lake Geneva.

Alexandre Dumas *Travels in Switzerland* (Owen o/p). Entertaining tales of Dumas's journeyings around Switzerland in 1832, at the age of 25.

Heinrich Harrer *The White Spider* (Flamingo). Classic mountaineer's tale of the first ascent of the North Face of the Eiger in 1938 by a four-man team from Germany. Full of thrills, spills and vivid writing.

Jim Ring *How the English Made the Alps* (John Murray). Comprehensive and well-written account of English involvement in Alpine travel and exploration, from the eighteenth century to the phenomenal growth in winter sports in the mid-twentieth. The evocation of Victorian imperial ambition, set against the backdrop of the conquest of Alpine peaks and the rise in tourism, is outstanding.

Mark Twain *A Tramp Abroad* (Oxford UP) and *Climbing the Rigi* (Hürlimann). Wry, witty and hugely enjoyable tales of mountain climbing and exploration in the Alps when such a thing was the height of fashion.

Edward Whymper *Scrambles Amongst the Alps* (Dover). Modern reprint of the nineteenth-century mountaineer's original account of the conquest of the Matterhorn, amongst many other epic tales of adventure.

Modern travellers and expat life

Paul N. Bilton *The Perpetual Tourist: In Search of a Swiss Role* (Bergli). A diary of an Englishman living in Switzerland, documenting the author's various attempts to bridge the cultural divide. The author quote on the back says it all: "The British look for humour in everything; the Swiss are brought up not to expect it." His *Laughing Along With the Swiss* (Bergli) is in much the same vein.

Dianne Dicks (ed) *Ticking Along With the Swiss, Ticking Along Too* and *Ticking Along Free* (Bergli). Entertaining collections of

personal stories from travellers to Switzerland and various expats living and working there – light reading that offers a sidelong glance at the people and the culture.

Eugene V. Epstein *Once Upon an Alp* (Bergli). Wry vignettes of life in Switzerland through American/Swiss eyes, out of print since the 1960s and now republished.

Shirley Eu-Wong *Culture Shock! Switzerland* (Kuperard). Slim, chatty trawl through the idiosyncracies of Swiss society, written more for arriving expats than tourists, though with handy bits and pieces for all.

David Hampshire *Living and Working in Switzerland* (Survival). A complete rundown of rules and regulations for those planning to emigrate, either permanently or just for the winter ski-bum season, along with a raft of useful tips on how to avoid the worst of the bureaucracy.

Margaret Oertig-Davidson *Beyond Chocolate: Understanding Swiss Culture* (Bergli). Outstanding dissection of the country and its mentality – one of the most insightful books on Switzerland available in English. Ostensibly targeted at expats and long-term visitors, this is nonetheless invaluable for anyone wanting to get a handle on how the place works beneath the stereotypes and the touristic images.

Susan Tuttle *Inside Outlandish* (Bergli). Brief little book that playfully tries to bridge the expat gap, explaining the Swiss to outsiders and outsiders to the Swiss.

Vitali Vitaliev *Little is the Light* (Simon & Schuster). Subtitled "Nostalgic travels in the mini-states of Europe", this is a trail through Luxembourg, San Marino, the Isle of Man, and various other statelets by an award-winning Russian journalist – the chapter on Liechtenstein is an especially witty and engaging portrait of the country, and one of the few to take the place at least halfway seriously.

Guidebooks

Peter Habicht *Lifting the Mask* (Bergli). Unassuming little volume that dissects the Basel *Fasnacht* (carnival) in minute detail. Written by a local historian and Fasnachtler, it gives unprecedented insight into this odd event.

Marcia & Philip Lieberman *Switzerland's Mountain Inns* (Countryman, US). Lovingly folksy walking tour of many isolated *Berghäuser* tucked away in the remote Alps, along with plenty of tried and trusted advice for hikers looking to get away from it all. Their *Walking Switzerland The Swiss Way* (Mountaineers, US) is a quality guide to walks throughout the country, with full background, plus plenty of trail information and practical guidelines.

Kev Reynolds *Walking in the Alps*, *The Valais*, *The Bernese Alps*, *Central Switzerland*, *The Jura* (with R. Brian Evans), *The Engadine*, *Walking in Ticino*, *The Alpine Pass Route*, and *Chamonix to Zermatt: The Walker's Haute Route* (all Cicerone, UK; some Hunter, US, others Interlink, US). The classic Swiss walking guides,

vividly and knowledgeably written, containing detailed route descriptions and sketch-maps. *Walking in the Alps* is the largest, an amalgam of several long-distance routes with new trails; all the others are neat little volumes concentrating on particular areas or hikes.

Ian Robertson *Blue Guide: Switzerland* (A&C Black/Norton). Encyclopedic historical and architectural tour of the whole country, packed with detail on virtually every historical building and a wealth of sketched-out mountain walks and climbs.

Alexander Schwab *Lake Thun* (Bergli). Coffee-table tome (in English), packed with photos, evoking this most beautiful of Swiss lakes.

Peter Studer, et al *Berne: A Portrait of Switzerland's Federal Capital, of its people, culture and spirit* (Bergli). Another interesting, photo-laden coffee-table book, written by Bernese insiders.

Elisabeth Upton-Eichenberger *Vaud* and *Zermatt* (Upton-Eichenberger, UK). Excellent self-published guides to two of the country's most celebrated corners, full of tales, historical odds and ends, and other delightfully long-winded material that gets edited out of most orthodox guidebooks.

History and society

Joy Charnley & Malcolm Pender (eds) *Images of Switzerland: Challenges from the Margins* (Peter Lang, Bern). Slender collection of essays published by the Centre for Swiss Cultural Studies at Glasgow University, including a review of historical attitudes towards the Jews before World War II, and assessments of themes of marginalization in recent

Swiss-German, -French and -Italian literature.

Clive H. Church *The Politics and Government of Switzerland* (Palgrave Macmillan). A learned work, targeted at students of comparative European politics but fascinating for providing a digestible one-stop take on the make-up of the Swiss body politic.

Walter Dettwiler *William Tell: Portrait of a Legend* (Swiss National Museum). Fascinating little study of the web of tales surrounding the Swiss national hero, and the many different ways the story has been told over the centuries to suit the concerns of each particular age.

Dieter Fahrni *An Outline History of Switzerland* (Pro Helvetia). Compact 130-page overview of the main events in Swiss history from Julius Caesar to the Nazi gold scandal, a little gushing on recent events and accomplishments (this is, after all, published by the official Arts Council of Switzerland) but nonetheless valuable for its clarity and simplicity of approach. Available free from Swiss embassies worldwide.

Caroline Moorhead *Dunant's Dream* (HarperCollins). Subtitled "War, Switzerland and the History of the Red Cross", this is a massively detailed trawl through the previously closed archives of the Red Cross, documenting the history of the organization and the sometimes hesitant entanglements of its well-intentioned bureaucrats in the nastiest wars of the twentieth century.

Mitya New *Switzerland Unwrapped* (I.B. Tauris). Fascinating delve into the country's skeleton-rich cupboards, presenting eye-witness accounts of Swiss treatment of Jews and gypsies, attempts to solve Zürich's drug problems, traditional Swiss culture and how it fits into modern society, and more, well written by a Reuters journalist with an eye for a story.

Joachim Remak *A Very Civil War* (Westview Press). Illustrated chronicle of the Sonderbund war of 1847 that draws many parallels with the events of the American civil war that followed within fifteen years.

Jonathan Steinberg *Why Switzerland?* (Cambridge UP). Outstanding overview of Swiss society, history and culture, a learned yet anecdotal account of the country that is rich with detail but maintains a superb grasp of the wider picture. Manages to give profound insight into how Switzerland works, and why it is the way it is, while remaining easily readable and digestible. Perfect train-journey reading: if you buy only one book about the country, buy this one.

John Wraight *The Swiss and the British* (Michael Russell o/p). Comprehensive study of relations between the two countries – political, cultural, sporting, military and more – in the form of an exhaustive chronology from the earliest times until the present day. Currently out of print, but scheduled for a new edition.

Jean Ziegler *The Swiss, The Gold and the Dead* (Harcourt Trade/Penguin). Of all the flood of books that jumped onto the bandwagon of the Nazi gold scandal once the depth of Swiss collaboration became clear, this was the most hard-hitting, written by a highly qualified academic at the University of Geneva and former parliamentarian – hounded and now politically ostracized for remaining uncowed by the storm of protest his revelations unleashed. His calm condemnation of the entire Swiss establishment for their role in funding the Nazis, prolonging the war and refusing to help the Jews is devastating.

Literature

Switzerland in foreign fiction

This is necessarily a tiny bite at a very large apple, a handful of personal selections that omits much more than it includes.

Anita Brookner *Hotel du Lac* (Penguin). A romantic novelist runs away from her impending marriage to spend a season at a grand hotel in a genteel lakeside resort (Vevey in all but name), and there finds what seems to be the start of a new life of freedom. Beautifully crafted prose, the best of Brookner's usually rather dry offerings, and winner of the 1984 Booker Prize.

Graham Greene *Dr Fischer of Geneva* (Penguin). Apocalyptic novella set in and around the lakeside residence of a rich misanthrope who decides to take his revenge on the fawning socialites who crave his money. A fluent and compelling read, published when Greene was 76.

Patricia Highsmith *Small g: a Summer Idyll* (Penguin). Highsmith – who spent her last years living in a Ticinese village – is best known for *Strangers on a Train* (made into a film by Alfred Hitchcock in 1951), along with her many works of crime fiction centred on Tom Ripley. *Small g* is focused on the characters who frequent a Zürich bar during one summer, with a story of love, sexuality and generosity expertly plotted around them. She died a month before its publication in 1995.

Henry James *Daisy Miller* (Penguin). The novella that made James's name, a witty, insightful portrait of a young American tourist visiting Lake Geneva who flirts and teases, and then travels to the Château de Chillon unchaperoned and so gets her comeuppance.

Thomas Mann *The Magic Mountain* (Minerva/Random House). Seminal World War I novel of ideas that employs a group of patients in a Davos sanatorium to discuss ideas of love, war and death, the characters' ongoing tuberculosis symbolizing the sickness of European society as a whole. Although this novel is acclaimed as the author's greatest, it was received less than favourably in Davos itself, whose residents objected to the town's portrayal as a place of neglect where sufferers stood little chance of being cured. This and Mann's other books were later burned by the Nazis in his native Germany.

Mary Shelley *Frankenstein* (Penguin). The famous tale of an idealistic doctor's dabblings with the elemental forces of life, inspired by "a half-waking nightmare" and written near Geneva in the summer of 1816 as Mary Shelley's offering in a ghost-story-writing competition dreamt up by Lord Byron.

Swiss authors

This is a choice of the handful of **Swiss authors**, classic and modern, whose works have been translated into English. Almost all are German Swiss. The couple of 1930s novels by the Lausannois writer Charles-Ferdinand Ramuz that have been translated into English – *Terror on the Mountain* and *When the Mountain Fell*, virtually the only works by any French Swiss authors to be published in English – are now out of print. The array of writings by the great Ticinese poet and novelist Francesco Chiesa, who died in 1973 at the age of 102, have yet to find an English translator, as do any by Romansh writers (bar a single out-of-print anthology).

Reto R. Bezzola *The Curly-Horned Cow: Anthology of Swiss-Romansh Literature* (o/p). The sole translation into English of any Romansh writing, now out of print.

Michael Butler & Malcolm Pender (eds) *Rejection and Emancipation* (Berg). Study of writing in German-speaking Switzerland between 1945 and 1991, with lit-crit essays on Frisch and Dürrenmatt, as well as Meyer, Loetscher, Schriber and others.

Max Frisch *Man in the Holocene* (Harcourt Brace). The most striking of the six novels by Frisch, who was born in Zürich in 1911 and is acclaimed as one of the century's greatest writers. This is a haunting but moving meditation on mortality, illuminating the slow decay of an old man's thought processes as he approaches death. Frisch's other novels are *Bluebeard*, *Gantenbein*, *Homo Faber*, his acclaimed masterpiece *I'm Not Stiller*, and *Montauk*.

Jeremias Gotthelf *The Black Spider* (Knightscross). Stories, tales and morality pieces from the nineteenth-century Emmental, as told by Gotthelf, a cleric turned author.

Hermann Hesse *Steppenwolf* (Penguin). Hesse's best-known work, profound social deconstruction wrapped up as fantasy, which weaves strands of Eastern religion and mysticism into the compelling tale of a middle-aged misanthrope's progress towards social and spiritual maturity, "violently misunderstood" according to Hesse. Of his dozens of other works, *Siddhartha* is a graceful retelling of the legend of the Buddha; *Narziss and Goldmund* is a picaresque portrait of two monks, one a scholar, the other a bohemian; and *The Glass Bead Game* is a monumental utopian novel, set in a future where an elite group develops a game that resolves the world's conflicts.

Zoë Jenny *The Pollen Room* (Bloomsbury). An understated, mesmeric novel, translated from the German, poetically chronicling a marriage breakup through the eyes of a child. This is the first novel by Jenny, who was born in Basel in 1974.

Gottfried Keller *Green Henry* (John Calder). Massive tome of a novel, and a highly celebrated *Bildungsroman*, charting the Zürich-born author's country, youth and philosophy, written between 1846 and 1855 to a backdrop of unrequited love in Berlin.

Liselotte Marshall *Tongue-Tied* (Birds of Passage). Tender novel of reconciliation, set in Péniel, a fictional Swiss Alpine town once known for its sanatoriums that is now a tourist haven, and centred on Rachel, an interpreter, who is forced to confront her painful wartime past.

Johanna Spyri *Heidi* (Penguin). Perhaps the most famous book ever written about Switzerland, but a hopelessly moralistic, cloying tale for all that. Spyri expertly evokes the folksiness and stolid culture of the Swiss Alpine farmers and effortlessly pulls heartstrings for her cheese-munching, milk-quaffing heroine.

Beat Sterchi *The Cow* (Faber, UK). Translated epic first novel set in a dairy farm and an abattoir, focusing on the experiences of a Spanish guest worker in Switzerland – Heaney-esque in its superb evocation of rural life. Not easy to read, but ultimately highly rewarding, praised by the *Guardian* for its "uncompromising magnificence as a work of art".

Robert Walser *Masquerade and other stories* (Quartet). Improvised prose poems and poetic short stories from Walser's life in four cities (Zürich, Berlin, Biel and Bern) over the period 1899–1933, tracing influences on Kafka and other avant-garde modernists. *The Walk* (Serpents Tail) is the best collection of his short fiction. The novel *Jakob von Gunten* (published in UK as *Institute Benjamenta*, Serpents Tail; and New York Review Books Classics), the dream-like tale of a young man at a school for butlers, was filmed by Britain's Channel 4. After 1933, Walser spent his last 22 years in an asylum near Appenzell. "I wrote nothing more," he said. "What for? My world had been obliterated by the Nazis." It later transpired that he wrote a great deal, but what survives is in a tiny, almost indecipherable script: his strange, shifting novel *The Robber* (Nebraska UP) was published only recently, since it took decades for anyone to realize that the few pages of microscopic scribble comprised a complete novel. Hermann Hesse said of Walser: "If he had 100,000 readers, the world would be a better place."

Food and drink

Marianne Kaltenbach *Cooking in Switzerland* (Wolfgang Hölker, Münster, Germany). Friendly trot through some traditional Swiss recipes, heavy on the meat and cream.

John C. Sloan *The Surprising Wines of Switzerland* (Bergli). Best book by far on the variety of Swiss wines and viticulture, exploring each area – and virtually each vineyard – with enthusiasm and expertise.

Sue Style *A Taste of Switzerland* (Bergli). Finest of the handful of cookery books devoted to Switzerland, with informed cultural background to local festivals and food celebrations dotted in amongst the recipes.

Architecture

Christoph Allenspach *Architecture in Switzerland: Building in the 19th and 20th centuries* (Pro Helvetia). Dry but authoritative volume published by the Swiss Arts Council (available for free from Swiss embassies).

Mercedes Daguerre *Birkhäuser Architectural Guide: Switzerland 20th century* (Birkhäuser). Pocket guide with exhaustive coverage of twentieth-century Swiss architecture.

Jacques Lucan & Bruno Marchand (eds) *A Matter of Art: Contemporary Architecture in Switzerland* (Birkhäuser). Attractive book offering detailed insight into Swiss architecture in the last ten years through a selection of emblematic buildings and analysis by experts.

Language

Language

Swiss languages

For a relatively small country bang in the heart of Western Europe, Switzerland has an astonishingly complicated array of languages to have to come to terms with. The one crumb of comfort is that almost everyone you'll come across will speak at least a smattering of English, and some Swiss are disconcertingly multilingual: fluency in four or five languages isn't as rare as you might assume.

There are four national languages in Switzerland. Broadly, **German** is spoken in the centre and the east; **French** in the west; **Italian** in the south; and **Romansh** in a few small areas of the southeast. The dividing lines between them (see map) mostly stem from the movements of tribal peoples in medieval times, and generally have nothing to do with the cantonal boundaries, which were drawn up much later. Cantons Bern, Fribourg and Valais are all bilingual German/French, while Graubünden is trilingual German/Italian/Romansh. According to census figures, 63.7 percent of the Swiss population consider German their main language, 20.4 percent French, 6.5 percent Italian and 0.5 percent Romansh (the rest are "others", principally English-speaking expats and international officials). However, more than one in ten of the Swiss population use English regularly every day alongside their own mother tongue.

All the spoken languages of Switzerland have differences from the orthodox standard versions used elsewhere that you may already have a grasp of. The German spoken in Switzerland, for instance, is completely different from that spoken in Germany or Austria, and has its own unique vocabulary, grammar

L

LANGUAGE

and syntax. Its umbrella title "Swiss German" covers a multitude of regional **dialects** with marked differences both from each other and from standard German: the dialect of Basel is different from that of Zürich, which is different again from that spoken in the high valleys of Oberwallis. In addition, both the French and Italian of Switzerland have small but noticeable differences from the "pure" languages spoken over the borders. Romansh (see p.504) has detectably the same Latin roots as French and Italian, but is different from both of them.

Rough Guides' own *French, Italian* and *German* **phrasebooks** are handy (though you'll earn extra respect for attempting Swiss-German where possible), with dictionary-style listings as well as menu readers and grammar sections.

For **Swiss German**, *Hoi: Your Swiss German Survival Guide*, by Sergio J. Lievano and Nicole Egger, published by Bergli Books (Ⓦwww.bergli.ch), is the only work of its kind in English, with grammar and vocabulary explained in a light, accessible way, along with a dictionary section. The only **Romansh**-English/English-Romansh dictionary and phrasebook, by Manfred Gross & Daniel Telli, is published by Hippocrene (New York). Ⓦwww.mypledari.ch is a comprehensive online Romansh translation tool.

In 1998, Dynamicha, the movement for a multicultural Switzerland, published an invaluable comparative phrasebook of **all four Swiss languages** entitled *Schweizer Sprachen, Langues suisses, Lingue svizzere, Linguas svizras* (ISBN 3952132314), now regrettably out of print but worth searching out. There's not a word of English in it, so you'll need to be already grounded in at least one of the four in order to make sense of the rest.

German

Two forms of German are used in Switzerland. **High German** or *Hochdeutsch* (also known as *Schriftdeutsch*, "Written German") is the same language used throughout German-speaking Europe. **Swiss German**, or *Schwyzertütsch*, comprises dozens of regional dialects unique to Switzerland, and is unrecognizable to speakers of High German.

No one speaks High German in everyday situations in Switzerland: oral use of High German is restricted to school education, the mass media and public speaking. In all other situations, everyone naturally uses their own local dialect of Swiss German. And unlike in Britain or France, no one in German-speaking Switzerland strives to copy a Zürich accent or a Basel accent in order to gain greater credibility. Using the dialect of your home town is a source of pride.

However, Swiss German is hardly ever written. It's only relatively recently that a dictionary laying down agreed spellings has been compiled, and it's still open to some controversy: ask a Swiss person to write something in Swiss German and they'll probably struggle over the spelling. Everybody writes in High German (which is also the language of all signs and public notices) – but when reading out loud, they mentally transcribe the High German text into their own dialect of Swiss German as they're going along. People see the written word *Dienstag* (Tuesday), and say *tseeschtig*; or *Abend* (evening), and say *obik*. Many High German words simply aren't used: *guten Tag* (hello) is *grüezi* in Swiss German; *Straßenbahn* (tram) is *Tram*; *Fahrrad* (bicycle) is *Velo*; while regional differences mean that *Wiese* (meadow) is *Wise* in St Gallen but *Matte* in Bern. Add in a range of idiosyncratic regional **accents** that are much greater than the accent difference between, say, Munich and Hamburg; a tendency to stick the coy **diminutive** *-li* onto the end of nouns, and to use the throat-rasping **ch** (as in the Scottish *loch*) wherever possible; and a **stress pattern** that

Italian

In **Italian**-speaking Switzerland, written or High Italian is used less than the **Lombardic** dialect common to most of northern Italy. There are also about seven local **Ticinese** dialects, different again from each other and from Lombardic. Almost all Ticinesi are effectively **quadrilingual**: to friends and family, the language of intimacy is the home dialect; on the street, the language of friendly conversation is Lombardic; to strangers and where there's any element of reserve, the language of formality is High Italian; and, in addition, most Ticinesi are also proficient in German and/or Swiss German in order to communicate with the vast numbers of tourists from the north. English, although spoken by some, remains well down the list.

The upshot of this is that, even if you happened to be fluent in Lombardic dialect, everyone you met in Ticino would anyway instinctively speak to you – a stranger and a foreigner – in standard Italian, which is not excessively hard for English-speakers to master.

Italian pronunciation

Pronunciation is easy, since every word is spoken exactly as it is written and usually enunciated with exaggerated, open-mouthed clarity. The only slight difficulties come in the following **consonants**, which differ from English:

c before e or i is an English *ch*: "cioccolata" is *chokolata*

ch is an English *k*: "chiesa" is *kee-ay-za*

g before e or i is an English *j* – "Maggiore" is *madge-or-eh*, "giorno" is *jorno*

g before h as in gun

gli as in million: "figlia" is *feelya*

gn as in onion: "bagno" is *banyo*

h is silent

sci as in ship

sce as in shed

z as in bats

Words and phrases

The basics

	Swiss German	French	Italian
good morning	guete Morge	bonjour	buongiorno
good evening	guete Obig	bonsoir	buona sera
hello/hi!	grüezi! (grüssech in Bern; grüess Gott in the east)	salut!	salve!/ciao!
cheers! (toast)	proscht!	santé!	salute!
enjoy your meal	enguete	bon appétit	buon appetito
goodbye	of Widerluege	au revoir	arrivederci
bye!	tschüss!/ciao!	salut!	ciao!
yes	jo	oui	si
no	nei	non	no
OK	OK	ça marche	va bene
please	bitte	s'il vous plaît	per favore
thank you (very much)	merci/dunkcha (vielmol)	merci (beaucoup)	(molte) grazie
you're welcome	bitte	je vous en prie	prego

	Swiss German	French	Italian
excuse me	entscholdigong	excusez-moi	mi scusi
I'm sorry	es tued mer leid	je suis désolé	mi dispiace
do you speak English?	reded Sii Änglisch?	parlez-vous anglais?	parla inglese?
I come from...	ich be vo...	je viens de...	vengo da...
Britain	Grossbritannie	Grande-Bretagne	Gran Bretagna
Ireland	Irland	Irlande	Irlanda
the US/Canada	d'Schtaate/Kanada	États-Unis/Canada	Stati Uniti/Canada
Australia	Auschtralie	Australie	Australia
New Zealand	Neuseeland	Nouvelle Zélande	Nuova Zelanda
I (don't) speak...	ich rede (ned)...	je (ne) parle (pas)...	io (non) parlo...
High German	Hochdütsch	allemand	tedesco
Swiss German	Schwyzertütsch	suisse allemand	svizzero-tedesco
French	Französisch	français	francese
Italian	Italiänisch	italienne	italiana
I (don't) understand	ich verschtoh (ned)	je (ne) comprends (pas)	(non) capisco

Directions and travel

	Swiss German	French	Italian
here/there	hier/dött	ici/là(-bas)	qui/li
left/right	links/rächts	gauche/droite	sinistra/destra
straight on	graduus	tout droit	sempre diritto
near/far	noch/wiit	près/loin	vicino/lontano
quick/slow	schnell/langsam	rapide/lent	rapido/lento
broad/narrow	breit/schmal	large/étroit	largo/stretto
train	Zug	train	treno
station	Bahnhof	gare	stazione
information	Auskunft	renseignements	informazioni
ticket office	Schalter	guichet	sportello
ticket	Billet	billet	biglietto
day card	Tageskarte	carte journalière	carta giornaliera
departure	Abfahrt	départ	partenza
arrival	Ankunft	arrivée	arrivo
which platform for the train to Zürich?	uf welem Gleis fahrt de Zog noch Züri?	sur quel quai part le train pour Zurich?	da quale binario parte il treno per Zurigo?
when does the train arrive in Geneva?	wenn chond de Zog z'Genf aa?	à quelle heure le train arrive-t-il à Genève?	quando arriva il treno a Ginevra?
change at Olten	umsteigen in Olten	changer à Olten	cambiare a Olten
lost-property office	Fundbüro	objets trouvés	oggetti smarriti
toilets	Toiletten/WC (spoken: vaytsay)	toilettes	gabinetti
women's toilet	Frauen/Damen	dames	signore
men's toilet	Männer/Herren	hommes	signori
postbus	Postauto	car postal	autopostale

English	Swiss German	French	Italian
bus stop	Haltestelle	arrêt	fermata
when does the bus to Chur leave?	wenn fahrt de Bus noch Chur?	à quelle heure part le bus pour Coire?	quando parte il autobus per Coira?
supplement	Zuschlag	supplément	sovratassa
tourist bus/coach	Car	autocar	pullman
(rental) car	(Miet)Auto	voiture (de location)	automobile (a noleggio)
parking area	Parkplatz	place de parc	parcheggio
covered car park	Parkhaus	parking	autosilo
available/full	frei/besetzt	libre/occupé	libero/occupato
(steam-)boat	(Dampf)Schiff	bateau (à vapeur)	battello (a vapore)
breakdown	Panne	panne	panna
boat travel	Schifffahrt	navigation	navigazione
(rental) bike	(Miet)Velo	vélo (de location)	bicicletta (a noleggio)
mountain bike	Mountainbike	vélo tout terrain (VTT)	rampichino
airport	Flughafen	aéroport	aeroporto
police	Polizei	police	polizia
fire service	Feuerwehr	pompiers	pompieri
ambulance	Ambulance	ambulance	ambulanza

Hotels and shops

English	Swiss German	French	Italian
entrance/exit	Eingang/Ausgang	entrée/sortie	entrata/uscita
emergency exit	Notausgang	sortie de secours	uscita di sicurezza
push/pull	drücken/ziehen	poussez/tirez	spingere/tirare
reception	Empfang	réception	ricezione
do you have any rooms available?	händ Sii noh freii Zimmer?	avez-vous des chambres libres?	ha camere libere?
I reserved a room	ich ha es Zimmer reserviert	j'ai réservé une chambre	ho riservato una camera
have you got...?	händ Sii...?	avez-vous...?	avete...?
I'd like...	ich hätt gärn...	j'aimerais...	vorrei...
a single room	Einzelzimmer	chambre simple	camera singola
a double room	Doppelzimmer	chambre double	camera doppia
with a shower	mit Dusche	avec douche	con doccia
with a bath	mit Bad	avec bain	con bagno
with a balcony	mit Balkon	avec balcon	con balcone
with a mountain/ lake view	mit Blick uf d'Berge/ uf de See	avec vue sur les montagnes/sur le lac	con vista sulle montagne/sul lago
without	ohne/oni	sans	senza
how much is the room?	was choschtet s'Zimmer?	combien coûte la chambre?	quanto costa la camera?
with breakfast	mit Frühstück	avec petit-déjeuner	con prima colazione
with half board	mit Halbpension	en demi-pension	mezza pensione
dormitory	Massenlager	dortoir	dormitorio
campsite	Campingplatz	camping	campeggio
fully booked	voll/besetzt	complet	completo

Place names in Switzerland

German	French	Italian
Aare	Aar	Aar
Aargau	Argovie	Argovia
Basel-Land	Bâle-Campagne	Basilea campagna
Basel-Stadt	Bâle-Ville	Basilea città
Bergell	Bregaglia	Bregaglia
Bern	Berne	Berna
Biel	Bienne	Bienne
Bodensee	Lac de Constance	Lago di Constanza
Brig	Brigue	Briga
Chur	Coire	Coira
Delsberg	Delémont	Delémont
Freiburg	Fribourg	Friborgo
Genf	Genève	Ginevra
Genfersee	Lac Léman	Lago Lemano
Glarus	Glaris	Glarona
Gotthard	Gothard	Gottardo
Graubünden	Grisons	Grigioni
Greyerz	Gruyères	Gruyères
Jura	Jura	Giura
Konstanz	Constance	Constanza
Lausanne	Lausanne	Losanna
Lukmanier	Lukmanier	Lucomagno
Luzern	Lucerne	Lucerna
Mailand	Milan	Milano
Matterhorn	Cervin	Cervino
Murten	Morat	Morat
Neuenburg	Neuchâtel	Neuchâtel
Nidwalden	Nidwald	Nidvaldo
Nufenen	Nufenen	Novena
Obwalden	Obwald	Obvaldo
Ofen	Ofen	Fuorn
Österreich	Autriche	Austria
Pruntrut	Porrentruy	Porrentruy
Puschlav	Poschiavo	Poschiavo
Rhein	Rhin	Reno
Rotten	Rhône	Rodano
Sankt Gallen	St-Gall	San Gallo
Schaffhausen	Schaffhouse	Sciaffusa
Schweiz	Suisse	Svizzera
Schwyz	Schwytz	Svitto
Siders	Sierre	Sierre
Simplon	Simplon	Sempione
Sitten	Sion	Sion
Solothurn	Soleure	Soletta
Tessin	Tessin	Ticino
Thurgau	Thurgovie	Turgovia
Visp	Viège	Visp
Waadt	Vaud	Vaud
Wallis	Valais	Vallese
Zug	Zoug	Zugo
Zürich	Zurich	Zurigo

big/small	gross/chli	grand/petit	grande/piccolo
new/old	neu/alt	nouveau/vieux	nuovo/vecchio
hot/cold	warm/chalt	chaud/froid	caldo/freddo
clean/dirty	suber/dräckig	propre/sale	pulito/sporco
quiet/noisy	ruhig/lärmig	silencieux/bruyant	silenzioso/rumoroso
open/closed	offen/geschlossen	ouvert/fermé	aperto/chiuso
opening hours	Öffnungszeiten	heures d'ouverture	orari d'apertura
day off	Ruhetag	jour de repos	giorno di riposo
VAT (sales tax)	MWST	TVA	IVA

Numbers

	Swiss German	French	Italian
0	null	zéro	zero
half	halb	demi	mezzo
1	eis	un	uno
2	zwöi	deux	due
3	drü	trois	tre
4	vier	quatre	quattro
5	füüf	cinq	cinque
6	sächs	six	sei
7	sibe	sept	sette
8	acht	huit	otto
9	nüün	neuf	nove
10	zää	dix	dieci
11	elf	onze	undici
12	zwölf	douze	dodici
13	drizää	treize	tredici
14	vierzää	quatorze	quattordici
15	föfzää	quinze	quindici
16	sächzää	seize	sedici
17	sibezää	dix-sept	diciasette
18	achzää	dix-huit	diciotto
19	nüünzää	dix-neuf	diciannove
20	zwänzg	vingt	venti
21	einezwänzg	vingt et un	ventuno
22	zwöiezwänzg	vingt-deux	ventidue
30	driisg	trente	trenta
40	vierzg	quarante	quaranta
50	föfzg	cinquante	cinquanta
60	sächzg	soixante	sessanta
70	sibezg	septante	settanta
80	achzg	huitante	ottanta
90	nüünzg	nonante	novanta
100	hondert	cent	cento
101	honderteis	cent un	centouno

L

LANGUAGE — Words and phrases

200	zwöihondert	deux cents	duecento
1000	tuusig	mille	mille
2000	zwöituusig	deux mille	duemila
1st	erscht (1.)	premier (1er)	primo (1º)
2nd	zwöit (2.)	deuxième (2e)	secondo (2º)
3rd	dret (3.)	troisième (3e)	terzo (3º)
4th	viert (4.)	quatrième (4e)	quarto (4º)
5th	füüft (5.)	cinquième (5e)	quinto (5º)
once	einisch	une fois	una volta
twice	zwöimol	deux fois	due volte
three times	drümol	trois fois	tre volte

Telling the time

	Swiss German	French	Italian
what time is it?	was isch för Ziit?	quelle heure est-il?	che ora sono?
it's nine o'clock	es isch nüüni	il est neuf heures	sono le nove
1.05	füüf ab eis	une heure cinq	l'una e cinque
2.15	Viertel ab zwöi	deux heures et quart	le due e un quarto
5.45	Viertel vor sächsi	six heures moins quart	le sei meno un quarto
9.40	zwänzg vor zääni	dix heures moins vingt	le dieci meno venti
10.30	halbi elfi (ie half to 11)	dix heures et demie	le dieci e mezza
noon	Mettag	midi	mezzogiorno
midnight	Metternacht	minuit	mezzanotte
an hour	e Schtond	une heure	un'ora
half-an-hour	e Halbschtond	une demi-heure	mezz'ora

Days and months

Beware that abbreviations of the days (for opening hours posted outside museums or shops) can be confusing: "Di" in French-speaking areas means Sunday, but in German-speaking areas means Tuesday. Similarly, "Do" is Thursday in German, but Sunday in Italian.

	Swiss German	French	Italian
Monday	Määntig (Mo)	lundi (lu)	lunedi (lu)
Tuesday	Ziischtig (Di)	mardi (ma)	martedi (ma)
Wednesday	Mettwoch (Mi)	mercredi (me)	mercoledi (me)
Thursday	Donnschtig (Do)	jeudi (je)	giovedi (gi)
Friday	Friitig (Fr)	vendredi (ve)	venerdi (ve)
Saturday	Samschtig (Sa)	samedi (sa)	sabato (sa)
Sunday	Sonntig (So)	dimanche (di)	domenica (do)
day	Tag	jour	giorno
in the morning	am Morge	le matin	la mattina
in the afternoon	am Nomitag	l'après-midi	di pomeriggio
in the evening	am Obig	le soir	di sera
at night	i de Nacht	la nuit	di notte

yesterday	geschter	hier	ieri
today	höt	aujourd'hui	oggi
tomorrow	morn	demain	domani
week	Woche	semaine	settimana
month	Monet	mois	mese
year	Johr	année	anno
spring	Früelig	printemps	primavera
summer	Sommer	été	estate
autumn	Herbscht	automne	autunno
winter	Wenter	hiver	inverno
January	Januar	janvier	gennaio
February	Februar	février	febbraio
March	März	mars	marzo
April	Aprel	avril	aprile
May	Mai	mai	maggio
June	Juni	juin	giugno
July	Juli	juillet	luglio
August	Auguscht	août	agosto
September	September	septembre	settembre
October	Oktober	octobre	ottobre
November	Novämber	novembre	novembre
December	Dezämber	décembre	dicembre

Swiss menu reader

Food and drink basics

	Swiss German	French	Italian
knife	Messer	couteau	coltello
fork	Gabel	fourchette	forchetta
spoon	Löffel	cuillère	cucchiaio
plate	Teller	assiette	piatto
napkin	Serviette	serviette	tovagliolo
bottle	Flasche	bouteille	bottiglia
glass	Glas	verre	bicchiere
cup	Tasse	tasse	tazza
menu	Speisekarte	carte	carta
bread	Brot	pain	pane
butter	Butter, Anke	beurre	burro
ham	Schinken	jambon	prosciutto
bacon	Speck	lardon	pancetta
cheese	Käse	fromage	formaggio
milk	Milch	lait	latte

whole milk	Vollmilch	lait entier	latte intero
skimmed milk	Magermilch	lait écrémé	latte scremato
buttermilk	Buttermilch	babeurre	latticello
yoghurt	Joghurt	yogourt	joghurt
cream	Rahm	crème	panna
egg	Ei	oeuf	uovo
jam	Konfitüre	confiture	marmellata
honey	Honig	miel	miele
tap water	Hahnenwasser	eau de robinet	acqua di rubinetto
mineral water	Mineralwasser	eau minérale	acqua minerale
juice	Saft	jus	succo
ice	Eis	glace	ghiaccio
a beer	e'Schtange	une pression	una birra
red wine	Rotwein	vin rouge	vino rosso
white wine	Weisswein	vin blanc	vino blanco
dry	trocken	sec	secco
sweet	süss	doux	dolce
sugar	Zucker	sucre	zucchero
salt	Salz	sel	sale
pepper	Pfeffer	poivre	pepe
oil	Öl	huile	olio
mustard	Senf	moutarde	senape
"waiter!"	"Bedienung!"	"Monsieur/Madame!"	"Cameriere/-a!"
"I'd like…"	"Ich nehme…"	"Je voudrais…"	"Vorrei…"
with	mit	avec	con
without	ohne	sans	senza
to eat	essen	manger	mangiare
to drink	trinken	boire	bere
non-smoking area	Nichtraucherzone	espace non-fumeurs	sezione non fumatori
breakfast	Frühstück, Zmorge	petit déjeuner	prima colazione
lunch	Mittagessen, Zmittag	déjeuner	pranzo
dinner/supper	Abendessen, Znacht	dîner	cena
the bill	die Rechnung	l'addition	il conto

I am a vegetarian (m/f) Ich bin Vegetarier/-in Je suis végétarien/-ne Sono vegetariano/-a	Have you got any special dishes for vegetarians? Haben Sie spezielle Menus für Vegetarier? Avez-vous des menus spéciaux pour les végétariens? Avete menù speciali per vegetariani?

Snacks and starters

	Swiss German	French	Italian
starters	Vorspeisen	hors d'oeuvres	antipasti
sandwich	Sandwich	sandwich	panino
chips (french fries)	Pommes frites	frites	patate fritte
crisps (potato chips)	Pommes Chips	pommes chips	patatine
omelette	Omelett	omelette	frittata
olives	Oliven	olives	olive
soup	Suppe	potage, consommé	zuppa, minestra
prawn cocktail	Krevetten Cocktail	cocktail des crevettes	cocktail di gamberi
green salad	Grüner Salat	salade verte	insalata verde
mixed salad	Gemischte Salat	salade mixte	insalata mista

Main courses

	Swiss German	French	Italian
main courses	Speisen	plats principaux	secondi piatti
meat	Fleisch	viande	carne
veal	Kalb	veau	vitello
beef	Rind	boeuf	manzo
pork	Schwein	porc	maiale
lamb	Lamm	agneau	agnello
chicken	Poulet	poulet	pollo
horse	Pferde	cheval	cavallo
fillet	Filet	filet	filetto
a chop	Kotelett	côtelette	cotoletta
diced meat	Geschnetzelte	émincé	spezzatino
mincemeat	Hackfleisch	hachée	carne macinata
liver	Leber	foie	fegato
kidney	Niere	rognon	rognone
sausage	Wurst	saucisse	salsiccia
rice	Reis	riz	riso
boiled potatoes	Salzkartoffeln	pommes nature	patate bollite
pasta	Teigwaren	pâtes	pasta
noodles	Nudeln	nouilles	tagliatelle
mushrooms	Pilze	champignons	funghi
fish	Fisch	poisson	pesce
salmon	Lachs	saumon	salmone
trout	Forelle	truite	trota
tuna	Thunfisch	thon	tonno

Basic Romansh

There's a survey of the various dialects of Romansh on p.504. Some similarities exist with Italian as regards pronunciation, but there are a few significant differences:

c before e or i is pronounced as in ba**ts**
ch before a or o is a palatal sneeze-like *tya* sound lost in the middle of sta**tu**te, almost an English *ch* but not quite; if there's a preceding *s*, Romansh separates the two with a hyphen – the Engadine town of Chamues-ch is pronounced something like *tyamwesh-tyuh*

ch before e or i is pronounced as in **c**at

g before e or i is pronounced as in **g**eranium

g before h is pronounced as in **g**arlic

gl before i and at the end of a word is like sta**lli**on

gn as in o**ni**on

h is silent

j is like an English y

qu before a, e or i as in **qu**ack

s before any consonant is like an English *sh*

tg is like an English *ch*: "notg" sounds like *notch*

The basics

hello	allegra	pardon!	perdunai!
good morning	bun di	excuse me	perstgisai
good afternoon or		I am	jau sun
good evening	buna saira	I'm from...	jau vegn...
goodbye	a revair	I'm sorry	i ma displascha
bye!	ciao!	I (don't) speak	jau (na) cur (betg)
yes	gea	Romansh	rumantsch
no	na	I (don't) understand	jau (na) chapesch
OK	va bain		(betg)
please	anzi	Do you speak English?	Discurris Vus
thank you (very much)	grazia (fitg)		englais?

Travel, hotels and shops

train	tren	with a shower	cun duscha
station	staziun	with a bath	cun bogn
information	infurmaziuns	how much is the room?	quant
ticket	bigliet		custa la
Where can I get a	Nua partan ils		chombra?
postbus to Chur?	autos postals	with breakfast	cun ensolver
	per Cuira?	with half board	mesa pensiun
bus stop	fermada	dormitory	champ da
I'd like	jau avess gugent		massa
a single room	chombra singula	campsite	plazza de
a double room	chombra dubla		campar
with a basin	cun aua currenta	open/closed	avert/serrà
		day off	di da repaus

Eating and drinking

Could we have a table in a non-smoking section?	Pudessan nus ina maisa en ilsectur da nunfimaders?
bread	paun
butter	paintg
cheese	chaschiel
soup	schuppa
beef	bov
veal	vadè
pork	portg
chicken	pulaster

game	selvaschina
sausage	liongia
fish	pesch
potato	tartuffel
vegetables	verdura
fruit	fritgs
water	aua
white/red wine	vin alv/cotschen
a beer	ina biera
cheers! (toast)	viva!

Numbers

0	nulla		11	indesch
1	in		12	dudesch
2	dus		13	tredesch
3	trais		14	quattordesch
4	quatter		15	quindesch
5	tschintg		16	sedesch
6	sis		17	deschse.0t
7	set		18	deschdotg
8	otg		19	deschnov
9	nov		20	ventg
10	diesch			

Days and months

Monday	glindesdi		today	oz
Tuesday	mardi		tomorrow	damaun
Wednesday	mesemna		January	schaner
Thursday	gievgia		February	favrer
Friday	venderdi		March	mars
Saturday	sonda		April	avrigl
Sunday	dumengia		May	matg
day	di		June	zercladur
in the morning	la damaun		July	fanadur
at noon	a mezdi		August	avust
in the afternoon	il suentermezdi		September	settember
in the evening	la saira		October	october
at night	la notg		November	november
at midnight	a mesanotg		December	december
yesterday	ier			

Vegetables

	Swiss German	French	Italian
vegetables	Gemüse	légumes	verdure
tomato	Tomate	tomate	pomodoro
carrot	Rüebli	carotte	carota
cabbage	Chabis	chou	cavolo
cauliflower	Blumenkohl	choufleur	cavolfiore
corn	Mais	maïs	mais
cucumber	Gurke	concombre	cetriolo
asparagus	Spargel	asperge	asparagi
beans	Bohnen	haricots	fagioli
peas	Erbse	poix	piselli
sweet pepper	Peperoni	poivron	peperone
spinach	Spinat	épinards	spinaci
fennel	Fenchel	fenouil	finocchio
broccoli	Broccoli	brocoli	broccolo
onion	Zwiebel	oignon	cipolla
garlic	Knoblauch	ail	aglio

Cooking terms

	Swiss German	French	Italian
hot	heiss	chaud	caldo
cold	kalt	froid	freddo
smoked	geräuchert	fumé	affumicato
roast	gebraten	rôti	arrosto
rare	bluetig	saignant	al sangue
well done	gar	bien cuit	ben cotto
boiled	gekochte	bouilli	bollito
steamed	gedämpft	à la vapeur	al vapore
stuffed	gefüllt	farci	farcito
grilled	gegrillt	grillé	alla griglia
raw	roh	cru	crudo
baked	gebacken	au four	al forno
fried	gebraten, fritiert	frite	fritto
spices	Gewürze	épices	spezie
traditional cooking	gutbürgerliche Küche	cuisine bourgeoise	cucina casalinga
Swiss-German cooking	Schweizer Küche	cuisine suisse alémanique	cucina svizzero tedesca
Swiss-French cooking	Welsche Küche	cuisine romande	cucina romanda
Ticinese cooking	Tessiner Küche	cuisine tessinoise	cucina ticinese
Romansh cooking	Romanische Küche	cuisine romanche	cucina romancia
in the style of	art	à la	al/alla
home-made	Hausgemacht	fait à la maison	fatto in casa

Fruit and desserts

	Swiss German	French	Italian
fruit	Früchte	fruits	frutta
apple	Apfel	pomme	mela
pear	Birne	poire	pera
plum	Zwetschge	prune	prugna
peach	Pfirsich	pêche	pesca
cherry	Kirsche	cerise	ciliegia
grape	Trauben	raisin	uva
raspberry	Himbeere	framboise	lampone
strawberry	Erdbeere	fraise	fragola
apricot	Aprikose	abricot	albicocca
orange	Orange	orange	arancia
grapefruit	Grapefruit	pamplemousse	pompelmo
lemon	Zitrone	citron	limone
cake	Kuchen, Torte	gâteau, tarte	torta
chocolate	Schokolade	chocolat	cioccolata
ice cream	Glace	glace	gelato

Glossary

German

Abfahrt departure

Achtung! Beware!

Altstadt Old Town

Ankunft arrival

Auskunft information

Bach stream

Bahnhof station

Berg mountain

Bergführer mountain guide

Bergweg mountain path

Billets tickets

Blaue zone blue zone (city parking)

Brücke bridge

Deutschschweiz German-speaking Switzerland

Dorf village

Durchgang passageway

Fluss river

Fussgängerzone pedestrian zone

Gasse alley

Gefahr! Danger!

Gepäck baggage

Gipfel summit

Gletscher glacier

Gutbürgerliche traditional, solidly bourgeois

Hafen harbour

Hauptbahnhof main station

Hochsaison high season

Hof court or courtyard

Horn peak

Jass (*yass*) extremely complicated card game played in taverns by young and old using non-standard Swiss playing cards; suits are Rosen (roses), Schilden (shields), Eicheln (acorns) and Schellen (bells)

Jugendherberge youth hostel

Kantönligeist literally "little cantonal spirit": describes a stubborn Swiss parochialism, a blinkered pride in the attributes and culture of one's own town or canton above all others (with the same overtones as "Little Englander")

Kirche church

Kloster monastery or convent

Kulm summit

Kunst art

Kurverein tourist office

Massenlager dormitory

Matratzenlager dormitory

Mitenand friendly welcoming Swiss-German term for everyone in a group, with the same disarming overtones as "folks" in English: a hotel receptionist or maitre d' will greet a party with *grüezi mitenand* ("hello everyone"), a waiter will say *enguete mitenand* ("enjoy your meal, folks"), and so on

Münster minster or cathedral

Nachsaison post-season, low season

Nord north

Ober upper

Ost east

Platz town square

Rathaus town hall

Röstigraben informal name for the language border – a *Graben* is a military trench – between French-speaking Switzerland (where they don't eat the traditional potato dish *Rösti*) and German-speaking Switzerland (where they do)

Sammlung collection

SBB Swiss Federal Railways

Schloss castle or stately home

Schlucht gorge

Schweiz Switzerland

See lake

Strasse street

Sud south

Tal valley

Tessin Ticino
Tor gate
Tourismus tourist office
Touristenlager dormitory
Turm tower
Verboten! Prohibited!
Verkehrsverein tourist office
Vorsaison pre-season, low season
Wald forest

Wanderweg footpath
Welschland informal name for French-speaking Switzerland (the Swiss-German word *Choderwelsch* means "gobbledygook")
Westschweiz formal name for French-speaking Switzerland
Zeughaus arsenal
Zwischensaison between-season, low season

French

Auberge de jeunesse youth hostel
Basse-saison low season
Billettes tickets
Bois woods
CFF Swiss Federal Railways
Château castle or stately home
Chemin pédestre footpath
Col mountain pass
Église church
Est east
Forêt forest
Gare station
Haute-saison high season
Hôtel de ville town hall
Interdit! Prohibited!
Nord north
Office du tourisme tourist office

Ouest west
Pont bridge
Randonnée hike
Renseignements information
Romandie French-speaking Switzerland
Rue street
Ruelle alley
Sud south
Suisse Switzerland
Suisse alémanique German-speaking Switzerland
Suisse romande French-speaking Switzerland
Tessin Ticino
Tour tower
Vieille ville Old Town
Zone pour piétons pedestrian zone

Italian

Albergo hotel or inn
Alloggio accommodation
Alta stagione high season
Arrivo arrival
Bassa stagione low season
Biglietti tickets
Bosco forest or woodland
Capanna alpine hut
Castello castle
Centro storico Old Town
Chiesa church
Ente turistico tourist office
Est east

FFS Swiss Federal Railways
Fiume river
Ghiacciaio glacier
Grotto rustic country tavern
Lago lake
Nord north
Ostello per la gioventù youth hostel
Osteria rustic country tavern
Ovest west
Palazzo civico city hall
Partenza departure
Pericolo! Danger!
Piano floor or storey (in a building)

Piz peak
Ponte bridge
Rifugio alpine hut
Sentiero footpath
Sud south
Svizzera Switzerland
Svizzera romanda French-speaking
Switzerland

Svizzera tedesca German-speaking
Switzerland
Torre tower
Vetta summit
Via street
Vicolo alley
Vietato! Prohibited!
Zona pedonale pedestrian zone

Art and architecture

Apse semi-circular termination at the east
(altar) end of a church
Baroque exuberant architectural style of the
seventeenth and early eighteenth centuries,
characterized by ornate decoration, complex
spatial arrangements and grand vistas. The
term is also applied to the sumptuous style
of painting of the same period
Biedermeier simple, bourgeois style of
painting and decoration practised throughout
the first half of the nineteenth century in
German-speaking Europe
Capital the top of a column, usually ornate
Carolingian mid-eighth- to early tenth-century
style of art and architecture named after
Charlemagne
Chancel part of a church in which the altar
is located
Choir part of a church where the service is
sung, usually beside the altar
Fresco mural painting applied to wet plaster,
so that the colours immediately soak in
Gothic architectural style of the thirteenth and
fourteenth centuries, with an emphasis on
verticality, characterized by pointed arches,
ribbed vaulting and flying buttresses
Neoclassical late-eighteenth- and early
nineteenth-century style of art and
architecture which returned to Classical

styles as a reaction against Baroque and
Rococo excesses
Oriel projecting bay window
Renaissance fifteenth- and sixteenth-century
Italian-originated movement in art and
architecture, inspired by the rediscovery of
Classical ideals
Rococo highly florid, light and graceful
eighteenth-century style of architecture,
painting and interior design, forming the last
phase of Baroque
Romanesque solid architectural style of
the late tenth to mid-thirteenth centuries,
characterized by round-headed arches and
a penchant for horizontality and geometrical
precision
Rood screen screen in a Catholic church
dividing the nave from the chancel (and thus
separating worshippers from clergy)
Sgraffiti exterior house decoration of the
Romansh-speaking Engadine Valley of
Graubünden whereby designs or mottoes are
etched into a white layer of plaster to reveal
a darker-coloured layer beneath
Spandrel the underside of an arch
Stucco plaster used for decorative effects
Trompe l'oeil painting designed to fool the
viewer into believing it is three-dimensional

Visit us online
www.roughguides.com
Information on over 25,000 destinations around the world

- **Read** Rough Guides' trusted travel info
- **Access** exclusive articles from Rough Guides authors
- **Update** yourself on new books, maps, CDs and other products
- **Enter** our competitions and win travel prizes
- **Share** ideas, journals, photos & travel advice with other users
- **Earn** points every time you contribute to the Rough Guide community and get rewards

ROUGH GUIDES   BROADEN YOUR HORIZONS

Small print and

Index

A Rough Guide to Rough Guides

Published in 1982, the first Rough Guide – to Greece – was a student scheme that became a publishing phenomenon. Mark Ellingham, a recent graduate in English from Bristol University, had been travelling in Greece the previous summer and couldn't find the right guidebook. With a small group of friends he wrote his own guide, combining a highly contemporary, journalistic style with a thoroughly practical approach to travellers' needs.

The immediate success of the book spawned a series that rapidly covered dozens of destinations. And, in addition to impecunious backpackers, Rough Guides soon acquired a much broader and older readership that relished the guides' wit and inquisitiveness as much as their enthusiastic, critical approach and value-for-money ethos.

These days, Rough Guides include recommendations from shoestring to luxury and cover more than 200 destinations around the globe, including almost every country in the Americas and Europe, more than half of Africa and most of Asia and Australasia. Our ever-growing team of authors and photographers is spread all over the world, particularly in Europe, the USA and Australia.

In the early 1990s, Rough Guides branched out of travel, with the publication of Rough Guides to World Music, Classical Music and the Internet. All three have become benchmark titles in their fields, spearheading the publication of a wide range of books under the Rough Guide name.

SMALL PRINT

Including the travel series, Rough Guides now number more than 350 titles, covering phrasebooks, waterproof maps, music guides from Opera to Heavy Metal, reference works on subjects as diverse as Conspiracy Theories and Shakespeare, and popular culture books from iPods to Poker. Rough Guides also produces a series of more than 120 World Music CDs in partnership with World Music Network.

Visit www.roughguides.com to see our latest publications.

Rough Guide travel images are available for commercial licensing at www.roughguidespictures.com.

Rough Guide credits

Text editor: Helena Smith
Layout: Jessica Subramanian
Cartography: Manish Chandra
Picture editor: Jj Luck
Production: Aimee Hampson
Proofreaders: Karen Paricer, Amanda Jones
Cover design: Chloë Roberts
Photographer: Helena Smith
Editorial: **London** Kate Berens, Claire Saunders, Geoff Howard, Edward Aves, Clifton Wilkinson, Alison Murchie, Ruth Blackmore, Polly Thomas, Richard Lim, Karoline Densley, Andy Turner, Keith Drew, Nikki Birrell, Helen Marsden, Alice Park, Sarah Eno, David Paul, Lucy White, Joe Staines, Duncan Clark, Peter Buckley, Matthew Milton, Tracy Hopkins, Ruth Tidball; **New York** Andrew Rosenberg, Richard Koss, Steven Horak, AnneLise Sorensen, Amy Hegarty, Hunter Slaton, April Isaacs, Sean Mahoney, Ella Steim
Design & Pictures: **London** Simon Bracken, Dan May, Diana Jarvis, Mark Thomas, Harriet Mills, Roger Mapp; **Delhi** Madhulita Mohapatra, Umesh Aggarwal, Ajay Verma, Amit Verma, Ankur Guha, Pradeep Thapliyal, Sachin Tanwar

Production: Sophie Hewat, Katherine Owers
Cartography: **London** Maxine Repath, Ed Wright, Katie Lloyd-Jones; **Delhi** Rajesh Chhibber, Jai Prakash Mishra, Ashutosh Bharti, Rajesh Mishra, Jasbir Sandhu, Karobi Gogoi, Amod Singh
Online: **New York** Jennifer Gold, Suzanne Welles, Kristin Mingrone; **Delhi** Manik Chauhan, Narender Kumar, Manish Shekhar Jha, Lalit K. Sharma, Rakesh Kumar, Chhandita Chakravarty
Marketing & Publicity: **London** Richard Trillo, Niki Hanmer, David Wearn, Demelza Dallow, Louise Maher, Jess Carter; **New York** Geoff Colquitt, Megan Kennedy, Katy Ball; **Delhi** Reem Khokhar
Custom publishing and foreign rights: Philippa Hopkins
Manager India: Punita Singh
Series editor: Mark Ellingham
Publishing Director: Martin Dunford
Reference Director: Andrew Lockett
PA to Publishing and Reference Directors: Megan McIntyre

Publishing information

This third edition published July 2006 by
Rough Guides Ltd,
80 Strand, London WC2R 0RL, UK
345 Hudson St, 4th Floor,
New York, NY 10014, USA
14 Local Shopping Centre, Panchsheel Park,
New Delhi 110017, India
Distributed by the Penguin Group
Penguin Books Ltd,
80 Strand, London WC2R 0RL, UK
Penguin Putnam, Inc.
375 Hudson Street, NY 10014, USA
Penguin Group (Australia)
250 Camberwell Road, Camberwell,
Victoria 3124, Australia
Penguin Books Canada Ltd,
10 Alcorn Avenue, Toronto, Ontario,
M4V 1E4, Canada
Penguin Group (New Zealand)
Cnr Rosedale and Airborne Roads
Albany, Auckland, New Zealand
Cover design by Peter Dyer.

Typeset in Bembo and Helvetica to an original design by Henry Iles.
Printed and bound at Legoprint S.p.A.
© Matthew Teller

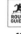

632pp includes index
A catalogue record for this book is available from the British Library
ISBN 13: 978-1-84353-668-0
ISBN 10: 1-84353-668-4

1   3   5   7   9   8   6   4   2

SMALL PRINT

Help us update

We've gone to a lot of effort to ensure that the third edition of **The Rough Guide to Switzerland** is accurate and up to date. However, things change – places get "discovered", opening hours are notoriously fickle, restaurants and rooms raise prices or lower standards. If you feel we've got it wrong or left something out, we'd like to know, and if you can remember the address, the price, the time, the phone number, so much the better.

We'll credit all contributions, and send a copy of the next edition (or any other Rough Guide

if you prefer) for the best letters. Everyone who writes to us and isn't already a subscriber will receive a copy of our full-colour thrice-yearly newsletter.

Please mark letters: **"Rough Guide Switzerland Update"** and send to: Rough Guides, 80 Strand, London WC2R 0RL, or Rough Guides, 4th Floor, 345 Hudson St, New York, NY 10014. Or send an email to **mail@roughguides.com**

Have your questions answered and tell others about your trip at
www.roughguides.atinfopop.com

Acknowledgements

The author would like to thank, **in London**, Evelyn Lafone, Roland Minder, Daniela Kiser, Anne Pedersen, Marcel Schoeb, Virginie Baeriswyl, Caroline Phillips-Pidroni and Russell Palmer at Switzerland Tourism for ever-present support, help and information; Greig Boyle at Swiss International Air Lines for enthusiasm, flexibility and understanding; Ursula Schneiter of the Information and Media Office of the Swiss Embassy, London; Kev Reynolds for inspiration, walking information and the flora and fauna article; John Collard, historian of skiing; and **in Milan** Lucy Ratcliffe and Luca Donadoni, for support, advice and encouragement, and the piece on architecture. **In Switzerland**, many thanks to Dianne Dicks of Bergli Books, Basel (@www .bergli.ch); Mike Evans, translator (@www .evans.ch); and tourist office staff around the country – especially Elena Pellandini of Ticino Tourism, Bellinzona, and Davide Caenaro of Zürich Tourism.

Many thanks, as always, to Christian Imdorf and Beat, Naama, Mica & Yonatan Vogt for food, wine, grappa and laughs in all kinds of odd places around Switzerland.

At Rough Guides, heartfelt thanks to my editor, Helena Smith, for her cool head and great photos, to Geoff Howard for great flexibility and understanding, and to Claire Saunders for putting so much into the first two editions of this book. Thanks also to: Jessica Subramanian for typesetting, Jj Luck for picture research, Maxine Repath and Manish Chandra for the maps, and Chloë Roberts for the cover. And thank you to Han, for everything.

Readers' letters

Many thanks to all those readers who took the time to write, email or contribute to the Travel Talk forums at @www.roughguides.com with comments on the previous edition, new discoveries in Switzerland or just an account of their travels. Apologies if we've misspelt or misunderstood anyone's name. Thanks to:

Steven Ainley, Richard Baker, Manuela Barrera, Vreni Bartschi, Ragnvald Bjelland, Jon Blythe, Nick Botham and Chris Lane, Praveen K. Chand, Daniel E. Coslett, Cathie and Tony Cox, Amy Eckert, Anne-Marie Elmiger, Angela Farnell, David Fowler, Tobin Fricke, Margaret Gallery, John Good, Niels de Groot, Tanja Haehlen, Mike Hewitt, Isabelle Holdener, Matt Horn, Frances Ilmberger, Marc Jones and Diane Sifis, Nicole Kruppa, Daniela Lauterjung, the family Majek, C.C. Mitchell, Mr A.P. Moore, Julie Paterson, Rob Patterson, Piergiorgio Pescali, Sue Poolman, Hilton Purvis and Loretta Jakubiec, Doreen Robb (Mrs), Samar Shamoon, Nicholas Straw, Ruth and Andrew Stuber, Roger Summers and Christo Mouton, K. Tan, Margot Timbel, Roger Tonge, Alicia Treppoz-Vielle, Alexia Wiasmitinow, Christof Wicki, Derek Wilde, Professor Jürg Willi, Barrie Wright, Gareth Wright, Laura Wuertz-Barac, the family Yakoubi.

SMALL PRINT

Photo credits

All photos © Rough Guides Pictures except the following:

Introduction
Crans Montana, Kanton Wallis Alpwiese © AURA/Crans-Montana, Bildrechte nur fÿr Presse im Zusammenhang mit Crans-Montana, http://www.crans-montana.ch
Swiss passport © Swiss Embassy, London
Appenzellerland, Appenzell, Kanton Appenzell Tradition Silvesterklaeuse in Urnaesch © Daisy Gilardini
Winter, Viadukt, Tannenwald, schnee © arosa tourismus

Things not to miss
02 Carneval, Basel © KEYSTONE Switzerland/AP/Winfried Rothermel http://www.keystone.ch
03 Aletsch, Kanton Wallis Klettersteig Aletsch © Belalp Tourismus http://www.aletsch.ch

04 Lake Luzern © LuzernTourismus
05 Bachalpsee, First © Jungfraubahnen
11 Isaac Hayes at the Montreux Jazz Festival © Antonio Marmolejo/Rezo
12 St-Saphorin, Lake Geneva © Lake Geneva Region Tourist Board
19 Rhätische Bahn © Peter Donatsch/swiss-image.ch
20 View from the vineyards of Mont d'Orge over the castle hills Tourbillon and Valere © Switzerland Tourism ST/swiss-image.ch

Black and whites
p.396 Monument to William Tell Altdorf © Gary Cook/Alamy
p.474 Castle Vaduz Liechtenstein © Jon Arnold Images/Alamy

Index

Map entries are in colour.

INDEX

INDEX

627

INDEX